HANDBOOK OF

INFORMATION
SECURITY

MANAGEMENT

H A N D B O O K   O F

INFORMATION
SECURITY

MANAGEMENT

Zella G. Ruthberg
Harold F. Tipton
Editors

AUERBACH
Boston and New York

Auerbach Publications
Warren Gorham Lamont
31 St. James Avenue
Boston, Massachusetts 02116

Contributors

Glenda Barnes
Partner, Z/B Associates, Boston MA

Steven F. Blanding
Senior EDP Audit Manager, Dean Witter, Discover & Co., Riverwoods IL

David Bonyun
President, Bunberry Philbert & Stokes Enterprises, Ltd., Nepean, Ontario, Canada

Robert J. Bosen
Senior Scientist, Enigma Logic, Inc., Concord CA

Dennis K. Branstad
NIST Fellow, National Institute of Standards and Technology, Gaithersburg MD

Nander Brown
Chief, Computer Security Unit, Resolution Trust Corp., Rosslyn VA

William E. Burr
Electronics Engineer, Computer Security Division, National Institute of Standards and Technology, Gaithersburg MD

F.J. (Phil) Dolan
Program Director of Information Security, IBM Corp., Armonk NY

Edwin A. Doty, Jr.
Associate Professor of Accounting, School of Business, East Carolina University, Greenville NC

Catherine Englishman
Member of Technical Staff, Computer Security, AT&T Bell Laboratories, Murray Hill NJ

Patricia A.P. Fisher
President, JANUS Associates, Inc., Stamford CT

Peter C. Gardiner
Associate Professor of Systems Management, Institute of Safety and Systems Management, University of Southern California, Los Angeles CA

CONTRIBUTORS

Gerald W. Grindler
President and Founder, Available & Secured Knowledge, Consulting, St. Louis MO

Cheryl W. Helsing
Manager of Information Resource Audit & Assurance, Sun Microsystems, Inc., Mountain View CA

Danny R. Hines
Professor of Accounting, School of Business, East Carolina University, Greenville NC

Gerald Isaacson
President, Information Security Services, Northborough MA

Sushil Jajodia
Professor of Information and Software Systems Engineering, Director of the Center for Secure Information Systems, George Mason University, Fairfax VA

Micki S. Krause
Program Manager, Information Security, Rockwell International Corp., Seal Beach CA

Stanley Kurzban
Senior Instructor (retired), System Research Education Center, IBM Corp., Chappaqua NY

Theodore M.P. Lee
Computer Scientist, Trusted Information Systems, Inc., Minnetonka MN

Jerome Lobel
President, Lobel & Associates, Phoenix AZ

Theresa F. Lunt
Manager of Computer Security Research, Computer Science Laboratory, SRI International, Menlo Park CA

Sally Meglathery
Director of EDP Audit, New York Stock Exchange, New York NY

William H. Murray
Executive Consultant to Deloitte & Touche, New Canaan CT

Melvyn Musson
Vice-President, Manager of Crisis Management and Business Continuation Specialty Group, Johnson & Higgins of Missouri, Inc., St. Louis MO

Peter G. Neumann
Principal Scientist, Computer Science Laboratory, SRI International Corp., Menlo Park CA

Donn B. Parker
Senior Management Consultant, SRI International, Menlo Park CA

William E. Perry
Executive Director, Quality Assurance Institute, Orlando FL

Zella G. Ruthberg
Security/Audit Consultant, ZGR Information Systems, Rockville MD

Ravi S. Sandhu
Associate Chairperson, Information and Software Systems Engineering
Department, George Mason University, Fairfax VA

Warren Schmitt
Independent Consultant for Small Businesses, Long Grove IL

Miles E. Smid
Manager, Security Technology Group, National Institute of Standards and
Technology, Gaithersburg MD

Mark Tantam
Coordinator of the Commercial Investigations Group, Touche Ross,
London UK

Mario Tinto
Senior Scientist, Office of Standards, Fort Meade MD

Harold F. Tipton
Program Director of Audit Coordination, Rockwell International Corp.,
Seal Beach CA

Charles Cresson Wood
Independent Information Security Management Consultant and President,
Baseline Software, Sausalito CA

Eddie L. Zeitler
Vice-President, Information Security Services, Fidelity Investments,
Boston MA

Contents

CONTENTS

Introduction

The adage that best defines the information age is "knowledge is power." Business success depends on information that enables organizations to take advantage of rapid changes in their markets. To be useful, this information must be accurate, timely, and in a form that can be readily understood. To protect the organization, however, proprietary or otherwise sensitive information must be made available only to those who are properly authorized.

Originally, the primary concern of information security—especially in defense-related organizations—was to protect the confidentiality of automated information. In today's computing environment, however, this narrow focus is no longer adequate. For business as well as civilian government, the integrity and availability of sensitive information are often of paramount importance. Security practitioners are called on to strike an appropriate balance between ensuring the availability of information and protecting its confidentiality.

As the requirements for protecting information have evolved over the years, so too has computing technology. Quantum leaps in the performance of microcomputers and in networking have given individual computer users a level of power and performance equivalent to that of the mainframes of the 1960s. Rapid technical advances have fostered the productive sharing of information across a worldwide network of data bases.

Unfortunately, these advances have made the work of security professionals more difficult. For example, the extreme complexity of networked computing architectures makes it difficult to ensure the integrity of shared information. Further complicating this situation, the development of information protection mechanisms has lagged behind innovations in information access and retrieval systems. Security practitioners find themselves in a constant scramble to adjust to new technologies and new threats to security. As a consequence, security organizations now require specialists with expertise in such diverse areas as communications, operating systems, systems and applications development, security investigation, and training.

INFORMATION SECURITY TRENDS

Changes in professional and technical standards, as well as advances in technology, are expected to have a major influence on the practice of information security in coming years. Information systems security has itself only recently evolved into a recognized profession. Security management has become increasingly concerned with ensuring that security personnel have the requisite knowledge and experience to effectively perform their jobs. To that end, several information security professional societies have banded together to develop a unified certification program for security professionals. This handbook is, in fact, based primarily on the common body of knowledge that has been developed as part of this effort to develop a common certification program.

It has also been recognized that a set of generally accepted systems security principles must be developed and promulgated. These principles would be used as guidelines to help vendors to design and manufacture secure systems and to assist users to select the most appropriate hardware and software products. An international committee is working to develop such common standards.

Historically, organizations have imposed a uniform set of controls (typically mandated by government or private sector policy) over all of the organization's computing systems. However, the same level of security is often not required for every system, and the expense of installing and maintaining such security is wasteful. Efforts are now under way to establish methodologies that tie specific security requirements to specific levels of information sensitivity and system risk. These efforts should make it possible to design and maintain system-specific controls for confidentiality, availability, and integrity.

In addition to developing professional and technical standards and methodologies, technological advances will also have a major impact on information security. For example, single sign-on capabilities are now being developed so that users who need to access multiple systems do not have to enter different user IDs and passwords for authentication on each system. This technical development complicates the problem of ensuring positive identification of system users.

Other technical developments are expected to provide security practitioners with improved tools for protecting the security of information resources. For example, partly in response to the success of hackers in subverting fixed password controls, dynamic password technologies have been developed. Intrusion detection systems are also being developed to assist in detecting and mitigating the impact of system abuse.

A BRIEF OVERVIEW OF CONTENTS

This handbook is divided into four parts; each part consists of one or more sections devoted to a specific security-related topic. Part I introduces the key issues in security management, with major sections that address how to establish an effective security program, how to analyze and manage risk, how to develop a business continuity plan, and how to develop security awareness.

Building on this information, Parts II and III focus on technical security issues. Part II covers data, applications, and systems security. This part begins with a section on the design and development of secure systems that describes the key components and processes of secure systems and the various tools, techniques, and methodologies that can be used to develop secure systems. The next section of Part II reviews physical and operations controls as well as technical controls appropriate for specific types of computer equipment and configurations. The third section of Part II addresses data- and application-specific controls, and the final section of this part describes access controls and various models and techniques for user verification and automated intrusion detection.

Part III is devoted to network and communications security. The implementation and management of network-based controls is discussed, as is the theory and practice of securing communications. The security of networks governed by the OSI and ISDN protocols is reviewed. Part III concludes with chapters on the use of cryptography to secure communications and on the control of EDI transactions.

Part IV focuses on security and the law. Methods of perpetrating, detecting, and investigating computer crime and abuse are covered. The final chapter of this part addresses a matter that should be of serious concern to all organizations—potential exposure to litigation based on claims of negligence in protecting information. In a future supplement to this handbook, we plan to cover state, federal, and international laws governing information privacy and security, as well as government and industry standards and regulations related to information security.

HOW TO USE THIS BOOK

Each part of this handbook begins with an introduction that briefly reviews the contents of its major sections. In turn, each section also starts with a brief overview of the chapters it contains. The introductions help provide an understanding of the relationship of ideas and topics that comprise information security. As such, readers are encouraged to read the relevant introductions before proceeding to specific chapters of the handbook.

Novices to the field of information security should begin by reading Part I on the fundamental issues in security management in its entirety before proceeding to the more technical sections of this book. Most newcomers would be best served by reading the book in sequential order of chapters. More advanced readers may choose to use this handbook as a reference tool; the index at the back of the book should help facilitate identifying specific topics and subtopics. The handbook also provides a detailed glossary of security-related terms and a list of recommended readings provided by contributors.

ACKNOWLEDGMENTS

The editors wish to thank all of the contributors to this handbook—the authors of chapters and the many other security practitioners who rendered assistance in suggesting improvements in specific areas. This document would not have been possible without the unselfish sharing of their expertise and experience. We would also like to thank the staff at Auerbach Publications for the development and production of this handbook, including Pamela Kirshen, who initiated this project, Kim Horan Kelly, who ensured its healthy development, and Robert Elliott, who guided the editors in the selection of chapters and who, with the able help of Deborah Schild, edited the final manuscript.

Zella G. Ruthberg
Harold F. Tipton

PART I

Information Security Management

Worldwide business and government communities depend increasingly on the use of automated information systems. As computer systems have become more prevalent, sophisticated, embedded in physical processes, and interconnected, organizations become more and more vulnerable to system design weaknesses, user errors and omissions, and attacks on the system. During the National Academy of Science study resulting in the "Computers at Risk" report, it was noted that the advent of networks and distributed systems has increased the risk of malicious attacks on computer systems and that many components commonly used in networked environments lack any intrinsic facilities to ensure security. It was further noted that the perils to be addressed by computer security are likely to be substantially greater in the future than in the past.

In response to this worldwide problem, this handbook is intended to help information security managers understand the key security issues and develop reasonable and cost-effective security programs for their organizations. This handbook encompasses the common body of knowledge that was defined by experts as the areas of knowledge that make up the field of information security. The common body of knowledge was developed as the basis for formal certification of information system security practitioners.

Part I of this handbook provides the information security manager with the fundamental philosophies, administrative guidelines, and functional orientation needed to make effective use of the more technical material that follows. One of the first challenges faced by the security manager is deciding what needs to be protected against which threats. Therefore, this introductory part of the handbook provides a discussion of the fundamental concepts of security management. Often user groups argue that security relates only to information confidentiality. How often have users been heard to complain that security is not necessary because all the information in their system is public knowledge and, therefore, does not require protection? They fail to realize that the integrity and availability of information must also be protected by security mechanisms. Without integrity of information and availability of the ability to use the system, a computer system is worthless to the user.

After gaining an understanding of the fundamentals of security management, security managers are ready to establish their organization's security program. Expert advice on how to accomplish this is provided in Section I-2. This advice is based on years of experience and offers proven practices to help security managers avoid making common mistakes.

Of course, it is impossible to develop a really cost-effective security program, tailored to the needs of a specific organization, without knowing the threats and vulnerabilities that a system is exposed to in its particular environment. To find out what protection is necessary, the security manager needs to perform a risk analysis. This may be an iterative process as systems or conditions change. Risk management guidance for the security manager is included in Section I-3.

Security managers recognize that there must be a balance between security measures and productivity. This balance is achieved by installing what is termed "reasonable security." Anything more—that which the user community perceives as unreasonable—will result in users subverting the security measures. This condition must be avoided; it is more dangerous to think security is in place when, in fact, it has been compromised than to know there is a vulnerability and monitor the risk.

Because security cannot be perfect, incidents will occur that may result in temporary loss of the data processing capability. Statistically, it has been shown that few organizations today can tolerate a loss in excess of one week of computing capability for critical systems. Therefore, it is vitally important that organizations plan for such a contingency. This planning for business continuity is addressed in Section I-4.

Although users will tolerate only the level of security that they consider reasonable, unfortunately, most user groups are not fully aware of the many threats and vulnerabilities that could disrupt their systems. They may have read about computer viruses and hackers in the media, but they probably do not realize the specific vulnerabilities in the computing equipment they are using. Also, they probably do not appreciate how easy it is for experienced intruders to break into systems—even those with no apparent weaknesses. Finally, they may not know what to look for to detect intrusions. The information that user groups need to appreciate the importance of information security is best obtained through an aggressive and effective security awareness program. This program must be ongoing in order to remind users of the threats and advise them of emergent vulnerabilities or risks precipitated by advancing technology. Section I-5, which concludes Part I, reviews the key components and strategies for implementing an effective security awareness program.

Fundamentals of Security Management

The management of information security affects virtually every function in an organization. Because of this broad scope, new security managers can easily be overwhelmed and uncertain about where to begin addressing the security problem in their organizations. Section I-1 provides the orientation needed to get a handle on the subject.

A good starting place is the discussion of the purposes of security management described in Chapter I-1-1. This chapter addresses the three basic goals of information security: the confidentiality, integrity, and availability of information considerations in an automated system. Included in the discussion is identification of the principal threats to achieving these goals that must be countered if a security program is to be successful. This chapter also includes a brief introduction to the various models that describe the controls used to ensure information confidentiality and integrity.

After this background in concepts, the process of establishing a framework for managing the security function is addressed. As described in Chapter I-1-2, this framework relates information security requirements to the mission, legal requirements, user needs, and policies pertinent to the organization.

Continuing the logical flow from concepts to framework to specific countermeasures, Chapter I-1-3 provides an overview of the types of information security controls that should be included. (More detailed discussions of these controls are found in Parts II and III of this handbook.) Types of controls are divided into two categories: those that are preventive and those that are detective. Preventive controls inhibit the free access to computing resources to ensure that only authorized users and programs can use them. The effectiveness of preventive controls is limited by the level of tolerance to such controls by authorized users. When this tolerance level is reached, it is necessary to resort to detective controls. Detective controls are typically passive and identify attempts at unauthorized access or other breaches of security policy. Therefore, they complement protective controls. The security program needs to achieve an appropriate balance between protective and detective controls. Experience in the field has been that this delicate balance is elusive and needs to be revisited frequently as changes in the types and uses of computing resources occur.

So far, Section 1 of Part I has introduced the whats and wheres of information security. Completing this section are the whys. Chapter I-1-4 on human behavior, with respect to computer security, provides insights based on actual experience and the compilation of thousands of security incidents reports. These insights focus on why computer users misbehave, the security-relevant expectations that people have of computer systems, and the expectations that system designers and administrators have with respect to system users. This chapter addresses issues of human behavior and potential measures to narrow the gap between expectations and realities of system security and use.

A serious concern related to human behavior and computer security is that of ethics. Chapter I-1-5 covers the ethical issues precipitated by technological advances that enable people to gain access to more and more vital information. Threats to individual privacy created by the increasing use of computer data bases to store personal information are addressed as well as the threats to privacy in the workplace by sophisticated electronic surveillance and monitoring devices. It is suggested that ethics education can help achieve a more constructive atmosphere for the use of computers. This chapter reflects efforts of various professional associations to develop codes of ethics.

The orientation provided in Section I-1 establishes the background and philosophy necessary to appreciate fully the information contained in the sections that follow. Thus, not only has an introduction to the field been provided but the stage has been set for the rest of the handbook.

Purposes of Information Security Management

HAL TIPTON

Managing computer and network security programs has become an increasingly difficult and challenging job. During the late 1970s and early 1980s, data processing was typically performed in a computing center with standalone mainframes. Security controls could be implemented centrally, at the data processing facility. Physical measures restricted computing center access to computer operations personnel, and access control software restricted computing system access to authorized users.

Dramatic advances in computing and communications technology during the past five years have redirected the focus of data processing from the computing center to the terminals in individual offices and homes. The result is that managers must now monitor security on a more widely dispersed level. These changes are continuing to accelerate, making the security manager's job increasingly difficult.

The information security manager must establish and maintain a security program that ensures three requirements: the confidentiality, integrity, and availability of the company's information resources. Some security experts argue that two other requirements may be added to these three: utility and authenticity (i.e., accuracy). In this discussion, however, the usefulness and authenticity of information are addressed within the context of the three basic requirements of security management.

CONFIDENTIALITY

Confidentiality is the protection of information in the system so that unauthorized persons cannot access it. Many believe this type of protection is of most importance to military and government organizations that need to keep plans and capabilities secret from potential enemies. However, it can also be significant to businesses that need to protect proprietary trade secrets from competitors or prevent unauthorized persons from accessing the company's sensitive information (e.g., legal, personnel, or medical information). Privacy issues, which have received an increasing amount of attention in the past few years, place the importance of confidentiality on protecting personal information maintained in automated systems by both government agencies and private-sector organizations.

5

Confidentiality must be well defined, and procedures for maintaining confidentiality must be carefully implemented, especially for standalone computers. A crucial aspect of confidentiality is user identification and authentication. Positive identification of each system user is essential to ensuring the effectiveness of policies that specify who is allowed access to which data items.

Threats to Confidentiality

Confidentiality can be compromised in several ways. The following are some of the most commonly encountered threats to information confidentiality:

- Hackers.
- Masqueraders.
- Unauthorized user activity.
- Unprotected downloaded files.
- Local area networks (LANs).
- Trojan horses.

Hackers. A hacker is someone who bypasses the system's access controls by taking advantage of security weaknesses that the systems developers have left in the system. In addition, many hackers are adept at discovering the passwords of authorized users who fail to choose passwords that are difficult to guess or not included in the dictionary. The activities of hackers represent serious threats to the confidentiality of information in computer systems. Many hackers have created copies of inadequately protected files and placed them in areas of the system where they can be accessed by unauthorized persons.

Masqueraders. A masquerader is an authorized user of the system who has obtained the password of another user and thus gains access to files available to the other user. Masqueraders are often able to read and copy confidential files. Masquerading is a common occurrence in companies that allow users to share passwords.

Unauthorized User Activity. This type of activity occurs when authorized system users gain access to files that they are not authorized to access. Weak access controls often enable unauthorized access, which can compromise confidential files.

Unprotected Downloaded Files. Downloading can compromise confidential information if, in the process, files are moved from the secure environment of a host computer to an unprotected microcomputer for local processing. While on the microcomputer, unattended confidential information could be accessed by authorized users.

Local Area Networks. LANs present a special confidentiality threat because data flowing through a LAN can be viewed at any node of the network, whether or not the data is addressed to that node. This is particularly significant because the unencrypted user IDs and secret passwords of users logging on to the host are subject to compromise as this data travels from the user's node through the LAN to the host. Any confidential information not intended for viewing at every node should be protected by encryption.

Trojan Horses. Trojan horses can be programmed to copy confidential files to unprotected areas of the system when they are unknowingly executed by users who have authorized access to those files. Once executed, the Trojan horse becomes resident on the user's system and can routinely copy confidential files to unprotected resources.

Confidentiality Models

Confidentiality models are used to describe what actions must be taken to ensure the confidentiality of information. These models can specify how security tools are used to achieve the desired level of confidentiality.

The most commonly used model for describing the enforcement of confidentiality is the Bell-LaPadula model. It defines the relationships between objects (i.e., the files, records, programs, and equipment that contain or receive information) and subjects (i.e., the persons, processes, or devices that cause information to flow between the objects). The relationships are described in terms of the subject's assigned level of access or privilege and the object's level of sensitivity. In military terms, these would be described as the security clearance of the subject and the security classification of the object.

Subjects access objects to read, write, or read and write information. The Bell-LaPadula model enforces the lattice principle, which specifies that subjects are allowed write access to objects at the same or higher level as the subject, read access to objects at the same or lower level, and read/write access to only those objects at the same level as the subject. This prevents the ability to write higher-classified information into a lower-classified file or to disclose higher-classified information to a lower-classified individual. Because an object's level indicates the security level of the data it contains, all the data within a single object must be at the same level. This type of model is called a flow model, because it ensures that information at a given security level flows only to an equal or higher level.

Another type of model that is commonly used is the access control model, which organizes a system into objects (i.e., resources being acted on), subjects (i.e., the persons or programs doing the action), and operations (i.e., the process of the interaction). A set of rules specifies which operations can be performed on an object by which subjects. This type of model has the additional benefit of ensuring the integrity of information as well as the confidentiality; the flow model supports only confidentiality.

7

Implementing Confidentiality Models

The trusted system criteria provide the best guidelines for implementing confidentiality models. These criteria were developed by the National Computer Security Center and are published in the *Department of Defense Trusted Computer System Evaluation Criteria* (commonly referred to as the Orange Book), which discusses information confidentiality in considerable detail. In addition, the National Computer Security Center has developed a Trusted Network Interpretation that applies the Orange Book criteria to networks; the network interpretation is described in the *Trusted Network Interpretation of the Trusted Computer System Evaluation Criteria* (commonly referred to as the Red Book),

INTEGRITY

Integrity is the protection of system data from intentional or accidental unauthorized changes. The challenge of the security program is to ensure that data is maintained in the state that users expect. Although the security program cannot improve the accuracy of data that is put into the system by users, it can help ensure that any changes are intended and correctly applied.

An additional element of integrity is the need to protect the process or program used to manipulate the data from unauthorized modification. A critical requirement of both commercial and government data processing is to ensure the integrity of data to prevent fraud and errors. It is imperative, therefore, that no user be able to modify data in a way that might corrupt or lose assets or financial records or render decision-making information unreliable. Examples of government systems in which integrity is crucial include air traffic control systems, military fire control systems (which control the firing of automated weapons), and Social Security and welfare systems. Examples of commercial systems that require a high level of integrity include medical prescription systems, credit reporting systems, production control systems, and payroll systems.

As with the confidentiality policy, identification and authentication of users are key elements of the information integrity policy. Integrity depends on access controls; therefore, it is necessary to positively and uniquely identify all persons who attempt access.

Protecting Against Threats to Integrity

Like confidentiality, integrity can be compromised by hackers, masqueraders, unauthorized user activity, unprotected downloaded files, LANs, and unauthorized programs (e.g., Trojan horses and viruses), because each of these threats can lead to unauthorized changes to data or programs. For example, authorized users can corrupt data and programs accidentally or intentionally if their activities on the system are not properly controlled.

Three basic principles are used to establish integrity controls: granting access on a need-to-know basis, separation of duties, and rotation of duties. These principles are discussed in the following sections.

Need-to-Know Access. Users should be granted access only to those files and programs that they need in order to perform their assigned job functions. User access to production data or source code should be further restricted through use of well-formed transactions, which ensure that users can change data only in controlled ways that maintain the integrity of data. A common element of well-formed transactions is the recording of data modifications in a log that can be reviewed later to ensure that only authorized and correct changes were made. To be effective, well-formed transactions must ensure that data can be manipulated only by a specific set of programs. These programs must be inspected for proper construction, installation, and controls to prevent unauthorized modification.

Because users must be able to work efficiently, access privileges should be judiciously granted to allow sufficient operational flexibility; need-to-know access should enable maximum control with minimum restrictions on users. The security program must employ a careful balance between ideal security and practical productivity.

Separation of Duties. To ensure that no single employee has control of a transaction from beginning to end, two or more people should be responsible for performing it—for example, anyone allowed to create or certify a well-formed transaction should not be allowed to execute it. Thus, a transaction cannot be manipulated for personal gain unless all persons responsible for it participate.

Rotation of Duties. Job assignments should be changed periodically so that it is more difficult for users to collaborate to exercise complete control of a transaction and subvert it for fraudulent purposes. This principle is effective when used in conjunction with separation of duties. Problems in effectively rotating duties usually appear in organizations with limited staff resources and inadequate training programs.

Integrity Models

Integrity models are used to describe what needs to be done to enforce the information integrity policy. There are three goals of integrity, which the models address in various ways. The goals are:

- Preventing unauthorized users from making modifications to data or programs.
- Preventing authorized users from making improper or unauthorized modifications.
- Maintaining internal and external consistency of data and programs.

The first step in creating an integrity model for a system is to identify and label those data items for which integrity must be ensured. Two procedures are then applied to these data items. The first procedure verifies that the data items are in a valid state (i.e., they are what the users or owners believe them to be because they have not been changed). The second procedure is the transformation procedure or well-formed transaction, which changes the data items from one valid state to another. If only a transformation procedure is able to change data items, the integrity of the data is maintained. Integrity enforcement systems usually require that all transformation procedures be logged, to provide an audit trail of data item changes.

Another aspect of preserving integrity relates to the system itself rather than only the data items in the system. The system must perform consistently and reliably—that is, it must always do what the users or owners expect it to do.

National Computer Security Center Report 79-91, "Integrity in Automated Information Systems" (September 1991), discusses several integrity models. Included are five models that suggest different approaches to achieving integrity: Biba, Goguen-Meseguer, Sutherland, Clark-Wilson, and Brewer-Nash. The following sections discuss these five models.

The Biba Model. The first model to address integrity in computer systems was based on a hierarchical lattice of integrity levels defined by Biba in 1977. The Biba integrity model is similar to the Bell-LaPadula model for confidentiality in that it uses subjects and objects; in addition, it controls object modification in the same way that Bell-LaPadula controls disclosure.

Biba's integrity policy consists of three parts. The first part specifies that a subject cannot execute objects that have a lower level of integrity than the subject. The second part specifies that a subject cannot modify objects that have a higher level of integrity. The third part specifies that a subject may not request service from subjects that have a higher integrity level.

The Goguen-Meseguer Model. The Goguen-Meseguer model, published in 1982, is based on the mathematical principle governing automatons (i.e., a control mechanism designed to automatically follow a predetermined sequence of operations or respond to encoded instructions) and includes domain separation. In this context, a domain is the list of objects that a user can access; users can be grouped according to their defined domains. Separating users into different domains ensures that users cannot interfere with each other's activities. All the information about which activities users are allowed to perform is included in a capabilities table.

In addition, the system contains information not related to permissions (e.g., user programs, data, and messages). The combination of all this information is called the state of the system. The automaton theory used as a basis for this model predefines all of the states and transitions between states, which prevents unauthorized users from making modifications to data or programs.

The Sutherland Model. The Sutherland model, published in 1986, approaches integrity by focusing on the problem of inference (i.e., the use of covert channels to influence the results of a process). This model is based on a state machine and consists of a set of states, a set of possible initial states, and a transformation function that maps states from the initial state to the current state.

Although the Sutherland model does not directly invoke a protection mechanism, it contains access restrictions related to subjects and information flow restrictions between objects. Therefore, it prevents unauthorized users from modifying data or programs.

The Clark-Wilson Model. The Clark-Wilson model, published in 1987 and updated in 1989, involves two primary elements for achieving data integrity: the well-formed transaction and separation of duties. Well-formed transactions, as previously mentioned, prevent users from manipulating data, thus ensuring the internal consistency of data. Separation of duties prevents authorized users from making improper modifications, thus preserving the external consistency of data by ensuring that data in the system reflects the real-world data it represents.

The Clark-Wilson model differs from the other models that are subject and object oriented by introducing a third access element—programs—resulting in what is called an access triple, which prevents unauthorized users from modifying data or programs. In addition, this model uses integrity verification and transformation procedures to maintain internal and external consistency of data. The verification procedures confirm that the data conforms to the integrity specifications at the time the verification is performed. The transformation procedures are designed to take the system from one valid state to the next. The Clark-Wilson model is believed to address all three goals of integrity.

The Brewer-Nash Model. The Brewer-Nash model, published in 1989, uses basic mathematical theory to implement dynamically changing access authorizations. This model can provide integrity in an integrated data base. In addition, it can provide confidentiality of information if the integrated data base is shared by competing companies; subjects can access only those objects that do not conflict with standards of fair competition.

Implementation involves grouping data sets into discrete classes, each class representing a different conflict of interest (e.g., classified information about a company is not made available to a competitor). Assuming that a subject initially accesses a data set in each of the classes, the subject would be prevented from accessing any other data set in each class. This isolation of data sets within a class provides the capability to keep one company's data separate from a competitor's in an integrated data base, thus preventing authorized users from making improper modifications to data outside their purview.

Implementing Integrity Models

The integrity models may be implemented in various ways to provide the integrity protection specified in the security policy. National Computer Security Center Report 79-91 discusses several implementations, including those by Lipner, Boebert and Kain, Lee and Shockley, Karger, Jueneman, and Gong. These six implementations are discussed in the following sections.

The Lipner Implementation. The Lipner implementation, published in 1982, describes two ways of implementing integrity. One uses the Bell-LaPadula confidentiality model, and the other uses both the Bell-LaPadula model and the Biba integrity model. Both methods assign security levels and functional categories to subjects and objects. For subjects, this translates into a person's clearance level and job function (e.g., user, operator, applications programmer, or systems programmer). For objects, the sensitivity of the data or program and its functions (e.g., test data, production data, application program, or system program) are defined.

Lipner's first method, using only the Bell-LaPadula model, assigns subjects to one of two sensitivity levels—system manager and anyone else—and to one of four job categories. Objects (i.e., file types) are assigned specific levels and categories. Most of the subjects and objects are assigned the same level; therefore, categories become the most significant integrity (i.e., access control) mechanism. The applications programmers, systems programmers, and users are confined to their own domains according to their assigned categories, thus preventing unauthorized users from modifying data.

Lipner's second method combines Biba's integrity model with the Bell-LaPadula basic security implementation. This combination of models helps prevent contamination of high-integrity data by low-integrity data or programs. The assignment of levels and categories to subjects and objects remains the same as for Lipner's first method. Integrity levels are used to avoid the unauthorized modification of system programs; integrity categories are used to separate domains that are based on functional areas (e.g., production or research and development). This method prevents unauthorized users from modifying data and prevents authorized users from making improper data modifications.

Lipner's methods were the first to separate objects into data and programs. The importance of this concept becomes clear when viewed in terms of implementing the Clark-Wilson integrity model: because programs allow users to manipulate data, it is necessary to control which programs a user may access and which objects a program can manipulate.

The Boebert and Kain Implementations. Boebert and Kain independently proposed (in 1985 and 1988, respectively) implementations of the Goguen-Meseguer integrity model. This implementation uses a subsystem that cannot be bypassed; the actions performed on this subsystem cannot be undone and must be correct. This type of subsystem is featured in the system's logical coprocessor kernel, which checks every access attempt to ensure that the access is consistent with the security policy being invoked.

Three security attributes are related to subjects and objects in this implementation. First, subjects and objects are assigned sensitivity levels. Second, subjects are identified according to the user in whose behalf the subject is acting, and objects are identified according to the list of users who can access the object and the access rights users can execute. Third, the domain (i.e., subsystem) that the program is a part of is defined for subjects, and the object type is defined according to the information contained within the object.

When the system must determine the kind of access a subject is allowed, all three of these security attributes are used. Sensitivity levels of subjects and objects are compared to enforce the mandatory access control policy. To enforce discretionary access control, the access control lists are checked. Finally, access rights are determined by comparing the subject domain with the object type.

By isolating the action rather than the user, the Boebert and Kain implementation ensures that unauthorized users cannot modify data. The use of domains requires that actions be performed in only one location and in only one way; a user who cannot access the domain cannot perform the action.

The Lee and Shockley Implementations. In 1988, Lee and Shockley independently developed implementations of the Clark-Wilson integrity model using Biba's integrity categories and trusted subjects. Both of these implementations were based on sensitivity levels constructed from independent elements. Each level represents a sensitivity to disclosure and a sensitivity to modification.

Data is manipulated by certified transactions, which are trusted subjects. The trusted subject can transform data from a specific input type to a specific output type. The Biba lattice philosophy is implemented so that a subject may not read above its level in disclosure or below its level in integrity. Every subject and object has both disclosure and integrity levels for use in this implementation. The Lee and Shockley implementations prevent unauthorized users from modifying data.

The Karger Implementation. In 1988, Karger proposed another implementation of the Clark-Wilson integrity model, augmenting it with his secure capabilities architecture (developed in 1984) and a generic lattice security model. In this implementation, audit trails play a much more prominent part in the enforcement of security than in other implementations. The capabilities architecture combined with access control lists that represent the security lattice provide for improved flexibility in implementing integrity.

In addition, the Karger implementation requires that the access control lists contain the specifics of the Clark-Wilson triples (i.e., the names of the subjects and objects the user is requesting access to and the names of the programs that provide the access), thereby enabling implementation of static separation of duties. Static separation of duties prevents unauthorized users from modifying data and prevents authorized users from making improper modifications.

The part of Karger's implementation that uses capabilities with access control lists limits actions to particular domains. The complex access control lists not only contain the triples but specify the order in which the transactions must be executed. These lists are used with audit-based capabilities to enforce dynamic separation of duties.

The Karger implementation provides three levels of integrity protection. First, triples in the access control lists allow for basic integrity (i.e., static separation of duties). Second, the capabilities architecture can be used with access control lists to provide faster access and domain separation. Third, access control lists and the capabilities architecture support both dynamic separation of duties and well-formed transactions.

The Jueneman Implementation. In 1989, Jueneman proposed a defensive detection implementation for use on dynamic networks of interconnected trusted computers communicating through unsecured media. This implementation was based on mandatory and discretionary access controls, encryption, checksums, and digital signatures. It prevents unauthorized users from modifying data.

The control mechanisms in this implementation support the philosophy that the originator of an object is responsible for its confidentiality and that the recipient is responsible for its integrity in a network environment. The mandatory access controls prevent unauthorized modification within the trusted computers and detect modifications external to the trusted computers. The discretionary access controls prevent the modification, destruction, or renaming of an object by a user who qualifies under mandatory control but lacks the owner's permission to access the object. The encryption mechanism is used to avoid unauthorized disclosure of the object. Checksums verify that the communication received is the communication that was sent, and digital signatures are evidence of the source of the communication.

The Gong Implementation. The Gong implementation, developed in 1989, is an identity-based and capability-oriented security system for distributed systems in a network environment. Capabilities identify each object and specify the access rights (i.e., read, write, and update) to be allowed each subject that is authorized access. Access authorizations are provided in an access list.

The Gong implementation consists of subjects (i.e., users), objects, object servers, and a centralized access control server. The access control server contains the access control lists. The object server contains the capability controls for each object.

This implementation is very flexible because it is independent of the protection policy (i.e., the Bell-LaPadula disclosure lattice, the Biba integrity lattice, the Clark-Wilson access triples, or the Lee-Shockley nonhierarchical categories). The Gong implementation can be used to prevent unauthorized users from modifying data and to prevent authorized users from making unauthorized modifications.

AVAILABILITY

Availability is the assurance that a computer system is accessible by authorized users whenever needed. Two facets of availability are typically discussed:

- Denial of service.
- Loss of data processing capabilities as a result of natural disasters (e.g., fires, floods, storms, or earthquakes) or human actions (e.g., bombs or strikes).

Denial of service usually refers to actions that tie up computing services in a way that renders the system unusable by authorized users. For example, the Internet worm overloaded about 10% of the computer system on the network, causing them to be nonresponsive to the needs of users.

The loss of data processing capabilities as a result of natural disasters or human actions is perhaps more common. Such losses are countered by contingency planning, which helps minimize the time that a data processing capability remains unavailable. Contingency planning—which may involve business resumption planning, alternative-site processing, or simply disaster recovery planning—provides an alternative means of processing, thereby ensuring availability.

Physical, technical, and administrative issues are important aspects of security initiatives that address availability. The physical issues include access controls that prevent unauthorized persons from coming into contact with computing resources, various fire and water control mechanisms, hot and cold sites for use in alternative-site processing, and off-site backup storage facilities. The technical issues include fault-tolerance mechanisms (e.g., hardware redundancy, disk mirroring, and application checkpoint restart), electronic vaulting (i.e., automatic backup to a secure, off-site location), and access control software to prevent unauthorized users from disrupting services. The administrative issues include access control policies, operating procedures, contingency planning, and user training. Although not obviously an important initiative, adequate training of operators, programmers, and security personnel can help avoid many computing outages that result in the loss of availability. In addition, availability can be restricted if a security officer accidentally locks up an access control data base during routine maintenance, thus preventing authorized users access for an extended period of time.

Considerable effort is being devoted to addressing various aspects of availability. For example, significant research has focused on achieving more fault-tolerant computing. Another sign that availability is a primary concern is that increasing investments are being made in disaster recovery planning combined with alternative-site processing facilities. Investments in antiviral products are escalating as well; denial of service associated with computer viruses, Trojan horses, and logic bombs is one of today's major security problems.

Known threats to availability can be expected to continue. New threats may emerge as technology evolves, making it quicker and easier for users to share information resources with other users, often at remote locations.

SUMMARY

The three basic purposes of security management—integrity, confidentiality, and availability—are present in all systems. Whether a system emphasizes one or the other of these purposes depends on the functions performed by the applications. For example, air traffic control systems do not require a high level of information confidentiality; however, a high degree of integrity is crucial to avoid disastrous misguiding of aircraft, and availability is important to avoid disruption of air traffic services.

Automobile companies, on the other hand, often go to extreme lengths to protect the confidentiality of new designs, whereas integrity and availability are of lesser concern. Military weapons systems also must have a high level of confidentiality to avoid enemy compromise. In addition, they must provide high levels of integrity (to ensure reliability) and availability (to ensure that the system operates as expected when needed).

Historically, confidentiality has received the most attention, probably because of its importance in military and government applications. As a result, capabilities to provide confidentiality in computer systems are considerably more advanced than those providing integrity or availability. Significant research efforts have recently been focused on the integrity issue. Still, little attention has been paid to · availability, with the exception of building fault tolerance into vendor products and including hot and cold sites for backup processing in disaster recovery planning.

The combination of integrity, availability, and confidentiality in appropriate proportions to support the organization's goals can provide users with a trustworthy system—that is, users can trust it will consistently perform according to their expectations. Trustworthiness has a broader definition than security in that it combines security with safety and reliability as well as the protection of privacy (which is already considered to be a part of security). In addition, many of the mechanisms that provide security also make systems more trustworthy in general. These multipurpose safeguards should be exploited to the extent practicable.

A Framework for Information Security Management

ZELLA G. RUTHBERG

To achieve a satisfactory level of information systems security, organizations must formulate a comprehensive set of information system elements, which help determine the functional requirements of the system. A set of control elements for the system should be generated in parallel with these system elements. A framework can be used to help organize these two sets of elements, thereby facilitating development and management of the information system.

Because there is no universally accepted framework for information security management, this discussion draws on concepts found in both the security and audit communities. The framework discussed is based on:

- The functional control areas derived from the organization's mission needs, the needs of users, and applicable laws and regulations.
- Senior management's view of the potential security risks.
- A control policy made up of control objectives and control standards.
- Implementation of the most cost-effective controls.
- Testing of the controls.

Organizations should adapt this framework to their own particular needs.

THE INFORMATION SYSTEMS FRAMEWORK

Every organization, whether public or private, has a basic set of information system elements. These elements consist of the organization's mission functions, the needs of the system users, applicable laws and regulations, and senior management's view of the organization's mission and assets. The organization uses these elements to develop a set of information system functions, an information system policy, and the functional requirements, implementation, and testing activities needed to develop the information system. The information framework presented in Exhibit I-1-1 helps clarify the relationship of these elements.

EXHIBIT I-1-1   Framework of Information System Elements

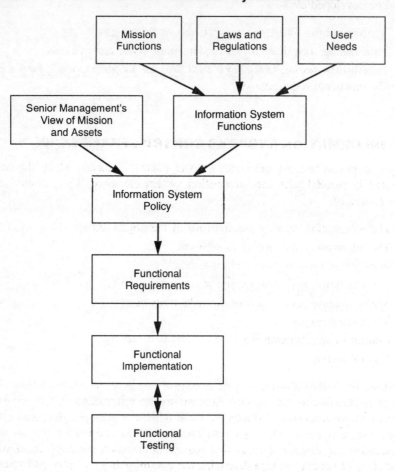

As shown in this exhibit, the organization's mission (e.g., banking, credit, or health services), applicable laws and regulations, and the needs of users (e.g., confidentiality, integrity, and availability) determine the information system functions, which are unique to each organization. The information system policy is an explicit statement of these functions, as affected by management's view of the organization's mission and assets. This policy describes the general rules of behavior that are expected of the information system. Unfortunately, many organizations do not write down their information system policy; as a result, these important rules of behavior remain vague and the system developed often does not meet the organization's needs.

Once the information system policy has been written, the information system should be developed by:

1. Writing out the functional requirements of the system.
2. Establishing specifications for implementing those requirements.
3. Establishing testing procedures to verify that the developed system meets the functional requirements.

THE INFORMATION SYSTEMS CONTROL FRAMEWORK

Every system can be associated with a set of control elements. which should be generated in parallel with the information system elements. These control elements consist of:

- The information security requirements of the organization.
- The information security needs of users.
- Information security laws and regulations.
- The functional areas that require information security.
- Senior management's view of the risks to its assets.
- The control policy.
- Control implementation.
- Control testing.

Exhibit I-1-2 illustrates the way these control elements relate to each other. The parallel relationship of the control elements to the information system elements may be seen by comparing Exhibits I-1-1 and I-1-2. For example, the organization and user security needs, along with the applicable laws and regulations, are used to determine the functional areas that require information security. These functional areas of security in turn determine the control policy, as affected by senior management's view of the risks to its assets.

The following sections discuss the major control elements in more detail.

Functional Areas that Require Information Security

To establish the control policy in an organized and comprehensive way, the organization should classify all of its information system activities in terms of functional areas meaningful to its mode of operation. There are many methods for accomplishing this; the method chosen depends on the functional areas important to the organization. The most comprehensive approaches to this classification are: The organizational chart structure (i.e., vertical groupings), which is useful for broad classifications; and the transaction structure (i.e., horizontal groupings), which is

EXHIBIT I-1-2 Framework for Information System Controls

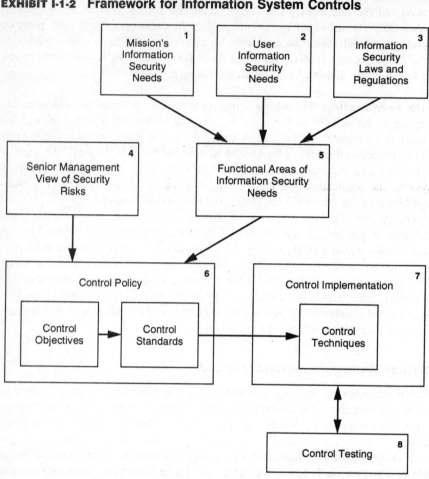

useful for systems and applications. The following sections discuss these two approaches in more detail. These approaches may be combined to tailor the information system to the particular needs of an organization.

The Organizational Chart Structure. In this approach, activities are classified along the vertical lines of authority within the organization; such classification can be derived from the company's organizational chart of staff and line departments. For example, at the staff level immediately below senior management, there might be internal audit, procurement, personnel, and security administration. At the line level, there might be several general divisions (e.g., operational ones for information systems project management, application program development and validation, and communications) and then an organizationwide set of data processing divisions (e.g., operations, data base administration, and system control). Exhibit I-1-3 illustrates this type of organization.

The Transaction Structure. In this approach, activities are classified according to the processing flows, which may cut across departmental lines of authority if a computer service or application is used by more than one department. For example, in the case of standalone systems within a department, the security concerns might include the data, the input procedures, the hardware, the operating system, the applications on the system, and the output procedures. The trustworthiness of the personnel involved would be another concern.

For systems that cut across more than one department, however, additional concerns might include the security of the local communications lines between departments within a single facility (i.e., the local area network) or the security of more distant facilities of the organization (i.e., the wide area network). For systems that communicate between organizations, on the other hand, the security of networks using either dedicated lines or public telephones (or both) could be added to the standalone system security concerns. Exhibit I-1-4 presents a transaction flowchart that illustrates these concerns.

Senior Management Involvement

Senior management must have a comprehensive view of the potential security risks to the organization. Senior managers can provide important input to development of a successful control policy, and their views must be taken into consideration.

If management does not consider security as important, other members of the organization are likely to feel the same way. Large losses may eventually occur as a result of security breaches. On the other hand, management may choose to undertake disaster recovery measures but consider a well-planned systems development methodology as unimportant; this approach typically results in security deficiencies in the information system, which could eventually cause irreparable losses.

The Control Policy

A successful control policy should consist of informal, easily understood descriptions of required system behavior for the set of systems found within the specific organization. The policy should be stated in terms of goals (i.e., the control objectives), their related standards (i.e., the control technique objectives), and the selected controls (i.e., the control techniques) used to carry out these objectives.

EXHIBIT I-1-3   Organizational Chart of Information System Activities

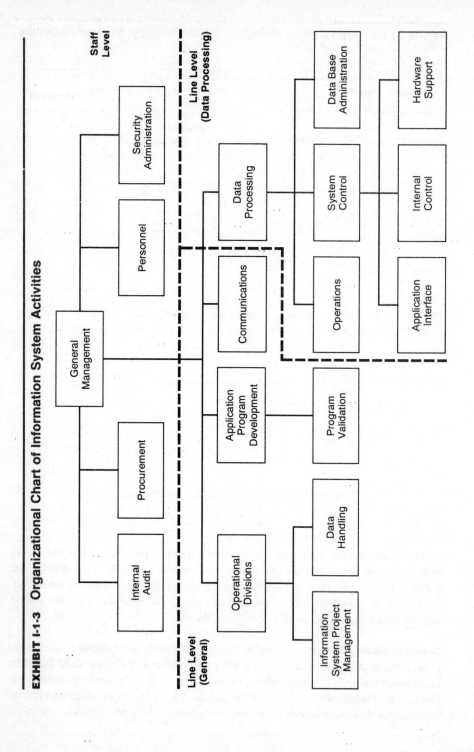

EXHIBIT I-1-4 Transaction Flowchart of Information System Activities

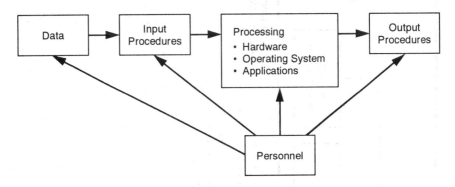

a. Standalone System Security Areas

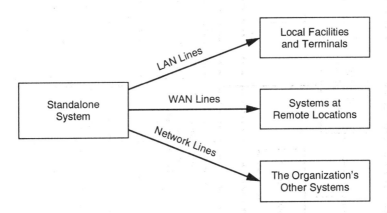

b. Adding Communications Security Concerns

The goals can be viewed as information security requirements at the policy level, whereas the standards are specific performance models for achieving the goals. For each goal there are usually several corresponding standards; some standards may be appropriate for more than one goal. The following sections discuss control policy goals and standards in more detail.

Control Policy Goals. It is useful to organize goals into organization-specific groupings. A comprehensive list of such goals can be found in the EDP Auditors Foundation document "Control Objectives—Controls in a Computer Environment: Objectives, Guidelines, and Audit Procedures" (April 1990). A modified table of contents for this document is presented in Exhibit I-1-5.

23

EXHIBIT I-1-5 Sample Control Objective Groupings

General and Application Controls

- Management controls
  —Planning for the information services department
  —Policies, standards, and procedures
  —Organizational responsibilities and personnel management
  —Information services department quality assurance
  —The organization's internal audit function
  —The organization's external requirements
- Information system life cycle controls (development, acquisition, and maintenance)
  —System life cycle methodology and responsibility
  —Project initiation
  —Feasibility study
  —Design phase
  —Programming, training, and implementation
  —Operations and maintenance
  —Postimplementation review
- Information system operational controls
  —Information services department resource planning and management
  —Computer operations
  —Operating system software
  —Logical and physical security
  —Contingency planning
- Application controls
  —Data origination controls
  —Data input controls
  —Data processing controls
  —Data output controls

Technology-Specific Controls

- Information system controls supported by the data base
- Distributed data processing and network operations controls
- Local area network controls
- Electronic data interchange controls
- Service bureau operations controls
- Microcomputer controls
- Expert system controls

One area of management controls, for example, focuses on the information services department. It discusses control objectives for such activities as long-range planning, short-range planning, and personnel. A control objective for personnel might be stated as, "Senior management should provide for a segregation of duties within the information services department, such as between systems development and operations, operations and data control, and data base administration and systems development." The objective would be to prevent employees from manipulating a system for fraudulent purposes.

Another important consideration in arriving at a comprehensive set of control objectives is to state the goals in terms of potential risks or exposures to be prevented. The advantage of this approach is that a menu of controls to prevent each exposure can then be drawn up and a direct correlation made between the controls and the risks they prevent or reduce. The following are business exposures that most organizations need to prevent:

- Erroneous recordkeeping.
- Unacceptable accounting.
- Business interruption.
- Erroneous management decisions.
- Fraud.
- Statutory sanctions.
- Excessive costs or deficient revenues.
- Loss or destruction of assets.
- Loss of competitive advantage.

These business exposures are then correlated to the functional areas of concern: applications, systems development, information processing, and communications.

Control Policy Standards. The organization develops its control standards from the control objectives. For example, one control objective might be to ensure the accuracy of data processed by the computer. Two control standards for achieving this goal might be stated as:

- Procedures should ensure that data is transmitted accurately to the computer center.
- Procedures should ensure that only valid files are used.

It is a major effort to write control standards that are explicit and comprehensive. This effort is well worth the organization's time, however, because the standards can provide the criteria against which to measure security performance. The control standards that an organization generates typically are a mixture of universal standards and those specific to the organization's activities.

Use of a systems development methodology is a standard that is crucial for the development of successful information systems. Such a methodology organizes systems development activities to guarantee that the resulting information system meets the requirements. Adequate documentation of the development process is another important standard. The more thorough the documentation of the information system elements, the more likely that the system will enjoy long-term success.

An interesting example of system security standards can be found in a 1985 US State Department document entitled "Security Standards for Unclassified Automated Information Systems in the United States." The functional areas addressed in this document are:

- Management responsibilities.
- Physical security.
- Personnel security.
- Administrative security.
- Technical and software security.
- Standalone microcomputers.
- Processing of official information that is targeted at a restricted audience.

Control standards are explicitly stated for most of these functional areas. Under personnel security, however, explicit standards are not provided; instead, a set of functional areas pertinent to the organization is defined, and performance standards for each of these areas are delineated.

Baselines for Control. Currently, no set of control objectives or standards is universally accepted as a baseline for control of information systems. On the basis of his research in this area, Donn Parker has subdivided objectives into baselines for information systems used by different types of industries. In addition, an informal survey, conducted for the committee that developed the 1991 National Research Council report entitled "Computers at Risk—Safe Computing in the Information Age" (National Academy Press), indicated that most corporate system managers and security officers want the ability to:

- Identify users.
- Limit times and places of access (particularly over networks).
- Watch for intrusions by recording attempts at invalid actions.
- Check for viruses on an ad hoc basis.

"Computers at Risk" addresses a closely related topic: the need for generally accepted system security principles. The report contains a set of elements that could be included in such principles. The elements listed include quality control, access control on code as well as data, user identification and authentication, security administration, data encryption, and independent audit capabilities. Much work is still needed, however, to develop a comprehensive set of generally accepted system security principles and then translate them into control objectives and standards.

Control Implementation

The security controls should be implemented during the systems development process or during operations. Controls should be selected on the basis of the control standards specified by the organization. If no such standards have been developed, the controls should be correlated with the organization's general control objectives.

Usually, several possible controls exist for satisfying the control standards or objectives. The controls should be selected on the basis of whether they are the most cost-effective—that is, the cost to implement them should be less than the estimated loss that could result without them. Senior management must determine the acceptable level of risk, on the basis of an overall consideration of the mission and budget. There are many ways of classifying controls, as discussed in Chapter I-1-3, "Types of Information Security Controls."

Testing the Controls

Controls should be tested periodically throughout the systems development process and as part of system operations. During the latter part of the systems development process, the system should be tested to determine whether it meets its functional and control requirements. A test plan of system controls should be developed and carried out, and alterations in faulty system controls should be implemented when necessary.

The functional requirements may change after the system is implemented, thereby changing the control requirements. Consequently, functional and control performance should be checked periodically during operations.

SUMMARY

A framework for information security management helps the organization articulate its information systems security requirements, identify the corresponding security controls, and arrange these controls in a structure that enhances systems management. To achieve such a control framework, the following two major steps should be taken in developing and operating the information systems:

1. Describe the information systems elements, including:
   —The mission statement.
   —Applicable laws and regulations.
   —User needs.
   —Senior management's view of the mission statements and assets.
   —Information systems functions.
   —The information systems policy.
   —The functional requirements.
   —Implementation of the functions.
   —Testing of the functions.
2. Describe the corresponding control elements, including:
   —The information security needs of the mission.
   —The information security needs of the users.
   —Information security laws and regulations.

—The functional areas that require information security.
—Senior management's view of the risks.
—The control policy.
—Implementation of the controls.
—Testing of the controls.

The information systems elements should be placed in a framework such as the one in Exhibit I-1-1; the corresponding control elements should be placed in a framework such as the one in Exhibit I-1-2. By establishing a controlled framework, management can better identify the control activities needed to secure the information system.

Types of Information Security Controls

HAL TIPTON

Security is generally defined as the freedom from danger or as the condition of safety. Computer security, specifically, is the protection of data in a system against unauthorized disclosure, modification, or destruction and protection of the computer system itself against unauthorized use, modification, or denial of service. Because certain computer security controls inhibit productivity, security is typically a compromise toward which security practitioners, system users, and system operations and administrative personnel work to achieve a satisfactory balance between security and productivity.

Controls for providing information security can be physical, technical, or administrative. These three categories of controls can be further classified as either preventive or detective. Preventive controls attempt to avoid the occurrence of unwanted events, whereas detective controls attempt to identify unwanted events after they have occurred. Preventive controls inhibit the free use of computing resources and therefore can be applied only to the degree that the users are willing to accept. Effective security awareness programs can help increase users' level of tolerance for preventive controls by helping them understand how such controls enable them to trust their computing systems. Common detective controls include audit trails, intrusion detection methods, and checksums.

Three other types of controls supplement preventive and detective controls. They are usually described as deterrent, corrective, and recovery. Deterrent controls are intended to discourage individuals from intentionally violating information security policies or procedures. These usually take the form of constraints that make it difficult or undesirable to perform unauthorized activities or threats of consequences that influence a potential intruder to not violate security (e.g., threats ranging from embarrassment to severe punishment).

Corrective controls either remedy the circumstances that allowed the unauthorized activity or return conditions to what they were before the violation. Execution of corrective controls could result in changes to existing physical, technical, and administrative controls. Recovery controls restore lost computing resources or capabilities and help the organization recover monetary losses caused by a security violation.

Deterrent, corrective, and recovery controls are considered to be special cases within the major categories of physical, technical, and administrative controls; they do not clearly belong in either preventive or detective categories. For example, it could be argued that deterrence is a form of prevention because it can cause an intruder to turn away; however, deterrence also involves detecting violations, which may be what the intruder fears most. Corrective controls, on the other hand, are not preventive or detective, but they are clearly linked with technical controls when antiviral software eradicates a virus or with administrative controls when backup procedures enable restoring a damaged data base. Finally, recovery controls are neither preventive nor detective but are included in administrative controls as disaster recovery or contingency plans.

Because of these overlaps with physical, technical, and administrative controls, the deterrent, corrective, and recovery controls are not discussed further in this chapter. Instead, the preventive and detective controls within the three major categories are examined.

PHYSICAL CONTROLS

Physical security is the use of locks, security guards, badges, alarms, and similar measures to control access to computers, related equipment (including utilities), and the processing facility itself. In addition, measures are required for protecting computers, related equipment, and their contents from espionage, theft, and destruction or damage by accident, fire, or natural disaster (e.g., floods and earthquakes).

Preventive Physical Controls

Preventive physical controls are employed to prevent unauthorized personnel from entering computing facilities (i.e., locations housing computing resources, supporting utilities, computer hard copy, and input data media) and to help protect against natural disasters. Examples of these controls include:

- Backup files and documentation.
- Fences.
- Security guards.
- Badge systems.
- Double door systems.
- Locks and keys.
- Backup power.
- Biometric access controls.
- Site selection.
- Fire extinguishers.

These are discussed in the following sections.

Backup Files and Documentation. Should an accident or intruder destroy active data files or documentation, it is essential that backup copies be readily available. Backup files should be stored far enough away from the active data or documentation to avoid destruction by the same incident that destroyed the original. Backup material should be stored in a secure location constructed of noncombustible materials, including two-hour-rated fire walls. Backups of sensitive information should have the same level of protection as the active files of this information; it is senseless to provide tight security for data on the system but lax security for the same data in a backup location.

Fences. Although fences around the perimeter of the building do not provide much protection against a determined intruder, they do establish a formal no-trespassing line and can dissuade the simply curious person. Fences should have alarms or should be under continuous surveillance by guards, dogs, or TV monitors.

Security Guards. Security guards are often stationed at the entrances of facilities to intercept intruders and ensure that only authorized persons are allowed to enter. Guards are effective in inspecting packages or other hand-carried items to ensure that only authorized, properly described articles are taken into or out of the facility. The effectiveness of stationary guards can be greatly enhanced if the building is wired with appropriate electronic detectors with alarms or other warning indicators terminating at the guard station. In addition, guards are often used to patrol unattended spaces inside buildings after normal working hours to deter intruders from obtaining or profiting from unauthorized access.

Badge Systems. Physical access to computing areas can be effectively controlled using a badge system. With this method of control, employees and visitors must wear appropriate badges whenever they are in access-controlled areas. Badge-reading systems programmed to allow entrance only to authorized persons can then easily identify intruders.

Double Door Systems. Double door systems can be used at entrances to restricted areas (e.g., computing facilities) to force people to identify themselves to the guard before they can be released into the secured area. Double doors are an excellent way to prevent intruders from following closely behind authorized persons and slipping into restricted areas.

Locks and Keys. Locks and keys are commonly used for controlling access to restricted areas. Because it is difficult to control copying of keys, many installations use cipher locks (i.e., combination locks containing buttons that open the lock when pushed in the proper sequence). With cipher locks, care must be taken to conceal which buttons are being pushed to avoid a compromise of the combination.

Backup Power. Backup power is necessary to ensure that computer services are in a constant state of readiness and to help avoid damage to equipment if normal power is lost. For short periods of power loss, backup power is usually provided by batteries. In areas susceptible to outages of more than 15 to 30 minutes, diesel generators are usually recommended.

Biometric Access Controls. Biometric identification is a more sophisticated method of controlling access to computing facilities than badge readers, but the two methods operate in much the same way. Biometrics used for identification include fingerprints, handprints, voice patterns, signature samples, and retinal scans. Because biometrics cannot be lost, stolen, or shared, they provide a higher level of security than badges. Biometric identification is recommended for high-security, low-traffic entrance control.

Site Selection. The site for the building that houses the computing facilities should be carefully chosen to avoid obvious risks. For example, wooded areas can pose a fire hazard, areas on or adjacent to an earthquake fault can be dangerous, and sites located in a flood plain are susceptible to water damage. In addition, locations under an aircraft approach or departure route are risky, and locations adjacent to railroad tracks can be susceptible to vibrations that can precipitate equipment problems.

Fire Extinguishers. The control of fire is important to prevent an emergency from turning into a disaster that seriously interrupts data processing. Computing facilities should be located far from potential fire sources (e.g., kitchens or cafeterias) and should be constructed of noncombustible materials. Furnishings should also be noncombustible. It is important that appropriate types of fire extinguishers be conveniently located for easy access. Employees must be trained in the proper use of fire extinguishers and in the procedures to follow should a fire break out.

Automatic sprinklers are essential in computer rooms and surrounding spaces and when expensive equipment is located on raised floors. Sprinklers are usually specified by insurance companies for the protection of any computer room that contains combustible materials. However, the risk of water damage to computing equipment is often greater than the risk of fire damage. Therefore, carbon dioxide extinguishing systems were developed; these systems flood an area threatened by fire with carbon dioxide, which suppresses fire by removing oxygen from the air. Although carbon dioxide does not cause water damage, it is potentially lethal to people in the area and is now used only in unattended areas.

Current extinguishing systems flood the area with Halon, which is usually harmless to equipment and less dangerous to personnel than carbon dioxide. At a concentration of about 10%, Halon extinguishes fire and can be safely breathed by humans. However, higher concentrations can eventually be a health hazard. In addition, the blast from releasing Halon under pressure can blow loose objects around and can be a danger to equipment and personnel. For these reasons and because of the high cost of Halon, it is typically used only under raised floors in computer rooms. Because it contains chlorofluorocarbons, it will be soon phased out in favor of a gas that is less hazardous to the environment.

Detective Physical Controls

Detective physical controls warn protective services personnel that physical security measures are being violated. Examples of these controls include:

- Motion detectors.
- Smoke and fire detectors.
- Closed-circuit television monitors.
- Sensors and alarms.

Motion Detectors. In computing facilities that usually do not have people in them, motion detectors are useful for calling attention to potential intrusions. Motion detectors must be constantly monitored by guards.

Fire and Smoke Detectors. Fire and smoke detectors should be strategically located to provide early warning of a fire. All fire detection equipment should be tested periodically to ensure that it is in working condition.

Closed-Circuit Television Monitors. Closed-circuit televisions can be used to monitor the activities in computing areas where users or operators are frequently absent. This method helps detect individuals behaving suspiciously.

Sensors and Alarms. Sensors and alarms monitor the environment surrounding the equipment to ensure that air and cooling water temperatures remain within the levels specified by equipment design. If proper conditions are not maintained, the alarms summon operations and maintenance personnel to correct the situation before a business interruption occurs.

TECHNICAL CONTROLS

Technical security involves the use of safeguards incorporated in computer hardware, operations or applications software, communications hardware and software, and related devices. Technical controls are sometimes referred to as logical controls.

Preventive Technical Controls

Preventive technical controls are used to prevent unauthorized personnel or programs from gaining remote access to computing resources. Examples of these controls include:

- Access control software.
- Antivirus software.
- Library control systems.
- Passwords.
- Smart cards.
- Encryption.
- Dial-up access control and callback systems.

The following sections discuss these controls.

Access Control Software. The purpose of access control software is to control sharing of data and programs between users. In many computer systems, access to data and programs is implemented by access control lists that designate which users are allowed access. Access control software provides the ability to control access to the system by establishing that only registered users with an authorized log-on ID and password can gain access to the computer system.

After access to the system has been granted, the next step is to control access to the data and programs residing in the system. The data or program owner can establish rules that designate who is authorized to use the data or program.

Antivirus Software. Viruses have reached epidemic proportions throughout the microcomputing world and can cause processing disruptions and loss of data as well as a significant loss of productivity while cleanup is conducted. In addition, new viruses are emerging at an ever-increasing rate—currently about one every 48 hours. It is recommended that antivirus software be installed on all microcomputers to detect, identify, isolate, and eradicate viruses. This software must be updated frequently to help fight new viruses. In addition, to help ensure that viruses are intercepted as early as possible, antivirus software should be kept active on a system, not used intermittently at the discretion of users.

Library Control Systems. These systems require that all changes to production programs be implemented by library control personnel instead of the programmers who created the changes. This practice ensures separation of duties, which helps prevent unauthorized changes to production programs.

Passwords. Passwords are used to verify that the user of an ID is the owner of the ID. The ID-password combination is unique to each user and therefore provides a means of holding users accountable for their activity on the system.

Fixed passwords that are used for a defined period of time are often easy for hackers to compromise; therefore, great care must be exercised to ensure that these passwords do not appear in any dictionary. Fixed passwords are often used to control access to specific data bases. In this use, however, all persons who have authorized access to the data base use the same password; therefore, no accountability can be achieved.

Currently, dynamic or one-time passwords, which are different for each log-on, are preferred over fixed passwords. Dynamic passwords are created by a token that is programmed to generate passwords randomly.

Smart Cards. Smart cards are usually about the size of a credit card and contain a chip with logic functions and information that can be read at a remote terminal to identify a specific user's privileges. Smart cards now carry prerecorded, usually encrypted access control information that is compared with data that the user provides (e.g., a personal ID number or biometric data) to verify authorization to access the computer or network.

Encryption. Encryption is defined as the transformation of plaintext (i.e., readable data) into ciphertext (i.e., unreadable data) by cryptographic techniques. Encryption is currently considered to be the only sure way of protecting data from disclosure during network transmissions.

Encryption can be implemented with either hardware or software. Software-based encryption is the least expensive method and is suitable for applications involving low-volume transmissions; the use of software for large volumes of data results in an unacceptable increase in processing costs. Because there is no overhead associated with hardware encryption, this method is preferred when large volumes of data are involved.

Dial-Up Access Control and Callback Systems. Dial-up access to a computer system increases the risk of intrusion by hackers. In networks that contain personal computers or are connected to other networks, it is difficult to determine whether dial-up access is available or not, because of the ease with which a modem can be added to a personal computer to turn it into a dial-up access point. Known dial-up access points should be controlled so that only authorized dial-up users can get through.

Currently, the best dial-up access controls use a microcomputer to intercept calls, verify the identity of the caller (using a dynamic password mechanism), and switch the user to authorized computing resources as requested. Previously, callback systems intercepted dial-up callers, verified their authorization, and called them back at their registered number, which at first proved effective; however, sophisticated hackers have learned how to defeat this control using call-forwarding techniques.

Detective Technical Controls

Detective technical controls warn personnel of violations or attempted violations of preventive technical controls. Examples of these include audit trails and intrusion detection expert systems, which are discussed in the following sections.

Audit Trails. An audit trail is a record of system activities that enables the reconstruction and examination of the sequence of events of a transaction, from its inception to output of final results. Violation reports present significant, security-oriented events that may indicate either actual or attempted policy transgressions reflected in the audit trail. Violation reports should be frequently and regularly reviewed by security officers and data base owners to identify and investigate successful or unsuccessful unauthorized accesses.

Intrusion Detection Systems. These expert systems track users (on the basis of their personal profiles) while they are using the system to determine whether their current activities are consistent with an established norm. If not, the user's session can be terminated or a security officer can be called to investigate. Intrusion detection can be especially effective in cases in which intruders are pretending to be authorized users or when authorized users are involved in unauthorized activities.

ADMINISTRATIVE CONTROLS

Administrative, or personnel, security consists of management constraints, operational procedures, accountability procedures, and supplemental administrative controls established to provide an acceptable level of protection for computing resources. In addition, administrative controls include procedures established to ensure that all personnel who have access to computing resources have the required authorizations and appropriate security clearances.

Preventive Administrative Controls

Preventive administrative controls are personnel-oriented techniques for controlling people's behavior to ensure the confidentiality, integrity, and availability of computing data and programs. Examples of preventive administrative controls include:

- Security awareness and technical training.
- Separation of duties.
- Procedures for recruiting and terminating employees.
- Security policies and procedures.
- Supervision.
- Disaster recovery, contingency, and emergency plans.
- User registration for computer access.

The following sections discuss these controls.

Security Awareness and Technical Training. Security awareness training is a preventive measure that helps users to understand the benefits of security practices. If employees do not understand the need for the controls being imposed, they may eventually circumvent them and thereby weaken the security program or render it ineffective.

Technical training can help users prevent the most common security problem—errors and omissions—as well as ensure that they understand how to make appropriate backup files and detect and control viruses. Technical training in the form of emergency and fire drills for operations personnel can ensure that proper action will be taken to prevent such events from escalating into disasters.

Separation of Duties. This administrative control separates a process into component parts, with different users responsible for different parts of the process. Judicious separation of duties prevents one individual from obtaining control of an entire process and forces collusion with others in order to manipulate the process for personal gain.

Recruitment and Termination Procedures. Appropriate recruitment procedures can prevent the hiring of people who are likely to violate security policies. A thorough background investigation should be conducted, including checking on the applicant's criminal history and references. Although this does not necessarily screen individuals for honesty and integrity, it can help identify areas that should be investigated further.

Three types of references should be obtained: employment, character, and credit. Employment references can help estimate an individual's competence to perform, or be trained to perform, the tasks required on the job. Character references can help determine such qualities as trustworthiness, reliability, and ability to get along with others. Credit references can indicate a person's financial habits, which in turn can be an indication of maturity and willingness to assume responsibility for one's own actions.

In addition, certain procedures should be followed when any employee leaves the company, regardless of the conditions of termination. Any employee being involuntarily terminated should be asked to leave the premises immediately upon notification, to prevent further access to computing resources. Voluntary terminations may be handled differently, depending on the judgment of the employee's supervisors, to enable the employee to complete work in process or train a replacement.

All authorizations that have been granted to an employee should be revoked upon departure. If the departing employee has the authority to grant authorizations to others, these other authorizations should also be reviewed. All keys, badges, and other devices used to gain access to premises, information, or equipment should be retrieved from the departing employee. The combinations of all locks known to a departing employee should be changed immediately. In addition, the employee's log-on IDs and passwords should be canceled, and the related active and backup files should be either deleted or reassigned to a replacement employee.

Any special conditions to the termination (e.g., denial of the right to use certain information) should be reviewed with the departing employee; in addition, a document stating these conditions should be signed by the employee. All terminations should be routed through the computer security representative for the facility where the terminated employee works to ensure that all information system access authority has been revoked.

Security Policies and Procedures. Appropriate policies and procedures are key to the establishment of an effective information security program. Policies and procedures should reflect the general policies of the organization as regards the protection of information and computing resources. Policies should cover the use of computing resources, marking of sensitive information, movement of computing resources outside the facility, introduction of personal computing equipment and media into the facility, disposal of sensitive waste, and computer and data security incident reporting. Enforcement of these policies is essential to their effectiveness.

Supervision. Often, an alert supervisor is the first person to notice a change in an employee's attitude. Early signs of job dissatisfaction or personal distress should prompt supervisors to consider subtly moving the employee out of a critical or sensitive position.

Supervisors must be thoroughly familiar with the policies and procedures related to the responsibilities of their department. Supervisors should require that their staff members comply with pertinent policies and procedures and should observe the effectiveness of these guidelines. If the objectives of the policies and procedures can be accomplished more effectively, the supervisor should recommend appropriate improvements. Job assignments should be reviewed regularly to ensure that an appropriate separation of duties is maintained, that employees in sensitive positions are occasionally removed from a complete processing cycle without prior announcement, and that critical or sensitive jobs are rotated periodically among qualified personnel.

Disaster Recovery, Contingency, and Emergency Plans. The disaster recovery plan is a document containing procedures for emergency response, extended backup operations, and recovery should a computer installation experience a partial or total loss of computing resources or physical facilities (or of access to such facilities). The primary objective of this plan, used in conjunction with the contingency plans, is to provide reasonable assurance that a computing installation can recover from disasters, continue to process critical applications in a degraded mode, and return to a normal mode of operation within a reasonable time. A key part of disaster recovery planning is to provide for processing at an alternative site during the time that the original facility is unavailable.

Contingency and emergency plans establish recovery procedures that address specific threats. These plans help prevent minor incidents from escalating into disasters. For example, a contingency plan might provide a set of procedures that defines the condition and response required to return a computing capability to nominal operation; an emergency plan might be a specific procedure for shutting down equipment in the event of a fire or for evacuating a facility in the event of an earthquake.

User Registration for Computer Access. Formal user registration ensures that all users are properly authorized for system and service access. In addition, it provides the opportunity to acquaint users with their responsibilities for the security of computing resources and to obtain their agreement to comply with related policies and procedures.

Detective Administrative Controls

Detective administrative controls are used to determine how well security policies and procedures are complied with, to detect fraud, and to avoid employing persons that represent an unacceptable security risk. This type of control includes:

- Security reviews and audits.
- Performance evaluations.
- Required vacations.
- Background investigations.
- Rotation of duties.

Security Reviews and Audits. Reviews and audits can identify instances in which policies and procedures are not being followed satisfactorily. Management involvement in correcting deficiencies can be a significant factor in obtaining user support for the computer security program.

Performance Evaluations. Regularly conducted performance evaluations are an important element in encouraging quality performance. In addition, they can be an effective forum for reinforcing management's support of information security principles.

Required Vacations. Tense employees are more likely to have accidents or make errors and omissions while performing their duties. Vacations contribute to the health of employees by relieving the tensions and anxieties that typically develop from long periods of work. In addition, if all employees in critical or sensitive positions are forced to take vacations, there will be less opportunity for an employee to set up a fraudulent scheme that depends on the employee's presence (e.g., to maintain the fraud's continuity or secrecy). Even if the employee's presence is not necessary to the scheme, required vacations can be a deterrent to embezzlement because the employee may fear discovery during his or her absence.

EXHIBIT I-1-6 Information Security Controls

PHYSICAL CONTROLS

Preventive
- Backup files and documentation
- Fences
- Security guards
- Badge systems
- Locks and keys
- Backup power
- Biometric access controls
- Site selection
- Fire extinguishers

Detective
- Motion detectors
- Smoke and fire detectors
- Closed-circuit television monitoring
- Sensors and alarms

TECHNICAL CONTROLS

Preventive
- Access control software
- Antivirus software
- Library control systems
- Passwords
- Smart cards
- Encryption
- Dial-up access control and callback systems

Detective
- Audit trails
- Intrusion-detection expert systems

ADMINISTRATIVE CONTROLS

Preventive
- Security awareness and technical training
- Separation of duties
- Procedures for recruiting and terminating employees
- Security policies and procedures
- Supervision
- Disaster recovery and contingency plans
- User registration for computer access

Detective
- Security reviews and audits
- Performance evaluations
- Required vacations
- Background investigations
- Rotation of duties

Background Investigations. Background investigations may disclose past performances that might indicate the potential risks of future performance. Background investigations should be conducted on all employees being considered for promotion or transfer into a position of trust; such investigations should be completed before the employee is actually placed in a sensitive position. Job applicants being considered for sensitive positions should also be investigated for potential problems. Companies involved in government-classified projects should conduct these investigations while obtaining the required security clearance for the employee.

Rotation of Duties. Like required vacations, rotation of duties (i.e., moving employees from one job to another at random intervals) helps deter fraud. An additional benefit is that as a result of rotating duties, employees are cross-trained to perform each other's functions in case of illness, vacation, or termination.

SUMMARY

Information security controls can be classified as physical, technical, or administrative. These are further divided into preventive and detective controls. Exhibit I-1-6 lists the controls discussed in this article.

The organization's security policy should be reviewed to determine the confidentiality, integrity, and availability needs of the organization. The appropriate physical, technical, and administrative controls can then be selected to provide the required level of information protection, as stated in the security policy.

A careful balance between preventive and detective control measures is needed to ensure that users consider the security controls reasonable and to ensure that the controls do not overly inhibit productivity. The combination of physical, technical, and administrative controls best suited for a specific computing environment can be identified by completing a quantitative risk analysis. Because this is usually an expensive, tedious, and subjective process, however, an alternative approach—referred to as meeting the standard of due care—is often used. Controls that meet a standard of due care are those that would be considered prudent by most organizations in similar circumstances or environments. Controls that meet the standard of due care generally are readily available for a reasonable cost and support the security policy of the organization; they include, at the least, controls that provide individual accountability, auditability, and separation of duties.

Computer Security and Human Values

PETER G. NEUMANN

Approaches to managing computer security require both technical and nontechnical solutions. Although the technical issues are generally complex, they are becoming better understood and better supported by newer computer systems. The nontechnical issues are exceedingly broad, involving social, economic, political, and other considerations.

Computer abuse is behavior that is different from what is desired or expected. Such behavior may be attributable to a combination of human, computer, and environmental problems—that is, not just system abuse by people but abuse of human rights through use of systems. There are three gaps that may permit computer abuse: a technical gap, a sociotechnical gap, and a social gap.

The technical gap is the difference between what a computer system is capable of enforcing and what it is expected to enforce (e.g., its policies for data confidentiality, data integrity, system integrity, availability, reliability, and correctness). This gap includes deficiencies in both hardware and software (for systems and communications) and deficiencies in administration, configuration, and operation. For example, passwords are expected to provide authentication of system users; in practice, passwords can be easily compromised. Instances of the technical gap may be accidentally or intentionally triggered by users, system malfunctions, or external events. The technical gap can be narrowed by proper development, administration, and use of computer systems and networks that satisfy their given requirements.

The sociotechnical gap is the difference between computer-related policies and social policies, including computer-related crime laws, privacy laws, ethical codes, malpractice codes, standards of good practice, insurance regulations, and other established codifications. For example, the social policy that states that a system user must not exceed his authorization level does not carry much weight when a system policy requires no authorization or when authorization is easily bypassed. The sociotechnical gap can be narrowed by creating well-defined and enforceable social policies; however, computer-based enforcement depends on the narrowing of the technical gap.

The social gap is the difference between expected human behavior as stated in security policies and actual human behavior; it includes hacker activity and misuse by legitimate users. For example, someone who is accessing a computer system from another country and who is determined to misuse that system may not be very concerned about local expectations of proper behavior. The social gap can be narrowed to some extent by narrowing the technical and sociotechnical gaps and through improved user education.

The burden of narrowing all three gaps must ultimately rest on better computer systems and computer networks as well as better management and self-imposed discipline on the part of information managers and workers. Detection of misuse can then further narrow the gaps—particularly when access controls are inadequate, making it easy for authorized users to misuse their allocated privileges.

(A detailed technical understanding of the different types of attack methods is not essential to this discussion. A classification of many types of system vulnerabilities and unintentionally introduced flaws that are subject to malicious or accidental exploitation is given in "A Summary of Computer Misuse Techniques," *Proceedings of the 12th National Computer Security Conference* (October 1989). This article, written by Peter G. Neumann and Donn Parker, provides useful background information on various attack methods.)

When computer abuse occurs, there is often a tendency to quickly place blame rather than determine the real cause of the problem. For example, it is common to blame the computer for mistakes that are ultimately attributable to people. Even computer-related misbehavior resulting from certain natural disasters and hardware malfunctions can in many cases be attributed to a deficiency in the system design, because the system should be designed to tolerate certain disruptions. Similarly, it is common to blame computer users for problems that should be attributed to system designers and, in some cases, to the designers of the user-system interface.

In many instances, the blame deserves to be shared widely. It would not be unusual to find that all three of the gaps previously discussed might be involved in a particular case of abuse. The following sections discuss user and system requirements as well as expected user behavior. Subsequent sections examine the ways the three gaps contribute to various types of computer abuse and suggest approaches to closing those gaps.

USER REQUIREMENTS

There are numerous security-relevant expectations that people may have of a computer system. A computer system may be expected to preserve human safety. In numerous disciplines (e.g., transportation, medical, utilities, and process control), computer systems play a key role in life-critical operations.

Computer systems are also expected to protect privacy rights, proprietary interests, and other attributes. For example, people should be notified when they are being subjected to unusual monitoring activities and should be given the opportunity to examine and correct erroneous personal data. In addition, the system must balance the rights of system users against the rights of system administration, particularly with respect to resource use and monitoring.

Computer systems are often relied on to prevent undesired behavior on the part of users. This includes malicious acts (e.g., sabotage, misuse, fraud, and piracy) as well as accidents. In addition, undesired system behavior (e.g., hardware- or software-induced crashes, incorrect results, fault tolerances, and excessive delays) must be prevented.

SYSTEM REQUIREMENTS

The user requirements discussed in the preceding section are typically related to computer system requirements, which include both functional and behavioral security requirements. Computer systems should dependably enforce certain agreed-on system and application security policies—for example, system integrity, data confidentiality, data integrity, system and application availability, reliability, timeliness, and human safety with respect to the system. These policies should be implemented as needed to enforce or enhance the socially relevant requirements discussed in the preceding section.

EXPECTED HUMAN BEHAVIOR

In addition to user and system requirements, there is a certain set of security-relevant behavior that system designers and administrators may expect of the people who use the computer system and applications. At one extreme are the expectations of presumably cooperative and benign users, all of whom are trusted within some particular limits. At the other extreme is the general absence of assumptions because of the possibility of random or unpredicatable human behavior (e.g., arbitrarily malicious or deviant behavior by unknown and potentially hostile users). It is convenient to consider both forms of behavior within a common set of assumptions.

Even in the presence of friendly users, assumptions of benign behavior are risky, particularly in light of masqueraders and accidents. In relatively constrained or nonhostile environments, it may be reasonable to make some simplifying assumptions—for example, that there are no external penetrators (as in a classified system that has no external access and only trusted users) and that the likelihood of malicious misuse by authorized users is relatively small—and then to make appropriate checks for deviations. If checks are not made, these simplifying assumptions may be dangerous.

Designing for random or unpredictable human behavior is an extremely difficult task. In a totally hostile environment, it may be necessary to assume the worst, including arbitrary malicious acts committed by intruders, possible collusions among hostile authorized users, and unreliability of hardware.

It may be difficult to develop a set of expectations for the user population, because the user population may not be so clearly defined (e.g., cooperative and uncooperative users, local and remote users, and authorized and unauthorized users). In this case, sensible security policies must be established and enforced, with default access attributes that support the user's needs and the administrator's demands for controlling system use.

DESIGN AND IMPLEMENTATION CONCERNS

System security requirements should properly reflect the relevant social requirements. System security requirements must be properly enforced by the system, because there are often flaws in system design and implementation. Systems administrators should monitor system use to ensure that the system is not being used in a fundamentally unsound way that permits violations of the desired behavior.

In addition, the intrinsic limitations as to what can and cannot be guaranteed must be determined. Nothing can be absolutely guaranteed; there are always possibilities for undetected exceptions. Systems should be designed so that if something undesirable does happen, it is possible to contain the problem, undo the problem, or compensate for it.

OPERATIONAL CONCERNS

Even a system that has been ideally designed and implemented can be compromised if it is not properly administered. One of the key issues relating to administration is the ability to recognize and eliminate in a timely fashion various system flaws, configuration vulnerabilities, and procedural weaknesses. Such problems tend to remain of little concern until they are actually exploited, at which point management may panic and allow a quick fix that solves only a small part of the problem.

The ability to react quickly to evident emergencies (e.g., massive penetrations or other computer system attacks) is another key administrative issue. Because it is difficult to prepare for unknown or unperceived threats, however, administrators should be well-trained in emergency response.

It is often helpful to communicate the existence of vulnerabilities and ongoing attacks to others who might have similar experiences. In some cases, corporate secrecy is important to those who fear a negative competitive result from disclosure of losses. In cases in which the community is unaware of global problems, exchange of information can be an enormous aid to effective management.

In addition, administrators must learn to recognize potential abuses (e.g., insiders privately selling off sensitive information or modifying base entries to remove outstanding warrants from criminal records). Dealing proactively with computer abuse may help ward off a catastrophic event.

MODES OF COMPUTER ABUSE

Whether misuse originates intentionally or accidentally, it can cause serious problems. A system may be misused by authorized users as well as unauthorized users. Serious problems can arise in either case, although in a particular application the effect of one type of abuse may be more important than the other, depending on the environment. What is actually authorized in any given application is often unclear and may be both poorly defined and poorly understood. In addition, the distinction between authorized and unauthorized users is sometimes hazy.

Trapdoors and other vulnerabilities represent serious potential sources of security compromise, whether by authorized or unauthorized users. Many systems have fundamental security flaws, and some flaws can be exploited by people who have only a limited amount of system knowledge.

In some system environments, misuse of authority by legitimate users is more likely than external intrusions (e.g., when opportunities for intrusion are much more limited because of the absence of dial-up lines and network connections). Authorized users do not need to have a full set of privileges in order to misuse a system. Users with a limited set of privileges can exploit a system if it is vulnerable.

One group of abusive system contaminants is often collectively referred to as pest programs. These include Trojan horses (e.g., time bombs, logic bombs, and letter bombs), viruses, and malicious worms. The distinctions among the various forms of pest programs are debatable—for example, viruses that infect personal computers are generally Trojan horse contaminants that are spread inadvertently by user activity. New strains of viruses continue to appear; stealth viruses, which can hide themselves and in some cases mutate to hinder detection, are just beginning to emerge.

The Consequences of Computer Abuse

The consequences of computer abuse can generally be viewed in two ways: damage to the system or the data on it, and violation of privacy and other human rights. Damage to the system is generally discussed in terms of loss of confidentiality, loss of integrity, or denial of service. There are many other types of misuse as well, including theft of services (e.g., computing time) or unethical use of applications (e.g., running a private business from the employer's facilities). The following sections discuss the main consequences of computer abuse.

Loss of Confidentiality. When information is viewed or obtained by someone who is not authorized to have access to that information, confidentiality is compromised. This can have serious consequences if the information is sensitive.

Information (e.g., data and programs) may be obtained directly, indirectly, or inadvertently. Information can be indirectly acquired by means of inferences derived contextually from available information. One form of inference involves aggregation, in which the totality of information is more sensitive than any of its component data items taken individually. Another form of indirect acquisition results from the exploitation of a covert channel, which involves signaling through a channel not ordinarily used to convey information (e.g., the presence or absence of an error message signifying the exhaustion of a shared resource).

Loss of Integrity. There are numerous relevant forms of loss of integrity. For example, user and system programs, data, and control information may be changed improperly, which may prevent the system from dependably producing the desired results. This type of integrity issue has to do with internal consistency.

External consistency is another serious problem. For example, the data in a data base may not be consistent with the real-world data it purports to represent. Erroneous information can have serious consequences in a variety of contexts.

Denial of Service. There are deleterious effects that involve neither loss of confidentiality nor loss of integrity. These include serious performance degradations, loss of critical real-time responsiveness, unavailability of data or resources when needed, and other forms of service denial.

Violation of Human Rights. Loss of confidentiality may result in a violation of privacy and other constitutional rights. Loss of integrity can be even more serious, in the sense of both internal and external consistency. In addition, theft of programs, data, documentation, and other information can result in loss of revenue, reliability, and accountability. Computer abuse may even have adverse effects on human safety. For example, misuse of a life-critical medical system could result in death or injury.

The potential legal consequences of computer abuse are quite varied. Lawsuits may be filed against misusers, innocent users, and system vendors. Although some of those lawsuits may be frivolous or misguided, they could nevertheless cause considerable damage for the accused. Computer crimes have already been a source of difficulties for law enforcement agencies as well as for both guilty and innocent defendants.

SYSTEM CONSIDERATIONS

Various techniques, architectures, and methods relating to system development and operation can help reduce the technical gap discussed at the beginning of this chapter. These measures include system security and administrative procedures. Crucial issues that must be addressed are system accountability, which involves user identification, authentication, and authorization as well as system and subsystem identification, authentication, and authorization; secure system design; implementing more comprehensive security policies and reducing security vulnerabilities; and judicious monitoring of system use. These issues are particularly relevant in highly distributed systems.

Some security professionals have attempted to make distinctions between intentional and accidental misuse. Even a cursory examination shows that it is essential in many systems and applications to anticipate both types of misuse, including system misbehavior (e.g., hardware faults) as well as human misbehavior.

Identification, Authentication, and Authorization

One of the most difficult security problems is determining what qualifies as authorized use. Computer fraud and abuse laws generally imply that unauthorized use is illegal. In many computer systems, however, no explicit authorization is required to use—or misuse—a system or application.

For example, the Internet worm exploited four mechanisms—the sendmail debug option, the finger program, the .rhosts tables for accessing remote systems, and the encrypted password file—none of which required any explicit authorization. If enabled by the system configuration, the sendmail debug option can be used by anyone. The finger program (relying on a flawed program, gets) permitted anyone to exploit a widely available program designed to give out information about another user. The .rhosts tables permit remote access to anyone without any further authorization than that required to log on to the system. Finally, encrypted password files are typically subject to offline or online dictionary attacks if any of the passwords are dictionary words.

The exploitation of each of these four mechanisms is clearly not what was intended as proper use, yet authorization does not always distinguish proper use from improper use. Perhaps the problem is that system administrators and users unwisely trust untrustworthy mechanisms, and vendors promote systems that are fundamentally flawed or otherwise limited.

Without the knowledge of who is doing what to whom (in terms of computer processes, programs, and data), authorization is of limited value. Therefore, a reasonably nonbypassable form of authentication (e.g., one-time passwords or biometrics) is essential to ensure that the presumed identity is correct.

In cases in which there is no meaningful authorization, the laws are often muddled. For example, the current computer abuse laws in California actually can be construed as making certain perfectly legitimate computer uses illegal. Prosecutors have said that this presents no problems, because no cases involving legitimate computer use would be prosecuted. Yet it highlights the difficulty that exists in closing the sociotechnical gap.

Access Controls

The technical gap is fairly pervasive in most computer and communications systems. Ideally, system access controls should permit only those accesses that are authorized; in practice, however, many undesirable forms of user behavior are permitted. System controls should permit authorized access only when that access supports desired behavior.

Encryption

Encryption has traditionally been used to achieve communications secrecy; it is now emerging as a partial solution for many other security-related functions. These new applications include providing encrypted and nonforgeable authenticators, transmitting encryption and decryption keys in an encrypted form, identifying and authenticating users, and providing digital signatures, tickets for trusted transactions (e.g., registry and notarization functions), nonforgeable integrity seals, and tamperproof date and time stamps. Unfortunately, government restrictions on research, use, and export of encryption techniques hinder the use of some of these applications.

Accountability and Monitoring

User identification and authentication are essential for adequate accountability. In the absence of adequate user identification, accountability cannot be assured. Typical restrictions permit reading only for information that is freely available while forbidding external modification. In addition, unless the system is to be used as a public bulletin board, the appending of new material should be restricted to prevent denial of service resulting from directory saturation.

Monitoring is itself a critical security issue. It must be generally nonsubvertible (i.e., nonbypassable, nonalterable, and otherwise noncompromisable) and must respect privacy requirements. Monitoring can serve many purposes, including detection of anomalies relating to confidentiality, integrity, availability, reliability, and human safety.

With respect to security monitoring, there are two fundamentally different but interrelated types: monitoring to detect intruders (which may benefit legitimate users) and monitoring to detect misuse by presumably legitimate users. Management must inform legitimate users as to what type of monitoring is in place. It may be desirable, however, to hide the detailed algorithms, because intruders may be able to use them to infer the existence of particular vulnerabilities.

Security remains an especially serious problem in highly distributed systems, in which accountability and monitoring play an even greater role. Systems can be designed to provide real-time audit trail analysis, with extensive restrictions on what can be audited and how the audit data can be controlled.

REDUCING THE GAPS

The pervasive technical, sociotechnical, and social gaps that contribute to computer abuse need to be narrowed. For example, better systems are needed to provide more comprehensive security with greater assurance. These systems must be easier to use and administer, easier to understand operationally, and more representative of desired security policy. Such measures would help reduce the technical gap.

Professional standards are needed as well. Existing professional associations have established ethical codes, which should be examined to determine whether they are adequate or adequately invoked. The appropriate ethical codes could help decrease the sociotechnical gap.

Another way to reduce the sociotechnical gap is to provide users with better education and training about ethics and values in relation to computer and communication systems. Users should be made aware of the social and technical risks of using computers improperly. A computing population—including designers, programmers, operations personnel, and general users—that is more intelligent and more responsible could help reduce the social gap, but only if the technical gap is narrowed.

A better understanding of the responsibilities and rights of system administrators and users would help reduce the social and sociotechnical gaps. In addition, the rights of computer abusers and penetrators must be clarified.

SUMMARY

Information security encompasses not only protection against computer penetration and internal misuse but protection against other types of undesirable system and user behavior. It is important to approach security from this perspective; attempts to address a narrower set of problems are generally shortsighted.

Overall, people are more aware of computer system vulnerabilities and security countermeasures than they were a few years ago. Computer security has been steadily improving, but so have the skills of hackers and other misusers. In addition, the potential opportunities for gains from insider misuse seem to be increasing. The technical gap has been reduced slightly in the past few years. The sociotechnical gap needs still more work, however, and the social gap remains a potentially serious problem.

Ethics and Computing Technology

MICKI S. KRAUSE

New technologies allow great social and economic progress, yet the consequences of technical advances are often paradoxical. Balancing the benefits and drawbacks of new ideas has always been a social dilemma—the fire that warms can also burn. In the same manner, computer and information technologies have enabled momentous advances but raise serious moral, legal, and ethical questions about their impact on society.

Society's increasing dependence on computers, especially in critical applications (e.g., national defense and health care) raises considerable concern for personal privacy, safety, and well-being. The more people rely on intricate computer technologies, the more dependent they become on the behavior of the people who operate the computers. Furthermore, as distributed computer processing becomes more widespread, human controls must be relied on rather than relying on technical controls alone. In essence, as information processing expands beyond the historical bounds of the mainframe, the people who operate computers must accept some of the responsibility for security.

Sociologists contend that human behavior is governed by law and ethics. Although law is relatively well defined, ethical conduct is often open to interpretation. Laws provide society with a framework for identifying appropriate and inappropriate behavior and the subsequent sanctions for misconduct. Ethical conduct, on the other hand, is an amorphous infrastructure that evolves in accordance with personal experience. It may be based on law and morality, but it typically differs from person to person depending on circumstances.

The far-reaching ethical implications of computer technology include threats to personal privacy, ownership of information, intellectual property rights, software piracy, equal access to information, ineffective computer software, computer viruses and worms, computer hacking, and the inappropriate use of computer resources. This chapter addresses the ambiguous relationship between computers and people and discusses the vital need to strike a balance between progressive technical advances and thoughtful consideration of the consequences of that progress.

THE THREAT TO PRIVACY

Privacy issues are becoming more important in information management as organizations use sophisticated technologies for marketing and to provide personal services. Enormous amounts of personal information on every individual in the US are being amassed in data bases operated by government agencies (e.g., the Internal Revenue Service and the Social Security Administration).

A few years ago, technology afforded only the largest mainframes the ability to store personal data on US citizens. Today, even the smallest marketing firm can acquire enough technology to store and process substantial amounts of personal data. Declining costs in technology promotes the proliferation of this personal data.

Increasingly, computer-based information is relied on for critical decision making. The potential for inaccuracy rises along with this increased reliance. For example, a consumer may be denied a loan because computer records incorrectly report a poor credit rating for that person. Thousands of consumer complaints about inaccurate information have led several states to file lawsuits against the credit bureau industry for violation of state consumer protection laws. According to the US Public Interest Research Group, the majority (79%) of those complaints allege that the consumer was denied credit because of errors in credit reports. There is clearly a critical need for effective control and management of information by invoking controls and safeguards that allow appropriate access to the information while maintaining integrity, privacy, and confidentiality.

In particular, safeguards are needed to provide control over access to sensitive information. Provision of information security can instill confidence among customers and help a company to portray an image of corporate and social responsibility. For example, a large insurance company has publicized its rigid policies with respect to the disclosure of customer data to third parties, thereby demonstrating its serious commitment to the privacy and confidentiality of its clients and their personal information.

Most companies, however, are still grappling with such issues as information ownership and accuracy and the questions of whether information can be sold to third parties. These issues become more intricate when data bases are interconnected, thereby providing more power to those with access to the data and substantially more inherent risk to data confidentiality and integrity. In addition, there are no standards for the control and protection of information. Therefore, the potential for invasion of privacy and misuse of information increases.

Privacy in the Workplace

Individual privacy, especially in the workplace, becomes more endangered as technology enables the widespread use of electronic surveillance and monitoring devices. Workplace surveillance is clearly an ethical issue.

A recent "Employee Privacy" study of US, European, and Canadian companies conducted by the New York–based Conference Board indicates that there is a growing need for reconciliation between a company's requirement for sensitive information about employees and the potential for invasion of privacy. In particular, companies continually demand data regarding the health and criminal records of workers. These needs raise such questions as:

- Can the information's accuracy be verified?
- Who can access this sensitive information?
- Does the employee know what information is on record?
- How are the rights of the individual balanced against the rights of organizations to conduct business?

It is already general practice for many companies to electronically monitor their employees, with the intention of collecting personal data, protecting company-owned information, curbing employee theft, or improving employee performance. Yet privacy issues in the workplace are not well defined. For example, it is not always clear how much a company needs to know about a worker or to what extent monitoring should be conducted. In addition, the employee's right to know that he is being monitored must be more clearly defined. Finally, once the surveillance information is stored in a company's computer, it must be protected.

Privacy advocates, civil libertarians, and others contend that electronic surveillance and monitoring threaten individual privacy. Companies maintain that active auditing of their employees is necessary, however—for example, to ensure compliance with policies and procedures established to secure computing resources and critical corporate assets. These companies contend that monitoring technologies can be used to improve security in the workplace. They use software, hardware, and biometric devices that monitor functions directly related to each individual (e.g., keyboard strokes) to collect detailed information about the activities of the employee. Experts predict that the use of biometrics will increase as the cost of these devices decreases.

In addition, systems are being developed that use artificial intelligence to detect patterns of system use, giving managers a clearer insight into irregular system activity. For example, a log-on at 3 A.M. under the employee ID of someone who usually accesses the system between 8 A.M. and 5 P.M. would alert management to a possible security violation.

These intrusion-detection programs go one step further than access control software (e.g., CA-ACF2 or RACF), provoking such questions as to what extent employee activity should be monitored and whether employees should be told that they are being monitored. Knowledge that an employee is being monitored may reduce morale and incentive to perform. In summary, electronic monitoring creates a dilemma: although it may protect the innocent user in cases of unauthorized system activity, it also negatively affects the already fragile expectation of employee privacy in the workplace.

Privacy Legislation

The extensive use of surveillance practices has already given rise to proposed legislation intended to prevent abuse of electronic monitoring. For example, California state representatives have written the Privacy Consumers and Workers Act (HR 2168), which would require companies to give employees prior notice of intent to monitor their activities.

Existing legislation provides electronic mail systems with the same kind of protection afforded to telephone calls. The Electronic Communications Privacy Act, enacted in 1986, makes it a federal crime to intercept and disclose electronic messages. However, the emphasis of much existing legislation is on public service systems, not internal company computer systems. Regardless, several lawsuits in California have recently been filed by employees claiming invasion of privacy because their electronic mail messages were monitored. The lack of a legal precedent clouds the issue and makes it a serious ethical concern.

Because of these lawsuits, legal experts have suggested that companies establish policies that dictate the appropriate use of computing resources, including computer-based electronic mail systems. Such policies would clearly define employee privacy rights so that they would not be left open to conjecture.

As technology continues to involve almost every aspect of life, people are becoming increasingly alarmed at the risk to their privacy. In a 1990 Louis Harris poll, four out of five Americans said they were fearful of the threats to their personal privacy in the computer age. Although 79% of those polled felt that privacy is a fundamental right of citizenship, 7 out of 10 Americans felt that they have lost all control over how personal information about them is circulated and used.

Government studies substantiate these fears. In late 1990, the US Government Accounting Office (GAO) report "Computers and Privacy: How the Government Obtains, Verifies, Uses, and Protects Personal Data," stated that federal agencies consistently violate the Privacy Act of 1974. The GAO asserts that there is a substantial amount of personal information in government data bases on every citizen. Citizens have no assurance that this information is either accurate or secure from theft.

The Fair Information Principles

The concern for personal privacy is certainly not new. In 1973, a government study was conducted on computers and the rights of citizens. Based on its research, the study committee developed the Fair Information Principles, which are presented in Exhibit I-1-7. The US Congress has also passed several privacy laws, including the 1966 Freedom of Information Act, the 1971 Fair Credit Reporting Act, the Privacy Act of 1974, the Right to Financial Privacy Act of 1978, the 1984 Cable Policy Act, the Electronic Communications Privacy Act of 1986, and

---

EXHIBIT I-1-7 Fair Information Principles

1. There must be a way . . . to prevent information about [a] person that was obtained for one purpose from being used or made available for other purposes without [that] person's consent.
2. There must be no personal data record-keeping systems whose very existence is secret.
3. There must be a way for a person to find out what information about [that person] is in a record and how it is used.
4. There must be a way for a person to correct or amend a record of identifiable information about [that person].
5. Any organization creating, maintaining, using, or disseminating records of identifiable personal data must ensure the reliability of the data for their intended use and must take [steps] to prevent misuses of the data.

SOURCE: National Research Council, *Computers at Risk: Safe Computing in the Information Age* (Washington DC: National Academy Press, 1991).

---

the Video Piracy Protection Act of 1990, all of which are based on the Fair Information Principles.

These laws were passed when most federal records were maintained on paper, however. Campaigns are currently under way to evaluate the applicability of the existing laws and to propose more up-to-date legislation. These efforts range from simple fixes to a full-fledged Constitutional amendment. One proposed bill would create a federal data protection board to oversee business and government use of electronic information. A second would apply the Freedom of Information Act to electronic files.

In 1991, Harvard University law professor Laurence Tribe proposed an amendment to the Constitution that would, among other things, protect citizens from having private data about them collected and shared without their consent. "Constitutional principles should not vary with accidents of technology," says Tribe. Moreover, he insists that an amendment to the Constitution is necessary because existing laws do not adequately address computer-related issues.

In Europe, privacy appears to be more sacrosanct. In 1990, the European Data Protection Commissioners recommended that the 1992 European Community (EC) charter include mandatory provisions for the enforcement of the Fair Information Principles throughout Europe. The EC has initiated a proposal that would also prevent the transfer of personal data from Europe to the US if US privacy laws are judged to be too weak.

ETHICS EDUCATION

It is widely accepted that in the future, wealth and power will belong to those who possess information. This transition from natural and material resources to technology brings with it increasingly complex ethical dilemmas and makes it more important than ever to strike a balance between access to information and control of that information (i.e., between use and abuse of information).

As previously discussed, several laws have been enacted that attempt to safeguard the use of new technologies. However, it is far more effective and practical to control and prevent computer abuse than to convict and penalize criminals after the fact.

In 1989, the National Institute of Justice sponsored studies on computer crime. The studies indicate that persons involved in computer crime often acquire their interest and skills at an early age. They are introduced to computers in elementary school, and their skills progress from copying software programs to telephone and credit card fraud.

For years, computer professionals have admonished the educational institutions for not educating students about the impact of computer technology. More recently, the 1991 National Research Council report, *Computers at Risk*, which addressed the computer security problems facing the US, recommended that security practices and ethics be integrated into the general process of learning about and using computers. Few schools teach computer ethics, however, and when such courses are offered, it is often only at graduate levels. It is important that all segments of the computer user population, even children, be taught about the ethical use of computer technology.

One effective instructional mechanism is to use ethical scenarios, stories about computer users engaging in acts that might be construed as unethical. Students and employees were asked to identify whether the behavior conforms to an appropriate personal or business standard of conduct and, if not, what strategies could be employed to satisfactorily resolve the conflict. Presenting ethical scenarios can help students and employees clarify and apply their ethical values as they encounter new, complex situations.

Professionals urge that lessons about socially acceptable and unacceptable behavior be taught when students first begin to use computers, alongside lessons about the technology. A 1989 survey conducted by James Madison University to ascertain the level of ethical awareness and practice by private industry indicates that 75% of the CEOs polled feel it is preferable to teach ethical behavior in a classroom rather than on the job, because there is often too much compromise in the workplace to remain competitive. For example, an employee who is pressed for deadlines but lacks adequate tools might decide to illegally copy a software package. In this situation, productivity and a strong work ethic override or conflict with other values.

Although universities have been slow to adopt ethics curricula, some programs are being established. For example, MIT's Project Athena, the university's computing facility, recently began holding open discussions on user accountability. In this way, MIT communicates a strong message that the university's standards of honesty and responsibility carry over to the use of computing resources. These standards define the appropriate use of computers, the confines of privacy and security, system integrity, and intellectual property rights.

ETHICAL STATEMENTS FROM PROFESSIONAL ASSOCIATIONS

Entire populations of users (e.g., the Internet Activities Board) have recognized the need to self-regulate and police their members' activities. The Internet, a large infrastructure of internetworked computers owned by government, industry, and the academic community, recognizes that its reliable operation depends in great part on the responsible use of its resources by its users, operators, and sponsors. Further, such organizations as Computer Professionals for Social Responsibility have publicly condemned irresponsible acts (e.g., the Internet worm), calling for the good will and common sense of computer users.

Many experts agree that the criteria for professional codes of ethics have been ill defined. Others contend that the generality of many of the codes diminishes their effectiveness. It appears that until more aggressive ethics education is adopted and professional codes of ethics are enforced, peer pressure must spur the ethical use of computing resources.

Several professional organizations have endeavored to define and develop guidelines for the appropriate behavior of their members. These ethical codes define the criteria by which professionals perform their duties and represent themselves. Organizations that have adopted ethical codes of conduct include the Information Systems Security Association (ISSA), the British Computer Society (BCS), the Association for Computing Machinery (ACM), the Institute for Certification of Computer Professionals (ICCP), the Data Processing Management Association (DPMA), and the Institute of Electrical and Electronics Engineers (IEEE). The following sections summarize the ethical codes of these organizations.

The Information Systems Security Association

The ISSA states that its primary goal is to promote management practices that ensure the confidentiality, integrity, and availability of the organization's information resources. To achieve this goal, ISSA members are required to uphold the highest standards of ethical conduct and technical competence. To help members accomplish this, the ISSA has established the following code of ethics and requires its observance to obtain and retain affiliation with the association.

Applicants for membership and members of the ISSA must state that they have in the past and will in the future:

- Perform all professional activities and duties in accordance with the law and highest ethical principles.
- Promote sound information security concepts and practices.
- Maintain the confidentiality of all proprietary or otherwise sensitive information encountered in the course of professional activities.
- Discharge professional responsibilities with diligence and honesty.

- Refrain from any activities that might constitute a conflict of interest or otherwise damage the reputation of employers, the information security profession, or the ISSA.
- Not intentionally injure or impugn the professional reputation or practice of colleagues, clients, or employers.

The British Computer Society

The BCS's code of ethics states that in the practice of their profession, members should to the extent possible:

- Keep themselves and their subordinates informed of such new technologies, practices, legal requirements, and standards are as relevant to their duties.
- Ensure that subordinates are trained to be effective in their duties and to qualify for increased responsibilities.
- Accept only such work as they believe they are competent to perform and not hesitate to obtain additional expertise from appropriately qualified individuals when necessary.
- Actively seek opportunities for increasing efficiency and effectiveness to the benefit of the user and the ultimate recipient of information or services.

In addition, members are reminded to keep up to date in the state of technology, because they are often expected to provide skills and advice. Members are told to take action to ensure that their knowledge and experience are passed on in such a way that those who receive them can not only improve their own effectiveness in their present positions but advance their careers and take on additional responsibilities.

The code advises members to always be aware of their own limitations and not knowingly imply that they have experience they do not actually possess. Finally, the code tells members that whatever the precise term of the task at hand, they should always be aware of the environment surrounding it and not work blindly toward completion of the defined task.

In addition, the BCS mandates certain principles of behavior. The code states that members must:

- Behave at all times with integrity.
- Act with complete discretion when entrusted with confidential information.
- Act with impartiality when purporting to give independent advice, and disclose any relevant personal interest.
- Accept full responsibility for any work they undertake, and construct and deliver that which they purport to deliver.
- Not seek personal advantage to the detriment of the BCS.

The Data Processing Management Association

Members of the DPMA are also required to keep their personal knowledge up to date and ensure that proper expertise is available when needed. They are advised to share their knowledge with others and to present factual and objective information to management to the best of their ability. In addition, they should accept full responsibility for work they perform; not misuse the authority entrusted to them; not misrepresent or withhold information concerning the capabilities of equipment, software, or systems; and not take advantage of the lack of knowledge or inexperience on the part of others.

The DPMA specifies obligations to fellow members and the profession, including:

- Taking appropriate action in regard to any illegal or unethical practices that come to a member's attention.
- Endeavoring to share one's expertise or knowledge.
- Cooperating with others in comprehending issues and identifying problems.
- Not using or taking credit for the work of others without specific acknowledgement and authorization.
- Not taking advantage of the lack of knowledge or inexperience on the part of others for personal gain.

In addition, the DPMA outlines certain obligations members have to society. The code states that members should:

- Protect the privacy and confidentiality of all information entrusted to them.
- Use their skills and knowledge to inform the public in all areas of their expertise.
- To the best of their ability, ensure that the products of their work are used in a socially responsible way.
- Support, respect, and abide by the appropriate local and federal laws.
- Never misrepresent or withhold information that is germane to a problem or situation of public concern, nor allow any such known information to remain unchallenged.
- Not use knowledge of a confidential or personal nature in any unauthorized manner or to achieve personal gain.

Finally, the DPMA code defines members' obligations to their employers. For example, members should make every effort to ensure that they have the most current knowledge and that the proper expertise is available when needed. They should avoid conflicts of interest and ensure that their employers are aware of any potential conflicts. In addition, DPMA members should not attempt to use the resources of their employers for personal gain or for any purpose unrelated to their work without proper approval, and they should not exploit the weakness of a computer system for personal gain or satisfaction.

The Association for Computing Machinery

The ACM sets forth five canons of ethical conduct. These state that ACM members should:

- Act at all times with integrity.
- Strive to increase their competence and the competence and prestige of the profession.
- Accept responsibility for their work.
- Act with professional responsibility.
- Use their knowledge and skills to help advance human welfare.

The Institute of Electrical and Electronics Engineers

The IEEE divides its ethical code into two articles. The first one states that members should maintain high standards of diligence, creativity, and productivity and should:

- Accept responsibility for their actions.
- Be honest and realistic in stating claims or estimates from available data.
- Undertake technical tasks and accept responsibility only if they are qualified by training or experience, or after full disclosure to their employers or clients of pertinent qualifications.
- Maintain their professional skills at the state of the art, and recognize the importance of current events in their work.
- Advance the integrity and prestige of the profession by working in a dignified manner and for adequate compensation.

The second part of the IEEE code states that members should:

- Treat fairly all colleagues and coworkers, regardless of race, religion, sex, age, or national origin.
- Report, publish, and freely disseminate information to others, subject to legal and proprietary restraints.
- Encourage colleagues and coworkers to act in accordance with this code and support them when they do so.
- Seek, accept, and offer honest criticism of work, and properly credit the contributions of others.
- Support and participate in the activities of their professional societies.
- Assist colleagues and coworkers in their professional development.

The Institute for Certification of Computer Professionals

The ICCP states that certified computer professionals, consistent with their obligation to the public at large, should promote the understanding of data processing methods and procedures using every resource at their command. Certified computer professionals have an obligation to their profession to uphold the ideals and the level of personal knowledge certified by the ICCP. In addition, they should encourage the dissemination of knowledge pertaining to the development of the computer profession.

The ICCP code further states that certified computer professionals have an obligation to serve the interests of their employers and clients loyally, diligently, and honestly. They must not engage in any conduct or commit any act that is discreditable to the reputation or integrity of the computer profession, and they must not imply that the ICCP certificate they hold is, by itself, proof of their professional competence.

The ICCP code specifies the following as the essential elements of conduct that identify a professional activity:

- A high standard of skill and knowledge.
- A confidential relationship with the people served.
- Public reliance on standards of conduct and established practice.
- Observance of an ethical code.

SUMMARY

The ethical dilemmas discussed in this chapter are complicated and lack immediate resolution. Moreover, as society becomes increasingly more complex, attributable in great part to rapidly evolving technologies, the ethical choices will become more complicated as well.

Technology has enriched society in countless ways. The benefits received from technology provide the ability to understand and manage an intricate, complex world. However, it is essential that everyone consider all circumstances and consequences so that the potential misuse and abuse of technology does not get out of control.

Establishing the Security Program

The fundamentals of security management discussed in Section I-1 are applied by implementing an information security program tailored to the needs of the organization. The program must be broad enough in scope to encompass all automated information systems and data processing activities in the organization from the smallest microcomputer to the largest mainframe. This is important because in this era of the network, standalone and isolated computers are heading rapidly toward extinction. A consistent level of security must be applied across all platforms to avoid inadvertently introducing a weak link into the network.

Key to establishing an effective security program is creating an appropriate security organization staffed with technically qualified people who have an interest in working security issues. Chapter I-2-1 of this section discusses how to determine the number and types of security personnel required to establish a security function for a specific organization. A discussion of responsibilities, job descriptions, mission and objectives statements, and reporting relationships is included to facilitate this startup process. Also provided are ideas on how to budget and allocate funds for the security function.

Chapter I-2-2 addresses how to find and select appropriate people to staff the security function. Once initial staffing is completed, attention must be directed toward ensuring that the staff obtains basic and ongoing training to enable them to perform their assigned functions. The field of data processing is rapidly advancing as technology makes it easier and easier for data to be shared among users who are widely dispersed geographically. Security personnel must thoroughly understand the threats and vulnerabilities precipitated by new technology so as to take proactive steps to ensure that data continues to be adequately protected. Training to enhance and maintain the quality of the security staff is also discussed in this chapter.

To complete the process of establishing the security program, it is necessary to create the appropriate organizational policies that advise users of management's attitude toward the security of information. These policies identify the goals of the security program and ensure that all personnel in the organization are aware of their responsibilities in this area. The final chapter in Section I-2, Chapter I-2-3, discusses how to create appropriate security policy as well as related standards, procedures, and guidelines.

In summary, Section I-2 provides the hows to go along with the whys and wheres of information security that were presented in Section I-1. It also addresses the whos and thereby has completed the presentation of the background and tools needed to get a security program started.

Organizing the Information Security Function

CHARLES CRESSON WOOD

Many people erroneously believe that information security is only a technical issue. In fact, it is also an issue that involves people. People problems, like the establishment of a suitable organizational structure, will make or break an information security effort. This section provides management-related ideas needed to achieve the mastery of an information security effort.

Issues of organizational structure must be dealt with when a company is establishing and changing the information security function. These include the resources required to properly handle information security and effective methods of defining information security responsibilities and establishing the relationship between the information security group and other organizational functions. (It should be noted here that the term information security group refers to the center of responsibility for information security within the organization. The security group may be composed of one part-time employee or a staff of full-time specialists, depending on the size of the organization.)

In general, there are no hard-and-fast rules to be found in this area: a relatively small number of approaches to organizational structure are used in the real world. This chapter addresses the most-often-encountered approaches and is based on the author's information security consulting experience with more than 70 different organizations.

DEFINING RESOURCE REQUIREMENTS

Obtaining sufficient resources involves convincing management that information security deserves a significant part of available organizational resources. There are many ways to do this. It is helpful to emphasize that information security is critical to the organization's success and may even be a source of competitive advantage. It is also important to note that information security is an ongoing business function, not simply a short-term project. The practitioner should also demonstrate that the information security group has made significant contributions to the organization and that it supports such nonsecurity objectives as cost reduction.

Determining Appropriate Staffing Levels

There is scant historical information on which to base judgments about what constitutes sufficient staffing levels for several reasons. Information security is a relatively new discipline; at many organizations, it is only during the past few years that specific individuals have been designated as responsible for information security. A recent survey of a small sample of member organizations of the Information Systems Security Association was conducted to determine the ratio of information security staff to staff in related functions.

The survey found, for example, that the ratio of full-time-equivalent employees in information security to those in information systems (IS) was between 1% and 5%, the average being slightly less than 3%. (These figures were corroborated by a separate study, which indicated that, on average, information security makes up 1.6% of data processing staff.)

The actual head-count ratios for information security relative to other functions such as information systems were shown to be a function of several factors. The more information intensive the organization's activities were, the larger the ratio was likely to be (and the more information security people there were likely to be). For example, banks are more information intensive than manufacturers and correspondingly have a higher percentage of information security people. Likewise, the ratio of information security to IS staff was correlated with the degree of regulation faced by different industries. Defense contractors, health-care organizations, and organizations in other industries with regulated information handling activities typically had a relatively larger information security staff than industries that were not regulated.

Staffing levels may also be a function of the number of years the information security group has been in existence. Different factors affect whether staffing levels increase or decrease. For example, if a group has been in existence for many years, management may understand the contribution that it makes and may staff the group at a higher level. If the group has just recently been organized, then it may not have yet made a convincing case for management support beyond an exploratory level.

In general, the longer an information security group has been in existence, the larger the number of people on its staff. However, if a group has been making a contribution for a number of years, it will be likely to need fewer people because it will have already established policies, standards, procedures, forms, and other elements of an infrastructure for information security. (For example, fewer people may be necessary because certain labor-saving technologies have been installed and because the staff has been trained over the years.) Management may, in these cases, take advantage of the perceived reduced need for information security people by reducing or constraining the growth of the group.

Obtaining Management Support. Public reports about computer crime and extensive discussions of security threats have not been sufficient motivation for many organizations to bolster the size of in-house information security staff.

Nonetheless, management is often open to discussing what other firms are doing and comparing the in-house level of investment in information security with the level of investment found at other similar organizations. Management is also open to discussing what constitutes the standard of due care and the minimum investment in information security that is necessary to avoid charges of negligence and breach of fiduciary duty. The practitioner wishing to increase the information security staff can successfully use these two topics in conversations with management to garner needed resources.

Performing a Risk Assessment to Evaluate Staffing Requirements. The security practitioner must evaluate the unique security needs facing the organization; these needs will determine the number and type of staff required. The most frequently employed method for evaluating these requirements is a risk assessment.

Risk assessments may be qualitative (e.g., scenario analysis, standard of due care comparative studies) or quantitative (e.g., threat analysis with estimates of expected loss, analyses of dollars lost from prior events). They may be developed using many sources of information, including an independent consultant's risk assessment report, internal audit reports, external audit management memos, and analyses of loss histories. To the extent that such documents are available, the practitioner should employ them to support staffing and budget requests.

Proposals for specific security staffing levels should be the product of a risk assessment project and stated as part of an action plan. Justification for specific numbers of people should be directly correlated with specific information security objectives.

The question of the type of staff needed is likewise a function of a risk assessment. For instance, if a risk assessment indicates that network security is in need of significant additional work, the organization may wish to hire an expert in local area networks and train this person about security. Similarly, if the work load for mainframe access control package administration is growing beyond the capacities of the existing staff, an experienced RACF or ACF2 administrator may be needed. Unfortunately, management often assigns these important tasks to persons who lack the appropriate background, because it fails to appreciate the importance of the security function.

Full-Time Versus Part-Time Staffing

No matter what the organization's size, someone should be designated as primarily responsible for information security. This person can devote a relatively small portion of his time to information security, if necessary. No matter how bad the organization's financial condition, there should always be someone who is responsible for information security.

As an organization grows larger and depends more on sophisticated information-handling technology, it should elevate the status of the information security function from a part-time activity to a full-time activity for at least one person. It is difficult to pinpoint exactly how large the organization must be before a full-time security specialist is warranted. In general, most organizations with more than 30 IS department employees probably require a full-time security specialist.

Increasing the amount of staff time and related resources devoted to information security has an observable positive effect on an organization's state of information security. By making at least one person a full-time information security specialist, management encourages professional training, professional society participation, and other information security activities in which the people responsible for information security might not otherwise engage. Full-time employees often take information security more seriously than part-timers. For example, they often work overtime; part-timers may not. Full-time staff may think more strategically with a longer-term perspective than part-timers. Full-time staff members are also more likely to have relevant experience than part-timers, and this fact understandably is likely to make them more effective.

Staff persons in a centralized information security group of a large organization are most often employed full time, while people acting as divisional or departmental liaisons will often be part time. On the other hand, a small organization may be able to afford only one centralized part-timer.

Establishing the Information Security Budget

The information security budget may actually comprise several budgets, depending on which units within an organization are responsible for information security. Just as staffing levels should respond to the unique needs of the organization, the budget should be responsive to the unique risks faced by the organization. The work that needs to be done should be reflected in an action plan, and it is this action plan that should drive a budget.

In addition to evaluating the unique circumstances found at the organization in question, the practitioner should review the amounts budgeted for information security at similar organizations. For example, several studies have attempted to determine the relative size of information security budgets to the overall data processing budget.

One 1989 study of Fortune 1000 corporations, conducted by Forrester Research of Cambridge, MA, indicated that information security accounted for 2% of the total information systems budget. Another survey in that same year found that the typical information security budget (regardless of how responsibilities were divided among organizational units) constituted 2.9% of the data processing budget. This study also found that, during the prior two years, the dollars devoted to information security grew at a far faster rate than the dollars devoted to IS. A German survey reported in 1990 also determined that the ratio of money spent on information security to the money spent on information systems had doubled from 1985 to 1989. This information may be useful in preparing information security budget proposals.

The security practitioner may find requests for additional funding more successful if they are directed to the industrial (i.e., physical) security department rather than to the IS department. At least one study in 1988 indicated that the typical security department allocated a greater percentage of its budget to information security than did the typical IS department. However, the relative attractiveness of the security department as a source of funding is diminished by the fact that security departments are often considerably smaller than IS departments.

Allocating the Budget

Staff costs are the primary constituent of the information security budget. Since user training and awareness efforts, access control package administration, contingency plan preparation, and related information security efforts require the extensive involvement of people, the emphasis of the practitioner should be on how many and what type of people are needed for an information security effort. One 1990 study found that, on average, in-house staff accounted for 68% of the security budget; such outside services as consultants and backup media storage made up 8%; software was 5%; hardware was 4%. The "other" category, making up approximately 15% of the budget, was composed of professional development, travel, and related expenses.

Although these figures may help the practitioner plan a budget, they may reflect an unnecessarily large reliance on people rather than technology. In the years ahead, it is expected that sophisticated information security programs will rely more heavily on technology. For example, organizations will use more software and fewer people to control and manage user access to information.

ESTABLISHING JOB DESCRIPTIONS

Establishing accountability for information security begins with the employee job description. It is not sufficient to focus on defining the responsibilities of security specialists only; all employees must share some level of responsibility for ensuring compliance with the organization's security objectives. Therefore, this section examines the development of job descriptions for both the general work force as well as for security practitioners.

Job Descriptions for the General Work Force

Job descriptions for workers—whether managers, staff, contractors, or consultants—who are not directly involved with information security do not typically involve specific mention of responsibility for information security. Nonetheless, progressive organizations have found that including responsibility for security in job descriptions effectively underlines the fact that every employee, contractor, and consultant is responsible for the appropriate handling of sensitive and valuable information. Taking this one step further, some organizations are making workers' performance evaluations contingent on compliance with information security measures.

Accountability and responsibility for information security is every worker's duty: accountability and responsibility for information security is not solely vested with the information security group. It is not sufficient to make these important points solely by means of job descriptions; they should also be made using training courses, awareness films, in-house newspaper articles, and management directives.

Job Descriptions for Security Specialists

Job descriptions of people working in an information security group vary considerably among organizations. In many respects, this is because the activities and tasks that go into being an information security specialist have not yet been formally defined in a generally accepted way. For example, in some organizations security practitioners are responsible for computer-related contingency planning; in other organizations it is handled by a computer operations group. Similarly, in some organizations, information security personnel are responsible for security-related compliance checking, while in others this is done by an EDP auditing group.

A job description for information security managers generally includes such activities as those listed in Exhibit I-2-1. Staff personnel who report to the information security manager typically perform a subset of these duties. Depending on their size, organizations may also have specialists in a number of areas within the security group's scope of responsibility, including systems development, personal computing, local area networking, access control administration, contingency planning, and training and awareness development.

DEVELOPING MISSION STATEMENTS

Mission statements (also called charters or objective statements) for an information security group describe how the security group fits into the organization, the role it plays, and the scope of its authority. Mission statements need not be long. They can include many of the activities contained in the information security manager's job description. Whatever the mission statement's content, it is very important that a mission statement be signed by a high-level executive within the organization to signify approval and support.

It is critical that the role and responsibility of the information security group be clearly communicated and understood within an organization. This is necessary to avoid political squabbles about who is responsible for performing specific functions and to prevent overstepping the bounds of their job. To illustrate this point, in-house information security staff at a major bank wanted to establish bankwide

EXHIBIT I-2-1 Activities Included in Job Descriptions for Information Security Managers

- Developing, presenting, and managing the dissemination of information security awareness and training materials.
- Evaluating the effectiveness, efficiency of, and compliance with existing information security control measures.
- Recommending control measures to improve information security (including evaluating and selecting products and services).
- Monitoring developments in the information security and information processing fields to identify new opportunities and new risks.
- Interpreting information security requirements emanating from external bodies, such as government agencies and standards-setting groups.
- Investigating alleged information security breaches and, if necessary, assisting with disciplinary and legal matters associated with such breaches.
- Developing security policies, standards, guidelines, procedures, and other elements of an infrastructure to support information security.
- Coordinating and monitoring information security activities throughout the organization, including the preparation of periodic status and progress reports.
- Serving as a liaison between various groups dealing with information security matters (e.g., with the legal department and the insurance department).
- Preparing implementation plans, security product purchase proposals, staffing plans, project schedules, budgets, and related information security management materials.
- Representing the organization on information security matters to external groups (e.g., participating in meetings to establish technical standards).
- Providing information security system administrative support (e.g., to maintain data bases for password access control systems).
- Performing research on new and improved ways to properly protect the organization's information assets.
- Providing consulting assistance on implementing information security controls (e.g., encryption system deployment and secure application system development procedures).

standards dealing with encryption. Because the role of the security group was not well understood, the group had to lobby more than 50 of the organization's managers to gain their support. Of course, building support by conferring with others is always a good idea, and the group would still have had to do some of this. However, it could have moved forward with the encryption standards with considerably more velocity if it had initially established a clear charter.

Content of the Mission Statement

A mission statement should be tailored to the needs of the organization, reflecting the risks faced by the organization and the division of responsibilities between the information security group and such other groups as EDP audit. Information security mission statements should include a set of objectives for the security group, a brief statement of background, and scope of activities.

Objectives Statement. Specific objectives should be carefully defined for an information security group because they will be used, in part, to determine whether the group has been successful. To ensure that management's intentions are consistent with the work being performed, there should be a direct correlation between the objectives appearing in the mission statement and the job descriptions of the people in the group. However, this does not mean that the tasks defined in a job description are simply reiterated as objectives in the mission statement. Objectives are high-level statements of the goals to which the organization aspires; for example:

- Establish, maintain, and customize management structures to ensure that information assets owned by or in the custody of the organization are adequately protected.

- Establish, maintain, and customize information security controls to provide the most cost-effective protection and to be responsive to the confidentiality, integrity, and availability needs of the information owned by or in the custody of the organization.

- Coordinate and oversee information security activities so that the organization's image with respect to information security reflects prudent management, efficiency, effectiveness, and responsiveness to community needs.

Background Statement. The statement of background for the information security effort is often used to sway management in the direction of approving the mission statement. For example, the background statement may discuss how information security is increasingly an issue in the organization's industry or how the use of new technology introduces new threats. Reference may be made to in-house risk assessments, new regulations, and other motivations for supporting the information security group. The background statement may also discuss improvements in previously initiated security projects and how such efforts have been incorporated in a newly reconstituted group.

Scope Statement. The scope of the mission statement is probably the most controversial part of the security group's mission statement. This part of the mission statement discusses the divisions or departments in the organization for which the group is responsible. The reporting relationship of the information security group should be clearly stated. This section also typically indicates the degree to which the group assists in implementing and administering controls, training users, supporting disciplinary actions, investigating security breaches, testing controls, preparing contingency plans, performing background checks, and attending to physical security. There is no hard-and-fast rule for developing the proper scope of an information security effort, although the more centralized the information security function is, the greater the potential economies of scale.

The scope section of the mission statement should also address the types of information for which the group is responsible. For example, it should discuss whether the group is responsible for all forms of information (e.g., paper, voice, graphics) or only computer-based information. It is recommended that the scope section state that the group is responsible for the security of information in all forms and in all stages of its collection, analysis, communication, processing, distribution, presentation, storage, and destruction.

Evolution of the Mission Statement

Practitioners should attempt to create a mission statement that will be appropriate five years in the future and that is not dictated by existing staff resources. A mission statement will typically be in effect for many years. Therefore, it should be written with a long-term perspective, so that the practitioner can later request additional support, whether in the form of additional in-house security staff, in-house auditors, or external consultants.

As an information security group matures, it typically takes on new duties. For example, at a large New York City bank, the information security group originally focused on controlling access to mainframes. But as the group became more sophisticated and as its contribution became more widely appreciated within the bank, it took on such tasks as controlling distributed systems and securing networks. The mission statement must evolve as the group grows, as new technology is deployed within the organization, and as business circumstances change.

The decentralization of information security means that user departments and other organizational units are increasingly taking on information security activities and responsibilities. The mission statements and other responsibility-related documentation of these distributed organizational units should address the responsibility for information security.

REPORTING RELATIONSHIPS

The information security group should be positioned within an organization so that it has significant power and authority to get its job done. Such organizational clout can be conveyed by association with a powerful member of the management team or by the relative position of the security group within the organization. For example, the information security group might report directly to the chief information officer, to the administrative services vice-president, or to the information resources vice-president.

Although many information security groups aspire to report directly to the chief executive officer in order to attain greater visibility, clout, and resources, this is clearly unnecessary and is in most instances inappropriate. A very high reporting relationship does not guarantee success for an information security effort. For example, high-level managers to whom the group may report may be too busy to pay sufficient attention to security issues, and the group may suffer from neglect. These managers may not be sufficiently knowledgeable about information security to understand what the members of the security group are saying, and the group may suffer from an inability to get its ideas accepted by management. In general, it is better to report to a middle- or upper-level manager such as the chief information officer.

The authority of the information security group may be largely influenced by organizational norms. For instance, if the organization supports a strict approach to compliance with controls, the group's mission statement might include such activities as preventing application systems from moving into production unless they first are shown to include sufficient controls. Although the clout of security groups has increased markedly over the past few years, the proper amount of power for any group is subject to debate. The debate exists because security is only one of an organization's objectives, and a supporting or subsidiary objective as well.

Independence of Reporting Relationships

The information security group should be relatively independent of those organizational units that are subject to significant security measures. For example, it is not appropriate for the security group to report to the systems programming department, because the activities of systems programmers are controlled by an access control package that the group administers. The information security group should also be independent of both the IS department and the internal audit department. If the security group reports to the IS department, security is likely to receive scant attention because such objectives as performance and customer service may be perceived as more important than security. If the information security group reports to the internal audit department, security-related activities cannot properly be audited without creating a conflict of interest.

Maintaining an independent stance can result in conflict. The more independent the group, the more able it is to provide unbiased information security support in the best interests of the organization as a whole. On the other hand, the most technical, controls-oriented people are often in the organizational units from which independence is sought (e.g., the IS department). If the information security group is independent, working with these people will be more difficult.

Conflicts may also arise over who owns responsibility for security-related functions. Some organizational units may claim that the information security group properly belongs in their unit. For example, the IS department may claim that because it knows more about the computer systems than any other group, it owns the information security function. Although ownership claims will need to be dealt with, they should not be an overriding factor in decisions about the organizational placement of an information security group.

Appropriate Reporting Relationships

Despite these concerns, at present information security groups typically report to their IS departments, often because the centralized security group must work with people in IS. However, the information security group is increasingly reporting to the industrial security department, which helps avoid problems of conflict of interest and ensures a proper focus on security objectives.

In some organizations, a centralized information security group reports to an IS standards group or another related department without day-to-day responsibility for information handling. Alternatively, the security group could suitably report to the risk management department, the information resource management department, or the systems planning department.

The absence of a standard department to which the security group reports reflects the fact that it is a relatively new function; management often does not understand the group's contribution or appreciate where the group should be placed within the organization.

Organizational Structure

An information security group is appropriate no matter what type of organizational structure an organization may have. Although some security-related activities are best performed on a centralized basis, a decentralized approach may also be successfully used. If the decentralized approach is taken, the need for activity coordination is markedly increased.

Since information security is an interdisciplinary field, the job of security manager naturally lends itself to matrixed positions. For example, in a matrix organization the manager of the security group might report to both the manager of the security department and to the chief information officer. In a hierarchical organization, the manager of the information security group might report to the manager of a standards and methods group, who in turn reports to the chief information officer.

OWNER, CUSTODIAN, AND USER RESPONSIBILITIES

Just as data classification simplifies and lowers costs associated with the handling of sensitive information, categorizing people within an organization simplifies and lowers the costs associated with security-related activities. People are generally categorized as owners (occasionally called sponsors), custodians, and users.

Owners are ultimately responsible for certain information on several fronts, including security. Custodians actually possess the information; they implement and administer controls over the information according to instructions from owners. Users access data on the basis of their need to know; they are obliged to comply with controls over information as determined by guidelines laid down by the owner.

In general, owners are middle-level managers, such as department or division heads. Custodians are lower-level managers responsible for computer or other information systems, such as the manager of computer operations. Users, of course, may be at any level within an organization.

Owner Duties

Such major types of information as payroll records or accounts receivable information should have a designated owner. After a major type of information has been assigned an owner, the owner is responsible for making decisions about the sensitivity and criticality of the information. This process typically involves ranking the information in question. For example, the owner may decide that payroll information is private and critical, while accounts receivable information is for internal use only and critical. These designations imply certain ways of handling the information in question. For example, if the information is critical to the business, a contingency plan to provide continued availability in the event of an emergency is likely to be necessary. Instructions for making these decisions are typically published by the information security group.

Joint Ownership Disputes. Because organizations use many types of information for different purposes, senior management may need to intervene to assign responsibility. If there are several potential information owners, senior management generally assigns ownership responsibility to the manager whose group makes the greatest use of the information or uses the information for the most important purpose. In practice, such decisions often involve political and subjective, personal considerations.

Multiple Roles. Information owners are generally not also information custodians. However, the IS department frequently owns operational computer information and is also the custodian for such information. Because different roles are implied by the designations owner and custodian, a potential conflict of interest may arise if a single person fills both roles. There are generally no problems associated with the combination of user and custodian roles or user and owner roles.

In a microcomputer environment, a single person is often called on to act as both custodian and user (if not owner as well). This lack of separation of duties can lead to a number of control lapses, such as failure to make regular backups, as well as other security problems. The security practitioner should pay special attention to the microcomputer area, making sure that compensatory controls are in place. For example, a local area network server may automatically backup a microcomputer's hard disk drive at night to compensate for the fact that the user is not likely to do this on a regular basis.

Custodian Duties

Just as each major type of information should have a designated owner, each major type of information should have a custodian. The custodian's job is to properly protect the specified information in keeping with the owner's decision about sensitivity and criticality of the information. Custodians are responsible for defining specific control procedures, administering information access controls, implementing and maintaining cost-effective information control measures, and providing recovery capabilities consistent with the instructions of information owners. For example, the custodian should ensure that proper off-site backups of critical information are made.

User Duties

Users are responsible for complying with the control requirements specified by the information's owner or custodian; users do not specify, evaluate, or otherwise manage control measures. A user who wants a certain type of access to information typically must have the owner's consent. Direct interaction with the information owner is generally not required, because the custodian in many cases has already prepared standard privilege profiles for specific job functions. If the user belongs to one of these categories of job functions, access may be granted without further review.

Assigning Responsibility

The categories of owner, custodian, and user are often ambiguous. For example, it may not be clear who is responsible for the enforcement of controls, investigation of security breaches, or design of controls in an application system. The information security group is responsible for defining the duties of owners, custodians, and users so that responsibility assignment is both clear and effective.

In some organizations, the security group acts as an agent of the custodian by administering access controls. These activities may involve administration of an access control package as well as encryption key management. However roles are assigned with respect to information security, it is critical that these roles be clear and that there be some mechanism to ensure that people perform in accordance with their designated responsibilities.

If an outsourcing firm has taken on the computer operations responsibilities previously performed in-house, it may also assume the role of custodian. It is generally inadvisable for an external third party to take the role of an owner, because this role entails the fiduciary responsibility to safeguard organization assets, which properly should be borne by in-house management. Third parties may also be users of information systems.

Information Security Staff Roles

The information security function works best when a centralized group of information security specialists is supported by a decentralized group of security coordinators. The centralized group includes people with expertise in such areas as access control package administration, contingency plan preparation, and personal computer security. The decentralized coordinators perform other jobs as well as security-related functions; they are not typically information security specialists.

Security staff, whether centralized or distributed, advise people about information security by, for instance, interpreting what is meant by an information security policy within a specific computing environment. They generally do not make line management decisions, such as which users can access certain data bases. Such access control decisions should be made by the owner of the information resources involved.

INTERDEPARTMENTAL RELATIONSHIPS

Information security is a multidisciplinary and multidepartmental activity that requires the participation of many groups. Many units within an organization have responsibility for information security. These may include the following departments:

- Internal auditing and EDP auditing.
- Communications.
- Legal.
- Risk management.
- Human resources.
- Security.
- Quality assurance.
- Computer operations.
- Computer technical support.
- Data administration.
- Information resource management.

The security practitioner must clarify responsibilities among these parties if an information security effort is to be effective. The practitioner is responsible for getting a team of people from various departments and divisions to work together in an effective way. This is not an easy task, particularly because it requires interactions in a horizontal manner across the organizational structure rather than more traditional interaction in vertical fashion. As a consequence, the practitioner needs to develop supporters in various departments by means of decentralized information security coordinators. Such coordinators typically have a dotted-line relationship with the manager of the information security group and a straight-line reporting relationship with their own department. Exhibit I-2-2 describes typical interactions between an information security group and the primary departments, committees, and functional areas with which it works.

EXHIBIT I-2-2   Joint Security-Related Activities

Functional Areas	Typical Joint Activities
Industrial Security Department	Establish standards for computer room access; perform investigations of computer crime; investigate backgrounds of candidates for computer positions.
Human Resources Department	Establish policies for employee discipline; develop policies for access control privilege handling at time of termination; establish standards for handling of private employee records.
Computer Technical Support Function	Install password-based access control package; develop computer contingency plans; develop log analysis programs.
Records Management Function	Develop procedures for secure storage of paper records; develop time table for retention of records by type of information; develop contingency plans.
Application Development Function	Build adequate controls into application systems; develop standard application testing procedures; develop standards for end-user programming.
Risk Management Department	Evaluate adequacy of computer-related insurance coverage; develop business contingency plans; establish computer emergency response team.
Board of Directors Audit Committee	Review overall status of an information security effort; review management report of external auditors; report about progress made in the information security area.
Internal and EDP Audit Functions	Investigate breaches of computer-related controls; design computer-related control measures; establish end-user self-assessment information security checklist.
External Audit Firm	Evaluate adequacy of financial information system records; review external audit management letter's sections dealing with internal controls; review overall status of information security (by means of management consulting department at external audit firm).

Information Security Management Committee

Many information security groups facilitate interactions with other departments by means of an information security management committee. Such committees are usually composed of middle-level managers or their designated representatives, chosen from a number of divisions or departments across the organization. The divisions or departments represented on the committee should either represent major computer users or have a significant responsibility for information security. For example, one large manufacturing firm had a committee made up of the vice-president of engineering, a middle-level manager from manufacturing, the vice-president of information resources, the director of internal auditing, the vice-president of research and development, a representative from the legal department, and—of course—the manager of the security group.

The goal of a management committee typically is to provide guidance for the information security group, by reviewing and approving the group's plans and activities. A committee is especially useful because it provides management-oriented reality checks for the security group's proposals. A committee can also facilitate interaction with senior management and the board of directors. In some cases, the committee also makes decisions about funding for the security group.

In many organizations, such committees are usually phased out after 5 to 10 years, once the security group has become well established and successful. After the committee has been phased out, the security group may obtain management feedback from other senior management committees (e.g., a risk management committee).

DOCUMENTATION

A large organization may develop many documents containing information about organizational structure and the information security group. These include policy statements, management memos, an information security manual, a systems development process manual, computer operations documentation, organization charts, and a standard operating procedures manual. The security practitioner should consult such sources of information to establish or redefine an appropriate organizational structure for information security. After it has been developed, the organizational structure should itself be documented in these and other places.

SUMMARY

Obtaining sufficient resources for an information security effort involves convincing management that information security deserves a significant part of available organizational resources. While there are many ways to do this, it is helpful to emphasize that information security is critical to the organization's success and may even be the source of competitive advantage. It is also important to impress management with the fact that information security is an integral business function, not a short-term project.

Another helpful approach to gaining additional resources involves demonstrating that the organization in question is not investing resources in information security at the same rate as comparable organizations. Comparisons can be made based on staffing levels, amount of money spent, and other business-oriented factors. Ultimately, the unique risks found within an organization should dictate the extent and nature of the resources devoted to information security.

With respect to organizational structure, it is essential that at least one person explicitly be assigned responsibility for information security. Many organizations use a full-time centralized staff in conjunction with a part-time decentralized staff. The duties of information security people should be fully specified in job descriptions, mission statements, and similar documents approved by management.

An information security group should be positioned within an organization so that it has the clout, independence, and resources to properly attend to information security. In many cases, the group is part of the IS department, although an increasing number of organizations are placing it in the security department.

Responsibility for information security should also be specified using the designations owner, custodian, and user. Each of these has specific responsibilities and roles to play. These designations underscore the fact that information security is a staff, not a line, function. These designations also indicate that information security is a team activity requiring the cooperation of many people from disparate parts of an organization. In many organizations, achieving a consensus about the security-related actions to be taken and obtaining senior management support for such action is facilitated by means of a management supervisory committee.

Determining the appropriate resources and establishing an appropriate organizational structure for information security are both significant and complex tasks worthy of the practitioner's extended study. Although the issues are numerous and the trade-offs difficult, fortunately several standard approaches already exist. The practitioner is well advised to approach these topics using generally accepted methods that have been shown to succeed. The practitioner's mastery of these areas will be directly reflected in the success of the security effort.

The Information Security Program: Staffing, Training, and Support

GLENDA BARNES • EDDIE ZEITLER

Information security has evolved from the simple file cabinet lock to the sophistication of cryptography. With this evolution has emerged the information security profession. Information security personnel are now responsible for developing and, in many instances, implementing and maintaining the programs that protect an organization's information assets.

In the past, the information security field has been narrowly defined and was found primarily in government- and defense-related industries. Now, however, the security professional's purview has expanded to include all segments of industry and information in all of its forms (i.e., written, oral, and electronic). Significant thought and effort have been devoted to specifying the function of information security and the strategies, policies, standards, and procedures that make up the information security program. However, the effectiveness of these strategies, policies, standards, and programs depends on the quality and knowledge of the information security staff. Therefore, significant attention must also be given to staffing this function with skilled professionals and providing them ongoing training and opportunities for advancement.

Recruiting and developing skilled information practitioners is critical to the implementation of a successful security program. A professional who is current with changing technology and the various classes of security problems can establish sound policies, identify important resources at risk, and recommend effective solutions. By hiring and developing capable security professionals, organizations can protect themselves from costly delays that impede the timely realization of their security goals.

This chapter provides guidance in the selection of security professionals. In addition, it addresses the support programs and training that are important to maintaining a skilled information security staff.

SELECTING QUALIFIED SECURITY STAFF

The information security professionals of the 1990s must be technologists, marketers, and diplomats as well as knowledgeable in the business that is being secured. Their background must support the responsibilities they will assume. As with other highly skilled professions, it is usually preferable to recruit experienced persons when possible. An experienced candidate should:

- Have hands-on security experience in the industry and should have developed or implemented security programs, technologies, and processes.
- Participate in security organizations and educational programs and should maintain a security professional's support network to augment and reinforce security skills.
- Maintain a broad and current understanding of security risks and controls and have an understanding of information security needs.
- Have a proven ability to understand business issues and should be able to develop and implement security mechanisms in a manner appropriate to management's business needs.
- Be a skillful diplomat and communicator who can communicate effectively with senior management, especially when sensitive issues are involved.

The demand for security professionals often exceeds the number available. Therefore, it may be necessary to assign information security responsibilities to staff members who have no previous experience in this field. Entry-level candidates should have strong oral and written communications skills, strong interpersonal abilities, and effective organizational skills (e.g., the ability to handle several tasks at once). In addition, the candidate should demonstrate integrity (i.e., the ability to maintain the confidence of others and to perform ethically) and a sound business sense (i.e., the ability to learn and apply the basic business concepts and requirements of the organization). Technical experience in a related field and the ability to quickly develop an understanding of hardware and software security systems may be required as well.

The increasing demand for security professionals places an added burden on the human resources staff assigned the task of recruiting them. There are four basic approaches to locating security staff; a comprehensive search should include all four. These approaches are:

- *Contacting local and national security organizations (e.g., the Information Systems Security Association and the Computer Security Institute).* Many organizations post job openings in their periodicals and newsletters.
- *Working with a search agency that specializes in security professionals.* If a senior security professional is required, this is the most expeditious approach. Although agency fees are usually incurred, the benefits of hiring a senior person often negate the expense.

- *Networking within the industry.* This is a valuable method when searching for security staff. Because the information security population in any given industry is relatively small, this method can provide not only potential applicants but a level of assurance as to the quality of that person's skills, which may not be as apparent in other search approaches.
- *Cultivating security professionals within the organization itself.* The following personnel may have experience in one or more disciplines that can lead to career paths in information security:
    —Auditors understand the need for controls and methods to establish and maintain control systems.
    —EDP auditors understand controls for information systems.
    —Systems programmers usually are technically knowledgeable and can identify exposures in systems software. In addition, they play a critical role in installing and implementing access control systems.
    —Data base analysts are technically knowledgeable, and they can identify exposures in data base system software.
    —Programmer/analysts are familiar with business applications and can identify exposures in application software.
    —Project managers can organize people and tasks to ensure timely completion of security projects.
    —Strategic planners have experience in setting long-range objectives that are compatible with overall business objectives.
    —Quality control analysts can evaluate systems for compliance and control.

Consultants

In organizations of all sizes, it is occasionally necessary to consider using outside consultant services. Securing modern data processing facilities, equipment, and software sometimes places a significant burden on an organization. For example, smaller organizations often do not have the resources or enough experienced staff members to perform a particular security project, and larger organizations with highly specialized projects do not necessarily have a full-time position in a particular specialty.

Consultants can be useful for such projects as business resumption planning, access control software implementation, and communications security risk assessment. Consultants are especially effective when used as a means for crossing management lines while remaining independent, to help overcome the political problems that sometimes hinder internal information security staff.

Selecting a competent information security consultant is not difficult, and it can be extremely important to the successful outcome of a particular security project. The most crucial step in this process is for the organization to define the project plan in the greatest possible detail. It is useful to first prepare a request for proposal, which describes the project plan and the expected results. After the plan has been well defined, selection of the appropriate consultant should begin. Consultants may be found through professional organizations, security conferences and seminars, and advertisements in trade publications.

It is extremely important to check the credentials of the consultants that apply. Past clients should be contacted to determine their level of satisfaction with the consultant's work, and the consultant's written proposal and rate structure should be evaluated. This information should be compared with that of the other applicants to choose the best consultant.

Temporary Employees

Because of the confidential nature of security work, it is not advisable to use temporary employees. However, temporary staffing is occasionally necessary to get a job done on time. Temporary employees should undergo the same level of background check as permanent employees. They should be required to sign non-disclosure agreements and security policy statements. Temporary employees should not be privy to conversations, data, or systems that are not directly related to their assignment. All documents and system accesses provided to a temporary employee should be monitored and immediately returned or terminated upon their departure.

Hiring Practices

In information security, a high degree of trust must ultimately be placed in the security staff. Therefore, it is imperative that the trustworthiness of new staff members be validated.

A thorough background investigation should be completed before a candidate is hired. Hackers are often attracted to work in information security—in fact, several organizations have only avoided hiring hackers because a sound background check was conducted. Background checks may be performed by an external agency or by the human resources function within the organization. A thorough background check should include the applicant's education, previous employment, military status, personal references, and criminal record.

At a minimum, three employment and three personal references should be checked. Consideration should be given to the source of personal references: applicants should be requested to give references with whom they have long-standing relationships, excluding family members. Professionals who have known the applicant for a long time (e.g., lawyers, doctors, dentists, and clergymen) are preferred over other acquaintances.

All employment references should be checked. Specifically, the applicant's work competence should be questioned as well as the applicant's work habits and honesty. Any discrepancy between information given by a reference and information given by the applicant should be carefully checked with the applicant. If it is determined that the applicant deliberately misstated any facts, regardless how trivial, the applicant should not be considered for employment. Any intentional misstatement on an employment application is an indication of the applicant's potential dishonesty.

Several reputable companies perform special checks on applicants for a fee. Litigation, court records, marital records, and all other types of public documents are checked to ensure that the potential employer has all pertinent information about the applicant and to ensure that the applicant has no negative records.

If the applicant has been in the military, a brief request for any information on the military record that might be deemed detrimental can be forwarded to the appropriate authorities. In addition, it may be possible to check with the appropriate law enforcement agencies to determine whether an applicant has a criminal record.

The applicant's educational background must be validated. Educational records often provide insight into the character and capability of the applicant, particularly when the applicant lacks sufficient work experience. In addition, professors and other school staff members may be interviewed for additional insights.

Job Descriptions and Responsibilities

Job descriptions are important for providing security staff members with the direction they need. Job descriptions must be clear, detailed, and current for all responsibilities and activities in the security organization. The job description should clearly delineate the employee's duties, responsibilities, and level of authority as well as the specific level of security access that the employee has been authorized.

TRAINING

The security staff is the key ingredient in the success of the information security program. Maintaining and improving the caliber of that staff provides long-term returns in program efficiency, successful implementations, and reduced security risks. It is equally critical that security staff members be educated and up to date in the business they are securing. Ultimately, security decisions are based on business objectives; lack of knowledge of the business may lead to foolish or costly security recommendations.

Choosing to minimize ongoing training for the security staff can quickly reduce employee morale. In addition, it weakens the staff's ability to react smoothly and efficiently when faced with a security emergency or questions regarding new techniques. The security staff must have the credibility that comes with having the most current information available when dealing with emergencies. These individuals must be able to react quickly and calmly in emergency situations; staff members who are well trained and informed are generally more level headed and confident.

In addition, training acts as a form of recognition and is an integral part of career path planning. It allows the company to advance security staff within the organization while providing the skills that the company will need for future projects.

Information security crosses all organizational boundaries, from clerk to CEO and from verbal to electronic information. The security staff must have and maintain all the skills required to work in this diverse arena. Training in the following areas should be a requirement for all security staff members:

- New approaches and techniques for addressing security risks and exposures.
- New security technologies, processes, and controls.
- Security awareness.
- Marketing and presentation skills. The security staff must be able to clearly explain security to senior and middle management as well as employees. They must be able to inform while they are demonstrating the value of security in relationship to the organization's overall objectives.
- State and federal security regulations. Training in this area prepares the staff to provide recommendations that will assist management in complying with government regulations.

Training can be provided in a variety of ways. Combining several training methods provides a broader scope of information to staff members and may help validate or enforce the information acquired from a single source. A combination of the following methods is recommended:

- On-the-job training teaches the staff about the business, the current information security program, and budget and expense control.
- Vendors can provide training for specific products and technologies.
- Many industry associations sponsor seminars and conferences specific to the industry, information security, or certain technical areas.

In addition, a variety of magazines, publications, and reference books do an excellent job of communicating current security events, technologies, techniques, and products. Appropriate periodicals and reference materials should be available within the security department for easy and immediate access. Senior security personnel should make a point of reading current publications that apply to their industry. Local and national security organizations can be contacted for recommendations on useful publications.

Support networks are another important part of keeping staff members up-to-date. Numerous agencies, organizations, conferences, and workshops are available to help the information security professional learn about new techniques and technologies, seek assistance, and build a support network. In most cases, the support network can help professionals stay current on changing technology and specific security-related events that may or may not be made public. The government agencies and industry organizations listed in Exhibit I-2-3 provide educational and networking opportunities. This is by no means an exhaustive list, how-

---

EXHIBIT I-2-3 Groups that Provide Networking Opportunities

Government Agencies
National Institute of Standards and Technology (NIST)
National Security Agency

Security and Private-Industry Organizations
American Society of Industrial Security (ASIS)
American National Standards Institute (ANSI)
Information Systems Security Association (ISSA)
Computer Security Institute (CSI)
American Bankers Association (ABA)
Bank Administration Institute (BAI)
SHARE
GUIDE

---

ever; security administrators should look within their own industry or area of business for support groups that specifically meet their needs.

Conferences provide an opportunity for staff members to immerse themselves in a particular security topic, to share ideas and develop new ones, and to expand or develop a support network. They provide an opportunity to identify solutions to problems and to be briefed on implementations. The information and network contacts acquired at conferences can benefit the entire security staff.

Conferences that focus on security and risk control are valuable sources of information. It is equally important that the security professional be involved in conferences with a business focus, however, because information security must reflect business objectives. Information security requirements should be practical in terms of their business impact; therefore, security decisions and recommendations must be based on a business approach that recognizes alternatives.

CONCLUSION

The decision to invest in a security program is a significant one. The return on that investment is limited, however, by the investment that is made in a quality security staff. For some businesses, a single security employee may suffice; for others, a full security department may be necessary.

The business of managing and implementing information security is now as specialized as that of managing information systems or the finance office. It is no longer adequate to rely on unqualified or untrained staff to develop a sound information security program.

Information security must be kept in perspective and must be consistent with long-term business strategies. This can be accomplished only with a quality, committed information security staff.

Commercial Information Security Policies

CHERYL W. HELSING

Information resources are typically considered a corporate asset, and as such they must be protected. To determine the level of information protection required, a framework should be developed that states the security policies and standards for the organization. This framework then serves as a foundation for creating the information security program. Cooperative development and ongoing monitoring, enforcement, and maintenance help make the security policies responsive to the organization's needs rather than a burdensome set of requirements.

In many organizations, the need for an information security program is realized only after a disaster or other event occurs. Usually, management responds by assigning an individual the task of implementing security—typically in the form of mainframe access control software.

The systems programmer assigned the implementation task soon runs into serious difficulty: decisions need to be made about what information to protect, to what degree this information must be protected, and who should be able to access and change that information. Because it is seldom clear who should make those decisions and on what basis, especially in large organizations, the computer security implementation may take several years. Even worse, some organizations believe they have protected their information when in fact they have only installed a security software package.

A successful information protection program does not seek to implement solutions until security objectives are agreed on, business needs are determined, and management direction is established. This management direction should be articulated in a formal policy statement, supported by underlying standards describing the organization's minimum protective requirements for its information assets (i.e., valuable or sensitive information in any form—written, verbal, or electronic). These policies and standards serve as the foundation for an effective organizational information security program.

INFORMATION AS A CORPORATE ASSET

Many organizations view information and information processing systems as critical business assets. For example, pricing decisions are made on the basis of management information, manufacturing processes are controlled by computer, cash flow depends on accounts receivable systems, and inventory is tracked and orders are generated automatically by computer when supplies fall below predetermined levels. The tremendous reliance of business on timely, accurate information has directly increased the need to protect that information from loss, wrongful modification, unauthorized disclosure, and unavailability.

In many business organizations, this increased importance of information as a corporate asset is evidenced by the emergence of the executive position of chief information officer (CIO). The CIO is responsible for managing the organization's information resources and planning to meet the organization's future information needs. Because of the organization's growing dependence on information systems, the role of CIO has become increasingly influential in charting the future of the organization.

There has been parallel growth in the number of firms that designate a corporate information security director, separate from the corporate security director responsible for physical security. The corporate information security director is charged with managing programs to safeguard information assets, just as the corporate security director is responsible for the protection of employees, premises, and physical assets.

A FRAMEWORK FOR INFORMATION PROTECTION

Confusion often surrounds use of terms that describe varying levels of protective requirement. For purposes of clarity, this article presumes that the internal framework for information protection in any organization consists of the following elements:

- *Policies*. These are high-level statements that indicate management's intentions. They provide broad direction or goals.
- *Standards*. These are more specific statements embodying control requirements suitable for achieving management's goals. Compliance with standards is expected. Standards should be general enough to be broadly applicable, yet specific enough to allow compliance in specific instances to be measured.
- *Guidelines*. These are suggestions about how to achieve compliance with protective standards. Guidelines are not binding; they are developed to provide assistance in complying with one or more policies or standards.
- *Procedures*. Procedures are step-by-step ways of obtaining an end result. Procedures are often established to satisfy control requirements, and they must be followed carefully to provide the intended level of control.

A body of internal policies and standards, supported by guidelines and procedures, are the primary means of instituting information protection programs in commercial business environments. Policies and standards are applied and observed throughout the organization. Deviation from a policy or standard should be approved only after an appropriate level of management has reviewed the risks, decided that compliance is not possible or cost-justified, and accepted the risk in writing.

Guidelines and procedures are often specific implementations of information security policies and standards. They are necessary when varying equipment, software, and office environments require different approaches to satisfy the control requirement. Guidelines are intended as suggested approaches and are not mandatory; procedures, on the other hand, must be followed and should be subject to regular management review.

Benefits of an Information Protection Framework

Establishment and observation of an internal framework of information security policies and standards provides the following important benefits to the organization:

- Standards provide cost-effective protection, with more stringent controls specified for more valuable or sensitive information. In the absence of such direction, information may be overprotected or underprotected.

- Internal standards ensure that similar information receives the same kind of protection wherever it resides. Information that exists in many forms and locations is thus safeguarded in a comprehensive, cohesive, and consistent manner.

- Standards guide employees' actions and help them apply measured protection to the information they handle in the course of their duties.

- The existence of policies and standards serves as an awareness tool and reminder that information is an important asset of the organization.

- Information security policies and standards help organizations safeguard their proprietary rights with regard to information ownership and trade secret protection. Trade secret protection is extended only when a company can demonstrate that it treated the information as secret, applying systematic controls to avoid disclosure to unauthorized individuals. If legal recourse is sought to protect trade secret information, internal information security standards regarding the protection of such information serve as valuable evidence that the organization acted prudently and therefore should be afforded legal protection of its ownership rights to that trade secret information.

- Other legal or regulatory requirements can be satisfied by information security measures. For example:
  —All US corporations must comply with the Foreign Corrupt Practices Act, which requires businesses to implement and maintain prudent management controls.
  —The Federal Financial Institution Examination Council requires that all federally chartered financial institutions establish controls over information processing.

—State and federal privacy laws, as well as international transborder data flow regulations, require protection of various types of personal information stored in computer systems.

MILITARY VERSUS COMMERCIAL INFORMATION SECURITY

Security in commercial information processing environments differs significantly from military or defense environment practices. It is essential to understand these differences in developing commercial policies and standards. Two areas in which the differences are most notable are information classification and the assignment of accountability for information security.

Information Classification

Information classification provides a means for separating information into categories with different protective requirements. Both the military and the private sector classify information, but with different motivations and goals.

The military generally classifies information on the basis of its sensitivity to disclosure. The most sensitive information is that which would most severely compromise the defense of the country if disclosed to enemies. Such an occurrence is considered totally unacceptable; therefore, cost is not an important consideration in designating safeguards for this very sensitive information.

Businesses are driven by profit and loss, which means that security must be cost-justified. Classification decisions in the private sector are driven by the consequences not only of unauthorized disclosure but of the destruction, modification, or unavailability of the information. Protection against loss, change, or delay may be far more important to the organization than protection against disclosure. Information is classified on the basis of the financial losses the organization would suffer should an undesirable event occur.

Some commercial firms classify information in two ways. One rating indicates sensitivity to disclosure or fraudulent manipulation, and the other indicates the information's criticality to the organization's operations. The sensitivity rating designates the required level of access control and other security safeguards, and the criticality rating determines backup procedures. Information designated confidential and noncritical, for example, would likely be subject to stringent access control but not to the rigorous backup provisions required for critical data.

Accountability for Information Security

Broad responsibility for information security in military and defense environments is often placed with specially designated security personnel. In commercial environments, responsibility is distributed in line with other dimensions of management authority. Ultimately, the protection of information assets is considered an integral part of managerial responsibility.

Business organizations with well-developed information security programs use the concept of ownership to designate decision-making authority for specific information. In its report "Good Security Practices for Information Ownership and Classification" (November 1986), IBM Corp. describes the role of owner in this way:

> The owner is that individual manager or representative of management who has the responsibility for making and communicating judgments and decisions on behalf of the organization with regard to the use, identification, classification, and protection of a specific information asset.

An organization's policies and standards are applied to specific information assets by the information owner (i.e., the individual with the responsibility of classifying, delegating access to, and specifying protective requirements for an information asset). The owner often must depend on others (e.g., the supplier of information processing services) to provide the means of implementing owner-specified controls.

Anyone other than the owner who has possession of the information is referred to as a custodian. The custodian is responsible for maintaining the continuity of protection while in custody of the information. The third role, that of the user, is anyone authorized by the owner to access, change, or delete the data. The user must abide by the security procedures approved by the owner. Owners, custodians, and users of information all fulfill their roles in accordance with the organization's overall information security policies and standards.

RESPONSIBILITY FOR THE INFORMATION SECURITY POLICY

The first issue an organization faces in addressing information security is assignment of responsibility for the information security program. As discussed in the preceding sections, all levels of management are responsible for information security in their sphere of influence. However, a source of leadership for the total information security effort is required. This responsibility is assigned on the basis of the internal delineation of boundaries for the information security function and several other organizational factors, as discussed in the following sections.

Establishing the Scope

The information security function has evolved considerably. In the early days of computer security, attention was focused primarily on physical security. As it became apparent that more value was represented by an organization's software and data than by the computer hardware, the focus shifted to data security and the implementation of automated controls (e.g., access control software).

Information security is now viewed as a broader discipline encompassing all aspects of information protection. It makes little sense to expend considerable amounts of time and money locking up information in a computer system if that information is treated carelessly once printed out and in the user's hands; many costly information security breaches occur outside the confines of the computer. This would argue for a cradle-to-grave view of information security, protecting information throughout its life cycle from origination until final disposition.

Despite the logic of a comprehensive information security effort, however, many organizations have developed narrower data security policies, restricted to the protection of electronic information. Most often, this is because the information systems department initiated the effort and did not have the functional authority to select a broader scope. In practice, the controls for securing information in the office environment are so straightforward and well understood that such an expansion of scope results in only a minor increase in the complexity of implementing the standards. There is, however, a dramatic difference in that every part of the organization and each employee needs to be involved. This makes the organizational placement of the information security function a critical success factor.

Proper Organizational Placement

Information security is a highly visible staff function that must influence the entire organization but rarely has any direct authority. Implementation of a corporate information security policy is driven by senior management and is most effectively managed by an organizational unit that has a corporate charter, business focus, and access to senior management. At the same time, the staff must have an in-depth understanding of the technological aspects of information security because of the complexity of securing the information systems environment. Areas that may be assigned responsibility for information security include the information systems, corporate security, risk management, and audit departments.

There is no ideal placement for information security that is best for every organization, because each function differs among companies. Each company must review the potential choices in light of the desired attributes of the department as well as the formal and informal factors that will influence the department's effectiveness in developing and implementing a meaningful information security program. Two key issues guiding the placement of responsibility for information are avoiding conflicts of interest and placing the function where it will receive strong visibility and support. The following sections discuss the advantages and disadvantages of placing responsibility for information security in the four areas just identified.

The Information Systems Department. The information systems department certainly has the technical expertise to install computer security controls;

however, this group is often ill-equipped to manage a comprehensive information security effort because it may have a limited charter and may be isolated from business managers. In addition, other departments may view issues outside automation as being outside the information systems department's sphere of influence. Most information security efforts led by this department do not completely address the protection of data in nonelectronic forms.

The Corporate Security Department. The corporate security department usually has a comprehensive charter to safeguard company assets. This charter already encompasses the necessary territory to initiate information asset protection programs, and many corporate security directors have sought to expand their functions to provide information security services. In addition, this group has the access to senior management needed to launch such an effort. Frequently, however, this department lacks a staff with the requisite business focus and knowledge of computer systems.

The Risk Management Department. Some organizations have assigned information security to a risk management department, with responsibility for loss control programs as well as insurance coverage. The risk management staff is usually business-oriented with senior management access. In addition, combining all types of risk management efforts in a single group may be beneficial. In some organizations, however, this department narrowly focuses on maintaining adequate insurance coverage and lacks strong ties to the rest of the organization. In addition, staffing may be inadequate to meet the demands of an effective information security effort.

The Audit Department. The audit department is sometimes asked to implement the information security policy. Its control orientation, access to senior management, and corporatewide charter are useful attributes. Most audit departments include EDP auditors with the necessary computer expertise and functional area auditors with in-depth knowledge of the business. The nature of the audit function results in a high level of visibility and influence. The main disadvantage to assigning the information security function to the audit department is the loss of independence that arises from making a review group responsible for implementation. It is difficult for the audit department to monitor and report on compliance with information security policy effectively when audit itself is responsible for the program.

POLICY DEVELOPMENT

The quality of the process for policy development greatly influences the usefulness and acceptance of the organization's information security policies and standards. Short-cutting the process usually backfires; investing extra effort during the early stages of policy creation, however, can pay large dividends over time. Factors to consider in developing a policy include gaining the support of senior management, reviewing various sources of information, getting business managers and staff specialists involved, and establishing the review and approval process to be used. The steps for developing an information security policy are discussed in the following sections.

Gaining Management Commitment

Most information security programs fail because they lack true management commitment. Implementation and maintenance of information security controls takes effort and often requires expenditure of funds. Without a strong executive mandate, middle managers have little incentive to provide the resources necessary to achieve compliance. The most important step in initiating an effort is to gain senior management support.

If executive support has not been obtained, a clear business case for information security must be developed and presented. The cost-effectiveness of the proposed program should be emphasized as well as the legal and regulatory requirements that would be satisfied by the implementation of internal information security standards. When presenting the proposal to management, the information security program manager should request specific actions needed to provide evidence of senior management support and should ask for the opportunity to provide status reports at milestones of the program implementation.

Forming a Policy Advisory Committee

The program manager might ask senior management to assign individuals to a policy advisory committee, which will provide input and guidance during policy development. The formation of such an advisory committee has several benefits. If individuals representing the major divisions of the organization participate in policy development, the results are more likely to be reasonable, business-oriented, and acceptable to the organization at large. The group should be chaired by the information security program manager and should comprise individuals representing the organization's various businesses, technological environments, and staff functions. For example, the following major operating units should be represented on this committee:

- Systems programming.
- Application programming.
- Data processing operations.
- The legal department.
- The human resources department.
- The finance department.
- The physical security department.
- The audit department.
- The risk management department.

Advisory committee representatives should be thoroughly knowledgeable about the business and operations of their departments. They should have enough seniority to effectively represent their group, and they should be able to devote the time necessary to attend meetings, review and circulate drafts, and perform similar duties. The advisory committee should begin its work with a charter from senior management and a common understanding of how the group will operate.

One of the most important responsibilities of the advisory committee members is to take draft information back to their functional areas, circulate it for review, and consolidate comments for reporting back to the committee. Committee members' time will be put to most effective use if their responsibilities are limited to reviewing and reworking draft materials prepared by the information security staff.

Drafting the Policies and Standards

Many sources of information are available as input when developing policies and standards: books, journals, conferences, seminars, information security and EDP audit professional associations, and the policies and standards of other organizations. From this information, a policy statement can be drafted. This statement should be reviewed with the policy advisory committee, and a consensus should be reached on its contents.

Some organizations choose to seek senior management approval and issue the policy statement at this point. This may be an appropriate step, depending on the level of detail contained in the policy. For example, if the policy statement requires supporting standards to be meaningful to the intended audience, it is probably advantageous to hold the policy statement until the standards are completed and then issue both at the same time. The policy statement may be printed in the information security policies and standards manual, included as a separate part of a corporate policy manual, or issued separately to all levels of management.

Two issues require resolution before development of the standards manual begins in earnest. First, the range of information processing to be covered by security standards must be determined. What will be included in the standards and who will be affected by them must be established.

Second, the desired level of specificity for the standards must be determined—that is, whether they will represent generic control requirements or be tailored to particular internal environments. Some organizations develop security standards that are independent of computer hardware; others develop separate sets of standards that apply to each type of equipment they use. A standard for secure destruction of sensitive documents could be written in different ways, depending on the situation. For example, one standard might specify a particular manufacturer and model of paper shredder, another would describe the shred size required, and a third could simply require that such documents be rendered unreadable by whatever means is chosen locally. The level of specificity desirable in security standards is primarily a function of the organization's size, geographic dispersion, and degree of operational centralization. Greater flexibility is needed for larger, more dispersed companies.

Developing overly specific standards increases the risk that they will not be applicable in many cases. One test of the quality of a standard is to determine how many respondents would reply that the standard is not applicable when queried about compliance; the best standards generate few such responses. If numerous exceptions to a standard are expected, the desirability of establishing such a standard must be questioned. An organization that does not follow its own rules may find itself in a position of liability.

With these issues resolved, a table of contents for the information security standards manual can be developed. Careful attention should be paid to organization, because poor organization can make it difficult to find all the pertinent information. As much as possible, the organization of the manual should reflect its intended audiences. A given segment of the audience should be able to find all the standards relating to its sphere of responsibility in one section. For example, a programmer should be able to locate all standards relating to application systems development in the same place.

The proposed contents and organization of the standards manual should be refined and approved by the policy advisory committee or other internal review group before work begins on actual standards development. Once agreement has been reached on the content and organization of the manual, the information security staff can begin writing the manual. Input should be sought from both internal and external resources throughout the draft process.

Useful internal information addresses such areas as the organization's culture regarding security, major types of valuable or sensitive information, management's perceptions of how much protection is reasonable, and current security practices. Possible sources of internal information include:

- Corporate policies.
- Current physical security practices.
- Personnel policies and procedures.
- The employee code of conduct.
- The amount and types of insurance coverage.
- Interviews with key managers.
- Records of operational losses.

The same external sources of information used in developing the corporate policy statement are also helpful in writing standards. Samples of other organizations' standards and general control publications and checklists are most useful. The recommended controls should be compared, analyzed, and tailored into statements of control requirements that suit the organization's needs. Any control requirements identified in the internal research phase should be included at this stage.

The practice of information security has matured to the extent that many control measures are now generally accepted baselines—for example, the issuance of individual user accounts for computer system use would be considered a baseline standard. This baseline theory argues that organizations that choose not to enforce these generally accepted practices may be placing themselves at an imprudent level of risk, regardless of established internal standards. Although there is currently no widely accepted source of baseline information security practices, policy and standards developers should be aware of generally implemented safeguards in formulating internal requirements.

Control Issues to Be Addressed. Although the policies and standards of each organization reflect its own unique business environment, there is a core of subject matter that should be addressed in every comprehensive information security program. These core subjects are described in Exhibit I-2-4.

EXHIBIT I-2-4 Core Subjects of the Security Program

Subject	Description
The policy statement	A brief directive regarding the importance of information as an asset and holding all employees responsible for its protection.
Responsibilities	The specific delineation of the security responsibilities of management, security staff, and employees.
Roles	How the roles of owner, custodian, and user are assigned within the organization.
Classification	A description of the information classification system to be employed by the organization.
Segregation of duties and need to know	The method for distributing sensitive combinations of duties among two or more individuals, and methods for ensuring that employees can access only the information or capabilities they need in order to carry out their job responsibilities.
Security standards for documents, electronic media, and verbal information	Protective requirements for all physical and verbal forms of information, keyed to classification.
Security standards for automated information	Protective requirements for electronic information, keyed to classification.
Security standards for systems development	Minimum control requirements to be included in information systems, and controls over the development process itself.
Security standards for data processing operations	The operational controls required in managing a production data processing operation.
Security standards for personnel administration	All people-related control requirements, such as security training requirements, inclusion of security responsibilities in job descriptions, identification of sensitive positions, special provisions for hiring and terminations, and requirements for contiguous vacation days.

Other topics may also be included, such as information on risk assessment procedures or compliance reporting, if required. The policies and standards manual should address all of the control issues appropriate for the individual organization.

Establishing a Review and Approval Process

The review process should ensure that all significant issues regarding standards content have been identified and addressed before senior management approval is sought. A two-stage review effectively serves this need.

During standards development, policy advisory committee members should have circulated each section for internal review; all input and conflicts should have been discussed and resolved by the committee. Upon completion of the policy and standards manual, a formal review copy can be sent to each functional area manager with a memo signed jointly by the information security manager and the advisory committee member who represented that functional area. The memo should briefly outline the manual development process and explain that all contents have been previously circulated for comments, perhaps adding the list of internal department reviewers. This should facilitate management review. Often, the information regarding the previous internal review process is all that is necessary to receive functional area management approval.

With this accomplished, senior management should be satisfied that the information security standards manual was developed in a manner that ensures a high degree of quality, usefulness, and pertinence to the business of the organization. Final approval typically can be obtained with little effort or delay, and implementation can proceed.

Establishing Procedures

In some cases, the information security policy statement clearly indicates the action required for compliance. More often, however, the policy or standard is stated as a control objective, which means there could be several ways to satisfy the requirement. Overly specific requirements typically result in an unacceptable number of compliance exceptions. For example, a requirement for controlling access to sensitive information can be more universally enforced than a requirement to use a specific computer hardware or software product.

This implies that procedural solutions must be devised to comply with many information security policies or standards. Some of these procedural solutions (e.g., employee hiring and termination procedures) can be centrally developed and implemented. Other procedures must be devised and applied within individual work groups—for example, a department might specify the procedures for personal computer data backup and storage.

THE IMPLEMENTATION PROCESS

Information security policy and standards can require significant change in systems and procedures. A plan should guide the process of implementing these changes, achieving them in a cost-effective manner that results in the least possible disruption to business operations. Training is required to ensure full understanding and acceptance of the new information security program. A temporary or permanent organizational structure may be desirable to support the program. Finally, a schedule for achieving and maintaining compliance, as well as permanent monitoring and reporting mechanisms, must be put in place.

Implementation Planning

The information security manager should develop a comprehensive plan for implementation of the policies and standards program. The plan should describe the implementation strategy recommended and the source and manner of funding. It should include a high-level description of the work that must be done to achieve compliance, specify who is responsible for completing the work, and provide an estimate of required resources.

Some level of management approval is recommended, depending on the implementation strategy. The greater the dispersion of effort required, the higher the level of approval needed. For example, if implementation responsibility is highly centralized, approval of only the immediate management is necessary.

The value in publishing a formal implementation plan is that it emphasizes that significant effort is required for a successful information security program. Approval by the appropriate level of management implies that resources will be made available for the implementation. The mere distribution of an information security manual to every manager's in-basket will not achieve the intended purpose.

Cost and Funding

The implementation strategy involves a trade-off between speed of reaching compliance and cost of implementation. If compliance is required within a relatively short time, the overall cost will tend to be higher than if a phased approach is taken. However, there may be counterproductive effects if a speedy implementation is attempted. Information security is a cultural attribute of the organization, and cultural changes are seldom achieved in short order. A long-term approach and commitment is probably a more effective strategy.

A speedy implementation typically requires special funding to underwrite the development of technical controls and training programs for achieving compliance with new security policies and standards. Special funds earmarked for such projects may help ensure that they receive the priority needed to meet their objectives in a short time; however, it is probably unrealistic to expect business managers to assign top priority to such projects on short notice.

A phased implementation can be built into the standard budgetary process and managed by means of routine planning mechanisms. This approach assumes that information security is part of the cost of doing business and should be included in the standard planning and budgeting cycle. High-priority security exposures should receive immediate attention.

The phased approach is particularly well suited to information processing applications. Rather than require immediate changes to all current systems to meet the new standards, an organization may choose to apply the standards only to new systems. A compromise would be to require security enhancements whenever changes are scheduled to be made to existing systems; alternatively, a compliance deadline could be established for the distant future.

Implementation Strategies

Many organizations adopt a decentralized approach to the implementation and maintenance of information security policies and standards. Just as a policy advisory committee consisting of major operating unit representatives can facilitate the development of standards, a similar network of individuals can speed and support the implementation process within their respective organizational units.

This structure of information security coordinators or contacts may be permanent or temporary, lasting only as long as the initial implementation. The disadvantage of a permanent group is that it may draw attention away from line manager responsibility for information security; an advantage is that having a dedicated information security resource at the staff level provides a focal point within the business area. A permanent function to implement and maintain information security is recommended; it must be recognized, however, that line management is ultimately responsible.

The larger the organization, the more advantageous it is to have individuals in place throughout the organization with specific knowledge of the business environment to monitor compliance, consult and assist in implementing security projects, and provide training. It is difficult for a centralized staff to understand the organization's business and have political sensitivity and the necessary influence to maintain the momentum of such an effort throughout a large organization. With a trend toward shrinking staff groups, a more decentralized information security staff may be more effective and less subject to staff reductions during less prosperous periods.

When a decentralized information security organization is established, the central information security manager may find that his primary job is the training and support of that group of individuals. Development of a spirit of cooperation and shared purpose is as important as fundamental training in information security. Such activities as seminars and regular group meetings help build the team. Input should be requested from this group regarding all corporate information security program activities as well as updates to the policies and standards. A regular communications vehicle (e.g., a newsletter) strengthens and enhances the relationship.

Training and Awareness

It is not enough to install security products and implement procedures; the human element is ultimately the decisive factor in the success or failure of the information security effort. Because most information security problems are people problems, a solid understanding of the organization's expectations is the most important objective of any information security program.

The initial training effort needs to reach every employee in some manner; the level of employee awareness should be maintained over time by periodic refresher training. A variety of media may be employed, from formal presentations to video and written materials. Training materials should be specifically designed for the intended audience. The following six audiences for information security awareness programs can be found in most organizations:

- Senior management.
- Middle management (i.e., business managers).
- Information systems staff.
- Mainframe and midrange system users.
- Microcomputer users.
- General information users.

The language, tone, type, and amount of information presented to each audience is determined by the role the audience plays in protecting the organization's information assets. Business managers need to recognize that they are accountable for carrying out information ownership tasks. Data processing staff members must understand their custodial responsibilities, and their training should include controls in information processing systems. General office staff members need to understand the organization's classification system and how to apply it to the information they generate, receive, or store. Senior management must be kept aware of the importance of the information security program.

MONITORING, ENFORCING, AND MAINTAINING THE POLICY

The compliance issue reaches to the heart of the information security policy effort. A specific schedule for reaching compliance with all security requirements should be established. A monitoring process should be designed and the compliance status periodically reported to senior management. Without firm expectations for reaching full compliance and rigorous enforcement, it is likely that information security will not receive serious attention.

Compliance measurement and reporting occurs in two ways: management self-assessment and external monitoring. Both are essential in reaching and maintaining a prudent level of control in the organization and should be built into the program implementation plan.

Management Self-Assessment. The management self-assessment process allows each functional area to review its own progress and status with regard to the information security policies and standards. For all areas of noncompliance, a plan of action and schedule must be developed for reaching compliance. Otherwise, a decision to accept the risk of noncompliance must be reached at an appropriate level of management. Because systems, procedures, and businesses change over time, the management self-assessment should be performed at least annually.

Functional areas often report overly optimistic self-assessment findings. In the early stages of implementation, more accurate results can be achieved by instituting a policy that no one will be blamed for current compliance violations. Honest evaluations are encouraged by alerting managers that they will be held accountable for unreported compliance violations that surface later through audits or other means.

A self-assessment checklist or other measurement tool should be developed by the information security manager and provided to those who are expected to perform the self-assessment. Such a tool ensures that a common methodology is used and will aid in achieving results that are consistent and comparable throughout the organization.

External Monitoring. External monitoring is needed to validate self-assessment results. External monitoring is usually performed by internal auditors in the course of regular audit reviews. Other indicators can also be used to provide an independent reading of the organization's information security status.

The audit department is an important ally to the information security effort, because there are generally a great many more internal auditors than information security staff members. Auditors should include information security standards in audit evaluations of business units. It would be counterproductive for negative audit findings to be reported with respect to information security before compliance objectives are expected to be met; therefore, the audit manager should be involved in developing the compliance strategy. On the other hand, if some groups choose to ignore information security requirements or postpone implementing required controls past the compliance deadline, audit findings can provide powerful motivation for taking appropriate action.

In addition, the organization should have a mechanism for providing feedback to the information security manager. These independent evaluations are vital in ascertaining what control weaknesses deserve greater emphasis and attention. Auditors are a valuable source of information in judging the effectiveness of the information security program and identifying new or unsatisfactorily addressed issues.

The internal information security group can also perform security reviews, serving as a consulting resource to the rest of the organization. Although similar in approach to audits, security reviews are most effective when used only to help business units ascertain how information security standards should be applied to their environments. It should be emphasized that the purpose of the review is to assist the department in identifying areas of concern and implementing safeguards. The provision of consulting services underscores the proactive, helpful nature of the information security group and is another way to gain insight into the true level of compliance in the organization.

Some information security professionals advocate the use of tiger team attacks. This technique involves attempts to bypass security measures in order to focus management attention on vulnerabilities. Although there are situations in which a tiger team attack can be of benefit, the technique must be used sparingly and carefully. If used extensively, the organization may be thrown into a reactive, firefighting mode rather than carefully planning and executing measured improvements to security. If done without explicit management approval, serious questions may arise about whether the attack was motivated by professional or personal concerns. If an internal attack on the organization's security defenses is to be carried out, it must be with full management understanding and approval and with stringent limitations on what actions may be taken if the attack is successful.

Management Reporting

Because the information security effort was originally chartered by senior managers, regular status reports should be prepared to keep them informed of program progress. When some areas are lagging in their implementation efforts, senior management attention may be appropriate. Often, the knowledge that status is periodically being reported at an executive level provides sufficient motivation to get information security projects back on schedule.

Reports to senior management must necessarily be brief and to the point. Status information gathered through self-assessments, audits, security reviews, and other sources require analysis and condensation into a succinct report of the issues of importance to senior management. Any actions requested of senior management should be explicitly stated in the opening paragraph of the report and supported by the content that follows.

The reporting frequently varies from company to company, decreasing as the program matures. As a rule of thumb, quarterly status reports for the first year of the information security program and annual status reports thereafter should provide senior management with sufficient information.

Occasionally, incidents occur that warrant reporting to senior management. Any breach of security that may bring serious loss or news media coverage should be brought to management's attention immediately. This should be done through the regular management channels in most cases.

Enforcement

As with any rule or law, information security standards must be enforced if they are to remain a meaningful and effective control mechanism. Enforcement is most effectively accomplished when information security is made an integral part of the individual's job at all levels of the organization.

Accountability is most directly achieved when individual job descriptions, objectives, and evaluations specifically reflect the performance of information security responsibilities. It is not unrealistic to request that senior management explicitly include implementation of the new information security standards as a performance objective for each of the managers who directly report to them. The level of detail of these objectives generally increases for less senior managerial positions.

Many positions in an organization have especially important roles with regard to information security. Whenever possible, those responsibilities should be incorporated into formal job descriptions. It is beneficial to identify specific positions that are considered sensitive so that background investigations, terminations, and vacation policies can be subjected to more stringent requirements, if necessary.

The information security manager should look for opportunities to build security into already existing company practices and procedures. For example, if systems development managers are rewarded for delivering systems under budget and ahead of schedule even though control requirements are bypassed, there is little incentive for project managers to include controls in future systems. If checkpoints are built into the systems development methodology for security requirements, however, new systems cannot be placed into production if these requirements are not satisfied.

Maintenance of Policies and Standards

Periodic updates to the organization's policies and standards serve a twofold purpose. Changes in the business environment and technology can be reflected in the organization's control requirements; at the same time, a powerful message is delivered that the policies and standards remain a meaningful expression of management intent.

When standards manuals date back several years, they tend to be viewed as obsolete. In companies that experience frequent organizational change, updates reinforce the currency of standards manuals and provide a subtle reminder that the subject is still important. Although an information security manual should be written in a manner that will not require frequent revision, periodic updates can help maintain attention on the program.

SUMMARY

Cost-effective information security programs that make an ongoing contribution to the organization are based on policies and standards. These policies and standards establish the organization's goals and articulate management direction regarding the protection of corporate information assets. A business orientation and cooperative development process help make the policy program responsive to the organization's needs rather than a burdensome set of requirements.

Implementation of the information security policy and standards must be carefully planned and executed, with consideration given to how the necessary funding and resources are provided. Mechanisms are needed to monitor and enforce compliance; periodic reporting keeps senior management informed of the organization's information security status. Continued maintenance of the policies and standards manual and related procedures should keep pace with organizational and technological change, serving as a reminder that management supports the information security program.

Risk Management

One of the basic problems in security management is how to determine the level and kind of security controls needed to adequately and cost effectively protect an organization's information systems. Organizations employ a variety of approaches to address this problem from a seat-of-the-pants methods that applies a bandage for each new threat to a formal risk analysis method that addresses each potential threat and vulnerability. Some use the due-care approach, which employs the same protection that other similar organizations use. Another facet of this topic is the emerging philosophy that it is not cost effective to continue to provide security mechanisms just because of general mandates. It is now recognized that not all systems in an organization need the same level of protection; therefore, protection requirements should be determined on the basis of a system-by-system risk analysis.

The first chapter of Section I-3 covers the techniques of risk analysis. It addresses both qualitative and quantitative risk analysis methods, including the determination of the annual loss expectancy for each event that might occur. The full spectrum of risk management is discussed. This chapter shows the interrelationship between potential losses, safeguards, and acceptance of risk. Also included in this chapter is a discussion of the use of expert systems in risk analysis operations.

Closely related to and used in conjunction with risk analysis is cost/benefit analysis. Cost/benefit analyses are used in information security to justify the cost of a safeguard to minimize a risk of loss. Applied to risk management, the techniques of cost/benefit analysis are applicable to the evaluation of proposed safeguards. Chapter I-3-2 provides a thorough discussion of cost/benefit analysis.

Chapter I-3-3 addresses the important subject of evaluating and selecting the safeguards to be used to minimize risk. The advice contained in this chapter is derived from information security research and experience. When evaluating a safeguard, management must consider not only its design and capabilities but also the likelihood of its being accepted and applied by all user personnel. This chapter presents principles for selecting information safeguards that can be used to facilitate the process of determining the best solution for an organization.

After the selection and installation of safeguards, the next step is to evaluate the ability of the installed safeguards to protect information in the system in accordance with organization policy. This process is called certification and accreditation. Certification is the technical evaluation of compliance with security requirements for the purpose of accreditation. Accreditation is official authorization for operation of the system in the environment used in certification. The process of certification and accreditation as well as the need for recertification and reaccreditation is detailed in Chapter I-3-4 of this section.

The final chapter of this section discusses the implementation of certification and accreditation for sensitive systems. Included is an explanation of sensitive systems and how to determine the relative level of sensitivity of systems. The 10 certification criteria are explained so that appropriate data can be collected to facilitate the certification process.

User groups often complain that information security controls are adversely affecting productivity. This does not have to be the case. Rather, properly selected and implemented security controls should improve productivity by minimizing the need to recover from user errors, the damage caused by malicious programs, or the actions of disgruntled employees. Section I-3 explains in considerable detail all of the activities involved in managing risk to ensure that properly selected security controls are effectively implemented.

Techniques of Risk Analysis

DAVID BONYUN

Risk analysis techniques have been used in the information security industry for many years. The role of risk analysis is to determine the position of the company with respect to the risks to its assets. Typically, each risk event is evaluated to determine the potential cost to the enterprise, should that event occur. This cost value can be combined with the likelihood of its occurring to determine the annual loss expectancy for each risk. The annual loss expectancies for each identified risk to the company are added together to produce the aggregated loss expectancy, which is often referred to as the risk profile of the company.

Because a certain amount of calculation is involved, this type of risk analysis is usually termed quantitative. In addition, there is a qualitative approach, in which the risk analysts help the asset owners understand the relative importance of the assets. A qualitative analysis is necessary when it is inappropriate or impossible to measure value in monetary terms.

The history of risk analysis is marked by a fair degree of controversy among those who practice it; one of the more contentious areas has been in the conflicting use of terminology. Individual users or sites often use different terms to convey the same ideas, or a certain term may be used to convey different ideas. The glossary at the end of this handbook provides definitions of some of the more common terms as they are used in this chapter.

This chapter examines the risk analysis process in detail and suggests areas in which expert systems may be used to facilitate the analysis. In addition, the requirements for computer-aided analysis are discussed.

METHODS AND SCOPE OF RISK ANALYSIS

When the analysis is quantitative, the primary result is the aggregated annual loss expectancy. Other answers include recommendations for safeguards and a statement about the cost-effectiveness of these measures. Should the analysis be qualitative, the answers are essentially the same except that the annual loss expectancy is not aggregated.

Of importance in both types of analysis is understanding those areas in which the company is most vulnerable, determining which assets are most likely to be affected, and determining how those assets will be affected. If an area could be easily or cheaply covered by means of appropriately selected safeguards, this should be noted. In all cases, the analysis must gauge the degree to which proposed safeguards reduce the expected risk as measured in terms that are prescribed by policy or convention.

It is virtually impossible for any analyst to foresee all the events that might happen. Consequently, there is a significant problem in achieving an acceptable level of completeness when the analysis is undertaken, whether it be quantitative or qualitative. One technique to help ensure that the analysis is as complete as possible is to categorize the risks.

For example, in a computer-based information system, the risks are frequently placed in categories of disclosure, contamination, and lack of availability. Disclosure is primarily a risk to intangible assets: data and software. It is particularly important to maintain data secrecy within government or industrial enterprises. Contamination is another peril that applies to data and software. It is typically a result of fraudulent or malicious modification of data bases or programs. Availability applies to both tangible and intangible assets. The availability of tangible assets (e.g., hardware, tools, and supplies) may be lost for different reasons than intangible assets (e.g., data, communications, and the complete system). It is often helpful when considering the risks that may compromise asset availability to distinguish between theft and destruction. With theft, the agent of the event acquires the asset, thereby denying it to the proper owner; with destruction, there is no such acquisition.

The internal environment (i.e., the company and its assets) and the external environment (which includes persons who may try to effect malicious acts against the company) together constitute the context for the risks and the required safeguards. Both must be examined during the course of the risk analysis.

Risk events may be intentional or accidental. Insiders (e.g., company employees) may cause intentional as well as accidental events, and they usually have a better opportunity to intentionally misuse the system than do outsiders. Accidental events may also include natural disasters (e.g., earthquakes or floods). A comprehensive risk analysis must account for both types of risk. In addition, the risk analyst should carefully consider such attributes as opportunity, motivation, ability, and knowledge with regard to the potential internal and external agents of risk events.

Quantitative analyses are concerned with original and replacement costs of the more tangible assets. Qualitative analyses, on the other hand, focus on the presence of already established safeguards. In both quantitative and qualitative analyses, the analysts must determine what the likely events are and what kind of impact each is likely to have on the company, as deduced from their knowledge about the company, its assets, and its practices and about the assumed external environment (e.g., whether someone may want commercial or military secrets or to defraud or embarrass the company).

Techniques for analyzing risk differ primarily in terms of perspective. Risks may be identified by first making a list of the company's assets and then identifying the risks that they may be exposed to. Another technique is to identify the types of risks (e.g., earthquake, fire, system failure, or attack by external agents) and then determine which pose the greatest threat to the company. A third technique is to identify the nature of the danger (e.g., disclosure or contamination). The perspective of the risk analysis is often dictated by the areas of greatest concern to management.

THE RISK ANALYSIS PROCESS

Before a formal analysis can be performed, a vast amount of information must be gathered. The company's various assets must be identified and evaluated with respect to costs (initial or replacement) and their role in the activities and functions of the enterprise. The potential risks must be anticipated so that the areas and levels of vulnerability can be determined. Finally, possible safeguards must be identified and evaluated. Once this information has been gathered, all potentially costly or dangerous events must be identified.

The risk analysis process may be divided into the following six steps:

- Defining the scope of the analysis.
- Identifying the company's assets.
- Evaluating the assets. This includes first determining whether the analysis will be qualitative or quantitative.
- Identifying the potential risks.
- Evaluating the risks and ascertaining the company's risk profile.
- Identifying and evaluating safeguards.

On the basis of this information, someone must then recommend safeguards that sufficiently cover the risk profile. For these suggestions to be appropriate, the level of coverage deemed sufficient must first be defined; this is usually included as part of the company policy.

The amount of human involvement in risk analysis is substantial. Computers can be used, however, to provide assistance in some of the steps. The following sections discuss the six steps in detail and suggest ways that the computer can be used to facilitate the process.

Defining the Scope of the Analysis

An essential first step in any risk analysis is to define which part of the company is to be the subject of analysis. This scope is usually defined by company authorities rather than the analysts.

Another management decision that is usually sought in the initial stages of analysis concerns the security policy that is to be enforced. This policy may include a great deal of detail or very little. For example, some policies state which safeguards are to be employed, whereas others may simply state the level of risk that is deemed acceptable. Frequently, the policy suggests ways of measuring levels of asset vulnerability to various threats and the means of determining the effectiveness of proposed safeguards in reducing these risks.

Both of these decisions are ultimately made by management. Often, the risk analyst must interview management to determine the appropriate scope and security policy. Computers are not of use in this step.

Identifying the Company's Assets

Once the scope of the analysis has been defined, the assets within that area must be determined. The best way to determine the company's tangible assets (e.g., hardware) and intangible assets (e.g., data and services) is to conduct interviews with users, information owners, and managers. In addition, the company's accounting department may be able to provide a list of the tangible assets, including their purchase value (which will be useful in the next step, evaluating the assets).

Identifying the company's assets is time-consuming. Although computers can help in recordkeeping, the interviews must inevitably be conducted by people. The data obtained in these interviews may be stored in the computer for future use. For example, an asset's attributes—including the degree to which it may be vulnerable to various risks in certain situations—can be saved for future analysis.

Evaluating the Assets

After the company's assets have been identified, they must be evaluated. It is in this step that the differences between quantitative and qualitative analysis become apparent.

If the goal of the analysis is to express the risk profile in terms of the annual loss expectancy, the common unit of measurement for quantitative evaluation is monetary. Other more qualitative units of measurement (e.g., expected downtime) are usually first encountered during the evaluation of assets.

One effective way to evaluate assets involves determining the role each plays in the overall functions of the organization. For example, if different parts of a data base play different roles in the operations of the company, they should be evaluated separately. Likewise, if the impact on the company changes when parts of a single asset become unavailable, the asset must be divided into its parts for purposes of evaluation.

Every company views its assets in a different light. For example, the same hardware might be critical to the operations of one company but of only minor importance to the operations of another. If the attributes of an asset are uniform and objective, this common set of information should be collected only once and reused; computers are effective at performing this task.

The value of assets can be determined for a particular company only by asking the correct questions of the appropriate people in the company. Again, computers can keep records of the information, but people must gather the information through interviews. It is efficient to gather information about the value of assets while conducting the interviews to identify the assets.

Identifying the Potential Risks

Once the company's assets have been identified and evaluated, it is appropriate to determine the potential risks to those assets. Assets can be violated intentionally or accidentally. There are generally only two sources of accidental events: natural disasters (e.g., floods) and elements of the internal environment (e.g., machine faults and human errors).

Intentional attacks can be the work of outsiders or disgruntled employees. If intentional attacks are of concern to a company, the risk analysis team should categorize the possible attackers according to such attributes as motivation, resourcefulness, opportunity, level of skill, and susceptability or sensitivity to deterrent measures (e.g., legally prescribed penalties or publicity of the event). These attacker attributes are discussed in a later section of this chapter on the evaluation of safeguards.

Compiling a list of possible risks is another time-consuming, human-intensive task. Usually, persons with experience in risk identification are required for successful completion of this step. The computer can be used for recordkeeping and to help check for completeness of the analysis. For example, common information about the attributes of the external environment (e.g., the presence of disgruntled former employees) can be stored and used as needed.

Evaluating the Risks

Risks, like assets, are best described in terms of their attributes. Some of these have already been encountered: the likelihood and potential severity of the event, the cause of the event, whether it is intentional or accidental, and the cost of the event should it occur. If the cost to the company can be assigned to specific risk areas, these areas can be evaluated separately.

Particularly when severity of the risk event is an issue, evaluation of the cost of an event can be difficult and time-consuming. This process requires skill and experience in risk analysis and identification of potential threat events. The reliability and credibility of the final results of the analysis depend on this step. Even so, guesswork is necessarily a part of this evaluation.

Some expert systems perform quantitative risk analysis by using formulae that take, as independent variables, the values of the assets, the values of the event (and possibly the cause of the event), and the severity of the event and determine the annual loss expectancy for that risk. The annual loss expectancy can be determined for each risk being studied to determine the company's risk profile. Expert systems are extremely useful in this type of analysis, which requires large amounts of mathematical computation.

When qualitative methods are being used, a variety of information is usually requested of the asset owner to determine the risk profile. The owner helps identify potential risks to information assets. The analyst then uses this information to define the risk profile. Although this is a human-intensive task, the information need be obtained only once and then stored in the computer for future use.

Identifying and Evaluating Safeguards

Once assets and risks have been identified and evaluated, the analyst should identify and evaluate safeguards that can reduce the risk. The gathering of information about commercial safeguards for specific risks is a significant task. It must be accompanied by a sound understanding of the risks each safeguard is designed to address and the means each uses to achieve its goal.

There is a wide range of safeguards, and information about most of them is readily available. After gathering this information, the analyst must assess how effectively each safeguard performs—that is, how it might reduce risks or the impact of risk events—in a variety of situations. At the heart of this assessment is the question of how much the safeguard improves the risk profile of the company. When the company is considering using more than one safeguard, each safeguard must be evaluated in the context of the other safeguards in the environment.

In addition to its benefits, the cost of each safeguard must be considered. The cost of a safeguard should not exceed its effectiveness for the company's particular environment and needs. Safeguards must be found that provide the necessary benefits and cost as little as possible. (Chapter I-3-2 discusses cost/benefit analysis at length and examines the ways this technique may be used in evaluating safeguards.)

The computer is extremely valuable for storing information that has been gathered about safeguards. In addition, if correct and sufficient data is available, expert systems can be used to evaluate the safeguards.

The end result is typically a list of suggested safeguards that have been determined to be the most cost-effective. Management then must decide which safeguards are to be implemented. This is discussed in more detail in the following section.

CHOOSING SAFEGUARDS

Although the final result of risk analysis is usually a set of recommendations for safeguards, there is a wide discrepancy in the techniques that lead to these recommendations and in the types of safeguards that may be recommended. Safeguards can be placed into four main categories according to their means of reducing risk:

- *Preventive safeguards.* These reduce the cost of the risk to zero by preventing the risk event from occurring.
- *Mitigative safeguards.* Should a risk event occur, these safeguards reduce its cost as well as its impact.
- *Detective safeguards.* These detect risk events after they occur, thereby reducing the cost and impact of the event.

EXHIBIT I-3-1 **Automated Risk Management Software Tools**

Product	Developer	Methodology
ANALYSIS 2000	Business Resumption Planners (San Carlos CA)	Quantitative and qualitative
Automated Risk Evaluation System (ARES)	Air Force Cryptologic Support Center (San Antonio TX)	Quantitative
Bayesian Decision Support System (BDSS)	Ozier, Peterse & Associates (San Francisco CA)	Quantitative and qualitative
The BUDDY Risk Analysis System	Countermeasures, Inc. (Hollywood MD)	Qualitative
Control Matrix	Nander Brown & Co. (Reston VA)	Quantitative
Control-It	Jerry Fitzgerald & Associates (Redwood City CA)	Qualitative
CCTA Risk Analysis and Management Methodology (CRAMM)	Executive Resources Association (Arlington VA)	Qualitative
CRITI-CALC	International Security Technology (New York NY)	Quantitative and qualitative
GRA/SYS	Nander Brown & Co. (Reston VA)	Qualitative
IST/RAMP	International Security Technology (New York NY)	Quantitative
JANBER	Eagon, McAllister Associates, Inc. (Lexington Park MD)	Qualitative
Los Alamos Vulnerability and Risk Assessment (LAVA)	Los Alamos National Laboratory (Los Alamos NM)	Quantitative and qualitative
Micro Secure Self Assessment	Boden Associates (East Williston NY)	Qualitative
MINIRISK	Nander Brown & Co. (Reston VA)	Qualitative
RA/SYS	Nander Brown & Co. (Reston VA)	Quantitative
RANK-IT	Jerry Fitzgerald & Associates (Redwood City CA)	Quantitative
RISKPAC	Computer Security Consultants, Inc. (Ridgefield CT)	Quantitative and qualitative
RISKWATCH	Expert Systems Software, Inc. (Landover MD)	Quantitative and qualitative
SOS	Entellus Technology Group, Inc. (Longwood FL)	Quantitative and qualitative

- *Recovery safeguards*. These help the company to recover from risk events that have occurred, thereby reducing the overall cost.

Several products are available for assisting in risk analysis and management. The National Institute of Standards and Technology (NIST) has established a laboratory to study these products; a list of those that have been studied is provided in Exhibit I-3-1. The results of the study are available from NIST. In addition, a Canadian government agency, the Communications Security Establishment, has performed a series of parallel experiments on six systems, which overlap with those studied by NIST.

RISK ANALYSIS AND EXPERT SYSTEMS

Expert systems are computer systems that provide users a certain amount of knowledge that might otherwise be available only from human experts in the domain covered by the system. Knowledge in this context may be either static or procedural. Static knowledge is made up of facts, conjectures, and beliefs, with varying degrees of certainty attached to each item. Procedural knowledge refers to the way experts perform their jobs, make decisions, and acquire new knowledge.

Because expert systems revolve around knowledge, this knowledge plays the role of data to the system and must be captured and maintained. The persons who gather and maintain this information are referred to as knowledge engineers.

Every expert system is concerned with a particular domain of expertise or knowledge—that is, there are boundaries to the information that may be found in or used by any particular expert system. In practice, expert systems are meant for use by experts knowledgeable in a given domain and not by people without sufficient background to comprehend the information processed by the system. For example, expert systems that assist in medical diagnosis are for use by physicians, not patients. The output of an expert system is usually in the form of advice or recommendations that may require further interpretation and analysis.

An important characteristic of expert systems is their ability to infer information. This so-called information (i.e., facts that were not explicitly stored as data) is implied from the original data put into the data base of knowledge, or knowledge base. For inferencing to occur, the knowledge base must contain not only facts (i.e., declarative statements) but rules for combining these facts to infer the new ones. Rules are essentially conditional if-then statements. The term "procedural knowledge" is used for this type of knowledge. Static knowledge is usually grouped under the term "factual knowledge," even though much of this knowledge is far from proven fact in the scientific sense. All expert systems must contain both procedural and static knowledge.

Some expert systems are rule-based, and others are frame-based. In addition, some expert systems mix these two paradigms. The difference is in the implementation of the systems and the relative emphasis placed on the two kinds of knowledge in terms of the way the knowledge is sought, stored, and manipulated. In rule-based systems, the primary knowledge is procedural, and new knowledge is inferred by chaining the conditional statements from either the starting point to the desired conclusion (i.e., forward chaining) or in the opposite direction (i.e., backward chaining). In frame-based systems, emphasis is placed on facts or statements about entities, their attributes, and the values that may be appropriate for particular entity-attribute pairs.

Every expert system contains an inference engine. The inference engines in rule-based systems permit forward and backward chaining. In frame-based systems, depending on how the procedural knowledge is stored and handled, there may be a wide variety of techniques available that allow the necessary inferencing to take place; the details are not pertinent to this discussion. The following characteristics of expert systems are important to this discussion, however, because they might play a role in risk management:

- Experts knowledge is the data of the system.
- The users of a system are expected to be knowledgeable in the domain of the system.
- Expert systems must contain both factual and procedural knowledge. These two types of data are combined to permit the drawing of inferences.

Currently, computer-aided systems are frequently used to facilitate risk analysis activities. These expert systems are extremely useful for organizing, storing, and analyzing certain data associated with risk analysis. A few organizations in the US are developing expert systems that support the risk analysis process; at the time of this writing, however, these efforts were not yet beyond the prototype stage.

REQUIREMENTS OF COMPUTER-AIDED ANALYSIS

There are several general requirements of risk analysis, including commitment on the part of company management, use of suitable software that has been evaluated by third-party testing agencies, and involvement by company personnel and experts.

There are additional requirements when expert systems are used in the risk analysis. These are discussed in the following sections.

A Risk Analysis Policy

A risk analysis policy is a formal statement issued by company management that mandates the risk analysis process and defines the ground rules for it. The degree of detail and emphasis varies from policy to policy.

It is advisable to have a policy even when expert systems and knowledge bases are not part of the risk analysis process. The policy is crucial, however, if there is to be meaningful output from a highly automated system. An expert system frequently advises users as to the safeguards that are the most cost-effective at providing adequate coverage of anticipated risks. However, because it is unlikely that any set of safeguards can totally eliminate all risks, the policy must state how much risk the company finds acceptable. On the other hand, the policy might state that only a certain level of investment in controlling risk is acceptable and that any recommendations based on a risk analysis must reflect these cost constraints. Alternatively, the policy might specify that certain risks must be prevented at all costs. In addition, some policies might state that certain safeguards must be employed. Whatever the specifics of the policy, it must clearly and explicitly define the boundaries that are to be placed on any recommendations of the expert system.

Knowledge Base Requirements

The knowledge in any expert system is usually based on a model of the domain of interest. In risk analysis, it is useful to construct a model of the domain of interest with these four divisions:

- The internal environment (e.g., assets, personnel, and services provided).
- The external environment (e.g., natural disasters and potential attackers).
- Potential risks, based on types of risks.
- The catalog of possible safeguards.

A risk has two fundamental relationship attributes: the agent or cause of the risk event and the collection of affected assets. Risks have several other attributes as well, including the impact of the risk event, the severity of the event, and the likelihood of occurrence.

A tremendous amount of data must be collected about the internal and external environments before any inferences about potential risks can be made. The virtue of expert systems is that once this information is compiled, the system's knowledge base can easily be maintained and updated.

User Interfaces

Because an expert system is a complex and often cumbersome piece of software and because it is more important for the user to be an expert in the system's domain rather than in the use and theory of expert systems, another essential feature of any risk management expert system is a reasonably simple user interface. All communication with the expert system (e.g., entering knowledge or using it to infer safeguard recommendations) must be done in the terms of the model. Therefore, the model should resemble the way users think as closely as possible.

Still, many expert systems force their users to recast the problems that the system is supposed to solve in terms of the system rather than in the natural terms of the problem. This can pose a real hardship, given the complexity of expert systems.

SUMMARY

The primary goal of risk analysis is to anticipate risks that may compromise the value of assets, either directly or indirectly, if the company is unable to maintain the environment at an acceptable state. Risk analysis activities are diverse and require an analysis team with different kinds of knowledge and experience.

In several phases of risk analysis, expert systems can be invaluable. There are two distinct drawbacks, however. First, gathering and organizing the information needed by the expert system takes as much effort (and possibly more) as is needed to gather and organize information for systems that do little more than bookkeeping. Although this information can be reused many times and is relatively easy to keep current, many companies are discouraged by the significant amount of work required to implement an expert system.

The second drawback is that a model is needed for the expert system domain, and there is no general agreement on what such a model should look like. There is not even any consensus on the terminology used to describe the elements of the model. This means that a sufficiently large volume of objective, reusable data will not become available until an agreement is reached as to data requirements; ideally, companies would then collaborate in gathering this data. Meanwhile, although computers can be used effectively for automation of bookkeeping and certain computational tasks involved in risk analysis, this remains primarily a human-intensive process.

Cost/Benefit Analysis

DAVID BONYUN

Government and industrial planners have used cost/benefit analysis techniques for many years—certainly for a longer time than computer security has been an issue. Security practitioners also find these techniques useful, however.

The goal of cost/benefit analysis is deceptively simple: to justify the expenditure of funds in terms of long-term financial advantage. The expenditure is known as the cost, and the long-term advantage is expressed as the benefits that are expected to accrue as the result of the costs. Because these benefits trickle in over a period of time (called the lifetime of the project), the benefits must be systematically discounted over the relevant time frame on the basis of the expected rate of inflation. The discounting indicates that the benefits exceed the costs when both are expressed in terms of present-value monetary units.

This implies that the analysis is a comparison between real expenditures and potentially realizable benefits. However, the comparison is not always legitimate—it might be a comparison of apples and oranges. Moreover, because the benefits are discounted according to anticipated (or guessed) future discount rates, there is always some uncertainty as to the accuracy of the results of the analysis, even if the comparison itself can be fully justified. This point is considered in depth in the section discussing the use of cost/benefit analysis during risk analysis.

The goal of cost/benefit analysis is somewhat complicated by two underlying issues. First, it must be assumed that the contemplated project is sufficiently worthwhile to justify performing a cost-benefit analysis. The cost-benefit analysis does not attempt to consider the basic question of whether the project is necessary. Second, owing to the uncertainties associated with the results of cost/benefit analysis, the analysis is generally best-suited for comparing versions of a project in order to determine if one version is more cost-effective than the others. For example, if a bridge is going to be built, those who will perform the cost/benefit analysis for this project should first be assured that the need for a bridge has been established. Because of the uncertainty of the results of comparing real present costs to possible future benefits, a number of locations for the proposed bridge ought to be considered. By doing this, the same amount of uncertainty can be said to apply to each of the analyses associated with the various locations. It therefore becomes possible to legitimately compare one project to another. In other words, the analysis can determine with relatively high assurance, that it is more cost-effective to place the bridge here than there. However, it should be remembered that the cost/benefit analysis itself does not consider at all the question of whether there ought to be a bridge in the first place.

This chapter examines the general principles of cost/benefit analysis and explains the techniques that are used. It then discusses the application of these principles and techniques to risk assessment and management.

GENERAL PRINCIPLES OF COST/BENEFIT ANALYSIS

Cost/benefit analysis is a form of mathematical evaluation that is applied to a proposed project to determine the cost-effectiveness of that project. The proposed lifetime of this project must be expressed as a number of time intervals—for example, n years. For the purposes of this discussion, the points on the continuum that delimit these intervals are designated as time (0), time (1), time (2), and so on to time (n), with time (0) representing the present time and time(n) representing the end of the project's lifetime.

The analysis enumerates the costs and anticipated benefits for each time interval; usually, the costs occur in time (0) and the benefits are first realized in time (1). When assets are disposed of at the end of a project, costs or major benefits may occur in time (n) as well. For example, it may be necessary to pay to have the asset removed (i.e., a cost is incurred), or it may be possible to find a buyer for whatever is unused or no longer desired (i.e., a benefit is realized). The following sections discuss the factors involved in cost/benefit analysis.

Present Values and Discount Rates

Each element in the time continuum must be converted to present-value units of measurement so that appropriate comparisons can be made. The discount rate is hypothesized but should reflect the expected rate of inflation. Because inflation causes the value of a monetary unit of measurement (e.g., the dollar) to decrease, the cost analysis must take this into account. For example, if the discount rate is 3%, the value V becomes $V \div 1.03$ after one year and $V \div (1.03 \times 1.03)$ after two years. In general, the present value of V occurring in time(j) is:

$$V \div (1 + D)^j$$

where:

D = the discount rate

Over the lifetime of the project, the costs and benefits are determined for each interval—from time (0) to time (n)—and then discounted according to the period in which they are expected to be realized. The results for each interval are then added together to give the total present value of the costs and the total present value of the benefits, and these two totals are compared. The comparison is usually expressed as a ratio of benefits to costs.

This ratio is a function of the discount rate that was used to calculate the present values. Often, more than one discount rate is used and the resulting ratios compared. This type of comparison is referred to as a sensitivity analysis, which is discussed further in the following section.

The benefit-to-cost ratio should be greater than one. The larger the discount rate becomes, the smaller the total present value of benefits becomes (assuming that the benefits are being accrued over time).

In many cases, it is possible to determine a discount rate that makes the total present value of the costs equal the total present value of the benefits, which makes the ratio equal to one. This discount rate is called the internal rate of return. If costs always exceed benefits, there is no internal rate of return.

Sensitivity Analysis

A sensitivity analysis may be conducted to determine the variability of the results of the analysis should there be changes in the originally selected values for costs and benefits. The costs and benefits associated with any project are placed into categories (e.g., according to the source or nature of the benefits or how the costs and benefits are measured). Each cost or benefit category is represented by a time series of values that have to be guessed or estimated independently. The sensitivity analysis, if applied to each of these time series, indicates those whose role in determining the final answer are the most important (or conversely, those to which the answer is the most sensitive).

Exhibit I-3-2 presents the data that would be analyzed if there were a single source of benefits and two sources of costs in a five-year project. If the discount rate is 10%, the data in this exhibit can be converted into present values by dividing all the entries in the Year 2 column by 1.1, all the entries in the Year 3 column by 1.21 (i.e., 1.1 × 1.1), and so on. The resulting present-value data is presented in Exhibit I-3-3. The benefit-to-cost ratio is the grand total of the benefits divided by the grand total of the costs; in this example, it is:

$$1{,}250.95 \div 781.69 = 1.60$$

EXHIBIT I-3-2 Raw Data for One Benefit and Two Costs

	Year 1	Year 2	Year 3	Year 4	Year 5	Grand Total
Benefit 1	300	300	300	300	300	1,500
Total Benefits	300	300	300	300	300	1,500
Cost 1	750	0	0	0	0	750
Cost 2	0	10	10	10	10	40
Total Costs	750	10	10	10	10	790

EXHIBIT I-3-3 **Present Value of Data in Exhibit I-3-2 at a Discount Rate of 10%**

	Year 1	Year 2	Year 3	Year 4	Year 5	Grand Total
Benefit 1	300.00	272.73	247.93	225.39	204.90	1,250.95
Total Benefits	300.00	272.73	247.93	225.39	204.90	1,250.95
Cost 1	750.00	0	0	0	0	750.00
Cost 2	0	9.09	8.26	7.51	6.83	31.69
Total Costs	750.00	9.09	8.26	7.51	6.83	781.69

EXHIBIT I-3-4 **Sample Cost/Benefit Analysis**

	Raw Data					Grand Total
	Year 1	Year 2	Year 3	Year 4	Year 5	
Initial Cost	750	0	0	0	0	750
Maintenance	0	10	10	10	10	40
Total Costs	750	10	10	10	10	790
Risk Reduction	300	300	300	300	300	1,500
Total Benefits	300	300	300	300	300	1,500
Benefits Minus Costs	(450)	290	290	290	290	710

	Total Present Values		
	5% Discount	10% Discount	15% Discount
Initial Cost	750.00	750.00	750.00
Maintenance	35.50	31.70	28.50
Total Costs	785.50	781.70	778.50
Risk Reduction	1,363.80	1,251.00	1,156.50
Total Benefits	1,363.80	1,251.00	1,156.50
Benefits Minus Costs	578.00	469.00	378.00

The sensitivity of the discount rate is evaluated by making an initial estimate of the discount rate based on realistic expectations and then creating two other values for purposes of comparison: the initial estimate of the discount rate plus 0.05, and the initial estimate minus 0.05. (This assumes that the expected rate of inflation is always greater than 5%.) These comparative calculations are taken together with the internal rate of return (if it is possible to compute this value) as a way of determining the sensitivity of the analysis to the discount rate used.

Exhibit I-3-4 illustrates a cost/benefit analysis that expands on the preceding examples. Three discount rates—5%, 10%, and 15%—are used. A cost/benefit analysis software product was used to calculate benefit-to-cost ratios of 1.74 at the 5% discount rate, 1.60 at the 10% discount rate, and 1.49 at the 15% discount rate. For all three discount rates, the total benefits are expected to exceed the total costs in approximately three years. The internal rate of return was calculated as 52.5%.

Units of Measurement

Perhaps the most important rule of cost/benefit analysis is to use the same unit of measurement for the total present values of the costs and the benefits. Otherwise, the benefit-to-cost ratio is not meaningful.

When cost/benefit analysis is used during risk assessment, it is possible that neither the costs nor the benefits can be expressed in monetary terms. Nevertheless, regardless of the units in which costs and benefits are measured, the ratio must be a quotient of like terms. Problems arise because safeguards cost money, even if they are primarily administrative in nature, yet the benefits they bestow can rarely be measured in monetary terms. The application of cost/benefit techniques to risk assessment is examined more closely in the following section.

COST/BENEFIT ANALYSIS IN RISK ASSESSMENT

Risk analysis consists of the following six steps:

1. Identifying the assets of the enterprise that are to be protected.
2. Evaluating the assets.
3. Identifying the risks to which the assets might be susceptible (e.g., disclosure, contamination, or unavailability).
4. Evaluating each risk to determine its potential impact on the company.
5. Proposing safeguards that prevent, mitigate, or detect risk events or that facilitate recovery from such events.
6. Calculating the cost-effectiveness of the safeguards, to facilitate selection from among those proposed. This step may also involve determining which combination of safeguards are capable of reducing risk to a point that is acceptable to the company.

Cost/benefit analysis techniques are most readily applied during the last step of risk assessment—calculating the cost-effectiveness of the proposed safeguards. The first five steps do not contain the two characteristics necessary for cost/benefit analysis: a proposed activity that has both identifiable, measurable costs and the potential to provide sufficient benefits to offset initial and ongoing costs. Some argue that evaluating the assets and risks implies the cost of doing nothing to protect against risk; however, there are no corresponding benefits. Therefore, this discussion focuses only on applying cost/benefit techniques to calculation of the cost-effectiveness of safeguards.

The proposed activity in this case is the adoption of a safeguard. Typically, several safeguards are proposed at the end of risk analysis, and one or more of them may be adopted. These proposed safeguards must be evaluated to determine which are the most cost-effective. Tangible costs are associated with each safeguard, and benefits are presumed to result from implementation of safeguards.

The following sections discuss the benefits and costs associated with safeguards. The benefits are discussed before the costs because the units used to measure benefits must be determined first in order to ensure that a valid comparison of benefits to costs is possible. If necessary, the units used to measure the costs of the safeguard can be either converted to the same units used for benefits or stated in terms that highlight any incompatibilities that may be present.

Benefits

The benefits that result from implementing a safeguard are stated in terms of the reduction of the impact of a risk event. Consequently, benefits are stated in the same unit of measurement as the impact of the risk event, which is likely to be the same unit of measurement used to evaluate the assets affected by that risk. For example, an asset is evaluated in a particular unit of measurement, and the impact of a particular risk event is stated as a reduction in the value of that asset should the risk event occur. The benefit of implementing the safeguard is a reduction in the impact of the risk event, which may be a full or partial reinstatement of the original value of the asset.

In most cases, therefore, the evaluation of assets is essential for calculating both the potential impact of risks and the benefits expected from safeguards. The principal unit of measurement is usually monetary, which is advantageous because the costs associated with safeguards are also usually monetary. The risk manager determines relevant costs and suggests possible safeguards for reducing risks. The amount by which the cost of the risk is reduced becomes the benefit of the safeguard; this benefit is compared to the cost of implementing that safeguard.

The impact of risks are not always stated in monetary terms, however. Difficulties arise when a risk has an impact that cannot be fully evaluated in monetary terms—for example, the loss of a corporate secret or the loss of goodwill if information embarrasing to a company is disclosed. In addition, a risk may have more serious or far-reaching impact, such as the tangible and intangible costs incurred when services (e.g., electrical power or online banking) become unavailable, the loss of lives as the result of unsafe operations, or damage to the environment as well as people's health should radiation leak from a power generator. If cost/benefit analysis is to be used to determine the cost-effectiveness of safeguards that prevent or mitigate such events, the costs and benefits of the safeguard must be brought into alignment.

Some have attempted to place monetary values on human lives, competitive advantage, goodwill, or damage to the environment. However, these values are only guesses and can be woefully misleading. It is possible to say that the benefit of a safeguard is a reduction in the number of lives that might be lost; in cost/

benefit analysis, however, this cannot be compared to the tangible, monetary costs of implementing a safeguard. The best solution is to evaluate the safeguards in a way that does not involve cost/benefit analysis, as discussed in a later section of this Chapter.

Costs

It is somewhat easier to consider the costs of a safeguard than the benefits. More may be involved than the initial cost of the safeguard (e.g., maintenance of the safeguard may be ongoing), and there may be a cost to the enterprise that is as intangible as the impact of the risk that the safeguard is designed to cover. However, it is unlikely that the intangible costs of a safeguard will be the same as the intangible costs of the risk—for example, lives will not be lost implementing a safeguard designed to improve the safety of employees. Rather, the cost may include such intangibles as a degradation of service owing to constraints imposed on the system by the safeguard.

Incompatible Comparisons

When cost/benefit analysis is applied to risk management, it is occasionally difficult or even impossible to have valid comparisons of the costs and benefits for certain safeguards. When costs and benefits are expressed in different, noncomparable units of measurement, it is not possible to compute a meaningful benefit-to-cost ratio. However, the cost/benefit analysis can still be worthwhile, because it can provide a wealth of useful information.

Even so, an alternative to the complete cost/benefit analysis must be used to evaluate the safeguard's effectiveness. The usefulness of safeguards may be stated in terms of whether or not they meet the requirements set forth in the company's security policy. Policies generally distinguish between various types of risks that assets (usually information) are exposed to. The policy should specify an acceptable level of risk reduction from the use of safeguards. The evaluation of safeguards should then state to what degree each safeguard meets these minimum requirements.

In addition, the costs of a proposed safeguard can include the degree to which it lessens the effectiveness of other safeguards that have been proposed or implemented. When more than one safeguard is to be used, it remains worthwhile to perform the initial steps in the cost/benefit analysis to identify any potentially counterproductive combinations.

SUMMARY

Cost/benefit analysis is useful in situations in which proposed courses of action involve costs and benefits that can be evaluated in the same unit of measurement. When applied to risk assessment, the techniques of cost/benefit analysis are often effective in evaluating proposed safeguards. However, cost/benefit analysis cannot be blindly used in risk analysis because of the variety of risks and units of measurement that may be used to evaluate their impact. Nevertheless, even when a benefit-to-cost ratio cannot be obtained, the earlier steps in the cost/benefit analysis can help determine the effectiveness of proposed safeguards in reducing the impact of various risks. In addition, the analysis can help determine whether the safeguard will incur intangible costs as well as monetary ones.

Selecting Information Safeguards

DONN B. PARKER

Most descriptions of computer security discuss methods for identifying and ranking or quantifying risk but provide little guidance on methods for selecting effective safeguards to reduce risk. This chapter provides a set of 20 principles that can be used to evaluate and select the best safeguards from the many that are available and to audit their effectiveness after they have been implemented. These principles have been expanded and formalized for use by computer security specialists and auditors. Each principle is described in detail with examples of its application. This chapter concludes with a discussion of risk acceptance and assignment.

PRINCIPLES FOR SELECTING SAFEGUARDS

Because new principles are still being discovered, the 20 principles presented here should not be considered an exhaustive list. Nonetheless, a safeguard that adheres to many of these principles will probably be more successful than a safeguard that does not. Some of these principles are mutually exclusive; total adherence to one principle could partially violate another. The experience and good judgment of the computer security specialist and EDP auditor therefore plays an important role in the successful application of these principles.

Cost-Effectiveness and Cost Savings

Security safeguards can incur a wide range of costs. There is no completely satisfactory standard that can be applied to all situations to determine how much should be spent for a safeguard, even when a potential loss is specified. Of course, limiting safeguard cost to the cost of the potential loss is important, but it is not enough. Many companies implement elaborate safeguards before addressing the basic principles of prudence and due care: safeguards should be effective enough so that if a loss is sustained, objective security specialists would agree that sufficient safeguards were in place to protect against the loss, and the custodians of the assets and those accountable for the assets would be held blameless.

The total cost of a safeguard must be identified by examining many factors, including the costs of selection and acquisition of the materials and mechanisms, construction and placement, modification of the environment, operation, maintenance, testing, repair, replacement, and any reduction in productivity or performance caused by the safeguard. Such factors as costs for materials and mechanisms are easy to evaluate. Others, such as the costs of degradation in performance, may be difficult to predict.

Many safeguards actually reduce costs through error reduction and increased performance and productivity. For example, access control can reduce the employee idleness that arises when employees wander into other areas to carry on personal conversations. Check digits can be used to correct input data as it is entered into the system; correcting data after it is entered is more expensive. The total cost of a safeguard is thus usually a net cost and can sometimes even generate savings.

Minimum Reliance on Human Intervention

A safeguard that requires little human intervention during its operation is usually superior to a safeguard of equal capability that requires much human involvement. For example, if access to a sensitive work area can be controlled through a simple algorithmic process with few or no exceptions, an automated access mechanism could be superior to stationing a guard at the door. Manual safeguard functions are generally weaker because they tend to deteriorate without frequent motivation reinforcement. The human element must be considered not only during the routine functioning of a safeguard but also when safeguards are violated or need servicing. In any event, auditing of safeguards, manual or automatic, is necessary to ensure their continued effectiveness.

Override and Failsafe Defaults

Safeguards that automatically react when attacked or violated usually require some automatic or human override capabilities. Safeguards that can be automatically reversed in case of failure are usually referred to as failsafe. Every safeguard should have a shut-down capability; no safeguard should have self-protective capabilities that completely prevent some form of human override to safely and cost-effectively shut it down. However, disabling of safeguards for maintenance or replacement must be limited to authorized personnel whose actions are audited. No safeguard should endanger humans unless human well-being is also at stake in the violation of the safeguard.

The default action of a safeguard in an emergency should result in reduced accessibility rather than loss of constraints. In a power failure, for example, a safeguard should automatically prohibit all access through a locked door activated by a card key rather than merely shutting down operation of the lock mechanism, possibly leaving the door unlocked. However, if there was an emergency in a controlled access area, a locked door that allowed those inside to exit might prevent access of firefighters or other safety personnel.

Human access controls and protection from natural disasters are the most common targets of this principle. Because human events and activities are unpredictable, failure of a safeguard should never detract from its life-saving functions.

No Reliance on Design Secrecy

A safeguard should not rely on the secrecy of its mechanism or algorithm for its effectiveness. An effective safeguard should meet its objective in spite of violators who know of its existence and how it functions. For example, a basic rule in cryptography is to assume that code breakers know as much about the cryptographic methods as do the designers. This ensures that the protecting of encoded data is not based on the secrecy of the encoding method but on code-breaking complexity and the secrecy of each key used. This principle might also be applied to the design of door locks; a potential violator will probably have purchased the same kind of lock and will have thoroughly studied it before attack. Safecrackers commonly spend significant amounts of money purchasing copies of the safes they intend to attack.

If a safeguard must rely on secrecy, periodic change of certain variables can thwart knowledgeable violators. For example, the floor limits of financial transaction values, above which a full audit is performed, can be readily discovered by perpetrators of fraud or embezzlement. However, if the floor limit can be frequently changed and the current limit made difficult to determine, this safeguard can become more effective. Although the perpetrator may know of the existence of the floor limit and how it is used, he will not know the current value. In automated, real-time systems in which the auditing of transactions is also automated, floor limits can be changed frequently. Periodic changes in important variables can also be easily performed in various types of door access controls, computer and terminal operations procedures, automatic identification procedures, and program intercommunication security procedures. Safety lies in the keys or parameters used in a safeguard (e.g., the number of characters in a password), not necessarily in the secrecy of the method or mechanism of the safeguard.

Some caution should be used in the application of this principle. Variation of system parameters can cause confusion among clerical employees and can make controlling and auditing functions difficult. In the example presented here, varying the floor limits by only small amounts can minimize interference with auditing processes while still achieving the goal of confounding the efforts of potential violators.

Least Privilege

The principle of least privilege (or need-to-know) has been commonly employed in national security for many years. This principle dictates that the least possible amount of information should be provided for a person or mechanism to carry out necessary functions effectively. For example, when a computer program calls a subroutine to perform a function, data is often passed to the subroutine. This procedure commonly involves passing the memory address of the needed data. The subroutine may thus have access not only to the required data but also to other, sensitive information that is not required. The calling program thus becomes vulnerable to the subprogram. The simplest solution is to impose least privilege by supplying the subroutine with only the data that it needs to perform its function.

This principle might at first appear to conflict with the principle of absence of reliance on design secrecy. Safeguard mechanisms should indeed be kept as confidential as possible. Their effectiveness, however, should not depend on that confidentiality.

No Overt Entrapment Characteristics

Entrapment is useful in organizations that have limited resources for making a multi-access, large-scale computer system secure or have more system vulnerabilities that can be treated with available resources. The strategy of entrapment is to make one or a few of the system vulnerabilities attractive to potential violators. These vulnerabilities are then heavily and regularly monitored to detect any attempts at compromise. Thus, a perpetrator attempting an attack will most likely choose one of these weaknesses and will be detected and stopped.

This strategy has several drawbacks. First, it is based on the assumption that the potential perpetrator is rational and has thoroughly studied a number of possible vulnerabilities before attacking. At least one of the vulnerabilities set up for entrapment must be chosen by the violator in order for this method to work. The success of this strategy requires that the perpetrator have the same sense of values, skills, knowledge, and level of access assumed by the security designers.

The second problem with this strategy is the possible unfairness of enticing an individual to engage in an unauthorized act. If the individual already has the intent and is merely looking for the vulnerability that best matches his needs and skills, then entrapment may be a reasonable method of preventing further violation. If, however, attractive vulnerabilities provide an incentive to otherwise innocent individuals, then this could be viewed as an irresponsible security strategy. Sound management principles dictate that an individual should never be assigned to a position of trust that exceeds his resistance to temptation. In summary, potential safeguards should be evaluated in terms of their entrapment possibilities, and overt entrapment characteristics should be reason to question the desirability of any safeguard.

Independence of Control and Subject

The controllers of a safeguard and those controlled by it should be independent and should come from different populations. If this principle is violated, a person who is meant to be constrained by a safeguard could also end up being responsible for assuring its effectiveness and making it work. Violation of this principle can result in rapid deterioration of the safeguard's effectiveness.

Many safeguards impose constraints that can hinder job performance. Workers naturally avoid constraints that interfere with their performance or make excessive work for them. For example, a tape librarian whose central function is maintenance of records of tape use will probably perform the task more accurately than computer operators who must log tapes in and out in addition to their primary duties. Similarly, standard protocols for programs calling subroutines are difficult to enforce among programmers if done on a voluntary basis without consistent monitoring. Protocol standards are likely to be ignored if they add complexity or extra effort to the programmer's job. However, if the compiler is configured so that it will not accept a program unless correct protocols are used, then control of the safeguard will be independent from the workers it constrains, and the safeguard will have a greater chance of success.

Separation of those responsible for safeguards and those subject to them can sometimes be impractical, especially in small organizations. Multiple control, a method that requires two or more people to be involved in each safeguard control, is an alternative that sometimes offers an advantage over total independence. For example, many banks control access to safe-deposit boxes by placing two locks on each box and assigning the two keys to different people. In this example, each key is a separate safeguard. The same concept could be applied to cryptographic key administration; two halves of a key could be placed in the custody of two different people. Dual control, in which two or more people control the same safeguard, is a weaker alternative.

Universal Application

Exceptions to rules and procedures have probably caused the failure of more safeguards than any other problem. Safeguards should be imposed as uniformly and completely as possible over their entire domain of function. The primary values of this principle are simplicity and methodical treatment of exceptions. For example, if a badging system is used for physical access control to sensitive areas, then it should apply universally to all people entering the area. No one should be allowed in the area without an authorized badge. A mixture of some people wearing badges and some not wearing badges soon causes the system to deteriorate, and the value of the safeguard is lost. As another example, the design of a computer system that was initially judged by many computer security researchers to be secure was modified during implementation to improve performance and reduce development costs. Subsequent introduction of errors and the failure to identify exceptions to safeguards results in security vulnerabilities in the delivered products. Compromises of this principle are difficult to avoid in practice. When exceptions are necessary, they should be clearly identified and kept to a minimum.

Compartmentalization and Defensive Depth

The concept of compartmentalization derives from ship design, which specifies that compartments should be built in the hull so that a breach can be easily located, causes minimal damage, and does not spread to other parts of the ship. Physical security for a computer system can be compartmentalized by installing dampers and exhaust fans in various ducts within a building to limit the spread of harmful gases and smoke in case of fire.

The defensive depth strategy involves planning a sequence of safeguards that will be serially encountered by a perpetrator working toward a specific target. The number of safeguards encountered should increase as the sensitivity of the asset increases. For example, physical access to the most sensitive computer areas, such as the magnetic tape library or input-output handling area, should require passing through the highest number of access control points in the building housing the data processing function. The violation of one control point should immediately alert and reinforce all connected control points. Serial safeguards can be a simpler, more flexible replacement for an elaborate, costly safeguard that causes significant constraints and performance degradation.

Application of this principle requires an analysis of the role of safeguards in relation to other safeguards and their environment. Perpetrators rarely perform only a single act or violate only a single safeguard to attain their goals. Violators often engage in many independent actions at once, in which sequences of dependent acts are performed. For example, a violator may make simultaneous attacks on the payroll and accounts receivable systems. Each of these attacks would require bypassing a sequence of dependent safeguards. An attack on a series of safeguards can occur at the beginning of the series, within the series, or at the end. Therefore, a safeguard must be evaluated in relation to all safeguards that are in the same environment or protect the same asset.

Isolation and Simplicity

Although the relationship among safeguards and safeguard series should be recognized and addressed, all safeguards must also be isolated from one another in terms of mechanical power, with as little dependence upon common mechanisms as possible. The failure of one mechanism should not cause the failure of all safeguards. A computer program that performs a sensitivity security function, for example, should be as self-contained and isolated from other systems programs as possible. The number of common subroutines that it shares with other security programs should be kept to a minimum so that failure of a subroutine has a minimal effect on security. As another example, the tape usage log maintained by a tape librarian during the first shift should be isolated from independent tape logging activities during other shifts.

The design of a safeguard should also be as simple as possible. In addition to reducing costs and increasing reliability, safeguard simplicity can reduce design and implementation errors and increase ease of testing and auditing.

Completeness and Consistency

Ensuring that a safeguard meets all of its specifications and is fully functional requires a complete, consistent set of specifications and operating instructions.

The specifications should state exactly what the safeguard is to do and also include limitations specifying what the safeguard is not supposed to do. For example, an underfloor CO_2 fire suppression system should be specified according to the space it is to fill with gas and the space that gas should not enter. In one computer installation, a CO_2 underfloor system that had never been tested was activated accidentally. The CO_2, which is heavier than air, seeped down through conduit openings in the base floor and nearly asphyxiated workers on the floor beneath the computer center.

Instrumentation

No safeguard is complete without instrumentation to regularly monitor its proper functioning and keep track of any performance failures or violations. A researcher designing secure computer operating systems recently indicated that his interest was in designing safeguards that absolutely prevented any form of compromise. Theoretically, a safeguard that is proved to consistently prevent all compromise eliminates the need for instrumentation. However, lack of instrumentation is not consistent with the general needs of a computer security program. IS management must be notified immediately when any safeguard has been violated, and records of past attempted violations are vital for performing audits. Even the most sophisticated safeguards can be neutralized by unanticipated events. One of the worst dangers to computer security is a safeguard that is assumed to be functioning effectively when it is not. This is called a negative safeguard and is worse than none at all.

Instrumentation is also valuable in keeping those accountable for a safeguard constantly aware of its correct functioning and immediately alerting them when a violation is attempted. The visible output of instrumentation must therefore be in a practical, usable form. If instrumentation output is in printed form, it should be as concise as possible so that those responsible for monitoring the safeguard do not become easily fatigued and distracted. If instrumentation produces voluminous data, then the data reduction capabilities of the computer can be used to produce summary data for human observation. The computer can be used to print or display detailed data when necessary for further study. Short summary reports can then be effectively reviewed by higher-level management.

Acceptance and Tolerance by Personnel

Safeguards are only as effective as the personnel involved allow them to be. Each new safeguard must be accepted by the people affected by it. Management must therefore convince all personnel that effective safeguards are in their own best interests. It should be noted that a safeguard that is seen as an attractive challenge to violate is more dangerous than none at all.

Automatic safeguards that function with little real-time intervention help avoid the problem of convincing and motivating people to accept them. Management-imposed constraints on a programming staff—for example, a policy to avoid the use of certain programming language features—are not as likely to be accepted as automatic constraints imposed through the compiler. Programmers are accustomed to being constrained by the computer system and tend to accept such constraints more readily, as long as the constraint does not represent a challenge for them to beat. However, no automatic safeguards in today's commercial systems are sophisticated enough to prevent ingenious and dedicated programmers from bypassing them without detection. Therefore, universal acceptance by the programming staff and tolerance for the constraints imposed must be achieved before a safeguard's effectiveness can be ensured.

An important aid to the acceptance and tolerance of safeguards is the willingness of management to be constrained by the same safeguards that apply to the personnel they supervise, which sets an example and provides an incentive for employees to follow suit. At the same time, the enforcement of safeguards should not impose an unreasonable or unacceptable burden on employees. For example, requiring computer operators to challenge the presence of unauthorized personnel in sensitive work areas usually fails because most employees feel uncomfortable about challenging coworkers. An alternative would be to instruct employees to report infractions to management rather than confronting violators themselves.

Sustainability

A safeguard should function properly several years after installation at the same level of effectiveness as on the first day. Usually, the more automated a safeguard, the more likely it is to function effectively over time. Safeguards that depend heavily on human activity will always be more subject to declining performance over time and require continual motivational efforts to remain effective. A common problem revealed by security audits is that manual safeguards specified in policies, procedures, and operating manuals have become almost nonexistent or ineffective in practice.

Auditability

Every safeguard must be able to be audited with respect to its performance and compliance with specifications. One of the first steps management should take after implementing a safeguard is to establish tests to ensure that the safeguard is auditable and that test criteria exist for it. Development of testing methods and criteria should be part of the design stage and should appear in the specifications of each safeguard. In addition, the cost of testing must be considered. For example, a CO_2 fire extinguishing system is relatively inexpensive to test, whereas halon gas systems can cost several thousand dollars to test. Safeguard testing can also help reveal unanticipated secondary effects or weaknesses.

Design and development staffs often discourage the involvement of auditors in the establishment of controls and safeguards, but it is important that auditors play a role in the evaluation of these controls and safeguards to ensure their auditability. The conflicts that arise when auditors are involved in both the design stage and the subsequent auditing process can be resolved by assigning one auditor to the design stage and another auditor to the auditing function.

Accountability

At least one person must be held accountable for each safeguard. Most often, this task is assigned to the person who is chiefly responsible for the operation of the safeguard and to his immediate supervisor. If an individual is responsible for too many safeguards, the principles of least privilege and sustainability will probably be violated. An individual's job performance should be directly associated with his safeguard accountability performance. Accountability for a safeguard often extends to the assets being protected by the safeguards. The person who is held accountable for both the safeguard and its associated assets will have a greater span of control, which helps achieve consistency in the protection of the assets.

Reaction and Recovery

Safeguards should be evaluated according to how they react to violations. In addition to denying access to violators, some safeguards may convey useful information to violators or even destroy the asset being protected. Some safeguards produce a hostile environment upon violation that delays or makes recovery difficult. The sudden or violent triggering of a safeguard, such as halon gas, can cause panic. In one company, a fire in a room adjacent to the computer room caused detection devices to be activated and armed the halon equipment to release in 30 seconds. Computer operators repeatedly overrode the release because they were terrified by the halon system. It had released accidentally on a previous occasion, frightening the employees with ear-shattering noise and blowing papers all over the room, and they did not want this to happen again.

The timeliness and appropriateness of safeguard responses are also important. A safeguard should not reveal information that could be used for further attack on a computer system. For example, access to a mainframe from a terminal usually requires the input of an authorized name and a password. If the name is valid, the password is tested. In some systems, if the name is not valid, the password is not tested and the terminal is immediately disconnected. A violator can thus determine whether a name is valid without entering a valid password. This safeguard would be more effective if it rejected both the name and the password if either were incorrect. This accomplishes the same goal but does not disclose whether the name is valid.

A safeguard should prevent loss or allow capture of a suspect without causing excessive reaction of the violator or other employees. For example, an alarm should not be so violent or pervasive that it causes overreaction and panic, which can result in other losses.

Residual Characteristics and Resetting of Safeguards

Before a safeguard is implemented, attention must be given to the residual conditions that the assets will be left in once the safeguard has been activated. The circumstances and needs for resetting or reactivating the safeguard should also be determined. After a safeguard has performed its function, the assets being protected should remain at least as secure as before. In many cases, however, additional protection may be necessary after a safeguard has been activated in response to an intrusion because the assets may be in greater danger. Resetting a safeguard that expends itself when activated may take significant time or effort, and assets must be protected by alternate means in the interim. For example, when materials are returned to a computer center from a remote backup facility to restore operations, copies of the material should be preserved in a safe place while recovery proceeds.

Violators can sometimes find sensitive information by scavenging for residual data. Well-designed computer programs erase residual data left in temporary storage locations (erasure of magnetic tapes and disks usually can be more effectively done manually). However, when a safeguard detects a fatal error in data or circuitry and causes an abnormal termination of program execution, residual data may not be erased. Violators can also scavenge through discarded output reports for sensitive data.

Safeguards should therefore be evaluated on the basis of postactivation characteristics and circumstances. Once a safeguard is implemented, its use may require extensive additional procedures. If these procedures are overlooked, the safeguard can actually increase vulnerability.

Trustworthiness of Vendors and Suppliers

If a safeguard is to be depended on, its reliability, integrity, sustainability, and adherence to specifications should be verified. If it is not possible or practical to test all of these characteristics, then the manufacturer, supplier, or maintenance service must be trusted. Cryptographic systems provide a good example of this dependence on vendors and manufacturers. Commercial devices that use the federally approved Data Encryption Standard (DES) are widely used. IBM developed the basic algorithm that was tested and adopted by the former National Bureau of Standards (now named the National Institute of Standards and Technology) with the assistance of the National Security Agency. None of these organizations has revealed the methods and results of its test; each states only that the algorithm used with a 56-bit key is adequate for all nonmilitary purposes. Users of DES must trust these organizations because they do not have the resources to sufficiently test the algorithm themselves. Users must also trust the manufacturers of the devices because their contents are complex and protected by tamper-resistant features. The suppliers must be trusted to deliver the devices in a consistent state of integrity, and the maintenance service must be trusted to preserve that integrity.

So far, efforts to determine the trustworthiness of manufacturers, suppliers, and maintenance services have been less than satisfying. The length of time in operation or the good reputation of a business is not as important as how long the present management has been in charge, whether recent adversities have occurred, and whether there is a record of good earnings. Even these factors are not as important as the individual people employed by the company who provide the products and services. The best strategy is to be informed and use good business practices (e.g., credit and reference checks, use of lawyers and accounts on contract negotiations).

Multiple Functions

A safeguard is almost always selected to serve only one primary security function: deterrence (e.g., enforcement through a code of ethics), prevention (e.g., guard at a door), detection (e.g., violation reporting), or recovery (e.g., remote backup storage). Selection of a safeguard for a specific risk reduction should be based on its primary functional value. However, two safeguards of apparently equal quality may prove to be different when secondary functions are evaluated. For example, most preventive safeguards have some degree of deterrent value. A uniformed guard at a door may be a stronger deterrent than an electronically locked door activated by a card key. On the other hand, a well-instrumented electronically locked door may have greater value for detection.

RISK ACCEPTANCE AND ASSIGNMENT

The acceptance and assignment of risk of information loss should be formally treated among the managers and owners of the information and the information security professionals. There are no absolute rules requiring that all risk of information loss be reduced or that some of the risk be eliminated in an enterprise. Risk of loss will never be totally eliminated. The only requirement is that the information security professional provide management and owners of the information adequate descriptions of the risks and other factors along with recommendations for dealing with them so that management can make informed decisions about the risks. Managers and owners of information must weigh the risks of exposure of information loss, cost to reduce them, and possible failure to meet a standard of due care with other business risks. They may reasonably decide to accept the risks and use the funds that would have been invested in controls for other more worthy purposes.

Managers and owners of information may, after careful consideration and some risk reduction, choose to accept residual risks or assign them to others who would then be accountable for them. Acceptance of risk means that the exposure and liability to loss would remain and be the responsibility of those who are accountable for the information and its required availability and utility, authenticity and integrity, and confidentiality.

Ideally, this acceptance of risk should be documented and signed by the managers and owners. In practice, this is rarely done. Therefore, it may be appropriate for the information security professional who provided advice on the risk to document the event and outcome, at least for the security records. Periodic follow-up should be conducted to evaluate changes in the circumstances of the risk, available controls, standard of due care, and other business risks that were considered in the original decision.

The assignment of retained risk to others is most often accomplished by insuring it. This means the risk is shared or transferred to an insurance company or to another function within the enterprise as self-insurance. In any case, the enterprise's insurance risk management department becomes involved. Another form of risk assignment is to give both the responsibility and accountability to another party more able and appropriate to accept the liability of the risk or to do something to reduce or eliminate it. For example, safely archiving information might better be done by a computer center or records management department rather than end users.

In summary, after informed consideration of reducing or eliminating the risk of information loss, the retained risk should be explicitly assigned to and accepted by the managers or owners of the information. Otherwise, it should be covered by insurance or assigned to other more appropriate parties. In addition, the risk and its acceptance and assignment should be documented in retained records and periodically reviewed by those responsible for information safekeeping with the assistance of information security professionals.

SUMMARY

The principles presented in this chapter contribute to the growing body of information security guidelines, which will continue to grow as the subject matures and agreement is reached by practitioners in the field. These principles are practical for everyday use in the performance of computer security reviews and IS operational audits. As more experience is gained in information security, it is expected that these principles will be expanded and refined.

System Security Certification and Accreditation

ZELLA G. RUTHBERG

Certification is the technical evaluation of compliance with security requirements for the purpose of accreditation. The technical evaluation uses a combination of security evaluation tools and culminates in a technical judgment concerning the extent to which safeguards meet security requirements. Accreditation is official authorization for operation (or, in cases of security deficiencies, for security corrections or suspension of certain activities).

This chapter describes the process of certification and accreditation and discusses the various technical tools used for evaluating systems security. Issues of scheduling and assigning responsibility for performing certification and accreditation activities are also addressed.

THE CERTIFICATION PROGRAM

The certification process is illustrated in Exhibit I-3-5. It is iterative in that, based on findings from each stage, previous stages might have to be reentered and work performed again. Typically, most or all of the stages are ongoing at the same time. The intent of the exhibit is to show the shift in emphasis as work progresses.

Two levels of activity are associated with security evaluation for certification: basic evaluation and detailed evaluation. Basic evaluation involves high-level, or general, evaluation and is essential to all certifications. Usually, basic evaluation suffices for most aspects of a system under review. Most certifications, however, also require detailed work in problem areas and therefore require some detailed evaluation as well.

Time and resources required to perform a certification vary widely from case to case. If potential loss or harm is low, certification cost must also be kept low. Risk analysis can help in deciding how much certification review is cost-justified. Resources for certification may vary from several person-days to many person-months. Minimum products required from certification and accreditation are a security evaluation report and an accreditation statement.

EXHIBIT I-3-5 The Certification Process

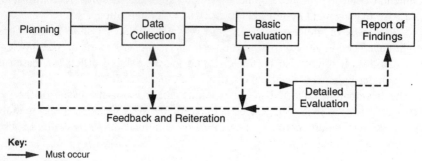

Feedback and Reiteration

Key:
──▶ Must occur
- - -▶ Usually occurs

The certification process described here is presented in functional form. It tells what must be done and presents a general view of how to accomplish it. Details of security evaluation differ widely from case to case and must be adapted to meet system needs. Such aids as detailed evaluation methods and checklists are helpful in the adaptation process, but no single detailed method exists that can be universally applied.

Since the certification process described occurs at a functional level, it can be applied both to systems under development and to operational systems. For example, the process for both could include review of such documentation as functional requirements and test procedure reports. Detailed evaluation methods differ for the two situations, however, because of differences in the types of data available, the time frame in which data is available, and the organization of the work.

The Planning Process

Because the planning process must anticipate problem areas and define needs for specialized skills, planners should perform a quick, high-level review of the entire system in order to gain an understanding of the issues involved. Additional planning tasks include defining the boundaries of the effort, partitioning the work, identifying areas of emphasis, and drawing up a certification plan.

For certification, system boundaries must be established to include all relevant facets of the system's environment, including the administrative, physical, and technical areas. Without this comprehensive review, certification gives an incomplete and perhaps misleading picture of system security. For example, excellent technical controls might be rendered worthless if administrative security duties are not properly defined.

Within these overall boundaries, partitioning of certification work is usually based on the specialized skills involved. For example, security evaluation responsibilities might be allocated among administrative security, operations, contingency planning, change control, data entry and output, the operating system, environmental controls, the development method, applications software controls, the data base management system, hardware, and communications.

Those areas of greatest potential loss or harm should be emphasized. These might have been identified in an earlier risk analysis or in reports of past problems or violations. It might also be the case that the accrediting official(s), based on management judgment, want a particular area emphasized.

The information collected in the planning phase forms the basis for the system's certification plan. Suggested sections for the plan include security requirements, the evaluation approach, the evaluation team makeup, a schedule, required support, and evaluation products.

Data Collection

The ideal source of information is system documentation. Critical documents include system security requirements; output from a risk analysis; a system flowchart showing input, processing steps, and output, along with complete transaction flows for important transaction types; and a listing of system controls. Unfortunately, few systems have complete documentation. Where such documents do not exist, the most efficient technique for gathering information is for system personnel to prepare the documentation and to provide supplementary tutorial briefings to the certification team. Reviews of the more common documents (e.g., user manuals) and interviews are also needed to expand on and corroborate the information in these documents.

Basic Evaluation

The basic security posture of the organization must be evaluated. For example, it might have to be decided whether authorization is needed for terminals as well as individuals and processes.

A basic evaluation comprises four tasks:

1. Requirements Evaluation. Are security requirements acceptable?
2. Function Evaluation. Does the design or description of security functions satisfy the security requirements?
3. Control Implementation Determination. Are the security functions implemented?
4. Methodology Review. Does the implementation method provide assurance that security functions are acceptably implemented?

Requirements Evaluation. Requirements evaluation is important because certification is only meaningful if security requirements are well defined. Unfortunately, this is often not the case. This task then critically examines any documentation of these requirements and compares it with federal, state, organizational, and user requirements. Where no such documentation exists, the security requirements implied in the system must be formulated.

In both formulating and evaluating security requirements, consideration is given to federal and state laws and regulations, organizational standards and policies, and the specific system needs. The four primary areas considered in defining system needs are assets, exposures, threats, and controls. Corresponding questions to be answered are: What should be protected? What might happen to assets if a threat is realized? What are assets being protected against? How effective are security safeguards in reducing exposures?

If a risk analysis has been performed for the system or its environment, many security needs might already be well defined. Other useful tools are computer security checklists and questionnaires.

Function Evaluation. Function evaluation determines whether the design or description of security functions, such as authentication, authorization, monitoring, security management, and security labeling, satisfy security requirements. With well-defined security requirements, function evaluation becomes the most important task in basic evaluation. The primary method is to use the stated requirements as a checklist. For example: Is individual accountability provided? Are subjects and objects identified and given security labels? Is an execute-only mode of access provided? Are all file accesses recorded? Are functions partitioned to provide separation of duties? Does a contingency plan exist and has it been tested?

An important concern in function evaluation is the appropriate level of detail. It is recommended that basic evaluations be complete (for all applicable control features) down through the logical specification level, as defined in (or appropriate for definition in) the functional requirements document. This recommendation applies to both internal computer controls and external physical/administrative controls (although the latter might not actually be defined in a functional requirements document).

This function evaluation approach is suggested in full realization of the difficulties in determining which functions to include in a functional requirements document and, when this document is incomplete or nonexistent, in examining other sources of system information (e.g., operating procedures, specifications). The logical specification level, however, is a legitimate, commonly used level that represents a complete picture of security functions and services with respect to the system environment. It can help ensure that major problem areas are not overlooked.

Control Implementation Determination. That functions are described in a document or discussed in an interview does not prove that they have been implemented. The existence of most physical and administrative controls can be determined by visual inspection. For controls internal to the computer, testing is needed. If the computer system incorporates products from the evaluated products list of the National Computer Security Center (NCSC) that satisfy specified internal computer security requirements, an important part of the needed testing will have already been done. (The NCSC's *Trusted Computer System Evaluation Criteria* (the Orange Book) established an ascending set of security levels for computer products, each of which satisfies increasingly stringent security measures.) Additional testing of the system containing these products would then be appropriate. In many cases, a short operational demonstration might suffice. For example, the existence of a password function can be determined by attempting to use the system and verifying that a valid password is required. If EPL products are not used, however, the controls in the computer system as a whole must be tested. Black box (external) testing is generally sufficient for control implementation determination.

Methodology Review. It is desirable to gain some assurance that controls are acceptably implemented. The best way to do this without becoming immersed in extensive testing or detailed analysis is to examine the methodology used to develop the system. This step applies whether the system is under development or operational.

Methodology review contributes to a confidence judgment on the extent to which controls are reliably implemented and on the susceptibility of the system to flaws. If review findings suggest that the implementation cannot be relied on, detailed evaluation is required to find specific flaws. Identification of specific flaws is far more preferable as certification evidence than a general judgment of low confidence.

Areas of concern in reviewing a systems development methodology for certification (some of which also apply to unevaluated security products obtained from vendors) are summarized as follows:

- Documentation. Is there current and complete documentation of acceptable quality? This applies to both development and operational documentation.
- Objectives. Has security been explicitly stated and treated as an objective? Have security requirements been defined?
- Project Control. Was development well controlled? Were independent reviews and testing performed and did they consider security? Was an effective change-control program used?
- Tools and Techniques. Were structured design techniques (e.g., modularization, formal specifications) used? Were established programming practices and standards (e.g., high-order languages, structured walkthroughs) used?
- Resources. How experienced were the people involved? What were the sensitivity levels or clearances associated with their positions?

Assurance by Detailed Evaluation

In many cases a basic evaluation does not provide sufficient evidence for certification. Examples include cases where basic evaluation reveals problems that require further analysis, the system has a high degree of sensitivity, or primary safeguards are embodied in detailed internal functions that are not visible or suitable for examination at the basic evaluation level. These situations require detailed evaluations to obtain additional evidence and provide increased confidence in evaluation judgments. Detailed evaluations analyze the quality of security safeguards. Primary tasks are to examine the application from the following four points of view and to establish illustrative examples:

1. *Functional operation*. Do controls function properly?
2. *Performance*. Do controls satisfy performance criteria?
3. *Penetration resistance*. How readily can controls be broken or circumvented?
4. *Detailed focusing*. What security components need detailed analysis? What are useful examples?

Tasks are performed as needed; it would be unusual for all four perspectives to be examined during one evaluation. Testing is the most common technique used. Other validation and verification techniques are also available and are becoming more widely used.

Functional Operation. This point of view is most often emphasized, since it assesses protection against human error and simple attempts at abuse. Tests of functional operation examine such areas as control operation, parameter checks, common error conditions, control monitoring, and control management. Software tools for program analysis and formal verification methods are also applicable.

Performance. There is much more to the quality of safeguards than proper functional operation. Performance factors relevant to security include availability, survivability, accuracy, response time, and throughput. Stress testing is a useful evaluation technique.

Penetration Resistance. This detailed evaluation assesses resistance against breaking or circumventing controls. This can be the most technically complex of the detailed evaluation categories. It can be used to establish confidence in security safeguards or to find and correct flaws, although the latter approach is inadequate for achieving security. The nature of the evaluation activity here differs widely depending on whether the penetrators are users, operators, application programmers, system programmers, managers, or external personnel. It applies not only to attacks against data, but also to attacks against physical assets and system performance. Areas for this detailed examination include the change control process, error handling, and access to residual information. Formal approaches have been developed for evaluating the penetration resistance of software, hardware, and both physical and administrative controls. Because penetration-resistance evaluation is different in kind from other forms of evaluation, it can play a useful role in certification.

Detailed Focusing. It is rarely feasible or desirable to examine everything in detail. In addition to evaluation from some or all of the points of view discussed thus far, two other strategies are especially useful for focusing on narrow portions of the security picture: one based on security components and one based on situational analysis.

Security-relevant components on which attention might be focused are assets, exposures, threats, and controls. A risk analysis may have already resulted in a high-level view of the relations among these elements. Examples of possible types of detailed analysis include asset value in relation to asset exploitation, threats in relation to classes of perpetrators, the impact of exposures (e.g., disclosure violations, erroneous decisions, and fraud) on primary security goals (e.g., integrity, nondisclosure), and control analysis (e.g., the work-factor needed to exploit a vulnerability, and trade-offs) among various counter measures. It is difficult to anticipate precise needs for such studies when planning certification, although it is safe to assume that some will be needed.

Situational analysis addresses the problem of system complexity, which limits not only the percentage of the system that can be examined but also the degree of understanding attainable for those portions that are examined. Two useful forms of it are the analysis of attack scenarios and the analysis of transaction flows. An attack scenario is a synopsis of a projected course of events associated with a threat (e.g., a penetration of the system). A transaction flow is a sequence of events involved in the processing of a transaction. Both can be used to complement the high-level completeness of basic evaluation by providing detailed, well-understood examples.

Report of Findings

The security evaluation report is the primary product of certification. It contains technical and management security recommendations and forms the primary basis for the accreditation decision. The report should:

- Summarize the security standards or policies applied.
- Summarize the controls in place.
- Summarize major vulnerabilities, recommending which should be corrected and which allowed to remain.
- Recommend and rank corrective actions, if warranted, along with anticipated costs and impact; recommend operational restrictions as necessary.
- Summarize the certification process, so the accreditor can determine how much confidence to place in the findings.
- Include a proposed accreditation statement (positive or negative).

EXHIBIT I-3-6 Sample Outline for a Security Evaluation Report

1. Introduction and Summary
2. Background
3. Major Findings
   3.1 General Control Posture
   3.2 Vulnerabilities
4. Recommended Corrective Actions
5. Certification Process
Attachment A: Proposed Accreditation Statement
Attachment B: Detailed Evaluation Reports

The certification process should produce the security evaluation report plus other documentation that can be used to support the findings and to evaluate the certification process itself. (See Exhibit I-3-6 for a suggested report outline.)

ACCREDITATION

Accreditors are responsible for evaluating the certification evidence, judging the acceptability of system security safeguards, approving corrective actions, ensuring that corrective actions are accomplished, and issuing the accreditation statement. Aids to be used to assist in this process include answers to questions on resources used (how much, who), processes used (review mechanisms, coordination of findings), and report content (reasonableness, support of findings). Accreditation responsibilities must be integrated into the normal decision-making process of the organization.

Since systems that warrant certification and accreditation are usually important to an organization's operations, most flaws will not be severe enough to remove an operational system from service. There are many intermediate accreditation alternatives available. The most common is to withhold accreditation pending completion of corrections. For example:

- Adding procedural security controls—Restricting use of the system to sites that have compensating controls.

- Restricting the system to processing only nonsensitive or minimally sensitive data.

- Removing especially vulnerable system functions or components (thus in a network environment possibly excluding a particularly weak node).

- Restricting the system to users with approved access to all data being processed or who have passed a background investigation.

- Restricting use of the system to noncritical situations in which the impact of errors or failures is less severe.

- Removing remote access (thus relying more on physical security).
- Granting conditional accreditation for a shakedown period before accreditation is finalized.

RECERTIFICATION AND REACCREDITATION

Once a system has been initially certified (whether during development or after becoming operational), the work is not over. As a system or its security environment changes, recertification and reaccreditation are needed.

It is not practical for the accreditor(s), who might be a senior official or a committee of officials, personally to approve every change. On the other hand, substantive changes do require reaccreditation. This gives rise to a need for levels of recertification and reaccreditation based on levels of change. The three levels suggested are: (1) major, affecting the basic security design; (2) intermediate, affecting two or more security software modules or a major hardware component; and (3) minor, within one security software module. The elements of the certification process and the organizational placement of the accreditor differ for each level, with more extensive changes requiring both more extensive evaluation and higher placement of reaccreditation responsibility.

Change control (configuration management) can provide important assistance to recertification and reaccreditation efforts, since it is required during both development and operation. Every change should be reviewed for its impact on prior certification evidence.

EVALUATION TOOLS

For certification and accreditation to be used properly, it is essential to know what tools are available and to which systems they should be applied. There are four groups of tools currently used in security evaluation that can be applied to certification, either alone or in combination. They differ from one another in their purpose as well as in the organizational entities that use them. The four groupings of methods are risk analysis; validation, verification, and testing; security safeguard evaluation; and EDP audit.

Risk Analysis

The primary purpose of risk analysis is to understand the security problem by identifying security risks, determining their magnitude, and identifying areas where safeguards are needed. It can be performed at the beginning of the system life cycle and, with user input and policy mandates, can provide the basis for system security requirements. When performed later in the system life cycle, it is useful for evaluating security when reliable data exists on threats (e.g., occurrences of fires and floods). Risk analysis is usually performed under the direction of personnel internal to the system in question. A good discussion of automated tools for risk analysis is provided in the NIST Computer Systems Laboratory report *Automated Risk Management Software Tools*, by Irene Gilbert (March 16, 1992).

Validation, Verification, and Testing

Validation, verification, and testing (VV&T) is a process of review, analysis, and testing that should be performed on a system throughout its life cycle but is particularly cost-effective when performed during its early stages. Validation determines the correctness of the system with respect to its requirements; verification checks the internal consistency and completeness of the system as it evolves and passes through different levels of specification; and testing, either automated or manual, examines system behavior by exercising it on sample data sets. VV&T provides a powerful quality assurance tool for systems, and when requirements include security, it becomes an important security evaluation tool. VV&T is usually performed by those responsible for developing the system; however, for critical systems it may be done by an independent body.

Security-Safeguard Evaluation

Security-safeguard evaluation methods are primarily concerned with assessing the security solution. They can be thought of as a specialized form of VV&T that involves validating security requirements, examining safeguards, and determining whether safeguards satisfy security requirements. These methods usually break the problem into manageable pieces that correspond with the different skill areas or organizational entities involved in the system or application. Numerous methods are being used for this type of evaluation. Examples of different approaches include checklists, control matrices, and partial quantitative analyses. This type of evaluation is typically performed by people independent of the system in question but internal to the organizational division within which the system resides. A security officer may head such an evaluation.

EDP Audit

EDP audit is usually broader in scope than security issues. Like security-safeguard evaluation, it assesses compliance with policies and the existence and adequacy of controls, but it might also address cost and efficiency in meeting mission objectives. Unlike security-safeguard evaluation, EDP audit is a tool external to the organizational division in which the system resides and is used by higher-level managers to manage the organization.

RESPONSIBILITIES AND SCHEDULING

Three important aspects of certification and accreditation remain to be summarized: Who does them, to which systems are they applied, and when are they done?

Accreditation Responsibility

The most important consideration in defining responsibilities is proper selection of the accrediting authority. This might be a high-level line official or a group of officials who are responsible for the system and who have authority to remedy deficiencies.

Certification Responsibility

Certification personnel are primarily technical, although every certification effort requires a manager. In addition, the organization might have a central coordinator or director for all certification activities. In some cases several certification efforts are performed in support of one accreditation decision. It is preferable to integrate such multiple technical certification findings into one final report.

Two points are noteworthy on technical support. First, it is often best to use both independent and internal people for security evaluation. Independent people provide necessary objectivity, though this is costly, since outsiders must take the time to learn details of the system. Internal people are typically less costly and less objective but can benefit greatly from the security training and increased security awareness they gain from participation. The second point is that certification makes much use of validation, verification, and testing findings and of reviews that are routinely performed during development and operation. It is not practical for certification to duplicate these activities. On the other hand, it is desirable for certification needs to influence them (e.g., by anticipating and recording these needs in VV&T planning).

Systems Requiring Certification and Accreditation

Certification and accreditation are only performed on those systems sensitive enough to warrant such attention (system sensitivity derives from the potential loss or harm associated with its operation). As mentioned, this information can be derived from a risk analysis. To be cost-effective, this process requires that an organization have a prioritized list of sensitive systems based on such factors as mission importance, asset value, and anticipated threats. Some organizations have sensitivity categorization schemes in use for this prioritizing activity.

Scheduling

The remaining issue concerns when this combined certification and accreditation process is performed. It begins with requirements definition and continues through development, operation, and maintenance of a system. It must be integrated into the life cycle management process. However, it is far more preferable to certify and accredit a system under development than one that has become operational, because a system under development is easier to change. Certification during development also permits the development process itself to be improved.

SUMMARY

The best way to view certification and accreditation is as a form of security quality control. Although to some they may appear to be unnecessary overhead functions, they are critically needed for sensitive systems. Security is too important and complex an issue to be without assurance of quality.

The keys to a successful certification and accreditation program follow:

- Formation of a ranked list of sensitive systems in order to scope and organize the program.
- Evaluation of new applications and changes to them that parallel development. Changes, including those required for security, are less costly and face less resistance at this point in the application life cycle.
- Proper assignment of accreditation authority. The official who authorizes the accreditation statement must possess authority to allocate resources both to achieve acceptable security and to remedy deficiencies. This typically requires that the accreditor be a high-level line manager or a group of officials.
- Accurate, complete, and understandable security requirements. Existing requirements must be critically examined; if they do not exist, they must be formulated.
- Capable and objective technical evaluators. Satisfactory technical evaluation requires people who understand both DP security and the technology associated with the system and who have no vested interest in the evaluation's outcome.
- Ready access to the personnel and documentation associated with the system; these provide the evidence needed for the certification and subsequent accreditation.
- Use of a comprehensive basic evaluation.
- Use of detailed evaluation where needed.

The certification of a sensitive system consists of a technical evaluation of the security safeguards in that system; the certification report is composed of a basic system evaluation plus detailed evaluations where needed. The accreditation statement for that sensitive system records the accreditors' acceptance of the satisfactory security safeguards, approval of any corrective actions to any unsatisfactory safeguards, and procedures for ensuring that corrective actions have been implemented.

The accreditation statement is an official document that records an explicit acceptance of responsibility for DP security. This acceptance of responsibility is a decision based on a judgment; it is not a guarantee. The statement culminates the certification and accreditation process. The true benefits, however, do not derive from the statement itself; they derive from the checks, balances, increased security awareness, and increased management control generated by the certification and accreditation process as a whole.

Implementing Certification and Accreditation of Systems

NANDER BROWN

The Office of Management and Budget (OMB) Circular A-130 mandates that federal agencies conduct security certifications of sensitive systems. The circular provides guidance that can be used by federal agencies and other organizations in specifying security requirements prior to acquiring or developing automated applications. Upon completion of the system test, an agency official certifies that the system meets all applicable federal policies, regulations, and standards, and that the results of the test demonstrate that implemented security and controls are adequate for the application.

Certification and accreditation are normally performed on systems that process sensitive information or perform critical support functions. Certification should be accomplished before a sensitive system becomes operational. Recertification should be performed after a designated period or after a major change or major security failure. Circular A-130 requires recertification at least every three years.

In most organizations, accreditation officials may consist of:

- Functional program managers.
- System owners.
- System project team leaders.
- Managers directly responsible for local area network (LAN) operations.
- Regional office managers responsible for local systems.

CERTIFICATION AND ACCREDITATION PROGRAM

In addition to prescribing the goal of certifying and accrediting a system, the certification and accreditation program should address the enhancement of the security capabilities of sensitive application systems. The primary objectives are to ensure that there is a minimum secure environment for computer applications and that sensitive data and financial resources are protected by a network of technical, physical, and administrative controls. These controls should ensure that:

- Sensitive transactions and data are limited to those individuals requiring access in support of official duties.
- Processing environments are equipped with security locks or other controls to prevent unauthorized destruction and disclosure of data.
- Security procedures are established and disseminated. They should include guidelines to classify systems as sensitive or nonsensitive.

The system security certification program should consist of the following:

- Assignment of system certification and accreditation responsibilities.
- Integration of security certification and accreditation into the system life cycle management process.
- Development and maintenance of an inventory of sensitive systems.
- Specification of security requirements commensurate with the sensitivity and risk of each system.
- Periodic certification and technical evaluation.

Exhibit I-3-7 summarizes the system certification and accreditation process.

SENSITIVE SYSTEMS DESIGNATION

The degree of protection afforded automated systems depends on the sensitivity of the data and the system to the mission of the organization. Sensitive data is data that require protection owing to the risk and magnitude of loss or harm that could result from inadvertent or deliberate disclosure, alteration, or destruction of the data. A sensitive system is an automated information system that requires protection because it processes sensitive data, or because of the risk and magnitude of loss or harm that could result from improper operation or deliberate manipulation of the system. Determination of sensitivity of systems is accomplished by assessing the impact of the system on operations, and by assessing the value of its data to the organization and its clients.

General Categories of Sensitive Information

Automated information systems or data that meet the following categories are considered sensitive:

- Data covered by the Privacy Act of 1974.
- Proprietary/business data that may be withheld under the provisions of the Freedom of Information Act.
- Financial information systems such as loan accounting and accounts receivable, accounts payable, payroll, personnel, and inventory control systems.

EXHIBIT I-3-7 **Sensitive System Certification and Accreditation Process**

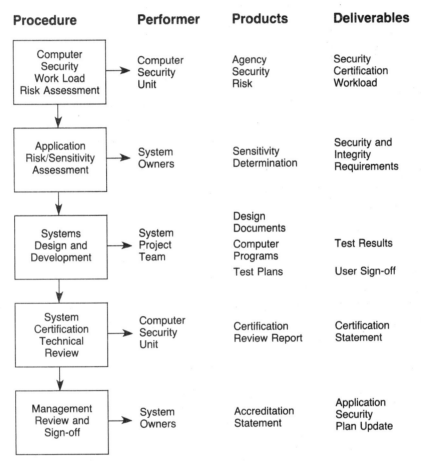

Procedure	Performer	Products	Deliverables
Computer Security Work Load Risk Assessment	Computer Security Unit	Agency Security Risk	Security Certification Workload
Application Risk/Sensitivity Assessment	System Owners	Sensitivity Determination	Security and Integrity Requirements
Systems Design and Development	System Project Team	Design Documents Computer Programs Test Plans	Test Results User Sign-off
System Certification Technical Review	Computer Security Unit	Certification Review Report	Certification Statement
Management Review and Sign-off	System Owners	Accreditation Statement	Application Security Plan Update

All applications and transactions that update information contained in such systems, including applications that produce checks, requisition supplies, or that perform critical management operations with limited human intervention (so-called automated decision-making systems) are similarly considered sensitive.

- Automated information systems considered essential or vital to the mission of the organization.
- Information processed by regional offices that fall within one or more of the categories above. This includes stand-alone systems and information systems that interact with the mainframe facility.

Sensitivity Levels

Some systems are more sensitive than others due to their high dollar value, their legal requirements, or their high impact on operations. Internal controls and computer security requirements will be more strenuous for these highly sensitive systems than for moderately sensitive systems. The overall objective is to provide sufficient security commensurate with the perceived risks of the system and not to overly secure a system. If this objective is achieved, the security and controls implemented will be cost effective and practical. Sensitive systems may be classified, for convenience, in one of five sensitivity levels as follows:

- Level 4—Very high.
- Level 3—High.
- Level 2—Moderate.
- Level 1—Low.
- Level 0—Not sensitive.

SYSTEM SENSITIVITY ASSESSMENT

Security and control requirements for new systems should be determined during the requirements analysis phase. These requirements should be incorporated in the overall functional requirements of new systems according to the risk of its environment. System documentation should include specific information pertaining to the system's security and control capabilities. System tests should be conducted to ensure that these capabilities are adequately implemented.

There is an economic advantage to addressing security and control issues during the system design and development stages. Installing controls at an early stage decreases system cost over the life of the system because subsequent corrective maintenance is minimized.

The following procedures describe the general steps that must be accomplished to complete the system sensitivity assessment and the security certification. Each step of this process is discussed fully in the following sections of this chapter.

- Perform application sensitivity assessment. Conduct interviews with the system owner and the project team leader, and perform an application sensitivity assessment.
- Determine sensitivity level. Calculate a risk score and determine the sensitivity level.
- Determine security requirements. Match the sensitivity level to the appropriate security requirements base set.
- Translate requirements into control objectives. Translate security requirements into specific control objectives based on the sensitivity level and the base security requirements.

- Prepare security and integrity specifications .
- Integrate security requirements into the design. Integrate security requirements with the overall user functional requirements, and include them in the design of the new system.
- Perform certification security review. Select an in-house team or contractor to conduct the certification review.
- Prepare the certification report. Prepare a certification report that describes the review procedure and recommendations to improve system security and integrity.

Sensitivity Assessment Criteria

Sensitivity assessment is a system-wide risk assessment with a specific focus on the risks and vulnerabilities specific to each application. After careful consideration of the combined ratings of all subcriteria listed in Exhibit I-3-8, risk ratings are assigned to each major criterion in the format shown in Exhibit I-3-9. The Delphi decision-making process is used to assist in determining an acceptable risk rating for pervasive risks. Application-specific risks are selected from a table that lists types of internal control risks; Exhibit I-3-10 is an example of an application-specific risk table.

The criteria listed in Exhibit I-3-8 are ranked in order of their relative importance. For example, for purposes of security assessment, the system functional attributes criterion is considered more important than the computer processing environment criterion. Subcriteria are also ranked in order of relative importance, as shown in Exhibit I-3-8. To determine the risk rating for each major criterion, the analyst checks off each subcriterion that presents a risk and sums up the number of check marks to determine the rating.

In addition to calculating a risk rating for each major criterion of pervasive risk, a risk rating is calculated for the three application-specific risk items that pose the greatest risk to the system; these three items are selected from the application-specific risk table (see Exhibit I-3-10 for a sample table).

A final risk score for all system risks (i.e., pervasive and application-specific risks) is then calculated using an algorithm that employs several sensitivity and weighting factors. As shown in Exhibit I-3-9, each risk criterion is assigned a weighting factor; for example, system functional attributes has a weighting factor of 3. At the top of Exhibit I-3-9, the analyst must also provide a sensitivity impact rating, reflecting the system's impact on the overall mission of the organization. Sample sensitivity impact ratings are provided in Exhibit I-3-11. It should be noted that in this exhibit, a system impairment is defined as any system problem that could result in a significant degradation of service or misrepresentation of data.

Exhibit I-3-12 shows the sensitivity impact rating and the risk ratings and weighting factors for a hypothetical system. With this information, it is now possi-

EXHIBIT I-3-8 **Sensitivity Assessment Subcriteria**

Rating		Relative Importance
	System Functional Attributes	
—	Regulations to comply with: Public laws OMB circulars Standard operating procedures	↑ High
—	Financial Data	
—	Privacy Data	
—	Agency proprietary data	
—	Total	
	System Integrity Requirements	
—	Data controls and data checks needs	
—	User Attitude and Security Awareness	
—	Perceived need for data integrity	
—	Special security and control needs	
—	Total	
	Data Confidentiality Requirements	Moderate
—	Privacy or proprietary data	
—	Degree of data sharing	
—	Special access requirements	
—	Interaction with other systems	
—	Total	
	System Availability Requirements	
—	System availability requirements	
—	Interaction with other systems	
—	Backup requirements (hourly, daily, weekly)	
—	Off-site backup storage requirements	
—	Total	
	Computer Processing Environment	
—	Geographic dispersion of users	
—	Number of users	
—	Complexity of automation operations	
—	Interaction with other systems	Low
—	Total	↓

EXHIBIT I-3-9 **Sensitivity Assessment Criteria**

Rating		Weight
—	**Sensitivity Impact**	
	Pervasive Risks	
—	System Functional Attributes	3
—	System Integrity Requirements	2.5
—	Data Confidentiality Requirements	2
—	System Availability Requirements	1.5
—	Computer Processing Environment	1
	Application-Specific Risks (Prerated in the application-specific risk table)	
—	Specific Risk 1	2
—	Specific Risk 2	1.5
—	Specific Risk 3	1

EXHIBIT I-3-10 Application-Specific Risk Table

Item Number	Specific Risk	Rating
10	No risk	0
11	Improper authorizations	7
12	Inefficient operation	8
13	Lack of management control	7
14	Loss of agency experience	7
15	Loss of assets	9
16	Lack of standardization	8
17	Low employee morale	2
18	Public loss of confidence	8
20	Ineffective reporting to management	8
22	Inability to meet goals/objectives	8
24	Inadequate communications capability	5
25	Legal violation	8
26	Potential for law suits	8
27	Ineffective monitoring	8
28	Improper financial decisions	8
29	Opportunity loss	7
30	Misstatement of financial data	8
33	Improper expenditures	8
34	Inadequate support	5
35	Potential for fraud	8
37	Destruction of data	9
39	Inability to meet agency procedural requirements	9
41	Integrity of information	8
44	Lack of systems development methodology	8
49	Continuity of operations—user areas	9
50	Inadequate internal/external audits	7
51	Potential disclosure of sensitive data	9
54	Control over output	8
55	Violation administration regulation	8
56	Misuse of computer resources	9
57	Integration of systems/technology	7
58	Documented policies and procedures	8
59	Development and maintenance of systems inventory	7

EXHIBIT I-3-11 Assessment of Mission Impact

Sensitivity Impact	Mission Impact
9	System directly supports the mission. A system impairment would adversely impact most agency operations.
8.5	System directly supports the mission. A system impairment would adversely impact major operations and the major program.
8	System supports the mission. A system impairment would adversely impact the major program only.
7	System supports the mission. A system impairment would adversely impact the local organization only.
6	System supports the mission. A system impairment would adversely impact the office only.
5	All other sensitive systems.

EXHIBIT I-3-12 **Sensitivity Assessment Criteria**

Rating
[8.5]   Sensitivity Impact

	Pervasive Risks	**Weight**
[7.5]	System Functional Attributes	3
[7]	System Integrity Requirements	2.5
[7]	Data Confidentiality Requirements	2
[8]	System Availability Requirements	1.5
[7]	Computer Processing Environment	1

Application-Specific Risks
(Prerated in the application-specific risk table)

[8]	Integrity of Information (41)	2
[7]	Lack of Management Control (13)	1.5
[7]	Improper Authorizations (11)	1

---

ble to calculate final system risk. The following algorithms can be used to accomplish this:

$$\text{PERVASIVE RISK} = \text{SUM } [W * [5(SI + R]]$$
$$\text{SPECIFIC RISK} = \text{SUM } [W * [5(SI + R]]$$
$$\text{FINAL RISK} = \text{PERVASIVE RISK} + \text{SPECIFIC RISK}$$

where:
  W = the weighting factor for each criterion
  SI = the sensitivity impact rating
  R = the risk rating for each criterion.

The total value for pervasive and specific risk is the sum of these calculated values for each criterion. For example, the calculated value for the system functional attributes criterion is: $3 * 5(8.5 + 7.5) = 240$. In this example, the final risk score is the sum of the scores for pervasive risk (790) plus specific risk (358.8), or 1,148.8.

The risk score can be normalized using the following algorithm:

$$\text{NORMALIZED RISK} = \text{FINAL RISK/MAXIMUM POSSIBLE SCORE}$$

In this example, the maximum possible score is 1,305; therefore, normalized risk score is 1,148.8/1,305, or .88. (The maximum possible score may change if there is a change in the number of criteria, weighting factors, or special risk factors.) The normalized risk score is used in subsequent analysis of security requirements. It should be noted that software packages can be used to calculate risk scores using similar types of algorithms.

EXHIBIT I-3-13 Sensitivity Level Security Requirements

Level 4
- User monitoring
- Reconciliation procedures
- Security test
- Special audit features

Level 3
- Application controls
- Enhanced audit trails
- Security report
- Error reports
- Test plan
- Segregation of activities

Level 2
- Audit trails
- System management
- Passwords
- Contingency plan
- Data validation

Level 1
- System test
- Data retention
- System documentation

Level 0
- Data backup

Security Requirements Selection

Security requirements, appropriate to the sensitivity level, should be included in the design specifications and the final system documentation. The system development team must integrate these requirements into the overall user functional requirements and develop computer algorithms to incorporate them into the design of the new system. The security requirements should be selected from one or more of the security requirements base sets illustrated in Exhibit I-3-13 according to the system's level of sensitivity. For example, a level 4 sensitivity (very high) requires all base sets, whereas, level 2 sensitivity requires only sets 0, 1, and 2.

Suggested ranges from which to select appropriate base security requirements on the basis of normalized risk scores are illustrated in Exhibit I-3-14.

Translating Security Requirements into Control Objectives. Security requirements consist of specific security control objectives necessary to protect designated control areas. Certification requirements consist of broader objectives that may consist of one or more security objectives. Thus, for adequate evaluation, security requirements must be translated into an appropriate set of safeguards and control objectives. A suggested translation based on sensitivity levels is shown in Exhibit I-3-15.

EXHIBIT I-3-14 Sensitivity Levels and Computed Risk Scores

Risk Scores	Sensitivity Level	Security Requirement Base Sets
.875–1.000	4—Very high	All Sets
.650–.874	3—High	Sets 0,1,2, and 3
.450–.649	2—Moderate	Sets 0,1, and 2
.150–.449	1—Low	Sets 0 and 1
.001–.149	0—Nonsensitive	Set 0

EXHIBIT I-3-15 Sample Control Objectives

	Sensitivity Level				
	4	3	2	1	0
Auditability					
• Audit trails	X	X	X		
• Special audit features	X				
Controllability					
• Systems management	X	X	X		
• Documentation	X	X	X		
• Test plans	X	X			
Identification					
• Passwords	X	X	X		
• Password administration	X	X	X		
Integrity					
• Data validation	X	X	X		
• Error reports	X	X			
• Control totals	X	X			
• Reconciliation procedures	X				
• System test	X	X	X	X	
Isolation					
• Segregation of activities	X	X			
Recoverability					
• Data backup	X	X	X	X	X
• Data retention	X	X	X	X	
• Contingency plan	X	X	X		
Surveillance					
• Enhanced audit trails	X	X			
• Error reports	X	X			
• User monitoring	X				
• Security test	X				

System Certification Criteria

The process of certifying that a computer system contains a properly functioning set of security safeguards and is operated under an appropriate set of controls and operational procedures is complex and difficult. The precise details of adequate certification procedures, including necessary tests and evaluations, are difficult to define. Once defined, they lack general acceptance. The procedural steps described in this section can be used to collect sufficient data to make a recommendation on whether a new system or existing system should be accredited.

Certification criteria for sensitive systems should include the following security attributes:

- Auditability of system operation and data handling.
- Controllability of system operation and performance.
- Identification of authorized users of the system.
- Integrity of system procedures and data entry and output processes.
- Isolation of system processes and segregation of duties.
- Recoverability procedures for data and system operations.
- Surveillance of error conditions and security violations.
- Specific risks of unique vulnerabilities of the system or its operating environment.
- Functional requirements unique to the system.
- Formal control objectives and regulatory policies that must be complied with.

Security and Integrity Requirements

This section provides a description of the security and integrity requirements that should be implemented for sensitive systems. The specific requirements are based on the system sensitivity level as discussed previously. Additional requirements may be implemented as warranted. The following sections describe the security and integrity requirements for the hypothetical XYZ system. This system is a payroll system rated at level 4 sensitivity.

Auditability. Auditability permits relative ease in examining, verifying, or demonstrating a system. Auditability's two prime objectives are to determine whether the proposed system contains internal controls adequate to ensure that system results will be reasonably accurate and reliable and to evaluate whether planned management reports and audit trails will satisfy management's need for periodic inquiry and enable auditors to perform an effective audit. The auditability requirements for the XYZ system are:

- Recording of all transactions and events.
- Recorded activity log.

- Auditable subsystems.
- Identified subsystem boundaries and interfaces.

Controllability. The objectives of internal control are to provide management with reasonable, but not absolute, assurance that financial and other resources are safeguarded from unauthorized use or disposition; transactions are executed as authorized; financial and statistical records and reports are accurate and reliable; applicable laws, regulations, and policies are adhered to; and resources are efficiently and effectively managed. The following requirements are applicable to the XYZ system:

- Systems administration controls.
- Systems design methodology.
- Project management controls and procedures.
- Management and user involvement.
- Standards.

Identification. A key element in data security is user identification, which enables an organization to hold authorized users accountable for their actions. To accurately identify users, security mechanisms need certain information concerning each attempted access. The following requirements apply to the XYZ system:

- Terminal or computer identification.
- Authorized user identification.
- Authorized level of access.
- Required level of logging and event tracking.

Integrity. Systems integrity is the property of a system that permits its effective and reliable development and use. A design methodology, structured development, and up-to-date operational procedures are usually required. The integrity requirements for the XYZ system are:

- Data base integrity.
- Software integrity.
- Processing integrity.
- System integrity tests.

Isolation. Isolation protects the system and its data from unauthorized disclosure. This is achieved by segregating functions and duties to specific activities on a need-to-know or a need-to-perform basis. The requirements prescribed for the XYZ system are:

- Segregation of duties.
- Segregation of processing.
- Documented systems interface and boundaries for the domain of access.

Recoverability. Recoverability of data and processing includes an emergency reaction capability, backup precautions, and the ability to fully recover any lost or damaged systems resource. File reconstruction and system fall-back procedures are major components of a recovery capability. Requirements for the XYZ system are:

- Recovery and reconstruction of files from backup.
- Data base logging and recovery.
- Source transaction retention.
- Systems documentation.
- Fault tolerance.

Surveillance. Surveillance enhances security by detecting potential threats and by accounting for all accesses and attempted processes by each user. It includes the recording of significant events in order to detect potential breaches and to raise an alarm. Surveillance requirements for the XYZ system are:

- Identification of required control mechanisms.
- Error detection routines.
- Overall system for logging and monitoring security events.

Formal Control Objectives. Formal control objectives refer to regulatory objectives that must be met. Regulatory objectives are addressed by security policy, control policy, accounting policy, and other directives. Requirements for the XYZ system are:

- Regulatory requirements, including OMB circulars and federal laws.
- Organization requirements, including management directives and policies.
- Measures to evaluate program effectiveness according to the requirements of the Chief Financial Officer Act of 1990.

Specific Risks. The system owner must identify three risk items from the table of application-specific risks. These items should be unique risks faced by the XYZ system. New items may be added to the specific risks table as needed.

Functionality. Functionality includes the minimum functions that must be performed to make the system successful. These are basic user requirements that the system must meet. The XYZ system must calculate accurate gross pay, taxes, other withholdings, and net pay.

Exceptions. Exceptions refer to constraints that are imposed upon the system owing to financial or technical considerations. Of primary concern are those constraints that may affect integrity and security of the system. Known exceptions that exist for the XYZ system are:

- Specific areas that should be excluded from consideration because of cost constraints or prior management decisions.
- Technical constraints owing to operational limitations of the system.

Security Certification Review

The scope of the certification review includes the assessment and evaluation of the security and integrity of the system, including its software and data. The certification process can be applied both to new systems and to existing systems. Detailed evaluation methods differ for the two situations, however, because of differences in the types of data available, the time frame in which data is available, and the organization of work.

The Security Certification Report is the primary product of the certification review. It should contain a summary of security and integrity measures and technical security recommendations. It is the primary basis for the accreditation decision. The certification report should be prepared by or at the direction of the computer security manager or the designated certification program manager. The final element in the certification report is the formal certification statement signed by the person in charge of protecting the system or application in question. The format of the certification statement is shown in Exhibit I-3-16.

EXHIBIT I-3-16 Security Certification Statement

We have carefully considered the security and integrity requirements and the vulnerabilities of the _____ [named] _____ system. Based on our review of the security requirements, vulnerabilities, and potential threats against the security and integrity measures implemented or planned, we have determined that the security capabilities are adequate for known risks, and that the statement of systems security and integrity requirements is a fair representation of the level of security and integrity of _____ [named] _____ system, except for the weaknesses noted in the security certification report.

Based on the report and our judgment, we hereby certify, subject to the corrections recommended in the security certification report that _____ [named] _____ system meets the documented and approved security requirements.

Weighing the remaining residual risks against operational requirements, we recommend that _____ [named] _____ be accredited for continued operation, and that the recommendations included in the security certification report be implemented.

Signed: _____
            Computer Security Manager

Date: _____

Certification and Accreditation Decisions

Based on the recommendations included in the certification report, accreditation officials issue the official accreditation. There are several accreditation alternatives available depending on results of the certification evaluation and the certification report. Conditional accreditation may be granted pending completion of corrections. Alternative accreditation recommendations include:

- Unconditional accreditation. Accreditation is granted without restrictions. There may be some minor security weaknesses; however, these weaknesses should not present significant risks to the system.
- Conditional accreditation. Accreditation is granted with certain restrictions. For example, continued operation under specific conditions or pending the correction of minor security weaknesses.
- Accreditation delayed. The implementation of procedures or safeguards to address major security weaknesses is required before accreditation can be extended.
- Accreditation denied. Design and development effort are required to implement required security measures. A new certification evaluation is required.
- Accreditation and system operation denied. The system presents a major risk to the organization. A major component of the system must be redesigned and implemented. A new technical certification evaluation may be required.

The Accreditation Statement (as shown in Exhibit I-3-17) contains the above accreditation recommendations. It should be signed by the person responsible for the appropriate security level of the system or application in question.

EXHIBIT I-3-17 Security Accreditation Statement

We have carefully considered the security and integrity requirements and the vulnerabilities of the _____ [named] _____ system based on the review of the requirements, vulnerabilities, and potential threats against the security and integrity measures that have been implemented or planned, we have determined that the security capabilities are adequate for known risks, and that the statement of systems security and integrity requirements worksheet is a fair representation of the level of security and integrity of the _____ [named] _____ system as of _____.
   We have determined that the requirements of _____ [named] _____ system dated _____, have been satisfied and the _____ [named] _____ system is in the best interest of the _____ [organization] _____ based on our authority and judgment, and weighing the remaining residual risks against operational requirements, we authorize operation (or continued operation) of the _____ [named] _____ system. We further authorize initiation of the following corrective actions to enhance security and integrity:

(Corrective Actions)

Signed: _____   _____

Date: _____   _____

SUMMARY

This chapter described the actions that must be performed to complete a system sensitivity assessment and obtain security certification and accreditation. The basic steps include:

- Performing the application sensitivity assessment.
- Determining sensitivity levels.
- Determining security requirements.
- Translating these requirements into control objectives.
- Preparing security and integrity specifications.
- Integrating security requirements into the system design.
- Performing certification security review.
- Preparing the certification report.

Certification should be completed before the targeted system becomes operational. The system should be recertified periodically or after a major system modification or a significant security failure.

Business Continuity

Even if all of the appropriate information security measures are properly implemented, a natural disaster (e.g., flood or earthquake) or human-engineered disaster (e.g., fire or bombing) could result in loss of data processing capabilities. Research has shown that most organizations can sustain an outage of a week or so using manual methods to work around the outage. However, a two-week outage could so cripple an organization that its very survival could become doubtful.

The answer to this problem is business continuity planning. Business continuity planning involves taking proactive steps to arrange for critical systems to be processed at an alternate site if the normal processing facility is not available for any reason.

The first chapter of this section provides an introduction to business continuity planning. It provides definitions of a disaster, critical system, and of a business continuity plan. The benefits of business continuity planning are discussed and the process of evaluating the operational and financial impact of an outage is explained. Included in emergency response procedures are life safety procedures and damage mitigation procedures. A thorough discussion of these important considerations is provided.

Chapter I-4-2 of this section addresses developing a business continuity plan to meet the needs of a particular organization. Legal and regulatory requirements related to this planning step are described, as is the process of forming a project team to ensure that the plan relates to all of the organization's functions. The five major elements of a business continuity plan are described and the scope is identified. This chapter provides a straightforward approach to developing an appropriate plan for any organization.

Business Continuity Planning

GERALD W. GRINDLER

The goal of business continuity planning is to specify a set of steps to follow in the event that a business function is lost or severely degraded. This discussion focuses on those business functions with significant dependence on computer operations. The recovery activities set forth in the business continuity plan, with the pertinent procedures and supply requirements, are specific to the business unit for which the plan was developed.

When properly produced, the business continuity plan mitigates the impact of an extended system outage on the company. A plan that is well prepared and tested reduces service disruption, maintains the company's market share, and helps reduce financial losses in the event of a disaster.

There are two basic types of disaster that may disrupt computer services. They are natural disasters (e.g., fires, storms, floods, and earthquakes) and human-caused disasters (e.g., arson, bombings, and vandalism). Human-caused disasters may be intentional and carried out by disgruntled employees or former employees, disgruntled customers, or terrorists. In addition, employees may unintentionally cause disruptions by using the system incorrectly. Within these two categories, technical disasters may occur. Technical disasters include power failures and failures of system software.

The company should have a policy that details the responsibilities of management in ensuring the timely resumption of critical business functions after a major disruption of information services. This policy could be incorporated into the organization's overall information security policy or issued as a separate policy statement. The policy might also be published in the form of memos from senior executives to staff members or other forms of notice that have been distributed. Acceptance of this policy is evidenced by inclusion of business continuity planning standards in strategic planning applications, capacity planning, systems development, and operations.

Once formal policies have been established, they must be communicated to the staff members who are concerned with the business continuity program. This communication should be consistent, conveying the same message to all staff members. Failure to be consistent results in confusion and may demonstrate a lack of commitment on the part of senior management.

An individual within the organization should be made accountable for administering the business continuity plan. The responsibilities involved should be clearly defined in the job description for this position. The qualifications and skill requirements for the position should be specified, and the assigned individual should possess the appropriate qualifications and experience. This position is supported by the necessary staffing and funding.

It is important that the business continuity plan be regularly reviewed to ensure that it is up-to-date and that maintenance procedures are in place for updating the business continuity program when needed. If changes are made to the information systems or to the business environment, the plan must reflect these changes.

All personnel should be educated about the organization's business continuity planning program. Employees who are to be involved in recovery strategies as part of the planning program should participate in regular training programs to keep them informed of their respective responsibilities and any changes that have taken place that could affect their recovery activities. In addition, there should be an overall training program for all of the organization's personnel to familiarize them with the business continuity plan.

All components of the business continuity plan should be tested at regular intervals. Without regular testing, the plan might not be up to date or operational when a disaster occurs.

A backup program for critical information and materials, including on-site and off-site storage, should be in place and effectively managed. Although many companies have comprehensive business continuity plans, it is still important to ensure that backup and off-site storage procedures are actually followed.

This chapter discusses the benefits of business continuity planning and various planning methods.

BENEFITS OF BUSINESS CONTINUITY PLANNING

After the organization's operations and its computing environment have been evaluated, several key issues must be closely examined to mitigate the impact of a disaster. The physical security of the company's premises is a key factor in reducing risks. The obvious operational components (e.g., computers and printers), as well as supporting data communications functions, must be physically secure. The quality of personnel who operate or manage the computing environment must be evaluated periodically.

This process is designed to locate any weaknesses in a computing installation and then take the appropriate steps to ensure that these weaknesses are kept to a minimum. Information access control plays an important part in risk analysis. Determining who can access what data, how authorized users access data, and when authorized users can access data are important aspects of information access control.

The goal of thoroughly analyzing and evaluating risks is to reduce the magnitude and duration of any service disruption in the event of a disaster. A well-documented business continuity plan gives management the computer resources needed to resume business operations within an acceptable time frame. The plan ensures the restoration of computer programs and computer-supported data files and data bases. It reduces disruption in the user department during an outage. Finally, a well-documented and well-tested plan reduces the possibility that further difficulties will arise during resumption.

In addition, the business continuity plan reduces the magnitude of a financial loss in the event of a disaster and helps control any loss of market share. It ensures that adequate production and distribution is maintained. By providing for the recovery of critical systems necessary to support customers, the plan ensures that adequate customer service is maintained. As with any functional business entity, the timely recovery of systems ensures that cash flow is preserved by supporting customer billing and accounts receivables, thus reducing the need to borrow operating funds on a short-term basis.

On the other side of accounts receivable, the prompt restoration of systems limits any payment penalties for outstanding accounts payable. Current computing systems perform complex financial modeling and tracking of company funds through institutional investment of surplus business funds. By ensuring timely recovery of the systems needed to support this function, investment interest is maximized and maintained.

DEVELOPING A BUSINESS CONTINUITY PLAN

When developing a business continuity plan, the organization must first determine what impact the loss of certain data or data operations would have on the business environment. Then a thorough risk evaluation must be performed to pinpoint those risks that most threaten the company's information assets. The following sections discuss these important activities in detail. (If the computing resource is for a government agency, the steps outlined in the following sections should be replaced with those outlined in Federal Information Publication 87, *Contingency Planning*, and the related Federal Information Publication 65, *Risk Analysis*.)

Business Impact Analysis

Organizations are placing increased reliance on information and information processing facilities to support their critical business applications and systems. It is therefore imperative to maintain the availability of this information and the associated processing facilities and to be able to promptly restore critical information processing systems in the event of an interruption of service. To help ensure the timely and controlled recovery of critical information systems, the impact that an interruption in information processing would have on the organization should be measured, system restoration responsibilities assigned, and contingency plans prepared, documented, and tested.

The operational and financial impact that could result from a disruption or disaster affecting a computing resource must be analyzed, evaluated, and documented. The impact of an outage must be analyzed to formulate cost-effective recovery strategies and to provide a basis for defining technical recovery resource requirements and integrating user contingency plans. Information regarding the effect of a disaster should be collected through interviews with managers of critical business functions.

This information should be analyzed and a sample outage scenario developed for each business function. These outage scenarios document the dependence of the business function on each computing resource application or system. They list alternative methods of support to be used during the outage, the impact of employing those methods, and the work backlog that could result from the outage. Conclusions regarding the point at which critical computing support should be restored are documented on the basis of the operational impact of the outage over time.

When all outage scenarios have been reviewed and approved by business function management, the operational (i.e., qualitative) impact analysis should be performed. This analysis identifies the point at which computing resource support should be restored for each critical business function. In addition, it dictates the type of recovery strategies (e.g., hot site versus cold site) that should be employed to restore application or system support within the required time frame.

Quantitative data contained in the outage scenarios should be extrapolated and used in calculations to estimate the financial impact of an application or system outage. An analysis of the financial impact provides cost-justification for implementing and maintaining a specific recovery strategy (e.g., a commercial hot site versus a private one).

The business impact analysis provides the basis for formulating the organization's business resumption strategies and a business continuity policy. Risk analyses and evaluations should be undertaken and compensating measures identified. These factors should be periodically reassessed to consider the impact of changes in the business and system environments. Recovery strategies and goals should be developed, consistent with the business impact analysis and risk evaluation, and should be approved by senior management.

The following sections discuss the steps in a business impact analysis. Many software tools are available for aiding in business impact analysis; these are discussed in more detail in Chapter I-3-1, "Techniques of Risk Analysis."

Classifying Critical Business Functions. Business operations should be reviewed with the appropriate managers to determine the importance of business functions to the continuity of the organization's critical operations. A general understanding of the services provided by computing resources should be gained through discussions with appropriate business managers and support personnel for each application or system. A high-level understanding of the computing resource facilities, support services, and interdependences of applications within the integrated system should be documented as a result of these discussions and reviews of appropriate documentation (e.g., application summaries and procedures manuals).

The business continuity concerns and priorities of senior management should be identified before establishing the scope of the computing resource's contingency plan and disaster recovery assumptions. This provides the context for the business impact analysis and subsequent contingency plan development.

Assembling Operational and Financial Impact Data. Each critical business function's computing resource support requirements must be understood. Data describing the operational and financial impact of a computing resource outage on the business should be gathered by interviewing managers and other representatives of each critical business function. Data collection forms and interview guidelines are helpful tools for collecting this data.

An overview of the business function as it relates to computing support should be developed. The nature and degree of application and system support required by the business function to maintain acceptable operational continuity should be established. This overview identifies the impact of the loss of application or system support for different time periods (e.g., a day, week, or month).

An outage scenario should be documented for each critical business function with the information gathered in business impact interviews. On the basis of the operational impact described in each outage scenario, a conclusion should be drawn as to the point at which computing resource support should be restored for that business function. Documented outage impact scenarios are distributed to appropriate business managers for review and approval; manager approvals should be documented. The approved scenarios provide the basis for overall operational and financial impact analyses.

Evaluating the Operational Impact. The next step is to identify the point at which computing resource support should be restored for each critical business function. This evaluation dictates the type of recovery strategies that should be employed to restore application or system support within the required time frame.

Information about computing resource recovery should be extracted from the approved outage impact scenarios. The extracted information should be sorted, evaluated, and analyzed to determine a minimum recovery time frame for each application or system. These time frames provide a basis for developing computing resource recovery strategies.

Evaluating the Financial Impact. The financial losses that could result from a computing resource outage must be identified to provide cost-justification for implementing and maintaining specific recovery strategies. As mentioned previously, quantitative data is extracted from the approved outage impact scenarios and used to determine the potential costs of an application or system, outage. Calculations should then be performed to estimate the costs that could be incurred during various outage periods as well as the corresponding costs to recover the work backlog. These estimates fall into the following categories:

- Additional expenses incurred to implement alternative procedures during an application or system outage or to eliminate the backlog resulting from a service area outage (e.g., employee overtime or the addition of temporary employees).
- The interest costs associated with delayed income (e.g., delayed invoice processing results in delayed customer payments).

These estimates should be considered to be direct costs—that is, they are directly attributable to events that would probably occur in the event of a computing resource outage. The direct costs are summarized by loss category (i.e., alternative procedures, backlog recovery, or interest expenses).

In addition, indirect costs accrue. For example, a significant contributor to indirect costs is the errors that occur as the result of a loss of computing resource support. Some errors can result in substantial losses, particularly during an extended outage. Indirect losses typically fall in the range of 2 to 20 times the direct costs; they are usually estimated conservatively at double the direct costs. The total single-event loss expectancy is the sum of the direct and indirect costs.

The single-event loss expectancies should be annualized to determine what expenditures are justified in reducing the financial loss exposure. The annualized loss expectancy for each outage period is calculated on the basis of the probability that each disaster may occur; these probabilities are presented in Exhibit I-4-1. From the data in this exhibit, it can be deduced that, on average, three disasters will probably occur every 100 years.

Annualized loss expectancies provide a quantitative basis for approximating the investment in contingency planning that will be justified on the basis of financial loss. An annualized loss expectancy should not be used to recommend the type of recovery strategy.

Developing Recovery Strategies. Recovery strategies should be developed and documented on the basis of the minimum recovery time frame identified for the application or system. The interdependences of applications and systems, business functions, and the outage duration limits established for the computing resource provide the basis for selecting which recovery strategies to implement.

The computing resource recovery strategies must accommodate the maximum acceptable outages established in the operational evaluation. Each recovery strategy should take into account the computing resource recovery assumptions developed in the preceding steps and should be based on a worst-case scenario.

Recovery strategies should consider the maximum time required to restore the

EXHIBIT I-4-1 Disaster Probability Occurrence Tables

Natural Disasters

Threat	Probability of Occurrence
Internal flooding	Once in 5 years to once in 100 years
External flooding	Once in 7.5 years to once in 100 years
Internal fire	Once in 6.6 years to once in 55 years
External fire	Once in 4 years to once in 40 years
Toxic spill	Once in 2 years to once in 20 years
Earthquake	Once in 5 years to once in 200 years
Wind storm	Once a year to once in 26 years
Snow and ice storms	Ten times a year to once in 200 years

Human-Caused Disasters

Threat	Probability of Occurrence
Data entry error	Ten to 50,000 times a year
Improper handling of sensitive data	Once a month to once in 5 years
Unauthorized physical access	Once a day to once a year
Malicious damage or destruction of physical assets	Once a year to once in 125 years
Malicious damage or destruction of software or data	Once a year to once in 125 years
Unauthorized access to data or theft of data	Twice a month to once in 66 years
Unauthorized modification of software or hardware	Once in 5 years to once in 20 years

Technical Disasters

Threat	Probability of Occurrence
Power failure or fluctuations	Once every 12 days to once in 10 years
Heating, ventilation, or air-conditioning failure	Once a month to once in 10 years
Malfunction or failure of CPU	Once a day to once in 5 years
Failure of system software	0.25 to 10 errors per 1,000 instructions
Failure of application software	0.25 to 10 errors per 1,000 instructions
Electromagnetic interference	Once a day to once in 50 years

SOURCE: **Available & Secured Knowledge (ASK), Consulting.**

computing resource if the computing facilities are destroyed. If a given application or system can be restored within an acceptable time frame, as determined by those who use the resource, restoration of the resource is the only reasonable recovery alternative. If the resource cannot be restored within an acceptable time frame, it may need to be replaced.

The business continuity policy must consider continuity requirements, strategies, and responsibilities and should address the specific continuity needs and concerns of the organization. This policy provides guidance and authority for developing and enforcing contingency plans. In addition, the policy specifies the applicability of certain risks and recovery strategies, the persons responsible for recovery activities, the scope of the contingency plan, and classifications of the organization's information assets based on the availability of those assets.

Risk Evaluation

The threats to which a computing resource is exposed must be identified to ensure that the physical security and environmental control devices and procedures, together with the emergency response procedures, reasonably address those threats. The probability of occurrence should be established for each threat (see Exhibit I-4-1) and the current annual loss expectancy associated with each threat calculated. This information provides a basis for a cost/benefit analysis of the proposed safeguards.

After the potential threats have been identified, the physical security and environmental control devices and procedures and the damage mitigation procedures should be analyzed to determine whether they reasonably address the potential threats. Recommendations for improvements in physical security and environmental controls should then be made.

Using current annual loss expectancies as a basis, the organization should estimate the risk reduction realized from each recommended improvement in physical security and environmental controls by recalculating the annual loss expectancies. The costs and benefits of each recommended improvement in protection methods should be calculated by comparing the present values of the risk reduction and the cost of the protection method.

Life safety procedures designed to protect personnel during an emergency should be evaluated to ensure that they reasonably address the potential threats previously identified. In addition, guidelines should be provided on developing computing resource emergency response procedures, including life safety and damage mitigation procedures. The following sections discuss the steps involved in analyzing risks and developing an emergency response plan.

Evaluating Threats to the Computing Facility. To assess or develop appropriate emergency response procedures for a computing resource, the significant threats to which the computing resource is exposed must first be identified and assessed. Relevant types or categories of threats provide a basis for determining appropriate safeguards (e.g., damage mitigation devices, alarms, and control procedures) for the computing resource.

The identified threats may be placed into categories to facilitate their assessment and help determine the appropriate emergency response procedures. The threat categories should be approved by management of the computing resource. Sample threat categories are presented in Exhibit I-4-2.

The threat categories and appropriate safeguards provide a framework for developing emergency response procedures. A cost/benefit analysis should be performed for recommended changes to existing safeguards.

An approximate probability of occurrence and annual loss expectancy for each identified threat should be established. Statistics should be obtained for each of the threats identified to establish the probability of occurrence. From the statistical probabilities of occurrence, the average duration of outages may be estimated for

EXHIBIT I-4-2 Sample Threat Categories

Extreme temperature or humidity conditions

Power failures

Fires

Explosions

Chemical spills

Toxic gas or waste spills

Noxious gas leaks

Water damage from overhead pipes, leaking roof, water coolers on roof, or rest rooms on floors above

Water damage from internal flooding (e.g., if computing facility is located below grade or is on a ground floor in a flood plain)

Hurricanes, tornados, or blizzards

Earthquakes

Construction nearby

Nuclear accidents

Intentional damage by employees

Intentional damage by persons outside the company

Bomb threats

Riots or civil disturbances

Strikes

each threat. All of this data should then be reviewed with and finalized by management.

The financial impact data developed in the business impact analysis and the estimated duration of each outage can be used to determine the single event financial impact of each threat. The probability of each threat is multiplied by the financial impact to arrive at the annual loss expectancy for each threat to the computing resource.

In general, statistics are readily available to establish probabilities for natural disasters. For example, the US hurricane belt is well defined, with records kept for nearly 100 years. However, the probability of such threats as explosions could be peculiar to the environment where the facility is located. The probability of occurrence of such environment-specific threats should be determined on the basis of recorded incidences at that specific location or similar locations. Several sources that may be contacted for probability statistics are listed in Exhibit I-4-3.

Evaluating the Physical Security of the Computing Facility. The physical security of the computing facility should be assessed to identify any areas that require improvement. This can help reduce the risk or impact of threats resulting from unauthorized physical access.

Physical security devices, alarms, and access control procedures should be

---

EXHIBIT I-4-3 Sources for Disaster Probability Statistics

Business risk management personnel

County emergency management agencies (e.g., for hazardous material routes)

Environmental Protection Agency, 401 M Street SW, Washington DC 20460; (202) 260-2090

Federal Emergency Management Agency, Federal Center Plaza, 500 C Street SW, Washington DC 20472; (202) 646-2500

Insurance companies

Libraries

Local fire and police departments

OMB Circular A-130

State and local weather bureaus

State departments of natural resources (e.g., flood statistics in flood districts)

US Army Corps of Engineers, 20 Massachusetts Avenue NW, Washington DC 20314; (202) 272-0660

US Geological Survey (e.g., for earthquake fault lines or sink holes), Office of Earthquakes, Volcanoes, and Engineering, Mail Stop 905, National Center, Reston VA 22092; (703) 648-6714

---

studied to determine whether they reasonably address the potential unauthorized physical access threats identified in the previous step. Available documentation on these safeguards should be reviewed and the appropriate employees interviewed to determine whether the documentation needs clarification or modification.

Existing physical security procedures should be reviewed to ensure that they cover the threats identified. In addition, the review should verify that employees have received adequate training in physical security procedures and that the appropriate maintenance and testing of physical security equipment is conducted. Some procedures may require improvement to increase asset protection and establish appropriate links to disaster recovery procedures. Any recommendations for improvement should be made to management.

Evaluating Environmental Controls. Environmental controls and procedures should be evaluated to determine whether they adequately address all of the potential environmental threats. Any recommendations for improvement should be made to management.

This review should verify that appropriate personnel have received adequate training in environmental control procedures. Maintenance and testing schedules should be reviewed to ensure that environmental control equipment is properly maintained and regularly tested.

Conducting a Cost/Benefit Analysis of Suggested Safeguards. All recommended safeguards or improvements to existing safeguards must be analyzed to verify that they are cost-justified and to set priorities. To determine whether an enhancement is cost-justified, the cost of implementing and maintaining the safeguard is compared to the benefits its provides (i.e., the reduction in annual loss expectancy). If the costs are greater than the benefits, the enhancement is not cost-justified.

Many organizations may want to implement all cost-justified enhancements but may be constrained by budgetary limitations. If all recommended enhancements are given priority according their cost/benefit ratios, the organization can easily determine which enhancements of safeguards should be implemented first.

When a cost/benefit analysis is being performed, the costs associated with each recommended enhancement must first be determined. Implementation and maintenance costs for devices and alarms can be obtained from appropriate vendors. The costs associated with control procedures can be determined by interviewing business managers.

The benefits of each enhancement are determined by first adjusting the annual loss expectancy to reflect the reduction in computing facility risk that can be realized by implementing the enhancement. The revised annual loss expectancy is subtracted from the original annual loss expectancy to determine the benefit of implementing the enhancement. When cost/benefit ratios have been calculated for all enhancements, the recommendations should be ranked according to priority, with the enhancements with the smallest ratios having the highest priority.

Analyzing Employee Safety Procedures. Emergency response procedures fall into two categories: those that mitigate damages, and those that protect the lives and safety of employees. Damage mitigation procedures have already been discussed. Employee safety procedures must also be reviewed, however, to ensure that they are adequate and effective.

The first priority of any emergency response procedure should be to ensure the safety of personnel. The second priority should be containing or reducing damages to the facility or its resources. Existing employee safety procedures should be reviewed to ensure that they adequately address the threats identified and to confirm that reasonable precautions have been included and documented. Any recommendations for improvements should be made to management.

Because little time is available in most emergencies for employees to read manuals to determine which procedures to follow, training in emergency response procedures are of utmost importance. Selected employees should be interviewed to verify that training has been received by appropriate personnel.

Developing Emergency Response Procedures. Emergency response procedures should be developed or enhanced to ensure the safety of employees, mitigate damage to company assets, and invoke appropriate recovery procedures. The procedures and enhancements recommended must be appropriate for the threats identified for the computing facility. In addition, employee training schedules and maintenance and testing schedules should be developed.

SUMMARY

Although business continuity planning might appear to be a technical issue, it must be approached as a business management issue. Otherwise, the security practitioner cannot overcome staffing and budgetary constraints imposed by senior management. To ensure that effective business continuity plans are developed, implemented, and tested, the security practitioner must use cost/benefit analysis to show that the plan is cost-justified. Well-developed policies, risk identification and evaluation, and a comprehensive business impact analysis are requisite steps toward convincing senior management of the importance of proactive planning to protect the company's information assets.

Developing a Business Continuity Plan

SALLY MEGLATHERY

Corporate business continuity planning specifies the methodology, structure, discipline, and procedures needed to back up and recover functional units struck by a catastrophe. Therefore, every functional unit must accept responsibility for developing and implementing the business continuity plan, and the plan must have the total support of management.

Strategically, senior management must ensure the development of a policy stating that the company will recover from any type of outage. Such recovery requires high-level commitment to the policy from all levels of management. Tactically, however, middle management implements the policy and the plan and is responsible for the daily operation of the plan. For management and the functional units to participate, they must have a comprehensive methodology to guide them in their actions and activities. This chapter discusses methods of developing a corporate business continuity plan.

PROJECT PLANNING

There are numerous reasons for developing a total business continuity plan. Some of the most compelling are legal and regulatory requirements. Consideration must be given to the following when developing the plan:

- Are there any federal statutes or regulations applicable to the business that would apply to disasters relating to the business?
- Are there any state statutes or regulations applicable to the business that would apply to disasters relating to the business?
- What contract requirements (e.g., labor contracts, insurance agreements, mortgages, loans, or other financial documents) should be addressed by the plan?
- Are there any common-law considerations, such as claims against directors and officers raised by shareholders and others? Could there by negligence claims against the company for property damage or injuries to customers or business visitors?

Before beginning development of the business continuity plan, management should identify a business continuity project team. The project team is responsible for developing the business continuity plan and designing procedures and reporting techniques to support overall project management. In addition, the project team should identify individuals from senior management to review and approve the work performed by the project team.

Although the makeup of the project team will vary among companies, the following departments should be represented on the team:

- Real estate and facilities.
- Security.
- Human resources.
- Information systems.
- Communications.
- Technology, planning, and development.

Additional departments may also be represented. A business continuity manager should be delegated for the team.

DEVELOPING THE PLAN

The plan that is developed must ensure that any disaster will have a minimum impact on the company. The plan should address the company's reasons for establishing the plan, the functional area of the company's business that the plan will cover, and what staff or materials are in place or should be in place for the plan to function. The following sections discuss the requirements of the business continuity plan, the various elements of the plan, and the scope of the plan.

Plan Requirements

Although most plans address the need to continue data processing operations and to support critical operations during a crisis, most plans fail to consider loss of other functional units within the organization. Data processing generally initiates the need for disaster recovery planning; however, it is now recognized that recovering data centers alone cannot ensure the continuing health of the organization. Companies must address corporate division and department business continuity planning as well. In fact, planning should be done for all essential functional units of the organization.

The plan must be comprehensive; it must deal with the broadest range of disasters possible. There should be a basic plan with additional procedures for specific hazards (e.g., earthquakes, fires, or exposure to hazardous materials). It should preserve the integrity of the business, not individual items or goals.

The plan must contain sufficient detail so that its users will know what procedures to follow, how to perform these activities, and the resources that will be available. The plan should contain action steps that have been decided on and agreed to in advance. Both the response to the immediate disaster and the recovery and continuance of business operations and functions must be specified.

The plan must be owned by the organization. Key personnel must participate in identifying priorities, determining alternative strategies, negotiating agreements, and assembling necessary materials.

The plan should be reviewed on a periodic basis or when circumstances change. It should be periodically tested with a defined testing program to ensure that it remains effective and up-to-date.

Plan Elements

The plan itself has five major elements:

- Risk and business impact analysis.
- Alternative analysis.
- Response and recovery planning and plan documentation.
- Plan publication and testing.
- Training and implementation.

These are discussed in the following sections.

Risk and Business Impact Analysis. Before the plan is written, the hazards that may affect the company's facilities must be identified and their potential impact determined. It is also necessary to identify and rank the major business functions and the resources necessary to carry out those functions and to identify the potential impact of the hazards on the critical business functions and operations. This helps determine the maximum allowable downtime for individual business functions and operations. From there, the minimum resource and personnel needs and time frames in which they will be needed can be identified. Finally, consideration of emergency operating procedures and strategies can begin.

Alternative Analysis. Using the risk and business impact analysis as a base, consideration is given to the internal and external alternatives available for continuation of each function within the necessary time frames. These alternatives should be chosen on the basis of their cost benefits, and feasibility. The alternatives considered should include not only those that are currently available but those that can be developed.

Response and Recovery Planning and Plan Documentation. This involves the development and documentation of the procedures to be used to activate the plan (by declaration or event), move specific functions to the alternative or backup facility, maintain operations at that site while the primary site is being restored or a new permanent site prepared, and return operations to the primary site or another permanent location. The plan must identify ways to procure alternative resources to carry out business activities; determine responsibilities and notification procedures for the company, vendors, customers, and others; and detail recovery strategies and responsibilities.

Plan Publication and Testing. The plan must be reviewed and agreed to by senior management and all departments. It must then be documented and distributed to key personnel with additional copies secured off-site. Individual sections of the plan should be distributed to those who will be involved with its activation and operation.

The plan should contain a schedule for periodic review and updating. The only way to assess the adequacy of the plan before a disaster occurs is with a program of periodic tests. The types of tests used will vary from conceptual walkthroughs to actual relocation of specific departments or business functions.

Training and Implementation. Employees should understand what is expected of them in a disaster and what their roles will be in the recovery process. This is achieved with a training and education program, which should be conducted before the plan is implemented.

The Scope of the Plan

All key personnel should be identified in the business continuity plan and given specific assignments. Common terminology should be defined in the plan document to avoid confusion at the time the plan is put into effect. In addition, the plan should interface with the information systems (IS) disaster recovery plan. Budgets should be prepared for the initial costs of developing the plan and for the costs of maintaining the plan. The scope of the business continuity plan should include the features discussed in the following sections.

A Vital-Records Program. The plan should help establish an information valuation program to determine which records should be retained and for how long. In addition, there should be a methodology for ensuring that critical records are retained off-site.

Security Requirements. The plan defines what security measures must be in place in the event of a disaster and what security measures are necessary for an off-site location. It also states who has access to each location.

Accounting Procedures. Procedures must be put in place to facilitate the acquisition of needed replacement parts and to properly account for the costs of recovery. This in turn facilitates the filing of insurance claims, among other benefits.

Insurance Requirements. The plan should define what insurance claims must be filed and give guidelines on working with risk managers to file a claim. One of the benefits of developing the business continuity plan is that insurance requirements are specifically defined.

Interdepartmental Interfaces. Interfaces between divisions and departments must be defined in the business continuity plan.

Backup, Recovery, and Restoration Strategies. All critical data, files, and documents should be backed up and stored off-site. Recovery procedures should be documented in the business continuity plan, defining the steps necessary to recover the information that was lost. Restoration may require recreating the lost data, files, or documents rather than recovering with a backup. Procedures for such restoration must be documented.

Plan Maintenance and Testing. Once implemented, the plan must be tested regularly to ensure that it is up-to-date. The plan should include a maintenance and testing schedule as well as a methodology for testing the plan to ensure that it is operating as expected.

IDENTIFYING CRITICAL RESOURCES

Not all activities within an organization are critical at the time of a catastrophe. The management disaster decision team identifies those operations that it deems critical to the organization. This determination is based on several specific factors, including the time at which the disaster occurs, legal and regulatory requirements, the amount of time that capability is lost, the company's public image, loss of market share, loss of revenue, the type of service loss (e.g., administrative, executive, or financial), and deadline requirements.

In addition, the plan should account for the facilities, equipment, materials, and supplies needed to adequately perform required tasks. Voice and data communications are particularly critical and should be given proper consideration.

For example, personnel are vital to the success of the recovery, and their comfort and support should be given special attention. Supplies and forms should be maintained off-site so that a supply is readily available in times of emergency. In addition, transportation can easily be disrupted in times of emergency, and transportation to an off-site location may not be readily available. Therefore, transportation to the main site or an off-site location must be planned if employees are to arrive at the designated stations in a timely manner.

Spare parts and units for power and environmental systems (e.g., air conditioners, fans, and heaters) should be available at the central business location. The engineering staff should have spare parts on hand for replacing broken parts. A backup unit should be available to replace the disabled units. When that is not possible or when the outage is outside the control of the company (e.g., the loss of a telephone company's central office or a power company's power station), the company must be prepared to move to its off-site location.

A vital record is any document that is necessary to ensure the survival of the business. To ensure the preservation and availability of vital records, all corporate documents should be classified as to their importance (e.g., essential, valuable, important, or nonessential). Corporate record-keeping policies as well as retention requirements based on legal or regulatory requirements should be documented. The source document should be controlled and protected. In addition, there should be backup procedures for the documents, and a copy of them should be maintained at the off-site location.

Documentation, policies, procedures, and standards should be available in hard copy and should be accessible in both main and off-site locations. A disaster recovery plan has no value if the disaster recovery team cannot locate a copy of it.

ORGANIZING THE PROJECT

The business continuity plan should be prefaced with a mission statement or purpose. This can be incorporated into the introductory section of the plan. All departments and functions involved in the project must understand the need for the plan, agree to participate in its implementation, and be committed to enforcing the plan.

The departments and functions that participate in the project vary among companies. In most companies, however, senior management must be kept up-to-date and is responsible for making most key decisions. The audit department oversees the entire process, ensuring that controls are enforced. When a disaster strikes, the building and facilities staff determines any losses and necessary repairs and the public relations and marketing staffs calm customers and reassure them that the company is all right. A legal staff helps protect the company from litigation, negotiates purchase contracts, and enforces contracts.

The human resources department is usually responsible for keeping all employees informed during and after a disaster, particularly in union shops. In addition, this staff often serves as the go-between for employees and management.

When it is necessary to replace equipment or parts, the purchasing department acquires the necessary components at the best possible price, and the financial or accounting department controls costs and purchases. The engineering department ensures that the components are properly ordered and installed.

At some level, all disasters have an impact on data processing. Therefore, the IS department must be kept up-to-date and should participate in the recovery procedures. The operations department ensures that the company continues to run as smoothly as possible.

Depending on the company's business, the following departments might also be included in the business continuity planning process:

- Manufacturing.
- Research and development.
- Warehouse and distribution.
- Customer service.
- Field support services.

Representatives from these business areas can identify the functional, management, and support operations of the company in the initial phases of the project, while gathering information for the plan. As a result, critical divisions and departments that support the organization in times of catastrophe are identified.

In any company, the business continuity plan cannot be developed without the commitment and assistance of management and departmental staff. A considerable amount of coordination is also required, both within the company and between any external resources or consultants and company personnel. To facilitate this, it is recommended that different planning teams and functions be created. The size, number, and type of teams used is determined by the size of the company and by the computing environment. The following are various options, ranging from senior-level management teams on down:

- *The management decision-making team.* This team consists of senior management. It is responsible for making major decisions about the continuity plan and about whether or not to move off-site after a disaster.
- *The business continuity steering committee.* This committee provides overall management of the project. It establishes and controls policies, standards, and procedures, and it defines the organization of departments and other participants to ensure cohesive planning. This committee should include members of operations, information systems, and finance. The actual composition of the team can be agreed on at the initiation of the project.
- *The business continuity planning coordinator.* This individual provides day-to-day coordination of the project and typically works with external resources or consultants. This person must be able to commit sufficient time to the project to ensure that it is completed within the agreed time frame.
- *The management operations team.* This team consists of line managers who are responsible for managing the day-to-day operations after a disaster occurs. They advise the management decision-making team and report decisions down through their respective areas.
- *Department coordinators.* These individuals are responsible for providing information on their department's operations, completing forms, and develop-

ing draft plans. Related departments can be grouped under one coordinator; other departments may have their own individual coordinators. The time required of these individuals increases with each phase of plan development.

- *The emergency operations team.* This team consists of those people who are responsible for ensuring that operations keep running in the off-site environment.

- *The damage assessment and postinvestigation team.* This team is responsible for evaluating damages to the facility and determining the cost to restore operations. It should consist of those people in charge of facilities and operations.

- *The reconstruction team.* This team consists primarily of facilities personnel. It is responsible for managing restoration activities.

It is recommended that at least a business continuity steering committee, a business continuity planning coordinator, and department coordinators be appointed.

It is important that departmental employees involved in developing the plan for their departments be aware of the reasons for developing the plan, the project organization, what is expected of them during the project, and the tools and information that will be provided to assist them in their work. This can be achieved by holding one or more group business continuity training meetings to discuss these points. During these meetings, any software that will be used should be demonstrated and all questionnaires and forms to be used in developing the plan should be explained in detail.

The following sections discuss the responsibilities of the various teams that may be involved in business continuity planning.

The Disaster Decision-Making Team

The disaster decision-making team is primarily responsible for notifying the board of directors, regulatory bodies, regional companies, local companies, international bodies, and the media, as required. This team may make these notifications itself or delegate the work.

In addition, members of this team make the final business decisions regarding whether the plan should go into effect, whether to move operations to the off-site location or continue business at the main site, and even whether to continue conducting business at all. Should the plan be put into effect, the team is kept up-to-date through management operations teams, the business continuity coordinator, and those functional areas reporting to the team that are in charge of handling areas of the disaster.

All recovery activities are submitted to this team for review; however, all disaster containment activities are handled on-site as the events take place. Steps taken to contain the disaster are reported back to this team through the management operations team, as they occur, if possible, or after the fact, if not. All major decisions regarding expenditures of funds are made by this team.

The Business Continuity Steering Committee and Planning Coordinator

The business continuity steering committee is responsible for establishing and controlling policies, standards, and procedures and for defining the structure of the project to ensure that the departments and other participants work together cohesively. In addition, the committee reviews, approves, and coordinates the plans developed by the participating groups.

In the event of a disaster, this committee serves as a facilitator, responsible for providing transportation to the backup facilities, if required; notifying affected personnel and families of the status of the disaster; providing cash for needed travel or emergency items; securing the affected areas, the business resumption control center, and the backup site; escorting personnel, if necessary; and presenting a carefully formatted release to the media and affected personnel as to the status of operations and personnel. Several areas are represented on the business continuity steering committee during the disaster, to ensure that basic necessities are made available to support those individuals working to recover the business.

The size of the business continuity steering committee depends on the extent of the disaster and the recovery needs. The following departments should be consulted in forming the committee:

- Purchasing.
- Human resources.
- Communications.
- Auditing.
- Finance and accounting.
- Transportation and amenities.
- Facilities.
- Security.
- Public relations.
- Risk management and insurance.
- Administrative services.
- Operations.
- Information systems.

The business continuity coordinator interfaces with the business continuity steering committee to ensure a smooth and successful transition to each phase of the plan. In addition, the coordinator acts as team manager for the management operations team, discussed in the following section.

The Management Operations Team

The management operations team is responsible for coordinating all emergency operations teams. When management decides that the business continuity plan is to be implemented, these team members (or their alternates) contact the emergency operations team members to advise them of the disaster declaration. They then report to the business resumption control center to begin damage assessment. Once at the disaster site, the management operations team monitors the emergency operations team's progress and acts as overall manager for all emergency operations teams activated with the operational group.

The management operations team forwards all requests for space, equipment, supplies, and additional human resources support to the department coordinator. The team members report daily on the status of all emergency operations to the business resumption coordinator for the management operations team.

The management operations team is primarily responsible for determining the extent of the disaster, relocating at the business resumption control center, and notifying emergency operations team managers and department coordinators. In addition, the team monitors recovery progress and compliance with the business resumption plan during recovery and reports on recovery status to the business resumption coordinator, who in turn reports to the company president as required.

The Department Coordinators Team

The department coordinators team is composed of members from all functional areas. Each department coordinator acts as chairperson for his department's emergency operations team. In addition, the department coordinator manages the management disaster decision team and the business continuity steering committee. He communicates all of the department's needs and the department's status.

Department coordinators have access to the business resumption control center and attend strategic planning meetings. When a disaster occurs, they contact all emergency operations team managers and coordinate recovery efforts. Department coordinators submit written requests for equipment or supplies as soon as needs are made known to the business continuity steering committee.

Perhaps most important, the department coordinators monitor recovery operations. In this capacity, they receive and communicate status reports, receive daily reports from all emergency operations team managers, request additional human resources support as necessary, and maintain a log of the department's status and progress. In addition, the department coordinators communicate all decisions made by the management disaster decision team to affected managers within the department.

The Emergency Operations Team

The members of the emergency operations team are responsible for the smooth transition to the prearranged emergency backup center, continued operations, emergency procedures, notification of users, requisition of equipment and supplies, and a return to normal processing. Each member of the team should designate an alternate in case the primary team member is unavailable when a disaster occurs.

The size of the emergency operations team depends on the extent of the disaster and the operating needs. The responsibilities of the team members include forwarding requests to the business continuity steering committee for transportation to the alternative facilities, if required, and for notification of key employees, affected families, and any employees who were off duty at the time of the disaster. In addition, the emergency operations team makes requests for first aid, supplies, mail or courier service, replacement software or equipment, temporary workers, additional security or communications measures, backup power, and documentation. Team members also work with the data processing operations and communications departments.

Each emergency operations team has a team manager and a backup manager, who report to the department coordinator. The team manager is responsible for coordinating the recovery effort. The managers participate in the damage assessment meeting to determine the extent of the damage. The manager gives daily status reports regarding recovery and ongoing operations to the business resumption coordinator.

The Damage Assessment and Postinvestigation Team

The damage assessment team reports directly to the management operations team and notifies it of the extent of damage. After damages have been assessed, this team functions as a postinvestigation team to determine the cause of the disaster. In some cases, the cause is obvious (e.g., an earthquake), but in many cases it is not. For example, in the case of a fire, the origin of the fire must be determined as well as how to prevent such a fire from happening again.

The Reconstruction Team

The reconstruction team is composed of those departments required to restore the damaged site. It should include all departments associated with building services as well as representatives from the damaged areas.

The reconstruction team's responsibilities include both temporary and long-term reconstruction efforts. From the initial damage assessment to final reconstruction of the damaged area, the reconstruction team directs and coordinates efforts to bring about a smooth, efficient reconstruction of the damaged areas.

PREPARING THE PLAN

In preparing the plan, members of the business continuity project team must assemble documentation about their specific functional area and operating environment. In addition, they must identify critical performance requirements and rank the tasks within their jobs according to priority.

Departments that rely heavily on computer processing must explain in detail how their operations interface with each other and are supported by data processing. The needed information can be gathered from:

- Organizational charts.
- Job descriptions.
- Procedures manuals.
- Technical support requirements.
- Existing disaster recovery or business continuity plans.
- Risk analyses.
- Business impact analyses.
- Vulnerability assessments.

Questionnaires can be used successfully to gather information that can provide a foundation for the strategies that must be developed in the planning process. Although questionnaires should be customized for individual projects, they should always provide the basic information presented in Exhibit I-4-4.

Departments should be asked to complete the questionnaire after the initial training meeting. The completed form should be returned to the department coordinator and any external consultants for review. The department coordinator and external consultants should review the answers with the department manager and the employee who completed the form to clarify, amend, and confirm the information.

The completed questionnaires should be compared to determine the priority of departmental functions, the impact relative to specific time frames, and the minimum resources needed to maintain the company's critical functions. This information is helpful when the team is considering alternative or backup sites that will be needed.

All of the information obtained in these early phases of plan development is integrated into the business continuity plan. Plan development is designed to integrate or provide interfaces between sections of the data processing plan and the corporate business continuity plan. In addition, the plan incorporates any emergency procedures and provides references to any applicable sections of existing data center and departmental standards and procedures manuals.

The prompt recovery of an organization's corporate and functional operations from a loss of capability depends on the availability of a broad spectrum of resources. The procedures necessary to restore operations—initially in temporary facilities and later in the original or another permanent location—are detailed in the plan.

Each of the functional units prepares its plan on the basis of the outline provided by the plan coordinators (see the sample outline provided in Exhibit I-4-5).

EXHIBIT I-4-4 Checklist of Basic Information Required on Business Continuity Planning

- [ ] Description of departmental operations.
- [ ] Functions that support departmental operations.
- [ ] Peak operating times.
- [ ] Impact of department downtime.
- [ ] Recovery priorities and time frames for departmental functions.
- [ ] Staffing requirements under normal circumstances and in an emergency.
- [ ] Computer support for both departmental operations and individual functions. (This should cover both centralized and decentralized computer operations.)
- [ ] Site requirements for both normal and emergency operations.
- [ ] Equipment needed (and the vendors of that equipment).
- [ ] Office and other supplies (and the vendors).
- [ ] Critical records needed and their backup and recovery requirements.
- [ ] Priority ranking of departmental functions.
- [ ] Name and address of alternative-site vendor.
- [ ] List of responsibilities and home telephone numbers of key personnel.
- [ ] Emergency telephone numbers (e.g., fire and police departments).
- [ ] Critical forms (number, names, and average use).
- [ ] Special equipment specifications.
- [ ] Area user list.
- [ ] Vendor backup contracts.
- [ ] Critical functions and assumptions (e.g., individuals might assume that they will have access to backup files).
- [ ] Minimum equipment and space requirements.

The outline can be modified to suit the needs of the individual units. Although the plan discussed in this section addresses disaster backup and recovery from a worst-case scenario, less severe or even short-term interruptions can also be planned for by using subsets of the overall plan.

BUSINESS CONTINUITY PLANNING SOFTWARE

Several contingency planning and risk analysis software packages are currently on the market. It is not practical to list and evaluate them because that list is constantly changing. However, there are certain criteria that should be used during the software package selection process.

For example, ease of use and the number of installations or users are important when the company is selecting any software package, as are the frequency and availability of updates, the quality of documentation and vendor support, the reputation of the vendor, and the amount of training the vendor provides. The usability

EXHIBIT I-4-5 Sample Outline of Business Continuity Plan

I. Introduction
   a. Executive overview or summary
   b. Organizational overview
   c. Minimum requirements
   d. General categories of disasters and contingencies

II. Responsibilities of the Disaster Decision-Making Team

III. Responsibilities of the Business Continuity Coordinator and the Business Continuity Steering Committee

IV. Responsibilities of the Management Operations Team

V. Responsibilities of the Department Coordinators Team

VI. Responsibilities of the Emergency Operations Team

VII. Responsibilities of the Damage Assessment and Post-investigation Team

VIII. Responsibilities of the Reconstruction Team

IX. General Issues
   a. Awareness of critical events
   b. Notification of relevant persons
   c. Diagnosis of the cause, severity, and expected duration of the event
   d. Coordination of emergency response
   e. Communications
   f. Investigation and analysis of the event

X. The Corporate Recovery Plan (corporatewide outage)*
   a. Organization and staffing
   b. Arrangements with vendors, contractors, and other organizations
   c. Backup and recovery plans
      1. Information and communications systems
      2. Hardware
      3. Site
      4. Location of business resumption control center

XI. The Operational Area Recovery Plan (based on functional areas)
   a. Responsibilities of the backup operations team
   b. Responsibilities of the emergency operations team
   c. Responsibilities of the reconstruction team
   d. General issues
   e. Priority ranking of functions
   f. Name and address of alternative-site vendor
   g. List of responsibilities and home telephone numbers of key personnel
   h. Emergency telephone numbers (e.g., fire and police departments)
   i. Critical forms (number, names, and average use)
   j. Special equipment specifications
   k. Area user list (ranked according to priority)
   l. Copy of vendor backup contract
   m. Critical functions and assumptions (e.g., individuals may assume that they will have access to backup files)
   n. Minimum equipment and space requirements
   o. Appendixes (same as Section XV)

XII. Emergency Notification
   a. General categories of disasters and contingencies
   b. Immediate evacuation
   c. Fire emergency procedures

Note:
*For simplicity, this section of the outline shows a general building outage recovery plan that is used for all locations. Some organizations may find it necessary to have a separate recovery plan for each location.

   d. Telephone bomb threat procedures
      1. Bomb search procedures
      2. General alert for bomb threats
   e. Medical emergencies
   f. Civil disorder
   g. Severe weather or threat of a natural disaster
   h. Extortion and terrorist threats
   i. Building and equipment emergencies (e.g., loss of power)
   j. Notification
      1. Company closings for a disaster
      2. Activating the business resumption control center
      3. Access control procedures
   k. Company closings for early release of employees (e.g., because of an impending storm)
   l. Major milestones in the notification process
   m. Backup sites

XIII. Testing the Business Continuity Plan
   a. Methodology for testing the plan
   b. Determination of frequency of testing

XIV. Business Resumption Plan Maintenance
   a. Procedures for updating the plan
      1. Areas that require regular review
      2. Areas that require occasional review
   b. Frequency of review for updates
      1. Areas that require regular review
      2. Areas that require occasional review

XV. Appendixes
   a. Special Resources for Business Resumption
   b. Special Guidelines for Managers Dealing with Disaster-Related Stress
   c. Disaster Recovery for Microcomputers
   d. Inventory Control Form and Instructions
   e. Equipment Requirements
   f. Decision Matrices
   g. Critical Time Periods (daily or seasonal)
   h. Cross-Training Requirements and Responsibilities Matrix
   i. Typical Resource Allocation Plan Charts
   j. Test Schedules
   k. Test Worksheets
   l. Preparedness Overview
   m. Network Diagrams
   n. Off-Site Storage Inventories
   o. Critical Functions
   p. Staff Emergency Contact Information
   q. Vendor Emergency Contact Information
   r. Vendor Contracts
   s. Emergency Organizational Charts
   t. Management Succession List
   u. Agreements for Alternative Work Space
   v. Temporary Agencies
   w. Functional Systems Overview
   x. Emergency Telephone Numbers
   y. Control of Building Contents (e.g., equipment and supplies)
   z. Special Salvage Vendors
   aa. Purchasing Department's List of Vendors
   bb. Procedures for Preserving Damaged Records
   cc. List of Personnel Who Need Access to the Plan
   dd. Notification Sequence
   ee. Organizational Chart for Business Resumption Command Center

(continued)

EXHIBIT I-4-5 *(continued)*

ff. Emergency Medical Information
gg. Emergency Housing Information
hh. Emergency Transportation Information
ii. Business Resumption Control Center Notification
jj. User Area Notification

of output should also be considered. Specific to contingency planning, the software should be evaluated in terms of whether it provides total business continuity planning assistance or simply data center recovery.

SUMMARY

For each company, every business continuity plan should cover all types of disaster situations. Procedures should be focused on getting the system running again within an acceptable time frame. The cause of the downtime is not important except in cases of regional disasters (e.g., earthquakes) or such specific hazards as a toxic spill. Special procedures should be included in the plan for these types of disasters.

The recovery strategies and procedures should be organized according to business functions. Strategies and procedures should be sufficiently detailed to enable company personnel to understand what is expected of them and how they should complete their responsibilities. However, strategies and procedures should be sufficiently flexible to permit changes should circumstances warrant them. Procedures should cover the maintenance of critical functions in an emergency mode as well as restoration of the primary facility or relocation to another permanent location.

The plan must specify the priority of recovery activities. It is impractical to determine during an emergency the order in which recovery procedures are to be conducted.

Personnel from the departments covered by the plan should be involved in its development from the start. These departments will be the users of the plan and therefore should play an integral part in its development.

The plan should be reviewed and updated on a regular basis; a plan is only as effective as its maintenance and updating program. Changes in departmental or company operations can quickly render a plan obsolete. A thorough maintenance and updating program prevents this.

Development of a business continuity plan may seem like a long and tedious process with no immediate benefit to the company. However, over the long term, a well-developed and well-maintained plan can help ensure that the company stays in business when a disaster strikes.

Security Awareness

This final section of Part I focuses on perhaps the most challenging as well as the most important element of a security program. It has been demonstrated repeatedly that the users of automated information systems must understand and support the need for information security or they will find ways to circumvent controls. This can create a very dangerous situation in which it is believed that appropriate controls are in effect when in fact they are being subverted. A security awareness program is the vehicle for keeping users and management informed of the need to implement and practice the principles of reasonable security.

The first chapter in this section addresses information protection awareness. It discusses the awareness program audience in relation to the content of an awareness program. Various tools and presentation techniques designed to ensure that each segment of the user population is reached are described. Presentation techniques are particularly important to ensure that the message is not distorted by the style in which it is given. Various media can be used to inform users about security risks and countermeasures. Some have proved to be more effective than others, but many are complementary to each other. Appropriate use of the various media is described.

Chapter I-5-2 in this section deals with strategies for developing security awareness. This chapter provides an insight into how to convince the various management personalities of the need to actively support the security program. Different management orientations are described to help the security manager understand differing management perspectives and develop methods of coping. In the final analysis, the success of a particular information security program hinges on the ability of the security function to relate to the management concerned and convince them that security can contribute to the productivity of their departments in a positive way.

Information Protection Awareness

CATHERINE ENGLISHMAN ▪ GERALD ISAACSON

We are now approaching a time when it is not only possible but probable that every employee will have the capabilities of a 1980s-era mainframe on his desk. Recent advances in information storage technologies allow users to capture all of an organization's sensitive data on media that will fit in a briefcase or pocket. It is no longer uncommon for the number of people who have authorized access to information to be greater than the total population of the organization. Raising security awareness in this far-flung and disparate group is a challenge for information security professionals.

Putting together an effective security awareness program requires the consideration of several elements: analysis of audience composition, determination of program content, development of awareness program tools and techniques, and finally, packaging and implementing the overall program. Each of these elements is covered in detail in this chapter.

SECURITY PROGRAM CONSIDERATIONS

Before an information protection or security awareness program is developed, four key points should be considered. They are the relationship of the awareness program to:

- A successful security program.
- Marketing, advertising, and public relations.
- Training.
- The skills of security professionals.

These are discussed in the following sections.

Relationship to a Successful Security Program

As information processing strategies change toward more distributed, client-server environments, the success of the security program will depend entirely on the success of the associated awareness program. In the early days of computing, when all of the resources were concentrated in one room, it was relatively easy to impart concerns over the protection of those resources to a very small, select population. Currently, however, the target audience for information security often extends beyond the walls of the organization to the organization's clients, customers, suppliers, and vendors, in addition to its staff. Therefore, the primary goal of the awareness program must be to ensure that anyone with access to the organization's information or processing resources understands the need for protecting those vital assets as well as his own responsibilities toward that end.

Relationship to Marketing, Advertising, and Public Relations

A security awareness program is nothing more or less than a marketing, advertising, or public relations program whose focus is on the protection of corporate information assets. An awareness program must convince its audience that its topic is important, that they are interested, that they consider the issue important, and that they want to participate in the program. Effective marketing techniques result in reaching the correct audience. Effective advertising makes customers of the audience, and solid program content develops strong grass-roots relationships between the customer or employee and the security organization.

Relationship to Training

A security awareness program is not a training program. Within the security profession, as is true of other disciplines, training and awareness programs serve two distinct purposes. Training programs teach those in specific job categories to perform their jobs properly. This training is directed at the specific individuals performing the given tasks. In contrast, awareness programs are directed at the more general population to ensure at least a minimal level of confidence, recognition, and ability to perform simple procedures while understanding the logic behind such requirements.

Relationship to the Skills of Security Professionals

Information security professionals should recognize that, of all their skills, they themselves may be weakest in the area of awareness program development. Security professionals do not necessarily lack the creativity required for this function; however, the ability to express that creativity in words and graphics and in voice and print—and the training to do it effectively—usually is not part of an information processing individual's technical experience and training. Still, this should not cause any more of a problem in implementation of an awareness program than the implementation of other security programs.

Very few security professionals are cryptanalysts, yet they regularly implement cryptographic solutions for appropriate problems. They rely on the accessibility of the expertise they need, both within and outside the organization, to accomplish that task. In their search for expertise, it is probably easier to find marketing assistance within the organization than it is to find the technical skills they might need to resolve a virus attack, for example.

REACHING THE AWARENESS PROGRAM AUDIENCE

To get the security message across to a wide, disparate audience, it is necessary to view the audience in terms of its individual demographic segments. The awareness program will work only if it is focused on these segments and if all messages are appropriate to the segments.

The population can be defined in various ways—for example, it can be divided into management and nonmanagement segments. These groups can be further segmented by management level (e.g., senior and line management), technical versus nontechnical managers, and local versus off-site managers.

The nonmanagerial categories can be further segmented into technical and nontechnical groups and skilled and unskilled groups. The segments could even focus on shifts, recognizing the general reduction in the number of supervisory personnel on second and third shifts.

The object of this segmentation process is to establish a target audience that will be receptive to or is in need of specific awareness enhancement. Once the target audience has been identified, appropriate awareness tools and techniques can be selected to get the message across.

It should be obvious that a presentation to an executive management group should be different from that to third-shift computer operations personnel or to clerical personnel in accounting. The message may be exactly the same throughout the organization, but the presentation cannot be. The presentations may use different language (e.g., a business orientation versus a more personal approach), different presentation media (e.g., in person versus a videotape), and different examples to bring home the point.

A key first step in putting together the awareness program is identification of the prospective audience. Some possible breakdowns that can be used are shown in Exhibit I-5-1. Within each of these categories, special consideration should be given to new employees, employees who have had no information security background, and employees who need a refresher program. It is particularly important to target new employees before they have the opportunity to develop habits that may be difficult to break or that may inadvertently compromise sensitive information.

CONTENTS OF THE AWARENESS PROGRAM

An initial step in developing the awareness program is determining its contents (i.e., what the audience needs to be aware of). Determining the contents of the

---

EXHIBIT I-5-1 Sample Audience Categories for the Awareness Program

Category	Subset
Management	• Senior management • Middle management • Line management
Staff	• Technical data processing staff members • Other technical groups • Administrative
Occupational	• Union • Unrepresented
Functional	• Production • Marketing • Sales • Support staff
Territorial	• Headquarters staff • Home office staff • Domestic personnel • International personnel
Quality Assurance	• Customer • Supplier • Service provider

program is a constantly evolving process because there are generally two broad categories of information that must be disseminated.

The first includes messages that present the broad, underlying principles of an information security program. Messages in this category include such basics as "Information is a valuable corporate asset," "Sensitive information should be protected," and "Do not duplicate copyrighted material." These messages are valid throughout the organization and even apply to those the organization does business with. These messages require continuous repetition to ensure that they become corporate habits that are hard to break. The presentation to different audiences may differ and the rationale behind the message may change for different groups, but the basic concepts are universal.

The second type of message is more specific to the organization or to security program initiatives. The awareness program raises security consciousness in general but can also be used to prepare the way for implementing specific aspects of security. For example, "Data should be backed up" is a message that can be focused on during the implementation of a business continuity planning program that addresses the user community. "Passwords should be kept secret" is a message that can accompany new access control initiatives.

The internal information protection program itself—that is, the organization's existing policies, methods, and procedures—is a directing force for the awareness program. The program should be fully integrated with the overall security implementation plan, and components of the plan should become security awareness tools.

For example, an information security policy is a tool for raising security awareness. It highlights senior management's concern and support for security, the business necessity, and the basic guidelines that employees will be expected to adhere to. A policy statement is an excellent tool, but only if it is widely disseminated. It does no good sitting on a manager's bookshelf.

Ideas and experiences resulting from other security programs can be used as awareness tools. For example, anecdotes can be used to report incidents that have occurred within the organization or to someone else in the same industry. Stories that are close to home are generally more effective at highlighting the need for security. When using this technique, it is essential to present solutions and preferred responses to the situation so that the anecdote provides a positive learning experience.

AWARENESS PROGRAM TECHNIQUES

A variety of techniques should be used to make the audience aware of the security program. The communications media selected will determine the effectiveness of the overall awareness program. The techniques selected should reflect the personality, traditions, and budget of the organization, as determined by the organization's established policy.

A wide range of communications techniques that are effective for awareness programs are shown in Exhibit I-5-2. As shown in the exhibit, the cost of any given technique ranges from expensive to minimal. In designing an effective program, both extremes should be used. Not only is the proposed program more easily accepted by management if all alternatives have been explored for content and expense, but the varied tools produce a more effective program.

Several companies provide services to develop awareness materials for clients or to provide such items as posters, booklets, and small handouts or trinkets. These services are of considerable advantage to small companies that do not have internal art departments. Most give smaller companies the benefit of bulk purchasing rates.

The following sections discuss the various techniques presented in Exhibit I-5-2.

Presentations

Direct, face-to-face discussions with employees are ideal for introducing and reinforcing information protection. There is no substitute for the interchange between the expert and the novice. This interchange is key; therefore, it is essential that the presenter be knowledgeable and enthusiastic about the subject and that the audience be encouraged to participate.

EXHIBIT I-5-2 Awareness Program Techniques

Technique	Development Time	Cost
Presentations	8 hours for 1-hour presentation	Moderate
Videos	2 to 4 months for 15-minute video	Expensive
Posters	1 month per poster	Expensive
Booklets	3 months	Moderate
Newsletters	1 month	Minimal
Articles in internal publications	1 week	Minimal
Special-alert memos	1 day	Minimal
Electronic bulletin boards	1 day	Minimal
Small handouts	1 month	Moderate

EXHIBIT I-5-3 Sample Presentation Agenda

Segment	Content	Duration
Introduction	References to company policy, executive support, and actual security horror stories (preferably internal incidents)	7 minutes
Video	Dramatization using company executives. Should emphasize a special topic being covered for this phase of the awareness program.	15 minutes
Summary	Reinforcement of policy, employee responsibility, and security contacts. Question and answer session.	8 minutes

Presentations should be limited to 30 minutes. This is sufficient to cover the material and hold the audience's attention. The presentation should be upbeat and dynamic and should involve a variety of media. The use of professional-quality slides or projection graphs, a video of no more than 15 minutes in duration, and a flip chart (i.e., something to write on) are the minimum requirements. The flip chart is used to encourage audience participation. The more the audience members participate, the more they will take back to the job. A presentation agenda might be developed as shown in Exhibit I-5-3.

In organizations with many remote locations, face-to-face presentations by the information protection specialist may not be possible. In such cases, knowledgeable employees at the remote site can be trained, either through seminars or conference calls, to give the presentation. The security specialist should prepare a presentation package for these remote-site presentations, including required slides with a proposed script to accompany each slide, a video with the appropriate introduction, copies of the policy documents, and information for obtaining further assistance to answer questions that arise during the presentation.

Caution must be exercised with remote-site presentations. For example, a very knowledgeable person may be chosen to give the presentation, and that person may sincerely follow the material and present the topic as well as the security specialist. On the other hand, the presenter may be a local enthusiast who feels more knowledgeable than the materials for the original presentation and may develop his own presentation. Although in some cases the result can be excellent, the security organization has lost control and may not realize that the desired result has not been achieved. In another situation, the presenter may be someone who is simply given the assignment because he has some time, regardless of his background or enthusiasm for the topic. The result may be an individual who simply reads the script—a fast way to lose the audience. The key to a successful presentation is the involvement of the speaker and the audience.

Videos

For emphasis and to ensure a consistent message, an appropriate video can provide the basis for presentations. In addition, it can be presented at remote sites as a standalone program, alleviating the need for a knowledgeable presenter. This multimedia tool gives depth and consistency to each presentation and ensures that key issues are covered by a standard approach.

Ensuring that a standard message is presented at remote sites or at sites with a small number of employees can be of particular value when a local expert cannot be readily identified. In addition, the use of a standalone video can reduce or eliminate travel expenses to remote sites because the headquarters representative does not have to be present. However, standalone videos should be used only when there is no other way to spread the message.

Two options are available: The video can be purchased or specifically developed. Purchasing an existing commercial video that has a generic message can be most cost-effective. However, the key to successfully selecting such a video is recognition of the target audience. More than one video may be needed to address a variety of audience segments. For example, the typical clerical staff person responsible for key input will not respond to a technical documentary.

The level of detail, the approach, and the background of all the videos available should be considered when the organization is evaluating videos for purchase. The approach of the video should match the general corporate climate. For example, are humorous dramatizations considered acceptable within the confines of general office behavior, or is a more serious tone required? Is it appropriate for videos to include introductions by executives? Such introductions may be effective only if widely recognized executives are used. Further consideration should be given to the background setting of the video. For example, does the audience being addressed work at a bank? If so, a dramatization set in a manufacturing plant may be distracting to them, resulting in a lost message.

The second option, that of producing the video in-house, has distinct advantages. Not only can the material be customized to address specific problems or issues within the organization, but it can be shot at a company site recognizable to the audience. In addition, this effort will reflect the concern and support of the organization's management for the issues presented. The video can refer specifically to the organization's own policy, provide hot-line numbers, and identify security personnel who can be contacted for further assistance.

The content of videos may very according to need. One approach is to use employee testimonials mixed with statements from experts within the security industry. Care must be taken with this approach to clearly identify the speakers, because the general employee body may not recognize the corporate data center director or the microcomputer guru. In addition, the audience probably will not appreciate the expertise provided by an industry specialist unless a preface is given to qualify the comments of the speaker. With the proper identification and presentation of credentials, the use of experts to support the issues presented can be very effective.

Dramatizations offer an easy way for people to remember issues. A story with a catchy theme, comic character, or unusual setting can leave a lasting impression. Voiceovers may be used to emphasize key issues highlighted by lists presented on screen.

Regardless of the technique used for producing the video, maximum impact is obtained when the video is part of an overall program. For a most effective ongoing awareness program, a variety of videos should be used. Each phase of the program should be represented with a video to emphasis that phase. For example, the program may start with a video discussing general information protection. Each phase after that might have a specific theme, such as information classification and protection, disaster recovery, microcomputer security, or mainframe security. A separate video for each theme provides effective emphasis.

Posters

Posters provide direct, daily contact with employees. Not only is the message delivered repeatedly, but the subliminal benefits of the presence of posters is enormous. For example, after seeing and reading the poster once or twice, employees may not actually read it again; yet whenever they see a poster anywhere in the office, subconsciously they will associate it with the topic of security.

One or two posters should be selected to illustrate the issues to be emphasized in each phase of the awareness program. For example, if there is a concern that employees are not properly backing up the data on their personal computers, the poster might remind them to back up. Different styles of artwork (e.g., photographs and cartoons) might be used to illustrate the topic. Effectiveness may be increased by using more than one style of art to attract the attention of different audience segments.

Effectiveness can also be increased by using a similar format for all posters in the series. Professional artists should be consulted for advice on developing a poster format that suits the organization. The security professional must take care, however, to keep the artist's creative suggestions related to the security topic being illustrated. The security professional must make the final decision regarding the intent of the message to be delivered.

As with videos, posters can be purchased from companies or developed internally. An element critical to this decision is the time available for development. As with videos, posters take time to develop; however, the benefits of internally developed or professionally customized posters may be worth the wait.

Commercial posters can help get the program off to a fast start. The first phases of a program may be completed more rapidly by using these posters. Customized posters may be developed for later phases. The use of commercial posters can be especially helpful to a company requiring only a small quantity of posters; it is generally very expensive to print small quantities of posters.

When an internal graphics department is available, it can be very effective to develop posters in-house. Posters can be designed to reflect specific problems or issues that surface within the organization. When developed in-house, consideration must be given to the size and weight of the paper as well as distribution needs. For example, because overseas shipping is expensive, a lightweight paper stock is more practical if the posters are to be shipped this way. In addition, some companies may require specific sizes for bulletin boards. The decision to develop posters internally or purchase commercial posters may be directly influenced by budget restrictions. Therefore, comparisons may be required for budget approval.

Posters should be replaced at regular intervals. If posters are released at the same time of the month or at the first of each quarter, for example, employees will become conditioned to looking for them. The release of a new poster each month or quarter allows employees to internalize the message before the next one is displayed. If two posters on the same theme are developed, they should be presented during the same period.

Booklets

When more detailed, long-term information needs to be distributed, booklets are an excellent medium for presenting ideas, stating policy, and documenting procedures. The booklet can then be retained for future reference. The topics presented in booklets, however, should be those not expected to change frequently.

The booklet should refer to existing policy and should review documented procedures. This format provides the opportunity to give more detailed implementation activities. It also provides a medium to answer frequently asked questions or to clarify misconceptions.

It is most effective to introduce the booklets with a letter from executive management demonstrating support for the topic covered. The introductory letter should then emphasize the employee's responsibilities. References to policy and to methods and procedures documentation should be clearly listed in the letter. In addition, it should include the names and telephone numbers of security contacts, along with a reminder of when such contacts are appropriate.

The booklet should be written in a clear, simple style. The amount of essay material should be limited. Bulleted lists are useful for clearly stating issues; they make the document cleaner and facilitate future reference.

During the design of the booklet, the security specialist should ensure that it follows the theme used for the overall program—that is, the theme used for the program's videos and posters. Color coordination, a logo, and a specific design for the cover similar to the poster layout help tie the program together.

In addition, the quality of the paper used for the booklet must be durable. The size of the booklet should be appealing if the audience is expected to retain the booklet. One consideration is to design a binder or cover to hold each booklet.

Once again, the program budget plays a primary role in the development of booklets. Unless a large quantity is to be distributed, it is unrealistic to consider having a booklet specially printed. In this case, consideration might be given to vendors who can provide small quantities of topical booklets. It should be noted that some vendors also customize this type of material, using the standard booklet as a basis and making modifications to personalize the booklet. Again, quantities to be printed determine whether this approach is practical from a financial position.

Booklets may be used to introduce the awareness program, or they may serve as a reference library of program information. Their versatility makes them a cornerstone of any awareness program. They can be mailed to employees to highlight the security topic of the month or to provide details on the topic. Having a ready supply of booklets on virus prevention and cleanup, microcomputer access controls and backup procedures, copyright and trade secret protection, or any other issue of particular importance to the company establishes the security manager as an information resource.

Newsletters

A short, regularly published newsletter can effectively provide timely information to employees. Such newsletters should be no longer than one page, front and back. If the newsletter is printed on a regular basis and printed on a distinctive paper stock, employees immediately recognize it. Employees will single it out for rapid consumption if the newsletter obtains a reputation for quality information. Newsletters should include current real-life stories of security issues, stories of internal incidents, a summary of the consequences incurred by violators, and an explanation of timely changes to policy before the revised policy is published.

If the newsletter is brief, informative, and timely, employees will not only read it but discuss it. There is no better element for an awareness program.

Articles

Existing company or agency magazines or newsletters have a ready audience. Timely articles regarding current security issues can be a hot topic for inclusion in these publications.

This medium can be used to introduce the overall awareness program. Distribution of posters should be timed to coincide with the appearance of the program article in the organizational publication. The article is most useful if it describes the poster, including a picture if possible, and explains the concept and importance of the posters and how they fit into the theme of this phase of the awareness program.

Another effective technique is to publish interviews in the internal publication. Interviews with security experts as well as executive management demonstrate support for the security program and its objectives.

The technical audience should not be overlooked when publishing articles in internal publications. There may be an internal publication aimed specifically at this audience. This medium may be used to discuss the more technical issues and implementation concerns of the program. Letters to the editor may be published as a followup to articles. This technique encourages employees to take an active role in the effort and offers them the opportunity to ask questions they may otherwise only complain about to coworkers. In addition, such letters demonstrate the day-to-day, real-world issues.

Articles should not sensationalize issues. They should be written with the primary goal of helping the audience understand the importance of security issues. A security program is much more effective if the audience understands the balance between vulnerability, risk, and countermeasures. The articles may be used to point out changes in technology that require changes in implementation. Articles with an appropriate focus will help prepare the audience to address security concerns with an understanding of their responsibilities and the possible consequences of not fulfilling those responsibilities.

Special-Alert Memos

A hacker has been identified in one of the corporate systems. An office fire has rendered several microcomputers unusable and access to the office temporarily unavailable. Real situations within the organization may be made known to employees through a special-alert memo. Such memos should be short but informative. They should not only describe the immediate problem but guide the reader through the procedures to fix the situation. In addition, they should highlight proactive steps to prevent or minimize damage in the future.

Special-alert memos should be reserved for genuine time-dependent situations. The security manager should be well prepared before a crisis occurs by knowing when a special-alert memo is appropriate, what information to include in it, and the best way to reproduce and distribute the memos.

Electronic Bulletin Boards

Electronic bulletin boards are now available in many organizations. This state-of-the-art communications technique is a most effective way to reach more technical organizations. The availability of a ready network to provide flash bulletins can be effective both as an awareness tool and to alert users of potential problems.

From an awareness perspective, a bulletin board can be used to store such reference material as policy references, security contact names and telephone numbers, and current known security problems. The periodic publishing of discussions regarding various security issues can be stimulated by employee requests for information through the bulletin board. Its use as an interactive tool is one of the best methods available for reaching the technical community.

Small Handouts

The use of trinkets for reinforcement round out a solid awareness program. Handouts that will be used repeatedly, that will be topics of conversation, or that generally grab attention help ensure that the awareness program is not forgotten. Trinkets and handouts that are periodically distributed can enhance the awareness program and reinforce the themes highlighted in each phase of the program.

MANAGING THE AWARENESS PROGRAM

Establishing a process for managing the security awareness program is the key to a solid, effective program. In addition, a planned management process serves as a presentation tool to management when requesting funding and is useful as an implementation tool. The following sections discuss important elements of this management process.

Using a Time-Bound Management Process

The use of a management process helps identify problems and solutions in an organized, documented, and time-bound way. A time-bound security awareness program presents a time line for the program and identifies milestones that should be met along the way. The initial time line should cover no less than the first year's milestones; additional key issues identified for further development should be noted but not discussed at length. This ensures that these remaining issues are developed within an acceptable time frame.

A well-managed awareness program helps create a proactive environment. The program should be kicked off with training for the coordinators and a development period for such activities as the design of tools, followed by actual field implementation. A simple overview of the awareness program schedule with specific key milestones is readily understood by managers and gives a quick picture to participating coordinators. This type of schedule leaves no question as to the ongoing nature of the program. As a result, future enhancements are anticipated.

Measurement of Effectiveness

The measurement of program effectiveness is another key to management acceptance, support, and funding. Therefore, a survey of employees that measures the effectiveness of the program should be included as a part of the initial first-quarter activities and at the start of the second year. The survey results should illustrate to management the success and necessity of the program. Such a survey of employees can also identify areas of concern and new issues requiring attention. The information gathered can help determine a level of compliance within the organization.

The results from the beginning of the awareness program can be compared with those of one year later to document the progress of the program. In addition, areas of weakness can be identified to develop a solid action plan for future improvement.

Surveys can be conducted in several ways. A written survey can be distributed to employees. However, this approach usually produces a low percentage of responses and can take an extended amount of time to complete. Electronic mail usually has a higher response level but may reach a limited audience. Random telephone surveys have proved the most effective. They also have the benefit of controlling the time invested in collecting responses. Regardless of the approach used, the number of questions must be kept to a minimum. In addition, the questions must be carefully developed and must be able to be reused in subsequent surveys to evaluate progress.

SAMPLE PROGRAMS

The golden rule for packaging a specific presentation is to know the audience. This same rule applies to the overall program developed for various targeted audiences. The following sections discuss sample programs developed for specific audiences.

Executive Programs

It is common to seek the support of executive management for the awareness program, and these managers are often asked to demonstrate their support to the general employee body. Therefore, the program presented to executive management must provide the background of the overall awareness program, its corporate needs, a proposed action plan, expected follow-up, and budget requirements. The initial meeting with executives should be short, because their time is limited. If they want more information, they will ask for it.

Executives deal in broad concepts. It is not necessary to present details, but detailed information should be available to answer any questions that may arise. In addition, executives typically want to know why an issue should be given their attention. This presents the opportunity to relate recent events that have happened elsewhere to occurrences within the company, a relationship that is key to illustrating the need for security awareness.

Once the need for security awareness is established, the next step is to present the action plan: the program schedule. Presentation of the schedule should include program objectives and expected results. The schedule becomes the guide to accomplishing the objectives and obtaining the desired results.

The executive program must be kept short, simple, and direct. Executives have little time for extremely detailed information, and the program should reflect a respect for their needs.

Staff Manager Programs

A staff manager can be considered a professional with no subordinates. This individual may be a systems analyst, accountant, engineer, or personnel specialist. Programs developed for these managers must reflect their particular job responsibilities. A group of staff managers should be introduced to the basic awareness program at a single meeting. However, the awareness materials and videos used with this audience should address specific professional concerns in relation to overall program requirements. Followup and guidance related to specific training should be provided, as required. The general awareness program alone may not be an adequate means to cover this group of managers; nevertheless, they must not be excluded from the program.

Line Operations Manager Programs

This category of managers should be prepared to enhance the program through sideline meetings, which may be supplemented with personalized handouts, for example. Line operations managers must convey their support to the employees on their staff and the staffs of company executives. Employees typically focus their efforts on the same areas that they perceive their bosses to support. If sufficient time is given in the early phases of these managers' programs to ensure that they are comfortable with the concepts and implementation of the awareness program, increased benefits will result.

Computer Professional Programs

Computer professionals' knowledge of security issues should already be reasonably thorough. The overall program for these employees must be maintained at a more technical level. The program for computer professionals should include a solicitation of their support in educating other employee groups and should emphasize the need for them to set a good example.

Researcher Programs

This group may need an individually implemented program. Because researchers may have unique work schedules and personalities, their manager should be given the freedom to organize a program appropriate for this particular environment. For example, reading a booklet may not be high in a researcher's job priorities. Scheduling one-on-one meetings or small project groups is probably a more effective way to introduce the awareness program to this group.

End-User Programs

Packaging for this group is critical. For example, end users include data entry clerks, who may not have a technical background. This lack of understanding can lead to careless mistakes and increases the possibility of errors and omissions, which are the most frequent cause of loss of data integrity. Therefore, in addition to the basic security issues, the end-user program should emphasize the importance of double-checking one's work to ensure that careless mistakes have not been made.

The program aimed at end users must be well planned and should be described to the audience before it is presented to them. This helps prepare the audience and shows that the program is not haphazard. The credibility gained by executing the program as laid out helps ensure a better understanding of the urgency and importance of the topic. In addition, this audience may need to attend awareness programs more frequently than may be necessary with a more management-oriented staff.

End users should be encouraged to conduct a meeting on each topic within the program. Time is well spent on details related to user responsibility, implementation tools and techniques, procedures that are specifically described, easily referenced user guides, and readily available information sources.

This type of audience generally responds well to seriousness mixed with humor. The awareness program should include frequently distributed handouts. In addition, positive reinforcement is most beneficial. For example, singling out an

---

EXHIBIT I-5-4 **Steps to Developing an Awareness Program**

1. Obtain senior-level management support.
2. Identify the audience.
3. Identify the basic program content and emphasis.
4. Develop the overall program.
5. Design awareness tools to enhance the program.
6. Measure the effectiveness of the program.
7. Evaluate problem areas and design the next phase of the ongoing program.

individual who has successfully backed up his data for the first week of the program may be more productive than showing several videos.

End users must have a solid appreciation for why security issues are important and a clear understanding of their role and responsibilities. In addition, they must be aware of exactly what they are expected to do.

GEOGRAPHIC ISSUES

When a company is highly departmentalized and widely dispersed geographically, it may be necessary to stagger the implementation of the program among locations. For example, the program may be implemented first in one location, then in another a quarter later. This approach permits consistent attention to each phase of the program. In addition, it allows feedback from the initial program to be reflected in later implementations. Specific decisions of this type reflect the availability of resources, the physical distance between sites, and the level of department decentralization.

SUMMARY

This chapter provides a solid background and specific guidelines for managing an information security awareness program. Exhibit I-5-4 outlines the specific steps that should be taken in developing the program, as discussed in this chapter.

In all of these steps, the key component is audience focus. Whether the awareness program is to address executive management or the clerical staff, the program and tools must focus on the audience members' primary concerns and job responsibilities. In addition, the message must be consistent for each audience presentation. Audience members must clearly understand why security is their responsibility and what they are expected to do. The success of the security program hinges on how effectively the security awareness program communicates with each of the audience segments.

A Framework for Developing Security Awareness

PETER C. GARDINER

One of the biggest challenges facing information security professionals has little to do with information security technology per se. Rather, the major challenge is getting the attention of line managers and their commitment to do something to improve information security.

In addition to the usual line-versus-staff problems, many line managers simply do not believe that security is an issue deserving their attention. Consequently, they only pay lip service to information security in their organizations. Moreover, they often have different ways of approaching and making decisions, which can complicate an information security professional's attempts to improve the security of the organization's information systems.

One of the complaints heard most frequently among information security professionals is that no one listens to them, and if people do listen, they still do not do anything about security. Knowing what to do to protect information confidentiality, integrity, and availability is one thing. Persuading line managers, who may or may not consider security a relevant issue, to follow the necessary procedures is quite another.

This chapter presents an integrated framework of methods for recognizing and dealing with some of the common problems information security professionals may encounter with line managers when trying to improve information security in an organization. The overall goal of this chapter is to help information security practitioners understand what they must do to convince line managers to follow information security procedures. In practice, this is a two-step process.

The first step is to get the attention of line managers. If they fail to pay serious attention to what the information security professional has to say, the prospects for improving the security of an organization's information system are grim, no matter how technically talented one is. The second step is to persuade line managers to commit to following or enforcing security procedures. Gaining attention but then failing to persuade the manager to take action produces results hardly different from failing to get attention in the first place.

In providing a background and framework for getting attention and action, this chapter can help the information security professional understand and, it is hoped, overcome what some perceive as a line manager's natural resistance to accepting anything recommended by any staff manager, let alone an information security staff manager. This resistance is a result of many factors, some related specifically to information security and others unrelated to security. Armed with the material that follows, a security professional can reduce a line manager's resistance to security and increase the chances of getting attention and action.

LINE MANAGERS

There is an important distinction between line managers and information security professionals, who are essentially staff managers. This distinction is not unique; it has long existed between line and staff managers in every organization. Likewise, the reluctance of line managers to take action on the recommendations of information security professionals is not new. In fact, staff professionals in other fields face similar problems. Many line managers simply do not like staff advice.

Some argue that there is an inherent tension between line and staff managers in any organization—some even argue that this tension is healthy. Regardless of its origin, there is a tension, and most believe it is caused by the different functions of line and staff managers. Line managers are directly responsible for an organization's production and operations system, which exists to produce output (i.e., a service or product). At all organizational levels, line managers are first and foremost responsible for managing their production and operation system so that it delivers the planned output of their system on time and within budget and so that it meets all performance requirements. Generally, everything that contributes to this task is welcome, and everything that hinders it is unwelcome.

Line managers are ordinarily very busy. Information security staff professionals have to persuade them to take time out to listen to a proposal on information security and then to spend money or change a production and operations procedure to implement security.

Line managers are key decision makers in any organization. It is the line manager who decides whether or not a staff suggestion is accepted or rejected. At all organizational levels, line managers are held responsible and accountable for meeting the cost, schedule, and performance targets for their production and operations system, as set by senior management.

When faced with staff recommendations that may or may not have to be adopted, they face a dilemma. If a staff recommendation is neither mandated by senior management nor legally required, the line manager must decide whether it should be accepted or not. From a line manager's perspective, if a staff recommendation has an adverse impact on production and operations, the impact will be noticed almost immediately by a higher-level manager. For example, an increase in cost can immediately be seen by anyone. Line managers who fail to meet cost targets are open to criticism.

On the other hand, if a staff recommendation is rejected, there may be no noticeable impact on that manager's production and operations system, at least in the short term. There might even be no impact in the long term—there may be no impact at all. These are the natural thoughts that run through a line manager's mind after receiving a staff recommendation. There is considerable pressure on most line managers to reject all nonessential staff recommendations or simply give them lip service.

STAFF MANAGERS

Staff managers, on the other hand, contribute only indirectly to a system's operation and output. Although the work performed by staff may be essential, it contributes indirectly to production. For example, by recruiting the right people, providing a safe work environment, and ensuring a secure information system for the line manager's production and operations system, the personnel, safety, and information security staffs contribute resources that help the line manager. These resources (and others) are integrated and molded by line managers into a smoothly running production system.

Information Security Professionals

The information security professional is one of many staff professionals who provide advice to line managers. Staff managers, such as the information security professional, have a different perspective of an organization's production and operations system and its output. Depending on the specialty area, staff members' efforts are often focused on a single area of expertise, such as safety, human resources, information systems, or information security. Often, this focus excludes all other areas.

Nevertheless, staff recommendations are driven by many legitimate factors, including legal requirements, a long-term organizational view, and various formal analyses that demonstrate a rational basis for a recommended action as opposed to the status quo. One important limit inherent in a staff position, however, is that staff managers cannot implement anything in the line organization, no matter how important or sound it is perceived to be. A staff manager can only make recommendations; it is the line manager who must determine whether to implement those recommendations.

CONFLICTS BETWEEN LINE AND STAFF MANAGERS

When a staff manager puts conditions and restrictions on the use of the resources it contributes to production and operations, the boundary between helping and hindering line management is often crossed. It is then that line managers begin to get uncomfortable with, if not downright hostile toward, staff.

A condition of use perceived as sound by staff may very well be perceived as hindering production and operations by line managers. Many staff recommendations or conditions of use are viewed by line managers as increasing costs, slowing schedules, and degrading the performance of an organization's operations. Unfortunately, the line manager's perception is quite often accurate.

As a result of the very different organizational perspectives between line and staff, there exists a natural tension between these two groups. Their views on managing an organization's production and operations system are typically in conflict. This tension is not necessarily good or bad, and it is unlikely that it will ever go away. Therefore, information security professionals must be aware of it and the role it inevitably plays in their interactions with line managers.

The use of information systems has spread widely with the advent of microcomputers and networks, which increase the productivity of users of production and operations systems. The major justifications for such systems is that they increase productivity and are user-friendly.

What happens, then, when an information security professional makes recommendations that increase the complexity of using computers, reduce user-friendliness, and reduce productivity? Security professionals rightly point out that if the confidentiality, integrity, or availability of information is compromised, an organization could face disaster. But the issue for line managers is whether to forego security for the sake of productivity or introduce security measures to reduce some probable risk and allow productivity to suffer. Unfortunately, many line managers would rather protect productivity and take their chances with security.

LINE MANAGEMENT AND INFORMATION SECURITY ISSUES

There are several factors that make the job of the information security staff professional more difficult when it comes to getting attention and action from line management. These complicating factors are the recent technological advances in and merging of telecommunications and data communications into what can be described as modern information systems, the new information security problems that are emerging as a result of this modernization and merging, and the almost total lack of significant knowledge about either on the part of most line managers.

The following sections discuss some of the main problems inherent in these recent changes.

Modern Information Systems

In many respects, the full impact of modern information systems have only recently begun emerging. These systems are starting to dramatically alter the shape, size, management, and productivity of organizations. Few line managers are well informed about such modern technology as integrated digital networks with megabyte data flows, which merge telephone systems with computers and connect various kinds of users inside and outside an organization.

What is emerging is a vast integrated digital network with local, metropolitan, wide area, and global interconnections and almost universal information service within an organization. It is expected that most users, wherever they are, will soon be able to connect to most computers. High-speed data paths will provide digital interconnections among users for all their voice, data, and video needs. Any user—friendly or unfriendly, insider or outside hacker—may attempt to access any and all of an organization's information.

With fiber optics and transmission rates approaching terabits per second, it is becoming possible to think about transmitting the entire contents of the Library of Congress in only a few minutes. There are now computer chips that have 10 to 20 million transistors; within 5 to 10 years, however, there may be one billion transistors on a chip. This will place computing power equivalent to one or two Cray supercomputers onto a chip that will fit in a microcomputer.

It is the emerging magnitude, power, pervasiveness, and interconnectedness of the modern information system that has dramatically changed the scope and context of information security. The rate of change in computing environments in general is accelerating rapidly. With this as a backdrop, many line managers are bewildered by the attention of security precautions.

Emerging Information Security Problems

The dramatic increase in risk as a result of modern information technology is altering the need for and methods of ensuring security. Early information security generalities about how much is at stake and the odds of a loss are no longer valid in most organizations. There are new and dramatically higher stakes, and the odds seem to be rapidly shifting against information security. Most line managers are unaware of these new issues.

Until fairly recently, most individuals could affect the confidentiality, integrity, and availability of information in only one or two computers, and the potential rewards to them and damages to an organization were relatively limited. Now, one person can affect the information security in thousands of computers throughout the nation or cause millions of dollars in damages in one computer.

A solid portion of the problems that information security professionals face as they attempt to influence line managers comes from these new security issues. An often vast and bewildering restructuring of many organizations is under way as a result of increasing uses of modern information systems. The advent of integrated digital networks, local area networks, and personal computers and the merging of the phone system with computer networks are producing fundamental changes in how line managers design and control their production and operations systems. It is often very difficult for line managers to adapt to the information age transformation itself, let alone cope with concerns about the information security aspects of that transformation.

CLASSIFYING THE NONBELIEVERS AMONG LINE MANAGERS

Most information security professionals fail to get the attention of nonbelieving line managers because they fail to recognize there are different kinds of nonbelievers. Rather than approach each nonbeliever with the same strategy, security professionals must recognize that each thinks differently, reacts differently, and therefore must be approached differently.

It is difficult to imagine one awareness approach or one information security program that will get the attention and action of every nonbeliever. Information security awareness programs and security program recommendations must be tailored for the type or mix of nonbelieving line managers who are to be persuaded to action. To tailor an approach, the nonbeliever types must be identified and an approach developed accordingly.

The following sections discuss several of the most common types of nonbelieving line managers.

The Know-Nothing. These are the line managers who know nothing about their information systems or information security. They are unaware that information systems can be compromised and that a compromise can be very costly. They simply assume that computers always work, that the computer specialists will take care of everything, and that they have no responsibility at all in this area. They have no idea that their own actions—or lack of them—can have an impact on information security.

The Do-Not-Want-to-Know. These are the line managers who not only do not know about security but do not want to know. Often, what little they do know on the subject is wrong. They might agree that information security is important but take the view that it is someone else's responsibility. These managers simply hope for the best and do not want to discuss information security.

The Bean Counter. These are the line managers who add up the costs of information security recommendations and immediately conclude that they simply cost too much and cannot be afforded. Information security recommendations almost always entail real and immediate costs. Money spent on information security often has to be taken from funds budgeted for other projects. Given the demands on an organization's budget, this may not be acceptable.

The Obsessive-Compulsive. These are the line managers who are so involved in meeting the cost, schedule, and performance requirements for which they are responsible that anything that tends to impede these goals is rejected as obstructions to the real mission at hand.

The Hyperactive. Every manager is busy, and making time for one more meeting on any subject tends to be difficult. However, this type of line manager tends to set a dizzying pace. Hyperactives are difficult, if not impossible, to pin down long enough to recommend anything. They rarely spend sufficient time to understand fully anything. No matter the subject, they always seem to have bigger fish to fry and are always late for the next meeting.

The Ostrich. Some line managers take the position that information security problems will simply not happen here. They typically argue that the company has never had security problems before or that the company has never taken security measures before. Like the ostrich, they simply stick their heads in standard operating procedures and refuse to acknowledge that information security problems can happen to them. This type of nonbelieving line manager recognizes only what has or has not happened in the past, not what may happen in the near future. At best, these line managers might be able to anticipate yesterday's threats to their current information systems.

The Pauper. A few managers take the position that the company does not have anything important enough to protect. Therefore, they argue, security measures are unnecessary.

The Propeller Head. These managers are information systems enthusiasts. They go to extremes to have the latest information systems technology and gadgets available for use. They insist on user-friendly systems. They insist that all employees have maximum access to the system and be free to explore it and use it. After all, they argue, that is why the system is there in the first place. They resist any recommendation that is viewed as getting in the way of users using the system.

The Eden Dweller. Diogenes was an ancient Greek philosopher who is remembered for searching with a lantern to find an honest human. Some line managers are convinced they have found lots of them. They take the view that their employees are all honest, hard working, and the finest that can be found. The suggestion that some employees might compromise information security and that therefore some information security recommendations should be implemented is often followed by a lecture about how honest the employees are and how unneeded an information security program is. They firmly believe this despite survey results that suggest that up to 25% of information security threats come from employee dishonesty and employee revenge.

The Procrastinator. These are difficult nonbelievers to deal with. They appear to agree with everything the security specialist recommends, but somehow nothing ever gets done about implementing the recommendations. Sometimes, these managers appear to have mastered the art of creative inertia, which is to avoid taking action on anything while giving the illusion of complete cooperation and action.

The Literalist. These are the line managers who are willing to protect the computer but not old notebooks, papers, printouts, or faxes or the trash cans, dumpsters, or telephones. They argue that these items have nothing to do with computers and therefore nothing to do with the information security program.

PERSPECTIVES ON DECISION MAKING

When developing recommendations to be presented to line managers for review and action, it is important for information security professionals to understand the audience of line managers to whom the ideas are being presented. Once the audience has been identified, recommendations and presentations can be tailored accordingly.

It is possible to get the attention of most nonbelievers regardless of type, and most can be persuaded to take action as well. However, each type must be approached and persuaded somewhat differently. There is no single best way to sell information security to every line manager.

Part of tailoring the right approach goes beyond recognizing which types of nonbeliever are in the audience; it also involves understanding how people approach and make decisions. There are three major perspectives people use in approaching and making decisions: the technical, organizational, and personal perspectives. A perspective shapes how a person looks at a situation, filters what is there, and then approaches a decision. The following sections discuss these three perspectives in more detail.

The Technical Perspective. When managers approach decision making from a technical perspective, their primary focus is on problem identification and rational problem solving. These managers use and are influenced by data, models, and other technical tools. They conduct formal analyses to help reach a decision.

The Organizational Perspective. For managers who approach a decision from an organizational perspective, the primary concern is not problem solving at all. The problem, as defined by those operating from the technical perspective, may in fact be irrelevant from an organizational perspective. When decisions are approached from an organizational perspective, therefore, the focus shifts from problem solving to a concern about how the organization will be affected by a decision. From this perspective, a good decision is one that has a favorable impact on an organization's rights, standing, stability, and parochial priorities and that preserves organizational stability, continuity, and standard operating procedures.

Managers operating from the organizational perspective use the art of compromise and bargaining to reach decisions. They have little interest in technical analyses. Incremental change and slow adaptation with bureaucratic red tape often are pervasive. Uncertainties are avoided, and there is a great fear of making a mistake. Data and models are not used to describe the environment; instead, a description is reached through organizational negotiations and consensus. After the facts and situation are agreed on as the result of negotiations among managers, other facts that contradict this negotiated reality are simply ignored or treated as exceptions to the rule.

The Personal Perspective. When managers approach a decision from a personal perspective, their primary concern is to maintain their own power, influence, and prestige. Most managers strive to maintain or increase their status. For managers with a personal perspective, however, problem solving and organizational stability are not important; intuition, personal experience, and personality are. Data and facts that can be compelling to managers operating from a technical perspective are often irrelevant in the personal perspective. Line managers operating from a personal perspective emphasize simple hypotheses and simple solutions.

AN INTEGRATED FRAMEWORK FOR GETTING ATTENTION AND ACTION

Understanding how line managers approach information security decision making and understanding what type of nonbelievers they are helps provide insight about how to get their attention (as well as how not to get their attention) and how to get action. There are three essential requirements that must be met to get a line manager's attention and action. These requirements form a basic framework for tailoring the way the managers should be approached. The following sections discuss these requirements.

Know and Speak the Line Manager's Language. The first requirement is to speak ordinary English when dealing with line managers. Better yet, the security professional should use terms familiar to line managers in the context of that manager's production and operation system and output. Security professionals should demonstrate that they understand how what they are saying fits into the overall environment. They should avoid heavy doses of information security jargon.

One common failure of many staff managers, including information security specialists, is that they do not speak ordinary English. Any manager will soon lose interest if someone walks in and begins to dole out information in a foreign language or jargon unless they themselves speak that language or jargon.

Most information security professionals are far better informed about information security than any line manager will ever become (or need become). It is a mistake to try to impress line managers with that fact. A line manager can lose interest during the first two minutes if the recommendations are not presented at a level the manager can fully and easily grasp. Every recommendation should be translated out of the jargon of a security specialist into a language and context the line manager can understand.

The advantages, disadvantages, and trade-offs on the manager's production and operations system and output should be clearly presented, in addition to reporting how information security will be improved. This is the first step in bridging the natural barrier between line and staff management.

Identify the Type of Nonbeliever. The second requirement, as discussed previously, is to correctly diagnose the type of nonbelieving line manager being addressed. Once diagnosed, any presentation made must be developed within the frame of reference of that type of nonbeliever. This is important because what may be an effective presentation and proposal to one type of nonbeliever probably will not work with another. If multiple types of nonbelieving managers are involved, it may be necessary to include some material in a briefing that appeals to each.

Correctly Diagnose the Manager's Approach to Decision Making. The third requirement is to correctly diagnose the perspective used by the manager to arrive at decisions. This requirement is similar to correctly diagnosing the type of nonbeliever. A briefing and recommendation that is prepared for a manager who approaches decision making from a technical perspective will likely fail if presented to a manager who approaches decision making from an organizational or personal perspective. Facts, figures, and rational conclusions are not important if organizational stability is threatened and the manager is operating from an organizational perspective or if the results of a formal analysis contradict strongly held beliefs of a manager who approaches decisions from a personal perspective.

Examples of Generic Approaches Using the Framework

Several generic strategies are available to the information security professional for getting attention and action from line managers. In each, the specific contents must be tailored to the individual line manager according to his decision-making perspective as well as what type of nonbeliever he is. For example, one generic strategy is a technical approach, and another is the use of horror stories. However, such generic strategies cannot simply be used at random, nor can a single generic strategy be singled out and used every time.

For example, it is a waste of time to prepare a detailed, formal risk analysis (an approach well suited for managers who approach a decision from a technical perspective) for a line manager who approaches all decisions from a personal perspective. It is far more effective to approach line managers who operate from a personal perspective with examples and horror stories that they personally can relate to and extend into their current situation. For a manager who makes decisions from a technical perspective and would react favorably to well-researched, formal risk analyses, it would be a mistake to attempt to gain attention and persuade to action using war stories and one-of-a-kind horror stories.

For example, if a know-nothing line manager approaches decisions from a technical perspective, a well-assembled risk analysis can sometimes achieve the desired result as long as it shows threats and threat frequency data, value and damage models, the estimated changes in risk as countermeasures are introduced, and the payback period for each recommended countermeasures computed. On the other hand, if a manager approaches decisions from an organizational perspective, such a technical analysis would probably languish in a pending basket. Far more effective in this case would be evidence about how a compromise of information security would upset that manager's organizational stability, continuity, and standard operating procedures. Finally, if the know-nothing line manager approaches decisions from a personal perspective, the best approach might involve focusing on an embarrassing loss of personal power, influence, and status that will surely occur if information is compromised. Equally effective might be a demonstration that helps reduce the fear of change and the unknown. Case studies and horror stories that hit home are much more likely to be effective for this type of manager than technical risk analyses.

The following sections discuss generic strategies that are available for approaching nonbelieving line managers.

The Technical Approach. In this approach, the information security professional emphasizes the use of formal analyses, risk analyses, annual loss estimates, threat probabilities, data, outside experts, and technical reports. This approach works well when managers, regardless of nonbeliever type, operate from a technical perspective.

Education and Awareness Programs. This approach is particularly useful for those managers and users who are considered the know-nothing or literalist types of nonbelievers. Attendees should be informed about sound policies and procedures. It is helpful to hold information security awareness briefings. Everyone should be encouraged to help with information security.

This approach works well with individuals operating from the technical perspective and can work with individuals operating from the organizational and personal perspectives as well, depending on the material included in the briefings and programs. For example, awareness programs that emphasize organizational stability and continuity produced by proper information security programs should work well with audiences that have an organizational perspectives.

Use of Horror Stories. The use of horror stories that reflect the personal and organizational experiences of others tends to work well with managers operating from the organizational and personal perspectives. In this approach, such incidents as virus attacks, compromised passwords, violations of confidentiality and their consequences, lawsuits filed, and insider computer crimes are told to the audience. Emphasis should be placed on the organizational turmoil, reorganizations, upheavals in standard operating procedures, loss of power, loss of influence, and loss of positions and status that followed information security compromises in these examples. Organizational-oriented horror stories should be selected for organizational audiences and personal-oriented horror stories for personal audiences.

The Legal Threat. In this approach, the strategy is to recruit attorneys in the organization's legal department as allies. In some instances, what the line manager is doing may be against the law or may expose the company to civil litigation (e.g., negligence). Enlisting the company lawyer to participate in the briefing may well get the attention of any reluctant manager, regardless of type or perspective.

The Organizational Detour. In some cases, it is extremely difficult to find a direct approach that will work. The managers who do not want to know about security are particularly difficult. In one case, a staff manager reported to a line vice-president that all signals on the microwave connection between corporate headquarters, where programmers worked, and the building housing the company's network hub mainframe were being intercepted and monitored. As a consequence, the data and passwords used on the mainframe were being read by outsiders. The vice-president's reaction was to tell the staff manager to go away and not bring that subject to his attention again.

In such cases, a given line manager may very well be impossible to reach and the information security professional faces a difficult decision. One approach is to detour the reluctant manager by seeking organizational allies who will support the proposed information security recommendations. This is a political maneuver and can be dangerous or may even lead to dismissal if not done well. Allies can be found and reluctant managers can be nudged along by an invisible organizational hand if the process is handled very carefully. However, the security professional must balance an obligation to the company and its security with the likelihood of strong organizational and personal sanctions for detouring the established chain of command. In many cases, this is simply not a feasible or satisfactory strategy. An effective alternative is gradualism, discussed in the following section.

Gradualism. Also known as the divine-patience approach, this is a strategy for wearing down nonbelieving line managers. This approach involves continually chipping away at the information security problems a little at a time. The idea is to think small and build on successes.

In addition, the security professional should enlist organizational support one person at a time, beginning with more sympathetic managers. The most obvious threats and those that are least expensive to counter should be tackled first. It is sometimes helpful to leave newspaper reports and technical reports (e.g., the National Research Council's 1991 report, *Computers at Risk: Safe Computing in the Information Age*) or books (e.g., *The Cuckoo's Egg* (New York: Doubleday, 1989) or *Cyberpunk* (New York: Simon & Schuster, 1991)) lying around for managers to read. Of utmost importance, however, is to preplan so that if an information security disaster occurs (which it probably will), the security professional can step in with a detection and recovery plan.

This is a very unsatisfactory approach for information security professionals who are impatient, action oriented, and committed to implementing sound information security programs in an organization. It works best when the information security professionals themselves follow an organizational perspective (regardless of whether or not they like the organizational perspective).

Experiments and Planned Penetrations. This approach involves getting permission to demonstrate for managers what the current vulnerabilities are by conducting a planned penetration. It is a useful approach for convincing managers operating from an organizational perspective and is often successful with managers operating from a personal perspective. It is an unnecessary though interesting strategy for managers operating from a technical perspective.

In one such penetration exercise, permission was given by a senior manager to penetrate the organization's large mainframe. The penetrators were in the operating system for 48 hours before anyone noticed and panic set in. Indeed, former members of the Legion of Doom, the group of young hackers who almost shut down BellSouth, have now formed a company that, for a fee, will run a penetration exercise against a company's system to discover and report its vulnerabilities. When asked, this group agreed that if information is online and there is an external link, they can break into it.

Properly done and with permission, penetration exercises can be quite dramatic and effective. Another version of experimentation might involve dumpster diving for computer printouts and discarded disks or using an automatic dialing program to find out all the organization's communications lines with modems and unprotected computers on them.

The Embedded Approach. This strategy has considerable merit and involves a longer-term view of how to implement successful information security programs in organizations. It suggests that computer systems should be ordered with technical features that make sound information security procedures part of their everyday use rather than something that requires an effort on the part of users. For example, the use of hand-held tokens with one-time passwords is accepted better than user-selected passwords. If the technology is in place systemwide, all managers and users simply use it as an accepted part of the system. Efforts to get the attention and action of managers and users need be performed only once, systemwide, rather than repeatedly in each organizational nook and cranny.

Striking While the Iron Is Hot. In this approach, the strategy is for security professionals to simply prepare themselves and wait until disaster occurs, then

237

strike while the iron is hot. It is much easier, for example, to advocate virus protection procedures after a virus has struck an organization than before.

A Mixed Approach. Many situations require a mixed approach. The strategy selected is mixed when several nonbeliever types who advocate different perspectives for decision-making are involved. Briefings and recommendations to such audiences should be tailored accordingly.

SUMMARY

This chapter suggests a framework that may help information security professionals get attention and action from line managers. The framework can be expanded and enhanced by integrating the security professional's personal experience to tailor a suitable approach. Selecting the right approach does not guarantee success, but it should increase the odds.

Because this chapter provides only a framework, the examples presented are illustrative rather than exhaustive. The underlying framework is far more important than the generic strategies presented.

Data, Applications, and Systems Security

To implement an effective information security program, it is essential to understand the various elements that constitute the data, the application programs, and the systems under consideration. Once this understanding is achieved, it is then necessary to determine the vulnerabilities of and risks to these data, application programs, and systems. It is only then that a comprehensive and effective set of controls for security can be devised. Part II of this handbook contains an in-depth discussion of the many administrative and technical issues that relate to the successful achievement of secure data, application programs, and automated information systems.

A fundamental area of concern is the design and development of secure application programs and information systems. Section II-1 deals with the major issues that need to be addressed for this endeavor to be successful. These include the importance of understanding system architectures and their accompanying vulnerabilities; using sound system development methodologies with appropriate controls; devising criteria for the achievement of secure systems; and developing suitable security evaluation procedures.

The more security practitioners understand the intimate operation of an information system, both administratively and technically, the more likely breaches of security will be avoided or, at the least, detected early. System development methodologies that recognize and document security requirements and explicitly tailor system control objectives to satisfy those requirements can also provide sets of both high-level and detailed criteria for evaluating system security.

Section II-2 describes the environmental issues that contribute to the administrative and technical vulnerabilities of a computer system. The use of physical controls (e.g., limiting access to the equipment) and operations controls (e.g., requiring timely backups of sensitive data) are essential ingredients for administrative security. Tailoring technical controls to the type of computer equipment used (e.g., microcomputers, mainframes, or a combination) is equally important, since vulnerabilities may change as equipment changes. The use of virus protection software on microcomputers, access tables for data and programs on mainframes, and data transmission controls for micro-mainframe connections are ways of achieving such technical controls.

Section II-3 discusses the controls needed for securing data and application programs. The use of information categorization techniques to classify data and of generally accepted standards of business practice provide administrative security controls, whereas data base access control mechanisms and data encryption standards for communications software provide technical solutions. All of these provide the practitioner with specific tools for achieving security in a more comprehensive manner.

A technical discussion of information security would be incomplete without detailed coverage of access controls, control policy, and control models. Section II-4 provides such a discussion by describing, at a fundamental level, the functions performed by access control (e.g., identification and authentication) and presenting the major control types (i.e., mandatory and discretionary controls) as well as the control models that implement them.

The security practitioner must be concerned not only with the achievement of secure systems, achieved by implementing control models and using sound system development methodologies, but with quickly detecting control breaches. Intrusion detection mechanisms are designed to identify illicit accesses by examining audit data, either online or after the fact. This approach to access control is still largely in the research stage but holds much promise.

Secure Systems Design and Development

This section treats the major considerations in the design and development of secure systems. The first two chapters take a tutorial approach so as to arm the security practitioner with a fundamental understanding of the way computer systems are organized and used. This understanding will in turn enable the security practitioner to assess how well a particular information system's security features satisfy its security requirements.

The first chapter discusses the general security problems caused by the complexity of today's systems and the sharing of hardware and data. Common vulnerabilities of modern systems such as contamination, unenforced restrictions, and covert channels are discussed, as are such methods of attack as browsing, Trojan horses, and viruses. This chapter also describes primitive architectural abstractions (e.g., domains and types of storage), many of which have specific security-related effects or uses. Chapter II-1-2 continues the tutorial, describing such basic control concepts as object of control and addressability, programs and processes, privilege and restriction, and the notion of trusted systems.

The next three chapters deal with how to develop secure information systems. Chapter II-1-3 describes in detail the primary analysis tools used to successfully develop such systems. The life cycle approach to system development is described, and a detailed suggested life cycle responsibility matrix is provided. The importance and content of documentation in the life cycle is also reviewed, as is the value and contribution of the audit function. These tools are needed not only to develop automated information systems in an orderly fashion but to direct particular attention to the vulnerabilities and risks at every stage of development.

It is particularly useful, from a security standpoint, for an organization to have a system development methodology that partitions the system life cycle into manageable phases and employs appropriate controls in each of the phases. One development methodology employs a set of six life cycle phases: initiation; definition; system design; programming and training; evaluation and acceptance; and installation and operation. Chapter II-1-4 reviews the first five of the six phases in the suggested life cycle matrix and presents, in the form of tables, a detailed list of controls for each phase. Chapter II-1-5 describes how security practitioners participate in the development process. This chapter emphasizes the importance of determining control objectives phase-by-phase for the information system under development. By reviewing security critical performance characteristics at each phase, management can make an informed go/no-go decision at the end of each phase.

During the mid 1980s, the US Department of Defense developed criteria for a hierarchical set of seven classes of trusted systems (i.e., systems that satisfy certain security requirements). This was published in a document called Trusted Computer Systems Evaluation Criteria (TCSEC). Chapter II-1-6 discusses the features of these security classes, ranging from the least secure, C1, with only discretionary security controls, to the most secure, A1, which includes mandatory security controls. It should be noted that these classes deal only with the broad control objective of confidentiality and not integrity or availability.

As a consequence of this effort, the US Department of Defense developed an evaluation methodology for testing computer industry products for compliance with the TCSEC criteria so as to assign a class or give an approval to the product. Chapter II-1-7 describes the current Evaluated Products List. Since the TCSEC criteria were developed and presented to the public, vendors have focused on developing products with specific ratings indicating confidentiality-oriented control levels. However, it is recognized that much future research is needed to provide for systems with satisfactory integrity and availability controls.

Secure Systems Architecture

WILLIAM H. MURRAY

Many security problems and the information system security procedures for solving those problems are rooted in the way that computer systems are organized and used. This chapter addresses several security vulnerabilities and the types of attacks that they expose systems to. It then discusses the basic elements of system architecture and explains how they may affect system security.

Information systems security attempts to account for problems presented by certain aspects inherent in the use of computers. For example, the sharing of hardware across computing processes presents a particular set of problems. The difficulties of information systems security began to be identified during the 1960s, when concurrent sharing of computers began. Computers had been shared among applications and users almost from the beginning. However, most of this sharing was serial rather than concurrent—that is, one job used all of the computer for a period of time, and upon completion, another would begin. This always presented a compromise to the confidentiality of data; if a job left any data in memory, that data could be captured by the subsequent job. Because few jobs used all of the resources of the computer and because of the very high cost of those resources, users immediately began to look for ways to better exploit their use by sharing the computer concurrently across multiple jobs or users.

Even if there were no economic reason to share hardware (and this motive diminishes as the cost and size of hardware decreases), it would still be necessary to share data. Data sharing permits information to be transferred from one individual to another. Although this sharing of data represents an increase in the value and utility of the data, there is a corresponding reduction in its confidentiality.

In addition, the power, generality, flexibility, scope, and complexity of the modern computer make it error prone and increase the difficulty of determining how it was intended to be used. Most of the behavior of a modern computer is controlled by its stored program. Because computer programming is very complex, the program may not always be a true implementation of the programmer's intention—even when the programmer has the best of motives and the highest of skills. For example, if the programmer fails to anticipate and provide for every possible input, the program may cause the computer to behave in an unanticipated way.

Because the behavior of the computer is so complex, it is often difficult to determine whether the computer is performing as intended. Sometimes the output is used so quickly that there is little time for checking it. In other cases, the output is such a complex transformation of the input that it is difficult to reconcile. Therefore, it is not always possible for users to know whether the information or programs they are using are accurate.

Hardware sharing, data sharing, and the complexity of computers are common aspects of computing. They present certain vulnerabilities to the information on the system, however, that the information security program must address. The following section discusses several of the vulnerabilities commonly encountered in computing environments.

TYPES OF VULNERABILITIES

The following sections discuss several types of security vulnerabilities inherent to many modern computing systems.

Contamination and Interference

Most computers are unable to distinguish between programs and other data. In many, a program is unable to recognize itself. Therefore, it is possible for a programmed procedure to overwrite itself, its data, other programs, or their data. This happens frequently by error; it may also be done deliberately.

It is possible for one process operating in the compute to interfere with the intended operation of another. Again, most of this happens by error but may be done deliberately. Most of it is obvious (i.e., job failure); a small amount may be subtle and difficult to detect.

Changes Between Time of Check and Time of Use

Conditions that are checked and relied on but not otherwise bound can be maliciously changed between the time of check and the time of use. This vulnerability can be reduced by increasing the number of checks, making them closer to the time of use, or by binding the condition so that it cannot be altered. (Binding is accomplished by resolving and fixing a meaning, property, or function so that subsequent changes are not supported and will be resisted.)

Unenforced Restrictions

Early systems, in which storage was costly, often relied on users and their programs to not attempt certain actions. Although modern systems can detect and prevent such actions, these early systems could not afford the storage and programs to do so. Most of these actions would produce unpredictable results and were not directly exploitable; however, a few produced exploitable results.

Similar problems appear in modern systems. For example, a UNIX user directory program, fingerd, may fail to enforce the restriction on the length of its input. The storage beyond the input area is occupied by a privileged program. An attacker can easily exceed the expected length of the input with a rogue program, which can then be executed under the identity and privilege of the overwritten program.

Covert Channels

The term "covert channels" is most often used to describe unintended information flow between compartments in compartmented systems. For example, although compartment A has no authorized path to do so, it may send information to compartment B by changing a variable or condition that B can see. This usually involves cooperation between the owners of the compartments in a manner that is not intended or anticipated by the managers of the system. Alternatively, compartment B may simply gather intelligence about compartment A by observing some condition that is influenced by A's behavior.

The severity of the vulnerability presented by covert channels is usually measured in terms of the bandwidth of the channel (i.e., the number of units of information that might flow per unit of time). Most covert channels are much slower than other intentional modes of signaling. Nonetheless, because of the speed of computers, covert channels may still represent a source of compromise.

The possibility of covert channels is of most concern when system management relies on the system to prevent data compromises involving the cooperation of two individuals or processes. Under many commercial processes, however, management is prepared to accept the risk of collusion. The system is expected to protect against an individual acting alone; other mechanisms protect against collusion.

The Department of Defense mandatory policy assumes that a single user might operate multiple processes at different levels. Therefore, the enforcement of label integrity might be compromised by covert channels. Under the mandatory policy, the system itself protects against such compromise.

TYPES OF ATTACKS

Attacks are deliberate and resourceful attempts to interfere with the intended use of a system. The following sections discuss types of potential attacks.

Browsing

Browsing, the simplest and most straightforward type of attack, is the perusal of large quantities of available data in an attempt to identify compromising information. Browsing may involve searching primary storage for the system password table. The intruder may browse documentation for restrictions and then test to identify any that are not enforced. Access control is the preferred mechanism for defending against browsing attacks.

Spoofing

Spoofing is an attack in which one person or process pretends to be a person or process that has more privileges. For example, user A can mimic behavior to make process B believe user A is user C. In the absence of any other controls, B may be duped into giving to user A the data and privileges that were intended for user C.

One way to spoof is to send a false notice to system users informing them that the system's telephone number has been changed. When the users call the new number, they see a screen generated by the hacker's machine that looks like the one that they expected from the target system. Believing that they are communicating with the target system, they enter their IDs and passwords. The hacker promptly plays these back to the target system, which accepts the hacker as a legitimate user. Two spoofs occur here. First, the hacker spoofs the user into believing that the accessed system is the target system. Second, the hacker spoofs the target system into believing that he is the legitimate user.

Eavesdropping

Eavesdropping is simply listening in on the conversations between people or systems to obtain certain information. This may be an attack in itself—that is, the information obtained from the conversation might itself be valuable. On the other hand, it may be a means to another attack (e.g., eavesdropping for a system password). Defenses against eavesdropping usually include moving the defense perimeter outward, reducing the amplitude of the communications signal, masking it with noise, or concealing it by the use of secret codes or encryption. Encryption is the most commonly used method of defense.

Exhaustive Attacks

Identifying secret data by testing all possibilities is referred to as an exhaustive attack. For example, one can identify a valid password by testing all possible passwords until a match is found. Exhaustive attacks almost always reveal the desired data. Like most other attacks, however, an exhaustive attack is efficient only when the value of the data obtained is greater than the cost of the attack.

Defenses against exhaustive attacks involve increasing the cost of the attack by increasing the number of possibilities to be exhausted. For example, increasing the length of a password will increase the cost of an exhaustive attack. Increasing the effective length of a cryptographic key variable will make it more resistant to an exhaustive attack.

Trojan Horses

A Trojan horse attack is one in which a hostile or unexpected entity is concealed inside a benign or expected one for the purpose of getting it through some protective barrier or perimeter. Trojan horse attacks usually involve concealing unauthorized data or programs inside authorized ones for the purpose of getting them inside the computer. One defense against such attacks is inspection (i.e., looking inside the Trojan horse). The effectiveness of this defense is improved if the data objects are kept small, simple, and obvious as to their intent.

Viruses

A virus is a Trojan horse program that, whenever executed, attempts to insert a copy of itself in another program, usually in order to perpetuate itself and spread its influence. Viruses exploit large populations of similar systems, sharing user privileges to execute arbitrary programs and to create or write to programs. To get themselves executed, viruses exploit the identity of the infected programs or automatic execution mechanisms, or the ability to trick part of a large user population. Defenses against viruses include differentiating systems along the lines exploited by the viruses and placing limits on sharing, writing, and executing programs.

Worms

A worm is a program that attempts to copy itself in nearby execution environments. Worms are distinguished from viruses by the fact that they travel under their own identity. Worms exploit connectivity with nearby execution environments. One worm spread within a large population of systems by looking for user IDs with null passwords or passwords equal to the ID. In this population, one system in five yielded to the attack. Defenses against worms involve limiting connectivity by means of well-managed access controls.

Dictionary Attacks

Dictionaries may be attacked to determine passwords. A short dictionary attack involves trying a list of hundreds or thousands of words that are frequently chosen as passwords against several systems. Although most systems resist such attacks, some do not. In one case, one system in five yielded to a particular dictionary attack.

Long dictionary attacks are used by insiders to expand their privileges. In this approach, a natural-language dictionary in the native language of the system users is encrypted under the encryption scheme used by the target system. The encrypted values of words in the dictionary are then compared to the encrypted passwords in the password file; a match occurs whenever a password has been chosen from the dictionary.

Three conditions are necessary to the success of a long dictionary attack. First, the attacker must be able to log on to the target system; this condition may be met by the use of a short dictionary attack. Second, the attacker must have read access to the password file; in many systems, particularly UNIX systems, this is the default access. Third, the attacker must know the mechanism and the key variable under which the passwords are encrypted; this condition is often met simply by using the defaults with which the system was shipped. Although these conditions may never be met in a well-managed system, dictionary attacks often work against several systems in a sufficiently large population of target systems.

THE BASIC ARCHITECTURAL ELEMENTS

The following sections discuss the basic components of computer architecture; these are the general ideas and abstractions used to describe computers. Most of these concepts apply to more than one type of computer; many have specific security-related effects or uses.

Domains

In general, a domain may be defined as a sphere of influence. With computers, it is useful to be able to talk about the extent of influence of various mechanisms and components.

Historically, the term "domain" was synonymous with "computer." In early single-thread computers, every application owned the whole machine, and that was its domain. In modern systems, multiple applications run asynchronously under the control of operating systems and monitors. Each of these processes may have a different domain. In early operating systems, the domain of the operating system was usually congruent with that of the hardware processor in which it ran; in modern systems, this may not be true. Some operating systems control multiple processors, and some processors run multiple operating systems.

In addition, the domain of early access control facilities was congruent with that of the operating system under which it ran; this is no longer true. Although few operating systems run more than one access control facility, it is not unusual for a single access control facility to serve multiple operating systems and even processors.

Although this flexibility is valuable, it may influence security. It may provide uniformity of control, yet in doing so, it may compromise the integrity of the implementation. The wider the domain, the more difficult it is to maintain its integrity.

States

Many computer systems offer separate domains called states. States are usually distinguished by the set of operations that are permitted to occur within them. For example, many systems are divided into two states called privileged and unprivileged, system and application, supervisor and problem program, or supervisor and user. System state is distinguished from application state by the fact that all operations are legal in system state, whereas only a subset of the operations is legal in application state. The instructions excluded from application state usually include input, output, and storage management instructions.

The Multics System (Honeywell Bull, Inc.) offered rings of domains. Rings are distinguished from states by the fact that there are more of them, they are not necessarily hierarchical, and each can be entered only from adjacent ones, and then only by means of a narrow portal called a gate.

It has been asserted that two states are inadequate for some purposes. For example, most modern hardware implements three or more states. Nonetheless, some large shared systems do not implement any hardware states.

Finite-State Machines

A finite-state machine is one in which all valid states can be enumerated and in which any operation takes the machine only from one valid state to another, equally valid state. For example, in finite-state architectures there may be no possibility of a data exception. One can contrast this concept to more traditional architectures in which it is possible for a defined operation to move the machine to an invalid state. By eliminating the possibility of invalid states, finite-state architecture eliminates much of the error handling that might otherwise have to be performed by programming or operator intervention.

Finite-state architecture limits and excludes much of the complexity that implementers, programmers, operators, and users might otherwise have to overcome. In addition, it limits the opportunity for mischief that such error-handling capability introduces.

Security Domains

A security domain is a single domain of trust that shares a single security policy and a single management. Historically, security domains have been used to define a single system. Modern networks often implement security domains that include many systems.

Storage

Storage refers to those computer components in which information can be recorded for later retrieval and use. It is typically classified by type. Storage is usually shared over time but allocated to only one use, user, or task at a time. The following sections discuss different types of storage.

Registers. A register is a primitive device for holding and operating on data. Some machines can operate only on data in registers, and many machines operate primarily on registers. Registers may be classified as special or general purpose.

Special-purpose registers are those whose function and identity are bound together. One such register is the current instruction register, which contains the instruction being decoded and executed. Another is the next instruction address register, which contains the address of the next instruction to be fetched, decoded, and executed. There is usually only one such register, and it is used only for this purpose. Because manipulating the contents of special-purpose registers alters the behavior of the machine and the results of program execution, their use is typically constrained so that they can be used only as intended.

General-purpose registers can be used for several functions. The identity of the register is independent of its function. The current purpose or function is determined by the context or operation; the identify or name of the register is arbitrary. For example, the IBM 360 (IBM Corp.) has 15 general-purpose registers. Depending on the context, these registers may be used for exchanging data between programs, holding address offsets, or inputting and outputting integer arithmetic.

State Vector. The state vector, or program status word, is a special register (i.e., reserved word and address) in which the system keeps critical information about what it is doing and what it will do next. Multiprogramming machines may have two or more such mechanisms. For example, the IBM 360 has a current program status word, which specifies what it is doing and what it will do next, and a previous program status word, which shows how it got to where it is. By swapping these words, it can return to what it was doing before the current interruption. The address of this program status is the range of normal addresses and can be specified by an application program.

A program might refer to the program status word to learn about its own identity or environment. It might refer to the previous program status word to determine by whom it was called and what it is expected to do. However, only privileged processes can alter the contents of the program status word.

Random Access Memory. Random access memory (RAM) refers to a primitive class of memory in which any portion of the memory can be read from or written to with the same facility and in the same time as any other. That is, each access is independent of the previous one. It is contrasted to sequential memory, in which each access is relative to the previous one. In this sense, a magnetic disk provides secondary RAM storage, whereas magnetic tape provides secondary sequential access storage.

In addition, RAM is contrasted to read-only memory (ROM), from which data can be read but not written. RAM is the kind of memory employed for primary storage (discussed in a later section). Procedures stored in RAM are vulnerable to accidental and intentional change.

Read-Only Memory. ROM looks to a system like RAM; however, its contents cannot be altered by the programmed functions of the system. ROM is typically used to hold stable procedures that are not intended to be altered. Procedures stored in this way are safe from interference and contamination and, to that extent, are reliable.

CD-ROM. Compact disk read-only memory (CD-ROM) records information optically on a small plastic disk. The disk is usually reproduced as an entity from a master. Information may be represented by the reflectivity of a spot. For use, the disk is placed into a drive and spun, and the data is sensed by bouncing a laser off of the disk into a photo-sensitive device. CD-ROM is well suited for publishing and distribution of programs and data bases. Because the data cannot be altered after being applied to the disk, it can be relied on as being the same as when shipped by the publisher.

Write-Once/Read-Many Storage. Write-once/read-many (WORM) storage can be written to only once but read forever. It is usually partly mechanical (similar to CD-ROM) and is often optical or photographic. Once written, the data is not subject to alteration and therefore is very reliable. This class of storage is useful for logs and journals.

Primary Storage. The procedures that the computer is to perform, the instructions it is to execute, and the data on which it will operate are stored in primary storage. Information in primary storage can be directly referenced or addressed. Arithmetic and logical operations can usually be performed directly on information in primary storage. (The exception to this rule is the few systems that can do such operations only on information in registers.)

Primary storage is typically all-electronic and very fast. On the other hand, it is also usually small, expensive, and volatile. As a rule, the more primary storage that is available to a system, the more concurrent operations it can perform.

Primary storage is usually organized into arbitrary groups of bits called bytes, characters, words, double words, blocks, and pages. These groups are defined in terms of the number of bits of data they can store. Each group is given a number (i.e., an address) by which it and its contents can be referenced.

Modern primary storage mechanisms usually include features to detect errors and control use. These features are often organized around the groups of bits into which the storage is organized. For example, there may be storage elements dedicated to holding redundant data, often called check-bits, one for each word, frame, or byte. These bits are set so as to make the bit count of the storage element conform to an arbitrary rule (e.g., odd or even parity). Whenever the element is used, the system automatically compares the count to the expected rule; variances indicate a failure. These mechanisms protect against data modification by providing for automatic error detection and, in some systems, automatic error correction.

Another such mechanism is called storage protection, which associate an arbitrary value with a block or page of storage. This value is called the storage protection key. The key currently associated with the block or page must agree with the value in the current program status word; otherwise, the program cannot use the storage. Changing either the key associated with the page or the key in the program status word requires privileges reserved from the active program. Storage protection is used to enforce process-to-process isolation.

Secondary Storage. Primary storage is supported by secondary storage, which includes magnetic disks and tapes. Secondary storage is relatively large and cheap; it may have mechanical as well as electronic components, but it is nonvolatile. Instructions or procedures cannot be executed directly from secondary storage. Execution of instructions or data operations kept in secondary storage usually requires that the instructions or operations first be moved to primary storage.

At a primitive level, information in secondary storage is referred to in terms of where it is stored. For example, one can specify a device (e.g., a drive), a device mechanism (e.g., a head), or a device abstraction (e.g., a cylinder, track, or sector). At a higher level, data in secondary storage is referred to in terms of such data abstractions as files and records or such language abstractions as get and put.

The lower the level (or closer to the hardware) at which the user or program accesses the data, the more difficult it is to control what the data does or to understand its intent. Therefore, for security, audit, and control of data, some systems allow users to access data only at the abstract or symbolic level, not at the hardware level. In other words, the user cannot access instructions that refer to the hardware, only those instructions that refer to the data by symbolic name.

Although nonvolatile and robust, secondary storage is not necessarily free of error. Errors are usually checked for and corrected by a combination of features of the secondary storage device, system-level code, and operator-initiated backup; they are rarely apparent at the application level. For example, modern tape drives have two heads. What is written by one is read by the other, and what is read is then compared to what was written. Variances are automatically corrected.

Virtual Storage. Virtual storage is an abstraction that a program process perceives as a very large and exclusive primary storage. It uses a combination of hardware address translation features, primary storage, and secondary storage to create this appearance. When a program process stores data in an address, a page of real storage is allocated to the page in which the address is located. When a request is made to read that data, the address is translated to point to the page previously allocated to it.

When the mechanism has no more real storage to allocate, it frees some by writing the contents to secondary storage, called paging storage, that has been reserved for that purpose. When referenced again, the page will be read back into primary storage from paging storage. It will be placed into any available page of real storage and the address of that page mapped to the virtual address of the data. This process is automatic and dynamic; it is neither necessary nor likely that the data will be returned to the same location in primary storage from which it was paged.

Virtual storage is a powerful mechanism for implementing process-to-process isolation within a computer. Because a request for data is always interpreted in the context of the local virtual store, there is no way for a program process to address data that it did not write or that belongs to another process. Exchange of data between processes using two virtual memories requires their mutual cooperation and in some cases may require the acquiescence of system management.

Buffers. Buffers are small stores used to speed the apparent movement of data from secondary to primary storage. The use of buffers is often automatic—that is, neither the user nor processes operating on the user's behalf are aware of the buffers. Because buffers are automatic and transparent, they represent neither an exposure nor a control.

Cache Storage. Cache storage is a special type of buffer that is placed between primary storage and the arithmetic and logical elements of a system. Like other buffers, cache storage is not a security exposure.

System-Managed Storage. Many otherwise modern systems implementing archaic architectures include a class of storage called system-managed storage. For example, IBM's 9000 Series, which for reasons of compatibility employs S/360 principles of operation, employs this class of storage to provide users the convenience of more modern architectures while maintaining all of the flexibility that is expected from older applications. Thus, an application that includes hardware-dependent programming can function as it always has. However, a newer application that employs only symbolic references and avoids hardware dependences can enjoy the advantages of single-level storage that are enjoyed by users of such modern architectures as IBM's AS/400 or Digital Equipment Corp.'s VAX/VMS.

Although the components of system-managed storage are similar to those employed for primary and secondary storage, its use and management are fully automatic. It is not managed by or visible to users or to procedures implemented in software. The automatic facilities may include paging, allocation, and backup. System-managed storage is accessed by means of symbolic addressing. As a consequence, data in such storage is usually immune from outside interference or contamination.

Expanded Storage. IBM uses a class of storage that it calls expanded storage, which has some interesting characteristics. This storage is implemented using the same kind of hardware as that used for primary storage. Unlike primary storage and like other system-managed storage, however, expanded storage is not visible to the operating system or application programs; it is visible only to the hardware.

Although it has almost as big an impact on performance as primary storage, it

253

is cheaper, partly because it can be addressed only at the page level and not at the word or byte level. This is possible because expanded storage does not need some of the control features required by primary storage. For example, because it cannot be addressed by processes implemented in software, it need not have any storage protection features.

Storage Objects

A storage object is an abstraction for containing data. In primary storage, the abstract object is usually a word or a similar, arbitrary group of bits. In the traditional Von Neumann architecture machine, the paradigm that is used to help the user understand storage objects is the bank of pigeon holes, which are stacked, orderly, symmetric, and the same size, inside and out. These pigeon holes are reusable; they are allocated to one process at a time, but they are used many times.

In more modern systems, it is not necessary for all storage objects to be the same size. The paradigm used for these machines is that of named boxes with locks. To use the contents, users must know the name of the box and have the key to the lock. Although all these boxes are the same size on the outside, the inside of each is an arbitrary size, as determined by the data object placed in it. Thus, a short vector and a large data base are each given their own numbered box.

Although these boxes are strong, they are so cheap that they are used only once. Users may remove the contents from the box, yet they can put the contents back only if the identity of the contents remains the same. If the identity is changed, the user must throw away the old box and use a new one. (The identity of data may be independent of its contents; however, the identity of a program changes when the program is changed as little as 1 bit. Therefore, the identity of the program and the name of the box are so bound that changing the program requires a new box.)

Data Objects

Data is information recorded and stored in symbolic form. In computer science, the term refers to information recorded in such a manner that it can be read by a machine. However, today's machines can read almost anything. Historically, data was used to refer to digitally encoded information as opposed to analog information (e.g., images or sounds). In modern systems, however, almost everything is digitally encoded.

In general, a data object is a named and bound collection of data that is dealt with as a unit, similar to a book. In computers, the most common data object is a file. Other data objects include bit, bytes, words, double words, messages, records, files, volumes, programs, data bases, tables, and views. The following sections discuss different types of data objects.

Typed Data Objects. A typed data object is a special data object on which only a limited and previously specified set of operations is valid. The procedures for these operations are implied by the name of the type. For example, program data is executable but may not be modifiable. Such systems as Digital Equipment's VAX/VMS and IBM's AS/400 manage all data in typed data objects.

Typed data is usually managed by a process known as type management. As a rule, typed data can be accessed only by means of the type manager, which is responsible for enforcing the rules of the type. Access to the data that bypasses the type manager presents problems.

Strongly Typed Data Objects. Strongly typed data objects assist in achieving the orderly and intended treatment of data while resisting any other use. The strongly typed data object is a special case in which both the type and the type manager are known to the environment. The environment provides protection to ensure that the type manager and its rules cannot be bypassed. The IBM AS/400 implements strongly typed objects. Currently, approximately three dozen object types have been defined.

Encapsulated Data Objects. The term "data object" is occasionally used in a more restricted sense. An encapsulated data object is a package containing data, its description, and a description of its manipulation. Because of the encapsulation, or data hiding, it is not possible to perform an arbitrary operation on these objects. For example, it is not possible to create an arbitrary copy of an encapsulated data object. The object must create the copy of itself and will do so only if that is consistent with its own rules. Because the capsule is a proper part of the object, a copy of the object is a separate object.

A local area network file server is both an instance and a paradigm for a data object: it is a capsule containing data, a description of the data, and the procedures for manipulating that data. Although, as with file servers, the capsule may be physical, the most general mechanism for achieving encapsulation is encryption.

Secure Data Objects. A secure data object is a special type of encapsulated data object. The rules about who is permitted what access to the data are included within the capsule. These rules are enforced in whatever environment is trusted to open the capsule. The capsule can be implemented in hardware or software (i.e., in secret codes). At the expense of performance or price, it can be made sufficiently strong for any application and environment.

The secure data object is the most general abstraction for enforcing information system security. It is independent of the media, the data, and the environment. The rules for using and changing the data move with the secure data object. It can be implemented so as to be independent of system or platform type. It may be used to implement seamless system-to-system access control in which the object is created in one system and its access rules move with it to other systems. Any system that can open the capsule may be relied on to enforce the access rules.

SUMMARY

This chapter surveys the field of computer science from a security, audit, and control perspective. It should be apparent from this discussion that most components and design decisions about a computer system will have some impact on the security, auditability, and control of the system and its applications.

Many of the requirements for security, audit, and control stem from the economics of computers and those steps that are taken to compensate for those economics. For example, in many computer environments, hardware or data is shared among a network of users. Hardware and data sharing expose the system to certain vulnerabilities, however, and mechanisms must therefore be in place to control the sharing. This chapter examines a generic set of vulnerabilities that are inherent in many computer systems.

In addition, this chapter reviews the control mechanisms, their origins, and their use. The emphasis is on primitive mechanisms and abstractions (e.g., storage). Because these primitive mechanisms have such broad influence, understanding them is essential to understanding how computers work and how they are secured. The discussion of these mechanisms is intended to provide a generalized and abstract view, a view that is broader than and independent of the existing implementations of those mechanisms. It is essential that security professionals be able to recognize, compare, and apply these mechanisms wherever they are found and without regard to specific implementations.

Objects and Processes of Control in Secure Systems

WILLIAM H. MURRAY

Data objects, programs, and processes are the building blocks of all computing systems. In a trusted computing system, privileges and restrictions are placed on access to these elements to provide a higher level of security than is found in most systems. This chapter describes the basic elements of computing systems and the concepts of privileges and restrictions. It then discusses the characteristics of trusted computing systems.

OBJECTS OF CONTROL

The objects of control are the class of data objects regulated by the access control facility. As a general rule, it should be possible to regulate the use of any resource that is dynamically allocated. However, few systems provide such control by default. For example, UNIX access control regulates the sharing of directories. On the other hand, although MVS permits the elaboration of file names with directory names and permits all objects with similar directory names to be controlled alike, the real object of control is the file. (This is discussed further in the section of this chapter on subsystems and type managers.)

Objects are referenced through the use of names and addresses. The following sections discuss specific cases of names and elements of address ability.

Names

Names are widely used in computers for referring to such abstractions as users and data objects. Special cases of names that are of interest from a security, audit, and control perspective include user names, variable names, constants, and addresses. These are discussed in the following sections.

User Names. Multiuser systems usually provide for users to be named. This name is typically called the user ID. It is assigned at the time that the user is enrolled as a user of the system. Each user must have a name; names should not be shared, and no user should have more than one name.

SECURE SYSTEMS DESIGN AND DEVELOPMENT

Variable Names. A variable is a quantity that may assume several values or a symbol for itself. In computer science, the term "variable" is often used to refer to a location in computer storage that contains the current quantity from the set.

A shared variable is one that is visible, usually by arrangement, between two or more processes. In some systems, such an arrangement may require the concurrence of management, so as not to provide a covert channel. The shared variable appears to each process as a data object within the process's space. The variable may be synchronously or asynchronously updated by either process (or by both). Synchronous updates usually involve a second shared variable, called a flag, for signaling that an update has taken place.

A shared variable may provide a highly controlled and very granular mechanism for sharing data. Unless it is known to management, however, it may also provide a covert channel for leaking data between compartments.

Constants. A constant is a single fixed quantity or value. It may have a symbolic name that refers to the location in storage that holds the value.

A special case of a constant is the address constant. Although not required in all languages or systems, the address constant is one that can be used in address arithmetic. This type of constant is necessary so that the process, compiler, or interpreter that translates or uses the constant can understand its intent.

Addresses. An address is the symbolic name of or reference to a storage location. It is used to refer to the number or value stored in that location.

A storage location can be referenced by both a physical address and a logical address. A physical address is the actual location within a storage device that the device itself is capable of recognizing and responding to. A logical address is a symbolic name that refers to a location in a program or data file; however, the device itself does not recognize a logical address. Logical addresses are often used at programming time and are translated into physical addresses at compile, interpret, or execute time.

Addressability

Addressability is the ability to reference a particular location by its name. Because it is a condition that must be met in order to retrieve information from storage and to identify that information, withholding addressability can be used as a data access control mechanism.

In most systems, a process can refer to any address in the address space. If it is not authorized to the contents, an exception or interrupt will occur. In some systems, however, a process cannot even refer to a storage location to which it is not authorized.

The following sections discuss different elements of addressability.

258

Address Space. An address space is a range of possible addresses. For example, a computer with an address of 24 bits can address 2^{24} bytes. Its address space is 16 million bytes; this is the maximum number of locations to which an instruction could directly refer.

Virtual Address Space. A virtual address space is an abstraction; it is a set of addresses that may not have any real storage or data directly associated with it. This range of addresses can be used in a program, because the program process sees an apparent address space. However, the address is interpreted, at execution time, according to rules implemented in the virtual memory facility.

Modern systems present very large virtual address spaces, some as large as 2^{24} bytes. In such a system, program processes need not know about the movement of data between primary and secondary storage. Indeed, for all practical purposes, such a space is infinitely large. Addresses are so cheap that they need never be reused. For example, a program can be given an address to go with its identity; if the identity changes, it is given a new address and the old one is never used again.

The security significance of a virtual address space is that it can be dedicated to a single process or use. Because each process can have its own virtual address space, separate from those of any other process, no process can reference data in another's space. Likewise, each address referenced by a process is interpreted in the context of its own space; it has no way to refer to an address in another process's space.

Single-Level Store. Single-level store is an architectural abstraction in which the existence of secondary storage is concealed from the user and any program processes running on the user's behalf. The user program process sees an infinitely large virtual storage space. All transfers of data between primary and secondary storage are automatic and not under user control. Thus, the identity of the data is under system, and not user, control.

Symbolic-Only Addressing. With this mechanism, all physical addressing is concealed from the user and any program processes subject to the user's influence. The user may refer to the data only by its name. Implementations of this mechanism make it more difficult for a user to exploit any special knowledge of the hardware to bypass controls or obscure any intent the user may have to exploit the system.

Symbolic-only addressing is often combined with single-level store so that all physical- or hardware-level addresses are concealed from the user. The user program process sees only data objects; all references to hardware-level mechanisms are concealed. Essentially, the user program process sees an orderly, simple, and secure environment in which things are referred to by the name that is most meaningful to the user. The user's ability to bypass control or conceal his intent is severely limited.

PROGRAMS AND PROCESSES

A program is a list of instructions for controlling the behavior of the computer. Instructions include the name of an operation and the names of one or more objects on which the operation is to be performed. These operands refer to storage locations or objects, devices, variables, or constants.

To direct the behavior of a computer, a program must be recorded in machine-readable form and stored in primary storage. Programs are assigned names, which are often associated with the function or behavior of the program.

Programs can be reproduced or modified. Two programs that produce the same results are equivalent; they are identical only if one is an exact copy of the other.

In general, a process is a computer executing a program, though often this term is used to include anything else that manifests similar behavior—for example, a user at a terminal or a service machine. A process may be identified by the system in which it runs, the user on whose behalf it runs, the program, or one of several copies of the program.

Because of the scale of modern computers, it is conventional to refer to subdivisions of the computer or program. For security and control purposes, the only subdivisions of the computer that can be used are those that are considered reliable. These come in two classes:

- Those implemented in hardware (e.g., states or rings).
- Those isolated domains provided by a trusted operating system or subsystem.

Isolated domains include such abstractions as virtual machines, memory space, regions, jobs, or tasks. When domains are effectively implemented, communication takes place between domains only through mutual cooperation (i.e., processes cannot unilaterally interfere with the operation of a process outside its defined domain).

A process usually takes part of its identity and name from its parent process (i.e., the process that spawns it). Part of the name and identity may be assigned arbitrarily simply to distinguish them from similar instances of the process.

In most cases, the termination of a program results in return of control to the parent process. For example, the termination of an application program running under MS-DOS will result in return of control to MS-DOS. This may create a compromise of security if the privileges of the parent process are greater than those of the child. A more secure alternative is for termination of a process to result in the system's being reinitialized from scratch, or in returning user control to the log-on program.

The Operating System

The root process within most systems is the operating system, which operates on behalf of system management. Its domain and privileges generally coincide with those of the hardware and the system manager. The operating system is usually loaded as part of the system initialization program. The operating system controls all other processes within the system.

Operating systems may be classified according to the kinds of subprocesses that they provide. Some operating systems are intended to supervise only one user and program at a time. Thus, they are characterized as single-user, single-tasking systems (e.g., MicroSoft Corp.'s DOS and IBM's VM-CMS). Others supervise multiple tasks but only for one user; these are classified as single-user multitasking systems (e.g., IBM's OS/2 and Digital Research, Inc.'s DR DOS).

UNIX, on the other hand, supervises multiple tasks for multiple users. Other classes include multiprogramming and multiprocessor systems (i.e., one operating system supervising multiple hardware processors) and combinations and variations of such systems.

Part of the reason management can rely on the operating system is that management chooses it. Therefore, the managers can ensure that it is the program they intended; this is called content control. Management may rely on the system to the extent that it is protected from outside interference or contamination. This protection may be provided in part by the hardware. When the threat is likely to exceed the strength of the hardware protection, however, the managers may rely on the additional protection provided by the physical environment or management supervision.

Managers can rely on the operating system to the extent that it conforms to a complete specification. In addition, they can rely on it to the extent of any warranty that is provided by the vendor. Although most operating systems are sold as is, some come with vendor warranties that the system will behave in a reliable manner. (However, such warranties are usually limited to repair.) Finally, managers can rely on the system to the extent that it is tested, either by themselves or an agent. However, many operating systems are of such scope and complexity as to make testing difficult or inconclusive. In such cases, use of the system will reveal most flaws.

User Processes

By definition, multiuser systems provide named processes for more than one user. Processes are provided that are dedicated to and exclusive to a user, and they usually share a name or ID with that user. These abstract processes act only on behalf of the user and inherit both the privileges and limitations of the user.

The parent process of the user process, usually the operating system, is typically responsible for providing user-to-user isolation or for preventing one user's process from interfering with or contaminating that of another. In addition, it is responsible for providing and mediating access to controlled resources.

Virtual Machines

A virtual machine is an abstract machine provided by a special operating system. The virtual machine appears no different to the user program than does the hardware itself. One characteristic of this appearance is independence: one virtual machine is as independent of another as two computers might be of each other.

Application Programs

Applications are uses of the computer; application programs, on the other hand, are those applications that run exclusively or primarily for a particular end use. Application programs are distinguished from system programs, which exist to manage the hardware and which are usually independent of any particular application.

Compilers

A compiler is a program process that takes a source program written in a high-level language and produces as its output a program, called an object program, in a code suitable for interpretation and execution by the machine. The compiler treats the program as an entity. It usually resolves all local symbols; all global symbols are placed in a table for subsequent resolution either by a linkage editor program or a loader program.

A compiler usually checks the input program for consistency and completeness. For example, it may check to ensure that all symbols are defined. However, they usually do not attempt to control intent, are not trusted, and do not run privileged.

There are important exceptions to this rule. There are some systems, usually those without hardware isolation features, in which the compiler is a primary control mechanism. Because the intent of the program is often more obvious in source code than in object code, the compiler has an advantage over the hardware in controlling the behavior of the program.

Subsystems and Type Managers

Many systems employ operating system extensions. Although not formally or originally part of the operating system, these extensions may run privileged and perform similar functions for the user. These extensions are optional and separately priced. They may implement abstractions that are not provided by the hardware or operating system, in which case they are usually considered the type managers for those abstractions. (A type manager is a process that presents typed data objects and enforces the rules of their behavior and access.) The subsystem defines and provides the application program interface for using those abstractions.

Perhaps the most obvious example of such a subsystem is the data base management system. Although operating systems usually know only about the identity of file objects, data base management systems may know about the identity of more granular objects (e.g., records, fields, tables, and views). Thus, these processes are able to provide more granular access control.

The Orange Book uses the term "data base manager" to refer to all subsystems. For the purposes of this discussion, however, there are several kinds of subsystems, as described in the following sections.

Monitors. A monitor is able to load and initiate programs, in which case it may be an alternative to the similar capability in the operating system. For example, if the operating system is optimized for batch processing, there may be an alternative monitor for transaction processing. Or if the operating system is optimized for online processing, the system may provide an alternative monitor for batch processing.

As with other subsystems, monitors often provide an alternative granularity of control to that provided by the operating system. For example, CICS provides an abstraction called the transaction type. Authorizing a user to employ a transaction type enables the user to execute a certain set of programs against a certain set of data. The definitions and extent of the programs and data are encapsulated in the identity of the transaction type and may not be defined in the context of the operating system alone.

A reference monitor is a process that mediates all data resource flow between subdomains within a system or security domain. For example, a reference monitor might mediate all sharing of data resources between users. It ensures that the data flow conforms to policy as expressed in access rules. These rules are usually expressed in triples, which are tables that relate the accessing subject, the data object, and the type of access.

Interpreters. An interpreter is a process that interprets a program in a high-level language for immediate execution. It may run as an application program or as a monitor. It usually treats each line or operator in the program as an entity rather than treating the program as a whole. Interpreters check syntax, ensure that symbols are defined, resolve the definition, and may confine or control the results. Some interpreters run as application programs and are not privileged. However, they are sometimes relied on to restrict the behavior of the interpreted program to prevent disorderly execution or to ensure that it adheres to management's intent.

Some interpreters access hardware primitives on behalf of the user and may run privileged. When they do so, they also act as a boundary layer to keep the user or program away from the hardware and to restrict behavior to prevent disorderly execution.

Some interpreters define the language that is used to communicate with them. Although some interpreted languages may be common across system types, the interpreter is usually specific to the system type. Thus, although a program written in BASIC may be interpreted on any system type, the BASIC interpreter usually runs only on the specific system for which it is intended.

Jobs and Tasks. A job is a process that is associated with a unit of work. It is usually large and can often be divided into smaller units. The abstraction of a job is most often used in those systems that operate in batch style, which record data in a separate step; the processing steps of the job do not begin until recording of all the input data is complete. Jobs may be spawned and owned by the operating system or by a special job or batch monitor.

A task is a process that corresponds to a small and indivisible unit of work. It may be spawned or owned by the operating system, a job, or a user.

PRIVILEGES AND RESTRICTIONS

Access control rules can be expressed in terms of privileges or restrictions. A privilege is a special right or power—for example, it may be the authority to use a particular data object. In computer systems, this term is often used to describe special control functions. The operating system is said to be a privileged process, and the system manager is often a privileged user.

Implicit in the concept of privileges is their opposite: restrictions. A restriction is a limit usually placed on a small number of people. Although any rule of access can likely be expressed as either a privilege or a restriction, it is often significantly shorter and easier to understand when both forms of expression are used than when only one or the other is permitted.

For example, in some systems it is possible to grant a privilege (e.g., the right to read a data set) to all the members of a named user group rather than to each named member of the group and to then explicitly restrict any named user from access to that data set. Using the two constructs in combination may minimize the amount of work required to grant access to a large number of named users.

Privileged State

A privileged state is one in which privileges can be exercised and in which restrictions may not apply. Privileged states may be expressed as system states or as problem program states.

The system, or supervisor, state is reserved for trusted and privileged programs. It usually includes the ability to perform all operations, specifically input and output operations.

The problem, or application, program state is used by unprivileged processes and programs that are not trusted. Many operations, specifically I/O instructions and those required for process-to-process sharing or cooperation, are not permitted in this state.

Rings

Rings are implementations of privileged states with the additional characteristics that a ring can only be entered from an adjacent one and only by means of a single narrow gateway or call.

Binding

To bind is to resolve and fix a meaning, property, or function such that subsequent changes are not supported and will be resisted. In many cases, binding is done so that users can rely on the meaning, property, or function.

For example, the meaning or function of a hardware instruction is fixed at the time the components are manufactured. Up until that time, the designer has the freedom to alter the function. After that time, however, the user (and anyone else for that matter) cannot change it. The meaning of a device address, on the other hand, is usually fixed at the time the components are configured into a system. Indeed, configuration time is defined in part by the fact that device addresses are set at that time. Any changes to device addresses can occur only at configuration time.

It is useful to speak of the time at which elements of the information system are bound and to bind elements at different times (e.g., early and late binding). In addition to the preceding examples, elements may be bound at initial program load, compile, link-edit, fetch, load, and execution times.

For example, in the trusted computer system (as defined by the *Trusted Computer System Evaluation Criteria*, commonly referred to as the Orange Book), the policy, usually thought of as static, is actually bound at system configuration time. User credentials are bound at enrollment time, data object classification is bound at creation time, and discretionary access is bound at authorization time.

Encapsulation

Encapsulation is the act of enclosing data in a protective and concealing cover. Data can be physically encapsulated in hardware storage or logically encapsulated in a secret code. Encapsulation hides the meaning of the data and preserves its confidentiality. In addition, encapsulation preserves data integrity by protecting data from unintended or uncontrolled changes.

Isolation

In multiuser or multitasking systems, isolation is used to protect one process from contamination by or interference with another. This is necessary to preserve the integrity of the process and its data and to maintain the confidentiality of the data.

Mediation

In the context of computer security, mediation is defined as the controlling of all data sharing to ensure that it conforms with the intention of the data owners (i.e., discretionary controls) or system managers (i.e., mandatory controls). Mediation is provided by such trusted processes as operating systems, subsystems, type managers, and reference monitors.

TRUSTED INFORMATION SYSTEMS

A trusted process or system is one whose behavior is sufficiently simple, coherent, consistent, and demonstrable that users can rely on it, at least for a special purpose. The telephone system, for example, meets these tests despite its enormous complexity. Although it is complex in structure, it is simple in behavior. Although it often fails, it works so well so much of the time that its failures are rarely noticed. Typically, a trusted computer system employs sufficient hardware and software protection and integrity measures to warrant its use for a particular sensitive application.

By definition, most computer systems have trusted processes. Despite their inherent problems, users do rely on them, at least to the extent that they use them. The purpose for which users trust such processes may or may not be related to security. For example, users trust a mathematics program to produce the correct results; security is not an issue. Still, there is a limit to the total number of processes that users can trust. A single user may trust a set of thousands of processes. For any population of users, however, the set that all users trust is much smaller—it may be as few as 10, depending on the application and environment.

Trusted Computing Bases

The Orange Book defines a trusted computing base as the totality of protection mechanisms in a computer system—including hardware, firmware, and software—to enforce a security policy. The trusted computing base creates a basic protection environment and provides additional user services required for a trusted computer system. The ability of a trusted computing base to correctly enforce a security policy depends on the mechanisms in the computing base and on the correct input of parameters (e.g., a user's clearance) as regards the security policy.

Therefore, a trusted computing base may be a complex process. However, it is trusted only for a limited portion of its behavior: its ability to enforce a security policy.

Kernels

A kernel is a special type of reference monitor that has been designed, implemented, and limited in scope in such a simple way that it is possible to easily demonstrate its effectiveness and correctness to an independent party (e.g., an auditor). Definitions of this process specify not only that the kernel must be protected but that it must protect itself. Therefore, according to this definition, the process must include both isolation and mediation.

Tokens

A token is an object used to symbolize or provide a privilege or capability (e.g., seals of office, subway tokens, driver's licenses, credit cards). Tokens usually lack any intrinsic value or meaning. However, they must be sufficiently difficult to counterfeit so as to discourage unauthorized persons from attempting to obtain the privilege they convey.

A token value is a symbol that is used as a token (i.e., it is not a tangible object). Token values are often used to convey privileges within information systems. As with physical tokens, they must be difficult to counterfeit. This is accomplished by choosing tokens from a large set and by concealing them so that they cannot be copied. Passwords and cryptographic keys are special types of token values.

In a closed system, token values are easily concealed through use of access controls. However, there is not much need for token values in closed systems, because there are simpler ways to convey privileges.

In contrast, the only way to conceal token values on an open system is to use secret codes (e.g., encryption), which are also useful in protecting against counterfeiting of tokens. To protect the token value from counterfeiting, it is encrypted under the private key of the originator. To protect the token value from being used by others, it is encrypted under the public key of the intended user; in essence, it is signed with the digital signature of the sender and put into a digital envelope that can be opened only by the intended user.

Capabilities

In the context of information systems, a capability is the capacity, privilege, and ability to execute a particular command, program, or procedure on an identified data object. In many information system, capabilities are specified in a list. In other systems, capabilities are represented by a token value. In such systems, the token value is sometimes viewed as synonymous with the capability; however, they are not synonymous.

In modern systems, a capability is required merely to address an object. Thus, instead of permitting a user to address any object and then restricting that user from those that the user is not authorized to, these systems permit the user to refer only to those objects for which the user has authority. Instructions in user programs cannot issue arbitrary physical addresses, only specific symbolic ones. They can use only those symbols that are defined for them and to which they have authority.

Labels

A label is descriptive information about an object that is attached to the object. In the context of information security, labels are used to describe the sensitivity of data objects. Such labels refer to the set of protective measures that should be used with the data.

In rule-based access control systems, the information in security labels is often used to make decisions about access to the data. Use of labels is specified in the US Department of Defense's mandatory access control policy, which states that a credential held by the using process must be equal to or greater than the label of the data. For example, if the data object is labeled secret, the user must have secret or top secret clearance.

Credentials

In contrast to labels, which contain descriptive information about data, a credential contains descriptive information about a user that may influence that user's right to access data. The credential is usually kept in a record called the user profile. Usually, the user's managers or an independent staff (e.g., human resources) provides the information stored in the credential.

In the Department of Defense's mandatory access control policy, credentials are granted by the security authorities on the basis of the extent and results of their own investigations. Therefore, only these authorities can modify the credential.

SUMMARY

This chapter discusses the basic elements of computing systems: programs, processes, and objects of control. The way a system uses these elements determines the level of security that is provided by the system. Trusted information systems employ hardware and software protection and certain integrity measures to protect sensitive applications or data. Thus, they have a higher level of reliability than most computing systems.

Systems Development and Security Analysis Tools

WILLIAM E. PERRY

Systems developers face two types of challenges: technical and business. The technical challenge involves using technology to meet user needs. The business challenge is to perform the technical work in a manner that addresses business risks. Many of these risks are not adequately addressed in systems development methodologies. The purpose of this chapter is to describe those risks and provide a process for addressing them.

In addressing the business risk, the security reviewer performs tasks similar to those performed by the auditor. These tasks may actually be performed by the security reviewer, the auditor, or both. Allocation of roles and responsibilities is determined by the specific responsibilities assigned to the security reviewer and the auditor for these activities.

This chapter examines three areas: the risk analysis process that should be performed by the security reviewer, the specific quality concerns that the security reviewer needs to address, and proposals for many of the solutions to those concerns through use of a life cycle methodology.

RISK ANALYSIS

The computer has substantially altered the methods by which processes (e.g., payroll and accounts receivable) operate and are controlled. The opportunity for personal review and clerical checking have declined as the collection and subsequent uses of data are automated. Automation of information systems produces new risks, however. Developing secure systems requires addressing these risks.

The two elements that generate risks in a computerized environment are its unique vulnerabilities and its unique set of threats. A vulnerability is a weakness or flaw in a computer-based system that may be exploited by a threat to cause destruction or misuse of assets or resources. Threats can be of natural origin (e.g., fire, water, damage, earthquakes, and hurricanes) or people-oriented (e.g., errors, omissions, intentional acts of violence, and fraud). When a threat materializes and takes advantage of a systems' vulnerabilities, a damaging event occurs that causes a loss. Although the risk of damaging events cannot be totally eliminated, the use of controls on vulnerabilities and threats can reduce such risks to an acceptable level.

The purposes of conducting a risk analysis of a computerized environment are to identify its vulnerabilities and the probabilities of threats that exploit these vulnerabilities and to calculate the damage to or loss of assets that could result from damaging events. Security practitioners should assess a computerized environment's vulnerabilities and set of threats to arrive at an estimate of possible damaging events. Such an assessment would also necessarily include reviewing the strength of existing controls.

Many organizations and federal agencies mandate that vulnerability assessments be conducted. The vulnerability assessment is a major evaluation of the adequacy of an organization's controls. Many tools are used to assess vulnerability, including part of the risk analysis. The organization must first identify vulnerabilities and threats and then determine whether controls are adequate to reduce the resulting risks to an acceptable level. If they are not adequate, the assessment identifies vulnerabilities that must be corrected and threats that must be guarded against. The following section discusses some of the specific risks that are encountered in a computing environment.

Risks in a Computerized Environment

The risks in a computerized environment include both the risks that would be present in manual processing and risks that are unique or increased in a computerized environment. The security reviewer (or EDP auditor) should identify these risks, estimate the severity of the risks, and develop audit tests to substantiate the impact of the risks on the application. For example, if the reviewer feels that erroneous processing is a very high risk for a specific application, he should devise tests to substantiate the correctness or incorrectness of processing. This could be accomplished in a variety of ways (e.g., use of computer-assisted audit techniques).

The use of a computer introduces risks into the processing environment that are either not present or present to a lesser degree in noncomputerized environments. These additional risks include problems associated with:

- Improper use of technology or inability to control technology.
- Inability to translate user needs into technical requirements.
- Illogical processing.
- Cascading and repetition of errors.
- Incorrect entry of data.
- Concentrated storage of data.
- Inability to react quickly to user needs.
- Inability to substantiate processing.
- Concentration of responsibilities.

Assessing Vulnerabilities Through the Security Review

Controls reduce the number and severity of damaging events to an acceptable level. To evaluate the effectiveness of controls, the security reviewer (or EDP auditor) must determine the vulnerabilities present in the computerized environment and the resulting risks. Until the risks are understood, the effectiveness of controls in reducing those risks cannot be evaluated. Therefore, if reviewers are going to rely on controls, they must both identify the vulnerabilities and determine the severity of those risks in the operating environment. It will be useful for reviewers, as they consider application system and data file risks, to be aware of the many undesirable events that can have serious consequences.

The list of potential vulnerabilities helps identify the additional risks that may be present in a computerized environment. To assist the security specialist in identifying unique risks, a brief description of the types of vulnerabilities found in information systems follows:

- *Erroneous or falsified data input.* Erroneous or falsified input data is the simplest and most common cause of undesirable performance by an application system. Vulnerabilities occur wherever data is collected, manually processed, or prepared for entry to the computer.

- *Misuse by authorized end users.* End users are the people who are served by the information system. Although the system is designed for their use, they may misuse it for undesirable purposes. It is often difficult to determine whether their use of the system is in accordance with the legitimate performance of their job.

- *Uncontrolled system access.* Organizations expose themselves to unnecessary risk if they fail to establish controls over who can enter the processing area, who can use the system, and who can access the information contained in the system.

- *Ineffective security practices for the application.* Inadequate manual checks and controls to ensure correct processing by the information system, or negligence by those responsible for carrying out these checks, result in many vulnerabilities.

- *Procedural errors within the IS facility.* Both errors and intentional acts committed by the IS operations staff result in improper operational procedures, lapsed controls, and losses in storage media and output.

- *Program errors.* Applications programs should be developed in an environment that requires and supports complete, correct, and consistent program design; sound programming practices; adequate testing, review, and documentation; and proper maintenance procedures. Although programs developed in such an environment may still contain undetected errors, programs not developed in this manner will probably be rife with errors. In addition, programmers can misuse the programs they are in charge of or deliberately modify programs to produce undesirable side effects.

- *Operating system flaws*. Design and implementation errors, system generation and maintenance programs, and deliberate penetrations resulting in modifications to the operating system can produce undesirable effects in the application system. Flaws in the operating system are often difficult to prevent and detect.

- *Communications system failure*. Information being routed from one location to another over communications lines is vulnerable to accidental failures and to intentional interception and modification by unauthorized parties.

Two key concepts are critical in developing secure systems. The first is a quality-oriented systems development life cycle, which institutionalizes the process of building systems so that adequate controls are incorporated into the process of developing systems. The second is review of the application by skilled security specialists at key points during the development process. The next two sections address these key concepts.

QUALITY ASSURANCE AND THE SYSTEMS DEVELOPMENT LIFE CYCLE

Because of the complexity of current information systems, maintenance of a consistent level of information quality, commensurate with stated corporate goals, requires a carefully planned and dedicated effort. An integral part of this effort involves setting up a formal quality assurance program. Establishing and running a formal quality assurance program is an effective way to reduce human errors and nonhuman faults and is as appropriate to information products as it is to products made on a plant line.

The labels, definitions, and activities of quality assurance can vary substantially among organizations. In fact, quality assurance, quality control, audit, and security control functions overlap in many organizations. The distinction is that quality assurance is responsible only for managing quality and raising the corporate consciousness about quality. Quality assurance is generally an IS staff function that involves analyzing, developing, and implementing control and review systems in all areas of information analysis and production. The IS staff does not usually perform the full quality review work itself but develops methodologies and oversees them.

In regard to systems development, the primary goal of quality assurance is to ensure quality in all parts of the system associated with acquiring, storing, manipulating, and reporting information. To this end, quality assurance generally involves:

- *Defining the various data processing workbenches*. Quality assurance must work with data processing management and staff to ensure that the various processing operations are defined in accordance with principles of quality.

- *Controlling the cost of quality.* The cost of nonconformance with standards or of inputting data incorrectly must be kept to a minimum through quality assurance programs.
- *Establishing quality improvement programs.* Quality assurance must work continuously to reduce and eventually eliminate the defect rate.
- *Building support for quality principles.* Quality assurance must work with and through data processing management and staff to build enthusiasm and support for the principles that permit data processing staff members to input data correctly the first time.

All people involved in producing a product share, to varying degrees, the responsibility of ensuring the quality of that product. To be effective, quality assurance must involve those same people, throughout the organization. End-user involvement during system development is key to attaining the right product, and their involvement in working with an implemented system is key to producing a quality product on a routine basis.

The following section discusses the quality assurance program as it pertains to systems development.

Scope of the Quality Assurance Program

With regard to systems development, the quality assurance function is primarily responsible for developing quality control methods for systems development, maintenance, and operations. These methods enable management to conduct quality control phase reviews of IS development projects to ensure adherence to established IS policies, procedures, standards, and operating schedules. In addition, management can conduct, on a scheduled basis, quality control reviews to verify adherence to established procedures and standards related to specific projects.

All functions in the information delivery chain should be subject to quality assurance policy and evaluations; the scope of the evaluation is dictated by the cost/benefit ratio of and the degree of risk to the organization inherent in the function. Management selects which systems are to be subjected to the evaluation process. This selection is based primarily on the significance of the system applications to business objectives, operations, or strategic plans.

The management of each IS development group helps select the quality control review objectives for that group, on the basis of the annual planned objectives of the group. IS management meets with senior management on a quarterly basis to review the quality assurance schedule and update it as necessary.

Management conducts the systems development reviews using a phased approach. A review should be conducted at the completion of each phase: systems requirements, systems design, systems program specifications, implementation, acceptance testing, and postimplementation. The following criteria are used in the systems developments reviews:

- The design should meet business, project, and economic objectives.
- The system should conform to standards and guidelines.
- Material presented should be clear.
- The system should operate efficiently.
- Controls and security considerations should be adequate.
- Restart and recovery needs should be considered.
- File and data retention procedures should be present.
- Conversion procedures should be in place.
- Test procedures should be in place.

The quality assurance staff should have reasonable access to all the information, records, and personnel related to the project or activities under review. Certain sensitive information may require user approval for access during the review; the systems department must determine the need for user approval before the start of the review.

The quality assurance staff should also be provided with the results from quality control tasks. This information should be transmitted to other parties only in the form of consolidated reports.

In addition to developing quality control methods for systems development, maintenance, and operations, the quality assurance function must:

- *Review standards.* Quality assurance develops and maintains programs and plans for conducting quality assurance reviews to ensure the adequacy of IS policies, procedures, standards, and operating guidelines. Any necessary changes should be reported to the appropriate IS group's management for approval and implementation.
- *Review audits, as necessary.* When audit reports include recommendations for the IS function, quality assurance should review the recommendations and submit a report to IS management. The responsible IS area then implements the changes or improvements.
- *Review key operations systems.* Annually, quality assurance should review selected key operations systems for adherence to standards, procedures, and operating guidelines. Data center or systems management may also request a review. Reviews are generally based on the volume and frequency of incidents requiring corrective action. Recommendations to upgrade hardware or software are occasionally warranted.
- *Help establish security standards.* The quality assurance manager should meet periodically with the data security officer to establish uniform information systems security standards and guidelines.

Organizing and Staffing the Quality Assurance Function

The organization of the quality assurance function should be tailored to meet the needs of the company. Some factors to be considered when organizing this function are:

- The company's business operating philosophy.
- The technical operating methods.
- The company's management style.
- The position and credibility of the technical support groups in the IS department.
- The level of maturity or growth of each of the technical support groups.
- The degree of responsibility and authority to be vested in the quality assurance function.

It should not be forgotten that quality assurance is essentially a managerial function and is most effective when it is given the necessary authority to act as such.

The quality assurance function can be managed by either a line group or staff group. As a line group, the function usually has the authority to stop development of a product that does not meet quality standards. As a staff group, it can only advise the IS manager to stop development of such products. It is recommended that the quality assurance function be a staff group because if the IS manager stops a project, that manager has the authority to initiate corrective action.

The quality assurance function is typically located within the company as follows:

- *Reports directly to the IS manager.* This is the best position for the quality assurance function. When placed elsewhere, quality assurance issues may not reach the appropriate level of management and therefore may not receive the necessary action.
- *Reports outside the data processing function.* This arrangement provides the quality assurance function with an independence not possible when the group reports directly to the data processing manager. This arrangement is more prevalent when applications are sold or used in locations other than where they were developed.
- *Reports to the computer operations manager.* This is another strong position for the quality assurance function because it usually prevents projects that do not meet quality standards from being run on the computer. However, when it reports to computer operations, the quality assurance function rarely has

the opportunity to influence applications during the development process; only the finished product is subject to review.

- *Reports to the systems or programming manager.* The quality assurance is typically weakest when it reports to the systems or programming manager, because most quality assurance reviews involve applications for which this manager is responsible.

To determine the effectiveness of the quality assurance function and its effect on review activities, several steps should be taken at the start of the systems development life cycle or during an early phase of the life cycle. First, the security specialist should determine what quality assurance mechanisms are in place. Management should be asked how they are assured that products have quality (i.e., other than personal assurances from systems personnel).

Second, the quality assurance mechanisms must be evaluated. There should be physical evidence that the mechanisms actually work. This evidence can be in the form of reports to management, documentation of reviews, or a prior audit of the process.

Third, review procedures should be modified when quality assurance is determined to be effective. For example, if it can be established that standards are effectively enforced, the security specialist may not need to review the adequacy of documentation.

Finally, if significant problems are identified within the quality assurance function, the security specialist should recommend improvements for the particular information system under development.

LIFE CYCLE RESPONSIBILITIES

Systems development life cycle (SDLC) methodologies provide formalized methods for developing automated systems. The following sections discuss practices that are generally accepted as part of an SDLC methodology:

Predefined Documents and Deliverables. All of the documents and deliverables to be developed during the creation of an automated information system must be defined. In the better design methodologies, these documents and deliverables are standardized. They are often preprinted forms or screens available to the designer on computer terminals. The sequence in which the products are created is predetermined. In most instances, the output from one product or set of products is needed before the next can be developed.

Life Cycle Phases or Checkpoints. The life cycle should be divided into segments defined by activities and outcomes or deliverables; each segment encompasses part of the developmental process. Having distinct phases or checkpoints allows decisions to be made regarding completion of the project, changes in direction, cancellation of the project, and authorization for use of more resources on the project at these points in time. In many organizations, management authorizes work (i.e., resources) on an IS project only through the next management checkpoint. This ensures that management can continually evaluate the project status and make the appropriate management decisions.

Completion of documents are tied to life cycle phase checkpoints. At each checkpoint, specified work—usually expressed as documents to be produced—is to be completed. Thus, when some reviews a project at a checkpoint, they know which products and documents are to be delivered at that time. In addition, this helps ensure that the project is on schedule and within budget. It is through the examination of these products that the status of work is determined.

Product and Document Reviews. The status of projects is determined by reviewing the products and documents produced by the project team. Therefore, it is important that these products and documents be produced in a standardized format. The National Institute of Standards and Technology, through its various publications, has issued standards for most of the documents produced during the developmental process. These reviews must be signed off upon completion, indicating satisfactory completion of the product or document and, consequently, the life cycle phase.

Training. The training program for people associated with development projects is centered around the products and documents to be produced. To properly review a project, security specialists involved in the developmental process should become familiar with the developmental products and documents. Although security specialists need not know how to develop them, they should understand the meaning of the information contained in those documents and how the documents fit together in the organization's SDLC process.

Project Administration and Control

Project administration and control are management tools for monitoring and directing the project during implementation. The life cycle methodology and the developmental products are designed to create a secure, accurate, and cost-effective system to meet user needs. Project administration and control produces documents that are used by management in administering the project. The developmental products are usually retained as part of the system documentation and become input to maintenance of the system. Because project administration and control documents generally are relevant for only a limited time, they are retained throughout the systems development life cycle but not for the life of the project.

The project administration and control documents can be used by the security specialist to determine the status of projects and to evaluate the performance of project management. Project status is determined by the products that relate actual work to scheduled or budgeted work as well as the project's ability to produce the specified work products in accordance with the project management plan.

The documents used for project administration and control include:

- *Budget status reports*. These identify the funds allocated for development of automated information systems and the internal budgetary reporting systems stating the use of funds against budgets.
- *Schedule status reports*. These reports divide systems development tasks into phases and deliverables, and then relate those phases and deliverables to specific time frames. These reports indicate whether the deliverables have been accomplished within the stated time frames.
- *Developmental project status reports*. These reports, prepared by the individual project members, indicate the status of deliverables under their responsibility. To be effective, these status reports must be able to definitively state the percent of work done as well as the amount of resources consumed.
- *Checkpoint review status report*. The results of a formal process for an independent group evaluating the completeness of work or product deliverables at specific system development checkpoints.
- *Resource usage report*. Status reports that are often automatically generated from statistical information collected about resources consumed during the development project. One such package is IBM Corp.'s job accounting system, System Management Facility (SMF).

In addition, project administration can be facilitated through use of project management software systems. Organizations use a variety of management software systems to control projects (e.g., a scheduling and status reporting system). Automated software development environments provide complete and self-contained software development, documentation, and test tools and techniques for systems analysts, programmers, and reviewers. In general, such environments automatically generate all the reports and code and provide mapping to high-level specifications.

In most systems development projects, more emphasis is placed on systems development than project management. Therefore, the security specialist is more apt to find well-defined developmental products than well-developed project administration and control documents. Many of the administrative documents are more quantitative (i.e., stating the amount of resources used) than qualitative (i.e., indicating percentage of project completion in relation to the development work products).

Life Cycle Phases

The security specialist should not expect systems to be developed in accordance with any single SDLC methodology. The six life cycle phases described in this section are intended to clarify the broad functions or activities that should occur during the development of an automated system. The phases cover activities commonly performed so that whatever development methodology the security specialist encounters, these phases encompass the activities likely to be required. The

278

activities and participants of these six phases are illustrated in exhibits, which can be customized to a specific review. All of the exhibits are intended to reflect, primarily, the roles and documents to be found in large, in-house development or redesign projects.

Phase 1: Initiation. The initiation phase begins with recognizing a problem or identifying a need. The need is validated and alternative functional concepts to satisfy the need are recommended, evaluated, and approved. The solution must be based on a clear understanding of the problem, a preliminary investigation of alternative solutions (including solutions that are not based on the computer), and a comparison of the expected benefits and costs (including design, construction, operation, and potential risks) of the solutions. At this stage, the risk or sensitivity of the data or information in the information system under consideration should be evaluated. The activities specific to the initiation phase are listed in Exhibit II-1-1, along with the individuals or functions who are responsible for those activities.

EXHIBIT II-1-1 Initiation Phase Responsibilities

Participant	Responsibilities
Information Resources Management Official	• Approves the needs statement
System Security Officer and Internal Control Officer	• Oversees or conducts the risk analysis • Helps evaluate system sensitivity
Auditor	• Reviews and evaluates the needs statement, feasibility study, risk analysis, cost/benefit analysis, and system decision paper • On the basis of review, determines scope of future involvement
Sponsor or User	• Identifies and validates need • Develops the needs statement • Directs the feasibility study, risk analysis, and cost/benefit analysis • Develops the system decision paper • Selects a project manager
Project Manager or Contracting Officer's Technical Representative	• Develops or oversees development of the feasibility study, risk analysis, cost/benefit analysis, and system decision paper
System Security Specialist and Internal Control Specialist	• Conducts the risk analysis, as appropriate
Contracting Officer or Contract Auditor	• If appropriate, awards contract and ensures contract compliance
IS Manager	• Provides consultation as appropriate, unless this office initiates system development
Quality Assurance Specialist	• Provides consultation on quality attributes of the needs statement

Phase 2: Definition. In this phase, the functional requirements are defined and detailed planning for the development of an information system is begun. Functional requirements and processes to be automated are documented and approved by an appropriate senior manager before a systems development effort is started. Requirements identification is iterative, as is the analysis of potential risks, involving those individuals who identify and solve problems. It is critical that internal control and specific security requirements be identified during this process. Requirements may be, and commonly are, modified in later phases as a better understanding of the problem is gained.

In addition, a project plan specifying a strategy for managing systems development, certification, and accreditation is prepared during this phase. This plan defined the goals and activities for all subsequent phases and includes resource estimates for each phase, intermediate milestones, and methods for design, documentation, problem reporting, and change control. Resource planning for validation, verification, and testing should be included here. In essence, the project plan describes the unique SDLC methodology to be used during the life of the project. During this phase, a review plan is also prepared so that the new information system can be reviewed from the start. The activities to be performed in the definition are presented in Exhibit II-1-2.

Phase 3: System Design. The activities performed during this phase (see Exhibit II-1-3) result in a specification of the solution. The solution provides a specific high-level definition, including information aggregates, information flows, and logical processing steps as well as all major interfaces and their input and output. The purpose is to refine, resolve deficiencies in, define additional details in, and package the solution. The detailed design specifications describe the physical solution (i.e., algorithms and data structures) in such a way that it can be implemented in code with little or no need for additional analysis. Companies should define and approve security specifications before acquiring or starting formal development of the applications.

In addition, the validation, verification, and testing goals are identified during this phase, and a plan for achieving these goals is developed. The project plan (e.g., schedules, budgets, and deliverables) and risk analysis are reviewed and revised as required, given the scope and complexity of the solution formulated. These activities are coordinated with the certification plan components.

Phase 4: Programming and Training. This phase results in programs that are ready for testing, evaluation, certification, and installation. Programming is the process of implementing the detailed design specifications into code. The completed code then undergoes testing, as described in the revised validation, verification, and testing plan, in phase 5. In addition to programming and training manuals, user and maintenance manuals are prepared during phase 4, as is a preliminary installation plan that specifies the approach to and details of installation

EXHIBIT II-1-2 Definition Phase Responsibilities

Participant	Responsibilities
Information Resources Management Official	• Approves system decision paper to advance to definition phase, in consultation with the sponser or user and data processing manager (occurs between initiation and definition phases)
System Security Officer and Internal Control Officer	• Reviews system security and internal controls components of the project plan, functional requirements documents and data requirements documents, on a select basis
Auditor	• Reviews and evaluates the system decision paper, project plan, functional requirements documents, and data requirements documents and participates in their development, as necessary • Prepares the audit program
Sponsor or User	• Approves the project plan and functional requirements documents • Updates the system decision paper
Project Manager or Contracting Officer's Technical Representative	• Develops the project plan and functional and data requirements documents, with user participation
System Security Specialist and Internal Control Specialist	• Provides consultation and review of system security and internal controls components of the project plan, functional requirements documents, and data requirements documents
Contracting Officer or Contract Auditor	• Ensures contract compliance
Data Processing Manager	• Reviews the project plan, functional requirements documents, data requirements documents. • As appropriate, provides technical support to the project manager the sponsor or user
Quality Assurance Specialist	• Reviews project definition to ensure compliance with the needs statement and data processing standards

of the information system. Exhibit II-1-4 illustrates the activities to be performed in this phase.

Phase 5: Evaluation and Acceptance. In this phase, integration and testing of the system occur. For validation purposes, the system should be executed on test transaction data and tested in one or more representative operational sites. If designated a sensitive system, an appropriate authority should certify the system for technical adequacy in meeting its security requirements, before accreditation

EXHIBIT II-1-3 **System Design Phase Responsibilities**

Participant	Responsibilities
Information Resources Management Official	• Approves updated system decision paper to advance to the system design phase, in consultation with the sponsor or user and the data processing manager (occurs between the definition and system design phases) • Enters system into the departments formal systems inventory
System Security Officer and Internal Control Officer	• Reviews system security and internal controls components of the system, subsystem, Program, and Data Base Specifications and the validation, verification, and testing plan and specifications
Auditor	• Reviews, evaluates, and possibly provides input for the risk analysis; system decision paper; system, subsystem, program, and data base specifications; validation, verification, and testing plan and specifications; and revised project plan • Updates the audit program
Sponsor or User	• Approves the revised project plan and updates the system decision paper • Reassesses the risk analysis • Approves the validation, verification, and testing plan and specifications
Project Manager or Contracting Officer's Technical Representative	• Updates the project plan • Develops the system, subsystem, program, and data base specifications and the validation, verification, and testing plan and specifications
System Security Specialist and Internal Control Specialist	• Reviews the system security and internal controls components of the system, subsystem, program, and data base specifications and the validation, verification, and testing plan and specifications
Contracting Officer or Contract Auditor	• Ensures contract compliance
Data Processing Manager	• Reviews the validation, verification, and testing components of the system, subsystem, program, and data base specifications and of the validation, verification, and testing plan and specifications • As appropriate, provides technical support to the project manager and the sponsor or user in developing specifications
Quality Assurance Specialist	• Reviews the system design and the validation, verification, and testing components and documentation for compliance with the system definition and data processing standards

EXHIBIT II-1-4 **Programming and Training Phase Responsibilities**

Participant	Responsibilities
Information Resources Management Official	• Approves updated system decision paper to advance to the programming and training phase, in consultation with the sponsor or user and the data processing manager (occurs between the system design and programming phases)
System Security Officer and Internal Control Officer	• Reviews the system security and internal controls components of the user manual, operations and maintenance manual, installation and conversion plan, and revised validation, verification, and testing plan and specifications
Auditor	• Reviews and evaluates the revised project plan, system decision paper, revised validation, verification, and testing plan and specifications, user manual, operations and maintenance manual, and installation and conversion plan • Updates the audit program
Sponsor or User	• Approves the revised project plan, revised validation, verification, and testing plan and specifications, user manual, operations and maintenance manual, and installaion and conversion plan • Updates the system decision paper • Initiates user training
Project Manager or Contracting Officer's Technical Representative	• Updates the project plan • Revises the validation, verification, and testing plan and specifications • Devleops the user manual, operations and maintenance manual, and installation and conversion plan • Is responsible for programming and testing
System Security Specialist and Internal Control Specialist	• Reviews the system security and internal controls components of the user manual, operations and maintenance manual, installation and conversion plan, and revised validation, verification, and testing plan and specifications
Contracting Officer or Contract Auditor	• Ensures contract compliance
Data Processing Manager	• Reviews the validation, verification, and testing components of the user manual, operations and maintenance manual, and installation and conversion plan • Provides technical support to the project manager and sponsor or user • May conduct data processing training
Quality Assurance Specialist	• Reviews program definition, program code, documentation, and training for compliance with design and data processing standards

EXHIBIT II-1-5 Evaluation and Acceptance Phase Responsibilities

Participant	Responsibilities
Information Resources Management Official	• Approves updated system decision paper to advance to the evaluation and acceptance phase, in consultation with the sponsor or user and the data processing manager (occurs between the programming and evaluation phases)
System Security Officer and Internal Control Officer	• Reviews the test analysis and security evaluation report and the system security and internal controls components of the revised installation and conversion plan
Auditor	• Reviews and evaluates the revised project plan, revised installation and conversion plan, and test analysis and security evaluation report • Updates the audit program
Sponsor or User	• Approves the revised project plan and installation and conversion plan • Updates the system decision paper • Oversees training • Accepts system for operation
Project Manager or Contracting Officer's Technical Representative	• Updates the project plan • Supports and oversees the test analysis and security evaluation report and certifies system security • Revises the user manual, operations and maintenance manual, and installation and conversion plan on the basis of the test results
System Security Specialist and Internal Control Specialist	• Reviews the test analysis and security evaluation report and documentation updates to the user manual, operations and maintenance manual, and installation and conversion plan for impact on system security and internal controls
Contracting Officer or Contract Auditor	• Ensures contract compliance
Data Processing Manager	• Directs tests • Reviews the test analysis and security evaluation report, and installation and conversion plan • Continues to provide technical support • May do technical evaluation for certification
Quality Assurance Specialist	• Reviews the test analysis and security evaluation report and advises responsible participants on ensuring that system adheres to the needs statement

and installation. Before certification, all validation, verification, and test results should be documented, and actual and expected results should be compared.

Security evaluation should be part of the broader test results and evaluation report. The accreditation statement, the last key activity of phase 5, is a statement from the responsible accrediting official (e.g., the sponsor or user) that the system is operating effectively and is ready to be installed. Any caveats or restrictions should be provided at this time. Exhibit II-1-5 lists the activities and responsible parties for phase 5.

Phase 6: Installation and Operation. The purpose of this final life cycle phase is to implement the approved operational plan (including extension or installation at other sites), continue approved operations, budget adequately, and control all changes and maintain or modify the system during its remaining life. Problem reporting, change requests, and other change control mechanisms are used to facilitate systematic correction and evolution of the system. In addition, periodic performance measurements and evaluations are performed to ensure that the system continues to meet its requirements in a cost-effective manner in the context of a changing system environment. These reviews may be conducted by the quality assurance staff or the internal audit unit, or by both. The activities involved in installation and operation are presented in Exhibit II-1-6.

SYSTEM LIFE CYCLE DOCUMENTATION

Reviews of systems under development are not practical unless well-defined documentation exists. The requirements for system documentation, however, present problems commonly encountered in the development of any automated system. Managers may find it appropriate to consolidate several requirements into a single document, move documentation requirements to an earlier phase, or make other changes that they deem necessary for the efficient and effective management of their program. What is critical is that the purpose and functions of the documents elaborated on in the following sections are achieved.

The following sections discuss the purpose and general contents of each of the documents or document types identified in the preceding exhibits. Exhibit II-1-7 describes the flow of these documents as the system project proceeds through its life cycle.

The Needs Statement

A needs statement should be prepared to describe the deficiencies in existing capabilities, any new or changed program requirements, and opportunities for increased economy and efficiency. It should justify the exploration of alternative solutions, including automation. An adaptation of the document should be used for systems not designated as major systems. The need for system security should

---

EXHIBIT II-1-6 **Installation and Operation Phase Responsibilities**

Participant	Responsibilities
Information Resources Management Official	• Approves final installation of system • Accredits all systems determined to be of critical sensitivity or importance to the department • Directs periodic reviews for continued need (all activities occur between evaluation and installation phases)
System Security Officer and Internal Control Officer	• Conducts periodic reviews • Promotes long-range system planning process
Auditor	• Conducts periodic reviews • Updates the audit plan and program as needed
Sponsor or User	• Oversees training • Directs periodic reviews of sensitive applications for recertification • Identifies need for changes to the system and revises the project plan accordingly
Project Manager or Contracting Officer's Technical Representative	• Directs implementation and updates the user manual and operations and maintenance manual as needed during implementation and operation
System Security Specialist and Internal Control Specialist	• Conducts periodic reviews
Contracting Officer or Contract Auditor	• If appropriate, continues to ensure contract compliance
IS Manager	• Conducts periodic reviews • Provides technical assistance • Maintains system documentation
Quality Assurance Specialist	• Reviews changes to the software system • Summarizes, analyzes, and reports on defects to responsible participants

be identified, on the basis of the system's anticipated level of the sensitivity or criticality. Because the needs statement is a management document, it should be no longer than four to six pages.

The Feasibility Study

The purposes of the feasibility study are to provide an analysis of the objectives, requirements, and system concepts; evaluate alternative approaches for reasonably achieving the objectives; and identify a proposed approach. This document, in conjunction with the cost/benefit analysis, should provide management with ade-

EXHIBIT II-1-7   SDLC Documentation Flowchart

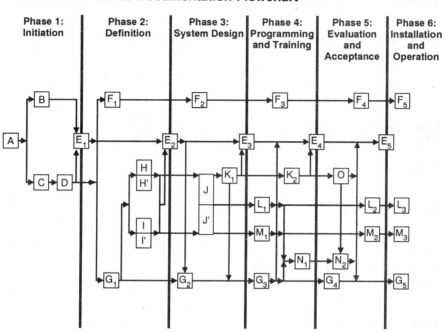

| Phase 1: Initiation | Phase 2: Definition | Phase 3: System Design | Phase 4: Programming and Training | Phase 5: Evaluation and Acceptance | Phase 6: Installation and Operation |

Documentation Codes

A	Needs statement
B	Feasibility study
C	Risk analysis
D	Cost benefit analysis
E	System decision paper
F	Audit plan
G	Project plan
H	Functional requirements document
H'	Functional security and internal control requirements document

I	Data requirements document
I'	Data sensitivity or criticallity description
J	System, subsystem, program, and data base specifications
J'	Security and internal control specifications
K	Validation, verification, and testing plan and specifications
L	User manual
M	Operations and maintenance manual
N	Installation and conversion plan
O	Test analysis and security evaluation report

Note:
Document subscripts refer to successive iterations of that document.

quate information to make decisions to initiate or continue the development, procurement, or modification of software or other processing-relating services. The feasibility study may be supplemented with an appendix containing details of a cost/benefit analysis, or it may be considered with a separate cost/benefit analysis.

The Risk Analysis

The purposes of the risk analysis are to identify the internal control and security vulnerabilities of an automated information system, determine the nature and magnitude of associated threats to data and assets, determine the resulting potential for loss, and provide managers, designers, and systems security specialists and auditors with recommended safeguards. These should be included during the design, development, and installation phases of a new or modified system to reduce the potential loss.

The system should be reviewed and revised, as necessary, during each phase of the development life cycle, to ensure that appropriate security measures are installed. The findings and recommendations of the risk analysis should be used by the review teams during the system security and certification reviews. The risk analysis should be prepared as a separate document and should be reviewed and updated as necessary (e.g., when a modification is made to the operational system).

The Cost/Benefit Analysis

The purpose of the cost/benefit analysis is to provide managers, users, designers, systems security specialists, and auditors with adequate cost and benefit information, including the impact of security, privacy, and internal control requirements on that information. These individuals use the cost/benefit data to analyze and evaluate alternative approaches to meeting mission deficiencies. This analysis, in conjunction with the feasibility study, should provide the information for management to make decisions to initiate or continue the development, procurement, or modification of software or other system-related components. The cost/benefit analysis may be prepared as a separate document, or details of the cost/benefit analysis may be appended to the feasibility study.

The System Decision Paper

The system decision paper provides the information and framework critical to the departmental and operating divisions' decision-making processes during system development. It is the principal document for recording the following essential information about the system:

- Mission need.
- Milestones and thresholds.
- Issues and risks, including security, privacy, and internal controls.
- Alternatives and their costs and benefits.
- The management plan.
- Supporting rationale for decisions.
- Affordability in terms of projected budget and funding.
- Decisions of the organization's CEO.

The system decision paper remains in existence throughout the life of a major system. It must be approved at the appropriate level when milestones for each life cycle phase are achieved. The final iteration of the system decision paper, which precedes system installation and operation, should include an accreditation statement by the responsible accrediting official. This statement verifies that the system is operating effectively; any caveats on its operation must be mentioned at this time.

The Audit Plan

Audit plans encompass all of the company's system activities. Systems under development may be selected for review on the basis of several factors, including the sensitivity or criticality of the system or the effectiveness of internal data processing management control (e.g., a verification and validation group, a formalized testing process, a quality assurance function, or a risk management function).

For those systems selected for audit review, a detailed system-specific plan is prepared. This plan clarified audit involvement, which may range from audit review of completed work products at each development stage to active review participation in each systems development phase. In any case, the overall objective is to assess the adequacy of internal audit controls and provide reasonable assurances to management.

The Project Plan

The project plan specifies the strategy for managing the software or system development. It defines the goals and activities for all phases and subphases of development. In addition, it includes resource estimates for the duration of systems development and such intermediate milestones as management technical reviews (i.e., those for security, privacy, and internal controls requirements); defines methods for design, documentation problem reporting, and change control; and specifies supporting techniques and tools.

Although the focus or emphasis of the project plan is on the developmental phases, the plan cannot omit consideration of the system's installation and operation, particularly the certification process the system must go through before entering the final life cycle phase. A formal certification plan should be included as a routine subsection of project plans for all systems designated as sensitive. That subsection contains clarification of responsibilities, a security requirements and evaluation approach, an evaluation schedule, and support required as well as identification of the evaluation products. The remainder of the project plan is to be reviewed and modified during each phase. The certification plan should be revised as needed, commonly on the basis of the updated risk analysis.

The Functional Requirements Document

The purpose of the functional requirements document is to provide a single, initial definition of the software or system under development, so that users and designers have a mutual understanding of it. The definition includes the requirements, operating environment, and development plan. The overview should include the proposed methods and procedures, a summary of improvements, a summary of the participated impact, security and privacy considerations, internal control considerations, cost considerations, and alternatives.

The requirements section should state the functions required of the software in quantitative and qualitative terms, as well as a description of how these functions will satisfy the performance objectives. In addition, it should specify the performance requirements for accuracy, validation, timing, and flexibility. Input and output must be explained as well as data characteristics. Finally, the requirements document describes the operating environment and provides or makes reference to a development plan.

The Functional Security and Internal Control Requirements Document

The purpose of the security and internal control requirements document is to focus the attention of the user and system designer on the security and internal control needs of the system, as determined by both the vulnerabilities identified during the risk analysis and the established internal control and security standards. This document should include requirements for general controls (i.e., management and environmental controls) at the computer installation, if additional controls are needed, and automated application controls. All security requirements must be defined and approved before formal development of the applications is begun.

The Data Requirements Document

The purpose of the data requirements document is to provide, during the definition stage of software development, a data description and technical information about data collection requirements. The data descriptions should be separated into two categories: static and dynamic data. Data elements in each category should be arranged in logical groupings (e.g., functions, subjects, or other groupings that are relevant to their use).

The document should describe the type of information required to document the characteristics of each data element and should specify information to be collected by the user and by the developer. Finally, procedures for data collection and the anticipated impact of the data requirements should be discussed.

A Data Sensitivity or Criticality Description

In the data sensitivity or criticality description, specific types of sensitive data and assets should be identified. Once sensitive or critical data have been identified, it may be necessary to determine the degree of sensitivity or criticality within the general grouping. Categories of sensitivity and criticality are organization dependent. The importance of this determination is that data sensitivity and criticality assessments must be known before the nature and magnitude of threats can be postulated.

System, Subsystem, Program, and Data Base Specifications

The purpose of the system and subsystem specifications is to describe for analysts and programmers the requirements, operating environment, design characteristics, and program specifications (if desired) for the system or subsystem. The purpose of the program specifications is to describe for programmers the requirements, operating environment, and design characteristics of a computer program. Both the system (or subsystem) and program specifications should have sections describing functions and performance requirements (in terms of accuracy, validation, timing, and flexibility) and the operating environment.

The purpose of the data base specifications is to describe the logical and physical characteristics of a particular data base. The section on physical characteristics should address storage and design considerations.

Security and Internal Control Specifications

By separating security and internal control specifications from the broader specifications papers, added weight is given to their importance. The details may be included as a separate but clearly identifiable subsection of the other specification papers. Its purpose is to set forth security and internal control specifications for meeting functional security and internal control requirements.

All specifications should be sufficiently precise to allow the design of tests that determine whether the requirement has been satisfied. The security specifications should be kept current throughout the entire life cycle of the system. No changes to the system should be permitted unless they either do not affect the security specifications or have been approved and entered as an official modification to this document. Security specifications should be reviewed by all organizations involved in the use or operation of the application. For any sensitive application, the specifications must be reviewed and approved by the party responsible for security and by the organization's internal auditors.

Validation, Verification, and Testing Plan and Specifications

The purpose of the validation, verification, and testing plan is to provide a method for evaluating the quality and correctness of software, including requirements and design documentation. The testing plan, which may be divided into two documents, also provides plans for the testing of software—including detailed specifications, descriptions, and procedures for all tests—as well as test data reduction and evaluation criteria.

A validation, verification, and testing plan document specifies a project's validation, verification, and testing requirements and the procedures needed to achieve them. Because general systems planning drives the validation, verification, and testing plan, in turn providing feedback to the overall system development, general project planning is closely integrated to planning for validation, verification, and testing. Once the general background, goals, and requirements of the system are clearly understood, validation, verification, and testing planning may begin.

The User Manual

The purpose of the user manual is to sufficiently describe the functions performed by the software in terminology that users can understand to determine the software's applicability as well as when and how to use it. The user's manual should serve as a reference document for initiation procedures, preparation of input data and parameters, and interpretation of results. In addition to general information, the manual should provide a full description of the application as well as a section on procedures and requirements, including those related to security, privacy, and internal controls. It should also describe error, recovery, and file query procedures and requirements.

The Operations and Maintenance Manual

Two separate manuals may be necessary for providing operations and maintenance information. The purpose of the operations manual provides computer operations personnel with a description of the software and the operational environment so that the software can be run. It includes an overview of the software organization, program inventory, and file inventory as well as a description of the runs and sections on nonroutine procedures, remote operations, and security requirements. The purpose of the maintenance manual is to provide the maintenance programmer with the information and source code necessary to understand the programs, their operating environment, and their maintenance procedures and security requirements.

The Installation and Conversion Plan

The installation and conversion plan is a tool for directing the installation or implementation of a system at locations other than the test site after the system, including its security features, has been tested. This plan may also be used to direct the implementation of major modifications of or enhancements to a system that has already been installed. Those parts of the document directed toward users should be presented in nontechnical language; those parts directed toward operations personnel should be presented in suitable terminology.

The Test Analysis and Security Evaluation Report

The purpose of the test analysis report is to document the test analysis results and findings; present the demonstrated capabilities and deficiencies (including the security evaluation report needed for certification of the system); and provide a basis for preparing a statement of system or software readiness for implementation. This report is reviewed by managers and users and, therefore, it should be prepared in nontechnical language.

The security evaluation report, which should be a large subsection of this document, should end with a certification transmittal letter and should contain a suggested accreditation statement for the responsible accrediting official. This statement authorizes installation of the system, possibly with qualifications or exceptions. Companies should conduct periodic reviews of sensitive applications once they are operational and recertify the adequacy of security safeguards.

CONCLUSION

By familiarizing themselves with the risks presented in this chapter before systems development is begun, security specialists have taken the first step toward ensuring that a secure system is developed. To adequately address these risks, the security practitioner must use a formal methodology for systems development. This chapter describes the systems development life cycle for reviewing, evaluating, and testing a system under development to verify that security controls adequately cover the identified risks.

Life Cycle Phase Controls

WILLIAM PERRY

To help ensure the success of a systems development project, the systems development life cycle (SDLC) can be broken down into phases that encompass specific activities. Although each systems development methodology may have its own set of phases, the following are the main phases generally encountered in a given project: initiation, definition, system design, programming and training, evaluation and acceptance, and installation and operation.

Chapter II-1-3, "Systems Development and Security Analysis Tools," describes the activities involved in these life cycle phases. This chapter examines the responsibilities of the security specialist in ensuring that controls are in place at the end of each development phase. A controls checklist is provided for each phase to help the security specialist meet this goal.

PHASE 1: INITIATION

The initiation phase begins with recognition of a problem or identification of a need. The need is then validated, and solutions that satisfy this need are recommended and, perhaps, approved. The decision to pursue a particular solution must be based on a clear understanding of the problem, a preliminary investigation of alternatives, and a comparison of their expected benefits and costs (including design, construction, and operations costs and potential risks). At this stage, the data in the system should be evaluated to determine its level of sensitivity and to identify the potential risks to that data.

The Initiation Phase Review

The initiation phase review focuses on the documents produced during this phase. Although the actual documents produced vary from company to company, depending on the systems development methodology used, the more common documents are:

- A needs statement.
- A feasibility study.
- A risk analysis.

- A cost/benefit analysis.
- A system decision paper.

In preparing for the initiation phase review, the security specialist must understand the work flow, gather the necessary documentation, and interview the responsible participants. Most of this background analysis can be performed by the team established to implement the project. The tasks that need to be completed during the review are to study the environment in which the project will be initiated, review the initiation phase plans, gather information on the initiation phase status, and verify information on the initiation phase status. These tasks are discussed in the following sections.

Studying the Environment. Before conducting the initiation phase review, the security specialist should become familiar with the developing organization's design methodology, particularly the initiation phase methodology. Specifically, the review should include:

- Determining whether any prior evaluations of this SDLC methodology have been made, and if so, how its effectiveness was evaluated.
- Determining whether the development team supports the SDLC methodology.
- Evaluating the effectiveness of the SDLC methodology, through inquiry and review of documentation.
- Comparing the SDLC methodology with that defined in this chapter and noting the differences, particularly where deficiencies might occur as a result of design deficiencies.
- Identifying the documents produced by the SDLC methodology.
- Determining through interviews whether the project team has been adequately trained in the use of the SDLC methodology.

In addition, the security specialist must become familiar with the organization's cost-justification process and with the appropriate regulations and policies relating to the area being considered for automation.

Reviewing the Initiation Phase Plans. The security specialist should become familiar with the problem that has been recognized and the need that must be satisfied. The plan to initiate the automated information system should be reviewed to ensure that it will result in the type of documents described in this subsection. In addition, the security specialist should verify that the individuals selected for participating in the initiation phase will in fact participate.

Gathering Information on the Initiation Phase Status. The security specialist should obtain and review the initiation phase documents to verify that they have been prepared, and if so, whether they have been prepared in accordance with the SDLC methodology. Next, the specialist must determine the status of the project—that is, whether it is on time, whether the needed tasks have been completed, and if not, when completion is expected. Finally, the security specialist should identify any changes to the recognized problem and need and should verify that any changes have been properly incorporated into the documents developed during this phase.

Verifying Information on the Initiation Phase Status. In fulfilling this task, the security specialist should review the documents produced during the initiation phase and interview key participants about their role in preparing those documents.

Reviewing the Documents. A computer project begins with a needs statement, which either includes or is supported by a needs validation and justification document. The needs statement becomes the basis for a feasibility study and a risk analysis. The objective of these parts of the initiation phase is to identify a proposed approach and the vulnerabilities associated with that approach. The risk analysis provides the additional input to supplement the needs statement so that a cost/benefit analysis can be prepared. This document, in conjunction with the feasibility study, provides the necessary information for management to make a decision to initiate or continue the development or to take other appropriate actions. Management's actions should be included within a system decision paper. This becomes the principle document, containing the essential information about the automated information system and serving as the basis for systems definition.

The documents to be completed during the initiation phase should be specified by the company's system design methodology. The security specialist, having already gained a familiarity with that methodology during the background analysis, can verify that all of the appropriate documents have been prepared. The security specialist should ensure that the appropriate information has been accumulated for the system decision paper to verify the correctness of that document.

Key Control Objectives

The key control objectives for each phase can be tied to the documents produced or updated during that phase. Each of the documents required should be listed and described in the company's system design methodology. If the described information is included in each document, the control needed to ensure a secure system should be present. Exhibit II-1-8 lists the information required for each document produced during the initiation phase.

The initiation phase controls checklist presented in Exhibit II-1-9 can be used by designers and security specialists to determine whether the key control objectives have been made during the development process. On all of the checklists presented in this chapter, a yes response indicates that the control objective has been adequately addressed by the system design. A negative response indicates

---

EXHIBIT II-1-8 Information Required in the Initiation Phase Documents

The needs statement should include:
- The need for the system, expressed in terms of the company mission.
- Deficiencies in existing capabilities.
- New or changed program requirements that are needed.
- Opportunities for increasing efficiency of user operation.
- The internal controls or security needed for the automated information system.
- Alternative methods of solving the need, with justification for the solution recommended.

The feasibility study document should include:
- An analysis of the objectives, requirements, and system concepts.
- An evaluation of alternative approaches for reasonably achieving the objectives.
- Identification of the proposed approach.
- Sufficient information in the three preceding areas to provide management with adequate information to make decisions to initiate or continue the development, procurement, or modification of software or other data processing services.

The risk analysis document should contain:
- Identification of internal control and security vulnerabilities.
- The nature and magnitude of associated threats to data and assets covered by the proposed system.
- Recommended safeguards to be included in the design to address the identified risks.
- A detailed review of all data and assets to be processed or accessed by the system, including the value and sensitivity of the data or assets.

The cost/benefit analysis should include:
- Costs to build the system.
- Benefits to be derived from the system.
- The impact the system will have on security, privacy, and internal control requirements.
- An analysis and evaluation of alternative approaches proposed in meeting the need, including a detailed cost/benefit analysis of the proposed alternatives.

The system decision paper should include:
- Information and framework critical to the decision-making process.
- The mission need.
- Project milestones.
- General business thresholds (e.g., cost, schedule, and resource constraints).
- Issues and risks.
- Cost/benefit analysis results.
- A management plan supporting rationale for decisions.
- Affordability in terms of projected budget and funding.
- The decision made (i.e., the alternative selected).

EXHIBIT II-1-9 Initiation Phase Controls Checklist

Control Objective	Yes	No	NA	Comments
1. The user needs statement clearly defines the need or problem and provides justification for implementing that need.				
2. User department management participated in the project initiation phase.				
3. The feasibility study document is clearly defined and documented.				
4. Internal control and security vulnerabilities have been determined, as well as the magnitude of any associated threats.				
5. The cost/benefit analysis includes all of the cost and benefit considerations associated with initiation, operation, and maintenance of the information system.				
6. Management has reviewed the feasibility study reports and decided whether or not to proceed. (When the decision is made to proceed, one of the alternatives should be selected as the starting point for the subsequent systems development phases.)				
7. An analysis was made before programming to determine whether the work could have been done more economically by either contracting the software or purchasing it off the shelf.				

that the control objective has not been addressed and an assessment must be made by the system users as to whether or not the resulting risk is acceptable. Not applicable (NA) indicates that this control objective is not applicable for the system being designed. A comments column is provided to clarify yes responses and to explain the risks associated with negative responses.

PHASE 2: DEFINITION

During the definition phase, functional requirements are defined and detailed planning for the development of an operational information system is begun. Previous government studies show that incorrect requirements are one of the major causes of defects in automated information systems. Because of the difficulty in defining correct requirements, requirement identification should be an iterative process involving both those who identify and those who solve problems.

Functional requirements and processes to be automated must be documented and approved by an appropriate senior manager before systems development is begun. It is critical that internal control and specific security requirements be identified during this phase. Requirements may be modified in later phases as a better understanding of the problem is gained. In addition, a project plan specifying a strategy for managing systems development, certification, and accreditation is prepared during this phase. The project plan defines the goals and activities for all phases and includes resource estimates for each phase and intermediate milestones as well as methods for design, documentation, problem reporting, and change control.

Individuals from user areas, data processing areas, and involved third parties (e.g., security personnel) participate in this phase. Data processing personnel play a much more active role during the definition phase.

The work performed during the definition phase is recorded on six definition phase documents: the audit plan, project plan, functional requirements document, functional security and internal control requirements document, data requirements document, and data sensitivity or criticality description. In addition, the system decision paper is updated as appropriate. Each phase of the system life cycle provides an opportunity to reevaluate the risks, cost/benefit ratio, and approach to be taken during implementation.

Audit Survey

The audit survey conducted during this and following phases primarily involves review of the documents produced in the previous phase, appropriate audit workpapers produced in the previous phase, and the documents produced in the present phase. The audit survey from the initiation phase requires the security specialist to examine the user area and appropriate policies, regulations, and design methodology. The specialist's observations should be documented in the audit workpapers from the initiation phase.

Each survey involves four steps. First, the security specialist must review the output documents produced during the previous phase as well as the appropriate audit workpapers. Second, the security specialist must review and become familiar with the plans to complete this phase. Third, the specialist gathers the documentation produced during this phase and evaluates the project status in comparison to the plan. Finally, the specialist verifies the documents produced during the definition phase by analyzing the documents and interviewing the participants in this phase. These four tasks are discussed individually in the following sections.

Reviewing Initiation Phase Output. The security specialist should review the five initiation phase documents (or the equivalent documents) produced by the developmental methodology used for the information system under development. The key document for review is the system decision paper, which includes a summation of much of the information in the other documents. The security specialist should refer back to the other documents as appropriate to get more detailed information.

In addition, the security specialist should review the audit papers prepared during the initiation phase. The main objective is to review the deficiencies uncovered during the initiation phase. The security specialist should ensure that those deficiencies have been adequately addressed during the definition phase, if they have not already been corrected and reviewed by the security specialist. One of the primary audit tasks during each review phase is to evaluate the adequacy of the actions taken on deficiencies from the previous phase that were identified by the security specialist.

Reviewing Definition Phase Plans. The system decision paper should provide the details of the plan for implementing each phase. The security specialist should be aware that many organizations maintain their schedules and plans through automated scheduling and project management systems. In these instances, the security specialist may need the output from the automatic scheduling system in order to review the plans.

The key plans from an audit perspective are the tasks that produce the needed documentation. Therefore, the security specialist should study the documents to be produced during the definition phase and then relate those to the plans to ensure that they will be produced. If it is uncertain that all the needed information will be produced, the security specialist should challenge the adequacy of the plans.

Gathering Information on Project Status. The security specialist should periodically check the project status to determine when reviews should occur. This can be done through inquiry to project management or using automated project status systems.

The security specialist must determine the status of three aspects of the project. First is the administrative status of the project, which involves the budget and schedule. This is necessary to determine the project's availability for review. Second, the security specialist must determine the status of documentation. If the schedule and budget are tight, the project team may decide to eliminate certain parts of documents in order to stay on schedule. When this occurs, the security specialist should note missing items as project deficiencies. Third, the security specialist must determine the status of changes. If there have been significant changes to the project, the security specialist should ensure that the schedule and budget have been adjusted accordingly and should verify that any required changes have been made to the documents produced in previous phases.

Verifying Information on Definition Phase Starts. This task involves reviewing documents produced during the definition phase and interviewing the key participants in producing those documents. The information used for the project's definition phase originates from the system decision paper developed during the initiation phase. This paper is expanded using the definition phase documents.

The document flow for the definition phase is determined by the SDLC methodology. The system decision paper is the source document for both the project plan and the updated system decision paper. Therefore, the security specialist must ensure that the system decision paper is kept up-to-date throughout the development process. The project plan specifies the strategy for managing the software development process and indicates how the system will be certified before installation and operation.

The system decision paper and the project plan are used as the basis for developing the functional requirements document, the functional security and internal control requirements document, the data requirements document, and the data sensitivity or criticality description. The preparation of these documents requires extensive interaction among the responsible participants—primarily the functional or operational participants, though the policy and oversight participants contribute expertise in special areas.

At the end of the definition phase, management again must decide whether to continue the project through the next phase, cancel the project, or propose modifications to the project. This may cause parts or all of the initiation and definition phase to be repeated.

Key Control Objectives

As with the initiation phase, the key control objectives in the definition phase can be tied to the documents. Exhibit II-1-10 lists the documents resulting from the definition phase and the key information to be included in each document.

The definition phase controls checklist presented in Exhibit II-1-11 can be used by designers and security specialists to determine whether the key control objectives have been addressed.

PHASE 3: SYSTEM DESIGN

The objective of the system design phase is to develop detailed design specifications that describe the physical solution to the system requirements developed during the definition phase. The challenge of this phase is to determine how the requirements can be satisfied using the computer. In addition, it may be necessary to resolve deficiencies and clarify requirements in more detail so that the computer solution can be finalized and documented.

The system design phase results in a specification that provides a high-level definition of the proposed system, including information aggregates, information flows, and logical processing steps as well as major interfaces and their input and output. The purpose is to refine the problem, resolve deficiencies, define additional details, and package the system. The detailed design specifications describe the algorithms and data structures in such a way that they can be implemented in code with little or no need for additional analysis.

The validation, verification, and testing goals are also identified during this

EXHIBIT II-1-10 Information Required in the Definition Phase Documents

The project plan should contain:
- A strategy for managing the software.
- Goals and activities for all phases and subphases.
- Resource estimates for the duration of the systems development process.
- Intermediate project milestones, including management and technical reviews.
- Methods for design, documentation, problem reporting, and change control.
- Supporting techniques and tools.

The functional requirements document should contain:
- The proposed methods and procedures.
- A summary of improvements.
- A summary of impact, security, and privacy considerations.
- Cost considerations and alternatives.
- The functions required of the software, in quantitative and qualitative terms.
- How the software functions will satisfy the performance objectives.
- Performance requirements (e.g., accuracy, validation, timing, and flexibility).
- Explanation of input and output.
- The operating environment.

The functional security and internal control requirements document should contain:
- Vulnerabilities identified during the risk analysis.
- Established internal control standards and general as well as application control requirements.

The data requirements document should contain:
- Data collection requirements (both static and dynamic data).
- Logical groupings of data.
- The type of information required to document the characteristics of each data element.
- Specific identification of the information to be collected by the user.
- Specific identification of the information to be collected by the developer.
- Procedures for data collection.
- Impact of the data requirement needs.

The data sensitivity or criticality description should include:
- Sensitive and critical data.
- Sensitive and critical assets.
- Degree of sensitivity.

phase, and a plan for achieving these goals is developed. The system tests should be able to verify that required administrative, technical, and physical safeguards are operationally adequate. The project plan (e.g., schedules, budgets, and deliverables) and risk analysis are reviewed and revised as required, given the scope and complexity of the solution formulated. These activities are coordinated with the certification plan components.

EXHIBIT II-1-11 Definition Phase Controls Checklist

Control Objective	Yes	No	NA	Comments
1. A project plan has been developed that specifies the strategy for managing the software or systems development.				
2. A detailed definition of existing and new information requirements is specified.				
3. All input requirements are defined and documented.				
4. All output requirements are defined and documented.				
5. Specifications for the processing steps are defined and documented.				
6. A plan for converting from the existing process to the new one has been documented.				
7. The impact of system failures are defined, and reconstruction requirements are specified.				
8. The level of service necessary to achieve the processing objective is defined and documented.				
9. The internal control and security requirements are defined and documented.				
10. The user requirements identify critical and sensitive data and assets and describe how those items should be controlled during computer processing.				
11. Security and quality assurance tools and techniques are planned for the system.				
12. The system decision paper includes all of the information needed by user management to make a decision on action to be taken regarding the system under development.				

The System Design Phase Review

During the system design phase, three new documents are created and three documents from preceding phases are updated. The three new documents are the system, subsystem, program, and data base specifications; the security and internal controls specifications; and the validation, verification, and testing plan and specifications. The three updated documents are the audit plan, the project plan, and the system decision paper.

For many data base systems, prototype systems, and skeletal code systems, programming commences after the definition phase. Therefore, the only parts of the design phase documents that the security specialist could expect to find are:

- Operating environment, design characteristics, and program specification portions of the system, subsystem, program, and data base specifications.
- The security specifications portion of the security and internal controls specifications. Although internal controls are important, they may not be included in this document because the control portion may not have been deemed necessary in the initial prototype version. This decision to develop without controls contains serious risks, because the subsequent inclusion of controls may introduce major alterations in system behavior and cost.

In the newer developmental methods, the sponsor or user may do the testing personally by examining the output to determine whether it meets the identified needs. However, if the system must fulfill a significant business role, the security specialist should expect to find at least a minimal test plan, regardless of the type of developmental methodology.

The extent of the background work to be performed by the security specialist depends on the specialist's level of participation in the earlier phases and on the project status as perceived by the specialist at the conclusion of the previous phase (i.e., definition). The better the security specialist's understanding of the system or the better controlled the system is, the less preparatory work the specialist must do during this phase. During the system design review, the security specialist must:

- Review the definition phase output.
- Review the design phase plans.
- Gather information on the design phase status.
- Verify information on the design phase status.

The specific work within these four tasks depends on the customized review objectives selected for this phase. These four tasks are discussed in the following sections.

Reviewing the Definition Phase Output. Before beginning the survey phase of project design, the security specialist should review the results of the definition phase review. This should include reviewing any workpapers and reports prepared during the audit survey of the definition phase plus the key documents produced during the design phase.

Reviewing the Design Phase Plans. The project manager should prepare and maintain a project plan. This document contains a work plan, a schedule, a budget, individual assignments, and work tasks to be performed by the project team. The security specialist should review this plan to determine which documents are to be produced during this phase, the sequence in which those documents will be produced, to whom the task of preparing the documents has been assigned, and the schedule and effort associated with each of the work documents. This information enables the security specialist to develop an appropriate audit work schedule.

Gathering Information on the Design Phase Status. The security specialist gathers the documents appropriate to the design methodology. During the background step of the design phase audit, the security specialist needs to obtain and review the system, subsystem, program, and data base specifications; the security and internal control specifications; the validation, verification, and testing plan and specifications; the updated risk analysis; the system decision paper (including the updated cost/benefit data and analysis); and the updated project plan. Specifically, the security specialist should determine:

- *The status of these documents.* If they are not complete, additional work may need to be undertaken to complete the documents. If so, a date for their completion must be established.
- *Whether the project has proceeded according to the project plan.* If not, the specialist must determine what action is being taken to get the project back on target.
- *Whether any changes have been made to the project's function or architecture.* If so, the security specialist needs to assess how they might affect the customized review objectives for previous audit phases and this phase.

Verifying Information on the Design Phase Status. The work done to verify the information on the design phase status is based on the customized review objectives selected.

Design Methodology Review Considerations

Design methodologies may vary significantly among companies or systems. Although the initiation and definition phases remain fairly constant, there are many methodologies for designing computer systems. Among the more common approaches (which can be used alone or in combination) are:

- *Life cycle–oriented design methodologies.* The discussion in this chapter is oriented toward the life cycle design methodology. In this concept, there are distinct phases during which the design evolves. Each phase produces deliverables (i.e., products or documents) that are input to the next phase.
- *Structured design methodologies.* These are similar to the life cycle methodologies except the documents produced are different. The structured design methodologies use Warnier-Orr diagrams to illustrate the logic paths throughout the design structure.
- *Data base management systems.* In data base systems, data design is per-

formed by data base administrators, and the use of that data requires a new series of documents.

- *Skeletal code.* This design methodology is usually oriented toward a data base structure. The key design concept is the partial construction of programs. In many instances, one-half or more of the program is precoded in a generalized or skeletal format. The designers can pick and choose among these skeletal programs for use in satisfying sponsor or user needs. In addition to the skeletal code, the designers may choose utility programs, general-purpose programs (e.g., data retrieval and analysis or report generators) and languages provided by data base and data communications software.

- *Prototyping.* Prototyping incorporates two new design principles. The first is an interactive design process. Prototyping recognizes that it is difficult to define requirements correctly the first time. Therefore, prototyping produces a system as quickly as possible so that the user can determine whether or not it meets the identified needs. If not, the prototyping process continues until the right system has been designed. The second characteristic of prototyping is the collapsing of design phases. After the basic requirements have been identified, the system design and remaining phases are collapsed into a single phase.

The security specialist must first determine what design methodology was used and then learn the functional aspects of that design methodology. The design phase documents identified in this chapter may vary significantly from those the system design group actually produces. For example, if prototyping or skeletal code is used, much of the information contained in the system design documents described in this chapter may not be necessary.

When security specialists encounter an unusual design methodology, they should compare the unusual design methodology with the life cycle design methodology described in this chapter. If the same basic information is produced, the audit programs outlined in this chapter are applicable. The security specialist need only customize the review approach for the specific design methodology.

If the actual design methodology cannot be reconciled to the one described in this chapter, the security specialist should study the design methodology sufficiently to see how the life cycle phases in this chapter are collapsed by the methodology and regroup the review programs to conform to this condensed life cycle. It is then a matter of judgment to decide which parts of the review programs are applicable to this situation.

During the detailed review process, the security specialist must emphasize the three new documents created during the design phase. In addition, the security specialist must verify that the three updated documents correctly reflect changes made during the design phase. The amount of validation required depends on the degree of risk associated with the application system. The greater the risk, the more extensively the security specialist should validate the documents.

EXHIBIT II-1-12 Information Required in the System Design Phase Documents

The system, subsystem, program, and data base specifications document should:
- Specify the design requirements.
- Specify the operating environment.
- Specify the design characteristics.
- Specify the program requirements.
- Specify the program operating environment.
- Specify the program design characteristics.
- Describe the functions and performance requirements. (These performance requirements should be stated in terms of accuracy, validation, timing, flexibility, and the operating environment.)

The security and internal controls specifications document should:
- Specify the security design.
- Specify the internal control design.
- State whether the security design meets the security requirements.
- State whether the internal controls design meets the internal controls requirements.
- Be in sufficient detail so that tests can be designed that will show whether or not requirements are satisfied.
- Verify that changes to the system have been evaluated to determine whether they affect the internal controls or security design. (If system changes do affect the design, the design must be changed accordingly.)
- Verify that sensitive applications have been reviewed and approved by the party responsible for security and control.

The validation, verification, and testing plan and specifications should:
- Include a plan for testing the software.
- Include detailed specifications, descriptions, and procedures for all systems.
- Include test data reduction and evaluation criteria.
- Be related to and driven by the system plan.
- Include general project background and information on the proposed solution to the mission need.
- Include validation, verification, and testing requirements, measurement criteria, and constraints.
- Include procedures to be applied during development in general, and by phase.
- Include supporting information for validation, verification, and testing selections.
- Include appendices that describe project and environmental considerations.
- Include appendices that define the testing technique and tool selection information.

Key Control Objectives

As with the preceding phases, the key control objectives in the system design phase can be tied to the documents. During this phase, the security specialist examines the documents to verify that they are complete, reasonable, and consistent. Verification can best be accomplished by using a checklist provided with the system design methodology. If verification has already been performed by a quality assurance or project review team, the security specialist may want to go directly to the validation step. Exhibit II-1-12 lists the essential information to be verified and validated in the three new documents produced during the system design phase.

The system design phase controls checklist presented in Exhibit II-1-13 can be used by designers and security specialists to determine whether the key control objectives for this phase have been addressed.

EXHIBIT II-1-13 **Design Phase Controls Checklist**

Control Objective	Yes	No	NA	Comments
1. The revised project plan is current and provides the direction needed to effectively and efficiently manage the project.				
2. The final system design has been approved by all appropriate levels of management as meeting all predetermined needs.				
3. Sufficient data processing and security controls are incorporated in the detailed design to ensure the integrity of the system.				
4. Rules for authorizing transactions are defined and documented.				
5. Documentation suitable for use as audit trails has been incorporated into the detailed design.				
6. A vulnerability assessment has been performed.				
7. The system, subsystem, program, and data base specifications provide the correct architectural solution to meet the documented requirements from the definition phase.				
8. The security and internal control specifications provide controls adequate for satisfying the control requirements defined in the previous phase.				
9. A validation, verification, and testing plan has been developed and documented.				
10. Audit and quality assurance tools and techniques have been included in the system design documents.				
11. The system design has optimized the use of technology.				
12. The decision to develop the system continues to be supported by documents.				

PHASE 4: PROGRAMMING AND TRAINING

During the programming and training phase, programs are developed and tested. The implemented programs should be based on the detailed design specifications prepared in phase 3. If the design was well specified, programming should not be technically difficult; if there are gaps in the specifications, however, the programming phase must address those gaps before the code can be written.

Much of the success of the system is directly attributable to how well the users are trained. For example, users typically do not use those features that they do not understand, or they use those features incorrectly. Both of these impediments to a successful system can be overcome through the proper development and use of training materials.

Training is often excluded from systems development methodologies. When it is included, it usually does not adequately address training issues. Therefore, the security specialist might find a very strong developmental methodology for programming but a very weak training methodology.

In addition to programming and training, phase 4 includes preparation of user and maintenance manuals and a preliminary installation plan that specifies the approach and details of installing the new system. This phase results in programs that are ready for testing, evaluation, certification, and installation.

The Programming and Training Phase Review

Three new documents are produced during this phase: the users manual, the operations and maintenance manual, and the installation and conversion plan. As the life cycle progresses, the length and detail of system documents increases. Review of the design documents is significantly more time-consuming than review of the documents from the initiation and definition phase. Therefore, it is important for the security specialist to focus the review on the key aspects of the design documents, particularly the security and internal controls specifications document and the validation, verification, and testing plan and specifications document. The role of the security specialist is heavily directed toward assessing the adequacy of internal and security controls. Therefore, the security specialist must understand the design specifications for those controls.

In the evaluation of security and internal controls, the security specialist has three activities to perform. The first is to identify the magnitude of the risks that the system faces. Second, the security specialist must determine which security and internal controls are in place. Third, the specialist must determine whether these controls work. On the basis of these activities, the security specialist makes an assessment as to whether the controls are adequate to reduce the risk to an acceptable level.

The validation, verification, and testing plan provides the standards against which implementation will be measured and defines the test conditions that will validate controls. In addition, this document indicates how the project team plans to implement the controls. Together, these two documents should define precisely how the controls should be implemented and thus provide the guidelines for conducting the programming review.

Projects that have firm implementation dates may need to make compromises to meet those dates. For example, if the project is late going into the programming and training phase, compromises are bound to occur. Two areas frequently compromised are implementation of security and internal controls and development of training programs. The elimination or curtailment of either of these areas may not directly affect the functional correctness of system output. The system may still be able to produce the desired reports, but not in a controlled manner or in an environment in which the users are trained. Many organizations plan to address controls and training after implementation.

The project plan should specify, in writing, who is responsible for controls and training and how they are to be implemented. In reviewing the plan, the security specialist must ensure that the necessary controls and training documents are included and that there is sufficient time and resources to accomplish them.

During the detailed review process, the security specialist must evaluate the adequacy of the programming effort by reviewing results from unit, integration, and system testing. First, the security specialist should evaluate the results of quality assurance reviews of testing efforts. This evaluation should determine the effectiveness of quality assurance reviews and thereby determine the nature and extent of audit involvement in this phase. Should there not be an effective quality assurance function, security specialists must evaluate the adequacy of testing efforts themselves.

In addition to evaluating testing, the security specialist must evaluate the adequacy of documentation (i.e., user, programming, maintenance, installation, and training manuals) and training. Again, the security specialist should review quality assurance efforts in these areas and should not duplicate the work done by that function. If there is not an effective quality assurance function, the security specialist must evaluate the adequacy of the documentation produced up to this point in the systems development. Security specialists can make a significant contribution to the evaluation of documents, because they must use this documentation to understand the system, just like any system user. In addition, the security specialist should attend training sessions on the system (just like any other system user) to determine the adequacy of training efforts.

There are several automated test tools that can be used during this and the final phase. The security specialist should review both phases concurrently to determine whether the tools used in one phase might be equally appropriate for accomplishing review objectives in the other phase.

Gathering Information on Programming and Training Phase Status. Controlling system change is particularly troublesome during the programming and training phase. It is during this phase that items are implemented on a very detailed level. Because a computer works in a binary mode, there is no room for vague implementation. Therefore, it is common for many design changes to be made during programming. The security specialist must ensure that these changes are received, logged, controlled, and implemented in an orderly manner.

During implementation, the security specialist should be particularly concerned about documents being improperly or partially produced or not produced at all. Therefore, the status review of this phase should examine not only the status of the project but the status of the completed documents.

The security specialist should gather the following six documents during the programming and training phase: the updated system decision paper; the updated project plan; the updated validation, verification, and testing plan and specifications; the users manual; the operations and maintenance manual; and the installation and conversion plan. Different methodologies may use different documents, but they should contain the same information as these six. If the security specialist becomes involved near the end of the phase, all of these documents should already have been completed. If the security specialist is involved throughout the phase, he may be able to review the documents as they are prepared.

The work flow must be compared against the development methodology in use. If additional documents are produced, they should be inserted; if indicated documents are not produced or updated, that too should be noted. When documents are not produced or updated, it usually indicates a potential problem in the application design.

Verifying Information on Program and Testing Phase Starts. After gathering this information, the security specialist must verify the project status by examining two general areas. First, the specialist must verify that security and internal controls are properly implemented; and second, that all of the design specifications are implemented.

Verification requires the security specialist to review the documents being produced to ensure that the appropriate information has been collected and recorded and that it is consistent with previous documents. Verification is primarily a quality control responsibility and should be performed by the project team. In some organizations, it is performed by the quality assurance function. If it has been performed by these other functions, the security specialist need only check to make sure the quality control function is working. If the project does not have a documentation verification procedure in place, the security specialist may need to do more extensive verification.

During the programming and training phase, the security specialist must verify three new documents and three updated documents. The verification tasks required on each document are listed in Exhibit II-1-14.

EXHIBIT II-1-14 Information to Be Verified During the Programming and Training Phase

The users manual should:
- Sufficiently describe the functions.
- Be written in terminology the users will understand.
- Indicate when and how the manual is to be used.
- Serve as a reference document.
- Explain how to prepare input data and parameters.
- Explain how to interpret output results.
- Provide a full description of the application.
- Explain all of the user operating procedures.
- Explain user responsibilities related to security, privacy, and internal controls.
- Describe how to correct errors.
- Describe how to recover operations.
- Describe how to perform a file query procedure.

The operations and maintenance manual should:
- Provide computer operations personnel with a description of the software.
- Provide computer operations personnel with the instructions necessary to operate the software.
- Provide computer operations personnel with sections on nonroutine procedures, remote operations, and security requirements.
- Provide computer operations personnel with error procedures.
- Provide computer operations personnel with recovery procedures.
- Provide maintenance programmers with the information and source code necessary to understand the programs.
- Provide maintenance programmers with an overview of the architecture of the system.
- Provide maintenance programmers with maintenance guidelines.
- Provide maintenance programmers with the design of internal controls and security procedures so that they can be individually maintained.

The installation and conversion plan should:
- Explain how to install the software.
- Explain how to activate security procedures.
- Explain how to connect the software with other related software packages.
- Explain how to install the software in the operating environment.
- Be written in nontechnical language in those sections directed toward staff personnel.
- Use appropriate terminology in those sections directed toward operations personnel.

The system decision paper should:
- Have been reviewed and approved by the responsible participants.
- Contain appropriate information to verify the correctness of this document.
- Have been updated to reflect changes in strategy occurring during this phase.

(continued)

EXHIBIT II-1-14 *(continued)*

The project plan should:

- Describe a strategy for managing the software.
- State the goals and activities for all phases and subphases.
- State resource estimates for the duration of the systems development process.
- Identify the intermediate project milestones, including management and technical reviews.
- Describe the methods for design, documentation, problem reporting, and change control.
- Identify supporting techniques and tools.
- Have been updated to reflect changes in strategy occurring during this phase.
- Confirm that controls are in place for determining whether or not milestones have been met.
- Confirm that appropriate actions have been taken if milestones were not met.

The validation, verification, and testing plan and specifications should:

- Include a plan for testing the software.
- Include detailed specifications, descriptions, and procedures for all system tests.
- Include test data reduction and evaluation criteria.
- Be related to and driven by the system plan.
- Include general project background and information on the proposed solution to the mission need.
- Include validation, verification, and testing requirements, measurement criteria, and constraints.
- Include procedures to be applied during development in general, and by phase.
- Include supporting information for validation, verification, and testing selections.
- Include appendices that describe project and environmental considerations.
- Include tests of security and internal controls.
- Include appendices that define the testing technique and tool selection information.
- Have been updated to reflect changes in strategy occurring during this phase.

Audit Involvement

The review of this phase must be customized on the basis of three factors: the current status of the system design, the type of methodology used, and certain technology integration factors. These are discussed in the following sections.

The Current Status of the Design. The fewer problems involved in this application, the less need for audit involvement during this phase. Generally, if the design is properly done, only minimal audit involvement is needed during this phase. Any problems can be readily detected by security specialists in the next phase.

The Type of Design Methodology Used. Audit involvement will change significantly depending on whether the software is developed in-house, contracted, or purchased. For in-house developed software, audit involvement should be at key management checkpoints, typically at the end of development phases. For contracted software, audit involvement must be specified in the contract. It should occur at the key management checkpoints specified in the contract. These checkpoints should coincide with the contractor's development phases.

For purchased applications, the only audit involvement is an assessment of the design methodology for the purpose of determining whether adequate controls were incorporated to develop an effective application. This should be done in preparation for a decision on whether or not to purchase a particular application. The audit assessment will change significantly depending on whether more traditional statement-level languages (e.g., COBOL) are used for development or whether fourth-generation languages are an output of the system design phase, thus requiring a minimal amount of work for the implementation team.

Technology Integration Factors. During the implementation phase, the risk attributes of technology integration can be reassessed to evaluate the implementation risk. The greater the risk, the greater the need for audit involvement. The technology integration attributes that must be considered in evaluating the scope of audit work and the objectives to accomplish include:

- The makeup of the project team in relation to the technology used (i.e., number, training, and experience of team members).
- Applicability of the data processing design methodologies and standards to the technology in use.
- User knowledge of data processing technology.
- The margin of error (i.e., there should be a reasonable time to make adjustments and corrections or perform analyses before the transaction is completed).
- Availability of automated error detection and correction procedures.
- Degree of dependence on the system.
- Criticality of interfaces with other systems and external organizations.

Key Control Objectives

The programming and training phase controls checklist presented in Exhibit II-1-15 can be used by designers and security specialists to determine whether the key control objectives addressed in this phase have been met by the development process.

PHASE 5: EVALUATION AND ACCEPTANCE

The objective of this phase is to ensure that the automated information system is acceptable to the users before the system is put into a production state. During this

EXHIBIT II-1-15 Programming and Training Phase Controls Checklist

Control Objective	Yes	No	NA	Comments
1. Program documentation and programming standards are enforced to ensure that documentation is maintained in accordance with management policy.				
2. Adequate test data has been prepared for each program to validate the functioning of the executable source code.				
3. Each program includes a detailed narrative description of the processing to be performed and the logic of that processing. (Documentation may be included within the program, maintained on electronic media outside the program, or prepared manually.)				
4. All of the source code was executed during testing.				
5. Operator procedures have been prepared and adequately documented in an operations manual.				
6. A maintenance manual has been prepared with adequate information on projected maintenance needs and problems.				
7. User manuals have been prepared and adequately documented.				
8. A training plan has been prepared and documented in detail. (This may be found within or based on the users manual and the operations and maintenance manual.)				
9. Effective programming practices have been employed to take advantage of modern software engineering and computer efficiencies.				
10. Each program has been tested to ensure that it correctly performs the functions assigned to that unit.				
11. An installation and conversion plan has been prepared and adequately documented.				
12. An updated system decision paper was produced at the start of this phase.				
13. A change control process is in place for the user manual and the operations and maintenance manual.				

phase, unit testing is completed and integration and system testing are undertaken. The results of these tests provide user management with the information necessary to make a decision on whether to accept, modify, or reject the system.

The evaluation of the automated information system should be conducted in accordance with the revised validation, verification, and testing plan. Generally, three types of program testing are performed: unit, integration, and system. If performed properly, unit testing will validate the functioning of the unit; integration testing will validate the interfaces between the units and the operating environment; and system testing will validate the interaction between the application system and the user area. It is recommended that unit testing be completed before integration testing commences and that integration testing be completed before system testing commences; however, this is often difficult to achieve.

It is important that adequate time be allocated to testing. Software testing is often an underplanned and undermanaged part of the development process. This occurs because if preceding phases are late in being completed and the operational date is fixed, the amount of time and effort that is allocated to testing deteriorates to the point that it is ineffective in accomplishing its objective.

After the review, analysis, and testing of the system, including execution of the programs on test data, the system should be field tested in one or more representative operational sites. For particularly sensitive systems, disaster recovery and business continuity plans should be fully documented and operationally tested. Using actual functional transaction data, sensitive systems should be certified for technical adequacy in meeting their security requirements by an appropriate authority, before accreditation and installation. Before certification, all validation, verification, and testing results should have been documented and a comparison of actual and expected results made.

A security evaluation should be part of the broader test analysis and security evaluation report. The responsible accrediting official (e.g., the sponsor) should provide an accreditation statement that the system is operating effectively and is ready to be installed. Any caveats or restrictions should be provided at this time.

Evaluation and Acceptance Phase Review

The security specialist evaluates the work performed in the evaluation and acceptance phase by reviewing the phase documentation. This phase produces one new document (i.e., the test analysis and security evaluation report) and three updated documents (i.e., the system decision paper, the project plan, and the installation and conversion plan). The security specialist must examine all of these documents but should focus on verifying that the test analysis and security evaluation report properly implements and accomplishes the test plan objective. In addition, the specialist must verify that the test results are properly reflected in the evaluation report.

The objective of this phase is to identify and remove defects from the completed system. This is accomplished through creation of a series of test conditions that, when processed against the executable code, produce the proper results. If the proper results are obtained, the system is judged correct, if the results are not appropriate, the system is deemed inadequate.

The security specialist may wish to review some of the documents from the earlier phases because they indicate what the system is supposed to do. For example, the programming phase documents are oriented toward what the system does to meet its objectives, whereas, the user manual explains how the system is to be operated by the end users.

It is important that the security specialist ensure that the test data and testing documentation are saved for use in validating subsequent changes to the system and for auditor use, as required.

This final development phase is frequently squeezed between the point at which the programs are complete and the date when those programs must be placed into production. If the production date is firm, insufficient time may be allocated to this phase. Therefore, it becomes essential that the security specialist review the plans to verify that at least the most critical system functions are tested.

It is unrealistic to expect exhaustive testing to occur, though it is certainly desirable. There are always compromises to testing because of budgets and schedules. In many instances, there are no options regarding when the system is placed into production, particularly when it is mandated by legislation. What is important is to optimize the test time available.

Gathering Information on Evaluation and Acceptance Phase Status. Reports should be maintained on the status of tests. The criteria for testing should be included in the validation, verification, and testing plan. This document indicates which functions are to be tested and what conditions will be used to test those functions.

Units or programs should be tested first. Once these have been validated as performing correctly, the integration or interfaces between the units or programs are tested. Once these interfaces have been validated, the acceptance test occurs, which validates the interfaces between users and the system.

The test status reports should indicate which functions have been tested, which functions work, which functions are in the process of being corrected, and when those functions should be retested. The security specialist should be able to determine how many functions have been validated and how many remain unvalidated. If this status information is not available, the security specialist should be concerned about whether the end product of testing will be able to indicate system performance before it is placed into production. Without this information, management cannot make a realistic business decision regarding whether or not the system should be placed into production.

During this phase, the security specialist should analyze the following documents:

- The test analysis and security evaluation report, including certification and accreditation statements.
- The updated installation and conversion plan.
- The updated users manual.
- The updated operations and maintenance manual, including change control.
- The updated project plan.

EXHIBIT II-1-16 Evaluation and Acceptance Phase Controls Checklist

Control Objective	Yes	No	NA	Comments
1. Unit, module, and integration testing were conducted according to the test plan and applicable test standards.				
2. Test results have been evaluated by data processing management and user management to verify that the system functions properly.				
3. Test results were recorded and retained as part of the system documentation.				
4. Circumstances under which a parallel run of both existing and new systems is desirable have been identified, and criteria for termination of the run are clearly stated.				
5. The conversion plan has been updated to include assignment of individual responsibilities.				
6. Adequate provisions have been made to ensure continuity of processing.				
7. Security evaluation, certification, and accreditation have been performed, and appropriate documents and statements have been prepared.				
8. The installation and conversion plan has been updated and represents the current status of the system.				
9. The users manual has been updated and represents the current status of the system.				
10. The operations and maintenance manual has been updated and represents the current status of the system.				
11. The project plan has been updated and represents the current status of the system.				
12. The system decision paper has been updated and represents the current status of the system.				

Verifying Information on the Evaluation and Acceptance Phase Status. By the time this phase commences, all of the work necessary to develop the application system should be complete and the organization should have an executable system. The security specialist must ensure, however, that the executable system meets the system requirements and specifications.

The work in the evaluation and acceptance phase is primarily a series of tests. Many modules (i.e., computer subprograms) are developed during this phase. Each module must be individually tested and then pulled together into programs. (Some of the programs may involve utility programs and other aspects of operating software.) The programs are then tested to validate that the modules work correctly together. Finally, the programs are all put together as an information system and that system is validated to ensure that it works in the operating environment when interfacing with other systems and to verify that it meets user requirements.

The security specialist must become familiar with the work flow of this phase, including the various types of testing and the expected results from those tests. As in other aspects of systems development, the exact flow of documents varies depending on the design methodology and the companies themselves.

Key Control Objectives

The evaluation and acceptance phase controls checklist presented in Exhibit II-1-16 can be used by designers and security specialists to determine whether the key controls in this phase have been met by the development process.

SUMMARY

This chapter describes in detail the steps the security specialist should take to ensure that security controls are not overlooked when a new system or application is being developed. By conducting a review of each development phase, the specialist can better evaluate the status of the project and confirm that the required controls have been provided. The checklists for each of the systems development phases should help the specialist verify that the controls associated with that phase have been addressed, thus ensuring that the final product meets security requirements.

Developing Secure Systems

WILLIAM PERRY

The best opportunity to build a secure system of internal control in a computerized application system is during systems development. During the development phases, changes and extensions to the system of internal control can be accomplished with considerably less cost and effort than after the system becomes operational. Once the system becomes operational, it may not be practical to make modifications. The participation of security specialists during the design phase helps ensure that the internal controls specified by the systems analyst provide adequate system integrity.

If security specialists are heavily involved in the development of computerized applications, they can review each aspect of the design as it is being considered. This is not an efficient use of security resources, however. In addition, it is often inefficient to have the systems developers' work checked every step of the way. The most feasible method for building a secure system is to have the security specialists perform a review at key points in the systems development life cycle (SDLC); these key points are called payoff points. This chapter identifies the payoff points in the systems development life cycle and provides guidance as to the appropriate steps to take at each of these payoff points in order to develop a secure system

THE ROLE OF SECURITY SPECIALISTS IN SYSTEM DESIGN

The security specialist's role in system design is twofold: first, to review and comment on the adequacy of the security features in computer applications; and second, to review and comment on the adequacy of controls over the systems development process. Because of the lack of control standards and the inability of most systems analysts to comprehend what is meant by internal controls, the security specialist must play a more active role than is desirable. In an effort to develop standards and to educate the systems analyst, many security specialists have been involved in designing security mechanisms. This is necessary because of the current state of the art in control and audit of computerized applications.

Ideally, the data processing department should have standards in both areas: the application security features and the controls over the systems development process. If this is so, the role of the security specialists is primarily in verifying compliance with these standards. The following sections discuss these two areas in more detail.

Application Security Features

The responsibility for the specification of application system controls rests with the user department. Responsibility for the implementation of these controls lies with the systems analysts and programmers. Although the user has responsibility for the total system of control, the data processing personnel must assume responsibility for implementing controls within the computerized application.

Security specialists should interact with both the user and the system designer during the developmental stage to evaluate the adequacy of audit provisions. If security specialists become involved at key points (i.e., payoff points) in the process, their effectiveness increases. By selecting payoff points within the SDLC, the security specialist can verify the adequacy of control at these points and, with minimum effort, ensure a system of adequate control.

Controls over the Development Process

The second function of security specialists is to monitor the development process itself. There appears to be a high degree of correlation between a well-managed developmental process and a well-controlled data processing application. If the data processing department has an effective systems management approach, there is greater assurance that the system of internal controls will also be adequate. A systematic approach to system design facilitates the work of the security specialist in checking the system at the payoff points.

SECURITY SPECIALIST QUALIFICATIONS

Security requirements in the systems development process call for assigning the most skilled security specialists to the task. Many organizations feel that the security specialist on the systems development security review should be as skilled in data processing as the lead systems analyst. As organizations adopt the payoff point approach, the skill levels required diminish to some degree.

At a minimum, the individual assigned to a systems development security review should have the following:

- An advanced knowledge of data processing fundamentals.
- Programming skills.
- System flowcharting skills.
- Advanced knowledge in data and file definition.
- Knowledge of data processing operations.

- Knowledge of the area in which the application will occur.
- Knowledge of the organization's policies and procedures.
- Advanced skills in data processing control techniques.

APPLICATION SECURITY AND CONTROLS

There are two distinct steps to designing an adequate system of internal controls. The first step is to determine an acceptable level of risk for the organization. The security specialist should determine whether the level of risk established by the user and data processing departments is in agreement with the policies, procedures, and long-range plans of the organization.

Once this has been verified, the second step is to implement a system of internal controls designed to ensure that acceptable level of risk. The security specialist reviews the control and feedback objectives established by the project team to determine whether they will achieve the desired quality of processing and maintain an acceptable level of risk. For example, if it is determined that orders will be accepted up to the authorized credit limit of any customer, the system should be designed to process all orders up to that limit and to reject all orders over the limit unless they have received additional approval.

The following sections discuss these steps in more detail.

Step 1: Determining the Acceptable Level of Risk

The key building block for secure systems is to determine the level of risk that management is willing to assume. Once this is known, all other steps in providing security for a computer application can be specified. The acceptable level of risk refers to the following types of conditions:

- The amount of loss an organization will accept on a transaction.
- The percentage of errors that will be tolerated before corrective action must be taken.
- The desired level of service.
- The tolerance that is acceptable between computer-generated amounts and actual amounts (e.g., when payments are within plus or minus $5 of amount due, the payment is accepted as correct).
- The acceptable types and levels of penetration.

It is uneconomical to operate a computer system without risk of loss and error; on the other hand, performance cannot degrade to the point at which the organization is threatened. Systems must perform at the highest possible level between these extremes. What is important is that management, rather than computer programmers, determine the acceptable level of risk.

In determining an acceptable level of risk, the major processing elements of a system must be identified, including:

- Control over the completeness and accuracy of input documents.
- Control over the receipt of input documents.
- The amount of time to process a transaction.
- The acceptable variance for each key data field in the system.
- The acceptable cost to process a transaction.
- The acceptable levels of error in processing each type of transaction.
- The point at which manual authorization must be received for override.
- A definition of the types of transactions that will not be processed (e.g., a shipment on credit to a foreign country).

Until management sets forth specifications for these processing elements, control objectives cannot be set. Security specialists are often accused of striving toward too high a level of control. On the other hand, many security specialists accuse users of trying to get by with too low a level of control. If management has established an acceptable level of risk, the process of setting control objectives and implementing controls will center on cost-effective methods rather than what controls should be implemented.

Step 2: Evaluating the Adequacy of Controls

The development of control guidelines has lagged behind the development of other data processing concepts. The fact that there are no generally accepted control guidelines has been cause for concern on the part of many, including executive management and customers, about the reliability and credibility of computer-produced information.

A checklist should be developed for each payoff point in the systems development cycle. (A sample checklist is presented later in this chapter.) Security specialists are encouraged to give these checklists to systems analysts to provide them with the security specialist's viewpoint of control. If the systems analyst tries to implement a system of internal control on the basis of these checklists, the security specialists' tasks will be greatly simplified. Security specialists then need only to assess the effectiveness of the implemented control, as opposed to the time-consuming process of first convincing the systems analyst of the need for a control and, second, working with the systems analyst on a method for implementing the control.

The security specialist has five areas of concern when establishing application control objectives:

- *Correctness of data handling and completeness of data.* This includes correct processing.

- *File integrity*. This includes correctness of data handling, completeness of data, auditability, and security of computerized files.
- *Error procedures*. This involves completeness of detecting and reporting errors to the proper level of management, together with the reentry procedures.
- *Data retention*. This includes having the necessary data for both audit and rerun purposes.
- *Audit trail*. This allows transactions to be traced from inception through the organization's books of accounts, and vice versa.

When setting objectives that provide these features, the security specialist must consider three elements: ensuring an acceptable level of risk, establishing a control methodology (including practices, tools, and techniques), and conducting a cost/benefit analysis of the controls. When available control methods and their costs are examined, it might be necessary to reexamine the stated acceptable level of risk.

Control objectives should be stated specifically. The best method of documenting a control objective is to develop a positive statement of performance, which may be seen as another way of stating the acceptable level of risk. Examples of statements of performance include:

- Payments within plus or minus $5 of invoice amounts will be accepted as paid in full.
- Stock should be on hand to fill 97% of all orders received.
- Of the orders received, 95% should be filled and shipped within 48 hours and 99% should be shipped within 10 working days.
- Of all keyed input data, 99.5% should be correct.
- Of all rejected transactions, 96% should be reentered within 24 hours.

When control objectives have been stated in such terms, systems designers can develop a system that meets these levels of control performance. In addition, these statements provide a means of evaluating the effectiveness of systems designers once the system becomes operational.

The remaining key element is the design and use of feedback mechanisms. For example, if 95% of all orders received are to be shipped within 24 hours, a monitoring mechanism must be established to ensure that this performance level is maintained. A feedback mechanism should be built into the application so that when performance drops below the acceptable level, management is notified.

OVERVIEW OF THE PAYOFF POINTS

When viewing the SDLC, the security specialist should focus on the payoff points to help determine how the controls should be developed, documented, implemented, and enforced. The five phases of an SDLC can be identified as initiation, definition, system design, programming and training, and evaluation and acceptance. In reality, one phase does not stop abruptly and another start; rather, the phases flow into one another, and many phases occur simultaneously. This is further complicated by the fact that problems encountered in a later phase may call for a reexecution of previous phases to correct the problems.

Exhibit II-1-17 shows the five phases of the system life cycle and the 18 recommended payoff points. The following sections briefly explain the management decisions that must be made during each of the five phases and describe the 18 payoff points. Later sections describe the payoff points in more detail.

Phase 1: Initiation

Senior management must determine whether there is enough merit in having a new system to warrant a study. When the project is first organized (the first payoff point), a team should be selected to conduct a study and make a recommendation as to whether or not a new system (or major extension to an existing system) should be undertaken. The security specialist should ensure that all parties with a vested interest in the new system are represented on the study team. The present system should then be reviewed to identify the methods by which the work is currently being accomplished. Even when a completely new system is being considered, an examination of the existing system can provide essential insight. The security specialist should make audit reports about the present system available to the study team, to make the team aware of known problems and strengths.

EXHIBIT II-1-17 Phases of the System Life Cycle

	Payoff Points
Phase 1: Initiation	• Project organization • Review of present system • Cost/benefit analysis • Project team formation
Phase 2: Definition	• Conceptual design of system • Output report design • Input screen design
Phase 3: System Design	• Data base and file design • Computer processing design • Equipment requirements • Communications network design • Error-handling design
Phase 4: Programming and Training	• System documentation • Detailed system design • System development • Operations and user controls
Phase 5: Evaluation and Acceptance	• System testing • Conversion

Next, a detailed cost/benefit analysis should be conducted to identify the costs of developing and operating a new system, the savings or extra expenses that may result from use of the new system, and the expected return on investment. The security specialist should conduct an independent review to verify that the costs have been properly collected and presented.

A project team should be formed, including systems personnel, users, and other interested parties that will help design the new system. The security specialist should verify that all the necessary parties are represented on the team and that the internal audit department has the opportunity to interact with the project team.

Phase 2: Definition

After management has agreed that a new system is warranted, system requirements must be defined. First, a conceptual design should be developed to show the general systems flow and associated data, illustrating how the new system will operate. This design should identify equipment components, processing times, general methods of operation, manual interfaces, and interfaces with other systems and accounting records. The security specialist is responsible for verifying that the audit and control needs have been considered in the design.

In addition, the required output reports must be designed. The security specialist should ensure that the necessary control data is being reported.

Input screens must also be designed to show how the input will be entered into the system. Input may be entered through manual preparation of forms or machine-readable documents, or it may be keyed into terminals. The security specialist must ensure that all the needed data is entered into the system and that appropriate controls exist over the input so that erroneous data and unauthorized entries are detected.

Phase 3: Systems Design

This detailed design phase reconfirms the plans developed in the preceding phase and authorizes implementing the next phase of development.

The first payoff point in this phase is to design the data base and files. The security specialist should verify that the custodial responsibility of the data processing function is fulfilled. The data trusted to the data processing department should be appropriately controlled and returned intact when needed.

Next, a detailed computer processing flowchart must be designed, showing how the transactions will be processed through the computer system. The specialist must verify that the audit and control requirements have been taken into consideration in the design of the system.

Detailed equipment requirements for operating the system must then be established. The requirements analysis usually confirms or rejects the estimates calculated during the cost/benefit analysis conducted during phase 1. The security specialist should review the system design to ensure that it conforms to the organization's policies and procedures. If financial calculations are involved, they should be reviewed independently.

The communications network used to transfer data between operating facilities must also be designed. This may be an in-house network or a network through public communications lines. The security specialist should evaluate network security to verify that transactions are not lost, that queues are controlled, and that unauthorized penetration of the network is detected. Finally, error-handling features must be designed to establish methods for detecting errors, rejecting them from the system with appropriate messages, and controlling errors through correction and reentry.

Phase 4: Programming and Training

The system design must be documented, including a field-by-field list of the information and acceptable values that can be contained in each field. The security specialist should learn the contents of the data file for potential audit uses and should provide an independent opinion as to the completeness of this documentation.

A detailed system design must then be developed to specify the programs contained in the system. The security specialist should be heavily involved in reviewing and specifying, as necessary, the control requirements of the system. (This is an area subject to strong negotiation with systems personnel, to ensure that the controls are economically installed and yet meet the control requirements.) System programming can then begin.

Finally, operations and user controls are identified to show how the operations segment of the system will be controlled and how users will control the system once it is in operation. This payoff point includes training both operations and user personnel. The specialist assists in and gives advice on the development of the procedures and methods by which the operations and user groups can determine whether the system is functioning properly.

It should be noted that in some fourth-generation languages and CASE tools, the definition, systems design, and programming phases, excluding training, may be combined through iterative development.

Phase 5: Evaluation and Acceptance

At this point, management and the user department approve the system and it goes into the test phase. This usually consists of acceptance testing conducted by the user; it may also include some integration and system testing within the data processing department.

The first payoff point in this phase is system testing. The security specialist must review the adequacy and type of test data (which may involve developing some test data). In addition, the specialist should independently review the results of the tests to determine whether the implemented system meets the specifications.

Data must then be converted from the old format to the new format. The security specialist must verify that controls are in place to ensure data integrity during the conversion process.

After all testing and conversions are completed, management, the user department, and independent parties must reach an agreement as to whether the system meets specifications and is ready to be put into production.

PROJECT MANAGEMENT

The security specialist must oversee the use of the organization's resources during the development project. The main concerns that security specialists have in reviewing project management are:

- Have adequate resources been assigned to the project?
- Are the individuals assigned to the project competent to do the job?
- Is sufficient time available to do the job properly?
- Do the objectives and goals of the project fit the long-range plans of the organization?
- Is the project on schedule?
- Is the project within budget constraints?
- Is management adequately monitoring and evaluating the project?

The payoff point checklists address these questions. After reviewing the system at one of the payoff points, security specialists should be able to give management information on these project management concerns and on the adequacy of the system of internal controls up to that point in systems development. Security specialists can use the payoff points to ascertain the status of both the system of internal application controls and the project itself.

The use of payoff points optimizes audit time. Rather than devote large amounts of resources to the systems development effort, security specialists can checkpoint those aspects of the system they deem important. If the system is progressing to the satisfaction of the security specialists, the time they spend on the project will be kept to a minimum. When problems occur, security specialist involvement will increase.

Security specialists should meet with systems analysts at the various checkpoints and:

- Ascertain the accomplishments since the last checkpoint.
- Review the questions on the appropriate payoff point checklist.
- Verify the authenticity of the reply to questions, as needed. This involves examining evidence.
- Make a judgment about the adequacy of the system of internal controls at this point and about the status of the project.

- Make any appropriate recommendations. If the system is encountering severe difficulties, a meeting with management may be required.
- Agree on the date for the next checkpoint review.

Security specialists must determine the amount of time that will be allocated to a particular systems development project. Once that has been determined, the hours can be broken down by the various checkpoints. Exhibit II-1-18 shows a suggested percentage of security specialist involvement in each payoff point. For example, if 100 hours were allocated to a particular project, one hour would be allocated for a review of the first payoff point, two hours to the second payoff point, and so one.

Although the largest amount of time is devoted to the detailed system design, system testing, and conversion phases, this is not necessarily indicative of the value received for time expended. The greatest value is achieved during the earlier life cycle phases. Although security specialists do not determine in the earlier phases how controls will be implemented, they can emphasize control philosophy. This enables the systems analysts to understand the objectives and may enable the security specialists to fulfill much of their mission. (The remaining part of the mission is to determine whether the implementation achieves control objectives.)

Security specialists face unique reporting problems when involved in systems development. The major problem faced by security specialists is determining how to work with the systems development personnel while reporting their weaknesses and problems to management.

EXHIBIT II-1-18 **Involvement in Phase of System Life Cycle**

Payoff Point	Security Involvement	Suggested Percentage of Total Review Time
Project Organization	Minimal	1%
Review of Present System	Minimal	2
Cost/Benefit Analysis	Some	3
Project Team Formation	Little	1
Conceptual Design of System	Minimal	2
Output Report Design	Some	3
Input Screen Design	Heavy	5
Data Base and File Design	Heavy	5
Computer Processing Design	Heavy	5
Equipment Requirements	Minimal	2
Communications Network Design	Heavy	5
Error-Handling Design	Heavy	10
System Documentation	Some	3
Detailed System Design	Very heavy	15
System Development	Minimal	3
Operations and User Controls	Heavy	15
System Testing	Heavy	10
Conversion	Heavy	10
Total		100%

PAYOFF POINTS CHECKLISTS

The payoff points concept is designed to make productive use of the security specialist's participation in system design. It assumes a methodical process for systems development. If the organization is unable to define the various phases of the process, the payoff point technique is difficult to implement. In this chapter, the five systems development phases have a total of 18 payoff points. This organization may be adapted to meet the needs of a particular company.

The security specialist in charge of an assignment should create a planning sheet at the beginning of the assignment. The purpose of the planning sheet is to schedule the 18 payoff point review dates. It should be recognized that setting dates for all five phases of the development cycle cannot be precise. The security specialist should instead provide approximate dates, to determine whether there will be resources available when the checkpoint date occurs.

The payoff points planning sheet presented in Exhibit II-1-19 provides a mechanism for scheduling and reporting on the payoff point reviews. At the beginning of the development of an application system, the security specialist in charge should list the 18 payoff point review dates as accurately as practical. In addition, the contact for each review should be listed; it may be the same individual for all 18 reviews, or it may be several individuals. After the review has been completed, a review score should be calculated and entered on the planning sheet together with any comments the security specialist cares to make on the checkpoint review. (The review score is discussed in the conclusion to this chapter.) As actual review dates near, they can be verified or changed to reflect actual review dates. The planning sheet (see Exhibit II-1-19) gives the security specialist in charge a quick synopsis of the scores from previous years. (The review process may last several months or years.) This score provides some guidance as to the required intensity of the next review.

The following sections describe the 18 payoff point reviews. The payoff points are grouped according to their respective life cycle phases.

INITIATION PHASE PAYOFF POINTS

Although the security specialist spends a relatively small amount of time on the four payoff point reviews during this phase, the time is extremely critical. The suggested allocation of total security specialist involvement time for these four payoff point reviews is only 7% (see Exhibit II-1-18), yet the influence the specialist can have on the system during this phase is more extensive than at any other phase.

During this phase, it is suggested that the security specialist:

- Explain to the project team what is meant by accounting-type internal controls.

EXHIBIT II-1-19 Payoff Points Planning Sheet

Payoff Point	Review Date	Contact	Review Score		Comments
			Key Questions	Other Questions	
Phase 1: Initiation Project Organization Review of Present System Cost/Benefit Analysis Project Team Formation					
Phase 2: Definition Conceptual Design of System Output Report Design Input Screen Design					

Phase 3: System Design
Data Base and File Design
Computer Processing
  Design
Equipment Requirements
Communications Network
  Design
Error-Handling Design					

Phase 4: Programming and Training System Documentation Detailed System Design System Development Operations and User Controls					
Phase 5: Evaluation and Acceptance System Testing Conversion					

- Provide the lead systems analyst with the questionnaire checklists for all 18 payoff point reviews.
- Explain the importance of controls.
- Explain the security specialist's involvement in the development process (including how and to whom reports will be made).
- Review with the systems personnel the typical control weaknesses in data processing applications, and explain how they can be improved through adequate control mechanisms.
- Discuss the approach of risk analysis and the setting of control objectives.
- Work with the systems analysts in risk evaluation and setting control objectives.

- Offer to make presentations on security and control to future members of the development team.
- Offer to provide the systems development team with literature on security and control.

At the conclusion of the four payoff point reviews in the initiation phase, executive management decides whether or not to go ahead with the development project. If the decision is to go ahead, the organization will commit considerable resources to the project. It is highly unlikely that the system will be scrapped after management decides to go ahead. Traditionally, extensions of schedule dates and budget increases are obtained, and system modifications are made to overcome shortcomings uncovered during later system life cycle phases. Therefore, security specialists should take an extremely critical look at the system by the end of the fourth payoff point and should be prepared to advise management not to go ahead with the project if either of the following conditions occur:

- Provisions have not been made to develop an adequate system of internal controls.
- Provision has not been made for an orderly plan, with sufficient resources, to implement the proposed system on time and within budget.

Project Organization

The checklist for this payoff point is provided in Exhibit II-1-20 to show what these checklists should look like. This particular checklist should be designed to evaluate the competency of the project team. It serves the purpose of introducing the team to the security specialist and the security specialist to the team. Ideally, this should be accomplished at one of the early status meetings held by the project team. At this point, the project team should have been selected and should have held an organizational meeting, in which responsibilities are assigned. Typically, the security specialist would develop answers to the questions in the checklist through discussions with project team members about their roles and responsibilities.

Review of Present System

If the security specialist assignments are made properly, the security specialist in charge of systems development should be knowledgeable about the present system. If not, it is desirable to have the security specialist conduct a review of the area in which the new system will operate. At the time of this review, the project team should have completed its analysis of the strengths, weaknesses, and procedures of the present system.

EXHIBIT II-1-20 Sample Payoff Point Checklist: Project Organization

Key Question	Control Evaluation				Comments
	Strong	Adequate	Weak	NA	
1. Have formal requests for the new or revised data processing applications been prepared and submitted with proper authorization signatures?					
2. Have adequate resources been provided to the project team so that they can successfully complete this phase of the project?					
3. Will executive management track the project so that they know whether or not the objectives and time schedules are being met?					
4. Has a list of project tasks to be accomplished been developed, as well as a schedule for accomplishing those tasks?					
5. Do the security objectives of the project fit within the long-range security plans of the organization?					
6. Can the security specialists assigned to the project spend sufficient time on this assignment?					
7. Has responsibility for the system been assigned to specific individuals, who are aware of the limits and scope of their responsibilities?					
8. Is there sufficient division of responsibility in the project?					
9. Will the project leader notify the internal audit department of important update and control meetings in which they should participate?					

It is possible that the new system application will encompass pieces of several existing systems. This may require some conceptual analysis of problems that would result from combining parts or all of two or more existing systems.

Cost/Benefit Analysis

Data processing is often accused of underestimating costs and overestimating benefits. It is difficult to validate this, however, because conditions typically change enough from the date of design to the date of operation to make comparisons difficult.

Security specialists should outline costs and benefits in enough detail so that a postimplementation review can validate these estimates. A review objective should be established to determine, after implementation, if both cost and benefit estimates have been met. Variations should be explained so that future projects can benefit from this experience.

If cost guidelines are available (e.g., the cost to write, debug, and document a program), they should be used by the security specialist to verify the reliability of estimates. Cost and benefit estimates should be compared with the results of previous systems as an additional check on their reliability. Currently, some organizations make managers responsible for their projections for new data processing applications. For example, if they state that a new application can handle X volume of work with Y workers, they are restricted to a budget that forces them to achieve those levels. If such a policy is clearly stated to responsible managers before they review system proposals, they will take a greater interest in the estimates of cost and benefits shown in these proposals.

Project Team Formation

If the project team has the necessary talent and resources, there is a high probability that a successful system will be developed. Although security specialists traditionally do not evaluate user personnel, their independent judgment as to the competence of the project team can be valuable to executive management. The security specialist is not expected to evaluate the detailed technical competence of the systems development team but can be expected to make some general judgments on attitude, ability, knowledge of the area, ability to get along with people, and ability to communicate with other members of the project team. The security specialist can interview others to confirm opinions as to the competence of project team members. If no one on the team possesses certain necessary knowledge or skills, additional people may be added to the team to compensate for this. For example, if no one on the team is knowledgeable about control techniques, the involvement of security personnel may be expanded to compensate for that weakness.

DEFINITION PHASE PAYOFF POINTS

The systems definition phase provides an overall framework for the system and offers control objectives. The security specialist's main interest and concern during the three payoff point reviews in this phase are:

- If time and budget constraints occur, will security requirements still be met?
- Will the control objectives be met through the design criteria?
- Are there adequate feedback mechanisms to determine whether controls are functioning correctly?
- Does the system monitor to determine whether action has to be taken by management to correct control problems?

The security specialist should ensure that users are involved in this phase so that their control requirements are included in the overall system design.

Conceptual Design of the System

The conceptual design created during the system planning phase usually contains the key elements of what the final system will look like. Security specialists should not assume that flaws in conceptual design will be corrected during the refinement of this conceptual design. All too frequently, systems analysts ignore control during the conceptual design phase, leaving the development of controls until the time when the system is implemented. They fail to recognize that implementers tend to follow these early blueprints closely.

The security review after the conceptual design is perhaps the key payoff point review for influencing design. If the security specialist were to expend extra time on any review, this would be the one. Within the conceptual design should be a methodology for controlling the application system. The plan should include commitment of resources to implement these controls.

Output Report Design

The usefulness of the system is related to the type of information the system can provide. A method of evaluating this is to analyze the completeness and usefulness of output reports. The type of information produced by a system is related to the information contained within the system. Therefore, the analysis of output indirectly evaluates the adequacy of input.

The concept of security specialists evaluating output instead of input has two advantages. First, it is difficult to analyze the usefulness of input elements in strictly an input context. Second, the security specialist is more familiar with using output information and therefore is better qualified to evaluate it. In examining output, the security specialist should be particularly concerned about reporting of error conditions, reporting of control information, reporting of override conditions, and usefulness of security report data to the system users.

Input Screen Design

This is one of the high-risk payoff points. Experience shows that most system manipulation occurs through input violations. The security specialist should ensure that only authorized transactions can be entered and that there is a high probability that unauthorized transactions will be detected.

The checklist for this payoff point should provide an overview of the type of controls the security specialist should look for. This checklist should be divided into batch input and online input. The security specialist is specifically concerned about:

- Are all input transactions controlled?
- Is there assurance that only authorized transactions will be entered?
- Are there controls to ensure that all appropriate input transactions are in fact entered in the system?
- Are there controls over transactions throughout the system to ensure that none are lost or manipulated?

SYSTEM DESIGN PHASE PAYOFF POINTS

These are the payoff points in which most of the security time is consumed: Approximately one-half of the review effort is expended in this phase. The time expended is extensive because the security specialists must become heavily enmeshed in the detail to verify that the security design and control criteria do what they were designed to accomplish. Although the previous phases can be handled on a conceptual basis, the design phase must be very specific.

During these payoff points, the security specialist must verify that the methods of implementation meet the control objectives. Too frequently, there is miscommunication. This is particularly true in the security area, because the systems designer and systems programmer may not be familiar with security practices. For example, in one case, a systems analyst did not realize that in accounting, debits must equal credits. In that system, it was possible to enter only half an accounting entry. It was not until several months after implementation that the flaw was discovered and the out-of-balance condition corrected.

During the system design phase, the main concerns to the security specialist are:

- The system implemented meets the system security specifications.
- The system implemented incorporates the control objectives.

- The system will be implemented on time and within budget. (Tight schedules may cause security tasks to be reduced or eliminated.)
- Adequate documentation has been developed.
- The user personnel will be adequately trained.
- User personnel will be satisfied with the system when it is designed.
- The user personnel will be involved in the system testing process.
- The conversion system is adequately controlled.
- The system is auditable.
- There is an adequate audit trail and backup facilities.

Data Base and File Design

This is a high-risk payoff point for the security specialist. The objective of many unauthorized transactions is to manipulate, change, delete, or add data to the data base or files. The security specialist's objective is to review the adequacy of data base and file controls.

Many of these controls are general controls. For example, applications may use organizational data bases. In those instances, the data base controls and the certification of security over those data bases may have been done in a general review. The controls placed in the checklist for this payoff point should apply primarily to data base management systems. However, many of these controls are also applicable to dedicated files. The sections dealing with input and output should also address control over dedicated files.

Computer Processing Design

The objective of the security specialist when evaluating the computer processing design is to determine whether the control objectives can be met by the design, whether the user security specifications will be met by the design, and whether the design is practical from a user's viewpoint (e.g., turnaround times, complexity of documents, and access controls). At this stage in the development cycle, the security specialist is still concerned about general objectives and specifications. The security specialist is trying to identify the approaches used by the systems designer to meet those design and control objectives. The questions on this checklist should be broad in scope.

Equipment Requirements

Data processing applications consume the resources of the organization. The security specialist's concern in this payoff point is the proper use of those resources. In some organizations, quality assurance groups have been established to concentrate on this area. In those cases, the security specialist merely verifies that the quality assurance function is being performed properly.

When quality assurance groups are not used, security specialists should assume that function. This involves determining whether the application is run on the right equipment, whether there is sufficient capacity within the equipment to run the system, or whether there are plans to increase capacity. In addition, the security specialist should ensure that unusual design criteria are not being proposed that would interfere with the overall efficiency of the total computer operation (e.g., larger than normal storage requirements).

Communications Network Design

Two general types of networks exist. One is local area networks (LANs), which are usually under the control of the organization but may come under the control of the common carrier. When common carriers are involved, the security risk increases.

The checklist for this payoff point should provide an assessment of the adequacy of communications controls. Like the data base, however, the communications controls may have been evaluated under a general control audit. If so, this step can be skipped by the security specialist when certifying to the adequacy of controls in a specific application.

Error-Handling Design

Another high-risk component of an application system is the error-handling routines. Many application systems only reject errors; they do not control them through the correction and reentry point. The security specialist should be specifically alert to how rejected transactions are controlled to avoid manipulation during the correction and reentry process.

The checklist for this payoff point should provide an assessment of the error-handling controls. This checklist should be divided into batch and online error handling, because the type of assessment will vary depending on whether the error has occurred in a batched entry or an online entry.

PROGRAMMING AND TRAINING PHASE PAYOFF POINTS

This phase involves implementation of the system according to the specifications created during the system design phase. If the system design phase has been effectively performed, implementation will not require extensive audit analysis. If the system design is vague, however, the security specialist may need to spend a lot of time reviewing the implementation.

During this phase, it is suggested that the security specialist:

- Ensure that documentation is complete and clear.
- Ensure that a training plan has been developed for the end users of the system.

- Verify that the security controls are implemented according to specifications.
- Ensure that end users have adequate operations manuals, including security procedural controls.
- Ensure that end users are adequately trained in using the application.
- Ensure that the completed programs and documentation are adequately safeguarded.

At the conclusion of this phase, the system is ready to go into final testing and operation. At this point, the data processing department should certify that the system has been built in accordance with specifications. The security specialist may be a member of the team reviewing the adequacy of security controls and may want to give an opinion on how effectively the controls have been implemented.

Definition of Data

Although the success of a system can be measured by the adequacy of the output, the accuracy and completeness of the system can be determined by the control over data input and storage. Therefore, the first step in implementation is to verify that data has been adequately defined. The definition of data includes:

- Types of data that can be included in a field (e.g., completeness of codes and types of information).
- Reviews to be executed on that data.
- Methods for handling rejected data.
- Who has responsibility for input of the data.
- Who has the responsibility for use of the data.
- Retention cycle of the data.
- Authorized uses of the data.
- Who will use the data (e.g., which programs, systems, or individuals).
- Security classifications of the data.
- Risk to the organization if data is lost, compromised, or modified.
- Places in which data will reside (e.g., input storage, data files, or such output usages as microfilm).
- Places where the data will be used.

Detailed System Design

This phase requires the heaviest review in terms of time expenditure. It is only through detailed analysis that the security specialist can determine whether or not design and control objectives have been met. The security specialist must review the details of a design to make a judgment on the implementation of the design and control criteria.

The checklist for this payoff point could be simply a list of questions. The review itself, however, may require examining program code or flowcharts to answer the questions in the checklist. It is highly probable that the systems programmers will not understand some of the objectives being implemented, because they will be following design instructions from the systems analyst and in this translation from design specifications to program code, there can be considerable misunderstandings. These misunderstandings often cause problems in operation.

System Development

The major functions of the security specialist should have been satisfied in the previous review. Within this payoff point, the systems programmer performs the actual coding and debugging. The function of the security specialist is to verify that specifications are not changed during the programming phase.

Frequently, systems programmers arbitrarily decide that new implementation methods can be used during this phase to enhance performance or reduce implementation time. Both are noble objectives if design criteria and control objectives are still satisfactorily implemented. Therefore, the key objective of the security specialist is to verify that the system design agreed on in the previous payoff point is implemented.

Operations and User Control

This phase of systems development provides operations personnel and users with instructions for using the system. The main cause of system failure is the inability of people to use the system effectively. Therefore, it is crucial to enable system users (including operating personnel) to make maximum use of the tools provided by the application.

Thorough documentation and training sessions can overcome most problems. The operations control personnel should be adequately trained in the type of input they are to receive, actions to take if input is not as they believe it should be, and procedures for verifying the controls over completeness and accuracy of input. The user must know how to use the reports, correct error conditions, determine whether the system is in balance, reenter corrections, and verify that corrections have been reentered properly.

EVALUATION AND ACCEPTANCE PHASE PAYOFF POINTS

This phase involves validating that the completed system meets the needs of the system users and that the controls are adequate. End users must validate that the system meets the needs; they may require guidance from the security specialist to validate the adequacy of security controls.

During this phase, it is suggested that the security specialist:

- Be involved in the testing process.
- Ensure that end users devote adequate time to testing.
- Ensure that end users create criteria for accepting the system.
- Ensure that the system is validated against those acceptance criteria.
- Prepare and run whatever tests are needed to validate the adequacy of security controls.
- Test to validate that the implemented system has been implemented in accordance with the design specifications.
- Validate that test conditions are adequate to validate the implementation of the security controls.
- Verify that end users will be involved in testing the application.
- Ensure that end users take responsibility for the system once the test has been completed.

At the conclusion of this phase, the new system is placed into operation. The security specialist may need to certify the adequacy of the security controls before the system is placed into production.

System Testing

The only means users have to ensure that the system performs as specified is to run extensive tests on the system. This step should not be cut short, and users should take an active involvement in system testing.

The security specialist's function is to verify that the system tests show the system to be functioning properly. If the security specialists can assure themselves that the test data is complete and that users are taking an active role in the testing process, the specialist's involvement in the review can be lessened. When the security specialists suspect that there are control conditions not being tested, however (e.g., entering data outside the normal system rules), they must become more active in the testing. Although the security specialists may run only a small group of transactions, if these transactions cannot be processed to their satisfaction, they must insist on modifications to the system before it can be accepted.

At the end of system testing, the security specialists should be able to provide executive management with an opinion on the adequacy of the system. The specialists must do enough work during the system testing to assure themselves that when the system is placed into production, it will perform as specified.

Conversion

Many organizations have not developed procedures for governing conversions. At least one large organization has suffered a major financial setback as a result of the loss of financial data during the conversion process.

During a conversion, the security specialist must ensure that:

- The procedures usually followed in systems development are followed in developing conversion routines.
- Controls over data are maintained during conversion.
- The conversion process is successful before using that data in starting up the new application system.

SUMMARY

As security specialists complete the payoff point checklists, they should put their own general reactions and opinions and any pertinent comments obtained from the individual being interviewed in the comments column of the checklists. This is helpful in writing up the evaluation of internal controls and in conducting additional tests. Notes in the comments column can be as extensive as time permits by using extra pages of notes.

In addition, the security specialist will have determined whether each control is strong, adequate, or weak. This evaluation typically requires intuition and judgment on the part of the security specialist.

Any questions on the checklist that are considered key questions in that review

---

EXHIBIT II-1-21 Key Payoff Point Questions: Evaluation of Controls

Control Evaluation Category	Number of Questions Checked	Score
Strong	_____ × 5 =	
Adequate	_____ × 3 =	
Weak	_____ × 1 =	_____
Total		

Total Score ÷ Total Number of Questions = Overall Rating

Evaluation Rating

1.0–2.75	Internal control is generally weak. Substantial effort needs to be taken to improve the overall system of internal control. Security specialists should recommend an internal controls study.
2.76–3.25	Internal control is adequate. There are most likely problems in various areas of internal control, which should be individually addressed and improved.
3.26–4.0	Ideal level of internal control; probably is cost-effective as well. Indicates that there should be few control weaknesses.
4.01–5.0	Superior level of internal control; however, it may not be cost-effective. Security specialists may wish to evaluate whether the organization is getting an adequate return on investment for the cost to operate the system of internal controls.

should be identified on the checklist. For example, all of the questions in the sample checklist in Exhibit II-1-20 are considered key questions. This offers the security specialist the option of using only the key questions in the review.

Exhibit II-1-21 is used to develop a numerical rating for each payoff point. The security specialist should tally key questions separately from the other questions. For example, for each completed checkpoint, the security specialist tallies the number of key questions marked strong, adequate, and weak. These totals are entered in the second column of the worksheet and multiplied by the corresponding factor to obtain a score for each evaluation category. The total number of key questions and the score should each then be totaled. The overall rating for the key questions in that checkpoint is determined by dividing the total number of questions into the total score. These steps are repeated on a separate worksheet for those questions not identified as key questions.

The security specialist now has an overall rating for both key questions and normal questions. Although the security specialist's judgment comes into this evaluation process, the rating of internal controls can be roughly interpreted as noted at the bottom of Exhibit II-1-21. This section of the exhibit provides the recommended course of action that the security specialist should follow for each of the various ratings.

Trusted Systems

THEODORE M.P. LEE

There are many methods of securing information being processed in a computer or handled over a network. One method is to use a trusted system, which is essential when the computer system itself is responsible for performing one or more critical security functions. This chapter discusses what a trusted system is, introduces the notion of differing degrees of trust, and summarizes the criteria used to judge what level of trust should be assigned to any given system. The specific threats to security that trusted systems are intended to resist are identified, and the historical motivation for building a trusted system to meet established standards is presented. In addition, the chapter discusses the key elements of a trusted system and the different classes of trusted systems in terms of their important features, what means of attack they can withstand, and what environments they are suitable for.

OVERVIEW OF TRUSTED SYSTEMS

Security of information can be provided by many means, whether an information processing system is involved or not. When an information processing system is involved, the system may or may not play a role in providing that security. For example, a system that is used by only one person, is not connected to a network, and never exchanges magnetic media with another system can handle sensitive or critical information quite securely and be regarded as secure, without the system itself performing any functions protecting the information. Protection of the information in this case can be provided by means external to the system—for example, through physical security over the system and its surroundings or by allowing only suitably trusted people to have access to it. In this case, it is not necessary to trust the computer system to perform any security role. On the other hand, most systems must be operated in such a way that the system itself, or at least part of it, has to play a role in protecting the information it is processing. In such cases, the system must be trusted to perform that role properly and adequately. In short, then, a trusted information processing system is one that is required to provide at least one function essential to protecting the security of information.

This distinction between trusted and secure systems emerged from the experiences of the US Department of Defense in trying to securely process classified information in computers, starting during the late 1960s. An important lesson learned in that experience is that it is necessary to have some means of knowing what a trusted computer system is trusted to do and to have some means for judging whether trusting it to behave that way is justified in a given environment. As a consequence, a series of standards, or criteria, for trusted systems have been developed, initially in the US and later internationally. (These are discussed in a later section of this chapter.) The criteria specify the functions that a system must provide to ensure information security and indicate what measures must be taken during the design and construction of the system to give adequate assurance that those functions do what they are supposed to do and cannot be subverted or by-passed.

Just as information comes in varying degrees of importance or sensitivity and must be protected from different kinds of threats in differing amounts, the criteria define a set of levels and classes of trusted systems, ranging from those that provide simple protection measures to those that provide a rich and strong degree of protection. It is somewhat unfortunate and misleading that the trusted systems criteria encompass such a broad spectrum of systems. Those at the highest levels of trust can be used with confidence to protect the most sensitive of national defense information; those at the lowest levels of trust are not strong enough to resist the attacks of a bored teenager and should only be used in environments in which all users are trustworthy and known not to be malicious. Technically, it is correct to call systems at both ends of the spectrum trusted, because their capabilities are well-characterized (i.e., both can be trusted to do what is expected of them).

Although the preceding definition for a trusted system is correct, it is often the case that a system is said to be a trusted system if and only if it has been evaluated as being in conformance with one or more of the trusted systems criteria, at a particular level and class. A distinction that is often ignored is the difference between whether a system needs to be trusted (because of the role it plays and the functions it is supposed to perform) and whether it deserves to be trusted (because it has met the appropriate criteria). Increasingly, systems are used in environments in which they need to be trusted and implicitly are but in which, by all objective standards and experience, they do not deserve to be trusted to the extent they are.

RATIONALE FOR ESTABLISHING TRUSTED SYSTEMS CRITERIA

Formal and informal requirements for security in information processing systems and networks have been around almost since the time when computers began to be used for handling sensitive information. It is natural to ask, then, why the various criteria for trusted systems emerged and, in particular, what shortcomings in the previous approaches they address. The following sections discuss the rationale for establishing trusted systems criteria.

Codification of Experience

Although much of computer security is based on common sense, important aspects of it are not obvious to someone without experience and training in the field. Casual intuition about what is easy and what is difficult, what kind of attacks a potential adversary might attempt, and how systems developers go about their business is often wrong. Although the analogy is not perfect, experience with amateur cryptography in contrast to that based on decades of theoretical and practical experience suggests how weak attempts at computer security can be if they are not grounded on a solid practical and theoretical foundation. A primary purpose of the initial trusted systems criteria was to attempt to capture the experience and knowledge of the experts in the field in such a way as to guide those who did not have that experience.

Known Characteristics

It is not very helpful for a user to simply say, "I want a secure information processing system." It is equally inadequate for systems developers or vendors to assert, justifiably or not, that they are providing a secure information processing system. In both cases, there is a need for standard language that defines what a secure information processing system is, because secure means different things to different people. Different people have different security needs and could benefit from a more effective way of communicating those different needs. Although the process is imperfect, the statement that one needs or provides a trusted system of a certain level or class conveys much more about the characteristics of the system in question. The trusted systems criteria, with the various nuances of meaning of the term "trusted" that they can convey, thus serve as a useful, concise vocabulary that identifies systems with known security characteristics.

Scarcity of High Levels of Trust

One of the goals of the trusted systems criteria was to reduce the wide but mostly inconsequential diversity of information security requirements to a small, focused number of consistent requirements. This goal does not seem to have succeeded, however. Despite the fact that the Department of Defense's *Trusted Computer System Evaluation Criteria* (the Orange Book) was issued in 1983 and directives and procurements requiring its use appeared within a few years, there is not a single, commercially successful, highly trusted system available as of this writing.

CAPABILITIES OF A TRUSTED SYSTEM

The purpose of a trusted system is to defend against a variety of specific technical threats to security with a justifiable, known level of confidence that it will succeed in doing so. All except the systems with the lowest levels of trust are intended to defend against almost all forms of attack, in varying degrees. The following sections describe each of the major threats that may be encountered by trusted systems. As discussed in the next section, some of these threats may need to be addressed by other means.

Threats Not Addressed by Trusted Systems

Information security encompasses protecting information from a broad variety of perils. In some cases, it is important that the correctness of a given piece of information not be compromised, though anyone can see it; in others, improper disclosure of the information must be prevented at any cost, but no extraordinary concern is placed on its correctness. In some cases, it is assumed that the user is trustworthy and not a concern; in others, it must be assumed that even those users entrusted with sensitive or valuable information may attempt to misuse the system for their personal gain, perhaps even to the extent of engaging in collusion with other users. Most current trusted systems also do not address the protection of information while it is being communicated over a network, though some do have trusted interfaces to cryptographically secure networks and some networks themselves have been evaluated as trusted systems.

Although trusted systems can protect against a variety of threats and forms of attack, there are both practical and theoretical limits to what they can provide. The following sections discuss several potential security problems that trusted systems in and of themselves usually do not and often cannot address very well.

Abuse of Authority. If a person is authorized to perform some set of actions (e.g., making particular kinds of entries in a data base), a trusted system cannot detect when that person exercises that authority in a way that ultimately is wrong and it cannot prevent this action from happening. The most a trusted system can do is ensure that users perform only those actions that they are authorized to perform; if that authorization is unwise or wrong, there is little the computer itself can do. However, a trusted system can record actions for later examination; still, if there is nothing a priori that defines a given action as wrong, the system cannot detect that it is wrong.

Data Entry Errors. For similar reasons, a trusted system usually cannot tell when someone has entered incorrect information in a data base. Although a system can be programmed to make as many discriminating reasonableness checks as its designers can devise, the responsibility for correct entry must ultimately rest with the user. (If a system could determine flawlessly whether any given entry is correct or not, there would be no need for a human to make the entry: the system would always know the correct entry and could make it itself.) This does not mean that a system cannot and should not play a significant role in attempting to ensure the correctness of information, if only by supporting verification by a second person when critical information is involved; it only means that the system cannot perform that role with the same level of confidence as when it performs other roles (e.g., preventing unauthorized disclosure of information).

Faulty Applications. As will be discussed later, only parts of a trusted system are actually trusted, in the sense that their behavior obeys known characteristics and is stringently evaluated using established criteria. This is in fact deliberate, because the less of a system that must be trusted, the easier it is to determine confidently whether it deserves to be trusted. A consequence of this narrow focus, however, is that most of what people think of as the computer system is in fact not evaluated against security criteria and is therefore untrusted. Although the functions of untrusted parts are strongly constrained by the parts that are trusted, there are limits to what those constraints can accomplish. A trusted system generally cannot force an application to exhibit correct behavior. However, it can constrain the payroll application, for example, to deal with only the payroll data base, ensure that only the payroll application can access the payroll data base, and ensure that only authorized payroll clerks and members of the accounting department access that application. It cannot ensure that the payroll application does what it is supposed to do with the payroll data base; the only way this can be done is to design and implement the payroll application as a trusted application in and of itself.

Threats Addressed by Trusted Systems

A trusted system is designed to resist a variety of technical threats to security. A technical threat is one that attempts to exploit flaws or oversights in the design, implementation, or configuration of the system. This is in contrast to physical threats to the system or ideological or coercive threats to a user of the system. The following sections summarize each of the major kinds of threats. A subsequent section characterizes how well each level and class of trusted system is expected to defend against these threats.

Accidents. Information is sometimes accidentally made available to someone not authorized to see it or may be accidentally altered or destroyed.

Browsing and Scavenging. Browsing involves looking at files one is not supposed to see, which can occur when files are not protected. Scavenging involves looking at information that has been left in supposedly deleted files, discarded buffers, or previously used memory.

Spoofing and Impersonation. Spoofing and impersonation involves pretending to be someone else or fooling someone into thinking he or she is communicating with a different part of the system. This tactic is often used to steal passwords.

Surreptitious Copying. In most systems, any program run by a user operates with the full authority of that user, even though the user does not necessarily know what the program is doing. Unless the system attempts to enforce an appropriate security policy, any such program can read any information accessible to its user and copy that information to another file or program, where it may be accessible to a user who is not supposed to see that information.

Exploitation of Protection Flaws. An attacker can write software to by-pass or subvert the security policy the system is attempting to enforce, thus allowing the attacker to access information in an unauthorized way. In principle, it should be impossible to exploit a trusted system. Any defect in the design or implementation of the system that directly or indirectly permits unauthorized access is a protection flaw. Following is a selected listing of the kinds of protection flaws that have been discovered in past systems:

- *Incomplete parameter checking.* This occurs when one part of the operating system acts on the understanding that its input has been checked for validity by another part when in fact it has not. The system thus can be made to perform a security-breaching act.
- *Time of check to time of use.* This occurs when security-relevant information (e.g., an address) is able to be changed by a malicious user after it has been checked for validity but before it is used.
- *System data in user space.* If it is security relevant, this data can then be changed by the user because it is not protected.
- *Addressing and indexing overflows with incomplete checking.* This is a hardware design error in which memory protection checks are performed before all address modifications have been performed (e.g., by an index register), potentially allowing improper accesses.
- *Incomplete protection checking on indirect addressing.* This is similar to the preceding problem. It occurs when proper memory protection checks might not be performed at every step of an indirect-addressing sequence.
- *Asynchrony and interlocking errors.* This is concurrent but incorrectly synchronized operation by different parts of the operating system, which causes security-relevant information to become vulnerable or be in an inconsistent state.
- *Puns.* This occurs when the same information is interpreted in different ways, such as a channel program started at two addresses.

An additional protection flaw is covert channels, which warrant more extensive discussion. A covert channel involves an aspect of the system, called the shared variable, that an unauthorized person can observe undetected while a program is being run by an authorized person. Sensitive information can be revealed by observing such innocuous system activity as the amount of available storage or the time it takes to fetch data from storage. In any case, trusted systems in higher classes are designed to reduce or eliminate these types of threats.

Exploitation of almost any protection flaw requires that specially written software be executed. That software can be written by an authorized but malicious user of the system, or it can be supplied from outside the system (e.g., as part of an application program from a commercial supplier). Some flaws require that the malicious software be run on behalf of an authorized user who has access to the information of interest to the attacker; others can be exploited directly by a malicious user. It is frequently suggested that one means of reducing the vulnerability caused by latent protection flaws is to not provide any means for doing programming on a system once it is operational. This is mostly an illusion, because there is so much software of unknown provenance on any system and because it is very difficult to remove all means of doing programming.

It is not always sufficient to be concerned just about protection flaws that might happen to be in a system as a result of design or implementation error or oversight. A system that is used to handle such sensitive information that it is an espionage target (either industrial, criminal, or foreign government) is always subject to the threat that the attacker will find a way of changing the system itself so as to insert a flaw that can later be exploited.

EVALUATION CRITERIA

A purportedly trusted system deserves to be trusted only if it is known to provide appropriate security features with enough assurance that they have been implemented correctly and cannot be bypassed or subverted. Several documents, all prepared under the auspices of one governmental body or another, have been issued to establish the criteria by which trusted systems are to be judged. Because the features and assurances appropriate for different environments are not the same, each of the documents defines different sets of criteria, one for each of about six classes of increasingly more trustworthy systems. The following sections discuss the various criteria documents and discuss their relationships. A later section summarizes the main requirements of the criteria.

The Orange Book and International Variations

The reference standard for trusted systems is the Orange Book. The first official version of the Orange Book was released in 1983, after several prior drafts and predecessors; it ultimately was adopted as a full US Department of Defense standard in 1985, after minor revisions. After release of these criteria, several other governments began developing their own criteria based on, but significantly expanding or revising, the US criteria. France, Germany, Holland, and the UK developed separate criteria, all published about 1989. Under the leadership of the Commission of the European Nations, these four documents were merged into the

Information Technology Security Evaluation Criteria (ITSEC), first issued as a draft in May 1990 with a major revision in June 1991. The ITSEC did not specify how to perform evaluations; a draft, *Information Technology Security Evaluation Manual*, was consequently developed and released for review in April 1992. In parallel, the Canadian Communications Security Establishment developed its own criteria, released in final form in April 1992.

The technical motivation for the development of the European and Canadian criteria was to correct what are viewed by many as two shortcomings of the Orange Book criteria. First, the Orange Book focuses, for all practical purposes, on protecting the confidentiality of information. This is understandable, given that the impetus for trusted systems development was the clear but narrow need of the Department of Defense to concurrently process information of more than one security classification on systems used by people with different security clearances. The newer criteria have added features concerning protecting integrity and availability.

Second, the Orange Book is quite rigid in the set of features it requires and in the way assurance is to relate to those features. The newer criteria permit more flexibility in the set of features a manufacturer may choose to include in a product and what level of assurance the product provides. This accordingly means that a purchaser (e.g., a government procurement office) has much greater flexibility in how it can specify its perceived computer security needs. There has been much argument over whether these changes are actually an improvement, and part of that argument is based on the differences between European and US computer manufacturers and the different economic climates.

Interpretations of the Orange Book

The Orange Book was written to address security in conventional multiuser, time-shared systems connected to nonintelligent terminals. As computer technology and use evolved from that limited model, several interpretations of the Orange Book were written to apply its principles to a broader class of systems. The following sections discuss three of these interpretations.

The Trusted Network Interpretation. In writing *Trusted Network Interpretation Environments Guideline* (August 1990), the National Computer Security Center (NCSC) applied the principles of the Orange Book criteria to computer networks. The primary insight in the trusted network interpretation is the recognition that a network can be regarded as a single trusted system with components distributed over the network. Each component need not contain all the features that the Orange Book requires of a complete system. In fact, the trusted network interpretation provides a way for individual components to be evaluated and given a rating.

The Trusted Data Base Management Interpretation. Despite its title, most of the NCSC's *Trusted Database Management System Interpretation of the*

Trusted Computer System Evaluation Criteria (TCSEC) (April 1991) has little specifically to do with data base management systems. It addresses a broader problem: how to evaluate a trusted system built out of layers of trusted applications, each of which may enforce different parts of an overall security policy. The term "data base" in the title reflects that the technical concepts in this interpretation were initially developed to permit trusted data base systems to be built and evaluated; however, in the end the criteria had much broader applicability.

The Trusted Virtual Machine Interpretation. The virtual machine is a type of system architecture that has proved useful for a variety of particular applications, especially those involving the allocation of a large mainframe to a small number of isolated or loosely connected projects or sets of users. A literal reading of the Orange Book does not apply well to such systems. Trusted Information Systems, Inc., developed *A Proposed Interpretation of the TCSEC for Virtual Machine Monitor Architectures* (August 1992) to indicate how the underlying principles of the Orange Book (and some from the trusted network interpretation) could apply to virtual machines. It has not yet been adopted as an official standard but is being accepted as a guideline.

Usage Guidelines

All of the criteria discussed in the preceding sections identify various classes of trusted systems. Those of the Orange Book are ordered into a simple hierarchy, each class more trusted than the one preceding it. The other criteria documents provide for a richer set of classes of systems—some more or less trusted than others, some simply with different sets of features. In any case, none of the criteria give much indication of exactly which classes of trusted system are necessary or appropriate for which applications.

The Department of Defense has issued two sets of guidelines for determining which class of system or network is appropriate for certain specific environments. These two documents—*Computer Security Requirements: Guidance for Applying the Department of Defense Trusted Computer System Evaluation Criteria in Specific Environments* (CSC-STD-003-85, June 1985) and *Technical Rationale Behind CSC-STD-003-85* (CSC-STD-004-85, June 1985), sometimes referred to as the Yellow Books—specify what class of trusted system to use as determined by the risk range of the environment for the system. In simple terms, the risk range of a system is the difference between the person with the lowest security clearance who can have access to the system and the highest classification of information in it. The Yellow Books also make a distinction between whether all the application software on the system has been written by people with sufficient security clearances (to minimize the likelihood of their containing malicious code) or whether some have been written by uncleared programmers. Systems in which all unevaluated (and therefore untrusted) software has been written by cleared people are said to be operating in a closed environment; the rest are said to be operating in an open environment. This distinction may not be of much practical importance, because almost all useful systems contain off-the-shelf software written by un-cleared and hence potentially malicious programmers.

The *Trusted Network Interpretation Environments Guideline* attempts to set similar guidelines, though it is less precise. This document and the Yellow Books are the results of reasoned professional judgment about whether a given level of trust provides adequate protection for classified information in a given environment; all three are subjective and may be either too conservative or too liberal for a specific situation.

Revisions in Progress

Although the Orange Book was first published in 1983, it is based on work several years older than that. In 1991, a joint effort was started by the US National Security Agency (NSA) and National Institute of Science and Technology (NIST) to completely revise the Orange Book. That effort is planned to culminate in the release of federal criteria applicable to all parts of the US government. A draft of some of the criteria for low-risk environments, titled *Minimum Security Functionality Requirements,* was issued in January 1992, and an initial draft of the complete federal criteria was released for public review in January 1993. Although the final form and content may change, the initial drafts do not render either the Orange Book or the ITSEC obsolete.

ELEMENTS OF A TRUSTED SYSTEM

A trusted system is based on a three-legged foundation: policy, mechanism, and assurance. The security policy of a system is the set of rules it is supposed to enforce, governing who is to have what kind of access to any given information or resource of the system. The security mechanisms of a system are the measures and techniques used in the hardware and software to enforce the policy. (Whether a particular feature of a system is considered mechanism or policy is occasionally somewhat arbitrary, but the distinction is still useful.) Security assurance is all the measures, mostly consisting of software development procedures and practices, used to generate confidence that the mechanisms correctly and robustly enforce the policy in the face of all credible threats the system might be exposed to. It is generally recognized that once the appropriate policy for a system has been determined, which can vary considerably depending on the kind of information involved, the most difficult and controversial aspects of trusted systems are deciding what level of assurance is needed for a given environment and evaluating whether the system provides that assurance.

An important concept that pervades all trusted systems in the higher classes is that of a security kernel. Because the concept is so central, even though it is part of the set of assurance measures required, it deserves separate mention. An examination of computer systems reveals that large parts of a system have no security-related role. Furthermore, both prototypes and finished systems have demonstrated that systems can be designed and built so that the parts not related to security can be constrained such that even if they misbehave (through errors or malicious use), they are sufficiently isolated from the security-relevant parts of the system so as not to cause a problem. The security-relevant parts of a system are called the security kernel of the system and are the only parts of the system that need to be trusted. One goal of trusted system design is to make the security kernel as small as possible, to minimize the amount of the system that needs to be trusted.

The following sections summarize the major aspects of the policy, mechanism, and assurance foundation required for a system to be trusted.

The Security Policy

The first general decision that has to be made in choosing or designing a trusted system is to define the set of security rules it is supposed to enforce. The criteria require that the intended policy be precisely stated and, for the higher classes, given in the form of a mathematical model. Five general forms of policies are prominent in the literature of the field and show up in various trusted systems. These five models are discussed in the following sections.

The Bell-LaPadula Model. This model and the policy it represents include the governmental need-to-know and lattice-based or security-labeled policies protecting classified information from unauthorized disclosure. The important part of the classification policy is that, apart from residual flaws and covert channels, it is possible to easily design a system such that untrusted software cannot violate the policy and such that the correctness of the design can be demonstrated with a great deal of confidence. In the way it is typically implemented, however, the need-to-know policy can be easily violated by malicious Trojan horse programs.

The Biba Model. This model and policy, which have several variations, represent what is called a dual of the Bell-LaPadula policy for the integrity of information. Whereas the Bell-LaPadula policy allows information to be read only by people with proper clearances and approvals, the Biba policy allows information only to be written or modified by people and software with proper clearances (i.e., labels). The two policies may be found combined in a single system. As with the Bell-LaPadula model, the Biba model allows strong statements to be made about who or what can change or write a given piece of information.

The Clark-Wilson Model. This model and policy is an attempt to represent common commercial practices for preserving the integrity of information. It is based on two key concepts: the well-formed transaction and the access control triple. A triple is a mechanism that shows the relationship between the user, a resource (e.g., programs and data), and the access rules that govern their connection. The idea of the triple, which is only occasionally found in systems, is that a given class of data item can be accessed (i.e., read or written) only by a particular set of programs (i.e., transactions), and then only when those transactions are exercised by particular people or classes of people performing particular roles.

Interference Models. Several general-purpose models of security have been developed that focus on demonstrating that less-trusted users and programs cannot possibly interfere with more-trusted ones. The results of these kinds of models are stronger than some of the other kinds of models because they do a better job of identifying potential covert channels.

Separation Models. The simplest form of security is to prevent any communication or interference between users of different security levels. In most trusted systems, for example, users and their programs operating at higher security levels can read but not write information at lower levels. In a system that supports a separation security policy, however, users at a given security level are completely isolated from users (and their data) at a different level. This model is used for certain types of networks and virtual machines.

Protection Mechanisms

A protection mechanism is anything used to help support the security policy of a system. The criteria for trusted systems deliberately state very few requirements about any particular protection mechanisms, especially those close to the hardware. The following sections discuss various protection requirements and mechanisms.

Accountability. Although not strictly speaking protection mechanisms, means for individual accountability are a prerequisite for any protection at all. Each user of a trusted system must be individually and positively identified by a secure means. In a trusted system, the mechanisms that perform secure identification usually decide whether someone can use (i.e., log on to) the system at all. Once a user has been identified, it is the access control mechanisms that decide exactly what, if any, resources and information that user can have access to.

The security-relevant actions of individual users must be securely audited, because auditing is the only means of analyzing behavior that cannot be determined ahead of time as being unauthorized, exceeding authority, or malicious. Any system that can determine whether an unauthorized access or action has been requested can prevent that action from occurring. The problem, especially in commercial systems, is that it is difficult or even impossible to characterize all possible actions ahead of time as being proper or not. For example, at what point does authorizing a funds transfer within the approval limits constitute embezzlement?

Access Control. Although later de facto revisions to the trusted systems criteria permit additional access control policies and mechanisms to support them, the initial versions require that a trusted system support both a discretionary access control policy and a mandatory (also known as nondiscretionary) access control policy. In a discretionary access control policy, the person responsible for information (e.g., the creator of a file) is able to grant or deny anyone access to that file and can control what kind of access (e.g., read or write) each is allowed. The difficulty with most discretionary access control policies is that any program run by a user can typically also grant access to other users, without the knowledge or consent of the original user.

In a mandatory access control policy, however, information and users are given security labels, which are used as the basis for granting or denying access. Once assigned, those labels cannot be changed by ordinary users. Mechanisms are required that prevent information from being copied into a place with a label that would permit access contrary to that permitted by the label on the information being copied. This means that untrusted programs cannot copy information and place it in a location where an unauthorized user can access it.

Assurance Measures

Although the protection measures required of a trusted system (especially mandatory access control) may seem novel to those not familiar with them, the heart of a robust trusted system lies in the measures required to ensure that the protection mechanisms enforce the security policy of the system. Those assurance measures are found in two areas: operational assurance, which comes into play during daily system use, and life cycle assurance, which governs how the system is designed, implemented, and maintained. The following sections discuss these two assurance areas.

Operational Assurance. The primary assurance that a system operates correctly is found in the requirements for how the trusted parts of a system are structured, which is called the system architecture. At the lower levels of trust, the primary requirement is that the trusted parts of the system be separate from the untrusted parts and protect themselves from external interference and tampering. At the higher levels of trust, this alone is not sufficient; detailed requirements on how the trusted parts of the system are internally structured are imposed, including the requirement that they use the protection mechanisms of the system itself to enforce that structuring. In addition, a trusted system must periodically validate that it is working correctly. Reduction or elimination of covert channels is included within the required assurance measures.

Life Cycle Assurance. The primary requirements for life cycle assurance, which also become more stringent the higher the level of trust, address the procedures used for designing, developing, testing, maintaining, and documenting the system. At almost all levels of trust, strict control over who can change the system (including the supporting documentation) is required. At the higher levels, the design of the system is subject to increasing scrutiny and rigor—including, ultimately, partial use of mathematical proofs of correctness. Also at the highest levels, the manufacturer must impose effective controls to ensure that the copy of a system delivered to a customer, including any new versions or modifications, is what was evaluated and shipped.

SYNOPSIS OF EVALUATION CLASSES

The Orange Book criteria define seven classes of trusted systems, designated by a letter and number and a distinctive title:

- C1: Discretionary Security Protection.
- C2: Controlled Access Protection.
- B1: Labeled Security Protection.
- B2: Structured Protection.
- B3: Security Domains.
- A1: Verified Design.

The following sections contain a subjective characterization of all but one of the classes; C1 has been omitted because there is little interest in that class. The characterizations summarize the primary features and assurance measures required of each class and describes which threats each class is expected to resist. Finally, the typical environments each class would be appropriately used in are identified. Unfortunately, only the Department of Defense has attempted to put forth an objective definition of use environments, and this definition is in terms of the security classification of the information involved and the clearances of the users.

Level C2: Controlled Access Protection

This level features individual accountability and authentication, audit trails, controls (e.g., access control lists) suitable for enforcement of need-to-know, and elimination of residue. Its attributes are that the operating system is isolated and protected from users, has been tested enough to discover and correct obvious flaws, and involves minimum documentation standards.

Systems at this level are defenseless against Trojan horse attacks and are likely to have exploitable technical flaws that can be discovered by anyone with average computer literacy. In addition, development and maintenance processes are easily subvertible. Another weakness is that all classification marking must be done manually or by untrustable application software. The strengths of systems at this level are that casual browsing is unproductive, security awareness is encouraged, and user behavior is extensively audited.

A C2 system is useful only in a benign, dedicated environment. Its main purposes are to encourage individual accountability in the handling of sensitive information and to encourage effective security practices in such areas as password management. Nonmalicious people who engage in poor practices are identified by the auditing mechanisms. The auditing mechanisms should also be useful in assessing the damage of a defection, provided that the defector had ceased to have access to the system far enough in advance or did not have the modest skills or information needed to technically subvert the mechanisms.

Users are required to specify who is to have access to particular files of information. However, there is nothing in the system—other than auditing—to discourage or otherwise prevent a user (or a program he uses that does the same) from making copies of information and passing those copies on to someone else. It is unlikely that a nonmalicious user could gain access to information others did not intend the user to have or accidentally give someone else information or access to information. Furthermore, an overzealous but basically honest person would not be able to access information he or she was not supposed to see by browsing or scavenging. Still, the system is almost certain to have technical flaws that could be discovered by a person of average computer literacy (e.g., high school computer exposure) and exploited by anyone, with little chance of detection. A C2 system has absolutely no defense against Trojan horse attacks, viral or otherwise.

Level B1: Labeled Security Protection

B1 systems feature security labels (i.e., classification and compartmentation as well as clearances and access approvals) used to enforce access control and physically and electronically mark most media. Untrusted software is not allowed to downgrade information in a B1 system. Users are isolated from each other.

B1 systems are likely to succumb to a moderate technical attack (less than six labor-months) by someone knowledgeable about the source code of the system. High-bandwidth leakage channels are exploitable by Trojan horses, which are likely to be present, and not all data is marked or controlled. B1 systems have the same vulnerability of development and distribution process as C2 systems. Other weaknesses are an illusory sense of security and security compromises through nonmalicious misuse of the system. Among the strengths of B1 systems are that they encourage secure handling and marking practices, keep the honest person honest, enforce proper design constraints on applications software, and help users grow accustomed to security procedures.

A B1 system is intended to operate in a relatively benign environment; a B1 system is not strong enough to protect even confidential data from uncleared users, because it has not been built with enough assurance to prevent it from being easily penetrated. The anomalies in the Yellow Books notwithstanding, a B1 system should be used only in a system-high environment. (A system is operating in system-high mode if all users are cleared for all information on the system but at least one user does not meet need-to-know requirements for all information on the system.) The purpose of having security labels at the B1 level is to encourage and assist people to mark material properly, but it is not expected to enforce access controls in the face of any conscious competent technical effort to defeat them. The access and flow control (*-property) features at the B1 level are intended only to force people to adopt operational and applications programming habits and styles that will be required at B2 and higher levels.

A B1 system cannot defend against Trojan horse attacks because it has covert storage channels and may even have direct channels through system objects not controlled by the trusted parts of the system. Although the object reuse requirement means that data used as intended cannot be accidentally left around, there are places in the system where classified data could be put, albeit intentionally, so it would be readable by an unauthorized person.

A B1 system has not been subject to penetration testing and, on the basis of past experience, would succumb to a moderate attack by someone knowledgeable about the system. Although all known design or implementation flaws have been corrected, there has been no systematic effort to search for others (e.g., time of check to time of use on system calls). There is no effective assurance that bugs, patches, or trapdoors have not been or cannot be implanted in the system during its manufacture or distribution.

A B1 system suffers from the flight-critical paradox, so named from the analogy that an airplane cockpit instrument is flight-critical if and only if a pilot relies on it, yet the pilot is supposed to rely only on those instruments that have been certified as flight-critical. In other words, if a B1 system is not intended to be trusted to control access to information, it is not likely that the opposition has bothered to try to subvert its development and thus it can probably be trusted. However, if the system is to be trusted, it is an easy target and must be assumed to have been subverted.

Level B2: Structured Protection

Among the B2 system features are that all data directly or indirectly accessible by users has security labels, a trusted path is provided to prevent log-on spoofing attacks, and all devices have labels indicating the minimum and maximum classification or compartmentation of data allowed on them. B2 systems have a well-structured system design. Leakage channels are identified and limited, and some penetration testing has been conducted. B2 systems also feature configuration management, detailed design specifications, and a formal model of security policy.

Still, sophisticated technical attacks are possible. Unless appropriate (but optional) protection mechanisms are included, data integrity is subject to viral attack. Unless development and maintenance processes are carried out in a cleared environment, B2 systems are still subject to attack, though it would probably require conspiracy to bypass the relatively strong configuration management process required at the B2 level. The primary weakness of B2 systems is the chance of exploitable residual design and implementation errors. Although not an intrinsic property, the user interface to B2 and higher-level systems can easily become unforgiving, which may lead to frustrations that in themselves may give rise to poor security practices.

B2 is the first level at which a system can be trusted enough to operate in a limited multilevel mode. There is essentially no risk that a user or a program can place classified data in a place where someone not cleared for it can directly read it. There is a bandwidth-limited risk that data can be signaled through covert storage channels by a Trojan horse program and an unknown risk that it can be signaled through timing channels.

The system has been subjected to a few worker-months of penetration testing by people trained in use of the system. It would likely succumb to approximately one worker-year of attack by a well-trained systems programmer with a year of system-internals experience on the system and access to a private copy of the system. Although the system design is clean, there is no particular guarantee (other than testing) that such classic attacks as time of check to time of use, hardware puns, or incomplete specifications would not succeed.

Configuration management, especially the ability to compare different versions and trace the reasons for change, is effective enough that it would take a conspiracy on the part of several people to subvert an existing copy of the system. According to the Yellow Books, a B2 system is not strong enough to protect secret data from access by uncleared users. However, it can span two or three security levels (e.g., secret and top secret).

Level B3: Security Domains

B3 systems must support access control lists, with the ability to explicitly specify those excluded from access. They feature a separate and limited security administrator role and the best conventional software engineering practices available, short of using any formal (i.e., mathematical) techniques. The size of protection-critical parts of the system have been reduced to a minimum, and the system enforces its own internal modular structure.

The B3 system has the same configuration management vulnerabilities as B2 systems. In addition, there is a slight, unquantifiable chance of residual design and implementation errors. Although the system has no obvious weaknesses, there has not yet been any real field experience with B3 systems. Because of this, it is not possible to quantify how much more secure a B3 system is than a B2 system

The strength of the B3 system is its forced simplicity of design. In addition, it is strong enough to protect secret data from unclassified users and top secret data from confidential users.

Level A1: Verified Design

A1 systems have no additional features over the B3 system. However, they have a formally (i.e., mathematically) specified and verified design, a trusted distribution process, and life cycle configuration management.

The vulnerability inherent in A1 systems is that there is a slight, unquantifiable chance of implementation errors. System weaknesses are the same as for B3 systems, except the technology is even farther from the state of the art.

An A1 system is just about the most secure available. There is essentially no chance for security-related design errors. A1 systems have a slightly broader range of use environments than B3 systems, but there has not been enough experience with A1 systems to determine whether they are appropriate for all applications.

SUMMARY

Because trusted systems support varying levels of security, the security specialist must understand the different classes of trusted systems and the criteria used to evaluate them. This chapter provides this information and identifies the threats that trusted systems are expected to resist. In addition, it summarizes the Orange Book classifications and examines the suitability of each class for specific environments.

The Evaluated Products List

MARIO TINTO

The Evaluated Products List is the vehicle by which the National Computer Security Center (NCSC) publishes the results of the evaluation of industry products against the Trusted Computer System Evaluation Criteria (TCSEC). Its purpose is to provide systems developers, managers, and users with an authoritative evaluation of a system's relative suitability for use in processing sensitive information. The Evaluated Products List is part of the Information Systems Security Products and Services Catalogue, which is published by the National Security Agency, and is updated quarterly.

A primary goal of the NCSC is to encourage the computer industry to provide, as part of its standard product lines, computer systems with features and attributes sufficient for the protection of sensitive information. This goal is pursued through a multifaceted program for advancing the technologies relevant to protecting information in shared-resource computer systems; working with industry to introduce security-relevant technology into computer systems; and evaluating the security capabilities of the resultant systems against the TCSEC. The availability of trusted products, as well as the status of ongoing evaluations are reported in the Evaluated Products List (thus providing advance indication of products that are expected to be available in the future).

THE EVALUATION PHASES

The various entries in the Evaluated Products List are closely related to the various phases of the evaluation program. These phases are described in the following sections.

Vendor Assistance Phase. During this phase, the NCSC plays an advisory evaluation role. The level of NCSC participation is relatively low, aimed primarily at providing consultative support for a vendor who has made an initial commitment to produce a product with the desired security attributes. This phase, upon mutual agreement of both the vendor and the NCSC, eventually leads to the design analysis phase.

Design Analysis Phase. In this phase, a sizable commitment of labor and time is made by both the vendor and the government. The product is expected to be largely completed, although some design and development activity may still be in progress. The NCSC evaluation team is responsible for becoming intimately familiar with the product, primarily by means of documentation. The evaluation team is also responsible for providing support to the vendor to minimize the risk that the product will not satisfy the requirements of the target evaluation class. The goal of the evaluation team's analysis is to gain adequate assurance that the vendor's design and implementation methods are likely to produce the desired results, and that all the evidence required for a detailed analysis is in place. This phase culminates in a detailed, formal analysis of the product's design and, if successful, a formal recommendation by the evaluation team.

Formal Evaluation. During this phase, the product is examined in considerable detail, the sufficiency and completeness of the vendor's product testing is assessed, and hands-on testing by the team is performed. Clearly, by this phase the product must be essentially complete and there must be a clear commitment by the vendor to market the product. This phase culminates in a Final Evaluation Report (FER) and the publication of the results of the evaluation in the Evaluated Products List.

EVALUATED PRODUCTS LIST STRUCTURE AND CONTENTS

The Evaluated Products List provides an index of all the entries (in alphabetic ordering by vendor), identifying the review status of each vendor's product by evaluation phase: vendor assistance phase, design analysis phase, formal evaluation, or completed. The first set of listings include products in the vendor assistance phase. For each product a vendor point of contact is provided, from whom further information about the product is available.

The next set of listings is for products in the design analysis phase. As noted previously, in this phase there has been a high level of commitment by both the NCSC and the vendor toward developing a product that complies with the TCSEC. When a product successfully completes the design analysis phase, a decision is made to move to the formal evaluation phase. This transition is marked by publication of an announcement titled the Product Evaluation Bulletin. This announcement formally recognizes that the indicated product is ready for a final evaluation, and that the vendor has made a serious commitment to bring to the marketplace a product with a well-defined set of TCSEC features and properties. The publication of a product bulletin ensures, short of extraordinary events, that a rating will eventually be assigned to the product and a final report will be published.

Exhibit II-1-22 provides an example of a product bulletin for a Honeywell

EXHIBIT II-1-22 Sample Product Evaluation Bulletin

REPORT NO.	CSC-PB-90/003
AS OF:	June 13, 1990
PRODUCT:	XTS-200 */STOP
VENDOR:	Honeywell Federal Systems Inc. (HFSI)
CANDIDATE CLASS:	B3

Product Description

The XTS-200 is a superminicomputer, based on the Bull HN Information Systems Inc. DPS 6 PLUS and DPS 6000. STOP is a multilevel secure operating system that runs on the XTS-200 hardware. The XTS-200 is a multiprocessing system capable of supporting up to four independent processors. It provides a two gigabyte virtual memory, and uses a hardware ring mechanism for protection. STOP is a multitasking system that can support multiple users. It supports much of the UNIX System V interface for application software.

STOP consists of four components: the Security Kernel, which operates in the most privileged ring and provides all mandatory access control, as well as discretionary access control for devices and processes; the TCB System Services, which operates in the next-most-privileged ring, and implements a hierarchical file system, supports user I/O, and implements the discretionary access control for file system objects; Trusted Processes, which provide the remaining security services and the user command interface to the TCB; and Commodity Application Services System (CASS), which operates in a less privileged ring and provides the UNIX-like interface. CASS is not a part of the Trusted Computing Base.

Product Status

XTS-200 uses the DPS 6 PLUS and DPS 6000 hardware, with firmware modifications developed by HFSI. STOP was developed by HFSI. XTS-200/STOP is marketed and supported by HFSI. STOP version 3.1 was released in September 1989.

Evaluation Status

A formal evaluation of XTS-200/STOP began in July 1990 and is scheduled for completion during the third quarter of 1991. XTS-200/STOP will be evaluated against the *DoD Trusted Computer System Evaluation Criteria*, DoD 5200.28-STD, December 1985.

The National Computer Security Center considers XTS-200/STOP a candidate for the class of products that provide security domains (i.e., class B3). At the completion of the evaluation, a final evaluation report will be produced by the National Computer Security Center and XTS-200/STOP will be placed on the Evaluated Products List with its assigned rating. A Product Bulletin does not assign any rating to a product. It merely establishes the candidate class that is the highest class the system could attain should the formal evaluation be completed. As with all evaluations, a system must complete the formal evaluation phase before being assigned any rating.

Environmental Strengths

XTS-200/STOP is designed to provide a high level of security for many kinds of environments, including office automation applications and those with specialized applications (such as message guards). The processor enforces a ring mechanism similar to that found in the Honeywell Multics system, which isolates the security mechanisms, and a virtual memory system based on segments. The system also supports a hierarchical file system similar to that of UNIX. Access control is provided by user-specified controls (i.e., discretionary access controls) through access control lists, with additional controls provided to properly separate sensitive information from unauthorized users (i.e., mandatory access controls). It provides for user identification and authentication through user IDs and passwords, and individual accountability through its auditing capability.

---

*XTS-200 is a registered trademark of Honeywell Federal Systems Inc.

product, which appeared in the Product and Services Catalog of January 1992. The bulletin shows the date that the bulletin was issued (in this case, June 13, 1990), identifies the vendor, provides the product identifier (XTS-200), and shows the TCSEC rating for which the product is targeted (i.e., B3). The bulletin provides some information about the device, and the paragraph titled "Evaluation Status" notes the scheduled completion date (at the time the bulletin was issued) for the evaluation.

The third set of product listings in the Evaluated Products List is for those products that are currently in the formal evaluation phase. For each product on the list, an accompanying product bulletin can be found, which provides a brief summary of the product, the projected TCSEC rating, and the scheduled completion date for the evaluation.

Finally, there is the listing for the set of completed evaluations. This represents the set of products that have successfully completed formal evaluation, and that have been assigned ratings. This section of the Evaluated Products List is actually the set of formal announcements about the products. These are short summaries, very much like the product bulletin that is issued at the initiation of the formal evaluation. Each summary identifies the product, shows the assigned rating, and provides a short description of the product as well as a summary of highlights of the security characteristics of the product. As part of the product summary, a chart is provided showing exactly which of the TCSEC requirements were satisfied. This chart may indicate that requirements were satisfied that exceed the minimum requirements for the rating assigned. This is because the rating is assigned on a "low water mark" basis—that is, the overall rating is that for which all requirements are satisfied. However, the summary chart allows the vendor to receive recognition for system features that exceed minimum requirements. A detailed Final Evaluation Report for each product listed in the summary is published separately and is publicly available.

A sample Evaluated Products List entry for the Trusted Information System's Trusted XENIX product is provided as Exhibit II-1-23. As in the product bulletin, the vendor and product name are identified. However, in this case the rating is final and applies to a specific version (i.e., version 2.0). The chart that is included in this announcement shows how the vendor fared in the evaluation against each of the TCSEC requirements. In this case, the product has been awarded a rating of B2, the highest level for which all the requirements are satisfied. Several aspects of the system did satisfy requirements for higher classes (e.g., the vendor has been given credit for satisfying the B3 statement of requirement for discretionary access control); however, other B3 requirements were not satisfied at the level required for a B3 rating (e.g., the requirement for design specification and verification). A prospective purchaser can use this listing to compare available products on the basis of security attributes as well as operational characteristics (e.g., the system designer may want a B2 product but may want a workstation rather than a mainframe).

EXHIBIT II-1-23 Sample Completed Evaluation

Serial No. CSC-EPL-91/003

Evaluated Product:	Trusted XENIX
Vendor:	Trusted Information Systems, Inc. (TIS)
Version Evaluated:	Trusted XENIX Version 2.0
Evaluation Date:	January 22, 1991
Overall Evaluation Class:	B2

Product Description

Trusted XENIX Version 2.0 (Trusted XENIX*) is a UNIX-like, multilevel secure operating system for the IBM Personal Computer AT (PC AT) and IBM Personal System/2 (PS/2) Models 50, 60, 70, 70T, 70P, and 80.** It is a multiuser, multitasking system that can support up to six concurrent users using currently available IBM equipment. Trusted XENIX contains many functional and security enhancements while maintaining binary compatability with programs developed under IBM Personal Computer XENIX versions 1.0 and 2.0.

Trusted XENIX is designed to provide a high level of security for environments requiring trusted desktop data processing. Trusted XENIX enforces a mandatory security policy based on the Bell and LaPadula security model. Discretionary access controls include traditional UNIX*** protection bits, as well as Access Control Lists. Trusted XENIX performs user identification and authentication, generates audit trail records, and provides a base upon which to build secure application programs. Evaluated hardware configurations include a range of disks, disk controllers, video configurations, and a cartridge tape unit for fast system back-up and restore.

Trusted Computer System Evaluation Summary Chart

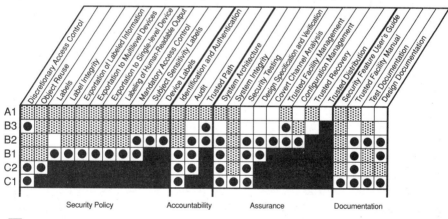

☐	Does Not Satisfy the Requirement For This Class
■	No Requirements For This Class
▨	No Additional Requirements For This Class
●	Meets or Exceeds the Requirements For This Class

Credit given above the overall rating recognizes mechanisms implemented beyond those strictly required within the assigned rating class. Security testing was not conducted above the rated level, and the reader should not infer any assurance above this level.

System Name:
Trusted Information Systems, Inc.
Trusted XENIX Version 2.0

Evaluation Date: 22 January 1991

(continued)

EXHIBIT II-1-23 *(continued)*

The system enforces the "principle of least privilege" (i.e., users should have no more authorization than what is required to perform their functions) for each of the four defined privileged user roles available in multiuser mode. These privileged users are assigned to one of the four following roles: System Security Administrator, Secure Operator, Account Administrator, and Auditor. This separation is supported by strictly limiting privileged users to predefined operations. In addition, all actions performed by privileged users can be audited, and the audit log cannot be modified by unprivileged users, the System Security Administrator, Secure Operator, or Account Administrator. In addition, there is also a Trusted System Programmer who is responsible for initial hardware and system configuration. This role only exists in single-user mode.

Evaluation Summary

The security protection provided by Trusted XENIX, configured according to the most secure manner described in the Trusted Facility Manual, has been evaluated by the NCSC against the requirements specified by the *Department of Defense Trusted Computer System Evaluation Criteria* [DOD 5200.28-STD] dated December 1985.

The NCSC evaluation team has determined that the highest class at which Trusted XENIX satisfies all the specified requirements of the Criteria is class B2. In addition, Trusted XENIX satisfies the functionality of the B3 requirements for DAC, Trusted Path, and Trusted Facility Management.

For a complete description of how Trusted XENIX satisfies each requirement of the Criteria, see *Final Evaluation Report, Trusted Information Systems' Trusted XENIX* (Report No. CSC-EPL-91/003). In addition, the report should also be consulted for the complete lists of evaluated hardware and software components.

---

*XENIX is a trademark of the Microsoft Corporation.
**IBM, Personal Computer AT, and Personal System/2 are registered trademarks of the IBM Corporation.
***UNIX is a registered trademark of AT&T Bell Laboratories, Inc.

An Overview of Evaluated Products

Of the nearly 90 products in the July 1992 issue of the Evaluated Products List, 36 products were evaluated (or were being evaluated) against either the TCSEC or one of its major interpretations (e.g., the trusted network interpretation or the trusted data base management systems interpretation). The bulk of these products were what would generally be considered operating systems—products that provide general-purpose computational services and thus enforce access control policies. Twenty-eight of the products listed represent completed evaluations, and thus there are Evaluated Products List entries for each and a reference to a detailed evaluation report. The remaining eight were products in the formal evaluation phase, whose evaluation was not yet completed. This version of the Evaluated Products List also included 12 products in the vendor assistance phase and another 10 products in the design analysis phase.

Of special interest is the number of UNIX and UNIX-like products, especially among the more recent entries. This is significant, especially with the growing consumer interest in open systems. With the move toward POSIX, there is now the strong potential for the availability of standard security capabilities in a popular and easily portable general-purpose system. In turn, this allows users to look forward to interoperable security products that may be hosted on and ported to a variety of hardware bases.

EVALUATION OF SECURITY DEVICES

In addition to evaluations of general-purpose computer systems, the Evaluated Products List also contains information about the availability and capabilities of commercially available security devices and packages that may be added to a system to augment or improve its security status. These include hardware or hardware-software combinations, such as a dialback modem or a smart-card based authentication device, as well as software packages that can be added to a system to provide a security capability that is not normally provided (e.g., auditing).

The July 1992 issue of the Evaluated Products List listed 29 subsystems that provide a security service. As an example, there are several devices that provide user authentication via a challenge-response mechanism. Such products could be used to provide user authentication for a system for which user authentication is either nonexistent or insufficient. Alternatively, they could be used to provide a redundant authentication mechanism to an existing password system in cases where particularly strong user authentication was deemed necessary.

This information is provided in the section of the Evaluated Products List titled Subsystem EPL Entries. The products in this section are evaluated against the Computer Systems Subsystem Interpretation (CSSI), which was developed as an extension of the TCSEC to allow the evaluation of special-purpose security products. All of the products listed in the subsystems section represent completed evaluations. That is, there is a final Evaluated Products List entry and a separately available final evaluation report for each of the products. Exhibit II-1-24 provides an example from the Evaluated Products List of a hardware-software package, marketed by Security Microsystems, Inc., that provides general protection capabilities to a large class of MS-DOS and PC-DOS products.

RELEVANCE OF EVALUATION RESULTS

Computer products continue to evolve even while they are being evaluated; as the evaluators are assessing a current version of the system, the developer is working on fixes and enhancements to the product. Coupled with the time it takes to complete an evaluation and publish the results, it is not unusual for the evaluation to have been performed on a version of the system that is no longer current. That is, by the time the evaluation has been completed and the results made available a later release of the system is issued. Even if the results of an evaluation could be made available concurrent with the release of the product, the fairly rapid evolution of computer products (a 6- to 18-month release schedule is common in the industry) would not solve the problem. Thus, the consumer is faced with the quandary of deciding the relevance of the published evaluation results to the current version. This may be especially difficult if several versions have been released since the one that was the subject of the evaluation. Clearly, such uncertainty undermines the effort of both the government and the developers. Just as

EXHIBIT II-1-24 Sample Subsystem Evaluation

Serial No. CSC-EPL-91/001

Evaluated Product: LOCKIT Professional 2.10

Vendor: Security Microsystems, Inc.

Version: LOCKIT Professional 2.10

Evaluation Date: March 27, 1991

Overall Evaluation Class: I&A / D
DAC / D
AUD / D
OR / D

Product Description
LOCKIT Professional 2.10 is a microcomputer hardware and software package that operates on an IBM PC, PC/XT, PC/AT, or compatible microcomputer under MS-DOS or PC-DOS. The product is a combination of a hardware board and a software package that allows many users to share a system, one at a time. The package provides a friendly user interface, a manual for the System Administrator, and a user's manual.

Evaluation Summary
The Trusted Product Evaluations and Network Security Evaluations Division of the National Security Agency (NSA) has evaluated the security protection provided by LOCKIT Professional 2.10. The security features for Identification and Authentication, Discretionary Access Control, Audit, and Object Reuse were evaluated against the CSSI of the *Trusted Computer Security Evaluation Criteria*.

LOCKIT Professional 2.10 is a subsystem which provides Identification and Authentication, Discretionary Access Control, Object Reuse, and Auditing. The user is confined within a menu driven environment that must not be exited if security is to be maintained. Identification and Authentication is accomplished within a separate domain before MS/PC-DOS is brought up.

Discretionary access control is obtained by defining a limited access area for each user and by providing access to that area only through that user's menu. Object reuse functionality for both memory resident objects and disk resident objects can be set up so that it is automatically invoked. Auditing capabilities are very limited. There are limited checks to determine if any part of LOCKIT Professional 2.10 was tampered with. LOCKIT Professional 2.10 receives a D rating in auditing because it does not meet all of the functional requirements for a higher rating.

In addition to meeting the functionality requirements defined in the CSSI, subsystems must also meet the assurance and documentation requirements. LOCKIT Professional failed to satisfy the assurance and documentation requirements, and therefore receives a composite rating of D for the Identification and Authentication, Object Reuse, and Discretionary Access Control features. For a complete description of how LOCKIT Professional satisfies each requirement of the CSSI, see *Final Evaluation Report, Security Microsystems, Inc. Lockit Professional* (Report No. CSC-EPL-91/001).

clearly, neither the government nor the vendors can invest in a completely new evaluation process each time a new release of the system is developed.

In response to the clear need for a program to maintain the relevance of the evaluation results, the NCSC instituted the Ratings Maintenance Program. This is essentially a configuration management program focused on maintaining the currency of a rating across versions of a product. A key element is a vendor representative who acts, in essence, as a quality assurance agent for security issues. As a product goes through its normal evolution, the vendor's existing configuration management system and related procedures are expected to identify, or be amended to identify, proposed changes that are relevant to the evaluation rating (i.e., those changes that have the potential for affecting the rating of the product). The vendor representative is provided with training by the NCSC to acquaint him with the particulars of the evaluation criteria and evaluation issues. The representative is expected to protect the vendor's investment by assessing the impact of changes on the product's rating.

In short, a well-defined process is currently in place for extending a rating to new versions of a product. The Evaluated Products List indicates which products are participating in the ratings maintenance program, and there is a separate section of the Evaluated Products List that discusses the extensions of the ratings to later versions.

A related issue involves products that may be considered obsolete—that is, products that are no longer supported by the manufacturer. It could be asked whether it is necessary or useful to keep such products on the Evaluated Products List. Certainly, one option is for the NCSC to determine periodically which products are to be deleted from the Evaluated Products List. However, it is argued that even though a product may no longer be purchasable, users may still be using the product and may thus profit from information about it. It is certainly possible that, from time to time, a determination may be made that some entries are no longer useful, and thus selected Evaluated Products List entries may be deleted. However, as of this writing, this has yet to occur; the decision is to avoid making essentially arbitrary determinations about the deletion of products from the list.

SUMMARY

The Evaluated Products List provides a variety of information about general systems and security products including the security properties of currently available products and of future products. System planners who need to satisfy a current or near-term requirement can refer to the listing of completed evaluations to determine which products are candidates for the system. After determining which products meet or exceed the security needs, they can then determine which of these also satisfy the operational requirements. System planners who must respond to mid- to far-term requirements will be able to determine the general availability of trusted products for the time frame for which they are planning. If, for instance, a system planner has identified a need for a B3 capability, a glance at the set of products in the vendor assistance and design analysis phases will indicate what the relative availability of such products is likely to be at the time the target system is to be implemented.

This discussion has presented the goals and essential characteristics of the Evaluated Products List. However, information in the Evaluated Products List is more complex and detailed than described in this relatively brief overview. Therefore, the reader is encouraged to obtain a current copy of the Information Systems Security Products and Services Catalog to obtain a more complete understanding of the information it contains. The catalog is available from the Government Printing Office and may be obtained by addressing orders to:

Superintendent of Documents
US Government Printing Office
Washington DC 20402

Further information or assistance can be obtained by writing to:

Director, National Security Agency
Attn: INFOSEC Office of Customer Relations
Fort Meade MD 20755

SECTION II-2

Systems and Operations Controls

Section II-2 addresses physical security and controls, operations security and controls, and the security requirements of specific types and configurations of hardware (i.e., microcomputers, mainframes, or a combination of both). Chapter II-2-1 discusses data center security—the first line of defense for maintaining secure application systems. This category of protection is directed against all types of hazards, whether accidental or intentional. After determining the physical risk exposure of the center, the security practitioner should ensure that cost-effective controls have been installed and are maintained and tested on a regular basis.

Common exposures in today's computer environments range from such natural disasters as fire, earthquake, and flood to such crimes as vandalism and internal sabotage. With a realistic view of such elements as site selection and location of the computer center, many of these risks can be minimized. Within the computer room, further protections can be afforded by proper construction, installation of electrical facilities within code, and mechanisms to protect against fire hazards. Access controls to the equipment and comprehensive backup procedures round out the list of needed protections.

In Chapter II-2-2 the next line of defense is discussed—operations security within the data center. Here the concern is with data and information resident in the computers or within the center. Security practitioners should ensure that a plan has been drawn up that protects all computing resources, such as storage and communications, from risks in the environment. Violations processing and analysis is an important aspect of this planning. Privilege control is another key element in safeguarding data and information, because privileged users are able to modify control functions. Certification and regular recertification of privileges should be an integral part of any protection plan.

The remaining three chapters of Section 2 discuss security concerns specific to microcomputers and mainframes. Chapter II-2-3 addresses microcomputer security. Limiting access to machines that process sensitive information, instituting regular backups of sensitive data, using virus protection software, and having at least two people familiar with each critical business process are major controls the security practitioner can use to enhance the security of microcomputers. It is clear that training users and sensitizing them to the vulnerabilities and risks of this environment is a significant factor in the secure operation of microcomputers.

When microcomputers connect to host computers, a key security consideration is the control of data transmissions. Chapter II-2-4 on micro-mainframe security reviews the use of such protective measures as hash totals, record sequence checking, transmission logging, transmission error control, and retransmission control. Clearly, the security practitioner must understand a great deal about communications technology as well as computer technology to successfully secure such interconnected systems. In addition to transmission controls, the security practitioner must ensure that access controls, backup and recovery controls, and change controls have been properly introduced at both the microcomputer level and the mainframe level.

Software security on a mainframe involves controlling access to programs and data, restricting use of utility programs used for systems management, and general protection of systems programs and hardware components. Chapter II-2-5 addresses the security of mainframes, primarily from the perspective of the IBM Multiple Virtual Systems (MVS) and Virtual Machine Facility (VM) operating systems. Many of the recommendations provided in this chapter, however, are relevant to other types of mainframe operating systems as well.

Security control elements consist of programs and data sets that perform or support the access control functions of permitting or denying access, logging of activity, and detecting violations. Restricted utilities are programs or commands that perform specific system tasks and usually must run in privileged mode. These must be reviewed systematically for possible misuse of privilege. Possible system vulnerabilities introduced by such special software elements as the system control program, data base management systems, communications systems, and installation-developed programs must also be critically examined so that proper controls can be devised to prevent misuse. The control elements, restricted utilities, and vulnerable software in the MVS and VM operating systems are discussed in detail in Chapter II-2-5.

Physical Security and Control of the Data Center

MELVYN MUSSON

Physical security and control is the protection of the computer room against human-made and natural hazards, whether accidental or intentional. Data center equipment can be damaged and its operations interrupted because of inadequate controls or because a potential hazard was not considered. For example, it is often incorrectly assumed that it is impossible to control for earthquakes or hurricanes; computer rooms can be designed to withstand such hazards. Also, it is inadequate to focus only on potential hazards originating in the data center. Threats to the area around the data center can also affect computer operations and must be considered. This chapter therefore focuses on the types of threats that can affect the data center, whether originating inside or outside the computer room, and discusses the controls that can be implemented to eliminate these threats or mitigate their effect.

RESPONDING TO THE THREAT

Physical security controls are intended to protect assets that are essential to the successful operation of computer and telecommunications systems, including equipment and facilities, essential utilities, software and data, processing services, and employees. Controls should be designed to protect the key processes of information collection, processing, storage, transmittal, and retrieval.

The types of threats that must be protected against include:

- *Physical damage*. This is damage to the computer room and its equipment and software, as a result of such hazards as fire, smoke, and explosion.
- *Natural hazards*. Assets can be damaged by earthquake, lightning, windstorm, hurricane, tornado, flood, or volcanic eruption.
- *Environmental hazards*. Computer operations can be damaged as the result of flammable, toxic, or corrosive chemicals within or outside the data center.
- *Threats to supporting utilities*. These may include loss of electrical power or communications lines inside or outside the computer facility or loss of climate control in the computer room.

- *Crime*. Computer operations can also be threatened by such criminal activities as vandalism, sabotage, or terrorist acts.

It is important to assess adequately the potential losses that can result from such hazards to the data center as part of an overall assessment of risk. Control measures should cover:

- *Protection requirements*. Requirements for protecting against natural and human-made hazards should be specified for such areas as construction, fire protection, and access control.
- *Maintenance and testing*. Requirements should be determined for maintaining and testing all protection equipment.
- *Employee responsibilities*. Employees may engage in actions that can cause or contribute to a loss. Work practices should be defined that help prevent such loss and limit human behaviors that expose the organization to risk.
- *Risk analysis and control plan*. The plan should identify risk exposures to the data center and specify the controls needed to eliminate these exposures or mitigate their impact.
- *Management responsibilities*. Responsibilities of managers for enforcing and maintaining the control plan should be defined.

FACILITY REQUIREMENTS

This section addresses the considerations that should be taken in selecting the site of the computer center, protecting hardware and related supplies, preventing and detecting hazards related to electrical and environmental support systems, and selecting and evaluating the materials used to construct the data center. Each of these areas presents a unique set of risks requiring the appropriate security response.

Site Selection

Physical protection begins with the selection of the site for the data center. Whether the center is to occupy a building of its own or share space in an existing building, the risks associated with its physical location must be assessed. The security practitioner should select a site that minimizes these hazards.

The natural hazards associated with the location should be evaluated. If the area under consideration is subject to earthquakes, tornados, or hurricanes, the potential damage must be assessed; the building should be designed and constructed to withstand such damage. The facility should not be located in a flood plain.

In evaluating potential sites, the security practitioner should also attempt to minimize the possibility of sabotage and arson. The building should be sited and constructed to minimize the possibility of penetration by explosive or incendiary devices, and access to the center should be restricted to authorized personnel.

The computer room should not be accessible from the street or ground level. In the past, some organizations placed their computer centers on the ground floor in order to showcase them to visitors. However, this also made them more vulnerable to sabotage and unauthorized penetration. It is now thought best to keep these centers as unobtrusive as possible.

The security practitioner should also carefully evaluate activities in adjacent buildings or floors, rating these activities according to their level of risk. The computer room should be kept away from areas deemed to be too hazardous. For example, the center should generally be well separated from manufacturing areas or storage rooms whose operations might expose the center to increased danger. In one case, a data center was located in a complex of buildings, one of which was used to repair and maintain auto parts. A highly flammable solvent stored in this building was ignited by sparks; the ensuing fire eventually spread to all buildings in the complex, including the data center. In another case, a bank's data center was shut down after a fire on the floor above. The center was spared the fire only to be flooded by the water used to fight the fire.

The data center should not be located in the basement of a building, if that can be avoided; basements are more likely to be flooded. If a basement must be used, it must have adequate drainage and storm sewers must have adequate capacity for current and future needs.

Protection of Hardware and Related Supplies

Data processing equipment—processors, consoles, disk memory units, high-speed printers, and communications equipment—are not inherently combustible. Fire can result from component malfunctions, but such fires can usually be readily detected by smoke-detection systems and brought under control quickly using hand-held fire extinguishers. The unit may have to be taken out of service until repaired or replaced; if there is sufficient redundancy of equipment, computer processing may not be interrupted by such an event.

In one case, for example, a column of smoke was observed coming from a processing unit in the computer room of an electronics manufacturer. After the system was shut down, the fire was located in a six-inch-wide area inside the processor's cabinet. The fire was extinguished with a hand-held extinguisher, and the air-conditioner was switched to exhaust to remove the smoke. The rest of the data center continued to operate throughout this episode. It was found that the fire had resulted from a short circuit in a memory card; the damaged system was repaired and back online that afternoon.

Although damage caused by fire can be contained reasonably well, computer equipment, tapes, and disks are very susceptible to heat and smoke damage. Furthermore, related storage media and supplies, including paper, microfilm, and various types of plastics, are highly combustible.

A major hazard stems from the fact that paper forms, records, and computer output as well as magnetic tapes and cardboard boxes are frequently stored in the area surrounding computer equipment. Many organizations store current tapes in the open in the computer room; others may use fire-resistant cabinets but keep the doors open to facilitate access. In other cases, storage areas for magnetic tapes and paper records face onto the computer room. And in some organizations, offices are actually part of the computer room itself; these offices may contain various combustible documents and supplies.

Although an equipment fire can usually be readily detected and controlled, the risk of extensive damage to the facility grows if paper and plastic materials are allowed to accumulate in proximity to computer equipment. A fire in the computer room can damage or destroy tapes and disks, even if the fire is quickly brought under control.

For example, a fire occurred in an airline reservations center that contained five computer terminals, two printers, several plastic disk cases, and thousands of diskettes. Although the fire was confined to the area around its source—a window air-conditioner—the resulting smoke and heat caused extensive damage to computer equipment, disks, and diskettes.

Electrical and Environmental Hazards

Electrical distribution systems are the major source of fires in data centers according to the latest study of computer center fires conducted by the National Fire Protection Association (NFPA) (see Exhibit II-2-1). This study found that 30.2% of data center fires involved electrical distribution systems, whereas 28.5% involved other types of processing and service equipment as well as unclassified electrical malfunctions.

Electrical fires can be caused by such factors as improper installation of electri-

---

EXHIBIT II-2-1 Causes of Computer Center Fires

Cause of Fire	Percentage of Fires
Electrical Distribution Systems	30.2
Other Equipment	28.5
Air-Conditioning Equipment	9.3
Suspicious Incendiary Events	7.9
Smoking	6.6
Open Flames	6.4
Heating Systems	3.5
Cooking Equipment	2.6
Exposure to Adjacent Occupants/Buildings	2.6
Unknown Cause	1.9
Natural Cause	0.7

Note:
The NFPA studied computer center fires for the period 1981–1985.

cal equipment, overloaded circuits, and the presence of large amounts of cabling in a confined space (typically under the floor). In addition, in many computer centers, electrical equipment is frequently changed; it may be incorrectly assumed that the existing electrical supply to these systems is adequate. Exhibit II-2-2 provides a checklist for evaluating potential electrical hazards.

Air-conditioning equipment accounted for 9.3% of the data center fires in the NFPA study. Special consideration must be given to the installation and operation of such equipment. Computer rooms should be equipped with their own air-conditioning units, and the electrical power supply should be adequate for the demand. Air filters, duct insulation, and linings should be made of noncombustible material. Automatic fire and smoke dampers should be provided in ducts if the ducts serve other areas in addition to the computer room; fire dampers should be installed in any ducts that pass through walls.

It is important that the temperature and humidity in the computer room be monitored routinely. (Computer rooms are usually maintained at about 70°F, with a relative humidity of about 50%.) If targeted levels are not maintained, the monitor should sound an alarm at a permanently staffed, central location. The detection system should also be able to automatically disconnect the air-conditioning system, if that becomes necessary. Moisture detectors and drains should be installed

EXHIBIT II-2-2 Checklist for Evaluating Hazards of Electrical Fire

	Yes	No
Is the electrical supply adequate for the demand?	☐	☐
Is wiring of the correct size? (There should be no temporary wiring arrangements.)	☐	☐
Is the power cable from the 415-volt power source to the mainframe less than 148 ft. long (the maximum length according to NFPA Standard 75)?	☐	☐
Has the wiring under the floor been kept to a minimum?	☐	☐
Are equipment cabinets and the area under the floor cleaned periodically?	☐	☐
Is the airflow sufficient to prevent heat buildup in equipment cabinets?	☐	☐
Is voltage sufficiently regulated to prevent power surges, voltage reductions, or other line disturbances that can affect computer equipment?	☐	☐
Are cable openings in fire-rated walls, floors, and ceilings fire stopped by approved material with the same fire resistance rating as the penetrated barrier?	☐	☐
Has an uninterruptible power supply (UPS) been provided?	☐	☐
Does the UPS disengage in the event of an emergency equipment shutdown?	☐	☐
Is there an emergency disconnect switch near the exit door?	☐	☐
Does the emergency disconnect system operate appropriately when the protection system (including detectors) is activated?	☐	☐
Has unused cabling been removed from the under-floor area? (New computer equipment has lower power requirements and needs less cabling.)	☐	☐
Has lightning protection been provided?	☐	☐

in the area under the floor of the computer room if liquid-cooled air-conditioning or computer equipment is installed or if the room has a sprinkler system.

Selecting and Evaluating Construction Materials

NFPA Standard 75, Protection of Electronic Computer/Data Processing Equipment, specifies that the building housing the data center should be composed of fire-resistant or noncombustible materials, supplemented by a sprinkler system. Specifically, the materials used in walls, floors, ceilings, partitions, finishes, and acoustical treatments must have a flame-spread rating less than or equal to 25. The fire-resistant characteristics of the walls of the computer room, as well as the general data center, are specified in this standard:

- Walls separating the computer room from other sections of the data center should have a fire-resistance rating of at least one hour, as should the walls separating the data center from the rest of the building.
- The fire-resistance rating of data center walls should be increased if warranted because of hazards present in other areas of the building or because existing fire-protection systems are deemed inadequate.
- Walls separating stored paper, records, and tapes from other areas should have a two-hour fire-resistance rating.
- All fire-rated walls should be constructed from the structural floor of the computer center to the structural floor above or to the roof. Doors should have a fire-resistance rating commensurate with the fire rating of the walls.
- Openings in walls should be kept to a minimum and be protected by automatic fire doors, fire dampers, or fire shutters.

In multistoried buildings, the floor above the computer room should be reasonably watertight to prevent water damage to equipment below. No drains should pass through the computer room or be located above it. If this cannot be avoided, moisture detectors should be installed in the area under the floor of the computer room. The structural floor of the computer center should support a live load of 150 pounds per square foot. A floor-to-floor height of 15 feet is recommended, and columns should be spaced at 30-foot intervals to provide for efficient configuration of computer hardware.

Typically, the computer room is designed to house computer processors and peripheral equipment and the supplies needed to maintain operations. The amount of paper stock and other combustible material housed in the computer room should be kept to the absolute minimum required for efficient operations. Such materials should be enclosed in metal file cabinets. Furniture in the computer room should be built of metal or other fire-resistant materials.

Similar attention should be given to the offices, work areas, and storage areas adjacent to the computer room. Printers and ancillary equipment for data output should be located in these areas adjacent to the computer room. Fire protection should be planned for the entire data center, not just the computer room.

Special consideration should be given to the safe storage of costly, preprinted forms (e.g., invoices) and other documents essential to business operations. Even if computer equipment is well protected, the organization may not be able to function if forms needed for computer output have been destroyed. Commercial printers typically require several weeks of lead time to produce these forms; the organization may not be able to tolerate such a delay.

ACCESS CONTROLS

Access to the computer center and computer systems should be restricted to authorized persons. Visitors to the data center should be required to sign in and sign out and should be accompanied at all times.

To control access, verification of personal identification is required. There are three basic techniques for verifying the identity of persons attempting to gain access: use of personal identification numbers, card-based systems, and biometrics.

The use of personal identification numbers can be easily compromised and may therefore actually threaten accurate verification. Card-based systems and biometrics offer advantages as well as disadvantages, as described in the following sections.

Card-Based Systems

A unique personal possession such as a coded card or key can be used to establish the identity of the possessor. Four types of cards are used.

Magnetic Stripe. Information identifying the card is encoded in a magnetic stripe on the back of the card. This information is read by inserting the card into magnetic readers at points of access. Although such cards are inexpensive and can store large quantities of data, the magnetic stripes can be damaged or erased. Cards are susceptible to counterfeiting. In addition, card readers require relatively frequent maintenance, and card slots are subject to vandalism.

Magnetic Dot. These cards store encoded information in particles of barium ferrite between layers of plastic; the information is read by means of magnetic card readers. Although such cards are economical, they are not very durable and can be erased. Card readers suffer the same disadvantages described for magnetic stripe devices.

Embedded Wire. Known as Wiegand cards, these cards contain small ferromagnetic wires embedded in plastic that react to magnetic pulses generated by the card reader. These devices are moderately priced and less vulnerable to wear and vandalism than are conventional card readers. The cards cannot be erased, because they are immune to external magnetic fields. However, these cards can become worn, and they may be incorrectly read if the card is not properly oriented while passing through the reading slot.

Proximity Card. Such reflected frequency cards emit radio signals that can be read by a reader without the need to insert the card in a slot. Such cards are durable, convenient to use, and difficult to duplicate. However, these cards are more expensive than magnetic cards and are susceptible to radio interference if another card is nearby.

Biometric Systems

Biometric devices can be used to identify either a unique physical characteristic, such as a finger or palm print or the retinal pattern of an eye, or a unique personal activity, such as the characteristics of a signature, voice, or keystrokes. Most of these methods of biometric identification involve expensive equipment. However, the expense may be justified depending on the value of the information being protected and the nature of the risks involved.

PROTECTION OF RECORDS

NFPA Standard 75 specifies the measures that should be taken to protect information records; its recommendations depend on the relative importance of the records to be protected. NFPA Standard 232, Protection of Records, provides a classification of records, as described in the following section.

Record Types

Two types of records are defined: vital and important records. Vital records are those that are irreplaceable or that must be available at all times to avoid serious legal liability or business loss. Such records include those for which a reproduction cannot be substituted for the original; records needed to sustain the business or recover monies to replace buildings, equipment, and material; and records needed to avoid delay in restoring production, sales, and service.

Important records are those for which a reproduction, though acceptable as a substitute for the original, can be obtained only at great expense or effort or only after a significant delay.

Minimum Protection Requirements

NFPA Standard 75 specifies that all vital or important records should be protected or duplicated; in some circumstances, it may be necessary to do both. Duplicate records should be stored in an area that is not subject to the same potential hazards as that for the originals. The following sections describe specific protection requirements.

Protecting Records Stored in the Computer Room. Vital or important records that have not been duplicated should be stored in approved Class 150 storage equipment with a fire-resistance rating of at least one hour. All other records should be stored in closed metal files or cabinets.

Protecting Records Stored Outside the Computer Room. Vital or important records that have not been duplicated should be stored in rooms with a fire-resistance rating of at least two hours. This rating should be increased if warranted by potential fire conditions.

Backing Up Records. It is important to store backup copies of the most current records at a reliable off-site location. A minimum of two generations of records should be stored; the first generation (i.e., parent) might be stored at the off-site location, with the second generation (i.e., grandparent) stored at the data center in an area separate from the computer room. This type of arrangement allows for a reasonable rotation of backup records, although the specific method used will vary according to the needs of the organization.

FIRE PROTECTION TECHNIQUES

Fire protection involves techniques and equipment for both detecting and suppressing fires. As shown in Exhibit II-2-3, damage to computer equipment and related materials can begin at very low temperatures. Therefore, to ensure the best possible protection, the fire detection system must issue an alarm quickly before damage can occur. Likewise, the suppression system must respond quickly to extinguish the fire. The following sections discuss the appropriate methods for fire detection and suppression.

It should be noted that NFPA Standard 75 provides additional information on how to determine the protection requirements of the data center, including special requirements of large or complex installations. Protection methods should be determined after a complete evaluation of potential fire exposures. Such factors as building construction and contents, equipment construction, business interruption, and security requirements should be considered. Exhibit II-2-4 provides a sum-

EXHIBIT II-2-3 Temperatures at Which Damage Occurs

Item Subject to Damage	Temperature
Computer Equipment	175°F
Magnetic Tapes/Diskettes	100°F to 120°F
Disks	150°F
Paper Products	350°F
Microfilm	225°F (in presence of steam)
	300°F (in absence of steam)

EXHIBIT II-2-4 Fire Protection Systems Recommended by NFPA Standard 75

PROTECTION SYSTEMS / AREAS	Automatic Sprinkler System	Automatic Smoke Detection System	Portable Fire Extinguishers and Equipment	Emergency Control Team	Automatic Gas-Based System (Halon 1301)
Equipment Areas	R	R	R	R	O
Record Storage Areas	R	R	R	R	O
Raised Floor Areas — Under 18" Depth	N	R	A*	A	O
Raised Floor Areas — 18"–36" Depth	R***	R	A*	A	R***
Raised Floor Areas — Over 36" Depth	R	R	A*	A	O
Special Equipment Units	**	O**	A	A	O**

Key:
R Required
O Optional
A Available (in the space above or nearby)
N Not Required

Notes:
* Floor Lifters Required
** Special Engineering Required
*** Either an Automatic Sprinkler or Automatic Halon 1301 (or its designated replacement) Required

mary of NFPA recommendations for fire-protection systems for each area of the data center.

Fire-Detection Techniques and Equipment

A smoke-detection system is required to provide early warning of fire. A heat-detection system is not suitable. Fixed-temperature heat detectors operate between 135°F and 165°F; as shown in Exhibit II-2-3, damage to tapes and disks can occur within this detection range. Heat detectors that measure the rate of temperature increase are also inadequate, because by the time the rate of increase triggers the detector it is probably too late to prevent damage to tapes and disks.

Modern smoke-detection equipment is able to sense smoke and gases before flames develop. Such detection equipment should be installed in the computer room and support areas, including areas critical to computer operations and human safety that contain air-conditioning and electrical equipment, uninterruptible power supplies, transformers, and switchgear. Detectors should also be placed in data entry and storage areas in which tape, paper stock, and other combustibles are frequently found in large quantities.

The detection system should be designed to both set off a local alarm and to transmit an alarm to a central security location staffed around the clock (e.g., a security guard station or the local fire department). The system should also indicate on a control panel exactly where the incipient fire is located. This should be by section within the computer room and, in other areas, by section or specific equipment. The ability to identify quickly the location of a fire can significantly decrease the time required to bring the fire under control and can also minimize any damage caused by suppression materials.

It is important that the fire-detection system be designed to deter tampering and to alert authorities if the equipment has been tampered with. Procedures should also be in place to prevent tampering. In one case, for example, the key to the system's control cabinet was kept alongside the cabinet so that maintenance people could readily open the cabinet for routine servicing. An arsonist used this key to gain access to the control cabinet and turn off the alarm before setting a fire in the computer room.

Fire-Suppression Techniques and Equipment

An automatic extinguishing system is needed to provide fast control of fires. There is considerable debate as to whether a sprinkler system or gaseous extinguisher should be used. The type of protection used should be directly related to the importance of computer operations to the company's revenue-producing capabilities. The decision should not be based solely on such factors as the size of the computer room or the value of the equipment. With equipment downsizing, for example, a small room may contain critical equipment essential for continued business operations.

NFPA Standard 75 specifies that sprinkler protection should be provided to protect the data center if:

- Materials used to construct the computer room have a flame spread rating greater than 25.
- Computer system units or enclosures are built using a significant quantity of combustible materials.
- Computer room operations involves use of a significant quantity of combustible materials.
- The building is otherwise required to have a sprinkler system.

The standard further states that whether or not the computer room is served by a sprinkler system, consideration should also be given to using a gaseous total flooding system if there is a critical need to protect data, reduce equipment damage, and facilitate return to service. In summary, it is recommended that a sprinkler system serve as the basic form of fire suppression, supplemented with a gaseous total flooding system if conditions warrant.

Sprinkler Systems. Sprinkler systems should be considered for use in any areas of the computer center containing significant quantities of combustible materials, including tape vaults and paper storage areas. Sprinkler systems can safely be used in rooms housing electronic equipment; water will not damage equipment that has been deenergized. (If energized equipment becomes wet, damaging electrical shorts and arcing can result.) Computer equipment that gets wet must be disassembled, dried out, and reassembled before it can be put back in service; this is the major drawback to sprinkler systems.

Gaseous Total Flooding Systems. Until recently, Halon had been the primary gas used to suppress fires in data centers. However, because of concerns about environmental damage caused by chlorofluorocarbons, the use of Halon will be prohibited in the near future. Research is being conducted to identify alternatives to Halon other than carbon dioxide.

Fire Extinguishers. An adequate number of portable water, carbon dioxide, or Halon 1211 fire extinguishers should be provided for the data center, and staff people should be trained in their use. A sign should be placed next to each extinguisher clearly indicating its contents and what it is to be used for. In most cases, such portable extinguishers are only capable of handling small, incipient fires. Foam and dry chemical extinguishers are not recommended for fires involving computer equipment: dry chemicals are corrosive and both types require extensive cleanup.

HOUSEKEEPING PRACTICES

Successful fire prevention is as much a matter of good housekeeping as it is the application of detection and suppression systems. Basic housekeeping considerations include:

- Minimizing the amount of combustibles in the computer area.
- Prohibiting smoking, eating, or drinking in the computer room.
- Using self-extinguishing trash receptacles.

The area under raised floors containing cabling, controlled air cooling, and other vital services should be inspected periodically. This area should be kept clean and free of extraneous materials.

SUMMARY

Effective physical security should be based on an analysis of the risk exposures to the data center and the impact of such exposures on both data center and overall business operations. Specific recommendations for data center construction, fire protection, access controls, and center maintenance should be developed and implemented on the basis of that analysis. These controls must be cost effective relative to the benefits they provide the organization.

This process can be broken down into five steps:

- Identifying areas at risk.
- Analyzing the identified exposures to the computer center.
- Estimating potential losses resulting from these exposures.
- Identifying the necessary controls for eliminating or mitigating these exposures.
- Implementing the controls.

History has shown that exposures originating outside the data center are more prevalent and often more serious than those from within the data center. Therefore, areas both inside and outside the center must be considered in developing a protection plan.

The protection program itself includes three components:

- *Control.* Automated and manual methods to help prevent an incident from occurring.
- *Emergency response.* A mechanism for quickly detecting and limiting the impact of an incident.
- *Disaster recovery planning.* A plan for timely recovery from an incident.

It must be remembered that physical security controls cannot be expected to eliminate completely all hazards; in some cases, they may be able only to reduce the impact of an incident. All controls should be reviewed periodically and updated as needed. Maintenance and testing procedures should be implemented for all protection-related equipment.

No security program can succeed without the cooperation and support of management and staff. Employee responsibilities for effective practices to reduce risks and help prevent loss should be clearly defined and enforced. The responsibilities of management for enforcing and maintaining the risk control program should also be well defined.

CHAPTER II-2-2

Operations Security and Controls

PATRICIA A.P. FISHER

Operations security and controls safeguard information assets while the data is resident in the computer or otherwise directly associated with the computing environment. The controls address both software and hardware as well as such processes as change control and problem management. Physical controls are not included and may be required in addition to operations controls.

Operations security and controls can be considered the heart of information security because they control the way data is accessed and processed. No information security program is complete without a thoroughly considered set of controls designed to promote both adequate and reasonable levels of security. The operations controls should provide consistency across all applications and processes; however, the resulting program should be neither too excessive nor too repressive.

Resource protection, privileged-entity control, and hardware control are critical aspects of the operations controls. To understand this important security area, managers must first understand these three concepts. The following sections give a detailed description of them.

RESOURCE PROTECTION

Resource protection safeguards all of the organization's computing resources from loss or compromise, including main storage, storage media (e.g., tape, disk, and optical devices), communications software and hardware, processing equipment, standalone computers, and printers. The method of protection used should not make working within the organization's computing environment an onerous task, nor should it be so flexible that it cannot adequately control excesses. Ideally, it should obtain a balance between these extremes, as dictated by the organization's specific needs.

This balance depends on two items. One is the value of the data, which may be stated in terms of intrinsic value or monetary value. Intrinsic value is determined by the data's sensitivity—for example, health- and defense-related information have a high intrinsic value. The monetary value is the potential financial or physical losses that would occur should the data be violated.

The second item is the ongoing business need for the data, which is particularly relevant when continuous availability (i.e., round-the-clock processing) is required.

When a choice must be made between structuring communications to produce a user-friendly environment, in which it may be more difficult for the equipment to operate reliably, and ensuring that the equipment is better controlled but not as user friendly (emphasizing availability), control must take precedence. Ease of use serves no purpose if the more basic need for equipment availability is not considered.

Resource protection is designed to help reduce the possibility of damage that might result from unauthorized disclosure and alteration of data by limiting opportunities for misuse. Therefore, both the general user and the technician must meet the same basic standards against which all access to resources is applied.

A more recent aspect of the need for resource protection involves legal requirements to protect data. Laws surrounding the privacy and protection of data are rapidly becoming more restrictive. Increasingly, organizations that do not exercise due care in the handling and maintenance of data are likely to find themselves at risk of litigation. A consistent, well-understood user methodology for the protection of information resources is becoming more important to not only reduce information damage and limit opportunities for misuse but to reduce litigation risks.

Accountability

Access and use must be specific to an individual user at a particular moment in time; it must be possible to track access and use to that individual. Throughout the entire protection process, user access must be appropriately controlled and limited to prevent excess privileges and the opportunity for serious errors. Tracking must always be an important dimension of this control. At the conclusion of the entire cycle, violations occurring during access and data manipulation phases must be reported on a regular basis so that these security problems can be solved.

Activity must be tracked to specific individuals to determine accountability. Responsibility for all actions is an integral part of accountability; holding someone accountable without assigning responsibility is meaningless. Conversley, to assign responsibility without accountability makes it impossible to enforce responsibility. Therefore, any method for protecting resources requires both responsibility and accountability for all of the parties involved in developing, maintaining, and using processing resources.

An example of providing accountability and responsibility can be found in the way some organizations handle passwords. Users are taught that their passwords are to be stored in a secure location and not disclosed to anyone. In some organizations, first-time violators are reprimanded; if they continue to expose organizational information, however, penalties may be imposed, including dismissal.

Violation Processing

To understand what has actually taken place during a computing session, it is often necessary to have a mechanism that captures the detail surrounding access, particularly accesses occurring outside the bounds of anticipated actions. Any activity beyond those designed into the system and specifically permitted by the generally established rules of the site should be considered a violation.

Capturing activity permits determination of whether a violation has occurred or whether elements of software and hardware implementation were merely omitted, therefore requirng modification. In this regard, tracking and analyzing violations are equally important. Violation tracking is necessary to satisfy the requirements for the due care of information. Without violation tracking, the ability to determine excesses or unauthorized use becomes extremely difficult, if not impossible. For example, a general user might discover that, because of an administrative error, he or she can access system control functions. Adequate, regular tracking highlights such inappropriate privileges before errors can occur.

An all-too-frequently overlooked component of violation processing is analysis. Violation analysis permits an organization to locate and understand specific trouble spots, both in security and usability. Violation analysis can be used to find:

- The types of violations occurring. For example:
  —Are repetitive mistakes being made? This might be a sign of poor implementation or user training.
  —Are individuals exceeding their system needs? This might be an indication of weak control implemtnation.
  —Do too many people have too many update abilities? This might be a result of inadequate information security design.
- Where the violations are occurring, which might help identify program or design problems.
- Patterns that can provide an early warning of serious intrusions (e.g., hackers or disgruntled employees).

A specialized form of violation examination, intrusion analysis (i.e., attempting to provide analysis of intrusion patterns), is gaining increased attention. As expert systems gain in popularity and ability, their use in analyzing patterns and recognizing potential security violations will grow. The need for such automated methods is based on the fact that intrusions continue to increase rapidly in quantity and intensity and are related directly to the increasing number of personal computers connected to various networks. The need for automated methods is not likely to diminish in the near future, at least not until laws surrounding computer intrusion are much more clearly defined and enforced.

Currently, these laws are not widely enforced because damages and injuries are usually not reported and therefore cannot be proved. Overburdened law enforcement officials are hesitant to actively pursue these violations because they have more pressing cases (e.g., murder and assault). Although usually less damaging from a physical injury point of view, information security violations may be significantly damaging in monetary terms. In several well-publicized cases, financial damage has exceeded $10 million. Not only do violation tracking and analysis assist in proving violations by providing a means for determining user errors and the occasional misuse of data, they also provide assistance in preventing serious crimes from going unnoticed and therefore unchallenged.

Clipping Levels. Organizations usually forgive a particular type, number, or pattern of violations, thus permitting a predetermined number of user errors before gathering this data for analysis. An organization attempting to track all violations, without sophisticated statistical computing ability, would be unable to manage the sheer quantity of such data. To make a violation listing effective, a clipping level must be established.

The clipping level establishes a baseline for violation activities that may be normal user errors. Only after this baseline is exceeded is a violation record produced. This solution is particularly effective for small- to medium-sized installations. Organizations with large-scale computing facilities often track all violations and use statistical routines to cull out the minor infractions (e.g., forgetting a password or mistyping it several times).

If the number of violations being tracked becomes unmanageable, the first step in correcting the problems should be to analyze why the condition has occurred. Do users understand how they are to interact with the computer resource? Are the rules too difficult to follow? Violation tracking and analysis can be valuable tools in assisting an organization to develop thorough but usable controls. Once these are in place and records are produced that accurately reflect serious violations, tracking and analysis become the first line of defense. With this procedure, intrusions are discovered before major damage occurs and sometimes early enough to catch the perpetrator. In addition, business protection and preservation are strengthened.

Transparency

Controls must be transparent to users within the resource protection schema. This applies to three groups of users. First, all authorized users doing authorized work, whether technical or not, need to feel that computer system protection requirements are reasonably flexible and are not counterproductive. Therefore, the protection process must not require users to perform extra steps; instead, the controls should be built into the computing functions, encapsulating the users' actions and producing the multiple commands expected by the system.

The second group of users consists of authorized users attempting unauthorized work. The resource protection process should capture any attempt to perform unauthorized activity without revealing that it is doing so. At the same time, the process must prevent the unauthorized activity. This type of process deters the user from learning too much about the protective mechanism yet controls permitted activities.

The third type of user consists of unauthorized users attempting unauthorized work. With unauthorized users, it is important to deny access transparently to prevent the intruder from learning anything more about the system than is already known.

User Access Authorities

Resource protection mechanisms may be either manual or automatic. The size of the installation must be evaluated when the security administrator is considering the use of a manual methodology because it can quickly be outgrown, becoming impossible to control and maintain. Automatic mechanisms are typically more costly to implement but may soon recoup their cost in productivity savings.

Regardless of the automation level of a particular mechanism, it is necessary to be able to separate types of access according to user needs. The most effective approach is one of least privilege; that is, users should not be allowed to undertake actions beyond what their specific job responsibilities warrant. With this method, it is useful to divide users into several groups. Each group is then assigned the most restrictive authority available while permitting users to carry out the functions of their jobs.

There are several options to which users may be assigned. The most restrictive authority and the one to which most users should be assigned is read only. Users assigned to read only are allowed to view data but are not allowed to add, delete, or make changes.

The next level is read/write access, which allows users to add or modify data within applications for which they have authority. This level permits individuals to access a particular application and read, add, and write over data in files copied from the original location.

A third access level is change. This option permits the holder not only to read a file and write data to another file location but to change the original data, thereby altering it permanently.

When analyzing user access authorities, the security practitioner must distinguish between access to discretionary information resources (which is regulated only by personal judgment) and access to nondiscretionary resources (which is strictly regulated on the basis of the predetermined transaction methodology). Discretionary user access is defined as the ability to manipulate data by using custom-developed programs or a general-purpose utility program. The only information logged for discretionary access in an information security control mechanism is the type of data accessed and at what level of authority. It is not possible to identify specific uses of the data.

Nondiscretionary user access, on the other hand, is performed while executing specific business transactions that affect information in a predefined way. For this type of access, users can perform only certain functions in carefully structured ways. For example, in a large accounting system, many people prepare transactions that affect the ledger. Typically, one group of accounting analysts is able to enter the original source data but not to review or access the overall results. Another group has access to the data for review but is not able to alter the results.

In addition, with nondiscretionary access, the broad privileges assigned to a user for working with the system itself should be analyzed in conjunction with the user's existing authority to execute the specific transactions needed for the current job assignment. This type of access is important when a user can be authorized to both read and add information but not to delete or change it. For example, bank tellers need access to customer account information to add deposits but do not need the ability to change any existing information.

At times, even nondiscretionary access may not provide sufficient control. In such situations, special access controls can be invoked. Additional restrictions may be implemented in various combinations of add, change, delete, and read capabilities. The control and auditability requirements that have been designed into each application are used to control the management of the information assets involved in the process.

Special Classifications. A growing trend is to give users access to only resource subsets or perhaps to give them the ability to update information only when performing a specific task and following a specific procedure. This has created the need for a different type of access control in which authorization can be granted on the basis of both the individual requesting resource access and the intended use of that resource. This type of control can be exercised by the base access control mechanism (i.e., the authorization list, including user ID and program combinations).

Another method sometimes used provides the required access authority along with the programs the user has authorization for; this information is provided only after the individual's authority has been verified by an authorization program. This program may incorporate additional constraints (e.g., scoped access control) and may include thorough access logging along with ensuring data integrity when updating information.

Scoped access control is necessary when users need access only to selected areas or records within a resource, thereby controlling the access granted to a small group on the basis of an established method for separating that group from the rest of the data. In general, the base access control mechanism is activated at the time of resource initialization (i.e., when a data set is prepared for access). Therefore, scoped access control should be provided by the data base management system or the application program. For example, in personnel systems, managers are given authority to access only the information related to their employees.

PRIVILEGED-ENTITY CONTROL

Levels of privileges provide users with the ability to invoke the commands needed to accomplish their work. Every user has some degree of privilege. The term, however, has come to be applied more to those individuals performing specialized tasks that require broad capabilities than to the general user. In this context, a privilege provides the authority necessary to modify control functions (e.g., access control, logging, and violation detection) or may provide access to specific system vulnerabilities. (Vulnerabilities are elements of the system's software or hardware that can be used to gain unauthorized access to system facilities or data.) Thus, individuals in such positions as systems programming, operations, and systems monitoring are authorized to do more than general users.

A privilege can be global when it is applicable to the entire system, function-oriented when it is restricted to resources grouped according to a specific criterion, or application specific when it is implemented within a particular piece of application code. It should be noted that when an access control mechanism is compromised, lower-level controls may also be compromised. If the system itself is compromised, all resources are exposed regardless of any lower-level controls that may be implemented.

Indirect authorization is a special type of privilege by which access granted for one resource may give control over another privilege. For example, a user with indirect privileges may obtain authority to modify the password of a privileged user (e.g., the security administrator). In this case, the user does not have direct privileges but obtains them by signing on to the system as the privileged user (although this would be a misuse of the system). The activities of anyone with indirect privileges should be regularly monitored for abuse.

Extended or special access to computing resources is termed privileged-entity access. Extended access can be divided into various segments, called classes, with each succeeding class more powerful than those preceding it. The class into which general system users are grouped is the lowest, most restrictive class; a class that permits someone to change the computing operating system is the least restrictive, or most powerful. All other system support functions fall somewhere between these two.

Users must be specifically assigned to a class; users within one class should not be able to complete functions assigned to users in other classes. This can be accomplished by specifically defining class designations according to job functions and not permitting access ability to any lower classes except those specifically needed (e.g., all users need general user access to log on to the system). An example of this arrangement is shown in Exhibit II-2-5.

System users should be assigned to a class on the basis of their job functions; staff members with similar computing access needs are grouped together in a class. One of the most typical problems uncovered by information security audits relates to the implementation of system assignments. Often, sites permit class members to access all lesser functions (i.e., toward A in Exhibit II-2-5). Although

---

EXHIBIT II-2-5 Sample Privileged-Entity Access

Class	Job Assignment	Class Access Privileges
A	General User	A
B	Programmer	B, A
C	Manager	C, A (sometimes B)
D	Security Administrator	D, B, A
E	Operator	E, D, B, A
F	System Programmer	F, E, D, B, A
G	Auditor	G, B, A

it is much simpler to implement this plan than to assign access strictly according to need, such a plan provides little control over assets.

The more extensive the system privileges given within a class, the greater the need for control and monitoring to ensure that abuses do not occur. One method for providing control is to install an access control mechanism, which may be purchased from a vendor (e.g., RACF, CA-TOP SECRET, and CA-ACF2) or customized by the specific site or application group. To support an access control mechanism, the computer software provides a system control program. This program maintains control over several aspects of computer processing, including allowing use of the hardware, enforcing data storage conventions, and regulating the use of I/O devices.

The misuse of system control program privileges may give a user full control over the system, because altering control information or functions may allow any control mechanism to be compromised. Users who abuse these privileges can prevent the recording of their own unauthorized activities, erase any record of their previous activities from the audit log, and achieve uncontrolled access to system resources. Furthermore, they may insert a special code into the system control program that can allow them to become privileged at any time in the future.

The following sections discuss the way the system control program provides control over computer processing.

Restricting Hardware Instructions. The system control program can restrict the execution of certain computing functions, permitting them only when the processor is in a particular functional state (known as privileged or supervisor state) or when authorized by architecturally defined tables in control storage. Programs operate in various states, during which different commands are permitted. To be authorized to execute privileged hardware instructions, a program should be running in a restrictive state that allows these commands.

Instructions permitting changes in the program state are classified as privileged and are available only to the operating system and its extensions. Therefore, to ensure adequate protection of the system, only carefully selected individuals should be able to change the program state and execute these commands.

Controlling Main Storage. The use of address translation mechanisms can provide effective isolation between different users' storage locations. In addition, main storage protection mechanisms protect main storage control blocks against unauthorized access. One type of mechanism involves assignment of storage protection keys to portions of main storage to keep unauthorized users out.

The system control program can provide each user section of the system with a specific storage key to protect against read-only or update access. In this methodology, the system control program assigns a key to each task and manages all requests to change that key. To obtain access to a particular location in storage, the requesting routine must have an identical key or the master key.

Constraining I/O Operations. If desired, I/O instructions may be defined as privileged and issued only by the system control program after access authority has been verified. In this protection method, before the initiation of any I/O operations, a user's program must notify the system control program of both the specific data set and the type of process requested. The system control program then obtains information about the data set location, boundaries, and characteristics that it uses to confirm authorization to execute the I/O instruction.

The system control program controls the operation of user programs and isolates storage control blocks to protect them from access or alteration by an unauthorized program. Authorization mechanisms for programs using restricted system functions should not be confused with the mechanisms invoked when a general user requests a computing function. In fact, almost every system function (e.g., the user of any I/O device, including a display station or printer) implies the execution of some privileged system functions that do not require an authorized user.

Privilege Definition

All levels of system privileges must be defined to the operating system when hardware is installed, brought online, and made available to the user community. As the operating system is implemented, each user ID, along with an associated level of system privileges, is assigned to a predefined class within the operating system. Each class is associated with a maximum level of activity.

For example, operators are assigned to the class that has been assigned those functions that must be performed by operations personnel. Likewise, systems auditors are assigned to a class reserved for audit functions. Auditors should be permitted to perform only those tasks that both general users and auditors are authorized to perform, not those permitted for operators. By following this technique, the operating system may be partitioned to provide no more access than is absolutely necessary for each class of user.

Particular attention must be given to password management privileges. Some administrators must have the ability and therefore the authorization to change another user's password, and this activity should always be properly logged. The display password feature, which permits all passwords to be seen by the password administrator, should be disabled or blocked. If not disabled, this feature can adversely affect accountability, because it allows some users to see other users' passwords.

Privilege Control and Recertification

Privileged-entity access must be carefully controlled, because the user IDs associated with some system levels are very powerful and can be used inappropriately, causing damage to information stored within the computing resource. As with any other group of users, privileged users must be subject to periodic recertification to maintain the broad level of privileges that have been assigned to them. The basis for recertification should be substantiation of a continued need for the ID. Need, in this case, should be no greater than the regular, assigned duties of the support person and should never be allocated on the basis of organizational politics or backup.

A recertification process should be conducted on a regular basis, at least semi-annually, with line management verifying each individual's need to retain privileges. The agreement should be formalized yet not bureaucratic, perhaps accomplished by initialing and dating a list of those IDs that are to be recertified. By structuring the recertification process to include authorization by managers of personnel empowered with the privileges, a natural separation of duties occurs. This separation is extremely important to ensure adequate control. By separating duties, overallocation of system privileges is minimized.

For example, a system programmer cannot receive auditor privileges unless the manager believes this function is required within the duties of the particular job. On the other hand, if a special project requires a temporary change in system privileges, the manager can institute such a change for the term of the project. These privileges can then be canceled after the project has been completed.

Emergency Procedures. Privileged-entity access is often granted to more personnel than is necessary to ensure that theoretical emergency situations are covered. This should be avoided and another process employed during emergencies—for example, an automated process in which support personnel can actually assign themselves increased levels of privileges. In such instances, an audit record is produced, which calls attention to the fact that new privileges have been assigned. Management can then decide after the emergency whether it is appropriate to revoke the assignment. However, management must be notified so the support person's subsequent actions can be tracked.

A much more basic emergency procedure might involve leaving a privileged ID password in a sealed envelope with the site security staff. When the password is needed, the employee must sign out the envelope, which establishes ownership of the expanded privileges and alerts management. Although this may be the least preferred method of control, it alerts management that someone has the ability to access powerful functions. Audit records can then be examined for details of what that ID has accessed. Although misuse of various privileged functions cannot be prevented with this technique, reasonable control can be accomplished without eliminating the ability to continue performing business functions in an efficient manner.

Activity Reporting. All activity connected with privileged IDs should be reported on logging audit records. These records should be reviewed periodically to ensure that privileged IDs are not being misused. Either a sample of the audit records should be reviewed using a predetermined methodology incorporating approved EDP auditing and review techniques or all accesses should be reviewed using expert system applications. Transactions that deviate from those normally conducted should be examined and, if necessary, fully investigated.

Under no circumstances should management skip the regular review of these activities. Many organizations have found that a regular review process deters curiosity and even mischief within the site and often produces the first evidence of attempted hacking by outsiders.

CHANGE MANAGEMENT CONTROLS

Additional control over activities by personnel using privileged access IDs can be provided by administrative techniques. For example, the most easily sidestepped control is change control. Therefore, every computing facility should have a policy regarding changes to operating systems, computing equipment, networks, environmental facilities (e.g., air-conditioning, water, heat, plumbing, electricity, and alarms), and applications. A policy is necessary if change is to be not only effective but orderly, because the purpose of the change control process is to manage changes to the computing environment.

The goals of the management process are to eliminate problems and errors and to ensure that the entire environment is stable. To achieve these goals, it is important to:

- *Ensure orderly change.* In a facility that requires a high level of systems availability, all changes must be managed in a process that can control any variables that may affect the environment. Because change can be a serious disruption, however, it must be carefully and consistently controlled.
- *Inform the computing community of the change.* Changes assumed to affect only a small subsection of a site or group may in fact affect a much broader cross-section of the computing community. Therefore, the entire computing community should receive adequate notification of impending changes. It is helpful to create a committee representing a broad cross-section of the user group to review proposed changes and their potential effect on users.

399

- *Analyze changes.* The presentation of an intended change to an oversight committee, with the corresponding documentation of the change, often effectively exposes the change to careful scrutiny. This analysis clarifies the originator's intent before the change is implemented and is helpful in preventing erroneous or inadequately considered changes from entering the system.
- *Reduce the impact of changes on service.* Computing resources must be available when the organization needs them. Poor judgment, erroneous changes, and inadequate preparation must not be allowed in the change process. A well-structured change management process prevents problems and keeps computing services running smoothly.

General procedures should be in place to support the change control policy. These procedures must, at the least, include steps for instituting a major change to the site's physical facility or to any major elements of the system's software or hardware. The following steps should be included:

1. *Applying to introduce a change.* A method must be established for applying to introduce a change that will affect the computing environment in areas covered by the change control policy. Change control requests must be presented to the individual who will manage the change through all of its subsequent steps.
2. *Cataloging the change.* The change request should be entered into a change log, which provides documentation for the change itself (e.g., the timing and testing of the change). This log should be updated as the change moves through the process, providing a thorough audit trail of all changes.
3. *Scheduling the change.* After thorough preparation and testing by the sponsor, the change should be scheduled for review by a change control committee and for implementation. The implementation date should be set far enough in advance to provide the committee with sufficient review time. At the meeting with the change control committee, all known ramifications of the change should be discussed. If the committee members agree that the change has been thoroughly tested, it should be entered on the implementation schedule and noted as approved. All approvals and denials should be in writing, with appropriate reasons given for denials.
4. *Implementing the change.* The final step in the change process is application of the change to the hardware and software environment. If the change works correctly, this should be noted on the change control form. When the change does not perform as expected, the corresponding information should be gathered, analyzed, and entered on the change control form, as a reference to help avoid a recurrence of the same problem in the future.
5. *Reporting changes to management.* Periodically, a full report summarizing change activity should be submitted to management. This helps ensure that

management is aware of any quality problems that may have developed and enables management to address any service problems.

These steps should be documented and made known to all involved in the change process. Once a change process has been established, someone must be assigned the responsibility for managing all changes throughout the process.

HARDWARE CONTROL

Security and control issues often revolve around software and physical needs. In addition, the hardware itself can have security vulnerabilities and exposures that need to be controlled. The hardware access control mechanism is supported by operating system software. However, hardware capabilities can be used to obtain access to system resources. Software-based control mechanisms, including audit trail maintenance, are ineffective against hardware-related access. Manual control procedures should be implemented to ensure that any hardware vulnerability is adequately protected.

When the system control program is initialized, the installation personnel select the desired operating system and other software code. However, by selecting a different operating system or merely a different setup of the operating system (i.e., changing the way the hardware mechanisms are used), software access control mechanisms can be defeated.

Some equipment provides hardware maintenance functions that allow main storage display and modification in addition to the ability to trace all program instructions while the system is running. These capabilities enable someone to update system control block information and obtain system privileges for use in compromising information. Although it is possible to access business information directly from main storage, the information may be encrypted. It is simpler to obtain privileges and run programs that can turn encrypted data into understandable information.

Another hardware-related exposure is the unauthorized connection of a device or communications line to a processor that can access information without interfacing with the required controls. Hardware manufacturers often maintain information on their hardware's vulnerabilities and exposures. Discussions with specific vendors should provide data that will help control these vulnerabilities.

Problem Management

Although problem management can affect different areas within computer services, it is most often encountered in dealing with hardware. This control process reports, tracks, and resolves problems affecting computer services. Management should be structured to measure the number and types of problems against predetermined service levels for the area in which the problem occurs. This area of management has three major objectives:

- Reducing failures to an acceptable level.
- Preventing recurrences of problems.
- Reducing impact on service.

Problems can be organized according to the types of problems that occur, enabling management to better focus on and control problems and thereby providing more meaningful measurement. Examples of the problem types include:

- Performance and availability.
- Hardware.
- Software.
- Environment (e.g., air-conditioning, plumbing, and heating).
- Procedures and operations (e.g., manual transactions).
- Network.
- Safety and security.

All functions in the organization that are affected by these problems should be included in the control process (e.g., operations, systems planning, network control, and systems programming).

Problem management should investigate any deviations from standards, unusual or unexplained occurrences, unscheduled initial program loads, or other abnormal conditions. Each is examined in the following sections.

Deviations from Standards. Every organization should have standards against which computing service levels are measured. These may be as simple as the number of hours a specific CPU is available during a fixed period of time. Any problem that affects the availability of this CPU should be quantified into time and deducted from the available service time. The resulting total provides a new, lower service level. This can be compared with the desired service level to determine the deviation.

Unusual or Unexplained Occurrences. Occasionally, problems cannot be readily understood or explained. They may be sporadic or appear to be random; whatever the specifics, they must be investigated and carefully analyzed for clues to their source. In addition, they must be quantified and grouped, even if in an Unexplained category. Frequently, these types of problems recur over a period of time or in similar circumstances, and patterns begin to develop that eventually lead to solutions.

Unscheduled Initial Program Loads. The primary reason a site undergoes an unscheduled initial program load (IPL) is that a problem has occurred. Some portion of the hardware may be malfunctioning and therefore slowing down, or software may be in an error condition from which it cannot recover. Whatever the reason, an occasional system queue must be cleared, hardware and software cleansed, and an IPL undertaken. This should be reported in the problem management system and tracked.

Other Abnormal Conditions. In addition to the preceding problems, such events as performance degradation, intermittent or unusual software failures, and incorrect systems software problems may occur. All should be tracked.

Problem Resolution

Problems should always be categorized and ranked in terms of their severity. This enables responsible personnel to concentrate their energies on solving those problems that are considered most severe, leaving those of lesser importance for a more convenient time.

When a problem can be solved, a test may be conducted to confirm problem resolution. Often, however, problems cannot be easily solved or tested. In these instances, a more subjective approach may be appropriate. For example, management may decide that if the problem does not recur within a predetermined number of days, the problem can be considered closed. Another way to close such problems is to reach a major milestone (e.g., completing the organization's year-end processing) without a recurrence of the problem.

SUMMARY

Operations security and control is an extremely important aspect of an organization's total information security program. The security program must continuously protect the organization's information resources within data center constraints. However, information security is only one aspect of the organization's overall functions. Therefore, it is imperative that control remain in balance with the organization's business, allowing the business to function as productively as possible. This balance is attained by focusing on the various aspects that make information security not only effective but as simple and transparent as possible.

Some elements of the security program are basic requirements. For example, general controls must be formulated, types of system use must be tracked, and violations must be tracked in any system. In addition, use of adequate control processes for manual procedures must be in place and monitored to ensure that availability and security needs are met for software, hardware, and personnel. Most important, whether the organization is designing and installing a new program or controlling an ongoing system, information security must always remain an integral part of the business and be addressed as such, thus affording an adequate and reasonable level of control based on the needs of the business.

Security and Control of Microcomputers

ZELLA G. RUTHBERG

Because of their rapidly expanding processing, storage, and networking capabilities, microcomputers are fast becoming the focal point of many organizations' computing activities. The information security administrator intent on safeguarding these devices and the often-critical data they process must understand the major issues in microcomputer security: physical security, access control (both physical and logical), communications security, and virus protection. This chapter assists the data security administrator and the microcomputer user in determining both the need for security and the techniques and types of products that can best meet that need.

THE MICROCOMPUTER SECURITY PROBLEM

Although microcomputers provide essentially the same functions as large systems (i.e., they permit the rapid manipulation and examination of large amounts of data), there are some characteristics that present special security problems. In general, the differences are in the following areas:

- Physical accessibility.
- Built-in security mechanisms.
- Nature of data being handled.
- Users' responsibilities.

Physical Accessibility

Basic physical protection of a computer system is required to ensure operational reliability and basic integrity of hardware and software. Other security mechanisms (e.g., those implemented in systems hardware and software) rely on this underlying level of protection. However, it is seldom feasible to build a protective shell around an individual personal computer. This means that protection against damage, hardware modification, or unauthorized access is difficult to achieve. Because many technical security mechanisms (e.g., access control software and cryptographic routines) often depend on the integrity of the underlying hardware and software, these security mechanisms may no longer provide the intended degree of protection.

Built-In Security Mechanisms

Most microcomputers lack the built-in hardware mechanisms needed to isolate users from sensitive, security-related, system functions. For example, the typical microcomputer does not support the following important security mechanisms that have long been available on larger systems:

- *Multiple processor states*. This enables maintenance of separate domains for users and system processes.
- *Privileged instructions*. This control limits access to certain functions (e.g., reading and writing to disk) to trusted system processes.
- *Memory protection features*. These features prevent unauthorized access to sensitive parts of the system.

Without such hardware features it is virtually impossible to prevent user programs from accessing or modifying parts of the operating system and thereby circumventing security mechanisms.

Nature of Data Being Handled

Information processed and stored on microcomputer systems often can be more sensitive and accessible than that found on larger, multiuser systems. This is due to the facts that information on a given machine is often associated with one person or group; such information is likely to be in the readily accessible form of memorandums, reports, spreadsheets, or lists; and this information tends to be in relatively final form rather than unprocessed raw data. The microcomputer is the electronic equivalent of the desk or file cabinet and, for sensitive information, requires equivalent security measures.

Users' Responsibilities

Many of the information protection responsibilities for microcomputers now reside with inexperienced users rather than a well-trained central data processing staff. The problems of providing adequate training, ensuring consistent procedures (security and otherwise), and minimizing duplication of effect (while retaining necessary separation of duties) are significant problems in the microcomputer environment.

REQUIRED CONTROLS

In any computer system there are several major areas of potential vulnerability that can have risks reduced by judicious use of management and technical security controls. When the computer system involves the use of microcomputer (either standalone or connected to other microcomputers or larger host computers), the areas of concern remain the same but the vulnerabilities and needed controls may change. These areas for control measures are:

- Physical and environmental controls.
- System and data access controls.
- Software and data integrity controls.
- Backup and contingency planning.
- Communications security.
- Virus protection.
- Auditability.

The next several sections discuss the vulnerabilities of microcomputers in these areas and the controls needed to reduce risks. In view of these control needs, several vendors have developed products designed to protect the computers themselves as well as the data they process and store. This chapter describes how to determine what security measures are needed and the types of security products that can be used to protect system resources.

PHYSICAL AND ENVIRONMENT CONTROLS

Physical controls are designed primarily to protect against theft of computer equipment as well as physical damage to such equipment. Environmental controls are concerned with counteracting risks posed by the environment in which the computer system exists. These include such risks as fire and flood.

Antitheft and Antidamage Measures

Microcomputing systems are often easy to carry and have a high resale value. At a minimum, therefore, each microcomputer in the organization should be secured against theft. This can be accomplished by locating the system in a lockable room, equipping the microcomputer with an alarm that sounds when the equipment is moved, putting the system in a locking workstation, or attaching the computer to a desk.

In most cases, putting the microcomputer in a locked room is the least expensive option. Isolating the equipment, however, could prove inconvenient, and the room might be left unlocked. An alarm is an effective deterrent only if someone is close enough to hear and respond to it. Furthermore, certain alarms are easily defeated. For example, the detector may consist simply of a weight-sensitive pad on which the system rests; placing another heavy object on the pad could prevent the alarm from sounding.

Another option, a locking workstation, ideally should provide a comfortable work area and should be difficult to move. Heavy, bulky cabinets with locking front panels are preferable; castors should by avoided. A cabinet has the added advantage of providing protection for other valuable items such as documentation and diskettes.

Several products allow the microcomputing system to be attached to a desk or a heavy table. The most effective of these enclose the computer within a box that is attached to the desk with bolts or glue. This approach prevents an intruder from removing the back panel and stealing expansion boards. Products that would permanently damage the desk should be avoided. Those that allow for easy, authorized removal of the system for servicing are useful.

The same measures used to counter possible theft of the equipment also provide damage protection.

Environmental Protection

In general, the more critical the work of the microcomputing system, the more it must be protected from failure. If the user can continue to work without the computer for several days, environmental protection is not a concern. Should the machine fail, the user can simply wait until it has been repaired or replaced. If such a delay is unacceptable, however, the computer should be protected from environmental threats stemming from fire, water, power failure or fluctuations, heat and humidity, air contaminants, and static electric discharge.

Fire and Water Protection. Not much can be done to protect the microcomputer system from fire; the sophisticated fire protection systems installed to protect large computers are prohibitively expensive. It is prudent, however, to install the personal computing system away from combustible materials and to place near the computer a fire extinguisher capable of putting out electrical fires. A plastic cover protects the system from overhead water leaks.

Electrical Power Protection. Electrical power protection devices suppress surges, reduce static, filter power to prevent irregular current, and provide battery backup in the event of total failure. Surge suppression is critical because a sudden jump in power can destroy the system. Some devices combine a power filter with a surge suppressor, battery backup, or both. Because the cost of these products ranges from $25 to $1,000, price may be the main consideration in selecting one. The device under consideration should be checked for an Underwriters Laboratory rating.

Temperature and Humidity Protection. The temperature and relative humidity found in the typical office environment are well within the operating limits of most personal computer systems. However, if equipment is used in other environments (e.g., on a factory floor or an outside location), users should refer to manufacturer specifications for the equipment. If portable systems are being used, care should be taken to avoid drastic changes in temperature or humidity (e.g., transporting a system from the outside into an office). Before operation, sufficient time should be allowed for the equipment to adjust to the new environment.

Air Contaminants Protection. The general cleanliness of the area in which personal computer equipment operates has an obvious effect on the reliability of both equipment and magnetic media. Electronic equipment (including microcomputers) will naturally attract charge particles in the air, such as smoke and dust. Therefore, such contaminants must be eliminated.

Magnetic Media Protection

Particular attention should be given to the protection of magnetic media. Not only is this the primary repository of each user's information; it is perhaps the system component most vulnerable to damage. The following discusses hazards affecting the two primary types of magnetic storage media found in microcomputer systems—fixed and flexible disk systems—and some general hazards that can affect all types of magnetic media.

Fixed Disk Devices. Fixed or hard disk devices usually are self-contained sealed units that are relatively well protected from environmental contaminants. However, care must be exercised when these units are moved, because of the danger of damage to read/write heads and other internal components.

Diskettes. Virtually every microcomputer system has at least one diskette drive. Diskettes are the most prevalent medium for distributing software and data, and the handling of diskettes is an integral part of using almost any microcomputer. The actual magnetic disk is contained within a protective jacket. However, there must be openings in the jacket for access by the read/write heads of the drive mechanism. These surfaces are particularly vulnerable to damage. Smaller diskettes employ a rigid plastic casing with a retractable access cover, thus reducing the vulnerability to rough handling and contaminants.

Proper handling techniques for flexible disks include:

- Always storing in the protective jacket.
- Protecting from bending or similar damage.
- Inserting carefully into the drive mechanism.
- Maintaining an acceptable temperature range (i.e., 50°–125°F).

- Avoiding direct contact with magnetic fields.
- Not writing directly on diskette jacket or sleeve.
- Touching a grounded unit to discharge built-up static electricity before touching disks.

Most of these precautions are simply common sense. Nevertheless, many microcomputer users are quite careless in handling such media, and management has the responsibility of providing proper training in this area.

General Hazards. Exposure to ordinary contaminants (e.g., smoke, hair, liquids) is probably the major reason for failures in magnetic media. Therefore, particular care should be exercised to minimize such exposures. Direct contact with magnetic devices should be minimized. It is worth noting, however, that airport X-ray devices and magnets (kept six or more inches away from magnetic media) pose no danger, despite considerable concerns to the contrary.

Simple wear is another cause of failure. Therefore, it is important that backup copies be made of all important disks. Indeed, day-to-day operation should be conducted with a backup copy, and not the master copy of such diskettes.

SYSTEM AND DATA ACCESS CONTROLS

These controls are designed to restrict access to system resources, including software and data. Shared use of microcomputers poses a potentially significant threat to these systems and may require the use of such sophisticated security mechanisms as access control software and encryption.

System-Level Protection

A microcomputing system usually is bought for an individual or for several individuals who share job responsibilities. In most cases, each person authorized to use the system is authorized to access all the information stored on it. The only security required is that needed to prevent unauthorized use.

Some antitheft products deter unauthorized use. For example, a locking cabinet that encloses the system and requires use of a key to gain access to the power switch or keyboard can prevent an outsider from using the equipment—and thus accessing the information stored there. Not all antitheft products prevent access, however. A detector that sounds an alarm if the computer is moved does not stop an intruder from using the system in place. Furthermore, if the key to the computer is left in the system or nearby, anyone can gain access.

Products are available that specifically limit access to the microcomputing system. The simplest put a lock on the power switch so that only those with a key can turn on the computer. Other products require the user to log on and supply a valid user identification code and password.

Protection in a Shared Environment

If the microcomputer is shared by users with varying levels of security clearance, further security may be required. Some users, for example, may be allowed to enter data but not to read or change that data.

To ensure that appropriate access is granted, several products implement sophisticated access controls on microcomputers. These controls are similar to those in such mainframe-based products as RACF (IBM Corp), CA-ACF2 (Computer Associates), and CA-TOP SECRET (Computer Associates). To gain access to the microcomputing system, the user must supply a valid identification code and password. After signing on the system, the user is allowed to view only that information to which access has been granted.

Therefore, in addition to identifying the user, there must be a means of identifying the resources to be protected. These resources are usually files containing data or programs but can also be the ability to perform a certain function within a given application. Data or programs can be given external labels visible to all (e.g., diskettes with colored jackets) or, for very sensitive information, internal labels readable by the computer. The ability to perform certain functions within an application requires more elaborate permission tables.

The term "access control" is applied both to products that limit who may use the computer and to those that additionally limit what users can do after they sign on. If separation of users is important, the product must provide both forms of access control.

If highly confidential data is stored on the system, the security products should ensure that a file is actually deleted when a user so instructs the system. Unsecured systems, rather than erasing files, merely flag the space on the hard disk as available. Another user could open a new file and then read the information that has been marked for deletion into the file.

An access control product may have additional features that prove useful. Logging, for example, can produce an audit trail that notes how often the system is used and by whom. Other features may include preventing users from copying software or controlling what commands the user can issue.

File Encryption

Some microcomputer security products control access by means of encryption, a process that scrambles information through use of a secret code, or key. A user who does not enter the correct key cannot unscramble files. Encryption protects deleted files as well. The user who opens a new file over an old one will be using a different key and will be unable to read the leftover data.

Some products combine access control with encryption. Users log on with a valid user ID code and password, and this information points to a profile specifying what the user is allowed to access. The system maintains encryption keys for all users so that the process is transparent to the user. The product decrypts information for a user only if its records indicate that the user is allowed access to the information.

A consideration in selecting one of these products is its means of encryption: software, hardware, or a combination of both. Software encryption can create performance problems; while it is encrypting, the microcomputer cannot perform other tasks. Although this is usually not a serious problem, the hardware approach is preferred if two products are equal in all other respects.

Some products encrypt information on hard disks but allow unscrambled information, or cleartext, to be written on diskettes; others encrypt diskettes. Information that has been encrypted cannot be processed on another system unless that system is equipped with the same encryption product and the user knows the encryption key.

Data can be encrypted in many ways, some of which are more easily decoded than others. The novice will find it difficult to distinguish the effective encryption routines from the ineffective. Products that use the federally approved Data Encryption Standard (DES) or a method called RSA should be given priority. Both have a long track record and, to date, have resisted all attempts to decode them without using impractical, unreasonably long decoding procedures.

SOFTWARE AND DATA INTEGRITY CONTROLS

It has long been recognized that software and data integrity are critical in almost all phases of data processing. In most organizations, information produced on computer systems (usually large-scale systems) and the software used to handle such information has been subject to extensive critical review and error-checking, both during system development and during normal processing. This has enabled a great deal of confidence to be placed in the quality of resulting information.

The microcomputer has made powerful computational and analytical tools available to users throughout many organizations. Increasingly important decisions are being made based on information processed by such systems. Unfortunately, there may be a reluctance to apply the same degree of care (and cost) in integrity assurance as is routinely applied for larger systems. To the extent that microcomputers are used for routine personal work and are not being used for critical decision-making functions, the lack of formal quality and integrity controls may not be a significant problem. However, for applications that are critical to the organization, there must be commensurate quality controls.

Formal Software Development

When important functions are being performed on microcomputers, management should consider application of formal controls over software development, testing, and data integrity. This applies not only to situations where systems are being designed and programmed in traditional programming languages (e.g., BASIC or

Pascal). There is increasing use of generic software tools (e.g., spreadsheet and data base management system) to build complex applications. Even though many of the typical programming problems may be reduced in these situations, the need for careful analysis and control is just as important. This may very well require additional training of personnel or the use of specially trained personnel.

Data Integrity Controls

Even a properly functioning application program is of little value if the data it handles is corrupted. Most generic software tools do not provide built-in facilities for checking the integrity of input data. Therefore, it becomes the responsibility of the user to build in such checks. These should include data format and range checks and other redundant cross-checks of results. Managers should require supporting information and evidence necessary to ensure that calculations and other data handling operations have been performed properly. It is perhaps most important for managers to require individual accountability and auditability of results before relying on information generated by microcomputer systems.

Operational Controls

When a major application is implemented on a microcomputer, formal operational procedures are as critical as they are for a large-scale system. An important application is important regardless of where or how it is processed. Operational procedures should include:

- Data preparation and input handling procedures.
- Program execution procedures.
- Media (probably diskette or tape) procedures.
- Output handling and distribution procedures.

These are, of course, the same types of procedures needed for large-scale system applications. It is important to recognize, however, that the personnel performing such procedures probably will not have extensive data processing or operations training and will be performing these duties along with their other responsibilities.

Documentation

Documentation of all aspects of any repetitive activity is critical to its ongoing operation. Again, the use of generic software tools makes some believe that there is less need for documentation. In addition, it is often more difficult to prepare documentation for such systems, since the user interface is often not as simple and straightforward as it is for specially designed application programs. Rather, the user often must first understand how to use the generic application, then must learn procedures for each specific application. This problem can be alleviated somewhat with the use of facilities in many generic software tools to customize an application and thereby simplify the user interface.

BACKUP AND CONTINGENCY PLANNING

The problem of backup and contingency planning in a microcomputer environment is essentially the same as for other data processing activities. Indeed, for organizations with both microcomputer and large-scale systems, the backup and contingency planning should be an integrated process. However, there are special considerations for microcomputers, primarily because of the wide distribution of equipment and the number of people now involved. This section discusses some of these considerations.

Elements of Contingency Planning

Contingency planning consists of those activities undertaken in anticipation of potential events that could cause serious adverse effects. This, of course, could apply to individual users and their applications as well as to organizations. In a microcomputer environment, one of the key elements in the contingency planning process is the individual user, because there is no central staff to perform many of the important functions.

Contingency plans should consist of emergency procedures; backup preparations for such resources as hardware, software, and data; and backup operation plans. In addition, comprehensive contingency plans will include recovery and test procedures. The following material focuses primarily on the first three areas.

Emergency Procedures

In general, the introduction of microcomputers into an office environment should not require significant changes in emergency preparations. Any area in which people work and important information is handled should have basic emergency procedures, including:

- Alarm activation and deactivation procedures.
- Evacuation plans.
- Lockup procedures.
- Medical emergency supplies and procedures.
- Fire detection and extinguishing equipment.
- Bomb threat procedures.
- Computer emergency response teams.

If such precautions are not in place, the introduction of the microcomputers may emphasize the need, if for no other reason than to protect the investment in equipment.

File Backup

It often takes the loss of an important file before most users become "converts" to the need for regular backup. Fortunately, such backup can now be done centrally and systematically, as is possible with a large-scale system.

Backup Approaches. The method and frequency of backup must be determined by each user, based on the storage medium and the volatility of the data involved. For data stored on diskettes or other removable media, it is often easiest to make a backup copy of the entire volume (e.g., diskette) after each use or at the end of each day if a given volume is used frequently during the day. This approach eliminates the need to keep track of individual files. If the original volume is damaged, the backup copy is used.

For large-capacity, nonremovable storage devices, such as fixed disks, it is usually impractical (and unnecessary) to perform full disk copies on a daily basis. In this situation, two basic alternative approaches should be considered: incremental backup and application-based backup.

In an incremental backup, only those files that have been modified since the last full or incremental backup are copied to the backup medium. This of course requires a mechanism in the file system to set an indicator whenever a file is opened for writing. Most microcomputer operating systems designed to handle hard disk systems have such facilities. It should be noted, however, that full backups are still required (e.g., monthly), since no single incremental backup will contain all files.

Recovery from minor problems (e.g., a single file error) involves locating the latest incremental backup containing the affected file. Recovery from a major loss, however, requires first reloading from the last full backup and then reloading each successive incremental backup. This can be a very time-consuming and error-prone process if there are too many incremental backups between full backups. A reasonable schedule might be a full backup each month and incremental backup each week. However, the specific schedule must be determined for each system.

Because of the potential complexity of incremental backups and the impracticality of full-volume backup for large capacity volumes, it may be more appropriate to perform backups based on each application or file grouping. Examples of file groups might be individual file subdirectories. Certain file groups (e.g., generic software, which never changes) would need only one initial backup. Software associated with locally maintained applications needs to be backed up only when the software is changed. Data files can be backed up whenever updated. Although this approach may require more backup volumes (e.g., diskettes), it will generally be easier to organize them and to locate files for restoration than with incremental or full-volume backups.

Backup Media. The most common backup medium is diskette, since virtually every microcomputer has a diskette drive. For systems with hard disks, however, a full file backup may require more than 20 diskettes. Alternatives such as streaming cassette backup systems should be considered if incremental backups to diskette are too difficult or time consuming. In addition, several software products are available that speed the backup process, usually by compressing the data being backed up so that fewer bytes are written to the backup medium. Such products can reduce the time required for backups by as much as 75%. These products can also help manage the storage of backup copies by tracking the storage location of each file. If a backup diskette is damaged, a backup utility is available that permits users to retrieve files that do not reside on damaged sectors of the diskette.

Errors on backup copies can have disastrous consequences. The typical backup utilities available on microcomputer systems are basically just file copy functions; they do not contain redundancy mechanisms found in some larger-scale systems. Therefore, regardless of the type of backup, only high-quality media should be used. Additional assurance of successful backup can be achieved by performing file comparison of original and backup copies. Most microcomputer systems provide disk and file comparison utility programs. In addition, some operating systems provide a write-verification option (which usually may be turned on or off as desired), which reads each disk record immediately after it is written to verify its accuracy. Most backup, file copy, or file comparison utilities provide a display of files processed. This information should be directed to the printer and stored with the backup copies.

Storage of Backups. It is important for users to understand the threats addressed by backup procedures. The obvious reason for backing up files is to enable recovery of data after loss due to media or hardware problems or accidents (e.g., unintentional erasure of files). This causes users to store backup copies in a convenient, nearby location. The other threat of concern, however, is loss resulting from a fire, theft, or other event that might involve an entire office or building. In these situations, locally stored backup copies would be lost along with the originals. Therefore, careful consideration should be given to storing periodic archival copies at a location unlikely to be jointly affected by such emergencies as fire or flooding. In situations where microcomputers are connected to a data communications network, it may be possible to establish procedures to make backup copies on a separate device, such as a remote host or a file server. This may provide the physically separate storage needed for disaster recovery purposes.

Backup of Equipment and Facilities

One advantage of widespread use of microcomputers is built-in equipment backup. If one machine is damaged or lost, it may be easy to find a replacement. However, not all systems are compatible. As application systems on microcomputers become more complex, it becomes more difficult simply to move to another microcomputer. Different equipment options, installation variations, and piracy-protection mechanisms used in many popular software packages can make portability extremely difficult. It should also be recognized that a major disaster (e.g., a fire or water damage) may affect much more than a single machine or area. Therefore, planning is critical.

Software Backup

Application software should be protected in the same manner as data files. Backup considerations may differ, depending on the source of the application software.

Applications on microcomputers are often built around mass-marketed generic software, such as data base management systems, spreadsheet programs, or word processing systems. Licensed software is often costly to replace if not properly registered with the supplier. Much commercially available software was distributed with piracy-protection mechanisms that linked the software to a given machine or system disk. This caused considerable difficulties when personnel tried to conduct backup operations on different equipment or with alternative versions of the software. Currently there is a stepped-up effort to prosecute instead.

For locally developed or maintained applications, backup should include source program files and, optionally, loadable versions of all software. The required compiler or interpreter programs should, of course, also be backed up. (See the previous discussion on application-based file backup.)

Personnel, Procedures, and Documentation

Personal computer applications, especially those involving only one machine and only one person (or a small group), are often unique. Moreover, they are often developed in a much less structured environment than are large-scale applications. Nevertheless, they often require a detailed knowledge of procedures that may not be documented. If such applications have any long-term value, it should be clear that their operation should not depend on a single person or small group. In emergency situations, others should be able to understand and use the applications. This requires specific efforts to document procedures and, perhaps, cross-train personnel.

COMMUNICATIONS SECURITY

A prime motivation for linking microcomputers in a local area network (LAN) is to allow users to share information. Information files sent from one user to another can, however, be intercepted by others. If all users of the LAN have access to all information on the system, this presents no problem. When users have different security clearances, however, security becomes a major consideration in the selection of a LAN product. Only products that can prevent such eavesdropping should be considered. Currently, traffic analysis programs (e.g., sniffers) are being used to allow people to analyze LAN traffic for both legal and illegal purposes.

Microcomputer communications security is no different from mainframe communications security. Computing systems with a telecommunications connection are vulnerable to two kinds of attack: wiretapping and hacking. Wiretapping refers to a physical connection to the line for the purpose of intercepting information or introducing fraudulent data. Hacking refers to unauthorized entry to the computing system by an intruder who enters by dialing the system's communications line. The recommended safeguards for microcomputers are the same as those for a mainframe system.

Wiretap Protection

The only sure way of securing a communications signal is through encryption. As the cost of encryption devices continues to fall, this process is becoming a cost-effective way of protecting information. The sending and receiving systems both must have decryption hardware, and users must exchange keys. The more sophisticated systems automatically change keys at specified intervals to reduce the risk of their being discovered.

As noted, encryption can also be implemented with software. A message is first processed through a special program that performs the same functions as encryption hardware. The receiver can decrypt the message with hardware or software as long as the process chosen is compatible with that used by the sender. In general, a hardware implementation is more secure because there is no way to bypass the encryption process inadvertently. As with file encryption products, hardware implementations are more efficient and the purchaser should focus on DES and RSA products.

Encryption protects against both passive (i.e., listening in) and active (i.e., introducing a fraudulent message) wiretapping. Anyone eavesdropping on an encrypted line finds only scrambled data. Likewise, the receiver converts a fraudulent message into scrambled data during decryption when the fraudulent message is in cleartext (i.e., is not encrypted).

Intrusion Protection

An unauthorized outsider can access a computing system over telephone lines only if that system is equipped with automatic answering equipment. If a modem requires action by the user before the call is accepted, the attempted access can be monitored and an unauthorized call disallowed.

For cases in which auto-answering is required, several hardware systems provide protection. Until recently, these systems intercepted the call before it reached the computer and required callers to identify themselves by means of a tone signal. The system then disconnected the caller and called back at an authorized number to verify the caller's identity. After verification, the caller was connected to the computer. However, this protection is difficult to administer and, more important, call forwarding can nullify it. The use of dynamic passwords is now replacing this outmoded protection. In addition, encryption provides a further level of protection against intruders.

VIRUS PROTECTION

Computer viruses are a growing problem for microcomputer users. Security experts estimate that in the next few years, almost every microcomputer user will experience some sort of infection by one or more of these rogue programs.

Virus Definition

A virus is a piece of executable code that can make copies of itself and insert itself into legitimate programs. When a user runs an application program or system program into which the virus has copied itself, virus code will also execute. Usually, the virus searches the system for programs that are not already infected and, when possible, copies itself into those programs. Later, when the new host program executes, the virus code executes as well, sometimes destroying files or locking the system from further use.

Viruses typically are introduced to a microcomputer system when an infected program is loaded to the system from diskette and executed. The virus immediately plants a copy of itself on the hard disk. Any diskettes inserted in the future are likely to become infected if they contain executable code. If diskettes containing software are shared, the infection can spread to other systems in the organization.

Approaches to Virus Protection

The best was to combat viruses is to prevent infection in the first place. Software should be purchased from a reputable dealer and delivered in a shrink-wrapped package. If exceptions to this rule are necessary, the software should be run on a computer that is specifically designated as a test system; this computer should not be used for critical processing and should be isolated from other systems in the organization.

Several products can be used to prevent or detect virus infections. Some of these products are designed to detect and block viruses from writing to disks or diskettes; others detect and report changes in programs that have already been infected. An antiviral product should be installed on every microcomputer for the best assurance of noninfection.

Regular backups should be made to ensure the ability to recover in the event of an infection. If possible, only files containing data (i.e., not executable code) should be backed up to prevent backup diskettes from becoming infected.

Procedures for Recovery from a Virus

Recovery should be a relatively straightforward process. The data security administrator should first attempt to identify and eliminate copies of the virus using the appropriate antiviral software. If this does not work, the security administrator should then attempt to recover using backup copies. Specifically, the security administrator should:

1. Power down the system to disable any memory-resident virus code.
2. Boot the system using a system diskette with a write-protect tab.
3. Format the hard disk.
4. Reinstall software using the write-protected diskettes provided by the vendor. Software should not be restored or executed from backups; these copies are likely to be infected.
5. Check the system with an antiviral product as each program is installed to ensure that the program is not the source of the infection. If the source of the infection is already known, the infected product should not be reinstalled.
6. Restore data files from write-protected backup copies.

AUDITABILITY

Designers of important applications, whether on small or large systems, will require reliable audit trails. Organizations also may wish to monitor use of microcomputers by employees. A single-user microcomputer may need special audit trail facilities as an historical record and to aid in recovery from errors. The placement and use of audit trails in microcomputer systems, however, requires special considerations.

Placement of Audit Trails

Audit trail information can be recorded as part of an access control process such as those discussed earlier. However, designers should avoid dependence on the microcomputer to provide a safe environment for the storage of such data. It may be too easy for a user to modify or delete such data. If it is important enough to keep audit trail information on the microcomputer, the system should be provided with appropriate physical and access control safeguards to protect the integrity of that data. If access to a host system is involved, the host is the proper location for the placement of audit data capture mechanisms.

Use Monitoring

Organizations with substantial investment in microcomputer equipment may wish to monitor the use of such equipment. Although this is not primarily a security concern, effective monitoring can have security benefits. The types of events that may be of interest include:

- System startup.
- User session initiation and completion.
- Program initiation and completion.
- Access to certain data files.

It is possible to develop or acquire software that records basic system use information. This requires, at minimum, the use of AUTOEXEC-type routines and may involve modifications to operating system functions to ensure that all relevant activity is logged. In addition, it requires a reliable source of date and time information (e.g., an internal clock-calendar) and methods to protect the log information from modification or destruction. Management must decide whether the user constraints needed to meet these requirements are justified by the information on system use that will be obtained.

SUMMARY

Effective security for microcomputing systems is readily achieved if the right controls and products are installed. This chapter has reviewed the recommended controls and the categories of products currently available. With the following checklist, the data security administrator and user can determine when such controls and products are needed:

- Is the microcomputer located in a room that is always locked when the system in not in use? If not, an antitheft product should be purchased.
- Could the users get by without the system for one or two weeks? If not, electrical power protection should be installed, because a power surge could permanently damage a CPU.
- Is creating backup diskettes for critical information taking longer than two hours each week? If so, the purchase of a backup software product or a tape drive for high-speed backup should be considered.
- Does the microcomputer process confidential information? If so, system access should be limited through an antitheft or access control product.
- Is the system shared by people who should not have access to all files? If so, an access control or encryption product should be installed.

- Is the computer attached to a LAN in which not all users have equal access to information? If so, the LAN must contain adequate separation safeguards.

- Does the system transmit sensitive or confidential information to another system? If so, line encryption devices should be installed on both systems.

- Does the system automatically accept dial-up connections from other systems? If so, line encryption devices or a dynamic password system should be installed.

- Is software from outside sources ever run on this microcomputer? If so, an antiviral software product should be used.

- Is all copyrighted software licensed? If not, a license should be purchased or the software should be removed from the system.

- Is the system used for critical business processes? If so, each process should be documented and at least two persons should be trained to perform the functions related to that process.

Micro-Mainframe Security and Control

STEVEN F. BLANDING

Micro-mainframe systems are made up of microcomputers, communications lines, modems, and a host computer, which is usually a mainframe but may be a minicomputer or even a large microcomputer. Configurations can be quite complex, depending on the sophistication of the micro-mainframe software link. As a result, the microcomputer can become an extremely versatile device when linked to a host system. The capabilities of link software must be evaluated to determine the adequacy of controls for communications, data access security, and application systems.

Standalone and networked microcomputers have proliferated in corporate environments because of the tremendous demand for local information processing and data sharing. To operate as a terminal, a microcomputer requires emulation software. The type of emulation program needed depends on the terminals the host computer supports. With additional program logic, the emulator can allow the microcomputer to act as an intelligent device and issue online execution commands, submit batch jobs for processing on the host, and upload and download data files to and from the host.

The host computer contains centralized data files, which the microcomputer can access. The microcomputer can also send data to and can change existing data on the host computer. Because microcomputers can function as intelligent devices when communicating with the host, unauthorized users can program their microcomputers to enter sign-on and password combinations to the host system repeatedly until access is granted. To ensure that adequate security is maintained, online system controls must safeguard against risk. Guidelines for the security review of micro-mainframe systems are summarized at the end of this chapter.

THE COMMUNICATIONS LINK

Communication between the microcomputer and the host can be established only by the appropriate linking software. The emulation program executes either on a microcomputer under the control of the microcomputer's operating system or as a function of terminal control devices attached to the mainframe. Regardless of how the emulation feature is controlled, it executes as a task during the terminal session.

Microcomputers can also emulate remote job entry (RJE) devices. This type of link is especially useful when an application's requirements for processing and transferring data exceed the microcomputer terminal's capacity. For example, with this configuration, the microcomputer RJE can write downloaded files on a disk or print output on microcomputer printers while the microcomputer terminal maintains communication with the host to process online commands.

Depending on the application, emulators can be used with communications software to automatically process, upload, or download data after communications have been established. These applications require strong security measures and must be reviewed closely. Microcomputers with this capability perform offline functions, whereas the communications link between the microcomputer and the host remains established. If the execution environment is on the mainframe, a program residing on the microcomputer will be passed to the communications software, which then transmits the program to the mainframe for execution. The communications software performs the downloading of any output that is to be returned to the microcomputer.

Some communications software products can provide seamless access to data files on either the mainframe or the microcomputer. Such products as IBM's Data Interpretation System link the mainframe and microcomputer so that it is not apparent to the user where the data resides or the software executes.

CONTROL OBJECTIVES

The data security administrator must determine whether the established controls are adequate for a microcomputer network environment. Special attention should be given to the following controls:

- *Application system controls*. Because data can be downloaded, processed, and uploaded, the data security administrator should review applications controls for programs that execute on the microcomputer.
- *Data transmission controls*. Because data files can be uploaded and downloaded between the microcomputer and the host, the data security administrator should review controls to ensure the integrity of these transmissions.
- *Data access controls*. Because sensitive corporate data can be downloaded to the microcomputer, the data security administrator should reevaluate access controls to data residing on the host computer and review access controls to data on the microcomputer system.
- *Backup and recovery controls*. Because host data may be subject to processing after it is downloaded to the micro, the data security administrator should evaluate the backup procedures for data.

- *Program change controls.* In a micro-mainframe system in which application program development is performed by a central support group and then distributed to microcomputer users, the data security administrator should review program change controls.
- *Management controls.* Because microcomputers are used by people who are not IS professionals, the data security administrator should review management policies regarding microcomputer procurement and use.

The control objectives of a micro-mainframe system depend on the sensitivity of the data, the types and means of communication, and the types of application systems. The data security administrator should review application systems documentation and operations to decide which control objectives apply and should review the micro-mainframe system to determine whether:

- Data input, processing, and output controls are adequate.
- Communications software controls provide accurate and complete data transmission.
- Access to data is adequately restricted.
- Backup and recovery controls for programs and data are adequate.
- Application and communications programs are adequately controlled, maintained, and secured.
- Management policies exist to control the acquisition and use of microcomputers.

APPLICATION SYSTEM CONTROLS

Application system controls vary significantly, depending on the application. Controls for input, processing, and output should be in place at both the microcomputer and mainframe level. The data security administrator should evaluate the strengths and weaknesses of these controls within the framework of each application.

DATA TRANSMISSION CONTROLS

Data transmission controls, which are designed to prevent data alteration or loss, are an integral part of an effective security scheme. A well-controlled system usually employs several transmission control features, including the use of hash totals, record sequence checking, transmission logging, transmission error correction, and retransmission controls.

Many application systems that transmit data between the microcomputer and the mainframe use vendor-supplied data communications control software. These software products should provide the control features described in the following sections. The data security administrator should evaluate the control features of such communications software before procurement.

Hash Totals. The hash totals control technique is effective for identifying errors and omissions in data transmissions. Its use requires an algorithm to provide a hexadecimal summation of the data in a transmission, which is tested for accuracy on the destination computer. The hash total is stored in a field on the record before transmission occurs. To allow checking of both uploaded and downloaded data files, the communications software on both the host and the microcomputer must incorporate the same algorithm. Therefore, communications programs must be developed on a centralized basis and distributed to the microcomputer systems. The hash totals control technique can be strengthened by using a different algorithm for each type of data file transmitted.

Record Sequence Checking. Sequence checking tests the accuracy and completeness of a transmission. The source computer's communications program assigns and stores a record sequence number for data, and the sequence is tested on the destination computer to ensure that all data has been transmitted. As with the hash totals control technique, both computers must have this feature on their front-end communications programs.

Transmission Logging. The transmission logging function can be built into a front-end communications program, allowing such specific information as transmission, date, time, origin, and type to be recorded for audit trail purposes. A logging feature is useful in a large microcomputer network as a source of data for reporting network efficiency and capacity and for planning purposes. During the audit of a specific application system, the log serves as an audit trail to substantiate that transmissions actually occurred. Transmission logging is usually performed on the host computer but can be incorporated on the microcomputer to meet application system control requirements.

Transmission Error Control. Extensive edit controls should exist in the front-end communications program to identify the hardware and software errors that can occur during transmission, including invalid log-on, modem error, lost connections, CPU failure, disk error, and line error. The edit controls should provide as much detail as possible so that errors can be quickly identified and corrected. As each error is identified, it should be recorded in an error log, which can be used to perform a trend analysis of error types and to identify chronic error problems. Error control is especially useful with large microcomputer networks.

Retransmission Control. Depending on application system requirements, transmission controls may be used to detect and prevent duplicate transmissions of data. The front-end communications program detects duplicate data transmission within a file by examining successive records during a transmission. Duplicate transmissions of files are much more difficult to identify; a downstream application program may be needed to detect them.

426

ACCESS CONTROLS

The introduction of the microcomputer into network systems with host computers has had a profound impact on the effectiveness of data access controls. In this environment, the data security administrator must ensure that data access controls are applied consistently on both mainframe and microcomputer platforms. Some systems use access control facilities defined on both the mainframe and microcomputer platforms, whereas other, more advanced systems use a central access control facility defined only on the mainframe; this facility controls access on both platforms. The access control features described in the following sections must be reviewed for effectiveness.

Access to Microcomputer Data

Access control to the microcomputer involves both physical and logical controls. Physical access controls reduce exposure to theft or destruction of data and hardware. Logical access controls reduce exposure to unauthorized alteration and manipulation of data and programs recorded on microcomputer storage media.

When sensitive data is being downloaded from the host computer to a disk or diskette, access to microcomputer equipment is an important control issue. The simplest and most effective way to secure data and software in a microcomputer is to remove the storage medium (i.e., the diskette, cassette tape, or disk) from the machine when it is not in use and lock it in a desk, file cabinet, or safe. Microcomputers with fixed disk systems may require additional security procedures for theft protection. Vendors offer lockable enclosures, clamping devices, and cable fastening devices that help prevent equipment theft. The computer can also be connected to a security system that sounds an alarm if equipment is moved. This is most effective when the alarm is tied into a building security network monitored by a guard station. A clever thief may remove only memory chips or circuit boards; however, vendors offer devices to secure the hardware cabinet to prevent this problem.

Preventing the theft of data residing on diskettes is virtually impossible. The medium itself is inexpensive, but the data recorded on the diskettes may be vital to the company. An employee could slip a diskette into a briefcase, make a copy on a home microcomputer, and return the diskette the next day. Placing signaling devices in diskette jackets prevents the removal of important diskettes; however, it would not stop someone from using an unprotected diskette to copy the data at the office. A more practical solution is to record all sensitive data on removable disks, which are more easily secured than fixed disks or diskettes.

Software can also be used to control access to microcomputer data. The basic software approach restricts access to program and data files with a password system. The password facility, which is usually a feature of the microcomputer operating system, using a hashing algorithm to store the scrambled passwords with the operating system files. Nevertheless, software security has its limitations. A determined individual with access to the diskette containing the password information can dump the password data and hashing algorithm, determine the password, and thus circumvent the password access control feature.

To provide stronger controls, microcomputer software vendors offer a variety of products, including hardware devices (e.g., expansion boards) that contain access security software. Physical access to these devices must be restricted for them to effectively limit data access.

Access to Host Data

Access security to data on host computer systems can be incorporated into the front-end communications software on the host system; however, all terminal network systems, including those incorporating microcomputers as terminals, should restrict data access through a comprehensive data access security package on the host system. Because the microcomputer can be used as an intelligent device when communicating with the host and is capable of uploading and downloading data, such access security facilities as sign-on IDs, passwords, data access profiles, and security logs should be reviewed for consistency.

The type of micro-mainframe link can vary from a terminal-emulation link to an apparently seamless micro-mainframe link. With terminal emulation, the user must have user authentication and access authority defined on both the microcomputer and mainframe systems. With seamless links, the user is subject to only one log-on procedure and one set of data access rules.

All terminal network systems should assign a unique sign-on ID to each user; group sign-on IDs should not be allowed. The sign-on ID should be the basis for establishing a data access security profile that defines the data files to which each user is allowed access. For data base systems, access can be defined to the data record or data field level. Access can be further defined as read only (download) or read and update (download, change, and upload).

Administration. Depending on the type of micro-mainframe system in use, access control may be defined either independently at both the microcomputer and mainframe levels or centrally at the mainframe level only. To minimize the effort required for administration of access security, defining security at one point in the system is optimal because it prevents the introduction of access incompatibilities that can occur when administering independent access security tables. The data security administrator must consider this function when procuring a vendor-supplied system or when developing a system internally.

Large micro-mainframe systems are likely to extend over large organizational and geographic boundaries, which can add to the complexity of performing security administration procedures. The security administrator must ensure that procedures for adding and deleting users and for granting and removing access authority are performed in a timely and consistent manner. The use of separate security tables on microcomputer and mainframe platforms can significantly increase the exposure to inconsistent and untimely administration of security access.

User Identification. Each user in a micro-mainframe application environment must be assigned a unique user ID. In order to maintain accountability, two or more users should never share the same identifier even if the access authority is the same for both individuals.

User Authentication. Each user should have an individual password to be entered when signing on in order to authenticate that person to the system. Passwords should have characteristics that reduce the possibility of disclosure. These characteristics include random assignment, frequent change in content, and a minimum length of six characters.

The system should automatically disconnect the communications line if the correct password is not entered after an established number of attempts. Without a limitation, unauthorized users can use their microcomputers to automatically and exhaustively try possible passwords until the correct one is obtained.

Passwords and data access profiles should be controlled by the host system's data access security software. This software should also provide a flexible logging facility that records attempted security violations and all data access transactions.

BACKUP AND RECOVERY CONTROLS

Backup and recovery controls have always been an important control area in mainframe systems. IS professionals understand the importance of being able to restore programs and data files from backup files when disasters or disruptions bring down the computer system, but microcomputer users often must be educated in the importance of performing a regular backup of their files. As part of the review of download and upload procedures, the data security administrator should verify that users are required to create backup files.

Downloading. Consideration should be given to making a backup copy of data before any changes are made to it. This practice eliminates the need to download data again if it is lost or destroyed on the microcomputer. The backup copy can be made by using the emulation of linking software on the microcomputer. The software can be designed to make backup optional or mandatory. Because microcomputer users seldom realize the importance of having a backup copy of data, however, the software should perform this function automatically.

Uploading. Uploaded files can be copied immediately to a tape file or copied as part of the mainframe data backup and recovery procedures. In determining the best backup system, the data security administrator should consider the size of the application system, the size of the uploaded and downloaded files, the subsequent processing of data, and the frequency of uploading and downloading.

PROGRAM CHANGE CONTROLS

Depending on the type of micro-mainframe system involved, the data security administrator may wish to review program change procedures as part of the system audit. For example, if microcomputer users employee proprietary software or software that they developed to process data before uploading it to the host, the application system controls and other controls should be reviewed in addition to the program change controls.

If the micro-mainframe system uses software that has been developed and distributed by a central programming group, however, the security administrator should review program change control procedures for microcomputer applications, because the software is uniform for all microcomputers in the network. In a large network, software development and modification must be subject to stringent program change control and quality assurance procedures.

The central programming group usually develops applications software for microcomputers on a mainframe rather than on microcomputers to take advantage of the speed and efficiency of the mainframe's cross compilers. Such languages as C have compilers for both microcomputers and mainframes. This compatibility allows C language programs to be developed and compiled on the mainframe and downloaded to the programmer's microcomputer for final recompilation and testing. Using the mainframe increases programmer productivity, and program changes can be made in a more controlled and secure environment.

Program change control procedures can be enhanced on IBM mainframe systems through the use of software products that manage and control source program libraries. Program changes usually involve the programmer changing the source code of a test version of a program and compiling and link editing the test code into an executable load module or program. The program is tested with test data and then reviewed and approved by a program manager. In a production JCL jobstream, the test code is copied to the production source library at this point, from which a production executable load program is generated. Programming personnel cannot access and change production programs without following an authorized program change control procedure. Comprehensive data security software products can provide access restrictions at the data set level for the production source and object procedure. With the using of this software, program changes on the mainframe can be subject to strong internal control procedures.

Microcomputer programs that are developed and compiled on a mainframe must be downloaded for test executions on the microcomputer before they can reach production status. Computer-generated data and time audit stamps can be used to designate program versions allowing for the tracing of downloaded programs back to mainframe program libraries. The program manager or supervisor should perform the final source program review, compilation, and test execution before granting program production status. At this point, the source and load versions should be subject to restricted physical access but should be made available for duplication and distribution to microcomputer users. The data security administrator should review the procedures used to ensure that the development, testing, and access security of microcomputer programs are adequate.

MANAGEMENT CONTROLS

Management's written policy regarding the acquisition and use of microcomputer hardware and software should be expanded to include microcomputer security procedures. This policy should be reviewed on a regular basis. The following security concerns should be taken into account:

- Procedures for microcomputer procurement.
- Responsibility for training staff in the use of microcomputers, including security issues.
- Provision of access security to microcomputer hardware, software, and data.
- Adherence to software copyright laws and licenses.
- Establishment of procedures for controlling access to the mainframe or other computer systems' data bases within the organization.
- Establishment of controls for data processing and for the disclosure of confidential information.
- Establishment of procedures for reporting the unauthorized, irregular, or fraudulent use of microcomputers.

SUMMARY

Increasingly powerful microcomputers have contributed to the complexity of networked micro-mainframe systems. As these networks become more sophisticated, the application of traditional control objectives must be reevaluated. The control guidelines presented in Exhibit II-2-6 can be used for this purpose.

EXHIBIT II-2-6 Control Guidelines for Micro-Mainframe Systems

Control Concern	Impact of Inadequate Controls	Control Procedures	Security Review
Application System Controls			
Errors in data entry transactions	Erroneous accounting and management reports from mainframe system Inaccurate data on mainframe data base	Authorize and approve data input to microcomputers Have the microcomputer software perform data verification Make sure batch controls are present	Enter test data to microcomputer system Review microcomputer software application programs
Errors in file maintenance transactions	Poor data integrity Inaccurate reports from mainframe system	Log all maintenance transactions to a control log Perform limit and reasonable tests on the microcomputer software	Enter test maintenance data to microcomputer test data files Review control log data and trace to microcomputer data file
Failure to process all input data and duplication of data	Insufficient or duplicate data on mainframe data base	Review reconciliation controls Review variance reports	Test reconciliation control procedure at microcomputer and mainframe level Perform trend analysis of mainframe data Review variance reports
Unauthorized access to host data and programs through microcomputers	Manipulation of data and programs Loss of data and programs Disclosure of sensitive data Embezzlement and fraud Computer system degradation and failure Theft of downloaded data	Assign individual sign-on IDs Assign individual passwords Establish data access security profiles Provide an access security logging system	Review sign-on tables and procedures to verify that only individual sign-ons are allowed Review password change procedures Review data access security profile tables and evaluate access needs Analyze the security log file for invalid log-on and data file access attempts

Control Concern	Impact of Inadequate Controls	Control Procedures	Security Review
Backup and Recovery Controls			
Loss of data and programs on the microcomputer	Inability to recover data or programs downloaded to microcomputers Repeated downloading of data or programs	Review the backup copy of data and programs on a regular basis Provide off-site storage of backup copies in a secure location Make backup copies immediately after downloading	Review backup procedures for microcomputer data Attempt to recover data and programs from backup copy Determine whether microcomputer software requires backup to be taken before further processing
Access Controls			
Theft of microcomputer hardware	Cost to replace equipment loss Loss in productivity Increased insurance premiums	Lock rooms during nonbusiness hours Install lockable enclosures, clamping devices, cable fastening devices Hire security guards during nonbusiness hours Have alarm systems connected to hardware	Review and evaluate procedures for the physical security of hardware Inspect microcomputer processing sites Review security guard activity reports
Theft of microcomputer data	Disclosure of trade secrets and proprietary information Loss of competitive position within the industry	Establish procedures that require data to be stored only on removable disks that are physically secured Install signaling devices in diskette jackets	Review and evaluate procedures for the physical security of microcomputer data Verify that data access security devices are in use Attempt to remove sensitive data
Unauthorized access to microcomputer data and programs	Embezzlement and fraud Manipulation of data and programs Loss of data and programs Disclosure of trade secrets and proprietary information Loss of competitive position within the industry	Provide for separation of duties Review microcomputer passwords and encryption techniques, including expansion boards Establish procedures that require data to be stored only on removable disks that are physically secured Install signaling devices in diskette jackets	Review procedures for microcomputer use, including physical security Review data ownership and access privileges

(continued)

EXHIBIT II-2-6 (*continued*)

Control Concern	Impact of Inadequate Controls	Control Procedures	Security Review
Data Transmission Controls			
Errors and omissions of data during uploading or downloading of files	Loss of data items or records within data files Loss of processing time and efficiency Additional cost to retransmit files Inaccurate accounting and management information reporting on the mainframe	Review hashing controls Check record sequence Identify, log, and correct transmission errors	Test hashing and record sequence checking by attempting to upload and download erroneous data Review emulator or front-end communications software on both the microcomputer and mainframe for code that performs hashing and record sequence control functions
Loss of transmitted file or duplicate transmission during uploading or downloading	Loss of processing time and efficiency Additional cost to retransmit files Incomplete summarization and reporting on the mainframe	Identify, log, and correct transmission errors Review reconciliation controls Review variance reports	Review transmission log error reports, and perform a trend analysis Test reconciliation control procedures at microcomputer and mainframe level Perform trend analysis of mainframe data Review variance reports Attempt to perform invalid transmissions, both upload and download, by introducing invalid conditions for transmission
Loss of data uploaded to the mainframe	Inability to recover data uploaded to the mainframe Repeated preparation and uploading of data	Review the backup copy of data on a regular basis Provide off-site storage of backup copies in a secure location Make backup copies immediately after backloading	Review backup procedures for mainframe data Attempt to recover uploaded data from mainframe backup data files

Control Concern	Impact of Inadequate Controls	Control Procedures	Security Review
Program Change Controls *(microcomputer programs)* Program errors and fraudulent programs	Inaccurate data Loss of data Duplicate data Inaccurate reports Inaccurate data uploaded to mainframe	Audit password control to program files Control physical security access to programs Have management review and approval of program changes Have management review of new programs Evaluate the use of date and time program version controls	Verify that all program files are password protected Review physical security access procedures Review program change control procedures Trace microcomputer programs back to mainframe program libraries
Management Controls No management policy regarding purchase and use of microcomputers	Incompatible hardware and software Redundant processing and storage of data Inefficient use of equipment Lack of security awareness Ignorance of copyright laws and regulations	Write a management policy for the procurement, use, and security of microcomputers Encourage management communication and monitoring of policies and procedures	Review the management policy regarding microcomputers Interview microcomputer users to determine their awareness of policies and the importance of security

IBM VM and MVS Mainframe Security

F. J. DOLAN

To safeguard software on a mainframe, the data security administrator must secure the following three system areas: security control elements, consisting of programs that run on the mainframe and their supporting data sets that perform access control functions; restricted utilities, which are programs used for system management that run in privileged mode but that could be misused by authorized users; and system programs or components that, if not installed and maintained carefully, can expose an entire system to security risk. This chapter describes these critically important elements and discusses ways to control them.

CONTROL ELEMENTS

A control element is a mechanism developed by management to measure the effectiveness of a particular business process either quantitatively or qualitatively. This chapter examines the control elements used to evaluate the effectiveness of computing services provided to users.

Control Element Concepts

Within a mainframe environment, effective control of a computing center is evaluated with respect to efficiency, effectiveness, and security. Efficiency measures how well information systems management uses the people, storage media, and computing cycles (e.g., is DASD use in the 80% range, or is a significant amount unused?). Effectiveness measures how well a computing center satisfies its users' needs (e.g., is the system available 99% of the time? Are 90% of batch processing runs completed on schedule?). Security determines how well the computing center protects the data and programs that are in its custody.

Definition of a Security Control Element. Security control elements, therefore, are programs and data sets that perform or support the access control functions of allowing or preventing access, logging activity, and detecting attempts at unauthorized access. Computing center management must establish adequate controls to ensure that control elements operate effectively and to initiate corrective action when they are not. Effective controls ensure that only authorized people use the system, that system resources (e.g., data sets, transactions, commands, and terminals) are accessed and used only by authorized people and in the prescribed manner and that unauthorized attempts to access a resource are identified so that appropriate action can be taken.

Components of a Security Control Element. In general terms, an access control element provides the facilities to:

- *Identify system users.* The company does not want individuals to use its systems or access its resources who are not authorized to do so.
- *Define system resources.* If there are system resources that should not be seen or executed by everyone with an ID on that system, the resources should be controlled to allow only authorized users to access, use, and execute them.
- *Relate users to protected resources through access lists or rules.* Only people with a need to know (i.e., to read, execute, or use resources) should be permitted to do so. This is most often accomplished with an access list or a rule defining access rights.
- *Log activity.* It is necessary to record when an unauthorized user tries to log onto a system, access a data set, execute a transaction, or use a restricted command or when any user successfully accesses the company's most important data or changes a program that is part of the trusted computer base.
- *Report activities.* It is important to understand the circumstances of the attempted access to determine what corrective action, if any, should be taken.
- *Manage people with privileged administrative authority.* Only employees explicitly authorized by their job requirements should be able to use privileged administrative authority. The data security department must ensure that people with such authority use it only for valid business purposes.

Control Element as a Black Box. Another way to understand a security control element is to view it as a black box between system users and resources. The box's owner, or manager, must:

- Define who can administer the black box.
- Define the users.
- Define the resources.
- Identify the appropriate relationship of users to resources (i.e., who is authorized to perform specific functions and access specific resources).
- Record successful and unsuccessful attempts to perform a function or access a resource.

EXHIBIT II-2-7 Control Elements Within the VM Architecture

VM Architecture	
Define users	Directory
Define resources	Directory
Map users to resources	Directory
Log activity	Accounting file
Produce report	User written
Manage administrative privilege	Directory updater

- Report these facts to the people affected by the authorized access or unauthorized access attempt.

VM Control Elements

Exhibit II-2-7 illustrates the components of a control element satisfied by IBM Corp.'s Virtual Machine Facility (VM) system architecture without benefit of additional security access control software. The VM directory is a key security mechanism for defining users to the system as well as for defining minidisks, the principal resource to be controlled.

When a LINK entry to a particular minidisk of virtual machine B is placed into the directory entry of virtual machine A, the minidisk of virtual machine B is made accessible to virtual machine A with various access authorities (e.g., read and write). Log records are written to the VM accounting file for LOGON and LOGOFF and for successful as well as unsuccessful linking to a minidisk; the installation must write a simple EXEC program to obtain the log events for analysis. The VM security administrator, the person with update authority to the VM directory, defines users, resources, and the mapping of one to another.

Access Control Software Added to the VM Architecture. Exhibit II-2-8 illustrates a configuration in which an external security product, the IBM Resource Access Control Facility (RACF), is added to the VM architecture. RACF enhances the security mechanisms of the architecture because it uses access lists instead of directory entries for minidisks as well as the other objects managed by RACF (i.e., unit record devices, Remote Spooling Communications Subsystem [RSCS] nodes, VM batch machines, VM/370 Control Program [CP] commands and terminals). RACF enables resource owners to permit other users to access their resources with various access authorities. The VM security administrator can perform this function as well. In addition to the logging provided by the VM accounting file, RACF provides a separate file for logging. It is really the same

EXHIBIT II-2-8 RACF Control Elements in the VM Environment

```
┌─────────────────────────────────────────────────────────────────┐
│ RACF │                                                            │
├──────┘                                                            │
│                                                                   │
│  Define users . . . . . . . . . . . . . . . . . . . . . RACF profiles       │
│  Define resources . . . . . . . . . . . . . . . . . . RACF profiles         │
│  Map users to resources . . . . . . . . . . . . . . Access lists            │
│  Log activity . . . . . . . . . . . . . . . . . . . . . . SETEROPS option   │
│  Produce report . . . . . . . . . . . . . . . . . . . RACF Report Writer     │
│  Manage administrative privilege . . . . . . . . . . Auditor                │
│                                                                   │
│  ┌───────────────┐                                                │
│  │ VM            │                                                │
│  │ Architecture  │                                                │
│  ├───────────────┘                                                │
│  │                                                                │
│  │ Define users . . . . . . . . . . . . . . . . . . . . . . . . . Directory │
│  │ Define resources . . . . . . . . . . . . . . . . . . . . . . . Directory │
│  │ Map users to resources . . . . . . . . . . . . . . . . . . . . Directory │
│  │ Log activity . . . . . . . . . . . . . . . . . . . . . . . . . Accounting file │
│  │ Generate report . . . . . . . . . . . . . . . . . . . . . . . . User written │
│  │ Manage administrative privilege . . . . . . . . . . . . . . . . Directory updater │
└──┴────────────────────────────────────────────────────────────────┘
```

format as the System Management Facility (SMF) file used in IBM's Multiple Virtual Systems (MVS) and contains log records of all RACF-relevant events. This file can be processed by the RACF Report Writer program to generate activity reports for subsequent analysis. With the introduction of RACF, an additional security administrator may have the privileged access authority SPECIAL which permits the user to modify any RACF profile, or OPERATIONS, which enables users to access the resource itself. Someone with AUDITOR privilege can log all the activities performed by these privileged users for subsequent analysis.

Control Elements in Service Machines. Many VM system functions are implemented as disconnected service machines—that is, machines that are always running, waiting for another virtual machine to send it a file—or as two virtual machines communicating with one another using the Virtual Machine Communication Facility or Inter-User Communication Vehicle protocols. These service machines perform such functions for the user's virtual machine as executing the RACF commands on behalf of the user.

Control Elements in Directory Maintenance Software. The IBM directory maintenance program (DIRMAINT), as illustrated in Exhibit II-2-9, is the service machine through which all users, including privileged users, access the VM directory. DIRMAINT contains an access control subsystem that is a control element. VM users invoke DIRMAINT to get information about their directory

EXHIBIT II-2-9 Control Elements in VM Service Machines

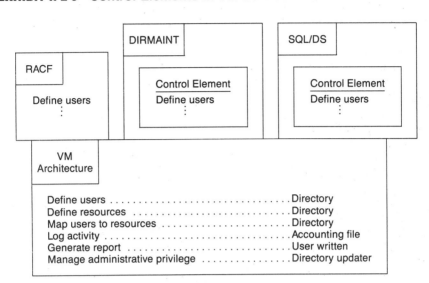

entries. However, only users defined to DIRMAINT as having STAFF authority can perform such functions as adding or deleting users and virtual machines, adding or deleting minidisk resources, changing passwords, and changing the configuration of components of the virtual machine in the directory.

Control Elements in the SQL/DS Data Base System. The IBM Structured Query Language/Data System (SQL/DS) is the relational data base management system used on a VM system and is also illustrated in Exhibit II-2-9. It contains an access control subsystem that is a control element. As with other IBM implementations of relational data bases. SQL/DS relies on a hierarchical structure of administrators that begins with the person having the most privileged authority, the data base administrator (DBA), and progresses to the owner of each table, who has all authorities for the table and the ability to grant the same or less access authority to another user ID. The SQL/DS Trace Facility provides for the recording of successful as well as unsuccessful access to tables, views, and other SQL/DS objects; the use of GRANT and REVOKE statements; as well as activity performed by the privileged user with DBA authority for subsequent analysis.

Control Elements in Network Software. Exhibit II-2-10 illustrates the control elements in network management software products. They include:

- The network management software product, IBM NetView.
- The VM networking product, RSCS.

EXHIBIT II-2-10 **Control Elements in Networking Service Machines**

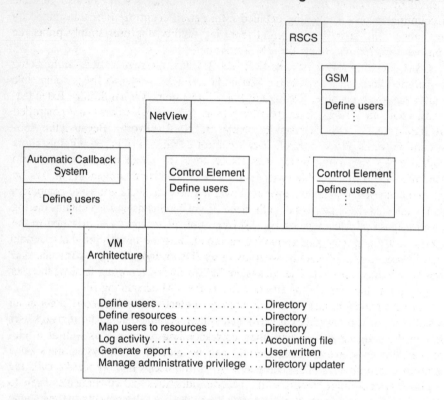

- The VM interenterprise connection subsystem, Gateway Security Module (GSM).
- One of the many automatic callback systems running external to the host system.

Each of these products contains an access control subsystem.

NetView enables a network operator to monitor that portion of the network defined to NetView. The NetView administrator has the privileged authority to define which commands can be executed by which operators. The administrator also defines which commands are logged for subsequent analysis. There is no formal reporting facility; a user simply prints the log. Formatted reports or extracts must be generated by user-written programs if they are required.

RSCS is a networking product that registers VM nodes capable of transmitting files between one another in a directory used by all participating nodes. Virtual machines specify to RSCS the user ID and node ID to which a file should be transmitted, and the RSCS service machines running on each node perform the transmission. Privileged RSCS administrators can manage links, files, and the service machine itself. The RSCS console file contains the log of activity performed by privileged users, as well as rejected traffic. RSCS can also generate accounting records containing detailed information about the files transmitted by the subsystem. There is no formal reporting facility; the user simply prints the console log file, or extracts the VM accounting file.

GSM consists of a set of exits to RSCS. It filters message and file traffic being transmitted between an enterprise VM node and a Network Job Entry compatible subsystem—for example, RSCS, Job Entry Subsystem, Virtual Storage Extended/ Priority Output Writers, Execution Processor, and Input Readers—not controlled by IBM (e.g., Harvard University on the BITNET network). Because this subsystem performs access control, it is a control element. Privileged administrators update tables specifying which user ID or node ID within the organization can send message traffic to which user ID or node ID outside the organization. Traffic between authorized pairs is transmitted over the link connecting the two computers and is rejected if the pair is not authorized. The RSCS console file contains the log of messages and files rejected by GSM because of improper authorization in the tables. GSM can generate accounting records telling the installation that a certain file, message, or command between two user IDs or node IDs on a particular date was accepted or rejected. The subsystem has no formal reporting facility; the user simply prints the console log file or extracts the VM accounting file.

An automatic callback system is used to protect dial-in telephone ports at an installation. It is managed by a privileged system administrator, who registers user IDs in the callback system with their corresponding passwords as well as a telephone number at which each user ID can be reached. This system runs on a microprocessor, not the host computer. When the user's microprocessor calls the callback system microprocessor, the program identifies and authenticates itself to the callback system, puts itself into receive mode, and disconnects the telephone line. After the callback system has identified and authenticated the user dialing in, it looks up the telephone number and makes an outgoing call to the user whose microprocessor has been set to receive mode. Once the connection is made, the microprocessor passes the connection from the remote user to a control unit on the host and drops out of the session. The remote user is now directly in session with the host. To accomplish its functions, the callback system has a mechanism to define users and resources that are control unit ports and telephone numbers. Updates are logged to the tables, and successful as well as unsuccessful accesses to the system can be displayed on demand. In choosing to use a callback system, the administrator should determine who should pay for the call.

Control Elements in System Management Software. Tape library management systems run as disconnected service machines, perform necessary system management functions at the installation, and have control element subsystems within them. Tape Control, which is illustrated in Exhibit II-2-11, refers to a tape management system that has a registry of users defined to it as well as an inventory of tape volumes. A privileged library administrator manages the system.

EXHIBIT II-2-11 Control Element in a System Management Service Machine

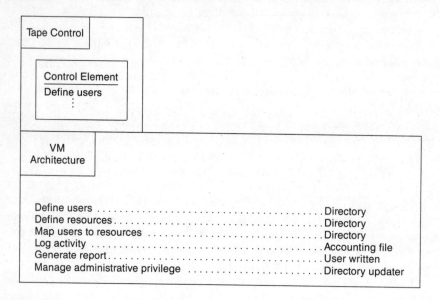

The system logs valid and invalid accesses to tapes, and its reporting function displays such activity for analysis.

MVS Control Elements

The security control elements in the basic control program of MVS, as illustrated in Exhibit II-2-12, are not as robust as those in VM. Users are defined to Time Sharing Option (TSO) through the mechanism of entries in the SYS1.UADS data set, whereas batch users are not defined at all. There is no mechanism for defining MVS resources, nor are there capabilities to map users to resources. However, some degree of security is achieved by the MVS password mechanism, which allows the password owner to access data sets in TSO or the operator to do so in a batch environment. The MVS SMF, on the other hand, is extremely robust, allowing logging of most relevant events on MVS. There is no mechanism native to the MVS architecture for report generation.

Access Control Software Added to the MVS Architecture. Exhibit II-2-13 illustrates a configuration in which RACF is added to the MVS architecture. RACF enhances the architecture's security mechanisms through its use of access lists to manage access to a large number of MVS objects (e.g., data sets, terminals, customer information control system (CICS) transactions, information

EXHIBIT II-2-12 Control Elements Within the MVS Architecture

MVS Architecture	
Define users	TSO users-SYS1.UADS
	Batch—none
Define resources	None
Map users to resources	Password facility
Log activity	SMF
Generate report	None
Manage administrative privilege	SYS1.UADS updater

management system [IMS] transactions and commands). RACF allows resource owners to give access to their resources to other users with various access authorities. The security administrator can also perform this function. RACF writes unique, security-relevant log records to the SMF file, which is the prime repository of logged events. The RACF Report Writer processes this file to generate activity reports for subsequent analysis. RACF allows security administrators sev-

EXHIBIT II-2-13 RACF Control Elements in the MVS Environment

RACF	
Define users	RACF profiles
Define resources	RACF profiles
Map users to resources	Access lists
Log activity	SETEROPS option
Produce report	RACF Report Writer
Manage administrative privilege	Auditor

MVS Architecture	
Define users	TSO users-SYS1.UADS
	Batch—none
Define resources	None
Map users to resources	None
Log activity	SMF
Generate report	None
Manage administrative privilege	SYS1.UADS updater

eral types of privileged access: SPECIAL authority permits the modification of any RACF profile: OPERATIONS authority permits access to the resource itself; and AUDITOR authority provides for the analysis of the logged activity of the other privileged security administrators. A privileged user can issue the RACF SET-ROPTS command to enable or disable a large number of global security options. Each of the MVS resource managers needing access control services invokes the RACF access control system.

Control Elements in the CICS Subsystem. CICS is a transaction-oriented subsystem that monitors terminals for input, executes transactions (i.e., typically, short, single-function programs) from those terminals, sends the answer back to the initiating terminal, and then returns to polling terminals that are waiting for the next transaction. CICS has an access control subsystem that is a control element (see Exhibit II-2-14). Privileged system administrators manage the CICS sign-on table to define users and map their access to transactions, programs, journals, queues, and files. CICS also supports such external security management software as RACF. Although CICS contains a comprehensive logging facility, its purpose is primarily for recovery management and not security. Log records written to the SMF log file are the primary source for logging and subsequent analysis of audit-relevant events. CICS security is significantly enhanced by using an external security manager as RACF.

Control Elements in the IMS Subsystem. IMS, the IBM Information Management System and ESA Transaction Manager (and, on earlier versions, the data communications system), is both a transaction- and batch-oriented subsystem. It receives transactions from a telecommunications access method, executes these transactions (typically short, single-function programs), sends the answer back to the initiating terminal, and waits for another transaction. IMS contains an access control subsystem that is a control element (see Exhibit II-2-15). The architectural mechanisms of IMS allow a privileged system administrator using the security maintenance utility to define transactions (including relationships between transactions and passwords), terminals, and commands. Although IMS contains a comprehensive logging facility, its primary function is recovery management and not security. Log records written to the SMF log file are the primary source for logging and analysis of audit-relevant events. IMS security is significantly enhanced by using an external security manager such as RACF.

Control Elements in the DB2 Data Base System. The IBM DB2 system is a relational data base management facility for use on an MVS system. DB2 has an access control subsystem that is a control element (see Exhibit II-2-16). As do other IBM implementations of relational data base systems, the DB2 control element relies on a hierarchical structure of security privileges assigned to administrators who define the physical data base and promote transactions and programs into production libraries. There are several levels of authority: SYSADM is the

EXHIBIT II-2-14 Control Elements in a CICS Subsystem

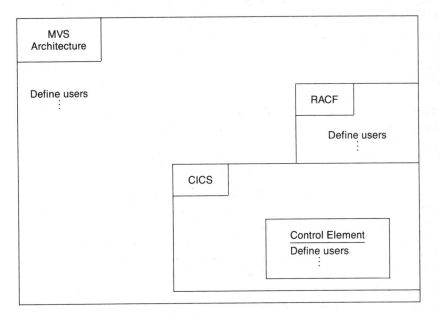

EXHIBIT II-2-15 Control Elements in an IMS Subsystem

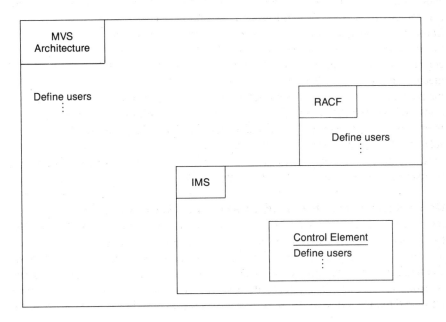

EXHIBIT II-2-16   Control Elements in a DB2 Subsystem

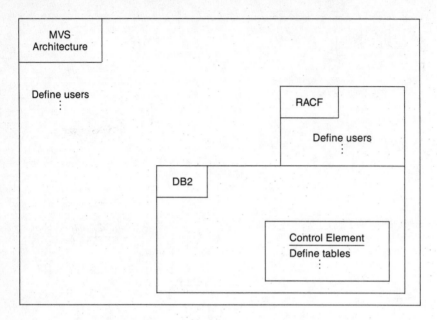

highest level of authority; SYSOPR permits the owner of each table or view of the table access authority for the table or view and the ability to grant the same or less access authority to another user ID. The DB2 Trace Facility allows the recording of successful and unsuccessful accesses to tables, views, and other DB2 objects, as well as the use of GRANT and REVOKE statements. These log records can be directed to monitoring routines or to either the SMF or Generalized Trace Facility (GTF) log file for subsequent analysis.

Control Elements in the IMS Data Base System. The IMS Data Base (IMS-DB) system provides the IBM Data Language Interface (DL/I), a hierarchical data base management facility for use on an MVS system in CICS, IMS, or batch environments. IMS-DB contains an access control subsystem that is a control element. IMS-DB relies on a hierarchical structure of security privileges assigned to administrators who define the physical data base, the programmer views of the data base, and the action control block and who promote transactions and programs into production libraries. SMF logs activity in its log records and the RACF Report Writer program is used to report on such activity.

Control Elements in User Applications. When developing application systems by using the IMS or CICS telecommunication functions in combination with IMS-DB or DB2 data base management systems, some application devel-

EXHIBIT II-2-17 Control Elements Within a User Application

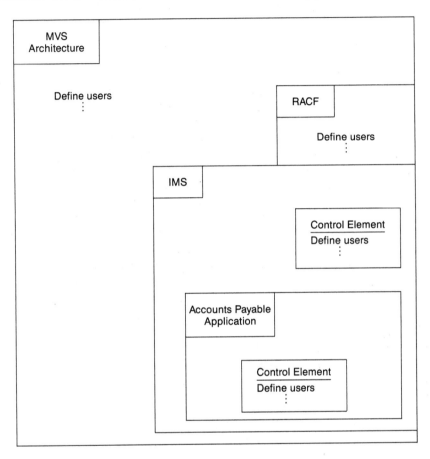

opers would rather write their own security subsystems than incorporate an external security manager. (Programmers developed these internal security subsystems because early external security products did not provide all the security mechanisms they felt were necessary.) Such access control subsystems within user applications are control elements (see Exhibit II-2-17). Although these security subsystems solved the access control problem in different ways, they generally provide the common functions required in a control element (i.e., identifying users and resources, mapping one to another, logging and reporting activity, and providing for privileged management of the security subsystem).

Control Elements in System Management Software. Tape management systems are used to manage the inventory and availability of tape volumes in

EXHIBIT II-2-18 Control Elements in a Tape Management Subsystem

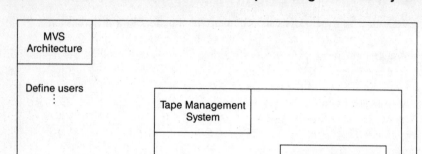

an installation. These systems often interact directly with the access methods for tape and intervene when scratch tapes are called for or when tapes are saved. System management software contains access control subsystems that are control elements (see Exhibit II-2-18). A privileged system administrator defines users of the media and manages the inventory of scratch and production tapes. Such systems usually log successful and unsuccessful use or access to tape volumes. A reporting facility may be provided for analyzing activity after it has been logged.

Control Requirements for Control Elements

A control element operates effectively when two conditions are satisfied:

- Data sets supporting the control element cannot be read, changed, or scratched except by authorized individuals.
- The components of the control element perform their respective functions to achieve the objectives of the control element.

This section reviews the components of a control element and analyzes the criteria that should be applied to determine whether each is performing its respective function to achieve the overall objectives of the control element.

Defining Users to the Control Element. There is no single way to define users to a system. However, because systems are a company asset, the requesting user's management should authorize access in order to maintain control. A formally defined process whereby a management-approved request form (either paper or electronic) is submitted to computing center management is best. An audit trail of such authorizations ensures control of the process. A formal process to remove authority is also necessary once the business need for access is over (e.g., when the accessing employee leaves the company or transfers to a different site). From the perspective of access control, an audit trail of removal is unnecessary.

Although significant progress has been made in the use of biometric technology to positively identify users, the user ID and password are still the primary mechanism for identifying and authenticating users to systems. The password is consequently the most important single mechanism available to protect the organization's systems. To prevent the use of passwords that can be easily guessed or to prevent someone from using a microprocessor to algorithmically guess passwords, a program for checking trivial passwords and a facility for locking out a user ID after a specified number of incorrect passwords have been tried is strongly recommended. It would be inappropriate only when the cost to develop and maintain one is greater than the benefits of ensuring secure passwords.

Defining Resources to the Control Element. Access must be controlled to such a computing resources as single files, sets of files (e.g., an MVS partitioned data set or a VM minidisk), terminal devices, control unit ports, and CICS and IMS transactions, commands, or communications facilities (e.g., RSCS on VM). Often, the person who defines the objects and classes of objects to the control element in effect defines security policy for the installation. Because this is critically important and is not simply a technical task, the security officer for the site should be involved in making such decisions, particularly as they relate to ownership and control of objects. The classes of objects protected at an installation should also be reevaluated on an ongoing basis.

Mapping Users to Resources Managed by the Control Element. Although most access control products enable resource owners to allow or disallow others from accessing the resources they own, security administrators are still needed to assist in this task. In such cases, an auditable process is necessary for resource owners to communicate their access requirements to installation management.

A major concern is keeping resource access lists current. When it is necessary to remove an individual from all access to system resources, user IDs make it more difficult to determine every resource to which a particular ID has had access than simply removing a user ID from membership in a group, thereby removing the user from access to any resource to which the group has access. Simply revoking a user ID does not accomplish the same objective, because all access lists continue to have the revoked user ID on them; should the user ID ever be reassigned, the new recipient would have all access authority that the former ID had. Installation management would typically be unaware of this access unless it was highly sensitive to security matters. Simply revoking the user ID, however, poses an unnecessary risk to the installation. When users initially require access to a resource, they are highly motivated to access it, but no such motivation exists for taking someone off access lists. The person in question is gone and has no further interest. Consequently, a formal process for periodically reviewing access lists is useful for reminding resource owners of all user IDs with access to their resources. A procedure should be followed to inform installation management that unauthorized users have been removed or to request the removal of IDs belonging to users who no longer require access.

Logging Activity Managed by the Control Element. Most mainframe systems employ mechanisms to define what events will be logged. Sometimes, as with VM, it is done as part of the system generation process; other times, as in MVS, a parameter in a table of system options is set. Some access control products also have optional facilities for specifying what kinds of events get logged, as well as special logging functions for privileged users or special classes of resources. This very important security area should not be viewed as a mere technical decision; the data security administrator should closely participate in the decisions made. The primary purpose for logging is to alert the appropriate people that unauthorized users have unsuccessfully attempted to access resources or to provide an audit trail of successful access to special classes of very important resources.

Monitoring of Successful Accesses. It is necessary to monitor successful accesses of critically important enterprise data sets, sensitive programs, restricted utilities, and privileged administrator activity because certain information is so valuable that it is important to know who accessed the information and when. The management responsible for the data should receive reports of successful access to such data at least monthly to initiate possible follow-up action.

In the context of this chapter, a sensitive program is an application program whose improper use could cause serious financial loss to the company and whose loss cannot be prevented by normal application system controls. Information on systems management should periodically inform owners of sensitive application programs of all updates to and executions of their programs. The frequency of such notification should be negotiated with the application owner.

Restricted utilities are specially privileged programs that could be misused by authorized individuals. Management should record and review every successful, unscheduled execution of a restricted utility. Because many restricted utilities are used routinely, management should focus on exceptions to normal use. Such exceptions should be so infrequent that a monthly review should be sufficient.

Within a particular control element, all activity of users with privileged administrator authority should be logged and reviewed by someone without such privilege. A monthly review is appropriate.

Monitoring of Unsuccessful Access Attempts. Information systems management should know about unsuccessful attempts to use certain user IDs so it can take action, if appropriate. Likewise, owners of such resources as data sets and sensitive programs should be informed if people have tried to access their resources. Owners could be informed either immediately or within some fixed time period. The attempted access of critically important data should be reviewed at least once a week.

Logging That Is Not Required. SYS1.PARMLIB, an important system data set, is neither a control element nor a restricted utility, yet it is an element of potential vulnerability like countless other system components. If, however, the usual system management control change management discipline is followed at the site and all system changes are understood, tested, and approved by management and are applied in a controlled fashion, there is no need to log every update to all system components unless that is explicitly defined as part of the change control procedure for that installation.

Reporting Logged Activity. Information systems management must communicate to responsible senior managers the security-related events that have been logged so that they can investigate and resolve the event, as appropriate. The events logged include:

- Successful events:
    - —Access to critically important data.
    - —Update or execution of sensitive programs.
    - —Use of privileged administrative authority.
    - —Execution of restricted utilities.
- Unsuccessful events:
    - —Failed log-on attempts.
    - —Failed data set access.
    - —Failed program, transaction, or privileged command execution.

Managing Users with Privileged Administrative Authority. A person without privileged administrative authority (e.g., someone with only RACF AUDITOR authority) should review the activity of users with privileged administrative authority (e.g., those with RACF SPECIAL and OPERATIONS authority). For example, it would be extraordinary for users with RACF SPECIAL authority to put themselves on an access list for a resource; only the owner of a resource should permit a person to be on an access list. The activity of people with privileged administrative authority should be reviewed for activity affecting critical or sensitive data and processes (e.g., did someone with OPERATIONS authority access a critically important data set or a restricted utility?). The reviewer should look for activity outside the normal domain of activity for the user. That a person with RACF SPECIAL authority also has AUDITOR authority is not necessarily a problem if the site ensures that the logging options in effect will never be turned off without management authorization.

RESTRICTED UTILITIES

Restricted utilities are programs or commands that allow computing installation personnel to perform specific, system-oriented tasks within a computing center. To accomplish their tasks, these programs must usually run in a privileged mode (e.g., Authorized Program Facility [APF] authorized in MVS or as a C class machine in VM). The key to securing restricted utilities is understanding that a person authorized to use a restricted utility could also use it for reasons never intended by the designer of the utility (e.g., to commit financial fraud or to steal, alter, or destroy programs and information).

MVS Restricted Utilities

It is important to offer a comprehensive list of restricted utilities that could run on an MVS system because new products are constantly being developed, support is withdrawn from others, and it is not possible to identify internally developed programs that fall into this category. It is wiser therefore to specify the principal classes of utility programs that should be considered restricted utilities, and to give some examples of each. For each restricted utility, it is important first to understand the function for which it was developed; it is also important to consider how the utility could be misused. (It would not be responsible to describe how specific programs could be misused; however, most systems programmers could provide credible scenarios.) Data security management must analyze the organization's restricted utilities to ensure that a due standard of care is applied in controlling them. Some of these programs, under standard MVS terminology and program names, and the functions they perform include:

- Writing an MVS standard label on a tape reel (e.g., IEHINIT).
- Changing a volume table of contents on a disk pack (e.g., AMASPZAP, IMASPZAP, and SUPERZAP).
- Rebuilding a volume table of contents on a disk pack (e.g., ICKDSF and IEHATLAS).
- Dynamically reading or changing some component of the executing operating system (e.g., COREZAP, INCORZAP, and OMEGAMON).
- Executing a program or command on behalf of a nonprivileged user with privileged authority. There is no example of a commercial product.
- Dumping or restoring whole volumes or specific data sets owned by individuals (e.g., ADRDSSU, DRWDASDR, and DFDSS).
- Turning off the operation of a control element (e.g., RVARY in RACF).

VM Restricted Utilities

Utilities under standard VM terminology and the functions they perform include:

- Writing a standard label on a tape reel. There is no available utility.
- Changing a volume table of contents on a disk pack. There is no available utility.
- Rebuilding a volume table of contents on a disk pack. There is no available utility.
- Dynamically reading or changing some component of the executing operating system (e.g., OMEGAMON).
- Executing some program or command on behalf of a nonprivileged user with privileged authority (e.g., PRIVCOM). PRIVCOM is a generic name for any service machine that has been set up with both privileged authority and a list of user IDs for which it will execute one or more privileged programs, CP or Conversational Monitor System (CMS) commands.
- Dumping and restoring entire volumes or specific data sets owned by individuals (e.g., VMDUMP). VMDUMP is a generic name for a disconnected service machine that either dumps all of the minidisks on one virtual machine or dumps specific minidisks on a particular virtual machine to backup files for the subsequent restoring. Each user ID can restore its own minidisks, and the privileged VMDUMP administrator can cause any volume or minidisk to be either dumped or restored. A log of successful and unsuccessful use can usually be displayed for subsequent analysis.
- Turning off the operation of a control element (e.g., RVARY in RACF).

Control Requirements for Restricted Utilities

Controls must be established to prevent the unauthorized use of restricted utilities. These controls have to ensure that only authorized people can execute the program and that authorized people use the program only for the purpose for which it was intended.

Because of the way some restricted utilities are shipped by the manufacturer (e.g., as part of SYS1.LINKLIB in MVS), the default option for universal access authority by nonprivileged users could be READ, thus allowing such users to EXECUTE. It is essential that these programs be identified and put within the domain of a control element (e.g., under RACF program control to restrict access to programs on an access list). In fact, there are few of these programs, and a program's documentation usually specifies the required security controls.

It is virtually impossible to programmatically restrict utility use to an authorized purpose. The only way to ensure this is to log all unscheduled executions of restricted utilities and to review that use.

Because monitoring unsuccessful access attempts is a normal part of the logging requirement, no special logging or reporting is needed for a restricted utility. Furthermore, because all updates to system components should be managed by the site's change control management process, no special logging of updates is required for a restricted utility. However, successful executions of the program should be logged, and all unscheduled executions should be reviewed. IS management sometimes resists this requirement, asserting that it is a burdensome task. Nevertheless, there should be very little unscheduled use of restricted utilities in a well-managed installation. Data security management should review the unscheduled use of each restricted utility periodically to determine why it was needed and why normal change control could not have been used. Management should review the logs to determine whether the individual who executed a utility was on the access list or used a privileged authority to access the restricted utility. If use is high, the review should occur frequently. If use is low, less frequent reviews are appropriate (e.g., monthly or quarterly).

SYSTEM VULNERABILITIES

In the context of this article, system vulnerabilities are system software components that—if not installed, protected, and maintained properly—could allow an unauthorized individual to either violate the integrity of the operating system or circumvent the system's access control elements. Such system vulnerabilities must be controlled and frequently reviewed to ensure a secure system.

Controls must be established to prevent the unauthorized modification of all operating system components. Consequently, when installing or maintaining system software, system programmers must address not only the efficiency and effectiveness of the system but security as well. They must ensure that inadequacies in the implementation of a software product do not allow the product to violate the integrity of the system or to circumvent its controls.

In the context of this chapter, operating system components include:

- The system control program.
- Subsystems.
- Job Entry Subsystem 2 (JES2), a functional extension of the HASP II program, or Job Entry Subsystem 3 (JES3), a functional extension of the ASP program.
- Data base management systems.
- Telecommunications systems.
- Program products that run as an extension of the operating system.
- Custom-developed programs that run as an extension of the operating system.

The operating system comprises all programs and associated data sets, with the exception of application programs and their data sets. Therefore, none of these components must permit access authority to update. These programs must be executed by systems users but must never be changed by an unauthorized user.

MVS System Vulnerabilities

It is impossible to list the vulnerabilities of all MVS system components, because new packaged and custom software is constantly being implemented and withdrawn from the system. It is wiser, therefore, to specify the principal classes of system vulnerabilities that should be considered and give some examples of each.

For each system vulnerability, it is important to understand the function for which it was developed and how it could be misused to commit financial fraud or to steal, alter, or destroy programs and information. Information systems management must understand the security implications of all products installed on site to ensure that they have been installed and are maintained exactly as recommended by the manufacturer and that every system change is applied under the change control process. A nonexhaustive list of system vulnerabilities using standard MVS terminology and library names is provided in the following paragraphs.

APF Libraries. APF libraries are a special set of load libraries containing code that is part of the trusted computing base of a system. If a program has been link edited into an authorized library as an authorized program, it can execute without having to further check authorization to execute. Very often, however, such program modules use some internal mechanism to check for authorization (e.g., as with RACF commands). If a user can identify a single authorized library that can be updated, this user could introduce a program into this library (which would place itself in supervisor state) and execute every command in the System 370 instruction set, thereby circumventing the integrity of the operating system and any control elements running on the system.

User-Developed Supervisor Calls (SVCs). Supervisor calls are programs that are privileged parts of the operating system and are intended to perform very important user functions (e.g., instead of issuing such input/output commands as START I/O, the user enters GET, which is mapped into the invocation of a supervisor call routine). IBM supplies users with many SVCs as part of the operating system, and in-house programmers can also write their own SVCs to perform privileged tasks for system management or user applications (e.g., reading or writing outside of one's own address space). Such SVCs must be written with extreme care to prevent an unauthorized user from using them. User-written SVCs must never return control to the invoking program in supervisor mode, only in problem program state. If privileged functions are required, they should be performed in the SVC in supervisor mode and control should be returned as a conventional problem program state.

SYS1.PARMLIB. SYS1.PARMLIB is a partitioned data set system library containing members that define the composition of a system (e.g., IEAAPFxx is a member of SYS1.PARMLIB used for defining which load libraries are authorized

457

libraries). The security vulnerability is obvious. A user who could update SYS1.PARMLIB could simply add the name and volume serial number of a personally owned load library; at the next Initial Program Load (IPL), that private library would be considered an APF library.

SYS1.LPALIB. SYS1.LPALIB is the system library containing load modules for most of the user exit code on the system (e.g., RACF and SMF exits). A user who updated SYS1.LPALIB could, for example, change the RACF exit code to always grant access to protected resources for a specified user ID or change the SMF exit code to suppress the writing of an SMF log record when a specified ID is used.

SYS1.LINKLIB. SYS1.LINKLIB is the system library containing the operating system's load modules. A user might update SYS1.LINKLIB with an unauthorized program that could violate the integrity of MVS or bypass the system's access control elements.

SYS1.PROCLIB. SYS1.PROCLIB is a partitioned data set system library containing sets of JCL statements for general use (e.g., procedures, called procs, for such functions as compiling and linking). A user might update SYS1.PROCLIB by adding an additional step to the default log-on proc, which is usually executed by a person with privilege that would invoke the RACF command to give an unauthorized person SPECIAL or OPERATIONS privilege and route the sysout listing to a nonexistent class thereby destroying any possible audit trail. If a nonauthorized user lacking SPECIAL authority executes this log-on proc, the step fails because the user cannot grant SPECIAL. But when an authorized person with SPECIAL authority executes the log-on proc, the step successfully executes, giving the unauthorized individual SPECIAL privilege.

SYS1.CLIST. SYS1.CLIST is a partitioned data set system library that is conceptually similar to SYS1.PROCLIB except that it contains CLISTs instead of procs. A CLIST is a set of TSO commands that execute successively in program like fashion. SYS1.CLIST is vulnerable in the same way as SYS1.PROCLIB. A user could find a CLIST used by someone with SPECIAL privilege, modify it to grant the user SPECIAL privilege, and wait until a privileged person executes it.

Bypass Label Processing (BLP). BLP is a job control language facility that allows a batch job to specify that the standard label on a tape should not be used by RACF to grant or restrict access to a tape volume. This facility is most often used when a tape of foreign origin is brought into an installation and the programmer needs to determine the tape's format. If someone bypasses label processing, the RACF product cannot determine whether the tape is a protected volume, because BLP processing bypasses access controls for tapes. This threat can be controlled by defining an RACF profile in the FACILITY class and placing the IDs of the few users requiring BLP on its access list.

VM System Vulnerabilites

System vulnerabilities can affect various VM components, including service machine default passwords, class authority within CP, disconnected service machines, and Cooperative Viewing Facility (CVIEW). These components and their associated vulnerabilities are discussed in the following paragraphs.

Service Machine Default Passwords. After a disconnected service machine has been installed by a systems programmer, the installer logs onto the ID of the service machine and provides the default password supplied by the manufacturer. Usually, the installation documentation directs the installer to change the password immediately. Unfortunately, such passwords are often not changed. These service machines often run in a privileged state because of the critical tasks they perform. If someone is able to access the log-on screen of a VM system before the passwords have been changed, this person could test various default passwords. Exhibit II-2-19 lists some common user ID and password combinations.

EXHIBIT II-2-19 Commonly Used Service Machines Default Passwords

User ID	Password	Service Machine Description
ADMIN	ADMIN	IBM Function Program (IFP) Administration
AUTOLOG	AUTOLOG	Automatically logs on the virtual machine
CMSBATCH	BATCH	Executes processor-intensive jobs
CMSUSER	CMSUSER	Example of a virtual machine
CPRM	CPRM	Optional product available with Release 3.1
CSPUSER	CSPUSER	Optional product available with Release 3.1
DIRMAINT	DIRM	VM directory maintenance
DISKACNT	ACNT	Collection of accounting information
EREP	IBMCE	Allows IBM customer engineer to execute CPEREP
FSFADMIN	FSFADMIN	File management system
FSFCNTRL	FSFCNTRL	File management system
IBMCE	IBMCE	Used by the IBM customer engineer
IBMUSER	SYS1	Initial user ID used by the RACF administrator
IIPS	IIPS	Controls interactive instructional presentation system
IPCS	PSR	Reserved for system support

(continued)

EXHIBIT II-2-19 (*continued*)

User ID	Password	Service Machine Description
ISMAINT	ISMAINT	Information system administration
ISPVM	ISPVM	Disconnected virtual machine for Interactive System Productivity Facility (ISPF)
IVPM1	IVPASS	Installation verification for programs after generation
IVPM2	IVPASS	Installation verification for programs after generation
LEV2VM	LEV2VM	Running a second-level VM system
MAINT	CPCMS	VM system programmers maintenance user ID
MONITOR	MON	Virtual Machine System Product (VM/SP) data collection facility
OLTSEP	IBMCE	Allows IBM customer engineer to run online test program
OPERATNS	IPCS	Disconnected virtual machine for problem management
OPERATOR	OPERATOR	System operations
OP1	OP1	System operations
OSVS1	OSVS1	User ID for a guest Operating System/Virtual Storage 1 (OS/VS1) operating system
PRODBM	PRODBM	Professional Office System (PROFS)
PROMAIL	PROMAIL	PROFS
PVM	PVM	VM/PASSTHRU facility
ROUTER	ROUTER	Disk Operating System/Virtual Storage Extended (DOS/VSE)
RSCS	RSCS	RSCS networking program product
SFBATCH	SFBATCH	PROFS
SFCAL	SFCAL	PROFS
SMART	SMART	System monitor
SQLDBA	SQLDBAPW	Virtual Machine Structural Query Language (VM/SQL) program product
SQLUSER	SQLUSER	VM/SQL program product
SYSADMIN	SYSADMIN	PROFS
SYSDUMP1	SYSDUMP	DASD volume dumps
VMBATCH	VMBATCH	Batch machine
VMBATCH1	VMBATCH1	Batch machine
VMAP	VMAP	Performance monitoring capabilities

EXHIBIT II-2-19 (*continued*)

User ID	Password	Service Machine Description
VMUTIL	VMUTIL	Disconnected virtual machine for privileged tasks
VSEIPO	VSEIPO	IBM System/370 Virtual Storage Extended (VSE) operating system
VSEMAINT	VSEMAINT	To tailor and service the VSE system

Class Authority Within CP. Virtual machines derive their ability to execute different sets of CP or Conversational Monitor System (CMS) commands from the CP class that has been assigned to the virtual machine in the directory entry for the user ID. Class authority applies to people as well as to disconnected service machines. The assignment of class authorities to systems programmers, operators, and disconnected service machines provides a granular way to assign privileged authority to people or service machines according to the need to perform tasks on behalf of installation management. These classes include:

- A—Primary system operator.
- B—System resource operator.
- C—System programmer.
- D—Spooling operator.
- E—System analyst.
- F—Service representative.
- G—General user.

A penetrator who gains unauthorized access to a disconnected service machine can execute any command permitted by the class of the service machine. For example, because a C class machine can alter real storage, it can grant itself any or all of the privileged class authorities A through F, thus enabling it to issue any CP or CMS command.

By maintaining the same user ID on a system even after their job responsibility has changed, many users retain significantly more authority than required. Data security management must continually monitor who has each class authority and reevaluate the continued need for this authority.

Disconnected Service Machines. User virtual machines must communicate with a service machine to tell it what service is required. This communication can be accomplished by sending a file to the virtual reader of the service machine or by a direct Inter-User Communication Vehicle (IUCV) or Virtual Machine Communication Facility (VMCF) communication between the machines. Many of these machines are privileged systems that run as C or E class virtual machines. Therefore, a penetrator with sufficient knowledge of what a service machine does with the data stream from the user's virtual machine could try to trick the service machine into performing a command on behalf of the user's virtual machine (e.g., trick an RACF service machine into giving a normal user SPECIAL or OPERATIONS authority). All service machines must carefully scrutinize the data streams sent to them and process these streams so that they cannot process any command sequences hidden within the data stream.

CVIEW. CVIEW allows consultants to help users remotely by permitting the consultant to view at a second terminal all activity displayed on the terminal of the user being helped. However, CVIEW could also allow an unauthorized user to view another person's display without that person's knowledge. This threat can be mitigated by displaying a message with sufficient frequency on the terminal of the person being helped (e.g., every 30 seconds) so that the user knows the session is being monitored.

Control Requirements for System Vulnerabilities

A control process is necessary to ensure that every operating system component is covered by an RACF profile and that the UACC (i.e., universal access authority) is never set at Update, Alter, or Control. An additional control process is required to ensure that the change control management discipline is followed during all system changes. Likewise, a process should be in place to regularly test system components to ensure that the necessary controls were installed correctly and are still operating effectively. At least one system programmer at a site should keep abreast of system testing and auditing and should communicate information as appropriate to the systems programming and operations departments to ensure their awareness of vulnerability problems and potential solutions.

Although there is no business need to maintain a list of system vulnerabilities, system testers and EDP auditors should have such a list to ensure that they thoroughly test the system. System testers and auditors should not test for a vulnerability that has just been uncovered without first explaining the problem to their colleagues.

Every installation should have a procedure for managing change control. (Change control is the process of planning, coordinating, and monitoring changes affecting system software resources. Such changes include those made to systems and network hardware and software, procedures, and environment.) There is no method for managing change control that necessarily applies to all systems environments. It may not be necessary, for example, to log and analyze all successful updates to system components. However, a controlled process must be followed to ensure that system changes are understood, tested, and approved by management. Whether the logging and reporting of such changes is part of the process depends on the totality of the control process developed and followed by the installation.

SUMMARY

To ensure that control elements operate effectively, data security management should be able to demonstrate that adequate controls exist to manage the process of:

- Identifying system users.
- Identifying system resources.
- Relating users to resources through access lists.
- Providing audit trails that log unauthorized access attempts and authorized accesses.
- Providing activity reports.
- Identifying and managing privileged users.

To control restricted utilities, data security management must ensure that only authorized persons can execute these utilities and that any unscheduled use of these utilities is logged and reviewed carefully.

To control system vulnerabilities, data security management must prevent unauthorized system modification, understand and control the implementation of software products, and control system changes. This requires an in-depth knowledge of the vulnerabilities of specific system components and a controlled process for monitoring system security.

Data and
Applications Controls

Section II-3 reviews the control mechanisms and techniques needed for secure data and application programs. Chapter II-3-1 addresses the need to categorize the sensitivity of data and programs in order to provide the proper level of protection. This categorization should be done from the perspective of each of the three general security control objectives: confidentiality, integrity, and availability. First, the organization must determine the value of the data to the organization. Then, by reviewing the risks to sensitive data and programs from each of the three perspectives, appropriate protective measures can be devised. A suggested set of categories for an organization's data is presented.

The data used by application programs can be organized so that a data base management system (DBMS) can be used to control access to that data, using identification and authentication techniques. Controls for DBMSs are discussed in Chapter II-3-2. It should be noted that DBMSs are capable of protecting the confidentiality of information much better than its integrity, but neither control objective is fully met by current commercial systems. The objective of information availability is poorly understood, and current products hardly address that control objective at all.

Chapter II-3-3 discusses generally accepted standards of business practice that should be followed to ensure effective control of applications. These include standards governing least privilege, separation of duties, assignment of privilege, and alternating roles.

The operating system provides process-to-process isolation among application level processes. However, whenever there are application-dependent definitions of entities that must be controlled, security depends on application-dependent processes. Access control to applications can be provided by the use of sophisticated password schemes, DBMS subschemas, and access control software products.

Information Categorization and Protection

WARREN SCHMITT

An effective information security program is based on the theory that the costs to protect an information asset should not exceed its value to the corporation. Most technical and nontechnical professionals would agree with this premise. However, although these professionals understand how much their hardware costs and, to a lesser extent, how much their software and applications cost, they often do not know the value of the information itself.

The seriousness of this problem is obvious in light of the fact the majority of major US corporations consider their corporate information the second most important asset next to their human resources. Although a great deal of work has focused on risk analysis theories and processes, practical means of determining the value of information has not yet been devised. This chapter discusses the major risks to information resources. It then presents a program for categorizing information according to its relative value to the organization and determining which protective measures are appropriate.

RISKS TO INFORMATION

Information is subject to three major risks: destruction, modification, and disclosure. In the past, work in the area of information security has addressed only one of these risks—disclosure. Increasing the scope of security to three dimensions greatly increases the complexity; however, there is no reasonable chance to properly manage information assets without taking each of the major risks into consideration.

Some information security practitioners suggest that by concentrating on these three major risks, thousands of risks may be overlooked. To some extent, this is true. However, these three major risk categories are broad enough to encompass all the known risks. Furthermore, this categorization approach permits the establishment of a framework that can identify the value of the information, the primary risks, the protective measures, and the individuals who are responsible for ensuring that a constructive and consistent approach is established.

A second premise is that not all information is subjected to these three risks to the same degree; in some cases, a body of information may be subjected to only one or two of the risks. For example, the airline guide used by the travel industry is not highly sensitive to disclosure except for the fact that the publisher wants it to be disclosed only to those who have paid the subscription fee. Maintaining the integrity of the online data base is of major concern, however, because if the customers who use this information lose faith in its accuracy—whether it is from improper data base updates or malicious access by a hacker—the value of the information will be greatly reduced.

An update error is a vulnerability that is best managed through implementation of a quality control program. On the other hand, access by a hacker is a vulnerability that the information security specialist should address. The value the publisher places on the information determines how much money will be spent to protect the integrity of the information through either quality or security controls.

Likewise, the availability of the online system supporting this airline guide information is highly critical. This aspect of information valuation dictates how quickly the online system would have to be restored should the host system be destroyed. If it is determined that the online system must be restored in a matter of hours, such controls as mirror images of the data base, operating systems, applications, and a hot site would have to be available within that specified time frame.

The value of the information to the corporation must be understood to determine which controls need to be in place to protect that information. In the preceding example, the emphasis should be directed toward preserving the availability and integrity of the information. Less effort would be expended on preserving the information's confidentiality.

This chapter discusses a program for establishing the categories that enable those responsible for the information to identify its value as it pertains to each of the three major risks. In addition, an approach is presented that enables the system designer, internal auditor, and IS personnel to identify the controls that are best suited to protecting information with varying degrees of value. By combining the knowledge and experiences of these individuals, it is possible to develop rational explanations for selecting certain controls and rejecting others. This decision process provides a means to justify installment of prudent controls and builds a basis for proper management of the information asset.

MANAGEMENT OF INFORMATION

To take the steps necessary to manage any asset, the security specialist must know, at the least, its value to the owner, the risks to which it may be subjected, and the measures that are available to protect it from the risks. If one or more of these three factors are not well understood, the specialist's ability to properly manage the asset is severely diminished. The more specialists understand about both the value of the information and the risks associated with it, the better they can properly protect that information. The following sections discuss these managerial aspects of information protection.

Establishing the Value of Information

The quickest, easiest way to identify the value of information is to ask the person who is responsible for the accuracy and integrity of the information. Some refer to this individual as the owner. In this chapter, however, the term "owner" is used to refer to the corporate entity, and the person responsible for the accuracy and integrity of that information is referred to as the guardian.

If the guardians are asked to rank the information for which they are responsible on the basis of its loss expectation, they could do so with little assistance, even if they do not know how it might be destroyed, modified, or disclosed. All applications that produce income, control the financial worth of the corporation, or contain proprietary information should be evaluated by the guardian for each of the three major risks (i.e., availability, integrity, and confidentiality).

This is a pragmatic approach to developing the value of information and does not provide a statistical analysis, because it relies on the guardian's judgment. Some guardians may select a value based on the controls associated with that value. For example, the guardian may intentionally lower the value assigned to the information to avoid installing more stringent controls. If this occurs, the protective measures would most likely be inadequate. To ensure that the guardian's evaluations are appropriate, the evaluations should be examined by a security review team, confirmed by the guardian's superiors, or possibly verified by the internal audit staff. This review process enables the security specialist to correct evaluations that are either understated or overstated.

Understanding the Risks and Identifying the Protective Measures

Once the guardian provides the security practitioner with the evaluation of the information, the risks that this application is exposed to must be identified and ranked and the best protective measures must be selected. The complexity of this task is usually in direct proportion to the complexity of the IS environment. To ensure the accuracy of this analysis, it is strongly suggested that representatives from systems development, the data center, network management, and internal auditing as well as internal or external consultants be involved.

The risks and exposures that information is subject to do not vary considerably within the business community. What is unique is the impact the same event may have on different business enterprises. For example, the impact of a long-lasting power failure may vary greatly depending on the type of business. The loss of power for several hours in the investment brokerage business may translate into millions of dollars of loss; the publisher of a monthly magazine, however, may suffer no more than a mild inconvenience.

Protective measures are seldom absolutes. They are installed to provide the ability to reduce the risk to an acceptable level and put the company in a position to properly manage the information asset. The overall objective of installing protective measures is to prevent threats from taking advantage of preexisting vulnerabilities, detect exposures if they cannot be prevented, and in some cases correct the malfunction and continue the processing.

To determine whether they are using the proper protective measures, security professionals must first establish their control objectives. Control objectives usually represent broad objectives that are expected to be accomplished. Identifying the control objectives enables the security specialist to determine, from a high-level perspective, whether all the risks and exposures are covered. It is helpful to consult the company's internal auditing staff, because they are usually familiar with these concepts and lay out their audit programs on the basis of preestablished control objectives. Input from the CIO, the head of internal auditing, and the major functional departments that are primary users of information systems should be obtained before determining which control objectives to address.

Once a comprehensive set of control objectives for the corporation has been identified and agreed on, the specific protective measures that will support each of the control objectives must be identified. This process produces an inventory of all the available protective measures, which are then ranked on the basis of their degree of effectiveness. This inventory should include all the measures the company currently uses as well as those that might provide a higher level of protection. For example, the most effective protective measure to ensure confidentiality currently used in the corporation might be a well-recognized electronic access control system. If a guardian identifies the need to protect several highly sensitive trade secrets, encryption might be an appropriate additional protective measure.

This inventory of protective measures should be reviewed with the appropriate technical staffs to help verify that all of the known risks and exposures have been reduced to an acceptable level. During this review process, it is likely that additional risks and exposures will be identified; these should be evaluated against the controls. This iterative process should continue until the security specialist is confident that the majority of the risks and exposures can be properly managed with the available protective measures.

INFORMATION CATEGORIES

This section establishes categories that provide a framework for affixing a relative value to information. The names assigned to each category are not particularly significant; they follow generally accepted usage to describe relative value. A later section explores the possibility of substituting the names with a number code.

The guardians are responsible for determining which category their information falls into and stipulating the potential loss (i.e., its value). As discussed previously, these assessments must be verified. The information security officer and IS manager then must identify and implement the measures necessary to protect against the potential loss.

Availability Categories

The potential for a corporation to suffer a loss varies greatly depending on the information that becomes unavailable. The following categories are useful for establishing information availability:

- *Vital*. Information that is essential for the continued operation of the corporation (e.g., life support systems, customer records, and on-line processing). The loss of this information may ultimately cause the corporation to cease to function or, at a minimum, suffer severe financial losses. In many instances, this information must be recovered within hours after the damaging event occurs.
- *Important*. Information that is essential for the continued operation of the corporation. This category includes the corporate data base, legal files and proceedings, research projects, and process control. A processing delay of several days to possibly a week would be acceptable.
- *Useful*. Information that, if destroyed, would cause the corporation some disruption in operations but would not prevent the continuation of the primary corporate or departmental operations. This category includes reference data, historical data, and departmental correspondence.
- *Nonessential*. Information of value that would not be reconstructed if lost (e.g., historical data older than three years).

Integrity Categories

The following categories are suggested to identify the varying degree of loss that might result should information integrity be compromised:

- *Critical*. Information that, if modified in an unauthorized manner, would cause the company to suffer a major financial loss, adversely affect the company's strategic business decisions, or otherwise cause a severe loss. This category includes financial records, the company's investment portfolio, and airline reservation systems.
- *Sensitive*. Information that represents dollar transactions, describes an employee's personal information, or identifies corporate income, expense, assets, or liabilities. Processing system data, research projects, corporate data, personnel records, and operating system data are some examples of information that would be considered sensitive.

- *Valuable*. Normal operating information would fall into this category. It may be represented by departmental plans or production results or accomplishments, corporate or departmental manuals or procedures, or correspondence or directives that are not categorized as either sensitive or critical.
- *Noncritical*. Information that is supplied from public sources and is not relied on to make business decisions (e.g., the company telephone directory).

Confidentiality Categories

Information can be placed in the following confidentiality categories:

- *Registered confidential*. Information that, if disclosed, would cause a severe loss from a financial or competitive advantage standpoint. This category might include such information as strategic plans, trade secrets, investment strategies, new products, and sealed bids.
- *Confidential*. Information that, if improperly disclosed, could be detrimental to an employee or customer. Included in this category would be corporate data, access security profiles, personnel records, and proprietary software.
- *Internal use only*. Information to be used only on an internal basis; appropriate approvals must be obtained for external use. This category includes corporate directives, organizational charts, and procedure manuals.
- *Public*. Information that is considered to be generally available (e.g., books and vendor manuals).

RISK AND PROTECTIVE MEASURES

The type of protective measure used depends not only on the risk it is to prevent but on the category of information and the potential for loss. The following sections discuss protective measures for ensuring availability, integrity, and confidentiality.

Availability Protective Measures

When substantial losses occur immediately following a damaging event, the key issues are how much time it will take to recover the information, how much time it will take to recover the processing capabilities, and how much time the security professional has to recover information and processing capabilities to prevent further losses. The severity of the expected loss determines the protective measures that must be employed. Protective measures must be in place before the damaging event occurs.

For example, if the security specialist has less than an hour to recover information and restore processing and the potential for loss is high, copies of all transac-

tions must be maintained off site, because there would be no time available to reconstruct the information. In addition, a hot site would have to be available within
the stipulated recovery time and would have to provide all the required networks,
operating systems, and system utilities. If the potential for loss were less—as it
might be for a customer data base that is used primarily for billing on a monthly
basis—an identified alternative processing site, off-site storage, and a pretested
contingency plan would be adequate protection measures.

Exhibit II-3-1 shows the relationship between the availability categories of information (with corresponding sample types of information), the potential for loss,
and examples of protective measures that might reduce the risk to an acceptable
level. This chart provides an overview of the factors that help determine the
proper actions to be taken to protect the information assets. Such charts help the

EXHIBIT II-3-1   Availability Categorization and Protection Chart

Type of Information	Category	Potential Loss	Protective Measures
Life support systems Customer records On-line processing	Vital	High ↑ Loss of income Customer service Management decisions Cost to reconstruct Customer confidence ↓ Low	Active hot site Backup copies Contingency plan (tested quarterly)
Customer records Corporate data base Legal files Research projects Process control	Important		Alternative processing sites Off-site storage Daily and weekly updates Contingency plan (tested annually)
Reference material Historical information (1–3 years old) Departmental correspondence	Useful		Retention schedules Locked desks, filing cabinets, and offices Physical and environmental controls
Historical information (older than 3 years)	Nonessential		Ordinary care

SOURCE: WR Schmitt & Associates.

guardians express their opinions about the value of the information, and security specialists can then determine which protective measures might be appropriate.

Similar charts should be developed for integrity and confidentiality, as discussed in the following sections. The examples used in the columns for types of information, potential for loss, and protective measures are but a small sampling of the possibilities that exist. It should be noted that some protective measures (e.g., encryption and electronic access controls) provide protection for both integrity and confidentiality categories.

Integrity Protective Measures

It is essential that the integrity of information be preserved to minimize erroneous management decisions, eliminate the ability to manipulate financial information for the purpose of committing fraud, and maintain customer and employee confidence that sensitive information about them will not be modified in an unauthorized manner. Unauthorized access and the ability to manipulate information have caused serious losses for many corporations. There are numerous examples in which the modification of information has permitted the diversion of millions of dollars, the shipment of goods to unauthorized persons, or the modification of information that in turn causes internal disruption.

The term "integrity," as used in this chapter, is not synonymous with accuracy or relevance. This is not to suggest that accuracy and relevance are not important; accuracy and relevance are simply not within the purview of information security. There are people within every organization who are charged with these responsibilities; information security practitioners do not have this responsibility unless they are the authors or originators of the information.

In most cases, the information security staff as well as the data processing staff have no way of knowing (nor should they know) if the information they process or protect is correct or relevant. In most large statistical data bases, there is a known error rate, which may include errors that have crept in over years of gathering the information. Decisions that are made on this information take into consideration that there is a base error rate; however, this does not materially affect the decisions that are made. The important consideration is that the integrity of the information remains unaffected (i.e., only authorized changes are processed). Helping ensure that only authorized changes are made is a condition with which information security can assist.

Exhibit II-3-2 shows the integrity categories of information, the potential for loss, and examples of protective measures.

Confidentiality Protective Measures

Confidentiality is the attribute most commonly thought of when information security is mentioned. Loss of competitive advantage is one of the major concerns of most corporations. Disclosure of new products, strategic plans, or investment strategies may result in the loss of market share, causing the loss of cash receipts

EXHIBIT II-3-2 Integrity Categorization and Protection Chart

Types of Information	Categories	Potential Loss	Protective Measures
Financial records Investment portfolio Airline reservation system	Critical	High ↑	Encryption Message authentication Dual approvals
Processing system Research projects Corporate data base Personnel records Operating systems	Sensitive	Fraud Customer confidence Management decisions Financial exposure Erroneous records	Individual accountability Segregation of duties Verification and monitoring Program change control
Time-keeping records Departmental directives Corporate procedures	Valuable	↓ Low	General access and need to know Update and change procedures Respect for copyright principles
Company telephone directories	Noncritical		Ordinary business controls

SOURCE: WR Schmitt & Associates.

or loss of net income. The right to privacy—for employees and customers alike—is generally held to be a high priority and a basic responsibility of well-run organizations.

Confidentiality of information can be maintained by the introduction of a variety of protective measures (see Exhibit II-3-3). The high end of the spectrum would include such measures as encryption, system and network isolation to ensure trusted processing and communications, and personal identification and authorization. The lower end of the spectrum might include nondisclosure agreements, audit trails, and locks on desks and filing cabinets.

CONVERTING THEORY INTO PRACTICE

Although most people agree that categorization is a reasonable concept, many reject it on the grounds that it is too large a task. They envision every piece of

EXHIBIT II-3-3 Confidentiality Categorization and Protection Chart

Types of Information	Categories	Potential Loss	Protective Measures
Strategic plans Trade secrets Investment strategy	Registered Confidential	High ↑	Encryption Individual assignments Isolation of computer systems and networks
Corporate data Access security profiles Personnel records Proprietary software	Confidential	Competitive advantage Financial exposure Fraud Conflict of interest Customer confidence Legal liability	Individual authorization Nondisclosure agreements Audit trails Locked desks, cabinets, and offices
Corporate directives Organizational charts Procedures manuals	Internal Use Only	↓ Low	Internal access Need to know Proper labeling
Books and vendor manuals	Public		Ordinary business controls

SOURCE: WR Schmitt & Associates.

information within a corporation: all paper files and all computerized and noncomputerized reports. Approaching it from this perspective would require a massive effort. However, categorization becomes plausible when the basic principles of computerization are employed (e.g., ensuring that all like records have the same format, all like transactions are processed in a consistent manner, and the same process is consistently repeated).

In most corporations, the major portion of the most valuable information is in electronic form, which enables the information security professional to readily place this information in categories. An entire application, including all of its subsystems, can occasionally support a single category of information for availability, integrity, and confidentiality. If, however, the application is very large and its protective requirements are diverse, it might be appropriate to categorize the major subsystems independently. For example, if a portion of an application must be recovered within one or two hours and the rest of the application must be recovered in several days, those subsystems should be categorized separately and should receive different protective measures that would support each of their recovery needs.

In large record-processing systems, the categorization process can occasionally be simplified by examining an individual record and assigning information to the appropriate categories (i.e., availability, integrity, and confidentiality). Because the other records maintained by the application are similar, this would enable the information security professional to identify the appropriate protective measures. This approach can be effectively used in large recordkeeping systems (e.g., hospital medical records, insurance policy records, and financial records). Depending on the size of the application, categorizing one record would permit the categorization of several thousand or even millions of records.

Translating Categorization Terminology into Numerical Codes

Earlier in this chapter, it was stated that the terms used to describe the potential for loss were not particularly important. An effective method of enabling the system users—from end users to technicians—to place information in categories is to assign values ranging from 0 to 9 to each of the major risks.

For example, in the risk category of availability, the values 9, 8, and 7 would be assigned to information considered vital; 6, 5, and 4 would be assigned to important information; the values 3, 2, and 1 would be assigned to useful information; and the value of 0 would be assigned to nonessential information (see Exhibit II-3-4). With this method, the guardian can more easily and accurately determine which information assets are more or less valuable than others. The same series of numerical values would be assigned to the other two major risk categories, as shown in Exhibit II-3-4.

In this manner, a simple coding system could be established that would identify the relative value of information in terms of its availability, integrity, and confidentiality. For example, if an information asset were coded A9 I9 C9, it would indicate that the application should receive the highest protective measures available in each of the three major risk categories. If the airline reservation system were coded, it would probably be coded A8 I8 C2, which would easily convey that maintaining the availability and integrity of the application is extremely important and maintaining its confidentiality is not a major security concern. This approach gives the guardian a standard way of communicating his value judgment as it pertains to each application.

EXHIBIT II-3-4 Assigning Numerical Values to Information Categories

Value	Availability Categories	Integrity Categories	Confidentiality Categories
9 8 7	Vital	Critical	Registered Confidential
6 5 4	Important	Sensitive	Confidential
3 2 1	Useful	Valuable	Internal Use Only
0	Nonessential	Noncritical	Public

Maintaining and Evaluating Categorizations

After the categorization process has been completed and approved, it should be maintained in a data base that would indicate the information or application that has been categorized, who was the approving authority, and when it was categorized. If, in the future, it is thought that the categorization is too high or too low, this should be reviewed with the approving authority and adjustments made if necessary.

Although the value of information does not change rapidly, the categorization should be reviewed periodically, possibly on an annual basis, to determine whether there has been any change. Any change in the categorization might indicate there is also a need to change the protective measures.

BENEFITS OF CATEGORIZATION

There are many benefits to be derived from the categorization process. First, a categorization program can help develop an overall awareness on the part of the employees and their managers that the company has a strong commitment to the proper use and protection of its information. Behaviorists contend that employees respond favorably when corporate management exhibits sound leadership and direction. Therefore, the process of information categorization and protection should become part of the organization's culture. In addition, the categorization process will make employees more sensitive to the need to protect confidential information and respect the right to privacy of others.

A second benefit is that such a program would clearly identify information that is essential to the operation of the business and would help provide the impetus to develop effective contingency plans. In addition, identification of the information that is sensitive to modification enables the end user and the systems developer to select the appropriate internal controls to help ensure the integrity of this information. A categorization program would also provide a basis for analyzing existing applications to determine whether they are adequately protected.

In addition to understanding the value of information, the categorization process helps identify the myriad protective measures available. It enables the corporation and specifically those charged with installing protective measures to understand why certain measures are selected and others are rejected.

SUMMARY

Categorizing information and specifying the appropriate protective measures are basic management responsibilities. They are neither trivial tasks, nor are they so large an undertaking as to prevent management from allocating a reasonable amount of resources to their accomplishment.

To many, the primary challenge comes from the fact that information has never been analyzed so definitively. Yet this analysis does not require sophisticated programs, analytical tools, or extensive training. This program can be employed using common sense and sound business judgment. Still, it is imperative that management accept primary responsibility for implementing the program and ensuring its success by providing their support and approval. Implementing such a program requires a little research, education, documentation, and testing to provide lasting results; however, it will afford many long-term benefits.

Data Base Security Controls

RAVI S. SANDHU ▪ SUSHIL JAJODIA

This chapter discusses data security and controls, primarily in the context of data base management systems (DBMSs), with an emphasis on basic principles and mechanisms that have been successfully used by practitioners in actual products and systems. When appropriate, the limitations of these techniques are noted.

The discussion focuses on principles and general concepts; it is therefore independent of any particular product (except for a later section that discusses a few specific products). In the more detailed considerations, the discussion is limited specifically to relational DBMSs, which store data in relations that have specific mathematical properties. All examples given are in SQL. It is assumed that readers are familiar with rudimentary concepts of relational data bases and SQL.

The chapter begins with a review of basic security concepts, followed by a discussion of access controls in the current generation of commercially available DBMSs. The problem of multilevel security is then introduced, including a review of techniques developed specifically for multilevel security. Next, the various kinds of inference threats that arise in a data base system are discussed, along with methods that have been developed for dealing with them. Inference poses a threat to security by allowing higher-classified information to be inferred from lower-classified information. Another section addresses the problem of data integrity, with a discussion of current practice in this area and its limitations.

BASIC SECURITY CONCEPTS

Data security has three separate but related objectives:

- *Confidentiality*. This objective concerns the prevention of improper disclosure of information.
- *Integrity*. This objective concerns prevention of improper modification of information or processes.
- *Availability*. This objective concerns prevention of improper denial of access to information.

These three objectives are present in practically every information system. There are differences, however, regarding the relative importance of these objectives in a given system. The commercial and military sectors have similar needs for high-integrity systems; however, the confidentiality and availability requirements of the military are often more stringent than those for typical commercial applications.

In addition, these objectives differ with respect to the level of understanding of the objectives themselves and the technology to achieve them. For example, availability is technically the least understood objective, and currently, no products address it directly. Therefore, availability is discussed only in passing in this chapter.

The security policy defines the three security objectives in the context of the organization's needs and requirements. In general, the policy defines what is improper for a particular system. This may be required by law (e.g., for confidentiality in the classified military and government sectors). However, the security policy is largely determined by the organization rather than by external mandates, particularly in the areas of integrity and availability.

Two distinct, mutually supportive mechanisms are used to meet the security objectives: prevention (i.e., attempts to ensure that security breaches cannot occur) and detection (i.e., provision of an adequate audit trail so that security breaches can be identified after they have occurred). Every system employs a mix of these techniques, though sometimes the distinction between them gets blurred. This chapter focuses on prevention, which is the more fundamental technique: to be effective, a detection mechanism first requires a mechanism for preventing improper modification of the audit trail.

A third technique for meeting security objectives is referred to as tolerance. Every practical system tolerates some degree of risk with respect to potential security breaches; however, it is important to understand which risks are being tolerated and which are covered by preventive and detective mechanisms.

Security mechanisms can be implemented with varying degrees of assurance, which is directly related to the effort required to subvert the mechanism. Low-assurance mechanisms are easy to implement but relatively easy to subvert. High-assurance mechanisms are notoriously difficult to implement, and they often suffer from degraded performance. Fortunately, rapid advances in hardware performance are alleviating these constraints on performance.

ACCESS CONTROLS IN CURRENT SYSTEMS

This section discusses the access controls provided in the current generation of commercially available data base management systems, with a focus on relational systems. The access controls described are often referred to as discretionary access controls as opposed to the mandatory access controls of multilevel security. This distinction is examined in the next section.

The purpose of access controls is to ensure that a user is permitted to perform only those operations on the data base for which that user is authorized. Access controls are based on the premise that the user has been correctly identified to the system by some authentication procedure. Authentication typically requires the user to supply his claimed identity (e.g., user name or operator number) along with a password or some other authentication token. Authentication may be performed by the operating system, the data base management system, a special authentication server, or some combination thereof.

Granularity and Modes of Access Control

Access controls can be imposed at various degrees of granularity in a system. For example, they can be implemented through the entire data base, over one or more data relations, or in columns or rows of relations. Access controls are differentiated with respect to the operation to which they apply. These distinctions are important—for example, each employee may be authorized to read his own salary but not to write it. In relational data bases, access control modes are expressed in terms of the basic SQL operations (i.e., SELECT, UPDATE, INSERT, and DELETE), as follows:

- The ability to insert and delete data is specified on a relation-by-relation basis.
- SELECT is usually specified on a relation-by-relation basis. Finer granularity of authorization for SELECT can be provided by views.
- UPDATE can be restricted to certain columns of a relation.

In addition to these access control modes, which apply to individual relations or parts thereof, there are privileges, which confer special authority on users. A common example is the DBA privilege for data base administrators.

Data-Dependent Access Control

Data base access controls are often data dependent. For example, some users may be limited to viewing salaries less than $30,000. Similarly, a manager may be restricted to seeing salaries for employees in his or her department. There are two basic techniques for implementing data-dependent access controls in relational data bases: view-based access control and query modification.

View-Based Access Control. A base relation is a relation that is actually stored in the data base. A view is a virtual relation derived from base relations and other views. The data base stores the view definitions and materializes the view as needed.

To illustrate the concept of a view and its security application, the following table shows the base relations of EMPLOYEE (the value NULL indicates that Harding has no manager):

NAME	DEPT	SALARY	MANAGER
Smith	Toy	10,000	Jones
Jones	Toy	15,000	Baker
Baker	Admin	40,000	Harding
Adams	Candy	20,000	Harding
Harding	Admin	50,000	NULL

The following SQL statement defines a view of these relations called TOY-DEPT:

```
CREATE    VIEW TOY-DEPT
AS        SELECT      NAME, SALARY, MANAGER
          FROM        EMPLOYEE
          WHERE       DEPT = 'Toy'
```

This statement generates the view shown in the following table:

NAME	SALARY	MANAGER
Smith	10,000	Jones
Jones	15,000	Baker

To illustrate the dynamic aspect of views, a new employee, Brown, is inserted in base relation EMPLOYEE, as shown in the following table:

NAME	DEPT	SALARY	MANAGER
Smith	Toy	10,000	Jones
Jones	Toy	15,000	Baker
Baker	Admin	40,000	Harding
Adams	Candy	20,000	Harding
Harding	Admin	50,000	NULL
Brown	Toy	22,000	Harding

The view TOY-DEPT is automatically modified to include Brown, as shown in the following table:

NAME	SALARY	MANAGER
Smith	10,000	Jones
Jones	15,000	Baker
Brown	22,000	Harding

Views can be used to provide access to statistical information. For example, the following view gives the average salary for each department:

```
CREATE    VIEW AVSAL(DEPT,AVG)
AS        SELECT     DEPT,AVG(SALARY)
          FROM       EMPLOYEE
          GROUP BY   DEPT
```

For retrieval purposes, users need not distinguish between views and base relations. A view is simply another relation in the data base, which happens to be automatically modified by the DBMS whenever its base relations are modified. Thus, views provide a powerful mechanism for specifying data-dependent authorization for data retrieval. However, there are significant problems if views are modified by users directly (rather than indirectly through modification of base relations). This is a result of the theoretical inability to translate updates of views into updates of base relations (discussed in a later section). This limits the usefulness of views for data-dependent authorization of update operations.

Query Modification. Query modification is another technique for enforcing data-dependent access controls for retrieval. (Query modification is not supported in SQL but is discussed here for the sake of completeness.) In this technique, a query submitted by a user is modified to include further restrictions as determined by the user's authorization.

For example, the data base administrator has granted Thomas the ability to query the EMPLOYEE base relation for employees in the toy department, as follows:

```
GRANT    SELECT
ON       EMPLOYEE
TO       Thomas
WHERE    DEPT = 'Toy'
```

Thomas then executes the following query:

```
SELECT   NAME, DEPT, SALARY, MANAGER
FROM     EMPLOYEE
```

In the absence of access controls, this query would obtain the entire EMPLOYEE relation. Because of the GRANT command, however, the DBMS automatically modifies this query to the following:

```
SELECT   NAME, DEPT, SALARY, MANAGER
FROM     EMPLOYEE
WHERE    DEPT = 'Toy'
```

This limits Thomas to retrieving that portion of the EMPLOYEE relation for which he was granted SELECT access.

Granting and Revoking Access

GRANT and REVOKE statements allow users to selectively and dynamically grant privileges to other users and subsequently revoke them if so desired. In SQL, access is granted by means of the GRANT statement, which applies to base relations as well as views. For example, the following GRANT statement allows Chris to execute SELECT queries on the EMPLOYEE relation:

GRANT SELECT ON EMPLOYEE TO CHRIS

The GRANT statements may be used to give additional privileges to users and even to grant these privileges to other users. For example, the following statement adds the ability to modify the salaries of existing employees in the EMPLOYEE relation:

GRANT SELECT, UPDATE(SALARY) ON EMPLOYEE TO CHRIS

The GRANT statement may also be used to allow a user to act as data base administrator, which carries with it many privileges. Because the data base administrator DBA privilege confers systemwide authority, no relation need be specified in the command. For example, the following statement allows Pat to act as data base administrator and, furthermore, to grant this privilege to others:

GRANT DBA TO PAT WITH GRANT OPTION

In SQL, it is not possible to give a user the GRANT OPTION on a privilege without further allowing the GRANT OPTION to be given to other users.

Accesses are revoked in SQL by means of the REVOKE statement. The REVOKE statement can remove only those privileges that the user also granted. For example, if Thomas has already granted Chris the SELECT privilege, he may execute the following command to revoke that privilege:

REVOKE SELECT ON EMPLOYEE FROM CHRIS

However, if Pat had also granted Chris the SELECT privilege, Chris would continue to retain this privilege even after Thomas revokes it.

Because the WITH GRANT OPTION statement allows users to grant their privileges to other users, the REVOKE statements can have a cascading effect. For example, if Pat grants Chris the SELECT privilege, and Chris subsequently grants this privilege to Kelly, the privilege would be revoked from both Chris and Kelly if Pat later revokes it from Chris.

These access controls are said to be discretionary because the granting of access is at the user's discretion—that is, users who possess a privilege with the GRANT OPTION are free to grant that privilege to whomever they choose. This approach has serious limitations with respect to confidentiality requirements, as discussed in the following section.

Limitations of Discretionary Access Controls

If a privilege is granted without the GRANT OPTION, that user should not be able to grant the privilege to other users. However, this intention can be subverted by simply making a copy of the relation. For example, the first example of a GRANT statement allows Chris to execute SELECT queries on the EMPLOYEE relation, but it does not allow Chris to grant this privilege to others. Chris can get around this limitation by creating a copy of the EMPLOYEE relation, into which all the rows of EMPLOYEE are copied.

As the creator of COPY-OF-EMPLOYEE, Chris has the authority to grant any privileges for it to any user. For example, with the following statement, Chris could grant Pat the ability to execute SELECT queries on the COPY-OF-EM-PLOYEE relation:

GRANT SELECT ON COPY-OF-EMPLOYEE TO PAT

In essence, this gives Pat access to all the information in the original EMPLOYEE relation, as long as Chris keeps COPY-OF-EMPLOYEE reasonably up-to-date with respect to EMPLOYEE.

Even if users are trusted not to deliberately violate security in this way, Trojan horses can be programmed to do so. The solution is to impose mandatory access controls that cannot be violated, even by Trojan horses. Mandatory access controls are discussed in the following section.

MULTILEVEL SECURITY

This selection introduces the issue of multilevel security, which focuses on confidentiality. Discretionary access controls pose a serious threat to confidentiality; mandatory access controls help eliminate these problems. Multilevel secure data base systems enforce mandatory access controls in addition to the discretionary controls commonly found in most current products.

The use of multilevel security, however, can create potential conflicts between data confidentiality and integrity. Specifically, the enforcement of integrity rules can create covert channels for discovering confidential information, which even mandatory access controls cannot prevent.

This section concludes with a brief discussion of the evaluation criteria for secure computer systems developed by the US Department of Defense. It should be noted that although multilevel secure systems were developed primarily for the military sector, they are relevant to the commercial sector as well.

Mandatory Access Controls

With mandatory access controls, the granting of access is constrained by the system security policy. These controls are based on security labels associated with each data item and each user. A label on a data item is called a security classification, and a label on a user is called a security clearance. In a computer system, every program run by a user inherits the user's security clearance—that is, the user's clearance applies not only to the user but to every program executed by that user. Once assigned, the classifications and clearances cannot be changed, except by the security officer.

Security labels in the military and government sectors have two components: a hierarchical component and a set of categories. The hierarchical component consists of the following classes, listed in decreasing order of sensitivity: top secret, secret, confidential, and unclassified. The set of categories may be empty, or it may consist of such items as nuclear, conventional, navy, army, or NATO.

Commercial organizations use similar labels for protecting sensitive information. The main difference is that procedures for assigning clearances to users are much less formal than in the military or government sectors.

It is possible for security labels to dominate each other. For example, label X is said to dominate label Y if the hierarchical component of X is greater than or equal to the hierarchical component of Y and if the categories of X contain all the categories of Y. That is, if label X is (TOP-SECRET, {NUCLEAR,ARMY}) and label Y is (SECRET, {ARMY}), label X dominates label Y. Likewise, if label X is (SECRET, {NUCLEAR,ARMY}), it would dominate label Y. If two labels are exactly identical, they are said to dominate each other.

If two labels are not comparable, however, neither one dominates the other. For example, if label X is (TOP-SECRET, {NUCLEAR}) and label Y is (SECRET, {ARMY}), they are not comparable.

The following discussion is limited to hierarchical labels without any categories. Although many subtle issues arise as a result of incomparable labels with categories, the basic concepts can be demonstrated with hierarchical labels alone. For simplicity, the labels denoting secret and unclassified classes are primarily used in this discussion.

When a user signs on to the system, that user's security clearance specifies the security level of that session. That is, a particular program (e.g., a text editor) is run as a secret process when executed by a secret user but is run as an unclassified process when executed by an unclassified user. It is possible for a user to sign on at a security level lower than the one assigned to that user, but not at one higher. For example, a secret user may sign on as an unclassified user, but an unclassified user may not sign on as a secret user. Once a user is signed on at a specific level, all programs executed by that user will be run at that level.

Covert Channels

Although a program running at the secret level is prevented from writing directly to unclassified data items, there are other ways of communicating information to unclassified programs. For example, a program labeled secret can acquire large amounts of memory in the system. This can be detected by an unclassified program that is able to observe how much memory is available. If the unclassified program is prevented from directly observing the amount of free memory, it can do so indirectly by making a request for a large amount of memory itself. Such indirect methods of communication are called covert channels. Covert channels present a formidable problem for ensuring multilevel security. They are difficult to detect, and once detected, they are difficult to close without incurring significant performance penalties.

Evaluation Criteria

The Orange Book established a metric against which computer systems can be evaluated for security. The metric consists of several levels: A1, B3, B2, B1, C2, C1, and D, listed in decreasing order of how secure the system is.

For each level, the Orange Book lists a set of requirements that a system must satisfy to achieve that level of security. Briefly, the D level consists of all systems that are not secure enough to qualify for any A, B, or C levels. Systems at levels C1 and C2 provide discretionary protection of data; systems at level B1 provide mandatory access controls; and systems at levels B2 or higher provide increasing assurance, particularly against covert channels. Level A1, which is most rigorous, requires verified protection of data.

In 1991, the Department of Defense published the *Trusted Database Interpretation of the Trusted Computer System Evaluation Criteria*, popularly known as the TDI. The TDI describes how a DBMS and the underlying operating system can be evaluated separately or in conjunction. Several efforts are under way to build secure DBMS products satisfying these criteria.

INFERENCE AND AGGREGATION

Even in multilevel secure DBMSs, it is possible for users to draw inferences from the information they obtain from the data base. The inference could be derived purely from the data obtained from the data base system, or it could additionally depend on prior knowledge that was obtained by users from outside the data base system. An inference presents a security breach if higher-classified information can be inferred from lower-classified information.

There is a significant difference between the inference and covert channel problems. Inference is a unilateral activity in which an unclassified user legitimately accesses unclassified information, from which that user is able to deduce secret information. Covert channels, on the other hand, require the existence of a secret process that deliberately or unwittingly transmits information to an unclassified user by means of indirect communication. The inference problem exists even in an ideal system that is completely free of covert channels.

There are many difficulties associated with determining when more highly classified information can be inferred from lower-classified information. The biggest problem is that it is impossible to determine precisely what a user knows. The inference problem is somewhat manageable if the closed-world assumption is adopted; this is the assumption that if information Y can be derived using information X, both X and Y are contained in the data base. In reality, however, the outside knowledge that users bring plays a significant role in inference.

There are two important cases of the inference problem, which often arise in data base systems. First, an aggregate problem occurs whenever there is a collection of data items that is classified at a higher level that the levels of the individual data items by themselves. A classic example from a military context occurs when the location of individual ships in a fleet is unclassified, but the aggregate information concerning the location of all ships in the fleet is secret. Similarly, in the commercial sector, the individual sales figures for branch offices might be considered less sensitive that the aggregate sales figures for the entire company.

Second, a data association problem occurs whenever two values seen together are classified at a higher level than the classification of either value individually. For example, although the list consisting of the names of all employees and the list containing all employee salaries are unclassified, a combined list giving employee names with their salaries is classified. The data association problem is different from the aggregate problem because what is really sensitive is not the aggregate of the two lists but the exact association giving an employee name and his salary.

The following sections describe some techniques for solving the inference problem. Although these methods can be extremely useful, a complete and generally applicable solution to the inference problem remains elusive.

Appropriate Labeling

One way to prevent unclassified information X from permitting disclosure of secret information Y is to reclassify all or part of information X such that it is no longer possible to derive Y from the disclosed subset of X. For example, attribute A is unclassified, and attribute B is secret. The data base enforces the constraint $A + B \leq 20$, and that constraint is known to unclassified users. The value of B does not affect the value of A directly; however, it does constrain the set of possible values A can take. This is an inference problem, which can be prevented by reclassifying A as secret.

Query Restriction

Many inference violations arise as a result of a query that obtains data at the user's level; evaluation of this query requires accessing data above the user's level. For example, data is classified at the relations level, and there are two relations; an unclassified relation called EP, with attributes EMPLOYEE-NAME and PROJECT-NAME, and a secret relation called PT, with attributes PROJECT-NAME and PROJECT-TYPE. EMPLOYEE-NAME is the key of the first relation, and PROJ-

ECT-NAME is the key of the second. (The existence of the secret relation scheme is unclassified.) An unclassified user then makes the following SQL query:

```
SELECT    EP.PROJECT-NAME
FROM      EP, PT
WHERE     EP.PROJECT-NAME = PT.PROJECT-NAME AND
          PT.PROJECT-TYPE = 'NUCLEAR'
```

The data obtained by this query (i.e., the project names) is extracted from the unclassified relation EP. As such, the output of this query contains unclassified data, yet it reveals secret information (i.e., names of nuclear projects) that is stored in the secret relation PT. Even though the output of this query is wholly contained in the unclassified relation EP, it reveals secret information by virtue of being selected on the basis of secret data in the PT relation.

Query restriction ensures that all data used in the process of evaluating the query is dominated by the level of the user and therefore prevents such inferences. To this end, the system can either simply abort the query or modify the user query so that the query involves only the authorized data.

Polyinstantiation

The technique of polyinstantiation can be used to prevent inference violations. Essentially, it allows different versions of the same information item to exist at different classification levels. For example, an unclassified user wants to enter a row in a relation in which each row is labeled either S (secret) or U (unclassified). If the same key is already occurring in an S row, the unclassified user can insert the U row without gaining access to any information by inference. The classification of the row must therefore be treated as part of the relation key. Thus, U rows and S rows always have different keys because the keys have different security classes.

The following table, which has the key STARSHIP-CLASS, helps illustrate this:

STARSHIP	DESTINATION	CLASS
Enterprise	Jupiter	S
Enterprise	Mars	U

A secret user inserted the first row in this relation. Later, an unclassified user inserted the second row. The second insertion must be allowed because it cannot be rejected without revealing to the unclassified user that a secret row for the Enterprise already exists. Unclassified users see only one row for the Enterprise—namely, the U row. Secret users see both rows. These two rows might be interpreted in two ways:

- There are two distinct starships named Enterprise going to two distinct destinations. Unclassified users know of the existence of only one of them (i.e., the one going to Mars). Secret users know about both of them.

491

- There is a single starship named Enterprise. Its real destination is Jupiter, which is known only to secret users. However, unclassified users have been told that the destination is Mars.

Presumably, secret users know which interpretation is intended.

Auditing

Auditing can be used to control inferences. For example, a history can be kept of all queries made by a user. Whenever the user makes a query, the history is analyzed to determine whether the response to this query, when compared with responses to earlier queries, might suggest an inference violation. If so, the system can take appropriate action (e.g., abort the query).

The advantage of this approach is that it may deter many inference attacks by threatening discovery of violations. There are two disadvantages of this approach, however. First, it may be too cumbersome to be useful in practical situations. Second, it can detect only very limited types of inferences—it assumes that a violation can always be detected by analyzing the audit record for abnormal behavior.

Tolerating Limited Inferences

Tolerance methods are useful when the inference bandwidth is so small that these violations do not pose any threat. For example, data may be classified at the column level, with two relations; one called PD with the unclassified attribute PLANE and the secret attribute DESTINATION, and another called DF with the unclassified attribute DESTINATION and the unclassified attribute FUEL-NEEDED. Although knowledge of the fuel needed for a particular plane can provide clues about the destination of the plane, there are too many destinations requiring the same amount of fuel for this to be a serious inference threat. Moreover, it would be too time-consuming to clear everybody responsible for fueling the plane to the secret level. Therefore, it is preferred that the derived relation with attributes PLANE and FUEL-NEEDED be made available to unclassified users.

Although it has been determined that this information does not provide a serious inference threat, unclassified users cannot be allowed to extract the required information from PD and PF by, for example, executing the following query:

```
SELECT     PLANE, FUEL-NEEDED
FROM       PD, DF
WHERE      PD.DESTINATION = DF.DESTINATION
```

This query would open up a covert channel for leaking secret information to unclassified users.

One solution is to use the snapshot approach, by which a trusted user creates a derived secret relation with attributes PLANE and FUEL-NEEDED and then downgrades it to unclassified. Although this snapshot cannot be updated automatically without opening a covert channel, it can be kept more or less up-do-date by having the trusted user re-create it from time to time. A snapshot or sanitized file is an important technique for controlling inferences, especially in offline, static data bases. It has been used quite effectively by the US Census Bureau.

INTEGRITY PRINCIPLES AND MECHANISMS

Integrity is a much less tangible objective than confidentiality. For the purposes of this chapter, "integrity" is defined as being concerned with the improper modification of information. Modification includes insertion of new information, deletion of existing information, and changes to existing information. Such modifications may be made accidentally or intentionally.

Data may be accidentally modified when users simultaneously update a field or file, get deadlocked, or inadvertently change relationships. Therefore, controls must be in place to prevent such situations. Controls over nonmalicious errors and day-to-day business routines are needed as well as controls to prevent malicious errors.

Some definitions of integrity use the term "unauthorized" instead of "improper." Integrity breaches can and do occur without authorization violations; however, authorization is only one part of the solution. The solution must also account for users who exercise their authority improperly.

The threat posed by a corrupt authorized user is quite different in the context of integrity from what it is in the context of confidentiality. A corrupt user can leak secrets by using the computer to legitimately access confidential information and then passing on this information to an improper destination by another means of communication (e.g., a telephone call). It is impossible for the computer to know whether or not the first step was followed by the second step. Therefore, organizations have no choice but to trust their employees to be honest and alert.

Although the military and government sectors have established elaborate procedures for this purpose, the commercial sector is much more informal in this respect. Security research focusing on confidentiality considers the principal threat to be Trojan horses embedded in programs; that is, the focus is on corrupt programs rather than corrupt users.

Similarly, a corrupt user can compromise integrity by manipulating stored data or falsifying source or output documents. Integrity must therefore focus on the corrupt user as the principal problem. In fact, the Trojan horse problem can itself be viewed as a problem of corrupt system or application programmers who improperly modify the software under their control. In addition, the problem of the corrupt user remains even if all of the organization's software is free of Trojan horses.

Integrity Principles and Mechanisms

This section identifies basic principles for achieving data integrity. Principles lay down broad goals without specifying how to achieve them. The following section maps these principles to DBMS mechanisms, which establish how the principles are to be achieved.

There are seven integrity principles:

- *Well-formed transactions*. The concept of the well-formed transaction is that users should not be able to manipulate data arbitrarily, only in restricted ways that preserve the integrity of the data base.
- *Lease privilege*. Programs and users should be given the least privilege necessary for them to accomplish their jobs.
- *Separation of duties*. Separation of duties is a time-honored principle for prevention of fraud and errors by ensuring that no single individual is in a position to misappropriate assets on his own. Operationally, this means that a chain of events that affects the balance of assets must be divided into separate tasks performed by different individuals.
- *Reconstruction of events*. This principle seeks to deter improper behavior by threatening its discovery. The ability to reconstruct what happened in a system requires that users be accountable for their actions (i.e., that it is possible to determine what they did).
- *Delegation of authority*. This principle concerns the critical issue of how privileges are acquired and distributed in an organization. The procedures to do so must reflect the structure of the organization and allow for effective delegation of authority.
- *Reality checks*. Cross-checks with external reality are an essential part of integrity control. For example, if an internal inventory record does not correctly reflect the number of items in the warehouse, it makes little difference if the internal record is being correctly recorded in the balance sheet.
- *Continuity of operation*. This principle states that system operations should be maintained at an appropriate level during potentially devastating events that are beyond the organization's control, including natural disasters, power failures, and disk crashes.

These integrity principles can be divided into two groups, on the basis of how well existing DBMS mechanisms support them. The first group consists of well-formed transactions, continuity of operation, and reality checks. The second group comprises least privilege, separation of duties, reconstruction of events, and delegation of authority. The principles in the first group are adequately supported in existing products (to the extent that a DBMS can address these issues), whereas the principles in the second group are not so well understood and require improvement. The following sections discuss various DBMS mechanisms for facilitating application of these principles.

Well-Formed Transactions. The concept of a well-formed transaction cor-responds well to the standard DBMS concept of a transaction. A transaction is defined as a sequence of primitive actions that satisfies the following properties:

- *Correct-state transformation*. If run by itself in isolation and given a consis-tent state to begin with, each transaction will leave the data base in a consis-tent state.
- *Serialization*. The net effect of executing a set of transactions is equivalent to executing them in a sequential order, even though they may actually be exe-cuted concurrently (i.e., their actions are interleaved or simultaneous).
- *Failure atomicity*. Either all or none of the updates of a transaction take effect. (In this context, update means modification, including insertion of new data, deletion of existing data, and changes to existing data.)
- *Progress*. Every transaction is eventually completed. That is, there is no indefinite blocking owing to deadlocks and no indefinite restarts owing to livelocks (i.e., the process is repeatedly aborted and restarted because of other processes).

The basic requirement is that the DBMS must ensure that updates are restricted to transactions. If users are allowed to bypass transactions and directly manipulate relations in a data base, there is no foundation to build on. In other words updates should be encapsulated within transactions. This restriction may seem too strong, because in practice there will always be a need to perform ad hoc updates. How-ever, ad hoc updates can themselves be carried out by means of special transac-tions. The authorization for these special ad hoc transactions should be carefully controlled and their use properly audited.

DBMS mechanisms can help ensure the correctness of a state by enforcing consistency constraints on the data. (Consistency constraints are often called integ-rity constraints or integrity rules.) The relational data model primarily imposes two consistency constraints:

- Entity integrity stipulates that attributes in the primary key of a relation can-not have null values. This amounts to requiring that each entity represented in the data base be uniquely identifiable.
- Referential integrity is concerned with references from one entity to another. A foreign key is a set of attributes in one relation whose values are required to match those of the primary key of some specific relation. Referential in-tegrity requires either that a foreign key be null or that a matching tuple exist in the relation being referenced. This essentially rules out references to non-existent entities.

Entity integrity is easily enforced. Referential integrity, however, requires more effort and has received limited support in commercial products. In addition, the precise method for achieving it is highly dependent on the semantics of the application, particularly when the referenced tuple is deleted. There are three options: prohibiting the delete operation, deleting the referencing tuple (with a possibility of cascading deletes), or setting the foreign key attributes in the referencing tuple to NULL.

In addition, the relational mode encourages the use of domain constraints that require the values in a particular attribute (column) to come from a given set. These constraints are particularly easy to state and enforce as long as the domains are defined in terms of primitive types (e.g., integers, decimal numbers, and character strings). A variety of dependence constraints, which constrain the tuples in a given relation, have been extensively studied.

A consistency constraint can be viewed as an arbitrary predicate that all correct states of the data base must satisfy. The predicate may involve any number of relations. Although this concept is theoretically appealing and flexible in its expressive power, in practice the overhead in checking the predicates for every transaction is prohibitive. As a result, relational DBMSs typically confine their enforcement of consistency constraints to domain constraints and entity integrity.

Least Privilege. The principle of least privilege translates into a requirement for highly granular access control. For the purpose of controlling read access, DBMSs have employed mechanisms based on views or query modification. These mechanisms are extremely flexible and can be as fine-grained as desired. However, neither one of the mechanisms provides the same flexibility for highly granular control of updates. The fundamental reason for this is the theoretical inability to translate updates on views into updates of base relations. As a result, authorization to control updates is often less sophisticated than authorization for read access.

Fine-grained control of updates by means of views does not work well in practice. However, views are extremely useful for controlling retrieval. For example, the following table shows two base relations, EMP-DEPT and DEPT-MANAGER:

EMP	DEPT	DEPT	MANAGER
Smith	Toy	Toy	Brown
Jones	Toy	Candy	Baker
Adams	Candy		

The following statement provides the EMP-MANAGER view of the base relations:

```
CREATE    VIEW EMP-MANAGER
AS        SELECT    EMP, MANAGER
          FROM      EMP-DEPT, DEPT-MANAGER
          WHERE     EMP-DEPT.DEPT = DEPT-
                    MANAGER.DEPT
```

This statement results in the following table:

EMP	MANAGER
Smith	Brown
Jones	Brown
Adams	Baker

This view can be updated with the following statement:

```
UPDATE    EMP-MANAGER
SET       MANAGER = 'Green'
WHERE     EMP = 'Smith'
```

If EMP-MANAGER is a base relation, this statement would create the following table:

EMP	MANAGER
Smith	Green
Jones	Brown
Adams	Baker

This effect cannot be attained, however, by updating existing tuples in the two base relations in the first table. For example, the manager of the toy department can be changed as follows:

```
UPDATE    DEPT-MANAGER
SET       MANAGER = 'Green'
WHERE     DEPT = 'Toy'
```

This statement results in the following view:

EMP	MANAGER
Smith	Green
Jones	Green
Adams	Baker

The first updated view of EMP-MANAGER can be realized by modifying the base relations in the first table as follows:

EMP	DEPT	DEPT	MANAGER
Smith	X	X	Green
Jones	Toy	Toy	Brown
Adams	Candy	Candy	Baker

In this case, Smith is assigned to an arbitrary department whose manager is Green. It is difficult, however, to determine whether this is the intended result of the original update. Moreover, the UPDATE statement does not explain what X is.

Separation of Duties. Separation of duties is not well supported in existing products. Although it is possible to use existing mechanisms for separating duties, these mechanisms were not designed for this purpose. As a result, their use is awkward at best.

Separation of duties is inherently concerned with sequences of transactions rather than individual transactions in isolation. For example, payment in the form of a check is prepared and issued by the following sequence of events:

- A clerk prepares a voucher and assigns an account.
- The voucher and account are approved by a supervisor.
- The check is issued by a clerk, who must be different from the clerk in the first item. Issuing the check also debits the assigned account.

This sequence embodies separation of duties because the three steps must be executed by different people. The policy has a dynamic flavor in that a particular clerk can prepare vouchers on one occasion and issue checks on another. However, the same clerk cannot prepare a voucher and issue a check for that voucher.

Reconstruction of Events. The ability to reconstruct events in a system serves as a deterrent to improper behavior. In the DBMS context, the mechanism for recording the history of a system is traditionally called an audit trail. As with the principle of least privilege, a high-end DBMS should be capable of reconstructing events to the finest detail. In practice, this ability must be tempered with the reality that gathering audit data indiscriminately can generate an overwhelming volume of data. Therefore, a DBMS must also allow fine-grained selectivity regarding what is audited.

In addition, it should structure the audit trail logically so that it is easy to query. For example, logging every keystroke provides the ability to reconstruct the system history accurately. However, with this primitive logical structure, a substantial effort is required to reconstruct a particular transaction. In addition to the actual recording of all events that take place in the data base, an audit trail must provide support for true auditing (i.e., an audit trail must have the capability for an auditor to examine it in a systematic manner). In this respect, DBMSs have a significant advantage, because their powerful querying abilities can be used for this purpose.

Delegation of Authority. The need to delegate authority and responsibility within an organization is essential to its smooth functioning. This need appears in its most developed form with respect to monetary budgets. However, the concept applies equally well to the control of other assets and resources of the organization.

In most organizations, the ability to grant authorization is never completely unconstrained. For example, a department manager may be able to delegate substantial authority over departmental resources to project managers within his department and yet be prohibited to delegate this authority to project managers outside the department. Traditional delegation mechanisms based on the concept of ownership (e.g., as embodied in the SQL GRANT and REVOKE statements) are not adequate in this context. Further work remains to be done in this area.

Reality Checks. This principle inherently requires activity outside the DBMS. The DBMS has an obligation to provide an internally consistent view of that portion of the data base that is being externally verified. This is particularly important if the external inspection is conducted on an ad hoc, on-demand basis.

Continuity of Operation. The basic technique for maintaining continuity of operation in the face of natural disasters, hardware failures, and other disruptive events is redundancy in various forms. Recovery mechanisms in DBMSs must also ensure that the data base is left in a consistent state.

SUMMARY

Data security has three objectives: confidentiality, integrity, and availability. A complete solution to the confidentiality problem requires high-assurance, multilevel systems that impose mandatory controls and are known to be free of covert channels. Such systems are currently at the research and development stage and are not available.

Until these products become available, security administrators must be aware of the limitations of discretionary access controls for achieving secrecy. Discretionary access controls cannot cope with Trojan horse attacks. It is therefore important to ensure that only high-quality software of known origin is used in the system. Moreover, security administrators must appreciate that even the mandatory controls of high-assurance, multilevel systems do not directly prevent inference of secret information.

The integrity problem, somewhat paradoxically, is less well understood than confidentiality but is better supported in existing products. The basic foundation of integrity is the assurance that all updates are carried out by well-formed transactions. This is reasonably well supported by currently available DBMS products (e.g., DB2 and Oracle). Other integrity principles—such as least privilege, separation of duties, and delegation of authority—are not as well supported. Products that satisfy these requirements are still in development. The availability objective is poorly understood. Therefore, existing products do not address it to any significant degree.

Applications Controls

STANLEY KURZBAN

Effective information security requires controlling access to system resources. A number of generally accepted standards of practice have been developed to guide administrators in controlling system access. These include such principles as least privilege, separation of duties, alternating roles (i.e., no one person should have sole responsibility for performing a critical task), and assignment of privilege (i.e., a specific privilege should be assigned to the smallest possible number of people). Many types of policies, standards, and control mechanisms can be used to protect system resources. This chapter reviews the roles of operating systems and applications in controlling access to resources and protecting information.

Before the issue of applications controls can be addressed, it is important to identify the types of assets that require such controls. Objects of interest can be defined by these criteria;

- Unauthorized access to the object might lead to harm.
- Access to the object can be controlled by the information system.
- The object has distinct access controls characteristics, as dictated by commonly accepted standards of practice. (For example, multiple data items that share the same access characteristics only need to be assigned a single file name.)

The first two criteria determine the types of assets to which access is controlled. Therefore, access may be controlled to various collections of data but not to such physical objects as cables and diskettes. Access to basic system services (such as a system function for reading records) might not be controlled because this type of service does not pose a potential hazard to security.

The third criterion determines the granularity of access control. For example, the organization can decide whether to protect data bases, files, records, or fields within records, according to applicable standards of practice. In essence, this specifies the granularity of the resource itself. It is also possible to define granularity as it applies to the type of access. For example, a distinction can be made between granting the right to execute a program and the right to copy it; it may even be decided that it is not necessary to make this distinction. The next section of this chapter defines the characteristics of key system resources; the following sections address operating system and applications controls over these assets.

CONTROLLING ACCESS TO RESOURCES

Access must be controlled to a variety of system resources, not just the data itself. Physical equipment may require such control—for example, a high-speed printer may be reserved for use by only selected individuals. Access to a terminal might be restricted on the basis of location (e.g., a terminal in an unsupervised location) or because of the capabilities associated with the terminal (e.g., system management). Access to services may also be restricted to prevent the use of specialized facilities for such functions as encryption or data base management. Control over access to services and physical resources may require controlling the use of certain system or application parameters, which are themselves forms of data. At some level, all controls over system resources must translate to controls over data.

The granularity of access controls must be based on a combination of factors, including generally accepted standards of practice and practical considerations of the targeted computing environment. For example, in a homogeneous organization like NASA, all system users may be granted access to the complete data base. At a hospital, on the other hand, accounting personnel may have access to billing information but not to medical data stored in the same data base; doctors may be restricted only to the medical data.

Certain applications may require a finer level of control. For example, only personnel management may have access to salary information. The degree of granularity ultimately depends on whether the benefit of a specific level of control outweighs its cost. Taken to an extreme, for example, the principle of least privilege might dictate that only administrators have the right to examine personnel records. The resulting burden on administrators may be too great to justify such a practice.

PROCESS-TO-PROCESS INTERFERENCE

An operating system is secure to the extent that people can use the system without interference by others. This means that others are unable to observe or modify the user's programs and data unless permitted to do so implicitly or explicitly. A secure operating system must provide the appropriate services to ensure that users can limit access to all system-defined units of data that they own.

Multiuser, multitasking, resource-sharing operating systems create the potential for process-to-process interference. Such operating systems must support the shared use of hardware components for multiple tasks in a secure manner; that is, these systems must prevent interference owing to the sharing of resources.

In summary, secure operating systems must be designed to prevent interference in the use of data and in the sharing of resources. Any interference between units of work that share underlying resources, including data resources, can result in a security breach. In order to prevent such interference, the operating system must provide process-to-process isolation among applications. This includes isolating the use of such resources as registers and primary and secondary storage devices.

The operating system must therefore mediate the sharing of data objects to ensure that sharing is consistent with the intent of the processes involved. The form of mediation depends on the type of sharing provided by the targeted system. For example, Smalltalk requires that all exchanges of data between processes be in the form of messages—the delivery of such messages as addressed may provide a sufficient control mechanism in this environment. MVS, on the other hand, which permits sharing of large numbers of data sets on secondary storage devices among large numbers of users, must provide list-based access controls. (It should be noted that MVS need not provide list-based controls when mediating cross-memory communications, as long as it ensures either that both processes cooperate and meet the intent of involved parties or that some policy-enforcing process is party to every communication.)

The operating system must mediate three types of sharing: sequential, interleaved, and simultaneous. Interleaving refers to the sharing of a resource by a process that does not require continuous use of the resource—that is, the process allows others to use the resource during periods when it does not need the resource. Simultaneous sharing implies that a process is able to share the resource while using it.

Sequential sharing is common in controlling use of such peripherals as printers. Interleaving applies to the allocation of physical page frames to main storage. Simultaneous sharing applies to read-only programs run on multiprocessing operating systems.

Defining Elements of Shared Processes

Shared units and resources are typically referred to as processes. (For purposes of discussion, a process refers to any instance of a program's execution.) However, what constitutes a process may differ among systems. For example, in MVS the unit of interest is the address space, whereas is OS/360 MVT it is the job.

It can become difficult to visualize the boundaries of a process in a multiprocessing environment. The boundaries of a process must be defined in the context of the architecture. However, given the lack of a general definition of process that spans all architectures, it may be safer to define these boundaries in terms of the concept of intent: process boundaries are what the architect intends them to be and what users expect them to be.

The sharing of resources manifests itself with respect to five elements that are common to an executing process:

- Control storage, wherein the status of the process is recorded.
- Logical addressed storage.
- Physical addressed storage, which contains the contents of logical addressed storage in physical storage objects that are logically, if not physically, in primary storage.

- Logical named storage, consisting of the named (secondary) storage objects that the process can access.
- Physical named storage, which contains the contents of logical named storage in physical storage objects that are logically, if not physically, in secondary storage.

Physical named storage and logical addressed storage are shared sequentially. In the case of sequential sharing, prevention of interference requires cleansing the resource between each pair of sequential uses. Without such cleansing, a read-before-write process would be able to obtain information about a prior use of the resource.

Preventing interference in interleaved and simultaneous sharing also requires the prevention of unauthorized modification. The sharing of control storage and physical addressed storage is interleaved in a multiprocessing operating system. Sharing of logical addressed and logical named storage that cannot be modified by sharing processes is simultaneous. (For example, under MVS this would include primary storage containing reentrant programs and data sets that are only being read.) In cases where modification is permitted, sharing by authorized users cannot simply be mediated by the system; all sharing entities must play a role in mediation.

Mediating Shared Processes

The specific methods for cleansing and for preventing modification depend on the type of resource or privilege involved. The mediation processes must be isolated effectively to ensure that the targeted processes are themselves isolated. Mediating processes must be capable of isolating all component elements of the targeted process, including both data and logic. The following sections discuss each type of resource or privilege whose sharing requires mediation by the operating system.

Protected Storage. Stored data and programs of mediating processes must be protected from modification. In addressed storage, this can be accomplished by associating them with a state reserved for them. For example, IBM 360 architectures define one state used for this purpose as a set of all storage protection keys that are less than eight; Honeywell's Multics system defines ring 0 as the protected domain.

In named storage, access control mechanisms are used to protect the appropriate units (e.g., system data sets under MVS). These units may be aggregated to support the selected security policies as long as the operating system permits control of each unit and supports the selected method of aggregation and the desired granularity of access type (e.g., read or write access).

Privilege States. Modification of the logic of mediation processes must be prevented. For example, under MVS the consequences of interruptions can be controlled by limiting the execution of mediating processes to programs that run in

504

supervisory state; the mediating processes themselves effect a software-mediated logical extension to that state called Authorized Program Facility. DEC's VAX system uses a distinct kernel state, whereas Multics and IBM's 8100 support analogous mechanisms that create hierarchies of rigorously isolated states for mediating processes.

Control Storage. Control storage contains the representation of a process's state at any instant. Operating systems maintain the integrity of control storage by reserving instructions for modifying its contents to mediating processes and to the process whose state is represented in control storage. The authority of the represented (i.e., nonmediating) process over control storage is limited by the operating systems mechanisms for isolating processes that do not participate in mediation. For example, under MVS a process can modify its own instruction counter to refer to any address within its address space, but it cannot modify its state of privilege unless it operates with the privilege reserved for mediating processes.

Logical Addressed Storage. A process's ability to address an area of storage is controlled by its representation in control storage. Whether or not an operating system supports virtual storage, this ability to address storage areas may be unlimited within main storage, limited to areas not reserved for mediating processes, or more narrowly restricted by the mediating processes. (With respect to the last condition, the manner in which the mediating processes can restrict the ability to address storage is more varied with virtual storage systems, as discussed later.)

Storage objects defined within the operating systems architecture are often determined by the underlying hardware structure. For example, IBM 370 mainframes support addressable storage objects that include bits, bytes, half-words, words, double words, segments, blocks, pages, and DASD extents; these are the units of control within the 370 operating system. It should be observed that these storage objects do not themselves convey a sense of what they contain (i.e., data or program). Control is independent of what is stored in the storage object. The only distinction based on whether the storage object contains data or programs is made during fetch operations.

More advanced systems architectures do provide a mechanism for identifying the type of stored object; that is, the name or address of the object includes a reference to what it contains. An analogy can be made to a box with a tag containing a unique name. The tag specifies the address of the box; without it, even the existence of the box is concealed. However, the tag is not sufficient to access the contents of the box; for that, a copy of its unique key is also required. The color of the box indicates the type of data object contained in the box (e.g., scalars, pointers, queues, and programs), thereby implying how the contents may be used. Certain processes use only specific types of data objects. For example, a load module handles only programs, a compiler processes only source code, and a link editor handles only object code.

A system architecture can be designed to run a specific program against a specific data item in a specific environment. (This is in contrast to, for example, running any program against a particular data item in a given environment.) In its simplest form, such a system can be thought of in terms of a single computer containing only one program and one data object. An operating system that can support such a capability would be able to provide sufficiently granular control for both isolating processes and mediating sharing of resources. By permitting confinement of a process's storage, this type of architecture can support a great variety of security policies.

Such architectures as the IBM System/38 have been implemented to support such a capability. Because the environment is typically fixed, only the names of the program and data object need to be specified. The enforcement mechanism requires typed storage objects in order to distinguish between programs and other data objects. It is important to recognize that because the enforcement mechanism is local to a specific environment, as are the names of programs, data, and associated permissions, this capability may not be valid in a new environment, even if brought to that environment with the data and programs.

Physical Addressed Storage. Physical addressed storage is typically shared sequentially or interleaved. If shared sequentially, mediating processes must prevent users from obtaining information about the prior use of a resource (i.e., scavenging). For example, when one person or process ceases to use a resource, a mechanism might be invoked to overwrite any residual data. Alternatively, this mechanism might be invoked just before use by the next sharer, providing data-free resources to each new sharing entity. In the case of interleaved sharing, the mediating processes must control modification. For example, IBM's 370 architecture supports prefix-protect and protection key mechanisms.

Virtual storage systems maintain data in control storage that restricts the process's ability to address logical addressed storage. The data may refer to data in physical addressed storage to which the privilege of modification has been limited to mediating processes. Isolation requires that nonmediating processes be prevented from modifying their own capabilities for addressing storage.

Logical Named Storage. Because logical named storage is shared sequentially, the security objective is to prevent scavenging. The operating system must overwrite data to prevent it from being reused.

Units of logical named storage include files and data sets. Applications are generally responsible for any further subdivision of these units into records, subschemas or views, and members of partitioned data sets. Such subdivisions are crucial to supporting least-privilege-based controls. Without them, it would be impossible to effectively limit users' privileges to only those data objects needed to accomplish their jobs.

It should be noted that the US Department of Defense standard for protecting information against disclosure requires that all data objects be labeled as to their sensitivity to disclosure and users labeled as to their security clearance. Access to data objects is granted only if the user has been explicitly granted access on the basis of his level of clearance. Although the standard infers that this policy must be implemented in the operating system, this is not a logically necessary condition.

Physical Named Storage. Physical named storage is typically shared sequentially or interleaved. If shared sequentially, mediating processes must prevent scavenging. This might involve overwriting residual data when the resource ceases to be used or immediately prior to its next use, thereby providing data-free resources to each new sharer. In the case of interleaved sharing, the mediating processes must control modification. For example, IBM's 370 architecture supports set-channel-mask and tape-write-protect mechanisms for this purpose.

The Application's Role in Security

Although this chapter discusses all aspects of control by mediating processes, it should be emphasized that control of logical named storage is of paramount importance for ensuring information security. Control of logical named storage requires the use of application-specific mechanisms.

The principle of least privilege requires control of entities that do not correspond to system-defined units; least privilege is an application-dependent concept that requires application-dependent definitions of the entities that must be controlled. Therefore, application-based processes must be used to enforce least privilege and other security objectives.

For this reason, it is as vital to protect the integrity of applications as it is to protect the system itself. Any products or methods that contribute to the effective development and testing of application programs also contribute to their integrity (e.g., code analysis and testing software).

CONTROLLING ACCESS

Granularity does not depend solely on aggregating data; access methods also provide an indispensable mechanism for ensuring the desired level of granularity. The most basic types of access involve observation (i.e., read access) and modification (i.e., write access). Functions to create and delete information can be viewed as variant forms of write access, although they are usually treated separately. Grant access is used to grant another person the right to access a resource in some manner.

For such resources as programs and procedures that embody algorithms, the right to execute the algorithm can be distinguished from the right to read it. This distinction can be implemented with relative ease in IBM AS/400 systems; it may be more difficult to enforce in others.

There can, in fact, be an infinite variety of types of access to algorithms. For example, a function called RUNTRANS, which processes a transaction against a financial file, may embody such generally accepted practices as double-entry bookkeeping, logging of transactions for audit purposes, performing certain reasonableness checks on all transactions, and printing confirmations of all transactions. RUNTRANS tightly controls the functions that can be performed on objects of a particular type. It therefore provides a greater degree of granularity than read and write access functions, although at the expense of the flexibility of those functions. In practice, users might be given RUNTRANS access, permitting them to modify data under generally accepted controls, but not the more global write access.

This same level of control can also be enforced in accessing such data base management systems as IMS and DB2. For example, administrators might restrict users to executing only specified IMS transactions and prohibit them from modifying transactions or defining new ones. Furthermore, administrators could use their ability to control access to IMS segments to limit a user's access to a particular subset of data.

IDENTIFYING OBJECTS AND SUBJECTS

For control purposes, it is essential to identify uniquely each object to be accessed and each user with access privileges. Unique identification of subjects and objects is not necessarily a simple task, as discussed in the following sections.

Identifying Objects

Conventions for naming objects can involve multiple layers of identification, depending on the type of system involved. For example, under MVS, the system generation (SYSGEN) process requires two files, each with the name SYS1.LINKLIB. The two files are distinguished by the name of the storage volume on which they reside—the volume's name is an integral part of the file's identifier.

A resource may be identified not only by its name but also by other elements, including:

- The name of an object to which it logically belongs (e.g., under MVS, the partitioned data set containing a member).
- The name of an object on which it physically resides (e.g., the SYSGEN example).
- The structure in which its name appears (e.g., a catalog of files).
- In a distributed environment, the name of the system through which access to the object is accomplished.

The specific naming conventions may vary according to the type of object (e.g., a storage volume's label or a system address).

Identifying Subjects

If individuals are to be assigned separate sets of privileges, they must be uniquely identified. This is essential to ensure accountability: two persons may share the same set of privileges, but if a security breach occurs, the security practitioner must be able to identify which one was responsible.

The method selected to identify users depends on the dual purposes of identification and verification of identity. For example, if there is a requirement to distinguish between personal and organizational actions, a user may be given two identifiers—one for personal use and the other for use in a professional capacity. Such dual identifiers could be useful for routing communications: if the user changes organizational roles, personal messages will continue to reach the correct recipient, while business-related messages will now be routed to the person who has assumed the business role that changed hands. To ensure separation of duties, however, multiple identifiers for a single individual must be monitored. It cannot be assumed that duties have been separated simply because they are assigned to different identifiers (e.g., where these identifiers are found to belong to the same person).

The selection of a form of unique identification can be difficult. Various privacy laws and regulations attempt to hinder the compilation of dossiers on individuals by limiting the use of certain forms of identification. For example, use of US Social Security numbers for identifying system users is considered by many to be an invasion of privacy. (Furthermore, Social Security numbers are not necessarily unique: in at least one case, numerous people used the same Social Security number to report earnings over several decades.)

Concern for work monitoring may also affect the identification of subjects. Legal requirements or union contracts may prevent employers from implementing access controls that associate specific acts with specific employees. In such an environment, the ability to identify an individual within a group of employees who share identical privileges might be restricted to union representatives. These representatives might agree to use their powers to track individual performance for purposes of discipline or reward, but to otherwise protect the confidentiality of this information. This type of arrangement may provide a compromise for meeting performance objectives without unduly invading the privacy of employees or creating unnecessary stress in the workplace.

CONTROLLING ACCESS TO RESOURCES

Access to resources can be controlled using password mechanisms and subschemas. A key issue involves the timing of the decision to allow access to a resource. Late binding of the resource, in which the decision is postponed as long as possible before the access attempt offers greater flexibility. Early binding, on the other hand, provides less flexibility but enhances performance and offers a greater level of protection against erroneous modification. The following sections illustrate the trade-offs between these two approaches using a sample access scenario. This scenario involves Pat's attempt to view Kris's salary; Kris's salary is stored in the SAL field in the record KRIS in the PAYROLL data base.

Late Binding

Under a late-binding access approach, when a program acting on Pat's behalf attempts to gain access to the SAL field in the PAYROLL data base, the system or application might request that Pat first demonstrate the right to access that field. For example, the application might prompt Pat to enter a resource-oriented password—that is, a password associated with this data item. (This type of password is distinguished from user-oriented passwords that are used to verify the identity of persons wishing to access a system.) Access would be granted only if the correct password were supplied.

There are several drawbacks to the use of such resource-oriented passwords. People are forced to remember resource-oriented passwords for each of the resources to which they have access privileges. In such an environment, it is likely that they will write down at least some of these passwords, thereby exposing the associated resources to the threat of unauthorized access.

In addition to having to remember various passwords, users are also required to enter a different password each time they access a different protected resource. This places an intolerable burden on users and may actually make them antagonistic to security measures in general.

Maintaining these passwords also places a significant burden on system management. For example, if managers need to withdraw or change a privilege, they must invalidate the existing password and replace it with another. They must then communicate the new password to all persons privileged to access the resource. Each communication creates the opportunity for an unauthorized user to learn the new password. Given that many people may legitimately share knowledge of a given resource-oriented password, it may be impossible to identify which privileged user is responsible in the event the password is leaked to an unauthorized user.

Last, in most installations, it is unlikely that Pat would be authorized to view only Kris's salary and no other fields in the PAYROLL data base. In fact, it is more likely that Pat would need to review many fields in rapid succession. A significant amount of system resources would be consumed checking Pat's authorization for each of these fields.

Early Binding

Under an early binding access approach, information indicating Pat's right to view Kris's salary is stored in the system and checked automatically when the access request is made. In this case, of course, the identity of the person requesting the information must be known, but this can be accomplished when the requestor begins the current job or work session rather than each time a resource is accessed.

There are several advantages to this approach. Users only need to memorize the single user-oriented password for verifying individual identity. Therefore, effective security can be achieved with a minimal burden on users. Password maintenance only requires the involvement of a single person (i.e., the administrator), which reduces the potential for passwords to be compromised. And if a password is obtained by an unauthorized user, the identity of the person responsible for the password can be easily determined. Use of a single password also reduces the amount of system resources required for checking authorization to multiple data items.

Subschemas

As an alternative to password-based access controls, it is possible to represent an individual's authority within a data base by means of data base views, also referred to as subschemas. (A subschema is a subset of the schema used to describe an entire data base.) In terms of the sample scenario, this works as follows: when Pat begins to use the PAYROLL data base, the data base management system binds the view Pat specifies to Pat's job or session, if Pat is authorized to use the view.

Three processes are involved in enacting this form of access control. An administrator must first record the user's access privileges to the view. The user begins a session, and his identity is bound to the session. The user requests a specific type of access to the view; access is granted or denied on the basis of the user privileges defined by the administrator for that view. Use of views provides an economical means for controlling access to resources.

Accountability Issues

It may be difficult to maintain accountability if a set of access privileges is assigned inextricably to a single person. For example, if Val substitutes for Jan when Jan is on vacation, controls must be established that anticipate the substitution. One solution is to assign Val all of the privileges owned by Jan as a special set of authorities in addition to Val's regular set. An administrator would be required to activate the special set of privileges when Jan goes on vacation.

A similar issue arises with surrogate relationships. For example, if Jan's electronic mail is sorted and routed by Jan's secretary, the system might be set up to automatically grant the secretary access to all mail that Jan creates or receives.

These solutions provide the substitute or surrogate with the necessary authority to perform the assigned task only when such authority is needed. In this way, accountability is ensured.

It should be noted that the preceding examples have all involved actions occurring within a session. However, in practice, some types of work are not associated with an ongoing, user-oriented session. For example, a terminal device might be dedicated to a printer and used to query and modify the printer's status. It may be desirable to route sensitive output files to the printer but then hold them until the system receives evidence that the recipient is physically present. In this type of dedicated environment, resource-oriented passwords may provide the best means for accomplishing this.

SUMMARY

Controls over system resources must be enforced to provide the appropriate granularity of access controls and to prevent process-to-process interference in systems where resources are shared. The operating system must mediate three types of sharing: sequential, interleaved, and simultaneous. The specific methods used to prevent unauthorized modification and disclosure of information depend on the type of resource or privilege involved. These mediating processes must be capable of isolating all components of the targeted processes, including both data and application logic. The mediating processes themselves must also be effectively isolated.

The control of logical named storage is of paramount importance for ensuring information security. Control of logical named storage requires the use of application-specific mechanisms.

Controlling access to resources can be accomplished using various methods. For example, access to resources can be controlled using user-oriented and resource-oriented password mechanisms and data base views. The timing of access control decisions must also be considered. Whatever method is used, however, it is essential that each object to be accessed and each privileged user be uniquely identified. The forms of identification reflect both technical concerns as well as legal and business constraints. To provide an effective level of security, it is essential that accountability be maintained, even in circumstances that involve substitute and surrogate relationships.

Access Controls

Access controls provide a very important set of security mechanisms for automated information systems. Physical controls, operations controls, hardware-specific controls (e.g., for microcomputers and mainframes), and controls for data and applications all involve access controls. Section II-4 provides an in-depth review of the essential components and methods of access control systems and also reviews automated techniques of intrusion detection.

Chapter II-4-1 provides an introductory tutorial on such basic access control functions as identification and naming of subjects, objects, groups, and roles, authentication, mediation, and logs and journals. The author observes that the closer to the data that the point of access control is exercised, the greater the security provided by the control. The importance of protecting the access control data itself (e.g., lists of privileges) is also addressed here.

It is crucial for an organization handling sensitive data to generate and implement an appropriate control policy. Such a policy may be based on categorizing data, compartmenting resources, and specifying types of access. A number of access control models have been developed, such as the lattice models, Bell LaPadula model, and the Clark/Wilson model, to more rigorously study access control policies. Administration of controls has become an important control in itself, and verification of identities is a very significant component of such administration. Identifiers can be categorized on the basis of user knowledge (e.g., passwords), user possession (e.g., artifacts such as tokens), and user characteristic (e.g., a biometric such as a signature dynamic). Security practitioners are using various implementations of these categories to protect sensitive systems. Chapters II-4-2 and II-4-3 discuss these access control policies, models, and techniques.

Although the use of access controls afford an automated information system a strong line of defense, it has become clear that more is needed when such preventive controls fail. Audit trails have been employed until recently to primarily measure performance and for accounting purposes. A good deal of work has been done in recent years to use automated analysis of security-oriented audit trail data for either after-the-fact or online intrusion detection. Some analytical schemes are based on detecting departures from the user's normal behavior patterns while others try to construct rules characterizing intrusive behavior. More recently developed schemes use a combined approach. Chapter II-4-4 discusses this active research area, which is already yielding practical intrusion-detection products and methodologies.

Introduction to Access Controls

WILLIAM H. MURRAY

This chapter introduces readers to the basic concepts of access controls, including access control functions for assigning access restrictions and permissions and mediation mechanisms for deciding whether access will be granted or denied. Such administrative activities as enrolling users, assigning roles and groups, describing rules, and changing passwords are also discussed. Monitoring and reporting mechanisms are reviewed, and a brief summary of common access control products and features is provided.

FUNCTIONS OF ACCESS CONTROL

Access control involves the interaction of a number of related functions. In order to restrict or permit access, for example, mechanisms must exist for identifying and naming both the users of data and the data itself. Various functions can then be employed to permit or restrict specific users or groups of users access to specific items of data.

Identification and Naming

Access control involves restricting or permitting subjects (e.g., users and system processes) to access named data objects. Access is granted based on the authenticated name of the subject or on a token held by the process.

Subjects. Multiuser systems support the ability to assign names to subjects that access data objects. User names are typically assigned at enrollment time, whereas names of processes are assigned at installation time. Names should be unique and not shared among users or processes. The name space should be sufficiently large to permit unique log-on names, and room should also be provided to associate the user's system and real names. Optionally, space may be provided to maintain other descriptive information about the user.

Objects. Most systems support the use of symbolically named data objects. The access control facility should be able to reference the names of all data objects of interest. These objects are typically allocated dynamically—that is, they are visible and available to the user only on request.

Groups. Subjects and objects can be grouped on the basis of such shared characteristics as department or project affiliation, system, or position. The manager should be able to define as many such groups as are useful for describing users.

Group information is used in the administration process to facilitate managing access authorizations. Rather than granting a privilege to each member of a group, a manager simply grants the privilege to the group. Thus, one command is issued instead of one for each member. By associating a new user with an existing group, the user is granted access to all of the resources accessible to the group. This function can save an enormous amount of administrative effort.

Roles. Such computer-related roles as end user, manager, operator, auditor, and security administrator can be used to describe an exclusive set of privileges, restrictions, and capabilities. A role is distinguished from other named groups of privileges by the fact that it cannot be added to or exercised in combination with others. For example, although it might be possible (and appropriate) for a user to simultaneously use his or her privileges as a member of the group of users of system A and the group of members of department B, he or she would not be permitted to simultaneously employ the privileges of the roles of general user and system operator. If authorized to both of the latter roles, he or she may alternate between these roles, but not join their privileges or exercise them in combination.

It should be noted that roles can be enforced only within a specific process and environment. If a user is able to log on to different processes simultaneously, he or she may be able to join the privileges of two or more roles regardless of the controls enforced in the target system.

As with groups, roles can facilitate administration of a system. In addition, carefully designed roles can be employed to implement separation of duties. In performing the duties associated with their roles, individuals act as checks upon the behavior of others. For example, IBM's RACF access control package implements roles named OPERATOR, SPECIAL, and AUDITOR. OPERATOR can access all resources but cannot change access rules; SPECIAL can change access rules but cannot access resources; both are subject to the logging and reporting of their activity. Logging and reporting is under the control of AUDITOR and cannot be interfered with by the other two roles. (It should be noted that much more sophisticated implementations are possible. It has been recommended that such structured roles be used to eliminate the need for omnipotent system managers.)

Authentication

Most closed systems are able to enforce and verify the integrity of data object names; they can also do so for internal processes. However, because the user identity is assigned outside the system, the system must collect and verify evidence that the user is indeed that person. This evidence takes the form of knowledge known only to the user (e.g., a password), a token held by the user (e.g., an electronic key), a unique but recognizable behavior of the user (e.g., speech or signature behavior), or a physical characteristic of the user (e.g., palm geometry or retinal pattern).

Mediation

Mediation is that part of the access control mechanism that decides whether an access is allowed or denied. This section describes some of the mechanisms and concepts employed in mediation.

Lockword. A lockword can be thought of as a secret extension to the name of the object that the user must have to access the object. Such keys provide access to a particular data object without regard to who is accessing the object. (This is in contrast to a password, which gives evidence about user identity and in which access is tied to identity.)

Lockwords work well for restricting the access of one person to a small number of objects. However, they do not work well for controlling the sharing of information, since they do not provide accountability, are easily compromised, and hard to change in a timely and nondisruptive manner. They also do not work well for controlling access to a large number of objects, since the user cannot remember very many. While residual lockword mechanisms persist in modern systems, few systems rely upon them exclusively.

Rule-Based Access Control. An access rule is a statement about which subjects may access which objects (e.g., access to this object is restricted to its creator). Optionally, such rules may also specify the conditions under which subjects may access objects. These rules fall into the two categories of discretionary access controls and mandatory access controls.

Discretionary access controls are the most widely implemented rules. They are created and administered by the owner or creator of the data, are locally applied to the owner's data, and are bound relatively late. For example, users may reserve write access to themselves, grant read access to members of their department or project, and restrict all access to the public group. Users may alter such discretionary rules whenever they choose.

Mandatory access controls, on the other hand, are created and managed by the system managers, are widely applied, and are typically bound quite early. System managers may require, for example, that in order to access a data object, the credentials of the user must dominate the classification of the object. This rule will apply systemwide. Although altering the classification of the object or the credentials of the user would change the access, in practice these controls are bound early and are rarely changed.

Rule-based systems provide a maximum of control for a minimum of administrative effort. They are effective in the sense that they are uniformly and consistently applied. Although some systems permit rules to be elaborated to the point where they approximate list-based controls, most do not. Thus, many rule-based systems may not provide appropriately granular control. For example, although such systems may permit owners to make rules about their own access, the access of members of their primary affinity group, and the access of users in general, they may not permit these owners to make rules for an arbitrary user or group of users.

Most modern systems provide some rule-based access controls; many provide nothing more. Rule-based mediation may be employed in combination with list-based mediation discussed in the next section. By detailed elaboration of the rules, rule-based systems can be made to approximate the effect of list-based systems, and may then be used in lieu of them.

List-Based Access Control. Many modern systems implement list-based access controls. List-based systems employ a list or table that associates subjects with objects by the type of access. For example, an entry might state "User A has write access to resource 1." Some lists are organized by user with a list of resources and types of permitted accesses; this is referred to as ticket-based or capability-based access control (e.g., MVS using CA-TOPSECRET). Others are organized by resource with a list of users and their accesses (e.g., MVS using RACF).

List-based systems may require a considerable administrative effort. The administrator may also need to have specific knowledge about resources. List-based controls are preferred for managing access on the basis of the user's need to know, while rule-based systems are preferred for access based on classification of the data and credentials or affinity of the user.

Administration

The access control administration function provides for the controlled creation and maintenance of access control data. Specifically it provides for:

- Enrollment of users.
- Assignment of roles.
- Definition and maintenance of groups.
- Classification of objects.
- Granting of user credentials.
- Description of rules.
- Granting and revoking of discretionary access.
- Changing of passwords.

These activities are described in the following sections.

Enrollment of Users. Multiuser systems usually include a command or procedure for enrolling new users. It is this function that defines the user name or identifier and associates the name with the identity of a particular user. Use of this function is generally reserved for the system manager, security administrators, or managers of user groups. (In the last case, the user may be automatically assigned to the group managed by that manager.) Use of this function is typically recorded in a log or journal with a reference to the enrolled individuals.

Assignment of Roles. Multiuser systems usually implement at least one privileged role (e.g., system manager). This role, which may be predefined in the system or software as shipped, is usually assigned to the individual who installs or initializes the system. If other roles are defined, they are usually assigned by this individual.

Definition and Maintenance of Groups. Systems that implement groups must first provide a function for naming and defining the group. Most systems provide that the individual who defines the group is its owner. Some systems support a hierarchical relationship of groups, while in others group names are purely arbitrary. The system must also provide a function for governing the membership of the groups. Since associating a user with a group may automatically confer privileges, use of this function must be reserved. It is usually restricted to the system manager or the managers of the groups.

Classification of Objects. Systems that implement labels for describing the sensitivity of objects provide functions for administering the labels. In some cases, the author or owner of the data object assigns the label; in others the labeling is a function of the classification of input. For example, the Orange Book states that the classification of the output must be at least as high as that of the highest classification of any input. On the other hand, one computer manufacturer's policy requires that unless the output involves a very simple transformation of the input, it must be classified on its own merits.

Labels are normally used for compartmenting information and may be arbitrarily selected. Typically, however, labels are chosen from a small hierarchical set agreed on in advance. For example, the Orange Book uses the labels Unclassified, Confidential, Secret, and Top Secret; IBM uses Public, Internal Use Only, Confidential, Confidential Restricted, and Registered Confidential. Each of these classifications has a specific set of protective procedures associated with it. They can be thought of both as directions about how the data is to be handled and as a decision by the classifying authority as to how much to spend to protect the data.

The authority to classify information may or may not include the authority to reclassify. In the business sector, the individual with the responsibility for creating, classifying, and destroying an object can also reclassify it. However, US Defense Department policy reserves the discretion to reclassify—that is, once a label is applied, special procedures usually reserved to the security staff must be employed to change it.

Granting of User Credentials. User credentials are usually granted at enrollment time. The ability to assign a particular credential may be reserved to either the enrolling manager or an independent party. For example, the mandatory access controls specified in the Orange Book call for the security function to assign credentials after ensuring that the appropriate background investigation has been successfully completed.

The ability to grant credentials usually includes the discretion to revoke them. Most systems that implement credentials provide a function to alter them dynamically. However, at least one system binds credentials at initialization and provides no capability to grant or revoke credentials while the system is operating. (It should be noted that although this is intended to ensure the integrity of the credentials, in a large and dynamic user environment the effect may be just the opposite.)

Description of Rules. Most systems that implement rule-based access controls employ a core set of default rules that are not subject to later change (e.g., systems that implement mandatory access controls). However, some rule-based systems (e.g., CA-ACF2 running under MVS) allow rules to be modified. In such cases, a privileged user typically maintains the rules table. To do so, this person must know the language in which the rules are expressed. Because of this requirement and because the modification process is error-prone, such rule-based systems are usually employed for controlling access to information that is not subject to frequent change. List-based systems are preferred for controlling access to information that changes frequently.

Granting and Revoking of Discretionary Access. In rule-based and list-based systems, the owner can grant discretionary access control to change the rules or lists. This requires that the owner be given a command for granting and revoking such access.

Changing of Passwords. Most current systems permit users to choose and alter their own passwords. It is assumed that it is easier for users to remember passwords that they choose themselves rather than one chosen by the system or systems manager. To prevent the user from choosing a weak password that might expose the system, some systems permit management to specify rules about password length, reuse, and content.

A password vouches for the identity of the user only to the extent that he is the only one who knows it. Passwords must therefore be protected from access by others, including the systems manager.

Older systems may permit the systems manager to choose, view, or modify the user password. Except in small and homogeneous user populations, this practice should be discouraged. Modern systems protect the password by storing it in encrypted form. Although this may not be effective against a sufficiently privileged user or manager—and it is not a substitute for also restricting access to passwords—encryption is a valuable control mechanism and its use should be encouraged.

Because users occasionally forget their passwords, the system must provide a remedy. Most systems do this by permitting the systems manager (or the user's manager) to reset the password to a known but expired value. This value is then communicated to the user, who must change it on the occasion of its first use.

Tools for Monitoring and Review

Logs and journals are chronologically sequenced records of system use, use or changes to data, enrollment of users, changes to authority or rules of access, use of privileged controls or roles, and variances from expected or intended results. Most systems use such logs and journals to establish accountability for the behavior, use, and content of the system.

In addition to keeping records of what has occurred, it is also necessary to get information into the hands of those managers who can recognize the need for corrective action and who have authority and discretion to initiate that action. Some systems may simply route all of this information to a single individual or device, relying upon this person to ensure subsequent follow-up. More sophisticated systems may route data to the user's manager, the manager of the terminal device, or the resource owner for reconciliation and corrective action.

Most systems also provide automated mechanisms intended to make the system more resistant to attack (most commonly, attacks against passwords). For example, some systems disable the terminal or line in response to failed log-on attempts; some disable the target user profile. A few arbitrarily increase response time. Many systems issue alarm messages that alert management so that timely corrective action can be taken. These measures raise the cost of attack while preserving the ability of a legitimate user to access the system.

PROTECTION OF ACCESS CONTROL DATA

Access control data is the information on which access control decisions are based. It includes user profiles and credentials. Access to this data must be rigorously controlled. Uncontrolled changes can result in unintended access to the system's resources. Unintended access to passwords may result in irremediable loss of system integrity. (This is true even if passwords are encrypted.)

The locus of access control is the point at which control is exercised. In a small number of systems, controls are maintained in the kernel and can be relied on to be uniform and consistent across all resource classes. However, in most systems, each resource or type manager may exercise local control.

The locus of log-on control is the point at which data about user identity is collected and verified. The closer this point is to the user interface, the fewer times it will be necessary for the user to log on and the more rational the system will appear to the user. However, the closer this point is to the application, the more confidence the manager of the application can have in it.

ACCESS CONTROL PRODUCTS

Access control software products offer flexible facilities for grouping users and resources to simplify administration. They also provide ways to implement additional code (by means of exits) to provide customized solutions not available with the products themselves. In general, access control products tend to be far more similar than different; the following sections therefore highlight only significant differences among these programs.

Resource Access Control Facility. IBM's Resource Access Control Facility (RACF) product runs under the MVS and VM families of IBM operating systems. RACF uses a list-based access control matrix as a control foundation, but it supports rule-based access control mechanisms as well. The basis for its implementation of triples, as defined by the Clark/Wilson model, is referred to as Program Access to Data Set (PADS).

Access Control Facility 2. (ACF2). Computer Associates' Access Control Facility 2 (CA-ACF2) product runs under the MVS, VM, DOS/VSE,VS1, and VAX/VMS operating systems. Rule-based access control is the foundation of CA-ACF2, but this product supports other control mechanisms as well.

TOP SECRET. Computer Associates' CA-TOP SECRET runs under the MVS, VM, and DOS/VSE operating systems. CA-TOP SECRET is primarily founded on ticket-based access control mechanisms, although it also supports other control mechanisms.

IBM OS/400 Access Control. Access control capabilities of the IBM AS/400 system are fundamentally ticket-based, but general list-based access controls are also supported, which helps eliminate the disadvantages of capability-based schemes. A specialized feature, referred to as adoption, is provided. This feature allows the specification of a set of permissions that is effective during the time a specific program is in control (that is, while the target program and any programs it envokes are active, but not before the target program is invoked or after it terminates). With use of adoption, it is relatively easy to implement triples as specified by the Clark/Wilson model.

UNISYS OS 1100 Access Control. The most distinctive feature of UNISYS 1100 access control is that it supports storage of passwords in a separate file that eliminates the need to encrypt passwords (unless they are off-loaded for backup purposes). This sensible feature is not duplicated in any of the other systems described here.

SUMMARY

Access control is perhaps the most important area of interest in information systems security. As discussed in this introduction to access controls, there are various methods for defining the users of data and data objects that can help simplify the creation and administration of access controls while ensuring a sufficiently granular level of control. The types of controls selected—whether discretionary or mandatory—depend on the control objectives of the organization and the resources available for implementing the controls.

Acknowledgments

The author acknowledges the contribution of Stanley A. Kurzban for the section of this chapter on access control products.

Implementation of Access Controls

STANLEY KURZBAN

The decision of which access controls to implement is based on organizational policy and on two generally accepted standards of practice: separation of duties and least privilege. For controls to be accepted and, therefore, used effectively, they must not disrupt the usual work flow more than is necessary or place too many burdens on administrators, auditors, or authorized users.

To ensure that access controls adequately protect all of the organization's resources, it may be necessary to first categorize the resources. This chapter first addresses this process and the various models of access controls. Methods of providing controls over unattended sessions are also discussed. Finally, administration and implementation of access controls are examined.

CATEGORIZING RESOURCES

Policies establish levels of sensitivity (e.g., top secret, secret, confidential, and unclassified) for data and other resources. These levels should be used for guidance on the proper procedures for handling data—for example, instructions not to copy. They may be used as a basis for access control decisions as well. In this case, individuals are granted access to only those resources at or below a specific level of sensitivity. Labels are used to indicate the sensitivity level of electronically stored documents.

In addition, the access control policy may be based on compartmentalization of resources. For example, access controls may all relate to a particular project or to a particular field of endeavor (e.g., technical R&D or military intelligence). Implementation of the access controls may involve either single compartments or combinations of them. These units of involvement are called categories, though the term "compartment" and "category" are often used interchangeably. Neither term applies to restrictions on handling of data. Individuals may need authorization to all categories associated with a resource to be entitled to access to it (as is the case in the US government's classification scheme) or to any one of the categories (as is more representative of how other organizations work).

The access control policy may distinguish among types of access as well. For example, only system maintenance personnel may be authorized to modify system libraries, but many if not all other users may be authorized to execute programs from those libraries. Billing personnel may be authorized to read credit files, but modification of such files may be restricted to those responsible for compiling credit data. Files with test data may be created only by testing personnel, but developers may be allowed to read and perhaps even modify such files.

One advantage of the use of sensitivity levels is that it allows security measures, which can be expensive, to be used selectively. For example, only for top-secret files might:

- The contents be zeroed after the file is deleted to prevent scavenging of a new file.
- Successful as well as unsuccessful requests for access be logged for later scrutiny, if necessary.
- Unsuccessful requests for access be reported on paper or in real-time to security personnel for action.

Although the use of sensitivity levels may be costly, it affords protection that is otherwise unavailable and may well be cost-justified in many organizations.

MANDATORY AND DISCRETIONARY ACCESS CONTROLS

Policy-based controls may be characterized as either mandatory or discretionary. With mandatory controls, only administrators and not owners of resources may make decisions that bear on or derive from policy. Only an administrator may change the category of a resource, and no one may grant a right of access that is explicitly forbidden in the access control policy.

Access controls that are not based on the policy are characterized as discretionary controls by the US government and as need-to-know controls by other organizations. The latter term connotes least privilege: those who may read an item of data are precisely those whose tasks entail the need.

It is important to note that mandatory controls are prohibitive (i.e., all that is not expressly permitted is forbidden), not only permissive. Only within that context do discretionary controls operate, prohibiting still more access with the same exclusionary principle.

Discretionary access controls can extend beyond limiting which subjects can gain what type of access to which objects. Administrators can limit access to certain times of day or days of the week. Typically, the period during which access would be permitted is 9 AM to 5 PM Monday through Friday. Such a limitation is designed to ensure that access takes place only when supervisory personnel are present, to discourage unauthorized use of data. Further, subjects' rights to access might be suspended when they are on vacation or leave of absence. When subjects leave an organization altogether, their rights must be terminated rather than merely suspended.

Supervision may be ensured by restricting access to certain sources of requests. For example, access to some resources might be granted only if the request comes from a job or session associated with a particular program, (e.g., the master PAY-ROLL program), subsystem (e.g., CICS or IMS), ports, (e.g., the terminals in the area to which only bank tellers have physical access), type of port (e.g., hard-wired rather than dial-up lines), or telephone number. Restrictions based on telephone numbers help prevent access by unauthorized callers and involve callback mechanisms.

Restricting access on the basis of particular programs is a useful approach. To the extent that a given program incorporates the controls that administrators wish to exercise, undesired activity is absolutely prevented at whatever granularity the program can treat. An accounts-payable program, for example, can ensure that all the operations involved in the payment of a bill are performed consistently, with like amounts both debited and credited from the two accounts involved. If the program, which may be a higher-level entity, controls everything the user sees during a session through menus of choices, it may even be impossible for the user to try to perform any unauthorized act.

Program development provides an apt context for examination of the interplay of controls. Proprietary software under development may have a level of sensitivity that is higher than that of leased software that is being tailored for use by an organization. Mandatory policies should:

- Allow only the applications programmers involved to have access to application programs under development.
- Allow only systems programmers to have access to system programs under development.
- Allow only librarians to have write access to system and application libraries.
- Allow access to live data only through programs that are in application libraries.

Discretionary access control, on the other hand, should grant only planners access to the schedule data associated with various projects and should allow access to test cases for specific functions only to those whose work involves those functions.

When systems enforce mandatory access control policies, they must distinguish between these and the discretionary policies that offer flexibility. This must be ensured during object creation, classification downgrading, and labeling, as discussed in the following sections.

Object Creation

When a new object is created, there must be no doubt about who is permitted what type of access to it. The creating job or session may specify the information explicitly; however, because it acts on behalf of someone who may not be an administrator, it must not contravene the mandatory policies. Therefore, the newly created object must assume the sensitivity of the data it contains. If the data has been collected from sources with diverse characteristics, the exclusionary nature of the mandatory policy requires that the new object assume the characteristics of the most sensitive object from which its data derives.

Downgrading Data Classifications

Downgrading of data classifications must be effected by an administrator. Because a job or session may act on behalf of one who is not an administrator, it must not be able to downgrade data classifications. Ensuring that new objects assume the characteristics of the most sensitive object from which its data derives is one safeguard that serves this purpose. Another safeguard concerns the output of a job or session: the output must never be written into an object below the most sensitive level of the job or session being used. This is true even though the data involved may have a sensitivity well below the job or session's level of sensitivity, because tracking individual data is not always possible. This may seem like an impractically harsh precaution; however, even the best-intentioned users may be duped by a Trojan horse that acts with their authority.

Outside the Department of Defense's (DoD's) sphere, all those who may read data are routinely accorded the privilege of downgrading their classification by storing that data in a file of lower sensitivity. This is possible largely because aggregations of data may be more sensitive than the individual items of data among them. Where civil law applies, de facto upgrading, which is specifically sanctioned by DoD regulations, may be the more serious consideration. For example, courts may treat the theft of secret data lightly if notices of washroom repairs are labeled secret. Nonetheless, no one has ever written of safeguards against de facto upgrading.

Labeling

When output from a job or session is physical rather than magnetic or electronic, it must bear a label that describes its sensitivity so that people can handle it in accordance with applicable policies. Although labels might be voluminous and therefore annoying in a physical sense, even a single label can create serious problems if it is misplaced.

For example, a program written with no regard for labels may place data at any point on its output medium—for example, a printed page. A label arbitrarily placed on that page at a fixed position might overlay valuable data, causing more harm than the label could be expected to prevent. Placing the label in a free space of adequate size, even if there is one, does not serve the purpose because one may not know where to look for it and a false label may appear elsewhere on the page.

Because labeling each page of output poses such difficult problems, labeling entire print files is especially important. Although it is easy enough to precede and follow a print file with a page that describes it, protecting against counterfeiting of such a page requires more extensive measures. For example, a person may produce a page in the middle of an output file that appears to terminate that file. This person may then be able to simulate the appearance of a totally separate, misleadingly labeled file following the counterfeit page. If header and trailer pages contain a matching random number that is unpredictable and unavailable to jobs, this type of counterfeiting is impossible.

Discussions of labels usually focus on labels that reflect sensitivity to observation by unauthorized individuals, but labels can reflect sensitivity to physical loss as well. For example, ensuring that a particular file or document will always be available may be at least as important as ensuring that only authorized users can access that file or document. All the considerations discussed in this section in the context of confidentiality apply as well to availability.

ACCESS CONTROL MODELS

To permit rigorous study of access control policies, models of various policies have been developed. Early work was based on detailed definitions of policies in place in the US government, but later models have addressed commercial concerns. The following sections contain the overviews of several models.

Lattice Models

In a lattice model, every resource and every user of a resource is associated with one of an ordered set of classes. The classes stemmed from the military designations top secret, secret, confidential, and unclassified. Resources associated with a particular class may be used only by those whose associated class is as high as or higher than that of the resources. This scheme's applicability to governmentally classified data is obvious; however, its application in commercial environments may also be appropriate.

The Bell-LaPadula Model

The lattice model took no account of the threat that might be posed by a Trojan horse lurking in a program used by people associated with a particular class that, unknown to them, copies information into a resource with a lower access level. In governmental terms, the Trojan horse would be said to effect de facto downgrading of classification. Despite the fact that there is no evidence that anyone has ever suffered a significant loss as a result of such an attack, such an attack would be very unattractive and several in the field are rightly concerned about it. Bell and LaPadula devised a model that took such an attack into account.

The Bell-LaPadula model prevents users and processes from reading above their security level, as does the lattice model (i.e., it asserts that processes with a given classification cannot read data associated with a higher classification). In addition, however, it prevents processes with any given classification from writing data associated with a lower classification. Although some might feel that the ability to write below the process's classification is a necessary function—placing data that is not sensitive, though contained in a sensitive document, into a less sensitive file so that it could be available to people who need to see it—DoD experts gave so much weight to the threat of de facto downgrading that it felt the model had to preclude it. All work sponsored by the National Computer Security Center (NCSC) has employed this model.

The term "higher," in this context, connotes more than a higher classification; it also connotes a superset of all resource categories. In asserting the Bell-LaPadula model's applicability to commercial data processing, Lipner omits mention of the fact that the requirement for a superset of categories may not be appropriate outside governmental circles.

Considerable nomenclature has arisen in the context of the Bell-LaPadula model. The read restriction is referred to as the simple security property. The write restriction is referred to as the star property, because the asterisk used as a place-holder until the property was given a more formal name was never replaced.

The Biba Model

In studying the two properties of the Bell-LaPadula model, Biba discovered a plausible notion of integrity, which he defined as prevention of unauthorized modification. The resulting Biba integrity model states that maintenance of integrity requires that data not flow from a receptacle of given integrity to a receptacle of higher integrity. For example, if a process can write above its security level, trustworthy data could be contaminated by the addition of less trustworthy data.

The Take-Grant Model

Although auditors must be concerned with who is authorized to make what type of access to what data, they should also be concerned about what types of access to what data might become authorized without administrative intervention. This assumes that some people who are not administrators are authorized to grant authorization to others, as is the case when there are discretionary access controls. The take-grant model provides a mathematical framework for studying the results of revoking and granting authorization. As such, it is a useful analytical tool for auditors.

The Clark/Wilson Model

Wilson and Clark were among the many who had observed by 1987 that academic work on models for access control emphasized data's confidentiality rather than its integrity (i.e., the work exhibited greater concern for unauthorized observation than for unauthorized modification). Accordingly, they attempted to redress what they saw as a military view that differed markedly from a commercial one. In fact, however, what they considered a military view was not pervasive in the military.

The Clark/Wilson model consists of subject/program/object triples and rules about data, application programs, and triples. The following sections discuss the triples and rules in more detail.

Triples. All formal access control models that predate the Clark/Wilson model treat an ordered subject/object pair—that is, a user and an item or collection of data, with respect to a fixed relationship (e.g., read or write) between the two. Clark and Wilson recognized that the relationship can be implemented by an arbitrary program. Accordingly, they treat an ordered subject/program/object triple. They use the term "transformational procedure" for program to make it clear that the program has integrity-relevance because it modifies or transforms data according to a rule or procedure. Data that transformational procedures modify are called constrained data items because they are constrained in the sense that only transformational procedures may modify them and that integrity verification procedures exercise constraints on them to ensure that they have certain properties, of which consistency and conformance to the real world are two of the most significant. Unconstrained data items are all other data, chiefly the keyed input to transformational procedures.

Once subjects have been constrained so that they can gain access to objects only through specified transformational procedures, the transformational procedures can be embedded with whatever logic is needed to effect limitation of privilege and separation of duties. The transformational procedures can themselves control access of subjects to objects at a level of granularity finer than that available to the system. What is more, they can exercise finer controls (e.g., reasonableness and consistency checks on unconstrained data items) for such purposes as double-entry bookkeeping, thus making sure that whatever is subtracted from one account is added to another so that assets are conserved in transactions.

Rules. To ensure that integrity is attained and preserved, Clark and Wilson assert, certain integrity-monitoring and integrity-preserving rules are needed. Integrity-monitoring rules are called certification rules, and integrity-preserving rules are called enforcement rules.

These certification rules address the following notions:

- Constrained data items are consistent.
- Transformational procedures act validly.
- Duties are separated.
- Accesses are logged.
- Unconstrained data items are validated.

The enforcement rules specify how the integrity of constrained data items and triples must be maintained and require that subjects' identities be authenticated, that triples be carefully managed, and that transformational procedures be executed serially and not in parallel.

Of all the models discussed, only Clark/Wilson contains elements that relate to the functions that characterize leading access control products. Unified access control generalizes notions of access rules and access types to permit description of a wide variety of access control policies.

UNATTENDED SESSIONS

Another type of access control deals with unattended sessions. Users cannot spend many hours continuously interacting with computers from the same port; everyone needs a break every so often. If resource-oriented passwords are not used, systems must associate all the acts of a session with the person who initiated it. If the session persists while its inhibitor takes a break, another person could come along and do something in that session with its initiator's authority. This would constitute a violation of security. Therefore, users must be discouraged from leaving their computers logged on when they are away from their workstations.

If administrators want users to attend their sessions, it is necessary to:

- Make it easy for people to interrupt and resume their work.
- Have the system try to detect absences and protect the session.
- Facilitate physical protection of the medium while it is unattended.
- Implement strictly human controls (e.g., training and surveillance of personnel to identify offenders).

There would be no unattended sessions if users logged off every time they left their ports. Most users do not do this because then they must log back on, and the log-on process of a typical system is neither simple nor fast. To compensate for this deficiency, some organizations use expedited log-on/log-off programs, also called suspend programs. Suspend programs do not sever any part of the physical or logical connection between a port and a host; rather, they sever the connection-maintaining resources of the host so that the port is put in a suspended state. The port can be released from suspended state only by the provision of a password or other identity-validation mechanism. Because this is more convenient for users, organizations hope that it will encourage employees to use it rather than leave their sessions unattended.

The lock function of UNIX is an example of a suspend program. Users can enter a password when suspending a session and resume it by simply reentering the same password. The password should not be the user's log-on password because an intruder could start a new session during the user's absence and run a program that would simulate the lock function, then read the user's resume password and store it in one of the intruder's own files before simulating a session-terminating failure.

Another way to prevent unattended sessions is to chain users to their sessions. For example, if a port is in an office that has a door that locks whenever it is released and only one person has a key to each door, it may not be necessary to have a system mechanism. If artifacts are used for verifying identities and the artifacts must be worn by their owners (e.g., similar to the identification badges in sensitive governmental buildings), extraction of the artifact can trigger automatic termination of a session. In more common environments, the best solution may be some variation of the following:

- If five minutes elapse with no signal from the port, a bell or other device sounds.
- If another half-minute elapses with no signal, automatic termination of the session, called time-out, occurs.

A system might automatically terminate a session if a user takes no action for a time interval specified by the administrator (e.g., five minutes). Such a measure is fraught with hazards, however. For example, users locked out (i.e., prevented from acting in any way the system can sense) by long-running processes will find their sessions needlessly terminated. In addition, users may circumvent the control by simulating an action, under program control, frequently enough to avoid session termination. If the system issues no audible alarm a few seconds before termination, sessions may be terminated while users remain present. On the other hand, such an alarm may be annoying to some users. In any case, the control may greatly annoy users, doing more harm to the organization than good.

Physical protection is easier if users can simply turn a key, which they then carry with them on a break, to render an input medium and the user's session invulnerable. If that is impossible, an office's lockable door can serve the same purpose. Perhaps best for any situation is a door that always swings shut and locks when it is not being held open.

ADMINISTRATION OF CONTROLS

Administration of access controls involves the creation and maintenance of access control rules. It is a vital concern because if this type of administration is difficult, it is certain to be done poorly. The keys to effective administration are:

- Expressing rules as economically and as naturally as possible.
- Remaining ignorant of as many irrelevant distinctions as possible.
- Reducing the administrative scope to manageable jurisdictions (i.e., decentralization).

Rules can be economically expressed through use of grouping mechanisms. Administrator interfaces ensure that administrators do not have to deal with irrelevant distinctions and help reduce the administrative scope. The following sections discuss grouping and administrator interfaces.

Grouping Subjects and Objects

Reducing what must be said involves two aspects: grouping objects and grouping subjects. The resource categories represent one way of grouping objects. Another mechanism is naming. For example, all of a user's private objects may bear the user's own name within their identifiers. In that case, a single rule that states that a user may have all types of access to all of that user's own private objects may take the place of thousands or even millions of separate statements of access permission. Still another way that objects are grouped is by their types; in this case, administrators can categorize all volumes of magnetic tape or all CICS transactions. Still other methods of grouping objects are by device, directory, and library.

When subject groupings match categories, many permissions may be subsumed in a single rule that grants groups all or selected types of access to resources of specific categories. For various administrative purposes, however, groups may not represent categories; rather, they must represent organizational departments or other groupings (e.g., projects) that are not categories. Although subject grouping runs counter to the assignment-of-privilege standard, identity-based access control redresses the balance.

Whenever there are groups of subjects or objects, efficiency requires a way to make exceptions. For example, 10 individuals may have access to 10 resources. Without aggregation, an administrator must make 10 times 10 (or 100) statements to tell the system about each person's rights to access each object. With groups, only 21 statements are needed: one to identify each member of the group of subjects, one to identify each member of the group of objects, and one to specify the subjects' right of access to the objects. Suppose, however, that one subject lacks one right that the others have. If exceptions cannot be specified, either the subject or the object must be excluded from a group and nine more statements must be made. If an overriding exception can be made, it is all that must be added to the other 21 statements. Although exceptions complicate processing, only the computer need be aware of this complication.

Additional grouping mechanisms may be superimposed on the subject and object groupings. For example, sets of privileges may be associated with individuals who are grouped by being identified as, for example, auditors, security administrators, operators, or data base administrators.

Administrator Interfaces

To remain ignorant of irrelevant distinctions, administrators must have a coherent and consistent interface. What the interface is consistent with depends on the administrative context. If administrators deal with multiple subsystems, a single product can provide administrators with a single interface that hides the multiplicity of subsystems for which they supply administrative data. On the other hand, if administrators deal with single subsystems, the subsystem itself or a subsystem-specific product can provide administrators with an interface that makes administrative and other functions available to them.

The administrative burden can be kept within tolerable bounds if each administrator is responsible for only a reasonable number of individuals and functions. Functional distribution might focus on subsystems or types of resources (e.g., media or programs). When functional distribution is inadequate, decentralization is vital. With decentralized administration, each administrator may be responsible for one or more departments of an organization. In sum, effective control of access is the implementation of the policy's rules and implications to ensure that, within cost/benefit constraints, the principles of separation of duties and least privilege are upheld.

IMPLEMENTING CONTROLS

Every time a request for access to a type of protected resource occurs in a job or session, an access control decision must be made. That decision must implement management's wishes, as recorded by administrators. The program that makes the decisions has been called a reference monitor because the job or session is said to refer to a protected resource and the decision is seen as a monitoring of the references.

Although the reference monitor is defined by its function rather than by its embodiment, it is convenient to think of it as a single program. For each type of object, there is a program, called a resource manager, that must be involved in every access to each object of that type. The resource manager uses the reference monitor as an arbiter of whether to grant or deny each set of requests for access to any object of a type that it protects.

In a data base management system (DBMS) that is responding to a request for a single field, the DBMS's view-management routines act as a reference monitor. More conventional is the case of binding to a view, whereby the DBMS typically uses an external, multipurpose reference monitor to decide whether to grant or deny the job or session access to use the view.

Whatever the reference monitor's structure, it must collect, store, and use administrators' specifications of what access is to be granted. The information is essentially a simple function involving types of access permitted as defined on two fields of variables (i.e., subjects or people and objects or resources), efficient storage of the data, and the function's values. However, this function poses a complex problem.

Much of what administrators specify should be stated tersely, using an abbreviated version of many values of the function. Efficient storage of the information can mirror its statement. Indeed, this is true in the implementation of every general access control product. Simply mirroring the administrator-supplied rules is

not enough, however. The stored version must be susceptible to efficient processing so that access control decisions can be made efficiently. This virtually requires
that the rules be stored in a form that permits the subject's and object's names to
be used as direct indexes to the rules that specify what access is permitted. Each
product provides an instructive example of how this may be done.

Because rules take advantage of generalizations, however, they are inevitably
less than optimum when generalizations are few. A rule that treats but one subject
and one object would be an inefficient repository for a very small amount of
information: the type of access permitted in this one case.

Access control information can be viewed as a matrix with rows representing
the subjects, and columns representing the objects. The access that the subject is
permitted to the object is shown in the body of the matrix. For example, in the

EXHIBIT II-4-1   Access Control Matrix

	SUBJECTS \ OBJECTS	A	B	C	D	E	F	G	H	J	K	L
Group 1	Alex	W	W	W	R	R	R	R	R	R	R	R
Group 1	Brook	R	W	W	R							
Group 1	Chris	R	W	W	R	R						
Group 1	Denny	R	W	W	R	W	R					
Group 2	Eddie	R	R	R	W	W	W					
Group 2	Fran	R	R	R	R	W	W					
Group 3	Gabriel	R	R	R			R	W	W	R		
Group 3	Harry	R						W	W	R	R	R
Group 3	Jan							W	W	W		
Group 4	Kim	R									W	W
Group 4	Lee	R									W	W
Group 4	Meryl	R									W	W

Notes:
R   Read
W   Write and read

EXHIBIT II-4-2 List-Based Storage of Access Controls

Object	User	Access
A	UACC	R
	Alex	W
	Jan	N
B and C	UACC	N
	GP1	W
	GP2	R
	Gabriel	R
D	UACC	N
	GP1	R
	Eddie	W
	Fran	R
E	UACC	N
	Alex	R
	Chris	R
	GP2	W
F	UACC	N
	Alex	R
	Chris	N
	Denny	R
	GP2	W
F	UACC	N
	Alex	R
	Denny	R
	GP2	W
	Gabriel	R
G and H	UACC	N
	Alex	R
	GP3	W
J	UACC	N
	Alex	R
	Gabriel	R
	Harry	R
	Jan	W
K and L	UACC	N
	Alex	R
	Harry	R
	GP4	W

Notes:
GP   Group
N   None
R   Read
W   Write and read

matrix in Exhibit II-4-1, the letter at an intersection of a row and a column indicates what type of access the subject may make to the object. Because least privilege is a primary goal of access control, most cells of the matrix will be empty, meaning that no access is allowed. When most of the cells are empty, the matrix is said to be sparse.

Storage of every cell's contents is not efficient if the matrix is sparse. Therefore, access control products store either the columns or the rows, as represented in Exhibits II-4-2 and II-4-3, which show storage of the matrix in Exhibit II-4-1.

In Exhibit II-4-2, a user called UACC, RACF's term for universal access, represents all users whose names do not explicitly appear in the access control lists represented in the matrix in Exhibit II-4-1. The type of access associated with UACC is usually none, indicated by an N. In addition, groups are used to represent sets of users with the same access rights for the object in question. For example, for objects B and C, GP1 (i.e., group 1) represents Alex, Brook, Chris, and Denny. Descriptions of the groups are stored separately. The grouping mechanisms reduce the amount of information that must be stored in the access control lists and the amount of keying a security administrator must do to specify all the permissions.

Exhibit II-4-2 shows access control storage based on the columns (i.e., the lists of users whose authorized type of access to each object is recorded), called list-based storage. Unlisted users need not be denied all access. In many cases, most users are authorized some access—for example, execute or read access to the system's language processors—and only a few will be granted more or less authority—for example, either write or no access. An indicator in or with the list (e.g., UACC in RACF) may indicate the default type of access for the resource. List-based control is efficient because it contains only the exceptions.

Exhibit II-4-3 shows access control storage based on the rows (i.e., the lists of objects to which the user is authorized to gain specified types of access), called ticket-based or capability-based storage. The latter term refers to rigorously defined constructs, called capabilities, that define both an object and one or more types of access permitted to it. Capabilities may be defined by hardware or by software. The many implications of capabilities are beyond the scope of this chapter. Any pure ticket-based scheme has the disadvantage that it lacks the efficiency

---

EXHIBIT II-4-3 Ticket-Based Storage of Access Controls

User	Object/Access
Alex	A/W, B/W, C/W, D/R, E/R, F/R, G/R, H/R, J/R, K/R, L/R
Brook	A/R, B/W, C/W, D/R
Chris	A/R, B/W, C/W, D/R, E/R
Denny	A/R, B/W, C/W, D/R, E/W, F/R
Eddie	A/R, B/R, C/R, D/W, E/W, F/W
Fran	A/R, B/R, C/R, D/R, E/W, F/W,
Gabriel	A/R, B/R, C/R, F/R, G/W, H/W, J/R
Harry	A/R, G/W, H/W, J/R, K/R, L/R
Jan	G/W, H/W, J/W
Kim	A/R, K/W, L/W
Lee	A/R, K/W, L/W
Meryl	A/R, K/W, L/W

Notes:
R   Read
W   Write and read

of a default access type per object. This problem can be alleviated, however, by grouping capabilities in shared catalogs and by grafting some list-based control onto a ticket-based scheme.

SUMMARY

Effective application security controls spring from such standards as least privilege and separation of duties. These controls must be precise and effective, but no more precise or granular than considerations of cost and value dictate. At the same time, they must place minimal burdens on administrators, auditors, and legitimate users of the system.

Controls must be built on a firm foundation of organizational policies. Although all organizations probably need the type of policy that predominates in the commercial environment, some require the more stringent type of policy that the US government uses, which places additional controls on use of systems.

User Verification

STANLEY KURZBAN

Access controls cannot be effective if it is possible for intruders to impersonate legitimate users. When access controls are not based on resources, it is necessary to verify that users are who they claim to be. This chapter examines user verification methods, with an emphasis on the use of passwords. Methods for limiting intruders' ability to guess passwords are discussed, as are methods for selecting effective passwords. Finally, the notion of password validity is addressed.

VERIFICATION METHODS AND CONSIDERATIONS

When users begin a job or session with an information processing system, they must provide a unique identifier. Systems require unique identifiers whenever functions (e.g., the right to modify salaries) are to be associated with particular individuals. Because unique identifiers are useful in many situations, they should be widely known. For security, therefore, a verification procedure that is not widely known or easily reproduced must be used to verify that the person who presents an identifier at the beginning of a job or session is the person to whom the identifier belongs.

The primary considerations associated with user verification are:

- People must be prevented from convincing the system that they are someone else (i.e., false positives must be avoided).
- The system must properly accept accurate statements of user identities (i.e., false negatives must be avoided).
- Verification procedures must impose a minimal burden on users (i.e., ease of use must be ensured).

There are several verification methods, each with its own strengths and weaknesses as concerns these considerations. The verification methods themselves fall into one of three categories, according to the type of information that is provided to the system:

- Information that can be read from a practically uncounterfeitable medium (e.g., a token).

- Information that can be mechanically sensed about a user's physical being or abilities (i.e., biometric information).
- Information the user can enter (i.e., a secret password).

Passwords are the most common medium of identity verification currently in use. Accordingly, this chapter discusses passwords in detail. The relative merits of other mechanisms deserve attention, however.

USE OF ARTIFACTS

Uncounterfeitable media are referred to as artifacts. Their intrinsic advantage over passwords is that users need not remember them, only carry them, which may be quite easy. A greater advantage is realized when (as is usually the case) the artifact produces a different value each time it is used. The different values render the mechanisms invulnerable to a playback attack, which occurs when an opponent intercepts and reuses a constant value. Disadvantages of using artifacts are that artifacts can be lost, stolen, or given away; they may be expensive because of per-port or per-user costs; and either the artifact or the reading device may be damaged.

USE OF BIOMETRICS

The chief advantage of biometric means of verifying identity is that users cannot give away or lose their identifying features. Its chief disadvantages are the cost of the reading devices, the risk of damage to the devices, and the costs associated with balancing false positive and false negative errors.

The most promising biometric mechanisms is signature dynamics, which has an error rate in the range of 0.5%. Other biometric mechanisms include retinal scanning, hand geometry, fingerprint identification, and voice recognition. Identification of facial images has been suggested. All of these methods suffer from the possibility that the biometric will change over time, but this disadvantage may be significant only in the case of voice recognition.

Some have suggested that keystroke dynamics are sufficiently distinctive to permit identity authentication. An authoritative study casts doubt on that hypothesis, with all error rates in excess of 5%. Nevertheless, its value and low cost, because no extra device is involved, might justify its use for continuous validation if an individual always uses the same keyboard, making use of this verification procedure a defense against exploitation of unattended sessions.

USE OF PASSWORDS

Although passwords are currently in most situations, they present a problem of structuring the secret information optimally with respect to following considerations, as mentioned at the beginning of this section:

- Users should be able to enter their secret passwords with minimal inconvenience.
- The probability that the system will accept the passwords from someone other than the associated user (i.e., false positive errors) should be minimal.
- The probability that the associated user will fail to present the password correctly (i.e., false negative errors) should be minimal.

The first consideration, ease of use, begins with the creation of the password itself. If users select their own passwords, ease is limited only by the constraints placed on their choice. If the system generates passwords, however, it may display them to users or send them to administrators. In the first case, people near the users may see the passwords. In the second case, passwords are explicitly made known to people other than their owners. The owners then can say, when accused of wrongdoing, that other people knew their passwords and may have impersonated them. Furthermore, the administrators must disseminate the passwords. Even careful procedures cannot compensate for the extra and needless risk that distribution entails. Distributing passwords over the telephone or distributing reentry passwords this way to users who have forgotten their passwords involves considerable risk because administrators may not be adept at identifying users by their voices over a telephone. If access to telephones is physically controlled, having an administrator return a user's call may provide an acceptably secure means of distribution.

Security may require the imposition of inconveniences associated with LOGON protection. For example, an intruder may try to deceive a user by writing a program that places a LOGON command on the display screen and captures the user's password as it is entered. The intruder then either passes control back to the system with a simulated LOGON or simulates a system failure and, possibly, a severing of the communications line. To defend against such an attack, the user should be required to press a hot key before logging on, which ensures that only the system's code controls the terminal's screen.

Another inconvenience associated with passwords has to do with separate attacks on a user ID and a password. An intruder trying to impersonate a legitimate user may not know any user IDs. If the system issues a distinct error message when given an invalid ID, opponents could try various IDs until they find one that does not evoke the error message. If instead the system issues the same error message whether the ID or the password is invalid, opponents must make many more attempts to achieve the same result. The problem with such security is the inconvenience to legitimate users, from whom the same useful information is withheld. The IDs themselves generally are not secret, because they are used freely as addresses for communication between users.

If users choose their own passwords, precautions against miskeying are needed.

The user should be asked to enter the chosen password identically twice in succession before it becomes effective. Keying the password in a second time helps the user remember it.

Both at selection time and at use, passwords entered from keyboards at display terminals should be obscured from view. If a daily suppression feature is available, it should be used whenever the password is entered. No other information should accompany the password, because the user will not be able to see it to verify correct entry. If there is no suppression feature, a field of obscuring characters, over which the user enters the password, should be provided.

Avoiding false-negative errors and ensuring ease of use raise two constraints. First, the number of possibilities, or combinations, for the secret password must be large enough so that a potential opponent cannot guess it by exhaustively trying all of the possibilities. (This constraint is affected by procedures that limit the rate at which an opponent can test guesses, as discussed further in the following section.) Passwords can be chosen from smaller spaces if they are augmented by artifacts. The second constraint is that the secret password must be selected in a way that an intruder would find difficult to reproduce or anticipate. These constraints have led, typically, to random selection of secret passwords. This increases the probability that a user will record, in an observable place, any hard-to-remember password, which imposes a further constraint—namely, secret information not chosen by the user must nevertheless be easy for the user to remember. This constraint also addresses the need to avoid false-positive errors.

LIMITING GUESSWORK ON PASSWORDS

Proposed solutions to the problems associated with use of passwords have addressed both limitations on the ability for intruders to guess or research passwords and the selection of appropriate passwords. Guesswork has been restricted by use of system responses to invalid password entries. After a predetermined number of consecutive or total entries of invalid passwords, the system does one or more of the following:

- Sends a message to an administrator or to a log.
- Severs the connection between the user and the system. This defense may not be possible if use of the terminal is vital to the organization.
- Delays the system's response to log-on attempts.
- Rejects all subsequent attempts to use the presented ID until administrative action has been taken. This defense has the disadvantage that an intruder can lock selected users or even all administrators out of the system by repeatedly entering incorrect passwords for their accounts.

One promising defense against successful guessing of passwords is to have the system retain all incorrect passwords entered consecutively within a single physical session and compare them with a correct password entered later during the same session. Unless all the incorrect passwords pass tests for likely errors in attempting to key the correct password (e.g., single added or deleted characters, transposition of two characters, or single-character errors, an alarm could be activated. Because most common causes of incorrect keying of passwords would not trigger alarms, administrative personnel would be justified in taking strenuous action (e.g., tracing activity) when alarms occur.

Confidence in measures that prevent opponents from making many guesses in trying to discover a password may lead to the use of smaller combination spaces. However, if the number used to trigger defensive measures is too low, forgetful legitimate users may be annoyed. If the number is too high, someone may succeed in guessing another person's password. If disconnection is possible and effected, the rate at which guesses can be entered has been reduced, but not necessarily below the threshold needed for security. If an account is invalidated, someone may enter incorrect passwords deliberately to prevent someone else from using the system.

In addition, the system may display to users the time that they last interacted with the system. If the time is incorrect, users should notify an administrator that an unknown individual has successfully impersonated them. With all but the most highly motivated users, this control is likely to have little practical value unless users are somehow rewarded for noticing improper log-on times or reprimanded for failing to notice them. Improper log-on times may be intentionally generated by the system at unpredictable intervals to test users' response to them.

The ability to research passwords is typically restricted by reducing the number of opportunities for intruders to observe the password in or on the system and by storing the password in an indecipherable form when such storage cannot be avoided. Passwords should be treated as confidential material whenever they are transmitted, and they should be changed frequently to reduce their vulnerability and their usefulness to an intruder.

Whatever representation of the password the system needs should be stored in a way that makes unauthorized access to it the most difficult. The password may be stored in an irreversibly encrypted form (i.e., one-way encryption) to prevent casual observation of its value. If encryption is slow, however, it is of limited practical value.

EFFECTIVE SELECTION OF PASSWORDS

Selection of passwords may take three paths:

- The system may randomly select passwords from a set of possible passwords believed to have properties that make them easy for users to remember.
- Users may select passwords, constrained by rules that are believed to prevent selection of passwords that an intruder might easily guess. Such rules typ-

ically include exclusion of vowels, so that common words and names cannot be used; required inclusion of numeral digits; or prohibition against inclusion of particular strings, such as common words, repeated letters, or consecutive letters either in the alphabet or on the keyboard.

- Users may select passwords from a set provided by the system.

The advantages and disadvantages of these three options are more or less obvious. Random selection of a password forces an intruder to try, on average, half of all possible passwords before finding the one sought. On the other hand, the owner of a randomly selected password may have difficulty remembering it and may therefore write it down where someone else can see it. User selection carries with it the inverse problem: users are more likely to protect passwords, but intruders are more likely to guess them. The third option is a compromise between the other two. A method that capitalizes on the strengths of the first option and reduces its weaknesses to a minimum is discussed in the next section.

Easily Remembered Passwords

The human mind appears to process data in chunks. In addition, people seem to remember sequences of digits most effectively by associating them with nondigital notions. A very simple picture may easily have as many as three distinct characteristics—for example, if something in a picture is active, the picture may be characterized in terms of the actor, a quality that it has (e.g., color), and the action it is performing. "Green dog runs," for example, may be as easy to remember as a number of three or four digits. If a different quality is substituted for green, a different actor is substituted for dog, and a different action is substituted for runs, the image remains just as memorable. This means that if the image is created from a pool of 100 actors, 100 qualities, and 100 actions, as many as one million (100 × 100 × 100) phrases can be created that are as memorable as a randomly chosen three-digit number.

These phrases are referred to as easily remembered password phrases. Users must be able to easily remember the phrase and quickly enter it into a computer. Therefore, the pool of words should contain short, syntactically similar, common words that are sufficiently dissimilar in appearance and meaning to yield distinct images in users' minds.

Concise, learnable, improved PINs (CLIPs) are another type of easily remembered password. With CLIPs, mnemonics are used to help users remember their three-digit PINs. The mnemonic aid is a data chunk that is easier to remember than the three-digit number to which it corresponds. The following sections discuss implementation of easily remembered password phrases and CLIPs.

Sample Implementations of Easily Remembered Password Phrases. The password phrases are randomly chosen by the system. They are formed by grouping words chosen from selected lists of words. For example, the

EXHIBIT II-4-4 **Sample Word List for Easily Remembered Password Phrases**

Number	Adjectives	Actors	Verbs	Objects
00	ANGRY	ACCOUNTS	ACT	APPLES
01	AUTOMATIC	ACTORS	ADD	ARCHES
02	BALD	ADMIRALS	AGREE	BAGS
03	BEAUTIFUL	ANALYSTS	AMUSE	BALLS
04	BLUE	ANIMALS	ANGER	BASKETS
05	BRIGHT	ANTS	ANSWER	BEDS
06	CALM	ARMS	APPROACH	BELLS
07	CERTAIN	BANDS	ARGUE	BERRIES

administrator may determine that security requires that the password be chosen randomly from a set of X possible passwords. The administrator need only find a power of a number—for example, M^n—that exceeds X. Then the administrator can use n lists that contain M words each. If the combination space is to contain one million password phrases, the administrator can use three lists of 100 words each, because one million is 100^3. Selection of a password consists of the random generation (e.g., by using the low-order digits of the system's clock) of a six-digit number and use of each pair of digits as an index into one of the lists of words. Each list might have 100 words, all of the same syntactic category (e.g., adjective or verb). The selected password phrase is the concatenation of the chosen words— for example, an adjective followed by a noun followed by a verb.

The user enters a complete password phrase, the corresponding $2n$-digit number, or a sequence of $3n$ characters formed by concatenating, in order, the first three categories of the n words that make up the password phrase, with or without embedded blanks. For example, two password phrases might be ADMIRALS ADD APPLES or BALD ACTORS ACT. The corresponding $2n$-digit number, as shown in Exhibit II-4-4, is 020100 for both phrases. The sequence of $3n$ characters for each password phrase is ADMADDAPP and BALACTACT, respectively.

The lists of words may be supplied by the system or chosen by the organization. The order in which the lists are used may be the order supplied, an order selected by the organization, or an order selected by the user. If the same lists are used in the same order for all users, the lists can be posted at each station as an aid to the user's memory, without representing any threat to security. Users who do not wish to take full advantage of the aid may be permitted to choose their own lists and the order in which the lists are used, as long as they accept a new randomly selected password phrase after each change to their lists and the lists have the required number (i.e., at least n) and uniqueness of entry abbreviations (i.e., no two words begin with the same three characters).

A user can specify with a command which lists of words are to be used in generating a new password phrase. The installation data field associated with the user is updated accordingly, and a new password is generated for the user.

The system security administrator can use a command to modify existing lists, delete one or more lists, or add new lists to the phrase variables. Because a modification or deletion could invalidate any or all existing passwords, the system permits these operations only if the system security administrator is the only person using the system at the time the command is issued; therefore, such a change might be made overnight. All users must be informed of changes to the existing lists. All requested changes are made in the phrase data set and in storage. When a list is added, activity on the lists is halted and a new set of lists is made effective before activity is permitted to resume.

The most important aspect of easily remembered password phrases requires almost no code for implementation. One need only implement a generator for random $2n$-digit passwords and post n lists of words at each terminal. The lists serve as the desired mnemonics; users can enter only the generated numbers themselves as passwords.

Sample Implementation of CLIPs. When systems use artifacts for verifying user identities, a supplemental scheme of secret passwords might be required as well, because people may lose their artifacts. Such a scheme need not be as secure as conventional passwords because it only supplements another mechanism and is not self-standing. In this case, personal identification numbers (PINs) of three digits may suffice. Conventionally, a PIN has four digits. CLIPs are proposed as a more easily remembered alternative to four-digit PINs.

CLIPs are randomly selected from a set with fewer than the 1,000 elements from which three-digit PINs are taken. In terms of effective security, however, the ease with which people can remember them fully compensates for the reduction in the size of the set from which they are chosen.

CLIPs employ a three- or four-letter word, abbreviation, or affix. Users enter their CLIPs from a PIN pad of digits with overlays showing the corresponding letters or from a standard keyboard using either all-digit or alphabetic form, whichever the user prefers. Alternatively, the correspondence of PINs and mnemonics can be posted at the keyboard without loss of security.

The system selects CLIPs by using a random variable (e.g., the low-order digits of the system timer) as an index into the list of possible CLIPs of the chosen size (i.e., three or four digits). The system's verification process and storage of CLIPs are as described for the easily remembered password phrases.

Because eight numbers correspond to triads of letters on the telephone dial and CLIPs have three digits, there are 8^3, or 512, possible CLIPs. A simple program could generate four-digit CLIPs from a dictionary of four-letter words. Security administrators can add or delete mnemonics or substitute alternative ones they judge better suited to their users.

Exhibit II-4-5 shows examples of mnemonics for 3-digit CLIPs based on the letters of the telephone dial, in which the first digit is 2 and the first character of the mnemonic is therefore always A, B, or C. For example, the suggested mnemonic for 224 is BAG, for 234 is BEG, and for 244 is BIG.

EXHIBIT II-4-5 Sample List of CLIPs

	ABC (2)	DEF (3)	GHI (4)	JKL (5)	MNO (6)	PRS (7)	TUV (8)	WXY (9)
ABC (2)	CAB	BEA	CHA	BLAh	BOB	BRA	CUB	CYC
DEF (3)	BAD	BED	AGE	ALE	COD	ARF	BUD	AXE
GHI (4)	BAG	BEG	BIG	ALI	COG	ASH	BUG	CYG
JKL (5)	CAL	BEL	AIL	ALL	COL	ARL	AUK	CYL
MNO (6)	CAN	ADO	BIN	BLOw	BOO	BRO	BUM	AWN
PRS (7)	CAR	ADS	AIR	ALSo	COS	ARR	BUS	CYSt
TUV (8)	CAT	BET	BIT	ALT	COT	ART	CUT	BYTe
WXY (9)	BAY	CEY	BIX	BLY	BOY	CRY	BUY	CXX

First Digit = ABC (2)

PASSWORD VALIDITY

If a password were compromised, ideally the intruder should be able to use that password for only a short time. Therefore, it is useful to make passwords valid for only a specific length of time. This period should not be so short that users must choose or receive assigned passwords too frequently. In practice, the length chosen is 30 to 60 days. Most sources suggest that the length of time be inversely proportional to the sensitivity of the data protected; however, if password protection is made more difficult by frequent changes, shorter periods may weaken rather than strengthen security.

When the specified amount of time has elapsed, the system requires users to change their passwords. If a user is masquerading as another user, the rightful user will be alerted to the deception because the rightful user will be locked out for lack of knowledge of the masquerader's new password.

Some administrators require that the system compare new passwords with old ones and reject those that resemble old ones. This requires that the system retain old passwords in a form that is not one-way encrypted. This not only exposes them to intruders but provides a defense for legitimate users who might be detected doing something wrong. For example, the accused user can claim that the misdeed was committed by a masquerader who saw the unencrypted password.

Control of expired passwords helps defend against attacks. For example, before the first publicized incident of hacking, IBM Corp. marked all passwords as expired that it distributed (for especially authorized system administrators) with its systems that include RACF. This requires the first person using the system-defined account to change the password before doing anything else. Other systems do not include this safeguard, and many of these systems have been mentioned in accounts of successful hacking.

Users occasionally forget their passwords, and there are many ways that systems can provide for this occurrence. RACF's mechanism is typical of the most useful method. In RACF, users who have forgotten their passwords must call their administrators to report the problem. The administrators may or may not check the callers' authenticity by returning the call, visiting the user in person, or another means. The exposure is rather limited in any case because all the administrators can do is set the users' passwords to the names of their default log-on groups (i.e., the name of the group of people they usually name when logging on to the system). The new password is marked as expired. Therefore, a masquerader can use it only once before being exposed, because the masquerader must provide a new password.

A common exposure related to passwords is the retention of accounts for people who should no longer be authorized to use the system. Such products as RACF permit administrators to revoke account privileges so that these people cannot continue to use the system after transfer or discharge or even while on vacation. In the case of temporary revocations, RACF permits reinstatement of accounts.

SUMMARY

Access controls depend on effective verification of individual identities commensurate with the organization's needs. No single means of verifying identities is best for all environments, however. Biometric means are most effective when users are not resistant to the inconveniences inherent in this approach and cannot be trusted to keep their passwords secret. Artifacts are most useful when the associated per-unit costs are tolerable. The likelihood of taps and playback attacks has a prominent role to play in the selection of verification mechanisms.

Automated Intrusion Detection

TERESA F. LUNT

Although a computer system's primary defense is its access controls, it is plain from numerous newspaper accounts of break-ins and computerized thefts that access control mechanisms cannot be relied on in most cases to safeguard against a penetration or insider attack. Most computer systems have security weaknesses that leave them vulnerable to attack and abuse. Finding and fixing all the flaws is not technically feasible, and building systems with no security vulnerabilities is extremely difficult, if not impossible. Moreover, even the most secure systems are vulnerable to abuse by insiders who misuse their privileges.

Audit trails can help ensure the accountability of users for their actions. Audit trails have been viewed as the final defense, not only because of their deterrent value but because in theory they can be perused for suspicious events and provide evidence to establish the guilt or innocence of suspected individuals. Moreover, audit trails may be the only means of detecting authorized but abusive user activity.

Although most computers in sensitive applications collect audit trails, these audit trails have generally been established for performance measurement or accounting purposes and, in practice, offer little help in detecting intrusions. Audit information is often too voluminous and detailed to be meaningful to a reviewer. Moreover, single items of audit information may not in themselves be indicators of an attempted or successful intrusion. In addition, such audit trails may omit information that is relevant to detecting intrusions. Nevertheless, even accounting audit trails provide information that can be useful for detecting intrusion attempts, including who ran a particular program at a given time, the files that were accessed, and how much main storage and disk space was used. To assist in the detection of suspicious events, automated tools are needed to support the analysis of the audit data.

Automated tools may serve several purposes. They may be used to screen the audit data to reduce the amount of data that a security officer must manually review. Alternatively, automated tools may attempt to pinpoint actual intrusions or security violations during analysis after the intrusion has occurred. More ambitious tools attempt to detect successful and attempted intrusions as they occur. In summary, the following types of audit data analysis are relevant for security purposes:

- In-depth analysis of audit data offline and after the intrusion has occurred.
- Real-time testing of audit data, so as to make possible an immediate protective response.
- Analysis of the audit data for damage assessment following an intrusion.

This chapter focuses on the first two types of audit trail analysis. Recent work in these areas has explored several approaches—for example, combining auditing with other methods for both assessing damage and gathering evidence against a discovered intruder.

DEVELOPMENTS IN AUDIT ANALYSIS

The past few years have been marked by a growing interest in automated security analysis of computer system audit trails and in systems for real-time intrusion detection. This section describes the evolution of various methods of intrusion detection.

The sources of intrusion that could be addressed by audit trail analysis are categorized as:

- External penetrators (i.e., persons not authorized to use the computer).
- Internal penetrators (i.e., persons authorized to use the computer but not authorized for access to the data, program, or resource). Such persons may include:
  —Masqueraders, who operate under another user's ID and password.
  —Clandestine users, who evade auditing and access controls.
- Misfeasors, who are authorized to use the computer and resources accessed but who misuse their privileges.

External penetrators can be detected by auditing failed log-on attempts, and some would-be internal penetrators can be detected by observing failed access attempts to files, programs, and other resources. Masqueraders can be detected by observing departures from established patterns of use for individual users.

The clandestine user can evade auditing by abuse of system privileges or by operating at a level below the one at which auditing occurs. Abuse of privileges could be detected by auditing use of functions that turn off or suspend auditing, change the specific users being audited, or change other auditing parameters. The third case could be addressed by auditing at a low level (e.g., auditing system service or kernel calls). To detect the clandestine user, such systemwide parameters as CPU, memory, and disk activity could be monitored and compared with historical norms for that facility.

Norm-Based Approaches

Several early research projects focused on developing procedures and algorithms that could serve as the basis for automated tools to help the security administrator assess the previous day's computer system activity. These studies provided the first experimental evidence that users could be distinguished from one another on the basis of their patterns of computer use and that certain behavioral characteristics could be used to discriminate between normal user behavior and a variety of simulated intrusions.

This work led to the development of real-time intrusion-detection systems that continuously monitor user behavior and detect suspicious behavior as it occurs. The Intrusion Detection Expert System (IDES) developed by SRI International takes the approach that intrusion attempts, whether successful or not, can be detected by flagging departures from historically established norms or behavior for individual users. Another real-time approach was taken by a group who measured certain characteristics (e.g., typing speed) of a user's keyboard activity; this approach is called keystroke dynamics. Keystroke dynamics has been found to be an effective means of continuously verifying the identity of the user who is typing.

Systems like IDES use different intrusion-detection measures appropriate to different classes of user. For example, for persons who almost always use the computer during regular business hours, an appropriate measure might simply track whether activity occurs during work hours or off hours. For users who frequently log on in the evenings as well but who still have a distinctive pattern of use (e.g., logging on between 7:00 and 9:00 PM but rarely between 5:00 and 7:00 or after 9:00), a measure that tracks whether the user is likely to be logged on during each hour would be more appropriate. For others who might work at any time of day, a time-of-use intrusion-detection measure may not be meaningful at all.

There are obvious difficulties with attempting to detect intrusions solely on the basis of departures from observed norms for individual users. Although some users may have well-established patterns of behavior—logging on and off at close to the same times every day and having a characteristic level and type of activity—others may have erratic work hours, may differ radically from day to day in the amount and type of work performed, or may use the computer in several locations and even time zones (e.g., at the office, at home, and on travel).

In addition, although detection methods based on observing departures from established norms might succeed in identifying penetrators and masqueraders, these measures may be less successful in detecting legitimate users who abuse their privileges, especially if such abuse is within the range of normal behavior for those users. Moreover, the approach is vulnerable to defeat by insiders who know that their behavior is being compared with a previously established behavior pattern; such users can slowly vary their behavior over time, until they have established a new behavior pattern within which they can safely mount an attack. Trend analysis on user behavior patterns—that is, observing how fast user behavior changes over time—may be useful in detecting such attacks.

Rule-Based Approaches

Because the task of discriminating between normal and intrusive behavior is so difficult, another approach has been to develop automated tools to assist in the analysis of audit data. Under this approach, expert systems technology is used to codify the rules used by the security officer to analyze audit data for suspicious activity. The obvious drawback to this approach is that, in practice, security officers have developed only limited expertise in analyzing audit data because of the length of time required to analyze such large amounts of data. Therefore, although automating these rules may help free security officers to perform further analysis of audit results, the rules cannot be expected to be comprehensive.

To establish more comprehensive solutions that avoid the limitations of norm-based detection methods, several other approaches have been proposed. One rule-based system encodes information about known system vulnerabilities and reported attack scenarios, as well as intuitively derived information about suspicious behavior. The rules do not depend on past user or system behavior. For example, a rule might specify that more than three consecutive unsuccessful log-on attempts within five minutes for the same user ID is a penetration attempt. Audit data from the monitored system is matched against these rules to determine whether the behavior is suspicious. This approach is limited in that it is capable of searching only known vulnerabilities and attacks. Because the greatest threat may be the vulnerabilities that are yet unknown and the attacks that have not yet been tried, the computer security industry is left in the position of playing catch-up with intruders.

Trap Doors

Trap doors can be used to catch intruders; with trap doors, bogus user accounts and passwords sound an alarm when someone attempts to use them. This technique could be extended to include "trip wire" files, phony passwords as bait on electronic bulletin boards, and similar decoys.

Monitoring Program Behavior

One novel approach has been to profile the normal or expected behavior of programs, files, and other objects. Profiles can be used to maintain statistics on such characteristics of program use as files accessed, CPU time used, elapsed time, and the number of input and output characters normally associated with use of the program.

A similar method involves using a knowledge-based name checker to compare the names and types of objects requested by a program (for reading, writing, creation, or destruction) with the names and types of objects expected for the program. For example, the name checker might expect a FORTRAN compiler to require read access to a file with a user-supplied name and a suffix of .FOR and to create or update files with the same name but suffixes of .OBJ and .LIS. If the compiler contained a Trojan horse that attempts to write a user's LOGIN.CMD file, the name checker would recognize that updating such a file is unexpected for the FORTRAN compiler. Other rules (e.g., for a UNIX system) could check whether a user program asks for set-uid privileges.

The name checker could also be used as a rule-based form of real-time intrusion detection. The rules for the behavior expected of commands could be obtained from information already known to the computer system; for example, from the command definition tables of the Command Definition Utility in VAX/VMS systems. For user programs and batch jobs, the user would encode the rules in a special directory tree, which would enumerate the objects on which the program is expected to operate.

At present, no single intrusion-detection method is sufficiently comprehensive to be used alone—each method addresses a different threat. A successful intrusion-detection system should incorporate several of the approaches described in this section. Even then, it is likely that more skilled penetrators will be able to disable audit mechanisms in order to work undetected. However, auditing and intrusion-detection mechanisms should help detect less-skilled penetrators, because they make it more difficult and time-consuming to penetrate systems. In fact, the use of auditing and intrusion-detection mechanisms may make it so difficult for penetrators to avoid detection that they may be forced to attempt other methods, such as bribing users.

SECURITY-SPECIFIC AUDITING

Although existing audit trails (i.e., those not designed specifically for security purposes) can be of some use in intrusion detection, specialized audit trails for security have the potential to be much more powerful. Existing audit trails collect far too much data to be usefully analyzed for intrusions and do not collect much of the information that is relevant to intrusion detection.

The particular data to be audited may depend on the application. For example, users may have identifiable patterns of access to data or of invocation of functions within an application. Because little is known about how to analyze large amounts of audit data for intrusions in a reasonable time frame, random sampling of users might be a reasonable audit approach.

Specialized audit trails for security purposes should report only data that is relevant to intrusion detection. In addition to the raw data, the following data can help distinguish between suspicious and normal activity:

- Such user-related information as changes in user status, new and terminated users, users on vacation, job assignments, and user locations.
- Information about files, directories, devices, and authorizations.
- Profiles of expected or socially acceptable behavior.

Correlation of audit data with such supporting information may help in detecting intrusion attempts. For example, data from electronic access systems that record the time and point of entry and exit of individuals to a building could be used to detect someone trying to log on from a hard-wired local terminal that is not physically in the building. Such information as vacation and travel schedules, job assignments, and unusual terminal locations can help in judging whether observed behavior is suspicious. The use of independent audit trails for each major system component or function (e.g., operating system, utility, data base management system, or application) can also make it more difficult for intruders to evade auditing.

Effective intrusion-detection systems will not come into widespread use until effective security-auditing mechanisms have been developed that make the relevant data available for analysis. Not only does the relevant data need to be captured, but the audit mechanisms should be made as tamper resistant and non-bypassable as possible. In addition, authentication of user identity goes hand in hand with auditing and intrusion detection: the audit trail is meaningless unless it is reliably known who the users are.

LEVELS OF AUDITING

There is considerable difference of opinion as to what is the appropriate level of auditing. Auditing can be performed at a low level by monitoring system calls; alternatively, the typing of commands at a terminal, keystrokes, and system responses could be audited. Different studies have used each of these levels of auditing, and some have used more than one. As discussed in the following sections, each level has its strengths and weaknesses with respect to the types of intrusions it can detect, the complexity and volume of the data, and the ability of the security officer to intuitively understand what the users intend.

Low-Level Monitoring

Users with direct programming access may operate at a level of control that bypasses auditing and access controls. To detect intruders operating at such a low level of system interaction, auditing should be performed at the lowest level possible. For example, monitoring system service calls rather than applications or command lines has been recommended, because user commands and programs can be aliased, it is difficult to ascertain what is really happening if auditing is performed at the command-line level. Because users can write programs to access files directly without leaving any trace in the application audit logs, auditing at the application level will not detect all user activity.

Command-Line Monitoring

Auditing at the command line makes it easier to define rules that characterize intrusive behavior, because it is generally easier to intuit intrusion scenarios at this level of system interaction. In addition, when an anomaly is detected, command-line auditing allows the system to provide an explanation of suspicious or abnormal activity in terms of what the user was doing. At this level of auditing, a security officer can scan a user's audit records to obtain a clear picture of the sequence of events that constitute the intrusion.

Application-Level Monitoring

An effective application-based audit subsystem can be implemented at three levels: operating system kernel calls, the interface between the user and the operating system, and within application programs. This application-level auditing, which is performed by certain trusted applications, can generate an audit trail that is reduced in volume and easier to comprehend than traditional audit trails. In the compartmented-mode workstation, such applications include the window manager and a data base management system. These applications perform their own auditing and are permitted to suspend the lower-level auditing of their activity.

At the level of the operating system interface, certain system calls are audited. In addition, certain kernel calls and their subroutines perform their own auditing, and any kernel routines that require a privilege to execute also perform internal auditing. The compartmented-mode workstation also has a program, called Redux, that selectively retrieves audit data on the basis of user ID, objects accessed, the classification of the objects accessed, and the event (i.e., the particular command, system call, or kernel routine). No analysis or intrusion detection is performed.

S-Gate Surveillance

A surveillance-gate, or S-gate, mechanism (sold by Raxco as a product for VAX/VMS called CONTRL) allows an investigator to link to a terminal and observe and record all information moving between that terminal and the processor. Neither the operating system nor the user being monitored can detect its presence. An S-gate can be dynamically inserted into the system during normal operation; no change to the operating system is needed. The S-gate's insertion and subsequent monitoring of the data path is transparent to the tasks that use the path. An S-gate can be inserted into the data path between a terminal user and the computer system, between a remote terminal and the computer system, between and I/O device and the computer system, or between a system service routine and the part of the operating system that makes service calls to the routine.

Other Useful Monitoring Features

The following audit features are important in investigating a suspected intrusion:

- Playing back a terminal session from the audit data exactly as it originally occurred.
- Obtaining a listing of all characters input and output on the affected communications line.
- Viewing a single user's audit records for a session contiguously.

The ability to play back a user session or gain an understanding of what has happened by viewing a user's audit records for a session requires auditing at the command line or application level. It has been argued, however, that effective investigation to confirm suspicion or establish innocence depends on evidence gathered at the keystroke and system response level.

In summary, the most effective auditing approach is to audit at a very low level, to allow detection of clandestine users, as well as at the command line or application level. Command-line and application-level auditing enables the analyst both to formulate expert system rules that characterize intrusions and to analyze the relevant events by scanning the audit records for a user's session.

ANALYSIS ON A SEPARATE COMPUTER SYSTEM

Implementing audit trail analysis and intrusion-detection mechanisms on a computer system separate from the system being monitored offers both performance and security advantages. By using a separate system, intrusion-detection analysis does not degrade the response time of the monitored system or otherwise affect its behavior. In addition, a standalone system can be made more tamper resistant from those being monitored; security flaws that may exist in the monitored system would not jeopardize the security of the separate intrusion-detection system.

Most computer systems collect vast amounts of audit data, only a fraction of which may be relevant to an intrusion-detection analysis. As a way to avoid flooding the intrusion-detection system with all of this audit data, the data could be preprocessed on the monitored system before being transmitted to the intrusion-detection system. This would drastically reduce both the storage and performance requirements of the intrusion-detection system. In preprocessing the audit data, the monitored system could also format the selected data into a generic audit record format established for the intrusion-detection system. This would permit the intrusion-detection system to monitor more than one system or even one type of system—any system capable of auditing the desired data and putting it into the desired format could be monitored.

COMMERCIAL APPLICATIONS

Intrusion detection may be most feasible in commercial applications in which the user interface of the system being monitored restricts the user to a tightly controlled set of functions. For example, automatic teller machines provide only a few functions (e.g., checking deposits, savings withdrawals, and account balance queries). The restricted user interface helps ensure that auditing cannot be disabled or bypassed by the user and makes it easier to enumerate suspicious events considered to be indicative of an intruder. Thus, the account holder's ability to withdraw funds through an automated teller machine will be suspended if too much money is withdrawn in too short a time period or if withdrawals are made at short time intervals from machines that are geographically distant from each other.

PRIVACY ISSUES

The use of monitoring for security purposes can itself create threats to privacy and the potential for increased computer abuse. Even such apparently benign security mechanisms as file backups, archives, and audit trails of user activity can be abused, threatening the privacy of the information they are meant to protect. Intrusion-detection mechanisms may actually increase the threat of computer abuse by engendering employee dissatisfaction, thereby contributing to the emergence of the so-called insider threat.

Real-time intrusion-detection systems may lead to an even greater degree of invasion of privacy as well as contribute to such potentially objectionable activities as employee performance monitoring. A recent study indicates that the use of computerized employee performance monitoring systems can lead to increased stress, lower levels of satisfaction, and a decrease in the quality of relationships with peers and management among the monitored workers. However, this same study found that workers were not opposed to computerized performance monitoring in principle but were concerned with how such information would be used by management.

These findings underline the need for ensuring the appropriate use of intrusion-detection technology, including defining limits on threat monitoring. It must also be recognized that many in the intelligence community believe that if would-be penetrators know there is an intrusion-detection system, they will be more careful about what they're doing because they know they are being monitored.

SUMMARY

All existing intrusion-detection systems share the same objective, though they attempt to attain it in different ways. Some systems attempt to detect departures from normal behavior patterns, whereas others evaluate observed behavior against a set of rules that characterize intrusive behavior. Many of these systems are now using both approaches.

The profile-based approach has the advantage of being potentially able to detect intrusive behavior that occurs in unforeseen ways; on the other hand, certain behaviors that are generally thought to be suspicious are not easily monitored with this approach. The rule-based approach has the advantage of clearly stating behaviors that are considered intrusive; however, it is able to detect only intrusions that can be foreseen—novel or highly sophisticated attacks may go undetected.

Therefore, to effectively detect intrusions, systems should offer a combination of intrusion-detection approaches. Combining the profile-based and rule-based approaches is only a beginning. Intrusion-detection systems need to be designed to make intelligent use of audit data gathered at several levels from the monitored system (e.g., system call level, command-line level, and application level). Profiling should be extended to files and programs to provide an added dimension for characterizing expected system behavior.

More research is needed also to determine which aspects of system and user behavior are most indicative of intrusions. To determine this, researchers must have access to examples of actual intrusions. A library of such examples needs to be developed.

As the computing workplace evolves, intrusion-detection systems will be introduced that are capable of concurrently integrating observations of user behavior as monitored on networks comprising different workstations and platforms. Improved audit facilities that support security analysis will also be developed.

PART III

Network and Communications Security

The networking of computers, particularly microcomputers in local area networks (LANs), has experienced explosive growth in recent years. Networks are being connected to other networks, LANs connect to public carriers to create wide area networks, which, in turn, use international links to create global area networks. User groups take advantage of connectivity to share common information, more efficiently use and manage storage media, communicate among workstations by means of electronic mail, and upload and download data between workstations and hosts. Maximizing connectivity has become a buzzword among IS professionals. Although networking has expanded the data access horizons of users, it has also greatly complicated access control problems for information security.

In its report, *Computers At Risk*, the System Security Study Committee of the National Academy of Sciences commented on the status of network and communications security:

> Interconnection results in weak links endangering other parts of an interconnected system. This phenomenon is particularly insidious when different parts of a system fall under different managements with different assessments of risk. . . . The design and the management of computer-mediated networks generate communication vulnerabilities. In these systems (e.g., Bitnet), messages travel lengthy paths through computers in the control of numerous organizations of which the communicants are largely unaware, and for which message handling is not a central business concern. Responsibility for the privacy and integrity of communications in these networks is so diffuse as to be nonexistent. Unlike common carriers, these networks warrant no degree of trust. This situation is understood by only some of these networks' users, and even they may gamble on the security of their transmissions in the interests of convenience and reduced expenses.

Initially, the focus of LAN vendors was on providing connectivity and network performance; little emphasis was placed on information security. Although security issues are now being addressed, security still lags far behind advancing systems technologies. Sensitive data, including user IDs and passwords, can be disclosed with the use of network analysis tools. These tools are readily available and can turn any node of a network into a monitoring station capable of reading all unencrypted network traffic, whether or not addressed to that node. In general, any link in a network can expose the entire network to attack. Once in through the weakest link, an intruder can proceed to attack other components from the inside, which is a much easier challenge.

Part III of this handbook provides the information security manager with an understanding of network and communications basics so that security issues can be discussed intelligently with communications experts. It begins the discussion of network and communications security with the subject of network security in Section III-1 and then proceeds to the more general topic of communications security in Section III-2. This provides the information security manager with an understanding of the terms, structures, and philosophies involved in network security and facilitates a transition into the discussion of more complex communications systems in Section III-2.

Network Security

Local area networks (LANs) are mainly composed of interconnected microcomputers working together as a single system. Other networks may consist of mainframes or minicomputers that act as hosts for the storage and processing of data; data can be downloaded from the host and processed locally on microcomputers, with the results being uploaded to the host. This is called distributed processing and is currently the fastest growing sector of networking.

There is a great deal of confusion surrounding basic issues of security and access control in LANs. Chapter III-1-1 attempts to clarify these issues by providing an overview of network architecture and security.

Chapters III-1-2 and III-1-3 discuss the process of implementing and managing network controls. These chapters also address network access control, documentation, training, performance, backup and contingency planning, and standards. Section III-1 concludes with a chapter on establishing network security controls in accordance with organizational policies. Such controls as one-time passwords, encryption, and node authentication are reviewed.

Introduction to LAN
Security

WILLIAM H. MURRAY

There is a great deal of confusion surrounding the issues of security and access control in local area networks (LANs). Some of this confusion results from misunderstandings about LANs, and some from projections onto the LAN of the characteristics of other multiuser (i.e., mainframe) computing environments. This last problem may be aggravated by the use of the term "LAN operating system" to describe the software used to implement the LAN. Finally, additional confusion results from misunderstandings about the way the access controls work in a LAN.

During the 1980s, the majority of computing environments changed from multiuser systems to single-user systems. Multiuser systems had come to include a set of controls to provide for their integrity and that of their data. System administrators and managers on these systems developed tools and procedures for using, configuring, and maintaining these security mechanisms. Such controls and procedures were not provided on the single-user systems. This absence of controls contributed, and may even have been essential, to the success and acceptance of single-user systems.

During the 1990s, single-user systems are being connected to form a new kind of multiuser system, the LAN. It is essential that they incorporate the appropriate controls and that these controls be properly applied.

Although controls of traditional multiuser systems provide some important concepts (e.g., user identification and authentication), it is important to recognize that they may not be sufficient for networks of peer computers. Indeed, a LAN system administrator or user must contend with a mix of issues that are unique to a LAN environment. For example, although programs execute on the workstation, many users believe that they run somewhere in the network. Although storage consists of a mixture of local workstation storage and LAN file-server storage, it all looks very similar. These subtle differences can quickly confuse. Nonetheless, the LAN administrator would be wise to try to learn from the experiences of traditional multiuser system administrators.

This chapter provides an overview of LAN security and access control issues.

TYPES OF NETWORKS

A network may be defined as a connecting infrastructure or as the collection of connected resources. The term is used to describe several ways to connect and use computers. The term "network" may be qualified by its particular use (e.g., microcomputer network) or by its scope (e.g., LAN). Some examples are discussed in the following sections.

LANs

LANs are so called because they are limited in scope, usually to a single site or campus. They can be contrasted to wide area networks (WANs), which connect two or more sites. Although LANs may use any combination of media, signaling, or topology, the term usually refers to continuous media arranged as a ring or a bus. This term is often used to describe a network of microcomputers.

Microcomputer Networks

A microcomputer LAN consists of two or more microcomputers connected by a LAN, usually for the purpose of sharing data or hardware (e.g., a hard drive or printer). This may be done either for efficiency or to facilitate cooperation.

At the media and signaling levels, the microcomputers are usually connected as peers, none dominating or controlling any other. The network is usually open in the sense that access to the media includes the right or ability to send a message to any computer already in the network. Small numbers of computers may also be attached as peers at the service level, with all able to act as either clients or servers to all the others. For larger numbers, however, each device is usually limited to one role or the other.

Client-Server Architectures

Most microcomputer LANs employ a client-server architecture. In this architecture, most computers in the network are client workstations, and a few are servers. The server machines provide various services (e.g., shared disk storage, shared printers, shared WAN facilities) to the clients. In practice, most such networks include file servers (i.e., shared disk storage), which appear to the workstation's operating system and applications as a disk drive, and print servers, which appear as printers.

Communications gateway services (which provide connections to other systems or networks) usually are not visible to the workstation operating system. Rather, the workstation runs a client application program that makes the workstation appear to the user as a terminal of the distant system.

Network Operating Systems

In addition to the primitive communications software, each computer in a client-server architecture must run client or server software, which runs as application software on top of the computer's normal operating system. This client-server software is known collectively as the network operating system. This terminology may be misleading to those who come from more traditional uses of computers, because the term "operating system" usually suggests a central point of control. It may also cause confusion between this client-server software and the machine's primitive operating system.

The workstation runs client software and the server runs server software. Applications run on workstations; both their programs and their data may be stored on servers. The user may cause an arbitrary program to execute on the workstation. However, programs that execute on the server are determined in advance, in support of its role as a server, and are not under the direct control of the user. The end user can neither cause these programs to run nor prevent them from running. Thus, the architecture provides for high-integrity process-to-process isolation. Programs running in either workstations or servers cannot easily or normally interfere with programs running in the other. Likewise, programs running in one workstation cannot easily or normally interfere with those running in another workstation.

LAN ACCESS CONTROL

Access to resources within a LAN is mediated by the servers. Access control may be accomplished by authenticating user IDs or by verifying which resources a user is permitted to access, as discussed in the following sections.

End-User Authentication

Most LAN servers are able to recognize their intended users and exclude all others. In most LANs, the user is enrolled to the server by a unique name or identifier, which is authenticated by a secret password chosen by the user. In some LANs, the password is encrypted by the client under a key known only to the server, to protect the password from eavesdropping during transmission. Some LANs provide that the password be encrypted for storage on the server, to restrict its use to the legitimate user.

The user must be known to and recognized by every server that the user employs. This usually means that the user must be enrolled to each of these servers, though some LANs provide a central name server.

Resource Access Control

Most servers are able to discriminate among their users and regulate or govern the services that each user receives. Because the file server is a shared device, it provides mechanisms that permit management and users to control who can use which file objects. The control is exercised in the server software and is resistant to being overridden by any action of the user or the client workstation. The control is usually independent of the primitive operating system running in the server. File access and sharing are mediated by the server software, not by its operating system. The functions of the server's operating system are not visible to its user, and the identity of the user is not visible to the operating system.

The object of control in the server is usually an abstraction that is familiar to the user and the operating system in the user's workstation. These abstractions include the device (i.e., the disk drive or printer), the directory, the subdirectory, and the file. Access rules are usually expressed in terms of access rights to one of these familiar objects. For example, users may be given read access to a file or directory. The access rules are stored in a file on the server that has been reserved for that purpose.

One interesting difference between LANs and traditional systems is that a user generally must be authorized to an object in order to see it. Servers are usually silent unless the user is recognized by them; users are shown only those directories and files to which they have authorized access. There are few messages that would allow attackers to distinguish between existing objects to which they are not authorized and objects that do not exist.

The access control mechanism may also limit the operations that can be performed on objects, as determined by each object's type. For example, object types may be expressed in terms of MS-DOS's file attribute abstraction. Some of the server mechanisms implement additional attributes over the limited set defined by MS-DOS.

Typical mechanisms permit server management or data owners to exercise very granular control over what a user can do with or to a file object. For example, a user can be permitted to copy or execute an object while being restricted from altering it. This control is more reliable than DOS attributes, because it is enforced in the server. However, the server cannot exercise any reliable control over copies of the software that are created in the workstation. Therefore, the ability to load and execute a program implies the ability to make a copy (even though this may be beyond the skill and special knowledge of most users) and to make modifications to that copy. Although the client software and workstation operating system may resist this, they are subject to the user control and may not be relied on by management.

Similar to other multiuser systems, some LANs anticipate the situation in which an application requires privileges that would be inappropriate for the user to have in any other context. They provide for the user to run with privileges equal to those of a specified profile other than their own.

In addition, servers can distinguish between workstations and permit management to restrict user activity by both workstation identity and time. What is actually recognized is the network adapter cared. The authenticity of this identity relies in part on supervision or physical access control of the card. For example, it is possible for a poorly supervised card to assume the identity of another.

Administration of LAN Access Controls

Access rules are created and maintained through the use of commands to the server. These commands are issued by invoking named procedures on the workstation. Therefore, to give a user access to a resource on a server, the administrator issues a GRANT command on the workstation. Some systems provide a full-screen menu-driven application or a graphics user interface for enrolling users, choosing options, and granting access.

Many LAN server access control mechanisms support the implementation of user groups. Employing this mechanism, administrators can group users together in such arbitrary and overlapping groups as MEMBERS OF THE PAYROLL DEPT. and USERS OF SERVERA. As with similar mechanisms in other multiuser systems, user groups can be employed to administer the rules properly with fewer commands. However, the capability presents the administrator with one more option to exercise and one more feature to understand. When properly used, the list of groups to which a user belongs (including groups of which there is only one member) becomes a detailed description of who the user is and what the user can do.

LAN WEAKNESSES

Microcomputer LANs have inherent weaknesses that do not appear in other multiuser systems. First, a user can run a program without having been authenticated. In LANs, simple access to a workstation is usually sufficient to run a program, whereas in traditional multiuser systems, users must be able to log on before they can do anything. This capability can be used to mount an attack against the server. For example, a user could run a program in the workstation to try hundreds of passwords, which may permit the user to log on to the server. This means that mechanisms that limit trial-and-error attacks are more important in LANs than they are in traditional multiuser systems, in which attackers must enter all of their attempts at the keyboard.

Because users may not know what programs are running, the capability to run a program without logging on can be employed against the user. For example, an attacker could install a password capturing program on workstations known to be used by others to capture the users' passwords without their notice.

A closely related problem is that all processes in the workstation—visible and invisible, known and unknown—assume the server privileges of the user logged on. Thus, files on servers have often been infected by viruses when privileged administrators have logged on to the server from workstations that were already infected by the virus. Tricking a privileged user into logging on from a workstation seeded with a malicious procedure is not too difficult.

The third inherent exposure in LAN systems is the potential for eavesdropping on the shared media. As contrasted to more traditional systems (in which each device is attached to its own dedicated cable, which carries only that traffic intended for it), in LANs most devices are attached to shared media, which carry all traffic. This exposure may be mitigated by adapters that pass to the device bus only the traffic intended for that device. However, this vulnerability is aggravated by adapters (primarily Ethernet adapters) that can be placed in promiscuous mode, in which they pass all traffic to the bus to be sorted out by the device. In addition, this vulnerability can be exploited through the use of protocol analyzers, which decode and display any selected traffic on the media. With an appropriate adapter or protocol analyzer, an attacker simply listens for records, and replays to the server any user ID and password pairs to assume the identity and privileges of the associated users.

The fourth vulnerability inherent in LANs is that server programming often runs at a single level of privilege and without compartmentation. Not only does this make the reliable behavior of the server dependent on the reliable behavior of any and all code within the system, but the privilege of modifying any code in the server includes the ability to change all of it. Thus, anyone who can install new services or maintain existing ones can install privileged code on his own behalf. This vulnerability can be exploited only by people who are already highly privileged. It should not introduce serious instability, because servers are fairly specific in function anyway. However, it does mean that a scheme for segregation of duties that works well on a mainframe is not as effective on a LAN.

Implementation-Induced Weaknesses

Microcomputer LANs often employ hardware that is less robust than that used in more traditional multiuser systems. Although this is partly compensated for by the fact that failures are more local and limited in their impact, the most successful applications often rapidly outgrow the inherent capabilities of this hardware.

As with traditional systems, the behavior of the file server is a reflection of the software installed on it. Management exercises control over the server, in part by managing its content. As with traditional systems, this content management relies partly on supervision and partly on control of access to the hardware and its privileged external controls. However, servers are often installed in environments that are at least somewhat more hostile than those of traditional systems (i.e., office space instead of computer rooms) and that are not usually subject to the same kind of continuous supervision that is typical of traditional systems. As with the traditional system, unsupervised physical access to the hardware is sufficient to install programming that acts on behalf of the attacker rather than on behalf of the owners and managers. Such access is somewhat more likely for file servers than for traditional systems.

One way in which any such vulnerability might be exploited would be to employ it to install an escape mechanism, or secret door, in the server. Attackers could subsequently employ this mechanism from a workstation to avoid controls to which they would typically be subject from a workstation. For example, it might be possible to alter the system in such a way that messages that should be handled by the file-server layer as server requests and subject to the server access rules would instead be passed through to the operating system, permitting access that avoids the server rules.

The inherent strengths of LAN software are often weakened and the weaknesses aggravated by the defaults with which these networks are shipped. For example, one popular system is shipped with the intrusion-detection alarm and the automatic remedy defaulted to off. The purpose of this choice is to avoid a deadlock during initial installation; however, this default is often never properly set.

SUMMARY

Security weaknesses can be subtle. Although most controls work as intended most of the time, when they fail they often do so in ways that are surprising to administrators and even to experts. In light of this potential for surprise and embarrassment, security administrators should:

- Hold users and managers explicitly accountable for use, results, and security. Users and managers should be given explicit guidance and direction. The security administrator should note variances and take timely corrective action.

- Train users and administrators in security; vulnerabilities are subtle and knowledge is low.

- Restrict access to clients, servers, and media. Both physical and logical access should be limited. Available workstation lockwords should be employed. The security administrator must maintain supervision over servers.

- Rely primarily on servers for access control; reliance on workstations should be avoided. The security administrator must ensure that code in servers is relied on, that vendor code is installed as shipped, and that installation code is authorized. Having multiple servers is preferable to having multiple uses per server.

- Rely on users to control machines. When relying on machines to control users, the users should be restricted to supervised workstations, hours, applications, and menus.

- Log on only from workstations that the administrator initialized from a known source (i.e., the administrator's own access-controlled hard drive or write-protected diskette).

- Prefer one-time passwords. Reusable passwords should be randomly chosen and at least five characters in length. In addition, reusable passwords should be changed often, at least every 30 to 60 days. Log-ons that do not require a password should be restricted.

- Employ the rule of least privilege. All access should be explicitly granted, never by default. Only that access required to get the job done should be granted.

- Restrict write privileges. Only one person at a time should have write access to any file or directory. No user should have write access to an executable system to which another user has read or execute access.

- Avoid the use of the supervisor profile or its equivalent. The system manager should be the only person granted this privilege. Applications that require privilege other than that of their users should be given equivalence to a profile prepared and used only for that purpose and that has only the required privilege.

- Avoid applications that require users to have the privilege of changing the application's programs.

- Keep a log of system activities, preferably on the servers. The use of add-on audit capabilities may be necessary.

- Encourage the use of alarms, report anomalies, and take timely corrective action.

- Keep multiple copies of server data. Backups should be made frequently and regularly. Mirroring of files, drives, and servers may be warranted, as indicated by the application.

Implementing Network Controls

JEROME LOBEL

This chapter discusses implementation of basic strategies for controlling networks. The strategies and types of controls for specific types of networks are presented first, followed by a discussion of issues influencing the design, development, installation and testing, and operation of secure networks. Network access controls and physical controls are also briefly discussed.

NETWORK PROTECTION STRATEGIES

Any node in a network or telecommunications systems can be vulnerable to physical or logical compromise. Therefore, the best defense is to install appropriate security mechanisms wherever called for in the network—a layered protection strategy. One network protection strategy calls for implementing network security administration and controls on the mainframe computer; another approach is to install such controls at specific microcomputer nodes located within the network.

Mainframe-Based Network Security

Mainframe-based controls reflect the fact that mainframe-controlled resources may be the ultimate target of a system compromise. For example, basic input/output functions (i.e., traffic to and from the communications network) is often controlled by mainframe software. One mainframe-oriented approach, therefore, might be to install system access control software (e.g., CA-ACF-2, RACF) on the mainframe as a last line of defense against attacks that might successfully evade network protection mechanisms. Encrypting the mainframe-associated data base is another tactic.

Another mainframe-oriented network security strategy involves using a centralized CPU security controller for an entire network or distributed processing system. In this use, all network accesses must first be processed or reviewed by the mainframe-oriented security controls (i.e., passwords, access control privileges) before successful connections are permitted. Security administration for either the entire network or a major part of it would reside on the host computer.

As more security functions and responsibilities are assigned to a host computer, the more critical it becomes to protect its protection mechanisms from all forms of compromise.

Microcomputer-Based Network Security

Distributing security throughout the network at specific microcomputer nodes is a practical, flexible strategy. It permits the installation of the right level of security at the right place for the right reason. It also makes it much harder to compromise the entire network, because different users may install different security mechanisms on their personal computers to protect the subnetwork or local system.

A disadvantage to this arrangement is the difficulty in maintaining access control standards throughout the network; this includes password and encryption, key management, and also periodic access control software updates and changes.

Numerous micro-based security products, protection mechanisms, and techniques are available for installation. The trend toward micro-based network security is strong because of cost advantages and flexibility. Using the personal computer as a protection tool in a network made up primarily of personal computers or mini-computers is technically convenient.

NETWORK TYPES

The types of risk associated with networks differ according to the type of network being secured. This section examines the security risks and controls associated with three network types: wide area networks (WANs), local area networks (LANs), and value-added networks.

WAN Security

The wide area or "long haul" network presents a number of significant security problems, not the least of which is distribution of network resources (i.e., up to and including intercontinental distribution). WAN topologies may include communication resources that are extremely insecure. For example, WAN facilities may broadcast through widely distributed electromagnetic transmissions or through cables where security cannot be guaranteed.

The lack of carrier-installed security mechanisms and lack of user control over these mechanisms creates an extremely insecure environment for WAN users. For this reason, the trend is to encrypt sensitive communications traffic that uses WAN facilities.

LAN Security

The security threat to a LAN is generally much more restricted than that of a WAN. First of all, most LANs are installed in a so-called campus, either within a building or in a limited manner between buildings. The physical and electronic environment is therefore much more controllable. Generally, a LAN connects devices that are only a short distance apart, usually not more than several hundred meters. For this reason, it may be easier to install physical and logical security mechanisms to protect a sensitive LAN.

Unfortunately, LAN security is often not given proper consideration either because it is considered too difficult to implement or because it is assumed that no security problem exists. LAN security should be given much more attention.

LAN security starts with the selection of an appropriate topology (e.g., star, bus, or ring configurations). For sensitive systems, a star-wired configuration that includes a secure controller may be appropriate. Depending on the sensitivity of the data going across the LAN, it may even be advisable to have every access to the LAN mediated by a host computer that contains user profile, permission, and password tables.

Different LAN products can be subject to unique vulnerabilities. For example, the Ethernet LAN is a case in point. Ethernet normally comprises a baseband mode of transmission, coaxial cable, bus topology, and the carrier sense multiple access with collision detection (CSMA/CD) protocol for interfacing to attached devices. It is vulnerable in several respects:

- It is easy to tap.
- Its operating mode allows any workstation with an adapter to join the network without detection.
- A workstation can intercept traffic going across the cable without detection or notification.
- LAN users can gain access to all packets going across the network including those going to other networks.

Numerous safeguards can be used to enhance the security of an existing LAN:

- Physical security for LAN hardware, including cabling and file servers.
- Protection for logged-in and uninstalled workstations.
- System controlled user authorization/permission tables.
- System boot protection for workstations and file servers.
- Use of one-time passwords and secure password generator systems.
- Use of encryption to protect network traffic.
- Use of encryption to protect passwords and encryption key management.
- Separation of cables to enhance security.
- Sensitive information stored offline on removable media.
- Callback modems installed or modems disconnected from the LAN.
- Downloading of sensitive data prevented by using diskless workstations or redirecting disk drives.

Commercial hardware and software products can be used to protect LANs. A careful review and analysis of these products should precede their selection and installation. In addition, careful attention should be paid to the appropriate use of conventional accounting controls and good manual operating procedures (including security awareness) to enhance LAN security.

Value-Added Network Security

Value-added networks add at least one more level of possible vulnerability to a WAN's own inherent potential for security compromise. A value-added network is a communications service (generally provided by a separate organization) that uses the network facilities of a common carrier. The value-added service usually includes the provision of additional equipment and system functions beyond the communications facilities and services provided by the common carrier or client organization.

As in the case of a WAN, the value-added network is not under the control of the user organization. Its facilities are often widely dispersed and geographically remote from both the facilities of the user and common carrier organizations. Users of value-added networks should evaluate the security of all value-added network components that transmit, store, or process sensitive data.

Client organizations should review the security controls included in their value-added network agreement. They should consider requiring the use of cryptography and enhanced password systems to protect sensitive information systems and communications. Some value-added networks customers even insist on annual audits or security reviews of the system facilities of their value-added network service providers to verify the existence and operational integrity of network security controls.

NETWORK SECURITY DEVELOPMENT, INSTALLATION, AND OPERATION

Network security involves the design, implementation, operation, and control of a network in a manner that complies with a predetermined level of systems protection and risk avoidance. There are five categories of resources associated with networks that require protection:

- *Data*. Data stored under the direct management of the network facilities.
- *Hardware*. Communications equipment (modems, switches, controllers, common carrier facilities, terminals) and network security equipment.
- *Software*. Network management software and network security software.
- *Documentation*. Network maps (current and planned), network management documentation, and network security documentation.
- *Processing results*. Network-related output (reports, displays, logs).

Information security experts agree that network security may be a more difficult problem area than computer security (i.e., host security). This is because so many communication hardware and software services are not under the control of information system owners but are operated by common carriers or other service organizations. In addition, transmission through wires, cables and air space (i.e., via radio, satellite, and microwave frequencies) make it especially difficult to protect sensitive data against all forms of compromise.

Network Security Development

In developing a secure network it is important to recognize the differences and similarities between information system security and network security. Whereas system security addresses the host, midrange, or microcomputer environments (which may be nodes in a network), network security addresses the remaining facilities (i.e., the hardware, software, and procedures) that provide communications or network services.

Because computer hardware and software are the core of both computer-oriented and communications-oriented subsystems, it should be no surprise that both classes of systems face similar categories of abuse, including unauthorized access (i.e., confidentiality compromise), integrity loss (i.e., unauthorized modification), and continuity interruption (i.e., denial of service). Therefore, network security design and development criteria should be similar to the criteria used in creating a secure host environment. These criteria will also need to address the physical and logical components of the network and its associated media and transmission facilities.

Design of comprehensive security controls for a large information network should be addressed from at least three perspectives:

- The overall network structure.
- Relationship of physical and logical components.
- The architecture or topology.

Network Structure. The information network must be evaluated in its entirety before the security design criteria can be established. There are many ways to go about doing this. The following approach is recommended although it is not the only way to accomplish this objective.

As shown in Exhibit III-1-1, a network structure consists of three primary components: physical, logical, and application. Although every network consists of all three components, the process of designing security into a network requires a separate view of the features and vulnerabilities uniquely associated with each component. Evaluating network structure in terms of these components provides several advantages:

- The overall security design effort is more systematic.
- Network complexities can be handled more efficiently.

577

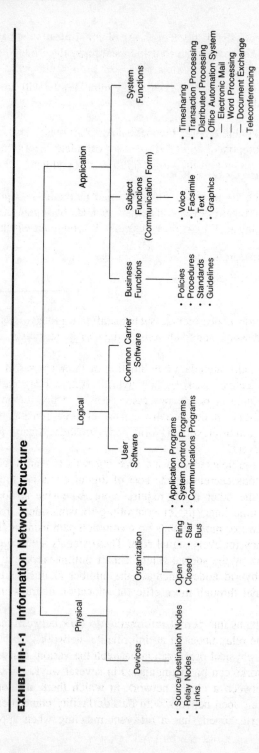

EXHIBIT III-1-1 Information Network Structure

- Separate checklists of problems and vulnerabilities (i.e., a questionnaire for each component) can be created and used to produce more complete network security requirements.
- The chance that a major weakness or vulnerability will be accidently overlooked is reduced.

It should also be noted that components are not mutually exclusive. A separate analysis of each component will produce more complete security requirements and does not preclude looking at the vulnerabilities of a complete subsystem or applications.

As shown under the heading "Physical" in Exhibit III-1-1, physical structure comprises both hardware devices and their manner of organization and connection. The typical physical network it made up of three components:

- Source/destination nodes.
- Relay nodes.
- Links.

Source/destination nodes include such mainframe processors as host, satellite, and network processors, and such remote devices as terminals and microprocessors.

Relay nodes usually include a combination of three classes of devices that can be referred to as active, passive, and hybrid. Active relay nodes may include front-end and remote network processors (often called communications processors). Passive relay nodes usually consist of time-division multiplexers and frequency division multiplexors. Hybrid nodes include "smart" multiplexers and statistical multiplexers.

Time division multiplexers allocate time intervals to transmissions in order to interleave them, thus decreasing the cost of digital circuitry. Frequency division multiplexers, on the other hand, require more expensive analog filter circuits. Instead of using time intervals for controlling transmissions, frequency division devices transmit two or more signals on a common path using a different part of a wideband frequency for every signal sent. These signals are then demultiplexed at the end of the line by the special filters. Smart multiplexers and statistical multiplexers, used in hybrid nodes, increase the number of devices that can be connected to a channel through more efficient allocation of transmission time intervals.

Links are the paths that permit information to flow between the source/destination nodes and the relay nodes of an information network.

Differences in physical organization between the various classes and designs of information networks can be distinguished in several ways. For example, there is the difference between a closed network in which there are not outside facility connections and an open network with outside facility connections. (It should be noted that the term "open" has a different meaning when applied to telecommunications vendors. If, for instance, the International Standards Organization [ISO] open systems interconnection [OSI] communications architecture is referred to, the design described is one in which devices manufactured by different vendors are compatible to the point where they may be installed in the same information network.)

LAN organization can also be distinguished on the basis of its configuration (depending on vendor equipment) in a ring, star, or bus design. (In addition, some LANs may use an architecture based on some combination of ring, star, and bus configuration.)

The logical network structure includes the different software or program logic that supports hardware devices and network applications. Typically this includes application, system control, and communications programs.

The application structure consists of business, subject, and system functions. Business functions include the policies, procedures, standards, and guidelines that encompass a specific organization or business activity (i.e., airline seat reservation systems). The subject function supports voice, facsimile, text, and graphics applications. The basic system function supports such processes as time sharing, transaction processing, distributed processing, office automation, and teleconferencing.

Relationship of Physical and Logical Components. Special attention must be paid to the relationship between the physical and logical components of the network architecture. For example, a company might implement a combination of software logic and hardware specifically to optimize the performance of its total physical communications facilities. This would be done to ensure that each application running on the network uses only those communications facilitates necessary to achieving its operational objectives.

Under these circumstances, the logical network can be defined only if enough is known about the application and its constraints to identify the specific physical and logical components of the communications network that will be used. This relationship is important to the network security designer because the scope of a security design is often limited to just a specific application running on the network—not the entire network.

Dial-Up Communications. The most vulnerable part of many networks are their dial-up communications. There are at least four important threats to these networks:

- Impersonation.
- Misrouting.
- Unauthorized system access.
- Interception.

The merging of voice and data in many networks adds to the problem. In particular, even though both voice and data may move through the same communications facility, the security problems and solutions are not identical. To begin with, it is generally conceded that there is no adequate protection against electronic surveillance of the conventional telephone system.

These communications vulnerabilities extend into the entire telecommunications network. For example, microwave transmission systems, which are used in routing most long-distance calls, are especially vulnerable to unauthorized interception—clandestine receivers may be located somewhere along the microwave path not directly under the control of system owners or managers.

Voice security problems at the local level are typically more common than those associated with WANs or long-distance communication lines because of the difficulty in identifying the long-distance call in the communications provider network. A local facility, therefore, is considered to be the primary target for voice interception. Outside of not locating a telephone in a sensitive location (because the line is available to transmit local conversations when the receiver is hung up), and instituting a personnel policy prohibiting discussion of sensitive subjects on a telephone altogether, most voice security assessments focus on three areas of concern. These are physical security of lines and equipment, transmission security, and personnel security.

Implementation of Pilot Systems

For large, complex, or sensitive networks it is important to implement major access control improvements on a test basis. This is done to ensure that the existing production system is not disrupted. The pilot system is not only useful as a test vehicle, it can also be used for training system operators and users.

The pilot system should be tested against preestablished specifications. For example, network access controls should be verified against all important design and performance criteria; network backup and recovery procedures should be thoroughly tested and reviewed against design specifications. The test plan itself must be carefully designed in order to fulfill its objectives. Pilot tests should precede any major product purchase (as is done with benchmarks before a major computer acquisition). Particular attention should be paid to the compatibility of all proposed network hardware and software components before a major purchase of network security products. It should be verified that security mechanisms do not compromise network integrity or preclude future changes or inhibit expansion.

Two test plans may need to be developed: one for the pilot test and one for an operational test. Ideally, after passing its pilot test, the new security processes or mechanisms should be given a thorough operational test before final acceptance. The purpose of the operational test is to make certain that existing business processes and functions will not fail or be degraded as a result of introducing new hardware, software, or procedures into a production environment.

EXHIBIT III-1-2 Security Implementation Schedule

	Implementation Phases	
Security Mechanisms	**Installation**	**Testing**
1. Modifications to Access Controls		
2. Log-on and Identification Functions		
3. Password System		
4. Access Control Software Package (If Any)		
5. Port Protection Devices		
6. Encryption System		
7. Communications Switches and Media (Link) Security Mechanisms		
8. Total System Integration Test		

Installation and Testing Phases

A phased access control implementation plan is appropriate if numerous logical and physical access controls need to be implemented in a relatively short time frame. In the phased approach shown in Exhibit III-1-2, control mechanisms are implemented one at a time, at a frequency that permits each new procedure or mechanism to be thoroughly tested before acceptance and before installing the next level of security controls.

Implementing a secure network based on a carefully constructed design specification can consume significant resources. For large organizations, this effort can include:

- Management review and approval.
- Policy creation or revision.
- Procedures creation or revision.
- Security product vendor meetings.
- Product demonstrations.
- Product evaluations.
- Technical reviews and reports.
- Documenting and mailing requests for proposals.
- Product selection reviews and approvals.
- Purchase order preparation and mailing.
- Implementation and testing.

Regardless of system size or configuration, implementation and testing of new or revised access control systems generally follows a standard pattern:

- Communication of security objectives and implementation plans to system users.

- Initial implementation of the components of the new access controls on a pilot or test basis.
- Fully integrated implementation of the components of the new access controls on a pilot or test basis.
- Thorough testing of all access control mechanisms in an operational environment.

In the case of a large network, this process may be quite formal and rigorous.

The major advantage of the phased approach shown in Exhibit III-1-2 is that by introducing only a few variables into the installation and test process at one time, problems can usually be pinpointed more easily. The final phase, systems integration, should test system safeguards with every plausible type of compromise, including multiple and simultaneous attacks.

Final Operations Testing

Testing new network mechanisms in the production environment must be done with considerable care. Tests should not be attempted during certain periods; for example:

- When new hardware or system or application software is being installed.
- When tests of system hardware or software are being performed.
- When vital communications operations are being executed.
- When sensitive data is being transmitted.

Operational testing should be performed by the most competent team of individuals that can be assembled. The team leader should tightly control all scheduled activities, test plans, and documentation. An external consultant should be considered to help with the final operational security integration test, if the required expertise is not available in-house. Before operational testing begins, the team members must be clearly informed as to the nature of the test plan, who is to perform each test, and how results are to be documented. System users should participate in operational tests, and their feedback should be included with test documentation.

Most networks continuously undergo change and enhancement. Even after a network has been thoroughly tested, new vulnerabilities might appear. Therefore, as new users enter the system, as new communications devices and lines are connected, and as new hardware and software modules are added, potential vulnerabilities may need to be reevaluated. Periodic reviews and tests should also be performed to protect against the intentional circumvention of safeguards by system users.

NETWORK ACCESS CONTROLS

Numerous protection mechanisms have been developed to prevent unauthorized use of communications networks. The problems addressed by these security mechanisms include:

- Preventing unauthorized network use where the objective is to obtain free network access (i.e., no payment for carrier services).
- Preventing someone from attacking a host computer system by first compromising one or more networks.
- Preventing an attack against the network intended to interrupt or intercept communications.

Three general classes of network control mechanisms are currently available to address these security concerns, including:

- Host access control mechanisms (i.e., where the host is a node in the network).
- Communications media control mechanisms.
- Node security control mechanisms.

These controls may include access control software, password generator and management systems, encryption systems, port protectors, call-up and answer-back systems, dial-up access control mechanisms, user authorization controls (e.g., profile and permission tables), and special log-in protection products.

Most network access control systems use the techniques of active monitoring, passive monitoring, or both. Active monitoring systems provide the ability to immediately detect an unauthorized activity and prevent its completion (e.g., successful log-on). Passive monitoring systems report violations after the fact, identifying possible network violations that should be investigated at a later time.

PHYSICAL NETWORK SECURITY

Physical network security addresses threats directed against such physical resources as computer hardware, offline media (e.g., tapes and disks), data links, documentation, power supplies, switches, and facilities that make up the network. It is important that all communication devices, including terminals, personal computers, modems, communications controllers, and concentrators (including carrier-supplied equipment) be protected from unauthorized access or use. A number of relatively simple physical protection measures can be effective; these include the use of guards, door and device locks, keyboard locks, concealment techniques, closed-circuit TV, and other electronic surveillance mechanisms.

In general, five key areas of the communications system may require physical protection and should therefore be evaluated:

- Relay node devices.
- Coupling devices that connect the source and destination devices to the interconnecting lines and trunks of the network.
- Distribution lines, trunks, and links that connect the different nodes of the communications network.
- Switches.
- Source and destination devices, including computers and terminals.

The security of the following network components should also be investigated: satellite and microwave links; certain LAN components; and such host or terminal-oriented communications facilities as front-end communications processors, concentrators, and modem devices.

The recent introduction of more advanced communications systems, LANs, and PBX systems designed to integrate voice and data communications make physical protection imperative. This new equipment is not necessarily more vulnerable than older systems, but these new systems tend to handle more sensitive data.

For the most part, existing manual procedures and electronic surveillance and alarm systems are more than adequate to protect sensitive communications facilities against all but the most sophisticated intruders. (For example, wiretap detection and prevention equipment can thwart most intruders.) In general, standard commercial electronic surveillance systems can adequately protect most on-premise communications facilities.

Local telephone cables are among the most vulnerable points in a communications network because it is relatively easy to sort out individual communications along the wires of a cable, thereby simplifying the job of monitoring transmissions. Existing security devices and electronic surveillance systems can solve this problem, although several levels of controls may have to be implemented depending on the vulnerability of the system. System owners may also want to consider installing underground cables and encrypting transmissions. Encryption is the ultimate protection measure. In some environments, such protection mechanisms as cable and device shielding (e.g., lead shielding, burying lines in concrete) and vacuum leak-detection equipment for sealed cables and facilities should be considered.

Microwave communications (i.e., high-frequency signals passed through terrestrial relay stations) and satellite communications (i.e., ultrahigh-frequency signals relayed via a device orbiting the earth) are also vulnerable to interception. These devices require the same level of physical protection afforded other communications facilities.

Despite the proven effectiveness of security technology, data communications users often fail to take sufficient measures to protect communications equipment and facilities, whether located on their own premises or on public or common-carrier property. There are two reasons for this: difficulties in justifying cost of solutions and in acquiring an intimate knowledge of the physical components of the communications system and their specific locations. To obtain an understanding of communications facilities, help should be sought from communications equipment technical service representatives. A complete inventory and layout of all communications-related facilities that can access the information system should be documented. With this information, it should be possible to design and implement an adequate protection system for on-premise communications facilities.

SUMMARY

A thorough understanding of the unique risks associated with each type of network is needed before the security practitioner can identify and implement appropriate control mechanisms. WANs, LANs, and value-added networks each pose a different set of issues that must be addressed. Furthermore, each network component must be evaluated with respect to the potential threats that can affect that component. Once a control strategy has been selected, a plan for developing and implementing the necessary controls should be created. It is important that controls be adequately tested to prevent disruption of the production system. If numerous logical and physical controls must be implemented in a short time frame, a phased implementation plan is recommended.

Managing Network Security

JEROME LOBEL

Because security controls must be implemented at several levels in a network environment, management of network security can be a complex task. For example, software controls must be implemented to protect data integrity, confidentiality, and availability. Network management-level controls must be implemented to ensure the operation and maintenance of communications and various network devices.

This chapter addresses the security issues specific to network software and network management. In addition, it discusses the necessary security documentation and training, security reviews, and network contingency planning. Finally, it presents network backup requirements and examines various network security standards.

NETWORK SOFTWARE SECURITY

Prevention of unauthorized access, unauthorized modifications, and interruption of network service should be the general security objective for network security software. These same issues are also relevant for nonsecurity-related software that drives the many devices that are directly or indirectly associated with the network. In recent years, however, it has become increasingly clear that the bottom line as far as security is concerned may be the attention that should be paid to protecting the security software itself.

Software security protection features may range from special code or logic inserted into network operating system software to extremely large and comprehensive security-oriented hardware and software systems inserted into key network nodes, which are designed to run in conjunction with other network components. Many categories and variations of commercial network security software are currently offered. Examples include data communications–oriented encryption packages, traffic analysis protection software, callback software and hardware, and terminal and user authentication systems (including digital signatures and network audit software packages).

In addition, packages may be internally designed, developed, and installed that serve essentially the same purpose as the commercial packages. Examples of security functions served by this software include encryption, utility system functional limiters, secure password managers, network violation reporting systems, terminal and screen deactivation and blanking modules, comprehensive access control software packages, internal system control modules, and software that supports a variety of hardware security devices and microprocessors.

The job of keeping a network secure is continuous and neverending. After system access policies and specifications have been defined and security mechanisms and procedures installed, the real job of maintaining network security has just begun. Both anticipated and unanticipated security problems can and do occur. Examples of events that can trigger these problems include:

- Errors or omissions in the access controls that have been installed.
- Network changes that result in new vulnerabilities.
- Legitimate users trying to circumvent controls for both harmful and benign purposes.
- External parties trying to test system safeguards or penetrate the network for a variety of unauthorized and illegal activities.

Access to the network is usually monitored through protection mechanisms built into special access control software packages or into basic computer hardware and software functions. A combination approach is often taken to add layers of security protection to the network. Examples of these multilevel network security mechanisms include:

- Mechanisms that disconnect users from the network after a certain number of attempts to log on with incorrect user IDs or passwords.
- Network user authorization tables.
- Security review of network use and telephone charge reports.
- Network use limitation constraints for each authorized user.

Although the monitoring and feedback system is in itself a key access control mechanism, it is far from being the whole of network security. For example, access control and violation reporting mechanisms are often built into encryption and port protection systems and communications front ends. In addition, there are numerous physical safeguards, backup procedures, program controls, and security mechanisms that play a part in total network security.

The access control monitoring and surveillance system is the key to preventing, detecting, and reporting of potential and actual violations. Even these systems are of limited use, however, without human interaction and intervention, for three reasons. First, access rules may change. At least one person (preferably two) must be able to make those changes to the access control system. Second, because unauthorized access is basically a human-oriented problem, serious violations must be dealt with personally by the appropriate people (e.g., managers, security officers, law enforcement personnel, and attorneys). And third, computer-generated violation reports often cannot interpret the difference between errors and intentional compromises, nor can they determine how serious the penetration was if one is identified.

The flow of a typical access control monitoring and feedback system includes compromise prevention, compromise detection, an automatic countermeasure response, and violation feedback and reporting. The typical full-feature access control software package provides all of these functions. However, there are important differences associated with the more comprehensive systems. For example, the design philosophy of some systems permits access only if the access meets predefined rules. Other systems deny access only if an illegal access attempt is identified. The general violation reports of some systems are of little value because it is difficult to detect errors from actual compromise attempts. The point is that if too many of the potential violation incidents included in the violation reports are not real system attacks or compromises but simply incidents of common human mistakes, the violation report will not be taken seriously.

Some access control monitors simply deny access, depending on how many times an invalid password or other transaction is presented to the system. Although undoubtedly a valuable security tool, this is a limited approach to access monitoring and surveillance.

Most comprehensive access monitoring and feedback systems provide both real-time access protection (i.e., compromise prevention and detection) and passive protection (i.e., violation reports). The objectives of this dual approach to access monitoring are to:

- Minimize unnecessary inconvenience to users through too many access denials for legitimate transactions.
- Establish a realistic approach to handling the large number of unintentional errors users make when logging on or using a system.
- Provide an adequate data base for violation reporting that should aid the successful investigation of a serious breach.
- Allow even suspected network transactions to occur if they cannot, for technical or other reasons, be canceled but can be dealt with immediately by human intervention.
- Allow time for management to authorize the implementation of a method for gathering more evidence for investigation or legal action.

System-default or access-denial mechanisms should replicate the organization's preestablished security policies. Unfortunately, many apparently illegal access attempts may only be user errors, and many apparently legitimate accesses to extremely sensitive objects may in fact be compromises. The problem of what to look for and how the system should react to the stimuli is an exceedingly difficult problem for both security designers and system users.

Not all system activity is initiated by a person using a computer, terminal, or console. Many system accesses can be triggered by automated decision-making mechanisms, which in turn generate computer programs or cause an existing program or device to perform a set of operations. These operations may require access to sensitive resources in the originating computer or even another network computer. Therefore, access monitors must include not only rules to follow when human users request access but rules that should be followed when processes request access.

As indicated earlier, because of frequent errors made by people in their attempts to access a system, it is difficult to distinguish between authorized and unauthorized activity. For this reason, the following transactions or events should be noted for possible inclusion in a violation report or investigation:

- All system access denials.
- Accesses to sensitive data or resources.
- All log-ons and log-offs.
- Unauthorized access to privileged instructions.
- Sensitive resource use.
- User profile or permission changes.
- System reconfigurations.
- Modifications to security parameters.
- All system user changes.
- All hardware or software changes.

A security violation investigation cannot be carried out successfully without this information. In addition to built-in controls designed to immediately block actual or probable system compromises, logging of sensitive events is the most important feature of an effective monitoring and feedback system.

NETWORK MANAGEMENT SECURITY

Network management includes the operation and maintenance of the various communications services, physical media, and devices in such a manner as to ensure efficiency, effectiveness, and integrity in the data and traffic flow and to ensure overall communications reliability. Network management functions also include control of user authorization, network configuration, priority definition, diagnostic checks, and failure correction.

The network management function for an organization may be internally or externally managed. Its continuous and dependable operation determines the continuity and integrity of the organization's communications and, in many cases, its eventual survival.

Network Management Security Considerations

Network management is responsible for determining the reliability and integrity of the network. A security exposure can be created because its centralized function typically permits operators and maintenance personnel to observe all but specially encrypted network traffic.

Ideally, network management and network security personnel should have a close and cooperative relationship. Under certain conditions, it may even be desirable for certain network security mechanisms to be installed in the same physical environment as the network management system. However, the independence of the security personnel should not be sacrificed for the sake of convenience or productivity.

NETWORK SECURITY DOCUMENTATION

The design specifications, network operating procedures, and test procedures of the network must be documented. In addition, an inventory of network components should be maintained, geographic and logical schematics should be kept up-to-date, and network security reports should be regularly reviewed by security personnel. The following sections discuss these documentation requirements.

Design Specifications. At a minimum, the design specifications for a secure network should contain:

- A complete description and inventory of the physical components that make up the network.
- A comprehesive description of the network objectives, functions, users, volumes, and priorities and relevant quantitative statistics and operating information.
- A description of network risks and vulnerabilities as well as selected protection mechanisms and controls (including control objectives).
- A description of how the network is organized, including logical and geographic schematics.
- A complete list of all network system software (by device run on).
- A complete description of all network applications (e.g., a funds transfer system or airline reservation system).

Operating Procedures. Network operating procedures should not only reflect standard and approved operating practices but describe all approved and recommended security rules and procedures.

Test Procedures. Documentation of test procedures should encompass:

- Network startup procedures (i.e., from technical hardware and software operating procedures).
- Network configuration and reconfiguration procedures (i.e., in conformance with system specifications and documented network management requirements).

- Network backup and restart procedures (i.e., a detailed description of specific backup and restart processes that meet organizational requirements, including emergency needs).
- Approved network hardware and software maintenance procedures (i.e., for both on-site and remote maintenance requirements).
- Approved customer engineering support requirements, in accordance with security requirements imposed on vendor support personnel and internal maintenance employees.

Component Inventory. A complete network component inventory should be maintained and kept up-to-date for all network facilities. For example, the following component list should be maintained for every geographic location in the network:

- Terminals.
- Personal computers (with modems).
- Satellite processors.
- Host computers.
- Communications controller (i.e., the network control processor).
- Switches (i.e., the channel interface switch and virtual switch matrix).
- Modems.
- Multiplexers.
- Concentrators and cluster controllers.
- Communications media (e.g., telephone lines, fiber optics, and coaxial cable).
- Special carriers (e.g., T1).
- Local area networks (by topology and transmission medium).

Schematics. Both logical and physical schematics should be kept current for all geographic locations associated with the network. In addition, appropriate communications carrier or provider network schematics should be maintained and kept current for emergency and planning purposes.

Network Security Reports. Network security and violation reports should be safeguarded and regularly reviewed and, when necessary, investigated by security personnel as well as appropriate levels of management. In addition, the appropriate managers should follow up on action item reports.

NETWORK SECURITY TRAINING

Both managers and network users should receive training in network security. The management security training program should be directed toward the highest level of management with information and communications system responsibilities. The program should receive senior-level management support and should include a computer and communications security awareness program. In addition to covering detailed security requirements, the training should include a clear picture of the physical scope and operation of the network and its importance to the profitability, survivability, and integrity of the organization.

The user security training program must address all of the duties and knowledge that an employee requires to support network security requirements. Security administrators should be careful to deliver the information in a systematic way. The program should be supported with appropriate written and approved security management policies. Operational manuals and instructions should be carefully documented, approved by management, and periodically reviewed for currency.

NETWORK SECURITY REVIEWS

Network security assessments and quality assurance reviews are essential for ensuring that network security remains adequate. Exhibit III-1-3 lists the procedural and technical components of an information system that should be assessed in the

---

EXHIBIT III-1-3 System Components to Be Assessed in the Security Review

Network Security Policies

Network Security Functional Procedures:

- Log-on processes
- Information transmission
- Communications line media
- Local area network
- Network host and nodes
- Network management
- Personal computers and terminals

Communication Types:

- Voice
- Facsimile
- Text
- Graphics

System functions:

- Time-sharing functions
- Transaction processing
- Distributed processing
- Teleconferencing
- Office automation systems:
  —Word processing
  —Electronic mail
  —Document exchange

Key Network Applications

security review. Information about these components should be obtained using questionnaires that are developed to support the security and control assessments. Each questionnaire should be integrated into a total security and control assessment procedure that includes the following review tools:

- Network security control objectives.
- A network security and control assessment.
- Risk impact analysis.
- Compliance tests.
- Recommended security and control measures.

The completion of a network security and control review is essentially a three-step process. The first step is the network and security assessment definition. This should entail the completion of a preliminary review that has as its objectives:

- A definition of the total scope of the network, including applications, control constraints, and geographic locations.
- A physical inventory of the network components that should be included.
- A schematic description of how the network is organized, including the physical and logical relationships.

The second step of the review is the network security and control assessment, which involves use of a network security and control assessment questionnaire. The completed questionnaire should:

- Identify relevant control objectives.
- Identify potential risks.
- Describe consequences of inadequate control procedures.
- Define appropriate control confirmation procedures (i.e., verification and test procedures).
- Describe appropriate risk reduction measures that could be implemented.

The third and final step of the review is writing the network security assessment report. This report should identify the review findings and conclusions, describe high-risk areas, recommended actions and priorities, and define the extent of compliance with industry standards.

Another essential method for maintaining network security is to conduct network security accreditations. The accreditation process is essentially a careful review or assessment of network operations to determine whether all approved and recommended security-related functions are operational and implemented. The purpose of network security accreditation is to ensure that no network or network change becomes operational without meeting management-approved security standards and procedures. A reaccreditation should be periodically required regardless of whether or not any network security violations have been reported since the last accreditation.

DISTRIBUTED NETWORK SECURITY

In a distributed network security environment, security controls may not be centralized; instead, they may be positioned in the most appropriate network nodes. Security monitoring, quality assurance, security system updating, use of passwords and encryption, key management, and regular assessments tend to be more difficult in this environment compared with centralized network security management. Although distributed network security controls are typically more acceptable and meaningful from a user's point of view, they are often much harder to monitor because they are geographically dispersed.

Security design changes and operational updates can be implemented in a distributed network environment only through a rigorous process that involves appropriate managers, network operations personnel, system users, security personnel, and frequently even the network management team as well as network product or service vendors. As difficult as this level of coordination may be, the advantage of distributed network security control is still desirable for many organizations.

NETWORK CONTINGENCY PLANNING

The most important objective of a network security plan is to provide for the survival of the organization in the event that the worst-case scenario occurs with regard to the operation of its communications network. Survival is usually measured in terms of the time it takes to restart the more important network facilities to meet the critical needs of the organization. The speed with which this must be done is usually determined by estimating the consequences of specific outages for given periods of time for defined critical applications. The typical components of a network disaster recovery or contingency plan usually include:

- Communications hardware recovery.
- Communications software recovery.
- Communications media or carrier recovery.
- A backup communications facility.
- Communications software backup.
- Off-site storage facilities.
- Alternative communications suppliers.
- A recovery plan and procedures.
- Recovery reliability and emergency testing.
- Power supply recovery.
- Redundant communications facilities.
- Contingency organization agreements.

Most large networks are vulnerable to single points of failure, which are critical components in the network that—if destroyed, damaged, or otherwise rendered unavailable—can create serious communications problems to the organization. With single points of failure, if a particular failure occurs, no recovery is possible within the organization's critical recovery or survival time. Severed communications and power cables are examples of single points of failure that can cause extensive service losses to major organizations, which could lead to severe business losses.

Therefore, one of the most important tasks in communications contingency planning is the analysis of possible single points of failure. This type of analysis usually involves having key system users, managers, and network operations personnel complete a questionnaire.

NETWORK BACKUP

The failure or loss of vital communications hardware systems may or may not be critical in a given system disaster. Although many factors can contribute to the impact of disasters, communications systems hardware clearly is an essential planning element.

Recent disasters have shown how extremely resilient and redundant communications systems are in the US. Many potentially destructive organizational losses have been avoided as a result of this redundancy. For example, redundancy was extremely beneficial during the aftermath of major earthquakes in California. In contrast, when communications lines were cut in the New York financial district, the costs of inadequate backup were huge, even though the outage was of relatively short duration.

Like hardware, inadequate communications software can be a serious problem in an emergency. However, organizations that do not have an adequate communications software backup program are probably guiltier of poor management or oversight than organizations that suffer seriously from a hardware loss, because the process required to back up critical communications software is probably less extensive and more controllable than certain redundant hardware decisions.

Although planning for an emergency may not be easy, it is important. A careful analysis of alternative communications suppliers, distributed system redundancies, geographic relocations, and satellite or microwave communications alternatives should be conducted for both economic and technical feasibility.

NETWORK SECURITY STANDARDS

Organizations are increasingly becoming more dependent on their state-of-the-art communications networks for critical business support functions. The security, integrity, and continuity of these systems is no longer a minor or low-level business consideration. Prime examples of heavily supported security activities can be drawn from such organizations as brokerage houses, charge card–oriented businesses, stock exchanges, and the airline industry.

With this in mind, more chief executives and their staffs are establishing firm, written policies that provide a clear signal to lower levels of management to create the kind of communications network that fully satisfies the organization's need to avoid unnecessary business risks.

Internal communications policies and manuals of standard practices and procedures must be created. These documents should include:

- Organizational network security objectives.
- Personnel security responsibilities.
- Penalties related to network abuse.
- Secure network access procedures.
- Violation reporting procedures and follow-up.
- Network security design requirements.
- Network application approval procedures.
- Secure network maintenance procedures.
- Network vendor approval procedures.
- Network disaster recovery and backup procedures.
- Network password protection requirements.

For many businesses, the question is no longer whether they can afford the cost of developing and maintaining a communications security program, but how they can afford not to. The management concept of due care can be applied quite appropriately to this area.

External and industry standards must also be addressed. Government and industry standards organizations are working to produce practical and comprehensive standards in the area of network security. In particular, the federal government's research into the security deficiencies of the TCP/IP protocol for MILNET and its interest in being able to procure compatible and connectable systems have led these efforts more in the direction of the International Standards Organization's open systems interconnection (OSI) architecture, including its security standards. Primary weaknesses in TCP/IP include deficiencies in the network management facilities and security authentication procedures.

The OSI standard has been implemented on many computer networks. This model of network communications consists of seven layers: application, presentation, session, transport, network, data link, and physical. Security standards are specified for each layer. Because each of the seven layers of the OSI model serves a specific function within network communications, security may be implemented to protect against different types of security threats.

SUMMARY

This chapter examines significant network vulnerabilities and the major technical issues surrounding network security. It provides a structure for building a secure network, from network assessment through implementation of network safeguards. The essential logical, physical, and procedural considerations are examined in such a way as to give readers insight into discovering, avoiding, and correcting possible deficiencies in their communications systems.

Establishing Network
Security Controls

ROBERT J. BOSEN

Compared with conventional centralized computing, computer networks present an entirely different set of challenges to the information security officer. Judicious application of policies and standards can help minimize these challenges; however, these policies and standards must be consistent with and compensate for the fundamental differences between networked and centralized computing. Simply trying to enforce old policies with new vigor does not work. Although a network-oriented interpretation of the old policies may help, distributed environments really require a fundamental redefinition of information security policies and standards.

Recognition of the need to fundamentally redefine security policies and standards leads to an immediate need to assess the basic goals and objectives of information security. Some basic questions must be asked—namely, the organization must determine what needs to be protected and who it needs to be protected from.

Neither of these questions is as trivial as might seem at first glance. Different organizations are likely to produce vastly different lists of answers. The information security officer must determine which answers are relevant to individual situations.

This chapter covers only the more predictable responses that might be expected. For example, physical equipment needs to be protected from theft and unauthorized activity. Computer programs must be protected from unauthorized use and copying, and sensitive information must be protected from unauthorized access. The people these resources must be protected from include amateur cryptographers or competitors, systems programmers, hardware maintenance technicians, and routine users.

This chapter identifies the most significant networking issues that affect information security and reviews the principles and methodologies that network professionals use when dealing with these issues. The security implications of major networking trends and options are discussed as well as suggested remedies for the major problem areas.

THE EFFECT OF NETWORKING ON SECURITY

Management must truly understand that networking fundamentally changes the information security environment. Only then can it support the information security officers in developing and implementing an effective security program.

Unfortunately, many managers lack the background to achieve the necessary understanding, and few managers have the time to study the issues seriously. Therefore, the information security staff must explain the principles of network exposures in a way that management can understand, remember, and communicate to others. Because senior managers often lack the time or enthusiasm for technical discussions, the security staff may have to rely on analogies and simple diagrams; in addition, the discussion should address only the broad principles, not the details.

Of all the issues that differentiate networking security from other aspects of security, one issue stands out: broadcast technologies. It is difficult to ensure the confidentiality of sensitive information traversing modern networks, because many local area networks (LANs) and most wide area networks (WANs) operate by broadcasting everything to everybody. Thus, broadcasting dramatically affects the ability to manage modern computing resources, maintain the privacy of sensitive information, hold users accountable for their actions, and establish or monitor the responsibilities of public and private institutions.

One way to help management visualize the ramifications of broadcasting is to use a simple analogy involving wiretaps to illustrate the problem. For example, the following scenario might be presented. One day the security manager uncovers a suspicious wire in the computer room. After investigating, the manager discovers that it leads to the engineering lab, where it is connected to various custom-built equipment. The engineering department has been using this connection to monitor all activity on the mainframe as part of an unauthorized project to develop a new type of storage device. The manager must face the possibility that such sensitive information as payroll and proprietary designs may have been compromised.

In a centralized environment, this type of wiretap would be considered an alarming breach of security. From a security standpoint, however, modern networks involve essentially the same type of connection.

Another helpful technique for explaining to management the effects of networking is to draw a diagram of the primary networks in the organization. The diagram in Exhibit III-1-4 uses a heavier arrow to bring attention to the broadcast segments of the network. The broadcast segment resembles a backbone connecting all of the network's computers, workstations, and servers to the hosts. This helps illustrate that all of the information sent from any network node is broadcast to all the other nodes. The connecting arrows can be highlighted to illustrate the most heavily trafficked network paths or the path that passwords traverse between users and the mainframe.

In addition, this diagram may help management understand that because the

EXHIBIT III-1-4 Sample Diagram of a Broadcast Network

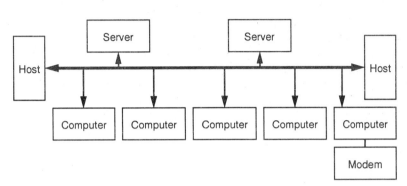

organization's computers are interconnected, they no longer function discretely. Users therefore require easier access to applications, regardless of the number or kinds of computers involved. Users and management may not even be aware of which computers actually store or execute the programs they rely on.

In providing users with the simple, uniform access methodologies they require, many of the de facto barriers to illicit penetration and compromise of sensitive information have disappeared. These de facto barriers have more to do with the difficulty of navigating primitive networks than the effectiveness of active security controls: in the early days of networking, it took a lot of effort to figure out how to access different applications across networks. Users correctly pointed out that these early networking systems were too cumbersome. Since then, networks have advanced tremendously, eliminating cumbersome access requirements and facilitating uniform access to networked systems.

Senior managers who understand networking are more supportive of efforts to provide uniform access. They realize the value in enabling users to spend more time working and less time navigating the pathways between their computers and the applications they need. Information security officers must help senior managers see the necessity of reworking security and access controls correspondingly.

Understanding Network Access

There are only four ways information can be extracted from networked computers. Once management understands what these four views are and, more important, realizes that there are only four views to worry about, it will be easier to elicit management support in obtaining and using the tools needed to control access to information. The following sections describe the four views to information.

The Application View. The application view is the only view that is understood by users who have not been trained in computer technology. Beginners start out with application views, and unless they become computer-literate, they stay with application views. This is the primary method by which applications programmers have systems deliver information to users. The most sensitive information is often best viewed through applications. For example, Lotus 1-2-3 spreadsheets are easier to access through Lotus 1-2-3 than any other way.

The File View. Sooner or later, nearly all users learn enough about their operating systems to access files directly using such commands as DIR, COPY, PRINT, or DELETE. Different operating systems use different command names, but this same capability is available in all modern environments. All of the information in networked microcomputers, workstations, mainframes, minicomputers, and servers is vulnerable to compromise through these powerful file commands.

The Sector View. This is the view that hardware service personnel and systems programmers use when they service disk drives, diskettes, caches, or controllers. Virtually all information in the entire network is subject to compromise through the sector view. In addition, routine users can easily gain access to sector views of disks running under popular operating systems through readily available tools (e.g., Norton Utilities from Peter Norton Computing or Mace Utilities from Paul Mace Software, both for MS-DOS). With these tools, users can bypass access controls and extract sensitive information from the sectors directly, or they can rebuild the sector view into the file view or application view. Although the names of the tools may differ, these problems apply to all operating system environments.

The Packet View. This is the view that network managers, network troubleshooters, data carriers, and systems programmers use when they service networks and network equipment and systems. All information traversing broadcast LANs and WANs is subject to compromise through the packet view. In addition, routine users can easily gain packet views of everything on the network by using a diskette containing network monitoring software.

The availability of the packet view destroys an organization's ability to certify the confidentiality of any information traversing the network. It also destroys the ability for users to be responsible for the care of confidential information, and unless steps are taken to authenticate user identity, it destroys management's ability to hold users accountable for their actions. For example, fixed passwords are automatically compromised when they traverse a broadcast network.

ASSET SHARING ON NETWORKS

Modern networks encourage sharing of assets. The security ramifications of networking are directly and profoundly affected by the assets that are shared on each network segment. The following sections summarize the state of the art of network sharing.

Shared File Systems

By far the most successful LAN application is file sharing. Indeed, most discussions about LANs and LAN operating systems center on the concept of the file server.

A shared file system allows users to behave as if the system's disk drives were merged. Taken to the extreme, a shared file system allows system managers to eliminate all local disk drives, including diskette drives, yet permits each user to operate from the disk operating system on a diskless workstation, almost as if the user had several disk drives. Regardless of whether or not the local workstation has any disk drives, the presence of one or more shared files on a central server is a flexible, powerful asset to the organization; information sharing becomes a simple process of storing files on the file server.

Shared Printers

The second most successful LAN application is printer sharing. The advantages of sharing a few printers among many users are obvious: economy and efficiency can be maximized. Nearly all LANs have one or more shared printers. Users can usually work as if the printer were attached to their local workstation, letting the network arbitrate who has command of the printer from moment to moment. The application software in the workstation is usually unaffected when printing is handled by a shared printer.

Remote Computing

Recent developments in WANs and technical support have resulted in wide availability of remote computing packages. These packages permit a user to hook up to a computer by means of a LAN connection, telephone line, or modem; the user can than control that computer from a remote location.

Two computers are always directly involved in this type of arrangement: the remote one that the user calls from, and the computer being called, referred to as the slave. Although this connection is active, the keyboards and screens of both computers are merged; anything typed on either keyboard is acted on by the slave. Anything displayed by the slave is seen on both screens.

This capability allows users at remote locations to work as if they were using the office workstation itself. All office files and programs are available in their familiar locations, and anything reachable though LAN or WAN from the office workstation is now reachable from the remote location in exactly the same way.

Popular software packages implementing this kind of scheme include Carbon-

Copy (Raxco, Inc.), CO/Session (Triton Technologies, Inc.), and BLAST (BLAST/Communications Research Group). A modem, telephone line, and MS-DOS-compatible workstation are the only other requirements.

Shared Windows

Widespread availability of the X-Windows system, developed in the public domain as part of Project Athena at the Massachusetts Institute of Technology, has created new commercial opportunities for companies that offer window-sharing packages for UNIX and other environments. With the window-sharing system, any workstation can act as a window into any X-compliant application anywhere on the network. X-Windows applications are now popular on UNIX workstations and are becoming available for MS-DOS and Macintosh systems as well.

Shared Mailboxes

It has recently become popular to share logical mailboxes on networks, which allows users to send messages back and forth very easily. Electronic mail (E-mail) has become a key aspect of operations in many modern organizations.

Shared mailboxes may rely on shared files; if they are not based on a shared file system, they need separate protection. It is often possible to institute policies that modify the way an organization uses E-mail so that measures that protect shared file systems also protect E-mail.

Network Data Bases

Data base servers are embodied in a network-aware application on the LAN, often in a separate process or dedicated to this one purpose. Protocols have been developed in the public domain to define vendor-independent ways of querying a network data base server (e.g., with SQL). Protection of this type of information as it traverses a LAN is almost impossible with currently available technology.

Distributed Processing

Recently, software tools have become available to facilitate use of otherwise idle computers that are connected to a LAN. Use of such computers is especially valuable when it is necessary to handle computer-intensive jobs (e.g., compiling data or generating graphics). Such jobs typically exchange information between LAN computers in cleartext, exposing it to compromise.

Often, however, it is easy to adapt this type of exchange to shared file systems. In this case, cryptographic measures that can protect shared files can also protect the information shared between distributed processors.

ESTABLISHING POLICIES FOR NETWORK SOFTWARE CONTROLS

If technologies developed before networking are adapted to networked environments, the systems may comply with policy and give the illusion that they are working, but in practice they will not control access to sensitive information or applications from all four views to the information (i.e., the application, file, sector, and packet views). As a general rule, operating system–based access controls fall into this category because they are effective only when the operating system is carefully administered. In a distributed network environment, administration of the operating systems is routinely handled individually by the users, at their computers. Because these users may not feel inclined to restrict their own access to information, an effective means of protecting sensitive information is required.

Encryption protects sensitive information that access controls cannot prevent users from accessing. If information is encrypted at its point of creation, it usually remains protected regardless of any administrative failures elsewhere on the network.

Although broadcast networks (e.g., Ethernet and IBM Token-Ring) lack fundamental security features, they remain popular. Therefore, information security personnel must learn to secure them, and encryption is the only known way to protect sensitive information traversing broadcast networks.

The OSI Model

Data communications experts have devised a sophisticated methodology for use in planning and installing networks. Network specialists developed sets of standardized layers in which networking equipment can be installed and through which cooperating modules interact. Security personnel must thoroughly understand this layered concept as the organization's plans for encryption develop and other security steps are taken.

The most common network layering methodology is based on a theoretical model proposed by the International Standards Organization (ISO), often referred to as the open systems interconnection (OSI) reference model. The ISO has proposed that all networks be described and implemented by mapping functions into the model's seven defined categories, called layers. However, many of the most popular network systems do not map cleanly onto this seven-layer model. Still, almost everybody is familiar with it, and most people can visualize how their particular network equipment differs from the OSI model.

The seven-layer OSI model as defined by the ISO is depicted in Exhibit III-1-5. Each of the seven layers is summarized in the following sections.

Although unusual, it is possible to configure large, sophisticated networks that contain no broadcast segments. If there are no broadcast segments in a network, many of the concerns discussed in the following sections are not applicable.

EXHIBIT III-1-5 The OSI Reference Model

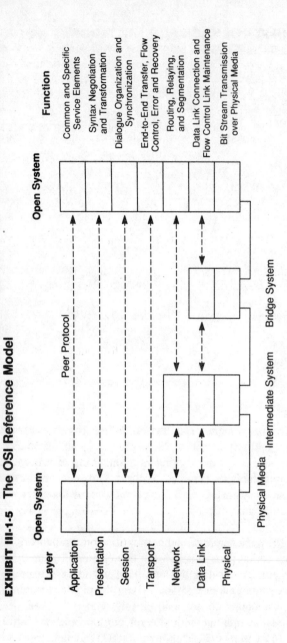

Layer	Open System		Function
Application			Common and Specific Service Elements
Presentation			Syntax Negotiation and Transformation
Session			Dialogue Organization and Synchronization
Transport			End-to-End Transfer, Flow Control, Error and Recovery
Network			Routing, Relaying, and Segmentation
Data Link			Data Link Connection and Flow Control Link Maintenance
Physical			Bit Stream Transmission over Physical Media

Peer Protocol

Physical Media

Intermediate System

Bridge System

Layer 7: The Application Layer. Security must first address the application layer, because this is where all information originates; in addition, it is where network applications run. The most common network applications are file servers, print servers, data base servers, and mail servers. Cooperative processes based on client-server architectures are also described under this layer. These network applications are fed by more conventional applications (e.g., word processors, spreadsheets, or file managers), which may not be aware of the existence of the network.

The application layer is often an ideal place to apply encryption, because the lower layers tend to be separated (both physically and logically) from the original location of the information needing protection. The network application layer is also an ideal place to apply access controls.

Layer 6: The Presentation Layer. When it is necessary to translate character sets (e.g., ASCII to EBCDIC) or to alter the representation of information so that it can be properly interpreted by the application layer at the other end of the network (e.g., to adapt to a different kind of display terminal), the ISO suggests grouping the necessary functions into what it calls the presentation layer. In practice, however, the presentation layer is not used extensively; applications tend to handle these functions without conforming to the OSI reference model. Standards bodies are trying to develop standards for conformance within networks, and conformant networking systems are emerging. Still, it is not yet clear whether the presentation layer, as described in the OSI model, will quickly be put into universal use.

Layer 5: The Session Layer. Network functions that bind communicating entities together are grouped into what the ISO calls the session layer. This is best illustrated by analogy. Without establishing some kind of session, networks would work a lot like postcards. A postcard can be mailed to any address; the permission of the addressee is not needed, and it may not even be known whether the address is valid. The sender may or may not get an acknowledgment that the postcard was received.

Establishing a session makes communications on the network more like a telephone call. The called party answers the telephone and joins in on the conversation until both parties say goodbye and hang up. Once this phone call has been established, everything either party hears over the phone is assumed to be for their benefit and to originate with the opposite party.

In conventional computing environments, log-on functions fulfill the role of the session layer. Most user identification and authentication systems function at this level.

Layer 4: The Transport Layer. Networks need a set of functions that are capable of reliably delivering arbitrary amounts of data to a specific destination, no matter what that data is or how much data must be delivered. The network tools that are prepared to receive that data and the instructions for its delivery are referred to as the transport layer in the OSI model.

Some encryption systems function at the transport layer. Although it is better to encrypt at this layer than to not encrypt at all, security personnel should be aware that encryption applied by the sending party at the transport layer will be removed by the receiving party at the transport layer. As a result, all of the equipment and software implementing the session, presentation, and application layers at both ends will see the data in cleartext. This could present unacceptable risks.

Layer 3: The Network Layer. Larger, more sophisticated networks require tools that can determine alternative routes between origin and destination to compensate for traffic congestion, system failure, scheduled maintenance of equipment, or conflicting priorities. The OSI model suggests that the equipment and software responsible for these functions should exchange data with the transport layer and should be called the network layer.

Encryption applied at this layer could be designed with sufficient intelligence to ensure that messages sent across routes with the highest risk of exposure used the strongest cryptographic algorithms; information sent across more trusted paths might be sent in cleartext. However, security personnel should be aware that any encryption applied by equipment or software at the originating station's network layer is automatically removed at the receiving station's network layer and would therefore traverse the transport, session, presentation, and application layers at both ends without protection.

Furthermore, intermediate switching nodes may remove encryption at their own network layers. It may be impossible to route encrypted information across network switching nodes without first supplying those nodes with the equipment and keys necessary to decrypt the information.

Layer 2: The Data Link Layer. To handle large volumes of data, networks need tools that divide large pieces of information into smaller packets for transmission and then reassemble the information after transmission. Each packet must contain enough information to allow reassembly in the proper sequence. The equipment and software used to perform these functions constitute the data link layer.

Many vendors offer products that encrypt individual packets of information and these would be grouped under this layer of the OSI model. Encryption applied at the originating station's data link layer is removed at the destination station's data link layer and therefore traverses all of the upper layers in cleartext. Furthermore, intermediate network nodes performing routing, buffering, or switching functions may not be able to handle encrypted packets unless they are equipped with the hardware, software, and keys necessary to decrypt the packets. This may create unacceptable exposures, especially with regard to the proliferation of cryptographic keys.

Layer 1: The Physical Layer. All networks need a physical means of transmitting and receiving information (e.g., telephone wires, coaxial cables, optical fibers, radio waves, or infrared beams). These components are the physical layer. Security equipment functioning at the physical layer includes tamper-resistant or tamper-evident connectors and fiber-optic backbones designed to make wiretapping difficult. This type of security equipment is usually oriented toward preventing wiretaps by unauthorized intruders; it generally cannot prevent abuse of workstations that are legitimately connected.

Analyzing the Networks

Security personnel must learn how to analyze large networks by dividing them into subnetworks. They then must test each subnetwork to identify the broadcast segments.

Although vendor literature identifies the broadcast segments, a more practical approach is to simply locate the physical layer of the network (usually a cable or set of cables) and follow it from end to end. If the same cable connects directly to two or more workstations or servers, it is probably a broadcast segment. If each network node is attached to its own separate cable, it is important to ensure that all the cables come together at a common point. Lack of a common connection point indicates that broadcast is probably not being used. If all of the separate wires come together, especially in a wiring closet or hub, broadcast is probably being used.

Security personnel should establish guidelines that outline the appropriate procedures to follow when broadcast networks are installed or when a broadcast segment is added to an existing nonbroadcast network. Encryption is recommended for broadcast segments and should be applied as close as possible to the point of creation of sensitive information.

TECHNICAL SOLUTIONS AND TOOLS

As of this writing, the best available technical means for securing networks of computers with critical applications or with sensitive information are:

- Nonreplayable user authentication technologies (e.g., dynamic password-generation systems).
- Software for encrypting information on shared file systems.
- Software for encrypting information on modems.
- Data link encryption boxes.
- Bulk encryptors.

These technologies fall under two categories—host-based controls and network-based controls—as discussed in the following sections.

Host-Based Controls

Most of the useful technical solutions currently available involve host-based controls. The two most commonly used host-based controls are nonreplayable user authentication and software for encrypting information on file systems. These two methods are not mutually exclusive; indeed, they are complementary. They are discussed in the following sections.

Nonreplayable User Authentication. Most user ID verification involves asking the user for a secret, memorized password. When any such password traverses a broadcast segment of a network, however, it becomes impossible to ensure that the password remains unknown to others. Because it is impossible to determine whether the password was compromised, user accountability is lost.

It is possible to identify users in ways that cannot be captured and replayed, even if the interchange takes place on a broadcast network. The most widely used method involves dynamic or one-time passwords, which are available in both hardware and software for most types of computers and networks. For example, users may be issued a hardware-based device that calculates passwords. When the computer or application needs to verify the identity of the user, it displays a short, random number and challenges the user to encrypt it with the user's password device and then send the encrypted password back. If the user returns the wrong password, access is denied. Authorized users equipped with properly registered password devices are easily able to encrypt the random number and return the correct response. Because the random number and the associated response are different every time, it is impossible for the password to be compromised and used again; old responses are instantly invalidated.

These systems are sometimes referred to as true one-time password systems to differentiate them from limited-duration password systems, which calculate a dynamic password that is valid for a predetermined period of time (e.g., 60 seconds). Limited-duration passwords provide excellent protection against intrusion from outsiders. However, extra measures must be taken to make them immune from unauthorized use by internal intruders; therefore, they are impractical when broadcast networks are used, if user accountability is required.

Encryption on Shared File Systems. Software for encrypting information on shared file systems automatically encrypts sensitive files as they are created; the files then traverse the networks in their encrypted form, safe from compromise even on broadcast segments. When these files are retrieved from storage, they again traverse intervening networks in their encrypted state and are decrypted only inside authorized workstations.

Network security officers should carefully evaluate the claims of vendors of encryption software to verify that sensitive information is encrypted as it traverses the network, not just while it resides on disk or tape storage devices. As a general rule, software for encrypting disk drives fails this test because disk systems generally enforce encryption at the disk sector or disk cluster level; sectors and clusters are fundamentally limited to the logic that is physically close to the disk drive being protected. Files stored on network file servers are usually redirected across the network at a higher level, before disk encryption software has a chance to encrypt them.

Encryption that is enforced at the file level can enforce encryption before network logic redirects the file for access across the network. Thus, it is much more effective at protecting sensitive information from exposure on broadcast LANs or WANs.

Encryption software for file systems is currently available for computers running MS-DOS and compatible operating systems and for Macintosh computers. Other operating systems (UNIX in particular) may soon be available with software for encrypting file systems. Interoperability between different file systems is limited, however, which complicates file sharing in some circumstances. In general, only files that are encrypted with the Data Encryption Standard (DES) can be shared across a network between hosts running different file-encrypting software. Some manual intervention is usually necessary to establish mutually agreeable cryptographic keys and DES modes of operation.

Network-Based Controls

Sometimes it is best to apply security inside individual hosts because that is where information originates and ultimately resides. However, certain security needs are better dealt with at the network level. At this time, two security controls dominate this area: end-to-end encryption and node authentication. These are discussed in the following sections.

End-to-End Encryption. It is possible to equip two or more network locations with a cryptographic network interface (either software or hardware) so that any information they exchange is automatically encrypted as it traverses the network but is decrypted on receipt at the destination. This arrangement, commonly referred to as end-to-end encryption, is especially useful when it is necessary to encrypt datagrams or data packets that do not form portions of files and therefore cannot be directly encrypted by the software on the file system. Examples include certain types of E-mail, especially older E-mail systems that may lack the flexibility available in newer E-mail applications.

In addition, certain types of network printing applications may send sensitive jobs directly to print servers through datagrams or transport mechanisms that are never treated as files. If it is impossible or impractical to have such systems use a file-level interface, the encryption software on the file system cannot protect them; end-to-end encryption asserted by network equipment may be the only feasible alternative.

End-to-end encryption is easy to understand. Its main advantage is that everything traversing the network between encrypted endpoints is encrypted. However, because everything is decrypted at the opposite end, nothing is encrypted beyond the endpoints. Therefore, all information is left unprotected inside the hosts (and sometimes inside network switching or routing equipment).

Another disadvantage of end-to-end encryption is that it tends to be expensive. It is usually necessary to use hardware modules to keep up with network traffic. In addition, existing network interface equipment often must be removed and replaced with more expensive encrypting units.

Another aspect of end-to-end encryption must be understood: installing end-to-end encryption hardware between a pair of nodes on a network may make those nodes incompatible with the rest of the network. Equipment operating at other network layers may become confused when asked to route or buffer the encrypted information. Therefore, it is usually necessary to install corresponding cryptographic equipment on many or all nodes in the entire network before information can be encrypted for network use.

Node Authentication. Universities with large networks have recently concentrated their security efforts on network-based node authentication. The best known of these efforts involves a sophisticated protocol called Kerberos, which was placed into the public domain by the Massachusetts Institute of Technology.

Most implementations of the Kerberos authentication protocol are compiled into UNIX-based network workstations. These work in cooperation with a UNIX-based network authentication server to access other UNIX-based hosts that have been similarly equipped with Kerberos-capable software. User name and password information is exchanged with the Kerberos server before any attempt is made to access another workstation or host.

By prior arrangements, the Kerberos server knows cryptographic keys with which it can carry on short dialogues with all protected workstations. (Each key is distinct from the others.) The workstations use these predetermined keys to persuade the Kerberos server of their authenticity; upon authentication, the server generates a certificate for the host that the user wants to access. Portions of this certificate are encrypted using keys known only to the requester, and other portions are encrypted using keys known only to the computer being accessed. By reading the portions of the certificate that it can read, the requesting node receives instructions on accessing the destination. By delivering to the destination node those portions of the certificate that only the destination node can read, the requesting node can assure the destination node that the authentication server has been involved in the dialogue for setting up the session. The destination node then grants access.

This mechanism provides excellent node authentication. However, the protocols involved are too complicated for users to carry out by themselves, even if they are equipped with a sophisticated, self-contained password-issuing device. The typical interface between users and the workstation consists of a simple user name and password protocol. Therefore, user authentication under this scheme is not as strong as the node authentication it provides. (Kerberos is fully compatible with the one-time dynamic passwords discussed previously, however.)

SUMMARY

Managing a network of interconnected computers requires an entirely different approach from managing a group of individual computers. From the security administrator's perspective, it is not so much the existence of the network that changes the administrative issues as the way most networks operate. It is therefore imperative that security administrators understand those portions of networking technology that affect information security.

Communications Security

The remote use of computers and related applications has increased rapidly in the past few years. The use of communications facilities to link users and computers brings with it a number of serious concerns. The most obvious is the need to protect sensitive data being sent over great distances from being disclosed to unauthorized persons intentionally or accidentally. However, just as important are such issues as knowing with certainty who sent the message, that it was received by the intended person, and that it arrived intact and unmodified. Such mechanisms and techniques as encryption, message authentication, and digital signatures can be used to provide the necessary assurances. It behooves information security managers to thoroughly understand the appropriate use of available controls so that they can adequately protect the information under their care.

Section III-2 begins with a discussion of the security of open systems interconnection (OSI) networks. This chapter describes how communications are performed between two information systems that conform to a certain set of international standards. The goal of OSI is to allow communications among a large number of geographically distributed computer systems produced by different manufacturers, including those manufactured or located in different countries.

Another service that is becoming available to users is the integrated services digital network (ISDN). ISDN provides switched communications capabilities for the world's public voice and data services, as well as packet-switched data services. Because of ISDN's potential importance in future communications, security of ISDN applications is a significant concern to information security managers. A thorough discussion of the security of ISDN is provided in Chapter III-2-2.

Encryption is generally considered to be the best method of protecting data in a network environment. Therefore, a handbook addressing network and communications security would not be complete without covering the subject of cryptography. Chapter III-2-3 provides a complete discussion of cryptography, including basic types of cryptographic algorithms.

Electronic data interchange (EDI) has become a powerful tool that can save organizations time and money by shortening lead times and reducing paper flow and inventories. However, reducing controls over source documents increases risks to the integrity of the information being communicated. Chapter III-2-4 provides a complete review of the internal controls needed to ensure secure communications in EDI environments.

Security of OSI-Based Networks

DENNIS K. BRANSTAD ▪ WILLIAM E. BURR

Open systems interconnection (OSI) specifies how communications are executed between two information systems that conform to a set of international standards. The goal of OSI is to allow communications among a large number of geographically distributed computer systems produced by different manufacturers (including those manufactured or located in different countries).

OSI provides a network architecture that designers can use as a common structure for building computer networks. It also gives network security designers a foundation on which security services can be defined and built. In addition, OSI provides a common vocabulary for designers and users in specifying the information communications that are desired and provided.

The OSI standards consist of two components. The OSI basic reference model (ISO 7498) provides a model for communications between open systems. The OSI security architecture, published as Part 2 of the basic reference model (ISO 7498-2), provides a security architecture for communications between open systems. This architecture has become the generally accepted standard in security for open systems.

Other efforts at developing open systems standards address security in a broader range of areas, including information processing and storage as well as communications. In this regard, the European Computer Manufacturers Association (ECMA) has been instrumental in addressing a broad scope of security issues relating to open systems. Although these efforts have focused on the security architecture, efforts are under way to develop security protocols that implement the architecture.

The seven-layer communications protocol specified by the OSI reference model is illustrated in Exhibit III-2-1. Each layer of the model communicates on a peer-to-peer basis between end systems or between an end system and an intermediate system. The interfaces between layers are defined by logical services that cannot be observed directly; only peer-to-peer entity communications can be observed externally.

EXHIBIT III-2-1 Open Systems Interconnection Reference Model

Layer	Function
7. Application	Services for user applications (e.g., file transfer, mail, directory)
6. Presentation	Code conversion and data reformatting
5. Session	Coordinates interactions between end-application processes
4. Transport	End-to-end data integrity and quality of service
3. Network	Routing and segmenting owing to subnetwork packet size limits
2. Data Link	Framing and error detection
1. Physical	Physical transport of bits

End System — Intermediate System — End System (layers 7–1)

OSI SECURITY GOALS

Use of a standard security architecture allows one OSI system to communicate with another while maintaining the desired security; it also facilitates the implementation of security services in commercial products. OSI security goals for communicated information include:

- Protection from unauthorized modification.
- Protection from undetected loss or repetition.
- Protection from unauthorized disclosure.
- Assurance of the correct identity of the data's sender.
- Assurance of the correct receiver of the data.

Achieving these security goals in the OSI architecture ensures that the data being transmitted from one OSI system to another will not be modified, disclosed, replayed, or lost in the network without the sender or the intended receiver being notified and that the participating parties in the transaction have been correctly identified. Achieving these security goals ensures protection of the data's integrity and confidentiality.

Other desirable security objectives include:

- Labeling data according to its sensitivity or source.
- Disclosing the identities of the sender and recipient and the quantity of data exchanged to only the sender and recipient.

- Providing security audit trails of network communications.
- Ensuring that data inside the OSI system cannot be transmitted using covert information channels.
- Proving to an independent third party that a communication did occur and that the correct contents were received.
- Obtaining explicit authorization for access to a system before connecting to the system.

Negotiated Security

To provide maximum flexibility for the users of OSI implementation, users should be consulted in selecting an optimum set of OSI services, including security services. Some organizations may not wish to allow negotiation of certain security services, however, especially if the negotiation could result in less than a predetermined minimum level of security. Other organizations may be willing to negotiate away all security services if those services are even temporarily causing operational problems. Still other organizations may choose to add to the security services provided in the base implementations and not allow other organizations to know about or use these additional services. A security architecture that can selectively support negotiated security services is necessary to provide special services without causing an unacceptable overhead on users not requiring those services.

Security Beyond the OSI Environment

OSI is concerned only with the interconnection of systems. To be effective, OSI security measures must be used in conjunction with security mechanisms that fall outside the scope of OSI. If such supporting security measures are not implemented, overall system security may be threatened. For example, information traffic between systems may be encrypted but may still be compromised if no physical security restrictions are placed on access to the systems themselves.

OSI SECURITY ARCHITECTURE

The OSI security architecture defines the following five basic security services for secure open systems communication:

- *Authentication.* This service provides a reliable answer to the question, "With whom am I communicating?" Authentication services are provided by an entity at one layer to the entity at the layer immediately above it.
- *Access control.* This service controls access to resources accessible through OSI communications as well as to the communications services themselves. Access controls rely on the authentication service to reliably identify the entity seeking access.

619

- *Data confidentiality*. This service protects data from unauthorized disclosure. Protection may be extended to all data sets or to specific data fields. Traffic flow confidentiality may also be provided to protect information generated by traffic analysis.

- *Data integrity*. This service protects against the unauthorized modification, insertion, deletion, or replay of all data sets or of selected fields. The integrity service may provide for recovery from integrity faults, or it may simply detect them.

- *Nonrepudiation*. This service prevents parties to a communication from denying that they sent or received it or from disputing its contents. It may provide either proof or origin or proof of delivery.

To implement these services, the ISO security architecture defines eight mechanisms:

- *Encryption*. Encryption protects the confidentiality of data. Two classes of encryption are defined: symmetric (i.e., secret key), and asymmetric (i.e., public key).

- *Digital signature*. This is the use of cryptographic technology to authenticate the identity of the originator of data and to protect the integrity of the data. A digital signature is produced using the private cryptographic key of the signer and verified using the public key of the signer. Therefore it can be proved that only the holder of that private information could have originated the signature. Asymmetric cryptography is used to produce the signature.

- *Access control*. Access control mechanisms grant or deny requests for access to cryptography resources by authenticated entities. Access control is based on authentication data bases, authentication information, security labels, the time of attempted access, the route of attempted access, and the duration of access.

- *Data integrity*. Data integrity mechanisms are used to protect the integrity of a single protocol data unit (PDU) (i.e., connectionless integrity) or a sequence of PDUs (i.e., connection integrity). The usual means of ensuring the integrity of a PDU is a check value, which is a function of the data in the PDU. The check value may then be encrypted or signed to prevent its alteration. The sequence of PDUs may be ensured by sequence numbering, time stamping, or cryptographic chaining.

- *Authentication exchange*. This mechanism is used to authenticate protocol entities. Passwords and cryptographic techniques, with suitable handshakes, provide either unilateral or mutual authentication.

- *Traffic padding*. Observation of traffic patterns, even when encrypted, may yield information to an intruder. This mechanism may be used to confound the analysis of traffic patterns.

EXHIBIT III-2-2 Security Services by OSI Level

Service	Physical	Data Link	Network	Transport	Session	Presentation	Application
Authentication							
Peer Entity			X	X		X	X
Data Origin			X	X		X	X
Access Control			X	X			X
Confidentiality							
Connection	X	X	X	X		✔	X
Connectionless		X	X	X		✔	X
Selective Field						✔	X
Traffic Flow	X		X			X	X
Data Integrity							
Connection with Recovery				X		X	X
Connection without Recovery			X	X		X	X
Selective Field Connection						X	X
Connectionless			X	X		X	X
Selective Field Connectionless						X	X
Nonrepudiation							
Proof of Origin						X	X
Proof of Delivery						X	X

Key:
X   Service may be provided
✔   Service will be provided

- *Routing control.* Routes can be chosen that use only secure links.
- *Notarization.* This mechanism ensures the authenticity of specific OSI layers in specific end systems through a trusted third party (e.g., a dedicated computer system) that verifies identities and records information about a communication that can be used to prove what transpired during the communication. This automated mechanism is equivalent to the process performed by a notary public, who is certified to legitimize certain legal transactions.

The ISO security architecture defines the appropriate protocol levels for each security service and the mechanisms that may be used to implement them. Exhibit III-2-2 illustrates the assignment of services to levels, and Exhibit III-2-3 shows the mechanisms used by each service.

EXHIBIT III-2-3   OSI Security Services and Mechanisms

Mechanism

Service	Encipherment	Digital Signature	Access Control	Data Integrity	Authentication Exchange	Traffic Padding	Routing Control	Notarization
Authentication								
Peer Entity	X	X			X			
Data Origin	X	X						
Access Control			X					
Confidentiality								
Connection	X						X	
Connectionless	X						X	
Selective Field	X							
Traffic Flow	X					X	X	
Data Integrity								
Connection with Recovery	X			X				
Connection without Recovery	X			X				
Selective Field Connection	X			X				
Connectionless	X	X		X				
Selective Field Connectionless	X	X		X				
Nonrepudiation								
Proof of Origin		X		✔				X
Proof of Delivery		✔		✔				✔

Key:
X   Service may be provided
✔   Service will be provided

OSI Security Service Calls

OSI security services can be implemented using service calls to software modules that perform the desired security service. The general format of a service call command line includes the name of the service, the names of the parameters provided to the service module, and the names of the results returned by the module. The following are examples of typical service calls:

- AUTHENTICATE (ID; authenticator) RETURN (result; status).
  This call verifies that the authenticator corresponds with the claimed ID by searching the local secure management information base and responding with the correct result and status.
- AUTHORIZE (ID; type; resource) RETURN (result; status).
  This call verifies the authorization of the user's ID with the indicated type for access to the requested resource and returns the correct result and status.

- ENCIPHER (PT; length; keyname) RETURN (CT; length; status).
  This call encrypts plaintext, beginning at PT, for the indicated length into ciphertext, beginning at CT, for the indicated length and sets the resulting status using the key associated with keyname.
- DECIPHER (CT; length; keyname) RETURN (PT; length; status).
  This call decodes ciphertext, beginning at CT, for the indicated length into plaintext, beginning at PT, for the indicated length and sets the resulting status using the key associated with keyname.
- COMPUTEMAC (data; length; keyname) RETURN (MAC; status).
  This call computes a message authentication code (MAC) on the data of indicated length using the key associated with the keyname and sets the resulting status.
- VERIFYMAC (data; length; keyname; MAC) RETURN (result).
  This call computes a test MAC on the data of indicated length using the key associated with the keyname and returns the correct result to indicate if the test MAC is identical with the input MAC.
- SIGN (data; length; ID; keyname) RETURN (signature; status).
  This call computes a signature on the data of indicated length for the user indicated by the user ID using the key associated with the keyname and sets the resulting status.
- VERIFYSIGNATURE (data; length; ID; keyname; signature) RETURN (result; status).
  This call computes a test signature on the data of indicated length for the user indicated by the user ID using the key associated with the keyname, compares it with the signature, and sets the correct result and status.

SECURE DATA NETWORK SYSTEM

The secure data network system (SDNS) was developed as a cooperative project between the US government and industry. The SDNS architecture and protocols can be overlayed on the OSI communications protocol.

The SDNS protocols work by encapsulating protocol data units (PDUs) for a given security protocol (e.g., SP3) in a security envelope, as illustrated in Exhibit III-2-4. A protected header for the data unit is placed in front of the PDU; this header optionally contains security labels, sequence numbers, and addresses. An integrity check value (ICV) is computed for the protected header and the PDU and is placed behind the PDU. The PDU, the protected header, and the ICV are then optionally encrypted. A clear header is then attached in front of the protected header. The primary use of the clear header is to identify the keys used to protect the PDU.

SDNS defines two somewhat similar protocols: security protocol 4 (SP4) at the bottom of the transport layer and security protocol 3 (SP3) at the top of the net-

EXHIBIT III-2-4 Security Encapsulation of a PDU

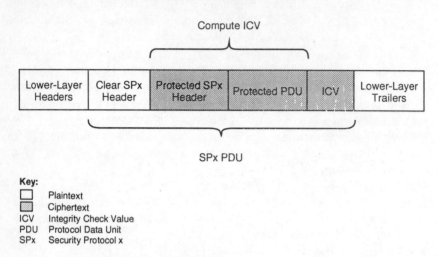

Compute ICV

| Lower-Layer Headers | Clear SPx Header | Protected SPx Header | Protected PDU | ICV | Lower-Layer Trailers |

SPx PDU

Key:
▢ Plaintext
▨ Ciphertext
ICV Integrity Check Value
PDU Protocol Data Unit
SPx Security Protocol x

work layer. SP4 provides cryptographic protection from end system to end system through the use of intermediate systems (see Exhibit III-2-1). A separate key can be established for each transport connection, even when the transport connections are between the same transport entities.

SP3 can be used from end system to end system, end system to intermediate system, or intermediate system to intermediate system. SP3 supports inclusion of source and destination addresses in the protected header. All connections between the same pair of end systems are protected by the same keys.

ISO SECURITY STANDARDS FOR OSI

There are several ongoing efforts to develop OSI security standards within the International Standards Organization (ISO). Two standards subcommittees are responsible for developing OSI standards, including security standards: ISO/IEC/JTC1/SC21 is responsible for OSI architecture layers 4 through 7 and SC6 is responsible for layers 1 through 3. In addition, an ISO subcommittee is responsible for development of technical security standards for information systems, and SC18 is responsible for X.400, the message-handling system and is developing security enhancements in conjunction with CCITT.

The SDNS SP4 protocol was proposed as an ISO standard and has evolved to a draft international standard (DIS) called the transport layer security protocol (ISO 10736). Similarly, the SP3 protocol has evolved to a proposed international standard called the network layer security (ISO 11577). The network layer security protocol and the transport layer security protocol are being developed by SC21.

The network layer security protocol supports two basic modes of secure operation, corresponding with connectionless and connection-oriented network services. The first is a mode of communication that uses independent packets to transfer information among communicating computers without first establishing a logical connection. The second establishes a logical connection between a pair of communicating computers, then passes data through the logical connection, finally terminating the logical connection when all the desired data has been received.

The transport layer security protocol also supports two basic modes of secure operation, corresponding with the connectionless mode transport service (ISO 8602) and the connection-oriented transport layer protocol (ISO 8073). The transport layer security protocol addresses a wide range of risk environments and can optionally implement confidentiality, integrity, authentication, and access control services as specified in ISO 7498-2.

Selection of which standard to use depends on several factors: granularity of security required, trust of the end system, implementation (integrated into the end system or in a standalone, in-line system), and cost. The transport layer security protocol provides improved security granularity between end systems while the network layer security protocol may be easier to implement in a standalone enhancement to an existing network.

In addition, work is under way to add needed security features to the X.400/ISO 8505-1 message-handling system and the X.500/ISO DIS 9594 directory services standards. Security services for message-handling systems are defined in ISO 10021 and CCITT X.400. The security services provide for authentication of message origin, confidentiality of message content, integrity of message content, and nonrepudiation of message origin and delivery. Security information (e.g., cryptographic algorithm identifier, cryptographic key identifier, and the security label) is contained in the header of the message. Additional security enhancements are being developed in other interpersonal messaging systems for special applications like military electronic mail and privacy-enhanced mail.

Security enhancements for the directory system are specified in ISO 9594 and CCITT X.500. Authentication and access control services are provided for directory entries. The directory may also be used as a repository for such security-related information as cryptographic keys and digital signature certificates.

General security techniques are being developed within three working groups of SC27. These techniques include key management, security criteria, security evaluation methods, digital signatures, authentication exchange mechanisms, and nonrepudiation techniques. SC27 also operates the International Register of Cryptographic Algorithms in accordance with the rules of registration contained in ISO 9979. The National Computer Centre in the United Kingdom is responsible for maintaining this international register.

IEEE LOCAL AREA NETWORK SECURITY STANDARDS

Local area networks (LANs) have particular security requirements, including secure broadcast messages. IEEE is developing standards for interoperable LAN security (IEEE 802.10). Three standards are addressed:

- Secure data exchange, a data link level protocol providing confidentiality, integrity, data origin authentication, and access control services.
- Key management protocol, a layer-7 service that supports secure data exchange.
- System/security management, which is a layer-7 set of services used to manage the security protocols.

SUMMARY

The objective of OSI standards and protocols is to enable secure communication among a diverse set of geographically distributed computer systems. The OSI network architecture provides a common foundation for building computer networks and supporting security services. The OSI security architecture provides an architecture for securing communications between open systems. SDNS protocols supplement the OSI communications protocols and form the basis for developing international standards.

Security of the Integrated Services Digital Network

WILLIAM E. BURR ▪ DENNIS K. BRANSTAD

At its conception around 15 years ago, the integrated services digital network (ISDN) was projected to be the universal network that would go everywhere and handle all voice and data applications. Developing one integrated network to serve nearly all voice and data applications was probably never realistic. As ISDN becomes a reality, it is proving to be somewhat less than universal. Nevertheless, it is an important development in the worldwide public network and will considerably extend its utility for data. The digital nature of ISDN also offers an opportunity to provide security services that were previously impractical.

ISDN will provide switched communications capabilities for the world's public voice and data networks in the coming decades. ISDN provides users with digital circuit-switched voice and data services as well as packet-switched data services. In addition to end-to-end digital services, ISDN supports interworking with existing analog voice circuits and equipment. Although the digital switching capability required for ISDN is now widely available in the public network, ISDN services are just beginning to become available to users.

Because of ISDN's anticipated importance in future communications, security of ISDN applications is a significant concern. This chapter focuses primarily on security for users of the public ISDN. It considers voice and data security in the general context of communications and open systems security and provides a broad discussion of user security needs and possible solutions. It does not attempt to prescribe specific detailed solutions.

ISDN USER SERVICE INTERFACES

ISDN provides digital voice and data services to public network subscribers. Two somewhat different service interfaces are offered by public network service providers. One is the basic rate interface, which provides a single physical line with two independent, circuit-switched 64K-bps B channels and one packet-switched 16K-bps D channel; this interface is often called 2B + D. The B channels may be used for digital voice or to provide a direct digital 64K-bps isochronous channel between computers or other digital devices. Service providers and independent networks also offer B channel packet services. The D channel is used for signaling—that is, for exchanging control information between an ISDN terminal and a network switch (e.g., to set up B channel calls). In addition, the D channel can provide packet-switched services to users. Because ISDN provides for conversion between the new digital voice services and existing analog terminals, it is possible to complete a voice call between a digital ISDN terminal and an analog telephone.

The other interface offered by public network service providers is the primary rate interface, which in North America bundles together 23 64K-bps B channels and one 64K-bps D channel (often referred to as 23B + D). It is equivalent to the established T1 1.536M-bps telephone carrier. The 23 B channels can be independently circuit switched through the network, and each can carry voice or data. The D channel carries signaling packets (e.g., to set up each of the B channels). It may also carry packet-switched user data packets. The primary rate interface is primarily used to connect a user private branch exchange (PBX) or multiplexer to the public network. Outside North America, the primary rate interface is usually 30 B channels plus one D channel (30B + D).

ISDN defines four interface points, as illustrated in Exhibit III-2-5. The U interface is used to connect the network transmission and switching equipment to the user premises. A network termination (NT1) converts the U interface to the T interface. The T interface in turn connects the NT1 to another network termination (NT2), which is a piece of customer-premises switching equipment (e.g., a PBX or multiplexer). The S interface connects the NT2 to terminal equipment or to a terminal adapter (TA). The terminal equipment is an ISDN telephone, a computer terminal, a fax machine, or similar devices. The terminal adapter adapts a pre-ISDN terminal for use with ISDN, at an R interface point (not shown in the exhibit). In many cases, the R interface is an RS-232 serial interface. In some cases, there is no NT2 and the S and T interfaces, which are electrically identical, collapse into an S/T interface. The S interface includes a provision for a passive bus, to which up to 8 pieces of terminal equipment may be attached.

EXHIBIT III-2-5   ISDN Interface Point Model

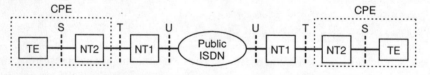

Notes:
CPE   Customer premises equipment
NT1   Network termination 1
NT2   Network termination 2 (typically a PBX or multiplexer)
S   ISDN interface point
T   ISDN interface point
TE   Terminal equipment
U   ISDN interface point

ISDN services are expected to be widely available from network services providers by the mid-1990s. There will be a transition period of more than a decade while ISDN gradually supplants the current analog services.

ISDN PRINCIPLES AND GOALS

The original principles of the International Telephone and Telegraph Consultative Committee's (CCITT's) ISDN standards are:

- The standardization of services offered to subscribers to enable services to be internationally compatible.
- The standardization of user-network interfaces to enable terminal equipment to be portable and to assist in standardizing services to subscribers.
- The standardization of network capabilities to the degree necessary to allow user-to-network and network-to-network interworking and to achieve standardization of services and user-network interfaces.

Portability of terminals and the ability to transport services internationally were the major goals; to accomplish this, user-network interfaces, services, and capabilities were standardized. Although network capabilities were standardized, internal network interfaces were not included, nor was portability of network switching equipment.

A secondary goal was to provide end-to-end digital connectivity. Although computer data traffic is a small part of the overall network load, it is growing quickly. Digital fax traffic is growing very rapidly. The digital B-channel service provides about a 4:1 improvement over the data rates that can ordinarily be achieved over analog voice circuits.

REFERENCE MODELS FOR ISDN

The protocols for the reference model for open systems interconnection (OSI) are peer-to-peer protocols, and its vertical interfaces are defined only as logical service primitives. An observer on the interconnection medium sees a series of nested, encapsulated protocol data units (PDUs), with the PDU of each layer encapsulated in that of its lower neighbor. For example, an application-layer PDU can be encapsulated six or more times. The OSI is a simple and powerful paradigm. Its major goal is broad interconnection of open systems. OSI can reliably get packets across many successive dissimilar networks. Although quality-of-service parameters may be specified, the OSI makes few performance guarantees, is in no sense real time, and does not include a concept of synchronism.

ISDN has a different paradigm. Although a packet D-channel service is provided for signaling and for user-to-user packet services, ISDN is primarily a circuit-switched network. The fundamental service is a 64K-bps, isochronous, full-duplex, circuit-switched, 8-bit byte–aligned, point-to-point B channel. It offers a modest and unvarying delay and a constant data rate. Provided that the rate is adequate, it is suitable for real-time applications and telemetry. Furthermore, because of the pervasive nature of the telephone network, if ISDN becomes universal in the telephone system, these B-channel circuits become available on demand from any place directly to any other place.

A rather complex reference model derived from the OSI model has been defined for ISDN (see Exhibit III-2-6). This model is primarily useful for circuit-switched B-channel connections. With seven layers and three vertical planes, it is somewhat difficult to follow. The front, or user, plane represents the circuit-switched B channel. Except in the end terminals, this plane never rises above the physical layer. The second, or control, plane deals with signaling and control of switching. This is defined between customer premises equipment and the network by the Q.931 signaling protocol. Between the public network switches, this function is performed by the signaling system seven (SS#7) protocol. The rear, or management, plane is concerned with the management of the network.

In OSI systems, the management function is usually conceived as an application-layer function with special access to the internals of each of the layers. There is no concept of a separate out-of-band signaling path for network control; all control is an in-band function of either the system management application process or peer-layer management protocols.

Some general texts on ISDN attempt to decompose the model presented in Exhibit III-2-6 into a single plane or into separate single planes for the B and D channels, making the model appear more like the OSI model. By isolating separate functions, these models may be somewhat easier to understand. However, ISDN does not map into the OSI model in an entirely satisfying way. OSI is defined in terms of peer-to-peer protocols, whereas ISDN is defined primarily in terms of interface points and highly asymmetric protocols between a terminal and the network defined at those points.

There are two fundamentally different modes of operation in ISDN, corresponding to the circuit-switched B channel and the packet D channel. The circuit-switched B channel roughly corresponds to the front, or user, plane of the model shown in Exhibit III-2-6, and the packet D channel corresponds roughly to the middle, or control, plane.

In usual operation, a terminal equipment device uses the D channel for signaling. Using an asymmetric protocol (Q.931), the terminal equipment sends packets to the network switch to which it is attached to set up a circuit connection on the B channel. The network uses the SS#7 protocol to communicate between network switches or separate networks, and the destination switch sends Q.931 packets to the destination terminal equipment. Q.931 packets, which effectively go from one terminal equipment device to another, are encapsulated in SS#7 packets while they cross the network. Other Q.931 packets are generated by the network switches and sent to the terminal equipment.

EXHIBIT III-2-6 ISDN Protocol Reference Model

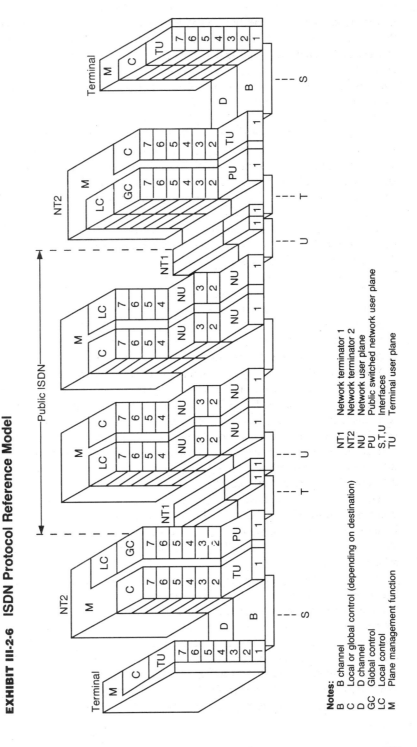

Notes:
B   B channel
C   Local or global control (depending on destination)
D   D channel
GC Global control
LC Local control
M   Plane management function

NT1   Network terminator 1
NT2   Network terminator 2
NU   Network user plane
PU   Public switched network user plane
S,T,U Interfaces
TU   Terminal user plane

If the destination terminal equipment accepts the call, a B channel connection is established between the two terminal equipment devices. Actual data transfer, be it data or voice, usually takes place on the B channel.

In recent years, there has been a trend to increase the integral user-to-user packet functions of ISDN. When user-to-user packet switching is applied to the D channel, this is in some respects straightforward; there is inherently a D-channel packet handler in every switch line card. There are two mechanisms for sending packet data from user to user over the D channel. One incorporates a user-to-user field in SS#7 packets and sends those packets through SS#7. The other routes D-channel packets to a separate user-to-user packet handler rather than to signal processing and SS#7.

When the B channel is to be used for packet data, it is circuit switched to a packet handler. Although service providers purport to provide B-channel packet services as a built-in feature of ISDN, there is logically no difference from a circuit-switched connection to a packet handler provided by an independent service provider.

For users, the major purpose of OSI is its application-layer services. Among them are the file transfer, access, and management (FTAM), directory services, and message-handling system electronic-mail protocols. Some of these applications, particularly the last two, are intended as much specialized teleservices that run directly on ISDN with X.25 as they are OSI applications. Therefore, the application itself can provide whatever end-to-end services may be needed in the application (including security services) and does not depend entirely on OSI end-to-end services. Moreover, the applications involve functions beyond the scope of data transmission, particularly data storage, with its own distinct security requirements.

In addition to the directory services and message-handling system protocols, which are intended to run directly on ISDN as well as the OSI stack, there are several other specialized services or teleservices defined for operation over ISDN, and more may be expected. The existing services are primarily derived from services defined for the analog telephone network, including fax, teletex, videotex, and telex. Standards for motion video over the B channel and for video conferencing are expected soon. Some of these services typically use the ISDN B channel as an end-to-end pipe, and the functions are embodied in the terminal equipment. However, some (e.g., mail or directory services) may rely on a service provider attached to the network. Many other specialized information services, though not necessarily fully defined by standards, may be attached to the network.

COMMUNICATIONS SERVICES

One of the major goals of ISDN is terminal portability. Current ISDN standards and products do not meet this goal. In general, current terminal equipment must be designed and tested to work with specific switch products. Indeed, some switch vendors maintain two models of terminals to work with different generations of their switches. Vendors of terminal equipment find that terminal equipment firmware must be updated whenever switch software is updated, and terminal equipment that used to operate properly with a switch may fail to do so when the software of the switch moves to a new release.

Part of the reason for terminal nonportability is the many options and features allowed by the ISDN standards. Different switch vendors select different sets of features. In addition, switch vendors implement many proprietary features that are not defined in ISDN. Many of these proprietary features are motivated by a desire to allow public telephone service providers to offer centrex services comparable to the advanced features of PBXs.

ISDN implementations are currently confined to small islands, typically only a single switch or a few similar switches. This is a far cry from the vision of a vast global ISDN. Bellcore is attempting to address these problem with a series of technical reports, including reports on the ISDN foundation and on end-user features. However, operation across international boundaries of any services beyond basic voice and 64K-bps circuit-switched data services is still uncertain.

ISDN was broadly conceived as a universal service for all network users. It was once thought that eventually, all subscribers in the network would be converted over to ISDN lines. For all practical purposes, this goal has been abandoned; network service providers recognize that there is no advantage to ISDN for many subscribers and that a forced conversion would be an untenable political and business proposition.

Indeed, there are several disadvantages to ISDN for residential and small-business subscribers, who may have little use for the 64K-bps digital service and who already have a large investment in their current terminal equipment and wiring. For example, although ISDN supports up to eight terminals on the same passive bus, two or three parties cannot simply pick up extensions on the same line and participate in the conversation as they do now. Another disadvantage to ISDN service for some purposes is that the terminal equipment is not powered by the network, as are analog telephones. With ISDN, a backup power supply is needed for terminal equipment; otherwise, an electrical service failure causes a telephone failure.

One way of viewing ISDN is strictly as a low-layer communications service, without concern for the applications it carries. This is not entirely satisfying from a security perspective. On the other hand, the set of applications that may be supported by ISDN is nearly unbounded; it would be difficult to consider the specific needs of all applications carried over ISDN. ISDN cannot itself satisfy the security requirements of such an application as electronic mail (which will operate over other networks as well as ISDN); still, it must provide the necessary security support that this application requires of any network.

USER SERVICES

Instead of pressing for universal ISDN service, service providers are installing the ISDN infrastructure in their networks but unbundling the ISDN features and making them available to analog subscribers. Call-waiting, call-forwarding, and calling-line ID features are now widely available to analog subscribers. They are supported by ISDN-capable switches and SS#7. It is more or less agreed that although only a small fraction of subscriber lines in the US will be ISDN lines in 1995, the majority of subscriber lines will be serviced by switches that support SS#7.

Eventually, the ISDN standards will provide the infrastructure for worldwide telephony. ISDN services will be available anywhere in the developed world. Full portability of ISDN terminals and switches may never be a reality, but the basic services will be transportable across national boundaries between terminal equipment devices. However, an all-ISDN worldwide telephone network seems improbable. Many users will continue to use analog terminals for the foreseeable future.

A development not originally anticipated by ISDN and not yet well integrated into ISDN is mobile cellular telephony, which experienced explosive growth during the 1980s. The current system uses digital control but analog voice channels. Work has recently begun on standards for an advanced digital cellular mobile telephone system. The data rate for this service will probably be 8K bps, which will require the development of inexpensive voice coders. With several 8K-bps channels assigned to one higher-rate carrier on a time-division multiplexing basis, broadcast spectrum use will be enhanced. In addition, there has been some speculation about using cellular radio to deliver voice services to private residences, perhaps as a competitive alternative to traditional wire line carriers or as a less expensive alternative to copper where densities are low.

SECURITY THREATS AND CONCERNS

The security threats posed by ISDN include:

- Denial of service.
- Intrusion into ISDN customer data.
- Use of ISDN to penetrate a customer system or for fraudulent activities.
- Violation of the confidentiality of data communicated across the ISDN.
- Modification of data communicated across the ISDN.

Denial-of-service attacks include physical damage to customer premises equipment, network links, and switches. Even if no actual attack is involved, accidents and disasters can cause loss of service. In addition, switches can be attacked by penetrating the switch software to either disable the entire switch or to affect a particular subscriber in some way, perhaps by diverting the subscriber's calls or disabling the line.

ISDNs can maintain certain data about subscribers, particularly records of calls made. This information is confidential to the subscriber and may be quite sensitive. If the network systems are penetrated, an intruder may obtain this information. Both the operational network, which collects the data, and the administrative system are possible points of attack.

Because the telephone network is the principal means of providing remote access to computer systems and networks of all sorts, it is an obvious vehicle for intrusion into these systems. Almost every outside penetration of a computer system begins with a telephone call. The purpose of the intrusion may be fraud, theft, sabotage, to obtain confidential information, or simply for the fun of it. Although the ISDN cannot prevent such attacks, it can support mechanisms the end systems can use to detect and thwart attacks.

The telephone network is one of the principle instruments of fraud in modern society. Although much of this fraud is petty, the total cost is undoubtedly substantial. Electronic fraud sometimes involves substantial funds transfers and may not always be detected or reported. Some telephone fraud involves obtaining confidential information, including credit records, law enforcement records, and telephone numbers. The network itself is often defrauded. Because the telephone network is a pervasive communications medium, this type of fraud is likely to continue. The inherent anonymity of callers in the current network is the great advantage of the telephone as an instrument of fraud.

Need for Security in ISDN

The need for routine security in wide area communications remains largely unsatisfied. Both the present pre-ISDN voice-oriented network and the ISDN that will replace it make little provision for security. There is no systematic provision for protecting the confidentiality of user communications, and in many cases, it is comparatively easy for intruders to intercept, understand, and alter communications or originate forgeries. The network itself is vulnerable to frauds of various sorts, and there is no standard, effective method for the authentication of network users by other users. Therefore, the network provides an excellent vehicle for committing frauds of all sorts while allowing the criminal to remain anonymous.

The need for strong security in communications is becoming urgent as the electronic documents replace paper in commercial transactions. Many of the traditional safeguards and practices that applied to paper have not been adequately replaced when electronic documents are used. Forgery or alteration of unprotected electronic documents is simple compared with forging or altering paper documents. It is often easier to tap a communications line and intercept all the traffic on that line than to intercept and read paper mail.

ISDN security is more than simple responses to specific deliberate threats, however. Much damage may be done by inadvertent errors, noise, accidents, confusion, and misunderstanding as well as by intent. However, the same signature, integrity, notarization, and authentication services may also apply in these cases as in cases of deliberate fraud. A digitally signed and notarized electronic document may settle a dispute caused simply by an error. The value of effective security practices is not limited to preventing deliberate attacks, and much security would still be sound business practice in a world free from deliberate fraud, theft, and intrusion.

There is now a stronger need for standards affecting the internal aspects of ISDNs, including internal network security (i.e., to protect the integrity of the network itself and to protect service providers against fraud, rather than to protect the security of user communications). With more diversity in the networks, there may also be more exposure to security vulnerabilities. Moreover, as the number of networks grows, the need for security standards between networks increases. When one monopoly service provider serves a nation, internal network security can be treated as an internal concern of that supplier and not properly the subject of standards. When that monopoly is replaced by many competing but interoperating networks, many aspects of network security can only be dealt with by broadly accepted standards.

Another consequence of the breakup of national monopolies is that it reduces any possibility of the user simply relying on the public network to provide secure communications, even within one nation. Whatever network security standards there may eventually be, there will be too many independent service providers for users to rely on the public network to provide strong, consistent security. Although it may be possible for network service providers to offer some security features and services, it will not be practical to simply secure the link to the network switch and then rely on the network thereafter. Users who wish secure end-to-end communications must rely on user-to-user protocols and standards.

The combination of digital communications over ISDN and evolving security technology offers an opportunity for significant improvements in user information security. When ISDN makes ubiquitous digital communication of voice and data a reality, the digital signals can readily be encrypted to maintain confidentiality and integrity of voice, data, and image traffic. The inclusion of a packet data facility for signaling offers the opportunity to implement digital security protocols even with fairly basic ISDN voice terminals. Public key cryptography makes key management practical on a large scale, allows electronic signatures that cannot be forged, and provides a means for reliable authentication without shared secret keys.

If implemented on a wide scale with suitable standards, the benefits of security are significant and the cost need not be excessive. If the market is sufficient, the cost of developing customized very large scale integration security devices is justified. It remains only to develop and implement the needed standards and to incorporate them in ordinary practice. The availability of pervasive security in the ISDN would provide a strong incentive for users to convert from analog service to digital service.

Security Policies and Domains

For effective communications security, an explicit and well-defined security policy must be enforced. A security policy is a systematic set of measures taken to ensure security. Measures to protect data include physical security (e.g., locks, guards, and perimeter alarms), procedural security (e.g., separation of duties and authority, review and release procedures), and cryptography. The set of users who share the same security policy is referred to as the security domain.

A security policy covers more than communications security. Data is stored, processed, and accessed as well as transported. Communications, however, often involves crossing boundaries between security domains. Each independent company or organization—or even each subunit of the same organization—may have its own security policy, suited to its needs and capabilities. Any confidential communications between these organizations crosses security domain boundaries.

Privacy and Confidentiality versus Accountability

Although the terms "confidentiality" and "privacy" share a common context of secrecy, the word privacy is used to describe the desire or right to be left alone and not have personal information divulged. Confidence implies trust resulting in the sharing of secrets—for example, a secret that is not shared with another is private, but not a confidence. In the context of ISDN security, the term "confidentiality" is used to describe the transmission of information between two or more parties without divulging that information to any unintended parties or intruders. Privacy in ISDN refers to the controlled capture, accumulation and release of information about subscribers, particularly when that information may enable intrusion on subscribers.

Balanced against the legitimate desire of subscribers for confidentiality and privacy is the need to hold them accountable for their use of the ISDN. When subscribers misuse the network, they should be held accountable. If commercial transactions are conducted over the network rather than with paper, the parties must be able to hold each other accountable. Achieving accountability, however, is to some extent in conflict with broad constructions of confidentiality and privacy.

Confidentiality involves both the contents of communications and the traffic flow (e.g., protecting the identities of the parties, amount of traffic, and length of transmission). Confidentiality can be compromised in several ways. For example, an intruder may be deliberately intercepting information. Deliberate intrusion may be easy in the case of cellular radio telephony or wireless telephones and local area networks (LANs), but signals can also be intercepted by intruders on copper wires, fiber-optic cables, and along either terrestrial or satellite microwave links. In addition, confidentiality can be compromised by crosstalk in the network, though all-digital transmission significantly reduces the likelihood of this.

Intrusions may or may not be illegal, depending on the circumstances. Federal laws forbid wiretaps on domestic private electronic communications by private parties and by law enforcement or other government agencies, except under limited circumstances as specifically defined by law. Nevertheless, illegal or not, it is usually easy to tap local communications loops.

Although confidentiality may be achieved to some degree by legislation forbidding the interception of communications, the most general and convenient means of ensuring confidentiality are cryptographic techniques. As more and more business transactions take place electronically over ISDN, the use of cryptography to protect the communications of private businesses and individuals will grow.

There are several current ISDN privacy concerns. The first involves the calling-line ID supplementary service. Unlisted subscribers pay to keep their numbers secret. If someone calls from an unlisted number and this number is revealed to the called party, the caller's privacy is allegedly infringed. Absent legislation forbidding this, calling-line ID can be used to build the network equivalent of mailing lists. The use of police tip lines, whistleblower lines, suicide counseling lines, and similar valuable services may be curtailed by public fears that anonymity is compromised by calling-line ID. The reporting of calling-line ID has been limited in some states by public utility commissions and in other states has been held by courts to be illegal. Some operating companies now offer blocking services, which block the calling-line ID service on selected outgoing calls; at least one state requires that calling-line ID be blocked on all calls from unlisted numbers.

Although calling-line ID has legitimate uses, it is dangerous in that it is at best a weak form of personal authentication. A strong personal authentication over ISDN terminals might be possible using D-channel user-to-user signaling; callers could be requested to be authenticated by the called party. A voluntary strong authentication would solve many security problems and the privacy concerns of calling-line ID.

Another privacy concern is the accumulation of data about subscribers. Systematic accumulation and analysis of regular telephone use may be regarded in the aggregate as infringing individual privacy. Thus, the call detail records legitimately kept by service providers may be held to be confidential between the subscriber and the service provider. Unauthorized release of these records to a third party, even (or perhaps particularly) a law enforcement or security agency, may be considered an intrusion of privacy.

ISDN SECURITY OVERVIEW

ISDN security must fit a broad environment, including LANs and wide area networks, public and private ISDN, specialized service providers, and multiple security domains. ISDN security must begin with the user, who may be a person, an organizational entity (e.g., the dispatcher), or a computer process acting on behalf of the person or entity. The user may not be bound to a specific line or terminal. Because people are used to operating telephones for a wide range of transactions, the reliable authentication of human users from any ISDN telephone is a major requirement.

People interact with the ISDN terminal equipment, which includes voice telephones, answering machines, integrated voice and data terminals, fax machines, and specialized terminals (e.g., automated teller machines). In many cases, the terminal equipment is a computer connected to the ISDN through an ISDN interface device or card. When this is the case, the user is a computer process acting as the agent for either a person or an organizational entity.

The terminal equipment may be connected directly to the ISDN or to a PBX, which in turn is connected to the public ISDN. In the ISDN jargon, a PBX is an NT2. Collectively, the terminal equipment and the NT2 equipment are called customer premises equipment.

The public network must be able to protect itself from fraud and threats to service availability. This is a business necessity for the service providers, who must also preserve the confidentiality of customer service records. The public network is too diverse to be expected to provide ubiquitous user-to-user security services, particularly confidentiality and authentication. There is no central authority capable of imposing and managing such a security program.

Application services, called specialized services or teleservices, may be provided to users through the ISDN. Specialized services include the directory service (X.500), packet message-handling service (X.400), and a variety of other value-added application services. The network service providers themselves may be specialized service providers, or the services may be provided by other service providers with access to the network switches. Some general teleservices, such as X.400, incorporate security into the more general application. The specialized service providers may also offer such security applications as key management. In this chapter, such a security-oriented application is called a specialized security application.

Users in different security domains communicate with each other over the same ISDN. In addition to the public ISDN, there are private ISDNs and a variety of data networks, including LANs, metropolitan area networks (MANs), and wide area networks, which may be connected to the public ISDN through gateways. Analog telephone service continues to be supported by the public network.

User-to-user security over ISDN must be a feature of the customer premises equipment. The security features chosen for the customer premises equipment should work not only for ISDN but for alternative communications networks.

The Human Component of ISDN Security

ISDN is both a telephone network and a data network. People interact with people, specialized machines, and computer systems over the ISDN. Computers also interact with each other. ISDN security must be considered in the context of human interactions, often unaided by computers, and of providing computer-based security functions to all telephone users whenever possible.

The fundaméntals of person-to-person interaction over the ISDN remain nearly the same as for analog telephone service, except that the called party may be given an indication of the caller's number. However, this is not equivalent to personal authentication. When parties known to each other communicate over high-quality telephone lines, they usually recognize each other's voice. In addition, challenge and response password authentication can be used over the telephone. Only simple authentication systems are practical for untrained humans. For the general public, memorizing and using a four-digit personal identity number (PIN) is the current accepted practice. An individual can be expected to memorize only two or three PINs. If more are needed, the individual generally writes them down, thus potentially compromising security.

OSI AND ISDN SECURITY SERVICES

In this section, the security services specified in the OSI model are examined as they apply to ISDN. In addition, the possibility of extending services to include additional services from European Computer Manufacturing Association (ECMA) standard 138 is discussed.

Integrity Services

Integrity services are generally provided for digital data by means of an integrity check value, which is a known function of all the protected bits in a packet. The integrity check value is then encrypted with a private or secret key. An intruder can modify a packet and compute the correct integrity check value of the modified packet but cannot then encrypt the integrity check value itself. Alteration of the packet can be detected, providing connectionless integrity. If the integrity check value covers an appropriate time-stamp field, connection replay attacks can be prevented. Integrity can be extended to connection integrity by including appropriate sequence number fields within the range of the integrity check value to detect the loss or duplication of packets.

Nonrepudiation Services

A message may be signed by encrypting the integrity check value of a packet or message with a private key known only to the originator of the message. If the message contains a date and time stamp and if the recipient checks the time of arrival and keeps a signed copy of the message, the recipient has nonrepudiation with proof of delivery.

The purpose of nonrepudiation with proof of delivery is to prevent a recipient from falsely denying that a message was received. A form of nonrepudiation with proof of delivery can be obtained if the recipient signs the received message and returns it to the originator. Although such a mechanism covers many needs, it is not a complete solution, because the recipient, having seen the message, can decline to confirm its receipt. If electronic communication is to substitute for registered mail or a process server, a mechanism that does not require the cooperation of the recipient is required.

Notary mechanisms have been proposed, involving a trusted third party who delivers the message to the recipient and keeps a copy or digest of the message. However, the recipient, having read the message, may falsely claim that the communications line was broken. Therefore, it may be useful to perform a test of the communications line, requesting a signed acknowledgment that it is working properly before the data is sent. This would serve as proof that the communications line was operational at least immediately before sending the message. If, however, a recipient is expecting the equivalent of an unwelcome subpoena, the recipient may not respond to the test communication. Legislation may be needed before nonrepudiation services can supplement or replace traditional mechanisms for provable communications.

Nonrepudiation is ordinarily considered a function within layer 7 of the OSI model and outside the scope of ISDN. However, voice or fax nonrepudiation services may appropriately be considered ISDN services. Modern digital signal and image processing allows undetectable alterations to be made to any electronic image or voice recording, unless the image is protected by a digital signature. To ensure that a voice call cannot be altered by either party to the call, a trusted voice notary service, for example, must be used to produce a signed digital recording of the call.

Confidentiality Services

Although it is possible to physically protect local links (e.g., within a building), the cost of physical protection increases with distance; therefore, physical protection of the entire public ISDN is infeasible. It is sometimes claimed that fiber-optic links cannot be tapped. Although noncryptographic means of protecting fiber communications exist, they are currently expensive and restrictive. It is often only marginally more difficult to tap fiber-optic links than electrical links.

Encryption is the principle mechanism for ensuring confidentiality in such wide area networks as ISDN for three reasons. First, its cost is independent of distance. Second, it provides both confidentiality and (in combination with an integrity check value and appropriate message sequence numbers) integrity services. Finally, it can provide end-to-end confidentiality and integrity through otherwise insecure channels, without any change to the network.

Authentication Services

Authentication is the verification of the claimed identity of the communicating party. International Standards Organization International Electrotechnical Commission (ISO/IEC) standard 9594-8 defines two classes of authentication: simple authentication and strong authentication. Simple authentication procedures rely on a secret password known only to the user. The name and password of user A are transferred to user B, possibly with a time stamp and random number. The passwords may be protected by a one-way hash function. In simple protected authentication, for example, user A sends user B an authenticator consisting of a time stamp, a random number, A's name, and a protection parameter generated with a one-way function from the first three parameters plus A's secret password. User B then accesses a local copy of user A's password to generate the protection parameter, which it compares with the protection parameter received from A.

Simple authentication is most useful for access to local systems and equipment. When access is restricted to ISDN terminal equipment or services, a simple user authentication process is appropriate. Simple authentication is less useful in cases in which user A wishes to be able to authenticate to any user B through the ISDN. Either B must have A's protected key, requiring that B be trusted by A, or a third party trusted by both A and B who knows the secret key must be invoked to check the authentication.

Strong authentication requires the use of public-key cryptography. Public-key algorithms used for strong authentication have the property that $X_p \times X_s = X_s \times X_p$, where X_p and X_s are the encryption functions using the public and secret keys, respectively. A certification authority produces certificates for users. These certificates include the name of the user, the validity dates of the certificate, and the public key of the user. The certificate is protected by the digital signature of the certification authority. That signature contains a summary of the certificate produced by a one-way hash function and encrypted with the secret key of the certification authority. The encryption ensures that the certificate cannot be forged.

Smart cards containing a public-key encryption function provide a portable means of providing strong personal authentication. To prevent use of a stolen smart card, activation of the private key contained in the smart card may require manual entry of a password memorized by the user.

Access Control Services

Access control in a communications network such as ISDN is not as complex as that required in a distributed computer system. There are three principal access control issues in ISDN security:

- Network access.
- Access to the terminal or customer premises equipment.
- Access to network data bases.

The ISDN access control issue is to determine whether the user has authorization to access a particular network service. For example, is the user authorized to place a long-distance call, an international call, or a secure call? In the case of an ISDN PBX, the PBX can enforce user access control checks. Although standards are not necessary for such services in PBXs, without them terminal inter-changability would be poor. The simplest solution is to bind the access privileges to the terminal. This changes the access control problem to one of controlling user access to terminals.

Control of access to the network data bases (including data bases maintained by PBXs) is vital. Because data bases containing records of calls are confidential, unauthorized users must be prevented from accessing them. Data bases maintained for routing and the management or maintenance of the network must be protected from unauthorized modification. An intruder might modify them to perpetrate a fraud (e.g., by deflecting calls from their proper destination) or to disrupt the operation of the network.

Effective access control requires effective authentication. A standard system for strong personal authentication (e.g., using smart cards) is first needed for identi-fication. The user's privileges could then be determined from a separate data base of privileges, and access would be either granted or denied in accordance with the security policy.

Security Services from ECMA 138

In addition to the five security services of ISO 7498-2 (i.e., confidentiality, access control, authentication, data integrity, and nonrepudiation), it is useful to consider extending the services for ISDN to adopt concepts introduced in ECMA 138. ECMA 138 deals with authentication and access control in the broad context of distributed computer systems and goes well beyond what is ordinarily thought of as communications security. However, it has application to two specific problems in ISDN:

- ISDN network data base access control.
- Interdomain security interworking.

In addition, ECMA 138 recognizes that security information must be collected and defines a security audit information service. This service automatically re-cords security-related events—for example, any attempt to access the data bases maintained by the network is a security-related event. In principle, any use of the network is potentially security-related. However, privacy concerns require that suitable criteria be developed for screening the events to be recorded in a public network, and probably only the time, parties, and network services used would be recorded (which are needed for billing as well).

ISDN SECURITY PROTOCOLS AND SUPPORT SERVICES

This section describes a general structure for ISDN security, which is composed of security protocols and security support applications. This structure allows imple-mentation of the security services listed in the preceding section. It includes some protocols and applications specific to ISDN but, as much as possible, uses the services now in the early stages of standardization for OSI.

For purposes of this discussion, a security protocol is a peer-to-peer process running at the transport layer (layer 4) or a lower layer and is intended to add security features to the overall protocol stack used in communications. Security protocols typically provide confidentiality, integrity, and security labeling during data exchange. Security support applications are processes at the application layer that support security protocols. The functions of security applications include authorization, authentication, and access control. Security applications may require a trusted specialized service application or third party. Security applications are ordinarily invoked as part of establishing or terminating a secure association or connection.

Security Protocols

The overall function of security protocols is the secure exchange of data. The first function of security protocols is to ensure integrity, which may be the only service required. The second major function is to ensure confidentiality. Both integrity and confidentiality are usually implemented with cryptographic techniques. Security labels may also be provided by security protocols, and the use of the correct key provides a means of authentication on a per-packet basis.

Security Protocols Above ISDN. The transport layer is the lowest end system—to—end system layer of the OSI reference model. A transport-layer security protocol can provide a powerful end-to-end confidentiality solution when ISDN or any other network technology is used to transport OSI data. When OSI is carried over an ISDN-based X.25 packet service, the X.25 packet network is reached through the ISDN B or D channels. An intruder monitoring the U interface point sees a network layer header as plaintext and the OSI transport PDU as ciphertext.

Network layer security protocols can encrypt B-channel data on the basis of subnetworks. This approach simplifies key management for terminals because only one key is used to protect communications with another specific secure packet network, whatever the end-host destination. It has the disadvantage that the entire packet network must be trusted, and packet switches must be trusted.

A practical disadvantage of network layer encryption for ISDN is that the secure gateway can become a bottleneck if traffic loads are heavy. X.25 protocol processing places limitations on performance, and a security protocol only increases the processing load. If frame-relay secure gateways are used, it is likely that the security protocol processing would have an even greater relative effect on the gateway's performance (because frame relay otherwise minimizes processing in intermediate systems) and would physically split the security protocol from the transport layer in end systems, where error recovery is intended to occur. When the terminal equipment is a dumb terminal, with no transport layer, the confidentiality service is logically a network layer protocol.

ISDN-Specific Security Protocols. Security protocols are possible at every layer of the OSI reference model. Some applications (e.g., X.400 message handling) incorporate security, including encryption, in the application itself. This provides consistent security for a service that can be accessed through many networks, including ISDN. Selective field confidentiality may eventually be provided in presentation-layer protocols. Transport-layer and network-layer security protocols are the most common OSI security protocols.

When appropriate higher-layer OSI security protocols are used, there may be no need for ISDN-specific security protocols, except to provide traffic flow confidentiality. However, many ISDN applications (e.g., voice or video) are not served by OSI protocols. In addition, much non-OSI data traffic is carried by the public ISDN. In these cases, appropriate ISDN security protocols must provide the needed security.

Security Support Services for ISDN

Although security protocols (e.g., key management) implement security services at layers 1 through 4, they require several layer 7 support applications for their operation. Other ISDN security applications (e.g., a notarization application, which provides nonrepudiation services to users) may provide services directly to users rather than to lower-layer protocols.

Security applications may require a trusted third party (e.g., a certification authority or a notary). When a trusted third party is required, that service may be provided by either the public network or an independent specialized service provider connected to the public network. Specialized service providers provide a variety of information services, such as message handling. Many security applications are not ISDN-specific and may be shared with those supporting OSI security. Possible supporting security applications include:

- *Key management.* A directory could contain certificates stating a user's public keys, and such keys could be used for authentication and to validate signatures. It is possible that session keys for confidentiality might be agreed on by the source and destination using a public-key algorithm.
- *Certification.* A trusted certification support service might supply or verify the security attributes of users. The attributes then would be used in accordance with local security policy to make access control decisions.
- *Notarization.* A notarization support application would provide nonrepudiation services. In some cases, the application might be fully distributed; this would generally require the explicit cooperation of both parties to the notarized communication. A trusted notarization support application might be required to prevent repudiation of voice or video communications or to assume the role of a process server, in the case of an uncooperative recipient of a message.
- *Secure conferencing.* A secure conferencing application for voice or video would probably require a secure conference bridge.

EXHIBIT III-2-7 Potential ISDN Security Interactions

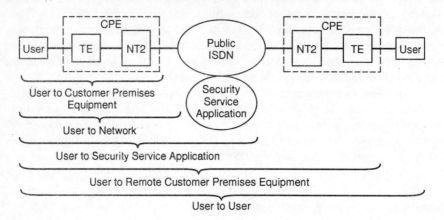

- *Secure mail*. Security provisions are being incorporated into the X.400 message-handling service. An analogous secure voice mail application would provide secure voice terminal users with similar voice messaging capabilities.
- *Trusted ISDN-to-analog conversion*. A large number of secure analog telephones now exist. A trusted conversion support application would be a trusted third party that performs conversion between secure analog and secure digital voice.

THE USER'S PERSPECTIVE OF ISDN SECURITY

There are several possible interactions between the user and the ISDN, as illustrated in Exhibit III-2-7. In this illustration, a user may be either a computer process or a human user. The terminal equipment is the initial point of connection to the ISDN. Users may be associated with a particular terminal equipment device, or they may be mobile. The terminal equipment may be connected directly to the public ISDN, or it may be connected through an NT2 (typically a PBX). The following sections discuss the possible interactions illustrated in the exhibit.

User to Customer Premises Equipment

The primary user-to-customer premises equipment security interaction is authentication and access control. (This discussion applies equally to interactions between the user and remote customer premises equipment.) If privileges are to be assigned to specific lines and terminals, access to the terminals must be controlled. In some cases, this may be by physical control of access to the terminal; in most cases, however, it will require that authentication and access control be built into the terminal or the PBX, or both.

A significant advantage of authentication and access control at this interface is that universal standards may not be required. Access control could be built into a terminal by requiring a personal token and perhaps a password to activate the terminal. This could be done as a proprietary feature of the terminal.

A weakness in access control provided by a terminal is that an intruder might physically remove the protected terminal and substitute another, unprotected terminal. Therefore, strong access control should extend to the next level of the network hierarchy: the terminal should be required to authenticate to the PBX or the public network. When terminal or user authentication is implemented in a PBX, standards are not strictly required; without standards, however, secure terminals are not portable to different PBXs. Currently, ISDN PBXs typically implement many proprietary features, and terminal portability is more a goal than a reality.

User to Network

The primary user-to-network security interactions are authentication and access control, for which standards are clearly required. Significant enhancements are needed in public network switches to implement user authentication. In the context of the public network, the primary access control consideration is user access to network services (e.g., 900 or long-distance telephone services). Such access control services might be offered to subscribers to prevent unauthorized use of business phones or to prevent children from making inappropriate use of home telephones.

In addition, public network service providers may provide improved authentication for the use of telephone calling cards to reduce fraud. To the extent that public networks allow dial-up access to sensitive resources and data bases, improved authentication would make a significant reduction to network vulnerability to fraud and denial of service attacks.

ISDN provides the telephone number of the calling party to the called party through a service known as calling-line ID (also sometimes called automatic number identification). In the absence of better authentication, the calling-line ID can be used for authentication and for inward access control. However, it does not provide true personal authentication.

User to Security Service Application

A large variety of interactions between the user and the security service application may eventually result. The major ones will probably be for key distribution, authentication, and access control, whereby the security application will be a trusted third party that supplies or verifies security attributes. Others may offer notarization services, secure conversion services (i.e., conversion of secure analog to secure ISDN digital voice), or secure mail services.

User to User

A great many ISDN security services will be implemented primarily on a user-to-user basis, perhaps with the assistance of a security service application for authentication or access control. There are three principle reasons for this:

- The provision of security functions in the network may not offer service providers a strong return on the investment required. Changes to ISDN switches require years to design, code, test, and deploy. Although current user investment in ISDN is minor, current service provider investment in ISDN is significant.
- User-to-user security is transparent to the network and can be implemented by users where and as needed much more quickly than features or services can be added to the network.
- Many security concerns are essentially end-to-end concerns, and it is desirable that only the end entities need be trusted. Several networks and service providers may be involved in a secure communication. In such cases, it would be difficult to ensure consistent security and trust except on a user-to-user basis.

Authentication, access control, and confidentiality are all likely to be addressed primarily on a user-to-user basis, with assistance in some cases from a security service application or the network.

STANDARDS FOR ISDN SECURITY

Although ISDN has been under development for many years and has been the subject of many standards activities, there currently are no standards specifically for ISDN security and few are in development. In contrast, the OSI community is actively pursuing standards for OSI security. When ISDN is used as a transport mechanism for OSI traffic, the OSI standards are applicable and should be reviewed for their adequacy in the ISDN environment. However, many ISDN applications and the ISDN itself may require specific security provisions that are not available in the OSI family of standards. This section discusses the security standards needed for ISDN, possible input and alternatives for the needed standards, and applicable standards under development.

ISDN-Specific Standards

ISDN has been depicted as both a data communications system and a broader set of applications that use that system. In addition, OSI has been presented as an architecture for communicating among peer and computer systems that may use the ISDN data communications system. The following sections deal with security standards that are specific to either of the two areas of ISDN outside OSI.

ISDN Security Architecture. The first standard that is needed in ISDN is a security architecture. This standard should select which alternatives should be developed as standards, and the architecture should support many security policies. The architecture would not dictate which policy would be followed, nor would it specify which security services and facilities are to be implemented in products. Security service and protocol specification standards are needed to provide these specifications.

ISDN Communications System Security Services. A standard is needed that specifies how security services would be provided in the ISDN communications system. The architecture specifies which services are required and where they would be offered.

ISDN Communications System Security Protocols. ISDN requires a simple physical layer confidentiality protocol operating on any circuit-switched ISDN channel octet stream using intrachannel security setup signaling. The protocol should support any circuit rate defined in ISDN (i.e., B channel, primary rate) and should provide confidentiality protection, including partial traffic flow confidentiality, for any use of the channel (e.g., voice, data, video, and facsimile). The protocol must allow for various cryptographic algorithms.

ISDN Application Security Services. There are several ISDN applications for which specific security standards are needed. Some of these overlap with OSI applications (e.g., electronic mail, electronic data interchange, and file transfer). The OSI security standards can be used for equivalent ISDN applications.

ISDN-specific applications, (e.g., voice conferencing) require special security services and special security protocols. A secure, or trusted, conference bridge is needed to allow several parties, each with a secure voice terminal, to hold a secure conference call. Voice and video conferences share some characteristics but will probably require different specific security services and definitely require different protocols.

Transition plans are required for conversions from secure analog telephone services to secure digital ISDN services. Although the basic security service providing confidentiality of the voice transmission will be the same, many supplemental voice services in ISDN require special security services and mechanisms. For example, call forwarding requires new and innovative security standards for authentication and supporting key management. There are now a large number of secure telephones that use digital encryption of a compressed speech signal; these devices require a standard interface to ISDN uncompressed digital speech.

Needed application security services include authentication and nonrepudiation as well as large granularity access control. Security support services include key management, auditing, and security fault recovery. Although these may be the same as application layer OSI security services, standards for implementing and supporting the services in an ISDN environment may be necessary. Authentication is a particularly difficult and important problem in the public ISDN. A universal means of strong personal authentication is badly needed in the public network.

ISDN Application Security Protocols. The application-specific security service standards outlined in the preceding section require security protocol standards between communicating entities to support and provide the security services. For example, the access control service requires specific protocols to obtain or transmit the personal access certificate containing identification, authentication, and authorization information. Access control in public networks requires authentication protocols for performing identity-based access control. Access control in closed or classified networks requires these protocols plus clearance (i.e., need-to-know) information for making rule-based access control decisions. Access control may be on outbound connections (e.g., to prevent children from accessing undesired advertising or pornographic services) or on inbound connections (e.g., to prevent unauthorized connections to classified computer systems or voice terminals).

In addition to application-specific security protocols, security support service protocols are needed. For example, protocols are required to make initial connections to key management centers to obtain the initial, or seed, key after proper authentication is performed. Signature certificates are required in addition to the seed key in commercial applications. Security officer protocols are required to manage the distributed security features in an ISDN environment.

Standard Security Mechanisms

Several security mechanism standards are needed for ISDN but need not be specific to ISDN. The OSI standards developed to provide the security mechanisms defined in International Standard 7498-2 should be used to the maximum extent possible. Specific security mechanisms are the subject of standards development efforts of the new JTC1/SC27. The following sections provide a brief overview of these security mechanisms.

Cryptographic Algorithms. Although not the subject of international standardization, several types of cryptographic algorithms are required for ISDN. First, data encryption algorithms are required to provide confidentiality protection to user and management data. Second, cryptography-based key establishment or distribution algorithms are needed to establish a data encryption key whenever necessary. Third, cryptography-based digital signature algorithms are needed for user and data authentication. Some of these algorithms may overlap to save implementation costs.

The Data Encryption Standard (DES) is currently the only recognized, publicly available standard for encrypting data and distributing keys. Although able to perform data authentication and limited personal authentication, DES is not satisfactory for signatures in open system environments. Digital public-key signature algorithms are needed, and simpler key distribution is possible with public key cryptography techniques. In addition, few symmetric-key algorithms may be necessary to support international commercial applications if DES devices are not exportable. These new algorithms may be faster when implemented in software or may satisfy other special requirements.

Cryptographic Modes of Operation. Standard modes of operation must be available for each of the standard cryptography algorithms. Interoperability and security require using the same mode that has been approved for an application with the same algorithm.

Mobile User Key Token Standards. Personal authentication and data protection standards rely on cryptographic methods that require a personal key for signatures and data protection. Standard key carriers, tokens, smart cards, and similar mechanisms are required to support a mobile user seeking access to secure distributed systems from multiple locations. Several ANSI and ISO standards activities are addressing standard tokens that may be used to provide access control and data protection keys.

SUMMARY

ISDN standards will provide worldwide digital communications service and will play a key role in the transition to electronic documents and business transactions. Because ISDN was developed with little thought to security, ISDN security will become a pressing concern for both government and business. Fortunately, ISDN's digital nature facilitates adding security. However, the deployment of ISDN in the public network is well under way, and the current investment in ISDN equipment as well as the commercial necessity to deploy ISDN in a timely manner constrain how security features may be added.

ISDN security standards should take advantage of and be compatible with emerging standards for OSI security. International Standard 7498-2 defines five security services for OSI: confidentiality, access control, authentication, data integrity, and nonrepudiation. The challenge of ISDN security is to extend these concepts to all ISDN applications, including voice use of the public network. Terminal-to-terminal link encryption provides a powerful ISDN security mechanism because of ISDN's ability to provide circuit-switched connections throughout the world. Standards for the reliable authentication of human users and simple B-channel link encryption are badly needed for ISDN security.

Cryptography

MILES E. SMID

The increase in distributed information systems has led to a corresponding increase in the need for cryptographic security services. For example, complete business transactions between buyer, seller, and banker can be performed electronically. Yet many electronic applications involve the transmission of data over unprotected communications lines, and the transmissions are often stored in unknown intermediate communications switches. Transmission between computers are often exposed to eavesdropping and alteration, and in most cases, cryptography provides the only effective means of protecting the transmitted data.

Cryptography may also be used to protect data within computers. Cryptographic algorithms may be used to protect large volumes of data stored on computer disks. For example, one user's data on a disk may be protected from unauthorized access by another user who uses the same disk. In addition, cryptographic algorithms may be used to assure a program user that the program is in its original, virus-free form.

Cryptography can even be used to control access to the computers themselves. Cryptographic mechanisms can be designed to offer significantly more protection that the traditional password systems, which have proved vulnerable to computer hackers. For example, a challenge-response system that transmits a randomly generated challenge and requires the response to be encrypted and returned offers a higher level of security than traditional password approaches. Unlike static password systems, the encrypted response changes for each challenge. In addition, the potential hacker has no knowledge of the randomly generated cryptographic key used by the encryption algorithm. Because the encryption is usually performed in the user's personal token, a hacker without the user's token has virtually no chance of being accepted by the system.

The cost of cryptographic equipment has dropped significantly over the past five years; however, cryptography is often not implemented because of its complex technical nature. As a result, many information systems today are inadequately protected. This chapter discusses the basics of cryptographic technology and the many services that cryptography provides. Implementation considerations are then addressed.

BASIC TECHNOLOGIES

There are two basic types of cryptographic algorithms: symmetric key algorithms (also called private-key algorithms) and asymmetric key cryptography (often called public-key algorithms). These are discussed in the following sections.

Symmetric Key Cryptography

Symmetric key cryptographic algorithms make use of a single key shared by both the originator and receiver of the data. If data confidentiality is provided, either party can encrypt or decrypt data with the shared key. If the data integrity service is provided, either party can generate an authenticated message. Symmetric key systems are built on the assumption that the two parties who share thc same key trust each other and are using the cryptography to protect against distrusted third parties.

The best-known symmetric key algorithm is the Data Encryption Standard (DES). Although the adequacy of the security provided by the algorithm has been questioned by some, DES remains the most widely accepted, publicly available cryptographic algorithm. Besides being the only published symmetric key algorithm approved for protection of the federal government's sensitive unclassified data, it has been widely adopted by the commercial sector. The American National Standards Institute (ANSI) has adopted the DES algorithm for commercial applications and has based several standards for integrity and key management on its use. Each week, electronic funds transfers worth trillions of dollars are protected by the DES algorithm.

Asymmetric Key Cryptography

With asymmetric key cryptography, a cryptographic algorithm employs two asymmetric keys: one to encrypt and the other to decrypt. It is not possible to derive the decryption key from the encryption key. A user can generate both keys and make the encryption key public while keeping the decryption key private. Anyone with the public encryption key can encrypt a message and send it to the owner of the private key. However, only the owner of the private key could decrypt the message. This arrangement offers advantages over symmetric key algorithms when providing nonrepudiation and key management services (which are discussed in a later section).

The best-known asymmetric cryptographic algorithm is the Rivest-Shamir-Adleman (RSA) algorithm. The RSA algorithm is notable not only because it is the first asymmetric key algorithm but because its security is related to a known mathematical problem—namely, the difficulty of factoring a number that is the product of two large prime numbers.

The RSA algorithm is considered versatile because it can be used to provide many security services; in fact, it provides all the services described in this chapter. Many applications of asymmetric key cryptography are designed to accommodate its features.

Hybrid Systems

Symmetric key algorithms have certain advantages over existing asymmetric key algorithms. The main one is computational efficiency. Most practical implementations of asymmetric key cryptography run at a few thousand bits per second, whereas symmetric key algorithms can process tens or even hundreds of millions of bits per second. Therefore, designers of cryptographic systems often use a symmetric key algorithm for bulk data encryption and an asymmetric key algorithm for automated key distribution. The asymmetric key algorithm uses the receiver's public key to encrypt the asymmetric key that encrypts the bulk data. This type of hybrid system provides many of the advantages of both symmetric and asymmetric key cryptography while minimizing the disadvantages.

CRYPTOGRAPHIC SERVICES AND MECHANISMS

A network designer must decide which cryptographic services are needed for the foreseen applications and then select the appropriate mechanisms to provide the desired services. Data may be encrypted for confidentiality, authenticated to protect its integrity, or both encrypted and authenticated to provide a combination of protective features. If the cryptographic keys are properly restricted, cryptography may be used to authenticate the identity of the sender and to provide an electronic analog of the written signature. Finally, all applications of cryptography require that the keys be managed in a secure manner. The following sections discuss these services and mechanisms.

Data Confidentiality

Data confidentiality can be provided by encryption and decryption algorithms. The encryption and decryption algorithms are designed so that only the desired receiver has the binary number, called the key, that is necessary to decrypt the data. Thus, secret messages may be sent from one party to another without fear of disclosing the data.

Data Integrity

In automated systems, it is not always possible for humans to scan data to determine whether bits have been dropped, added, or modified. Even if scanning were possible, the data might have been modified in such a manner that it would be very difficult for the scanner to detect the alteration. For example, *do* may be changed to *do not* or $1,000 be changed to $10,000. It is therefore desirable to have an automated means of detecting both intentional and unintentional modifications of data. Ordinary error-detecting codes are not sufficient, because if the algorithm for generating the code is known, an adversary could generate the correct code for any modification of the data. The modification would then go undetected. A cryptographic error-detection code is required to protect against individuals who might modify legitimate data into false data that looks legitimate.

Cryptographic algorithms can be used along with a secret key to calculate a cryptographic error-detection code, called a message authentication code, on data whose integrity must be maintained. The message authentication code is sent with the plaintext data to the receiver, who with the correct key can calculate the message authentication code on the received data and compare it with the received message authentication code. If the two agree, the data is considered to have integrity. Otherwise, an unauthorized modification is assumed. Any party trying to modify the data without knowing the key would be unable to calculate the appropriate message authentication code corresponding to the altered data.

Authentication of Message Originator

If a cryptographic mechanism is used to protect data and the key used by the cryptographic mechanism is shared only by the originator and receiver of the data, the receiver can authenticate the message originator provided that the key has not been compromised (i.e., released to an unauthorized party). For example, if parties A and B share a secret key and party B receives a message with a message authentication code that correctly validates using the shared key, party B may assume that the message was sent by party A. Therefore, authentication of the message originator is obtained as well as message authentication.

System User Authentication

With the growth of time-sharing and other forms of computer networking, the use of remotely accessed computers has become widespread. However, with this ease of access have come increased operational risks. Potential losses range from unauthorized use of computing time to theft of data or unauthorized use, modification or destruction of data. Perpetrators of such abuse may be otherwise honest individuals wishing to play a few games, or they may be sophisticated corporate or national spies hoping to obtain information of economic or political value.

Many access control systems permit the transmission of plaintext passwords to remote computers in order to authenticate the identity of the user and control access to the computer's resources. Cryptography can be used to encrypt passwords and other sensitive information sent to remote computers. In fact, passwords may not need to be sent at all. The user could authenticate identity by performing a cryptographic function with a unique cryptographic key, as previously discussed. Because the output of a cryptographic algorithm appears to be random, an unauthorized party could not easily predict or guess the result. A cryptographic handshake between the user and the host computer could be performed so that the computer is authenticated to the user as well as the user being authenticated to the computer.

Electronic Certification and Digital Signatures

Automated information processing systems enable companies to store and process documents in electronic form. Having documents in electronic form permits rapid processing and transmission and thereby improves the overall efficiency of information systems. However, approval of a paper-based document has traditionally been indicated by a written signature. There is a need for an electronic equivalent to the written signature that could be recognized to have the same legal status. Merely digitizing the written signature is not an acceptable alternative, because the digitized signature bears no relationship to the data that is being signed. In addition, paper-based documents offer some resistance to alteration and forgery. Modifying a paper document entails erasing and replacing text in an undetectable manner, and forging a written signature requires a certain degree of skill and practice. An electronic document with a digitized written signature would provide no such protection against unauthorized modifications. The document could be altered without changing the signature, and the digitized signature could be replicated on other documents without detection.

Cryptographic algorithms can provide protection against modification and forgery of electronic documents. These algorithms make use of a cryptographic key to generate a digital signature that is based on the key and all bits of the electronic document. The digital signature is verified by the receiver of the document. Changing a single bit of the document results in an unpredictable change to the signature. Therefore, when the digital signature is verified, any alteration is certain to be detected.

If a symmetric key algorithm is used to form the signature, the same key is shared by both the originator and the receiver of the message but is known to no other parties. If the signature is verified, the receiver knows that the document came from the originator and has not been modified. Such systems have been approved for use by the federal government as a replacement for written signatures on certain electronic documents.

Nonrepudiation

When an asymmetric digital signature algorithm is implemented, the private key of the signer is used to generate the signature and the public key of the signer is used to verify the signature. An additional property known as nonrepudiation is inherently provided. Because the private key used to generate the signature is known only to the signer, only the signer could have created the digital signature on a verified message. With symmetric key algorithms, the receiver as well as the signer can generate a signed message because they share the same key.

The receiver of a message signed by an asymmetric key algorithm is protected from repudiation by the signer because the receiver can verify the message to any third party by applying the signer's public key. This property is often called non-repudiation of message origin. The use of an asymmetric algorithm does not limit the transmission to only a single receiver, because anyone who has the signer's public key can verify the signed message. This feature is useful when distributing signed copies of virus-free software.

In 1991, the National Institute of Standards and Technology (NIST) proposed a new Federal Information Processing Standard for digital signatures. This proposed standard, which as of this writing is awaiting its second public comments review, specifies a public key–based Digital Signature Algorithm (DSA) appropriate for applications requiring a digital rather than a written signature. The DSA can be used to verify to a recipient the integrity of data and the identity of the originator of the data. DSA signatures can be used in proving to a third party that data was actually signed by the generator of the signature (i.e., nonrepudiation). In addition, it can be used to generate and verify signatures for stored as well as transmitted data. The security of the DSA is based on the difficulty of the discrete-logarithm problem, which is considered virtually impossible to solve when the values are large.

Among the factors that were considered during the DSA selection process were:

- The level of security provided.
- The ease of implementation in both hardware and software.
- The ease of export from the US.
- The applicability of patents.
- Impact on national security and law enforcement.
- The level of efficiency in both the signing and verification functions.

If adopted, the DSA will become the federal government's public key signature technique for all unclassified data. Anticipated applications include electronic mail, electronic funds transfer, electronic data interchange, software distribution, data storage, and other applications that require data integrity assurance and data origin authentication.

Key Management

Key management involves the secure generation, distribution, storage, journaling, and discontinuation of the cryptographic keys used by the cryptographic mechanisms. The security of cryptographically protected data depends on the protection afforded to the keys. Secret and private keys must be randomly generated and protected from disclosure and substitution. Public keys must be protected from substitution so that the correct owner of a public key can always be determined. Some networks provide for the automatic generation and transmission of new keys, encrypted under previously exchanged keys, and for the automatic discontinuation of keys when they are no longer to be used.

When communications between a large number of users is desirable, key management becomes crucial. Future networks will have key centers that help distribute or certify the authenticity of keys to parties who do not share any keys in common.

CONSIDERATIONS WHEN IMPLEMENTING CRYPTOGRAPHY

Cryptographic algorithms are implemented in a physical device called a cryptographic module. This section discusses several factors that should be considered by system designers when implementing cryptographic modules in information systems.

Security Services

Cryptographic algorithms are members of the class of security mechanisms that are used to provide security services. Security services are used to reduce the probability of specific security threats, thereby improving the security of the system. A system designer should conduct a risk analysis involving the probabilities that specific security threats may occur and the expected losses if the threats do in fact happen. By considering the risk of specific threats to the system, the designer attempts to determine which threats are relevant and which are impractical to guard against. Security mechanisms can then be used to protect against relevant threats, provided that the cost of the mechanisms does not exceed the expected loss that would result if the threat were exploited.

Cryptographic algorithms provide various security services—for example, data confidentiality, data integrity, authentication of message originator, user authentication, digital signatures, nonrepudiation, and automated key distribution. These services might be provided by encryption, decryption, authentication, digital signature, and other security mechanisms. A list of security services and the cryptographic mechanisms that can provide these services is provided in the International Standards Organization's open system's interconnection reference model. The designer must determine which security services are needed to meet the overall system design requirements and which security mechanisms best provide the needed services.

Cryptography Media

Cryptography may be implemented in software, firmware, or hardware. Software is generally less expensive, less secure, and less efficient than hardware. Hardware or firmware is often required for federal government applications.

659

Configuration

The following configurations should be considered in a cryptographic module that is being implemented:

- Inline.
- Offline.
- Embedded.
- Standalone.

These are discussed in the following sections.

Inline. Inline or front-end configurations require that the cryptographic module be capable of accepting plaintext data from the source, performing the cryptographic processing, and passing the processed data directly to the data communications equipment without passing it back to the source device. The cryptographic module may also be capable of accepting data (e.g., ciphertext) from the data communications equipment. The module processes (e.g., decrypts) the data and passes it on to an end system.

For inline configurations, the communications equipment is in the cryptographic module or external to the host. Data cannot leave the host without passing through the module.

Offline. Offline or back-end configurations require that the cryptographic module be capable of accepting data from the source, performing the cryptographic processing, and passing the processed data back to the source. The source controls storage or further transmission of the data and is responsible for maintaining the separation between protected and unprotected data.

Offline configurations are ideal for local file encryption. The host computer may contain both protected and unprotected data. When transmitting data, hosts in offline configurations must be designed or trusted not to transmit unprotected data. Offline configurations allow separate communications boards to be internal to the host.

Embedded. These configurations require the module to be physically enclosed within a computer and to interface with the computer. Embedded configurations may be either offline or inline configurations. Embedded configurations tend to be less expensive, but their physical security (i.e., tamper protection and detection) is often lacking.

Standalone. This type of configuration requires the module to be contained in its own physical enclosure outside a host computer. Standalone configurations may be either inline or offline configurations.

Physical Security

The security of a cryptographic module depends on the security of the keys and the proper functioning of the cryptographic algorithm. Because both the keys and the algorithm are contained in the module, it is important to protect the contents of the module from tampering.

NIST Draft FIPS 140-1, "Security Requirements for Cryptographic Modules" (July 1991), describes four levels of physical security. The first and lowest level requires no physical security beyond what is typically implemented in commercial-grade products. The second level requires tamper-evident features that indicate, on examination, whether the module has been tampered with. The third level requires tamper-responsive circuitry on any module openings or removable covers. When tampering is detected, the critical security parameters (e.g., the cryptographic keys) are filled with zeros. The fourth and highest level requires that the module have tamper-responsive circuitry designed to detect penetration even by drilling through the module enclosure.

Physical security is never 100% effective, and protective features can significantly increase the cost of the module. The designer must therefore be sure that the selected level of security offers a reasonable compromise between cost and security.

Networking Issues

When cryptography is implemented in a network, additional considerations must be made. For example, the system designer should consider whether encrypted data will pass directly to the ultimate receiver or travel through a switched network. In switched networks, a plaintext header containing the ultimate receiver's address must be sent with the data. If the cryptographic module is in the inline configuration, the module must have the capability of permitting the header to bypass the encryption process. Therefore, a more sophisticated module is required. When the module is offline, the communications software in the source host can append the necessary headers on the encrypted data, so that no cryptographic bypass needs to be performed by the module. However, the host must then be trusted to perform the function correctly.

Additional problems may occur when encrypted data is sent through a character-oriented network. Many network devices act on transmitted control characters. If these characters appear by chance in the encrypted text, some data may be garbled or lost. To circumvent this problem, the ciphertext can be filtered so that these control characters are never sent as cipher. For example, each eight-bit byte could be filtered as follows: the first four bits of the byte are coded in ASCII as a hexadecimal character. The second four bits of the byte are coded in ASCII as another hexadecimal character. The number of cipher bits is doubled, but only the ASCII characters 0 through 9 and A through F appear as cipher. To filter the data, the number of bits of filtered cipher is increased over the number of bits of the original encrypted data. The ratio of the two numbers is the efficiency of the filter.

Although inline cryptographic modules designed for such networks should have a filter, offline modules may leave the filtering to the communications software. This problem is much less significant with integrity-only modules, which transmit plaintext rather than cipher. However, certain data (e.g., the message authentication code, the digital signature, or transmitted encrypted keys) may also have to be filtered.

A third consideration when implementing cryptography in a network is that some network devices require that a particular character (e.g., a line feed) appear every so often in transmitted data. If that character does not appear in the cipher, it must be inserted so that the requirement is met. In this case, the cipher is blocked with the character in a regular manner and the receiver unblocks the data before it is decrypted. This blocking and unblocking can be built into the filters previously discussed.

A fourth network consideration concerns filters. Filters expand data and therefore reduce the efficiency of the communications system, but data compression techniques used on the plaintext can reduce the amount of the cipher that must actually be transmitted. The designer should consider the efficiency requirements of the system when choosing and implementing cryptography. However, care should be taken to neither overemphasize nor underemphasize the need for efficiency.

Key Distribution

Perhaps the most important consideration of system design is key distribution. Key distribution involves the secure movement of cryptographic keys from where they are generated to where they are used. If symmetric key cryptography is used, the designer must determine how the initial keys are manually distributed. If automated key distribution is also employed, the designer must consider whether to distribute keys on a direct point-to-point basis or whether to use a key distribution (or key translation) center to reduce the number of required manual keying relationships.

If asymmetric key cryptography is used, the designer must decide how public keys are to be distributed so that every user can identify the correct public key of all the other users. It may be necessary to establish a certification authority or a hierarchy of certification authorities to authenticate users and to sign credentials containing the user's identity and the user's public key to form a public key certificate. The problems of key distribution should be considered before expensive systems are purchased and the commitment to a particular method is made.

Built-in Test Functions

If the cryptographic module is not functioning properly, the user is not getting the intended security. The system designer must be satisfied that failures that could compromise security will not go undetected. Modules should have built-in test functions that detect major flaws in their proper functioning. Additional information on tests built into the cryptographic module can be found in Draft FIPS 140-1.

Standards and Validation

The cryptographic system designer must be familiar with the applicable security standards. Standards are useful because they provide a common level of security and interoperability among users. Some vendors offer proprietary cryptographic algorithms, thus requiring the customer to rely on the vendor both to design the algorithm and to evaluate its security. Designers are not always adept at finding weaknesses in their own work, however. Standardized algorithms are publicly known so they may be evaluated by any interested party. If a standard cryptographic algorithm is used with common communications protocols, there is a high probability that modules of different vendors will be able to communicate securely. The disadvantage of a standard algorithm is that if it is extensively used, it becomes a more likely target for attack because the potential payoff is greater.

Because a secure implementation involves much more than a secure algorithm, most cryptographic standards deal with the implementation of cryptography in particular applications or communications protocols. Networks conforming to the seven-layer architecture of the open systems interconnection (OSI) reference model have protocols for implementing encryption, data integrity, and authentication at several layers. Once these protocols are completely defined, vendors will be able to market cryptographic modules that can communicate with other cryptographic modules meeting the same standard. OSI networks also provide communications functions that minimize some of the network implementation problems discussed previously.

NIST maintains validation programs for certain of its critical federal information processing standards. Under these programs, vendors can have their products validated as conforming to the standard. The product must undergo a series of tests that compare the operation of the product with the results required by the standard. Once a product passes the tests, a certificate of validation is issued to the vendor. System designers and users generally have greater confidence that a validated product conforms to the standard. Vendors voluntarily validate their products because it shows that they have designed their products to meet accepted standards.

Because cryptographic algorithms are now used to provide a variety of security services that protect data of significantly differing sensitivity, Draft FIPS 140-1 permits flexibility in the design of cryptographic modules. Rather than limiting itself to a single security level that would be inappropriate for widely varying applications, the draft provides for multiple security levels. Each level offers a significant increase insecurity over the preceding level. All levels require that the algorithms be approved by NIST. However, the levels differ significantly in the requirements for physical security, user authentication, operating system security, and key management. This approach provides for cost-effective security because the user can select a product with the lowest security level satisfying the requirements of the application. The cost of unnecessary security features can therefore be avoided.

Product Availability

It is difficult to determine how large the market for cryptographic products is. Vendors are reluctant to release information on their customers or the dollar value of their sales. However, a wide variety of cryptographic products are available, many using the DES algorithm. The number of software cryptographic applications is impossible to determine because many users implement their own software cryptography.

Since publishing DES, NIST has validated more than 50 hardware and firmware implementations. Implementations range from firmware programmable read-only memories, which implement only the basic DES algorithm, to electronic chips that provide several modes of operation running at speeds up to 98 million bps. Most recently, DES has been implemented on single-chip integrated circuit (i.e., smart) cards, which may be carried in a person's wallet. Hardware DES chips, personal computer encryption boards, and standalone units are available.

SUMMARY

Although the study and practice of cryptography dates back to the ancients, new breakthroughs continue to occur. The development of computer systems and distributed processing networks has led to new cryptographic applications. These applications require sophisticated cryptographic algorithms to provide data confidentiality, data integrity, message authentication, access control, digital signature, nonrepudiation, and key management services.

Cryptographic-based security standards are being developed to provide a common level of security and interoperability. Designers of cryptographic systems must be able to match the cryptographic algorithm and its implementation to a diverse spectrum of security requirements.

Internal Controls in EDI Environments

EDWIN A. DOTY, JR. ▪ DANNY R. HINES

Electronic data interchange (EDI) usually refers to independent companies exchanging information electronically instead of by paper. Sample exchanges include letters, memos, and reports, but more significant from an accounting perspective are purchase orders, invoices, and receiving notices. Although EDI saves time and money by shortening lead times and reducing inventories and paper flow, replacing the internal control documents that pass between accounting systems with computer functions involves risks. EDI systems must therefore be properly controlled and monitored.

EDI risks can be controlled by two security responses. One of these addresses the physical aspects of data transmission, particularly data integrity; the other secures EDI users. The goal of EDI security is to ensure that information is transmitted completely, free of errors, and in a timely fashion. This chapter addresses the technical and human factors that must be controlled to secure EDI processing.

DATA TRANSMISSION CONTROLS

Data transmission is controlled by coding schemes, transmission techniques, and transmission speed, which are discussed in the following sections. EDI transmission on wide area networks is also addressed.

Coding Schemes

Coding schemes translate the standard characters and symbols found on a keyboard into the zeros and ones used directly by computers and indirectly by data transmission devices. One of the more widely accepted coding schemes is the American Standard Code for Information Interchange (ASCII), which translates characters into a seven-digit binary code. Other coding schemes, such as the Extended Binary Coded Decimal Interchange Code (EBCDIC) and the Baudot Code, are also used in various applications.

An additional zero or one is often added to each character code as a parity check. Parity checking is a summing technique that totals the seven digits in a character code and adds a last digit of either a zero or a one to create a total that is either an odd or even number, depending on the system designation. The receiver duplicates this summation to verify the correctness of the character code it received. When errors are detected, the data is retransmitted. Parity checking detects errors in bytes that have single-bit errors and provides a minimal level of control.

The last digit or bit is sometimes used to expand a potential character set to include the graphic characters found on many printed documents. In such cases, the safety of parity is compromised for presentation flexibility.

Transmission Techniques

Once characters have been encoded, they must be sent across wires to a receiver. The usual transmission method over long distances (i.e., more than 100 feet) is to send the characters as a series of bits signifying the presence or absence of an electrical signal. The next step is to know when one character stops and the next begins.

Two methods control character flow: synchronous mode and asynchronous mode. In synchronous mode, both the sender and the receiver carefully time the data flow. The data is usually put into a block that is sent as a package to the receiver. The package contains information about the size of the block, its error-detection methods, and its coding method. The package is a self-contained, verified piece of information with start and stop flags on both ends. After the receiver accepts the start flag, the transmission protocol dictates the exact meaning for each portion of the signal package on the basis of the timing of this reception. The data package can be any size that makes the technique efficient, as long as there is little noise on the communications lines to corrupt data. Synchronized transmission is very reliable and well controlled; most mainframes use it.

In asynchronous mode, each character contains the starting and stopping code signals for the receiver to interpret its bit flow. This mode provides a high level of data integrity but a slower data transmission rate than synchronous mode offers. Most microcomputers and bulletin boards use this technique.

Several integrity checking techniques besides odd or even parity attempt to determine whether strings of bits have been corrupted during transmission. One of the more effective techniques is the cyclic redundancy check, which applies a mathematical algorithm to a character's bits, retains the remainder from the process, appends the remainder to the character (or package), and sends the entire package to its receiver. The receiver strips the appended remainder, applies the same algorithm to the bits, and compares the result with the package's result to look for errors. When corrupt data is detected, it is retransmitted. This technique detects multiple errors that can slip through the parity filter; it is both effective and efficient.

Transmission of data in packages is an efficient use of transmission resources, particularly time. Packages can include error-checking procedures and allow flexibility in the choice of a transmission protocol. Protocol definition is important when different types of equipment are used at ends of a communications channel, as is often the case in EDI between independent companies.

Many communications protocols have entered into the public domain or are available at minimum cost. One of the most flexible and reliable techniques, when properly configured, is the Kermit file transfer protocol, developed at Columbia University. Its extensive error checking, data compression, and multiple file transfer capabilities; character code flexibility (it can accept seven- or eight-bit character strings); and renegotiation of the package arrangement for each transmission make Kermit a highly reliable protocol.

Transmission Speed

The speed of data transmission is measured by its baud rate, or signal duration. Transmissions with longer signal durations send fewer signals each second; short durations entail a faster transmission rate. Typical transmission lines limit speed, imposing a limit on how short the signal duration can be. To overcome this physical restriction, organizations often use a scheme that encodes a series of bits as one signal. Thus, the actual data flow is increased and the signal duration is not reduced below acceptable equipment tolerances. With this scheme, the baud rate does not always translate directly into the character transmission rate; therefore, bits per second can be a better measurement of a system's data transmission speed.

Modems funnel electrical signals from a computer into a communications network. A sending modem converts it digital signal into an amplitude-modulated signal for analog transmission; the receiving modem then demodulates the signal into a digital signal for its computer to interpret. To complete the transmission, each computer requires one modem.

Various devices increase transmission rates over a single set of wires. Multiplexers combine the signals from several modems and send the combined signal at a high speed to a receiving multiplexer, which reverses the process. This technique can significantly reduce transmission costs.

Wide Area Network Models

EDI between different companies occurs through wide area network (WAN) communications, which differs from the local area network (LAN) communications systems used in a single company that are controlled by its data processing and communications departments. Two architectural standards provide high-quality data integrity between remote WAN locations. The International Standards Organization developed the open systems interconnection (OSI) reference model for connecting equipment from different vendors in a standard fashion, and IBM Corp. introduced the System Network Architecture (SNA) model for connecting IBM equipment at remote locations.

The layered approaches used by SNA and OSI are roughly the same (see Ex-

EXHIBIT III-2-8 The OSI and SNA Models

OSI	SNA
7. Application	7. User
6. Presentation	6. Presentation
5. Session	5. Data Flow
4. Transport	4. Transmission
3. Network	3. Data Path
2. Data Link	2. Data Link
1. Physical	1. Physical

hibit III-2-8). Briefly, the layers begin with the physical control of media at the lower end and culminate at the user end with transaction or applications control. The intermediate layers control data links (synchronous or asynchronous), data path, transmission (i.e., data delivery and delivery acknowledgment), data flow, and presentation services (i.e., data conversions and transformations). Systems connected with these models have a high level of data integrity, network security, standardized interconnectivity, upward compatibility, and applications transfer. These guidelines ensure that output matches input and that corrective actions are taken when errors are detected.

CONTROLS ON EDI USERS

Users can introduce errors into EDI systems either intentionally or unintentionally, thus degrading system integrity. User interaction with EDI systems occurs in two ways: first, users are responsible for data entry, and second, they sometimes interfere during transmission (e.g., by breaking the communications link). These interactions may occur simultaneously if data is immediately transferred upon entry.

EDI applications increase the complexity of the processing environment, creating a higher level of risk—particularly for the organization's accounting system. The level of risk depends on the complexity and type of EDI application being implemented. The following sections review the controls needed to monitor EDI applications, including human interaction with these applications.

General and Applications Controls

The following general controls relate to all parts of an EDI installation:

- Organization and management controls.
- Applications development and maintenance controls.
- Computer operation controls.
- System software controls.
- Data entry and program controls.

These controls include such corporate-level controls as security policies and procedures, the segregation of incompatible functions, testing and development concerns, and documentation controls.

Applications controls apply to a system's particular functions and are therefore built into them and evaluated by security personnel. Applications controls include:

- Controls over input.
- Controls over processing and data files.
- Controls over output.

Usually, the input stage is controlled with preprocessing authorization, transmittal and conversion verification, and programmed controls. Error correction, recovery, and backup procedures and postprocessing review are employed during the last two processing stages. Output is controlled by restricting access to output and by ensuring its proper delivery to authorized personnel.

Microcomputers

The standalone microcomputer can accomplish much and sometimes all of the financial processing required by a firm, particularly if it is networked to other microcomputers or a mainframe. However, a microcomputer's simplified applications development, physical separation from the mainframe it accesses, and inexpensive initial investment often create a weakened internal control environment. Many of the controls required in a microcomputer may not be present. For example, segregation of duties, a general control, is usually sacrificed with a standalone microcomputer because relatively few people are required to operate it. More specific controls over software, files, input, processing, and output are compromised in the microcomputing environment because users often take a casual attitude toward the computer; such a lax attitude can be especially dangerous when the work environment changes.

Many microcomputer applications are manual operations that were computerized, yet microcomputer operators often lack significant security experience. Instruction and training, authorization to access programs, physical security and backup procedures, personal use policies, file organization, hidden files, passwords, and even cryptography are necessary controls that the security manager should consider. Many controls traditionally used with the central computer must be applied to small systems.

Online Computer Systems

With EDI, data is entered and transmitted without delay, which puts data integrity at risk. Online processing imposes an increased risk of fraud and errors in accounting and internal control systems. This risk occurs when terminals are located throughout a firm, when the opportunity exists for their unauthorized use, when communications failures cause processing interruptions, and when online access to data or programs is allowed. In addition, an EDI internal control system may be unable to provide an adequate audit trail: source documents may not exist, the results contained in existing source documents may be so highly summarized that the detail cannot be determined, or the system's hardware may not be configured to produce a printed document.

Online processing can be performed on terminals linked to a mainframe, intelligent terminals with minor local processing capability, or microcomputers with both local processing and significant storage capacity. However, those installations that involve mainframe access by programmers pose a significant risk because they can allow unauthorized access to programs and data files.

The five areas of internal control for online systems are:

- Access.
- Passwords.
- Systems development and maintenance.
- Programming.
- Transaction logs.

Particular attention must be given to access controls because they guard the door to a system. An opened door can allow unauthorized data or program modifications, transactions, users, or programs to enter. This door is usually protected by a password system and menu-driven processing. A password system requires conscientious control over the issue and maintenance of passwords. Passwords should be changed as employees change and at specific time intervals. Systems development controls include passwords and access controls, data validation, and recovery procedures. Programming controls prevent unauthorized alteration of program code; library and change procedures also assist in this. Finally, the transaction log creates the critical audit trail of transaction details, including the source and time of transaction entry and processing.

Particular attention must be given to controls over transaction authorization in the online and EDI environment. For example, EDI purchase orders to outside vendors establish a legal obligation to the firm that cannot be cleared by a simple reversing entry. Complications also occur in certain online data base systems when reversals cannot correct faulty transactions. To avoid this problem, terminal edit routines and validity checks must be incorporated in the input stage as part of the application.

EDI systems are designed for direct entry through terminals in a real-time environment. In real-time environments, data files are immediately updated, data is immediately processed, or information output is provided in time for decision makers to incorporate that information in their decision models. The immediacy of real-time environments makes it impossible to prescreen data or correct it during a presubmission review. This introduces a new set of concerns regarding the internal control objectives of reliability, adherence to accounting policies, and safeguard-

EXHIBIT III-2-9 Control Evaluation Framework for an Accounts Payable Analysis

General Objective	Potential Error	Impact on Transaction Processed	Control Technique
Completeness	Data lost (in-house)	Transaction not recorded	Preprocess review, use of hard copy
Completeness	Data lost (outside the organization)	Order not placed	Posttransaction review, echo checking, confirmation request, redundancy data, tickler file setup
Mechanical accuracy	Data duplication	False inventory growth request	Echo checking, confirmation, request reasonableness test, posttransaction review, batching (if appropriate), purchase order number analysis
Mechanical accuracy	Inaccurate data	Wrong liability	Preprocessing review
Classification	Improper classification	Inventory not authorized	Hard copy, echo checking
Posting and summarization	Wrong file processed	Wrong record processed	Reasonableness checking, echo checking, postprocessing edits, scheduling, processing security controls
Cutoff	Untimely procedures	Late or lost output	Preprocessing review, batching, cutoff procedures, scheduling
Authorization (or ownership)	Blanket authorization	Invalid payment could result	Preprocessing review

ing assets and records. To evaluate adherence to accounting policies, accounting records are examined at the end of each fiscal period and valuations are performed. Safeguarding techniques focus on unauthorized or invalid transaction entry during transmission. After these internal control objectives have been realized, the objectives of data completeness, validity, and mechanical accuracy must be pursued.

SUMMARY

An organization must establish a relationship among control objectives, potential errors, and control techniques. Analysis of the internal control system in an automated environment does not differ from analysis in a manual setting. A security administrator looks initially at the organization's financial statements for areas where significant errors could occur and then works back through the accounting system for the processing points where those errors or irregularities could be introduced. The administrator identifies where transactions are initiated, recorded, summarized, and posted—these are the points where errors can occur.

Next, the type of error and its potential significance are evaluated for each processing point. The administrator should implement a control for each error judged to be material. A relationship can be drawn between each potential processing error and its transaction by following this procedure. This mapping aids in evaluating the effect of errors on an organization's financial statements.

The next step is to create a chart that maps each potential processing error and the control technique used to achieve an internal control objective. Linking the objective, potential error, and control technique for each transaction ensures that each internal control has a purpose. This analytical format yields a clear map to each control objective and lowers the control risk associated with transactions.

Exhibit III-2-9 maps these relationships for the processing of purchase orders. This exhibit lists only those errors that can be attributed to EDI processing—for example, program code changes would be reviewed as part of the EDP audit and are therefore not addressed. By analyzing their EDI systems in this manner, security administrators can help their organizations realize the savings in time and money that EDI promises, without the risks that it poses.

The Legal and
Regulatory Environment

Up to this point, this handbook has dealt with the managerial, administrative, and technical issues involved with the security of automated information systems. An obvious motivation for an organization's interest in this subject is the prevention of serious losses to the organization of resources, money, reputation, and even human life. However, there exists another source of motivation—the laws, regulations, and standards that have been developed in this field. Part IV of this handbook focuses on computer crime and abuse and on the laws and regulations governing the use of automated information systems.

Computer crime and abuse, along with accidental loss, are fundamental problems for information security practitioners. A computer crime is any violation of the law that involves the use of computer technology for its perpetration. Computer abuse is any intentional act involving computer technology that allows a perpetrator to make an unlawful gain or a victim to suffer a loss. Computers can be the subject of a crime, the object of a crime, or the instrument of a crime.

Computer crimes can be placed in one of four main categories: introduction of fraudulent records; unauthorized use; alteration or destruction of information; and stealing resources (e.g., money or property). Computer crimes can also be classified by the types of information losses that occur, (e.g., loss of integrity and authenticity, loss of confidentiality, and loss of availability and utility).

Unfortunately, there are no valid statistics on computer crime, because of the reluctance of many organizations to report such crimes. Over the years, however, computer abuses have been reported in sufficient numbers to permit development of a profile of computer abuse methods, possible perpetrators, and methods of detection. Some of the better known methods of abuse involve masquerading, false data entry, Trojan horses and computer viruses, salami techniques (i.e., rounding up or down), trap doors, logic bombs, computer program piracy, and larceny of computer components. Chapters IV-1-1 and IV-1-2 provide a comprehensive discussion of the various types of computer crime and abuse and their methods of detection.

It is clear that new forms of computer crime will emerge as the technology evolves. Such actions as extortion using E-mail, fax graffiti, and repudiation of EDI transactions can be expected to add to the pantheon of computer crimes.

Eventually, all business crime will become computer crime; new laws will have to be written to address these new crime forms.

The investigation of computer abuse is addressed in Chapter IV-1-3. From an investigative point of view, there are three classes of computer abuse: the fraudulent removal of money, information, or other property; invasion of privacy; and malicious damage. A successful investigation of fraud may require only analysis of an audit trail. Investigation of malicious damage, on the other hand, is complicated by the fact that evidence may be destroyed inadvertently before a person becomes aware that a malicious act has been committed. Chapter IV-1-3 takes the reader through three case examples—one for fraud, one for hacking, and one for malicious damages—to illustrate variations in such investigations.

The failure of an information system to ensure, within reason, the confidentiality, integrity, and availability of the information in a computer system may lead to litigation. The law of torts addresses a class of wrongs involving negligence. A formula for determining negligence is based on proof of the existence of five elements: the duty to act to prevent harm to another, breach of such duty, conduct that causes damage, a traceable path between cause and damage, and actual losses that result from such damage.

Chapter IV-1-4 describes how these elements relate to cases of negligence in protecting computer systems and information. This chapter also reviews several other legal concepts that may form the basis for a lawsuit. These legalities have important implications for information security. For example, two of the elements needed to prove breach of duty are the foreseeability of threats requiring countermeasures and a standard of care based on what a reasonable and prudent person would do, regardless of industry practice. To avoid litigation based on negligence, organizations should assemble an interdisciplinary team (including an attorney) to design a program for identifying foreseeable threats and designing and implementing acceptable countermeasures that reflect a prudent standard of care. A recovery plan should also be developed and suitable insurance taken out so that an act of negligence by one employee does not threaten the entire organization. By implementing the measures described in Chapter IV-1-4, the organization should be able to significantly reduce its potential liability for negligence.

Introduction to Computer Crime

DONN B. PARKER

Computer crime and accidental loss are the fundamental problems that security practitioners must try to prevent. Business, economic, and white-collar crimes have rapidly changed as a result of the increasing use of computers for a wide variety of business transactions. Computers have engendered a different form of crime even though they are called by familiar names of fraud, embezzlement, larceny, and espionage.

The methods of committing crime have changed as well, for which a new jargon has developed. These methods are examined in Chapter IV-1-2, "Computer Abuse Methods and Detection." In addition, new methods are bound to emerge as the technology changes (e.g., digital imaging for forgery and wireless local area networks as targets of espionage), new applications arise, and criminal ingenuity advances.

The forms of many of the targets of computer crime are also different. Electronic transactions and money as well as paper and credit cards represent assets subject to intentionally caused, automated losses. For example, money in the form of electronic signals and magnetic patterns is stored and processed in computers and transmitted over telephone lines. Many other physical assets, including inventories of products in warehouses and of materials leaving or entering factories, are represented by electronic and optical documents of record inside computer systems. Electronic data interchange (EDI)—which connects trading partners for conducting contract negotiations, sales, invoicing, and collections—focuses traditional sources of business crime on computers and data communications.

In addition, the timing of some crimes is different. Traditionally, the time of criminal acts has been measured in minutes, hours, days, weeks, months, and years. Today, some crimes are being perpetrated in less then 3 milliseconds. Automated crime must be considered in terms of a computer time scale (i.e., milliseconds, microseconds, and nanoseconds) because of the speed of the execution of instructions in computers.

Furthermore, geographic constraints do not inhibit perpetration of computer crime. A telephone with an attached modem and computer terminal in one part of the world could be used to engage in a crime in an online computer system in any other part of the world.

All these factors and more must be considered in dealing with the crime of computer abuse. Unfortunately, however, the business community—comprising all businesses, government agencies, and institutions that use computers for technical and business purposes—is neither adequately prepared to deal with nor sufficiently motivated to report this kind of crime to the authorities. Although reliable statistics are not yet available to prove this, computer security studies within the business community and interviews with certified public accountants have indicated that few crimes of this type are ever reported to law enforcement agencies for prosecution.

Many businesspeople complain that even when they do report computer crimes, prosecutors frequently refuse to accept the cases for a variety of reasons, including their lack of understanding of the technology and their already-heavy case loads. In addition, many investigators are not sufficiently technically skilled. Prosecutors and investigators counter that the victim's records and documentation of crimes associated with computers are often inadequate for effective protection.

This chapter presents methods of defining and classifying computer crimes so that security practitioners can better understand the crimes their organizations may face. In addition, the history of computer crimes is briefly examined, and the ways the media have portrayed computer crimes are discussed.

DEFINING COMPUTER CRIME

Computers have been involved in most types of crime. Still, computer crime is not well understood in the criminal justice and computer-using communities, and no consensus on its definition exists, as evidenced by the diversity of computer crime laws. One definition is that it is a form of white-collar crime committed inside a computer system; another definition is that it is the use of a computer as the instrument of a business crime.

In general, computer crimes fall into three legal categories:

- Violations of specific computer crime laws.
- Computer-related crime (i.e., violations of criminal law that involve use of computers).
- Computer abuse.

For the purposes of this discussion, the term "computer crime" is used to refer to all three types of computer crime.

State and federal criminal codes in the US contain at least 52 statutes defining computer crime. At least nine other countries (including Australia, Canada, Germany, France, and Norway) have computer crime laws. Any violations of these specific statutes are computer crimes under the strictest interpretation of the term; in some contexts, it is also customary to include alleged violations of these statutes as computer crimes. In addition, some computer crimes may be prosecuted under older, better-tested laws.

Computer-related crimes, a broader category, are any violations of criminal law that involve a knowledge of computer technology for their perpetration, investigation, or prosecution. Although computer-related crimes are primarily white-collar offenses, any kind of illegal act based on an understanding of computer technology can be a computer-related crime. Computers can be used as tools in almost any crime that otherwise would not involve computers at all. They could even be violent crimes that destroy computers or their contents and thereby jeopardize human life (e.g., automated life support systems in hospitals).

Computer abuse encompasses a broad range of intentional acts that may or may not be specifically prohibited by criminal statutes. Any intentional act involving knowledge of computer use or technology is considered computer abuse if one or more perpetrators realized or could have realized a profit or if one or more victims suffered or could have suffered a loss.

Computer crime may involve computers not only actively but passively when usable evidence of the crime resides in computer storage. Any kind of telephone or credit card fraud falls under the realm of computer crime because both services are carried out through computers. The victims and potential victims of computer crime include all organizations and people who use or are affected by computer and data communication systems, including people about whom data is stored and processed in computers.

On the basis of all known and reported cases of computer crime, the computer can function in one or more of the following capacities to perpetrate a crime:

- *The object of a crime.* Cases include destruction of computers or of data or programs contained in them, destruction of support facilities, and destruction of resources that allow the computers to function (e.g., air-conditioning equipment and electrical power).

- *The subject of a crime.* A computer can be the site of a crime or the source of or reason for unique kinds of assets lost (e.g., pirated computer programs). A fraud perpetrated by changing account balances in financial data stored in a computer makes the computer the subject of a crime.

- *The instrument for committing a crime.* Some types and methods of crime are complex enough to require the use of a computer as a tool or instrument. A computer can be used actively (e.g., to automatically scan telephone codes to make unauthorized use of a telephone system) or passively (e.g., to simulate a general ledger in the planning and control of a continuing financial embezzlement).

- *A symbol for intimidation or deception.* This could involve an organization's claiming to use computers that actually do not exist.

Determining whether a specific crime is a computer crime can be a problem in some cases. If a computer is stolen in a simple theft, knowledge of computer technology is not necessary and it would not be considered a computer crime. Essentially, knowledge of computer technology must be integral to perpetration of the crime for it to be considered a computer crime.

CLASSIFYING COMPUTER CRIME

Computer crime is classified on the basis of a variety of lists and models. Efforts made during the mid-1970s to amend Title 18 of the US Criminal Code resulted in Article 1030, Chapter 47, stating that unauthorized acts in, around, and with computers were crimes. Four main types of computer crime were identified:

- The introduction of fraudulent records or data into a computer system.
- Unauthorized use of computer-related facilities.
- The alteration or destruction of information or files.
- The theft, whether by electronic means or otherwise, of money, financial instruments, property, services, or valuable data.

Computer crime has also been classified by types of information processing loss: modification, destruction, disclosure, and use or denial of use. This classification is deceptive, however, because many other types of loss have occurred, including acts of misrepresentation, delay or prolongation of use, renaming, misappropriation, repudiation, and failure to act. Therefore, a more comprehensive and usable classification is loss of integrity and authenticity, confidentiality, and availability and utility of information. These three classes define acts that are intrinsic to information (e.g., rearranging data or making it useless), extrinsic to information (e.g., changing access to properties the data is supposed to represent), and external to information (e.g., removing or copying the data).

Computer abuse studies have identified several methods for classifying computer crimes:

- By ways in which information loss occurs (i.e., loss of integrity or authenticity, confidentiality, and availability or utility).
- By type of loss (i.e., physical damage and destruction, intellectual property loss, direct financial loss, and unauthorized use of services).
- By the role played by computers (i.e., object, subject, instrument, and symbol).
- By type of act relative to the data, computer programs, and services (i.e., external abuse, masquerading, preparatory abuse, bypass of intended controls, passive abuse, active abuse, and use as a tool for committing a crime).
- By type of crime (e.g., fraud, theft, robbery, larceny, arson, embezzlement, extortion, conspiracy, sabotage, and espionage).
- By modus operandi (e.g., physical attacks, false data entry, superzapping, impersonation, wiretapping, piggybacking, scavenging, Trojan horse attacks, trapdoor use, asynchronous attacks, salami techniques, data leakage, logic bombs, and simulation).
- By skills required:
  —No programming skills required (e.g., physical scavenging, spying, masquerading, entering false data, and stealing data).

—Programming skills required (e.g., to release viruses, leak data, or use in criminal enterprises).

These classifications have been developed into sets of complete, detailed descriptions and models of computer crime. They are useful for a variety of research and practical purposes in providing security and in investigating and prosecuting computer crimes.

HISTORY OF COMPUTER CRIME

Computer abuse can be traced back to the emergence of computer technology during the late 1940s. The problem of abuse became especially acute, however, when computer technology began to be applied in sensitive areas (e.g., military systems). Computer abuse is now prevalent in engineering, science, business, and personal applications.

The first recorded computer abuse occurred in 1958. The first prosecution of a crime identified as a computer crime on the basis of US federal statutes occurred in 1966 and involved the alteration of bank records through use of a computer in Minneapolis.

No valid statistics on computer crime exist, though several surveys have been conducted and well-known organizations and professionals have quoted various statistics. Frequency, annual losses, the rate of increase or decrease, percentages of perpetrators within or outside victimized organizations, and the number of cases discovered and prosecuted are not known. (This is partly owing to the fact that victims typically hide or deny their losses, in an effort to protect themselves.)

No methods have been devised to apply uniform definitions, identify authoritative sources, or conduct surveys in any statistically valid way. For example, the American Bar Association Task Force on Computer Crime, Section of Criminal Justice, reported the results of an informal questionnaire survey in a report on computer crime, stating:

> One cannot extrapolate from the results of this limited survey to derive a valid "total annual dollar loss" figure for computer crime, a figure which has been sought by many, but which is elusive and unattainable given the current state of record-keeping. . . . It is also noteworthy that many of the largest organizations responding to the survey (those with annual revenues/budgets over $1 billion) reported no available system to monitor or estimate value of losses. . . . As various commentators have pointed out, valid and reliable statistics on the actual incidence of computer crime and actual losses sustained on any comprehensive basis are simply not possible until better reporting systems are in place.

As experience increases, valid statistics on rates of convictions among cases reported to the authorities should be obtainable, but only with respect to specific statutes.

Pursuit of the study of computer crime and computer abuse has been controversial. In 1970, several researchers concluded that the problem was merely a small part of the effect of technology on society and therefore was not worthy of specific, explicit research. However, the increase in substantial losses associated with intentional acts involving computers proved the fallacy of this view.

Efforts to research and develop preventive measures for computer crime suffered a similar fate during the mid-1970s. Researchers argued that the involvement of computers in crime should be subordinate to the study of each specific type of crime, both manual and automated. The uniqueness of the characteristics of computer crime as compared with all the other types of crime was not considered sufficient to warrant explicit research of computer crime alone.

The formal study of computer abuse began in 1971. The first national conference on computer abuse and a comprehensive report were completed in 1973. Since then, many reports, papers, articles, and books have been published describing the research.

The interest of the criminal justice community began in response to increasing numbers of cases and action by criminal justice organizations. In 1976, the FBI established a four-week training course in investigating computer crime for its agencies. The US Treasury Federal Law Enforcement Training Center at Glynco, Georgia is now the largest training facility for police officers that addresses computer crime.

In 1976, as a result of the increasing frequency of cases, Senator Abraham Ribicoff and his US Senate Government Affairs Committee recognized computer crime and the inadequacy of federal criminal law to deal with it. The committee produced tow reports on its research, and Ribicoff introduced the first Federal Systems Protection Act Bill in June 1977. These legislative efforts evolved into House Bill 5616 in 1986, which resulted in the Computer Fraud and Abuse Act of 1987 (established as Article 1030, Chapter 47 of Title 18 Criminal Code).

On the state level, Florida, Michigan, Colorado, Rhode Island, and Arizona were the first to have computer crime laws based on the Ribicoff bill. Current legislation on computer crime exists in at least 49 states. No legislative actions in other countries during this time were reported internationally. A computer hacker crime law has now been passed in the UK Parliament, however, and several other countries now have computer crime laws.

MEDIA PORTRAYAL OF COMPUTER CRIME

Computer crime has been portrayed fictionally in film and print. Several television news shows have run special segments on computer crime, and articles have appeared in major magazines and newspapers. Unfortunately, the public interest and sensationalism associated with computer crime has made folk heroes of the perpetrators and has embarrassed the victims.

The news media have done a great service in bringing public attention to the problem of computer crime; however, those who must deal with the real nature of the problem (as opposed to the reported nature) should not be influenced by the media's sometimes distorted representations. Since 1970, several computer crime issues have saturated and subsequently faded from news media attention, though the potential for loss grows more serious as technology advances. The primary issues have been:

- Invasion of personal privacy.
- Salami fraud techniques.
- Telephone toll fraud.
- Hacker computer intrusion.
- Trojan horse attacks.
- Software piracy.
- Interference with communications.
- Radio frequency emanation pickup.
- Computer virus attacks.

News reporters often ask victims, investigators, and prosecutors for information on these cases, especially as the issues become popular or if they are associated with well-known people or organizations. Criminal justice personnel and victims must be cautious to protect the privacy of victims, suspects, and witnesses as well as the confidentiality of their cases and findings. Fortunately, journalists, through their increasing experience with computer use and computer technology, are becoming more accurate in their reporting of computer crimes.

SUMMARY

This chapter presents an overview of computer crime, providing definitions and working classifications of this form of abuse. To place computer crimes in proper perspective, security practitioners would do well to understand the history of state and federal statutes on computer crimes as well as the way the media have influenced the public's perception of these crimes. Chapter IV-1-2, "Computer Abuse Methods and Detection," examines the various methods of computer crime in more detail.

Computer Abuse Methods and Detection

DONN B. PARKER

This chapter describes 17 computer abuse methods in which computers play a key role. Several of the methods are far more complex than can be described here in detail; in addition, it would not be prudent to reveal specific details that criminals could use. These descriptions should facilitate a sufficient understanding of computer abuse for security practitioners to apply to specific instances. Most technologically sophisticated computer crimes are committed using one or more of these methods. The results of these sophisticated and automated attacks are loss of information integrity or authenticity, loss of confidentiality, and loss of availability or utility associated with the use of services, computer and communications equipment or facilities, computer programs, or data in computer systems and communications media.

As discussed in Chapter IV-1-1, "Introduction to Computer Crime," the abuse methods are not necessarily identifiable with specific statutory offenses. The methods, possible types of perpetrators, likely evidence of their use, and detection and prevention methods are described in the following sections.

EAVESDROPPING AND SPYING

Eavesdropping includes wiretapping and monitoring of radio frequency emanations, Few wiretap abuses are known, and no cases of radio frequency emanation eavesdropping have been proved outside government intelligence agencies. Case experience is probably so scarce because industrial spying and scavenging represent easier, more direct ways for criminals to obtain the required information.

On the other hand, these passive eavesdropping methods may be so difficult to detect that they are never reported. In addition, opportunities to pick up emanations from isolated small computers and terminals, microwave circuits, and satellite signals continue to grow.

One disadvantage of eavesdropping, from the eavesdropper's point of view, is that the perpetrators often do not know when the needed data will be sent. Therefore, they must collect relatively large amounts of data and search for the specific items of interest. Another disadvantage is that identifying and isolating the communications circuit can pose a problem for perpetrators. Intercepting microwave and satellite communications is even more difficult, primarily because complex, costly equipment is needed for interception and because the perpetrators must determine whether active detection facilities are built into the communications system.

Clandestine radio transmitters can be attached to computer components. They can be detected by panoramic spectrum analysis or second-harmonic radar sweeping. Interception of free-space radiation is not a crime in the US unless disclosure of the information thus obtained violates the Electronic Communications Privacy Act of 1986 (the ECPA) or the Espionage Act. Producing radiation may be a violation of FCC regulations.

Intelligible emanations can be intercepted even from large machine rooms and at long distances using parametric amplifiers and digital filters. Faraday-cage shielding can be supplemented by carbon-filament adsorptive covering on the walls and ceilings. Interception of microwave spillage and satellite footprints is different because it deals with intended signal data emanation and could be illegal under the ECPA if it is proved that the information obtained was communicated to a third party.

Spying consists of criminal acquisition of information by covert observation. For example, shoulder surfing involves observing users at computer terminals as they enter or receive displays of sensitive information (e.g., observing passwords in this fashion using binoculars). Frame-by-frame analysis of video recordings can also be used to determine personal ID numbers entered at automatic teller machines.

Solutions to Eavesdropping and Spying

The two best solutions to eavesdropping are to use computer and communications equipment with reduced emanations and to use cryptography to scramble data. Because both solutions are relatively costly, they are not used unless the risks are perceived to be sufficiently great or until a new level of standard of due care is met through changes in practices, regulation, or law.

In addition, electronic shielding that uses a Faraday grounded electrical conducting shield helps prevent eavesdropping, and physical shielding helps prevent spying. Detecting these forms of abuse and obtaining evidence require that investigators observe the acts and capture the equipment used to perpetrate the crime.

Eavesdropping should be assumed to be the least likely method used in the theft or modification of data. Detection methods and possible evidence are the same as in the investigation of voice communications wiretapping. Exhibit IV-1-1 summarizes the potential perpetrators, detection, and evidence in eavesdropping acts.

EXHIBIT IV-1-1 Detection of Eavesdropping

Potential Perpetrators	Methods of Detection	Evidence
• Communications technicians and engineers	• Voice wiretapping methods	• Voice wiretapping evidence
• Communications employees	• Observation	
	• Tracing sources of equipment used	

SCANNING

Scanning is the process of presenting information sequentially to an automated system to identify those items that receive a positive response (e.g., until a password is identified). This method is typically used to identify telephone numbers that access computers, user IDs, and passwords that facilitate access to computers as well as credit card numbers that can be used illegally for ordering merchandise or services.

Computer programs that perform the automatic searching, called demon programs, are available from various hacker electronic bulletin boards. Scanning may be prosecuted as criminal harassment and perhaps as trespassing or fraud if the information identified is used with criminal intent. For example, scanning for credit card numbers involves testing sequential numbers by automatically dialing credit verification services. Access to proprietary credit rating services may constitute criminal trespass.

Prevention of Scanning

The perpetrators of scanning are generally malicious hackers and system intruders. Many computer systems can deter scanners by limiting the number of access attempts. Attempts to exceed these limits result in long delays that discourage the scanning process.

Identifying perpetrators is often difficult, usually requiring the use of pen registers or dialed number recorder equipment in cooperation with communication companies. Mere possession of a demon program may constitute possession of a tool for criminal purposes, and printouts from demon programs may be used to incriminate a suspect.

MASQUERADING

Physical access to computer terminals and electronic access through terminals to a computer require positive identification of an authorized user. The authentication of a user's identity is based on a combination of something the user knows (e.g., a secret password), a physiological or learned characteristic of the user (e.g., a fingerprint, retinal pattern, hand geometry, keystroke rhythm, or voice), and a token the user possesses (e.g., a magnetic-stripe card, smart card, or metal key). Masquerading is the process of an intruder's assuming the identity of an authorized user after acquiring the user's ID information. Anybody with the correct combination of identification characteristics can masquerade as another individual.

Playback is another type of masquerade, in which user or computer responses or initiations of transactions are surreptitiously recorded and played back to the computer as though they came from the user. Playback was suggested as a means of robbing ATMs by repeating cash dispensing commands to the machines through a wiretap. This fraud was curtailed when banks installed controls that placed encrypted message sequence numbers, times, and dates into each transmitted transaction and command.

Detection of Masquerading

Masquerading is the most common activity of computer system intruders. It is also one of the most difficult to prove in a trial. When an intrusion takes place, the investigator must obtain evidence identifying the masquerader, the location of the terminal the masquerader used, and the activities the masquerader performed. This task is especially difficult when network connections through several switched telephone systems interfere with pen register and direct number line tracing. Exhibit IV-1-2 summarizes the methods of detecting computer abuse committed by masquerading.

PIGGYBACKING AND TAILGATING

Piggybacking and tailgating can be done physically or electronically. Physical piggybacking is a method for gaining access to controlled access areas when con-

---

EXHIBIT IV-1-2   Detection of Masquerading

Potential Perpetrators	Methods of Detection	Evidence
• Authorized computer users	• Audit log analysis	• Computer audit log
• Hackers	• Password violations	• Notes and documents in possession of suspects
	• Observation	• Pen register and records of number dialed
	• Report by person impersonated	• Witnesses
		• Access control package exception or violation reports

trol is accomplished by electronically or mechanically locked doors. Typically, an individual carrying computer-related objects (e.g., tape reels) stands by the locked door. When an authorized individual arrives and opens the door, the intruder goes in as well. The success of this method of piggybacking depends on the quality of the access control mechanism and the alertness of authorized personnel in resisting cooperation with the perpetrator.

Electronic piggybacking can take place in an online computer system in which individuals use terminals and the computer system automatically verifies identification. When a terminal has been activated, the computer authorizes access, usually on the basis of a secret password, token or other exchange of required identification and authentication information (i.e., a protocol). Compromise of the computer can occur when a covert computer terminal is connected to the same line through the telephone switching equipment and is then used when the legitimate user is not using the terminal. The computer cannot differentiate between the two terminals; it senses only one terminal and one authorized user.

Electronic piggybacking can also be accomplished when the user signs off or a session terminates improperly, leaving the terminal or communications circuit in an active state or leaving the computer in a state in which it assumes the user is still active. Call forwarding of the victim's telephone to the perpetrator's telephone is another means of piggybacking.

Tailgating involves connecting a computer user to a computer in the same session as and under the same identifier as another computer user, whose session has been interrupted. This situation happens when a dial-up or direct-connect session is abruptly terminated, and a communications controller (i.e., a concentrator or packet assembler/disassembler) incorrectly allows a second user to be patched directly into the first user's still-open files.

This problem is exacerbated if the controller incorrectly handles a modem's data-terminal-ready signal. Many network managers set up the controller to send data-terminal-ready signals continually so that the modem quickly establishes a new session after finishing its disconnect sequence from the previous session. The controller may miss the modem's drop-carrier signal after a session is dropped, allowing a new session to tailgate onto the old session.

In one vexing situation, computer users connected their office terminal hard-wired cables directly to their personal modems. This allowed them to connect any outside telephone directly to their employer's computers through central data switches, thus avoiding all dial-up protection controls (e.g., automatic callback devices). Such methods are very dangerous and have few means of acceptable control.

Prevention of Piggybacking and Tailgating

Turnstiles, double doors, or a stationed guard are the usual methods of preventing physical piggybacking. The turnstile allows passage of only one individual with a

---

EXHIBIT IV-1-3 Detection of Piggybacking and Tailgating

Potential Perpetrators	Methods of Detection	Evidence
• Employees and former employees	• Access observations	• Logs, journals, and equipment usage meters
• Vendor's employees	• Interviewing witnesses	• Photographs and voice and video recordings
• Contracted persons	• Examination of journals and logs	• Other physical evidence
• Outsiders	• Out-of-sequence messages	
	• Specialized computer programs that analyze characteristics of on line computer user accesses	

---

metal key, an electronic or magnetic card key, or the combination to a locking mechanism. The double door is a double-doored closet through which only one person can move with one key activation.

Electronic door access control systems frequently are run by a microcomputer that produces a log identifying each individual gaining access and the time of access. Alternatively, human guards may record this information in logs. Unauthorized access can be detected by studying these logs and interviewing people who may have witnessed the unauthorized access. Exhibit IV-1-3 summarizes the methods of detecting computer abuse committed by piggybacking and tailgating methods.

FALSE DATA ENTRY

False data entry is usually the simplest, safest, and most common method of computer abuse. It involves changing data before or during its input to computers. Anybody associated with or having access to the processes of creating, recording, transporting, encoding, examining, checking, converting, and transforming data that ultimately enters a computer can change this data. Examples of false data entry include forging, misrepresenting, or counterfeiting documents; exchanging computer tapes or disks; keyboard entry falsifications; failure to enter data; and neutralizing or avoiding controls.

Preventing False Data Entry

Data entry typically must be protected using manual controls. Manual controls include separation of duties or responsibilities, which force collusion among employees to perpetrate fraudulent acts.

In addition, batch control totals can be manually calculated and compared with matching computer-produced batch control totals. Another common control is the

---

EXHIBIT IV-1-4 Detection of False Data Entry

Potential Perpetrators	Methods of Detection	Evidence
• Transaction participants • Data preparers • Source data suppliers • Nonparticipants with access	• Data comparison • Document validation • Manual controls • Audit log analysis • Computer validation • Report analysis • Computer output comparison • Integrity tests (e.g., for value limits, logic consistencies, hash totals, crossfoot and column totals, and forged entry)	• Data documents: —Source —Transactions • Computer-readable output • Computer data media: —Tapes —Disks —Storage modules • Manual logs, audit logs, journals, and exception reports • Incorrect computer output • Control violation alarms

---

use of check digits or characters embedded in the data on the basis of various characteristics of each field of data (e.g., odd or even number indicators or hash totals). Sequence numbers and time of arrival can be associated with data and checked to ensure that data has not been lost or reordered. Large volumes of data can be checked with utility or special-purpose programs.

Evidence of false data entry is data that does not correctly represent data found at sources, does not match redundant or duplicate data, and does not conform to earlier forms of data if manual processes are reversed. Further evidence is control totals or check digits that do not check or meet validation and verification test requirements in the computer.

Exhibit IV-1-4 summarizes the likely perpetrators of false data entry, methods of detection, and sources of evidence.

SUPERZAPPING

Computers sometimes stop, malfunction, or enter a state that cannot be overcome by normal recovery or restart procedures. In addition, computers occasionally perform unexpectedly and need attention that normal access methods do not allow. In such cases, a universal access program is needed.

Superzapping derives its name from Superzap, a utility program used as a systems tool in most IBM mainframe centers. This program is capable of bypassing all controls to modify or disclose any program or computer-based data. Many programs similar to Superzap are available for microcomputers as well.

Such powerful utility programs as Superzap can be dangerous in the wrong hands. They are meant to be used only by systems programmers and computer operators who maintain the operating system and should be kept secure from unauthorized use. However, they are often placed in program libraries, where they can be used by any programmer or operator who knows how to use them.

Detection of Superzapping

Unauthorized use of Superzap programs can result in changes to data files that are usually updated only by production programs. Typically, few if any controls can detect changes in the data files from previous runs. Applications programmers do not anticipate this type of fraud; their realm of concern is limited to the application program and its interaction with data files. Therefore, the fraud is detected only when the recipients of regular computer output reports from the production program notify management that a discrepancy has occurred.

Furthermore, computer managers often conclude that the evidence indicates data entry errors, because it would not be a characteristic computer or program error. Considerable time can be wasted in searching the wrong areas. When management concludes that unauthorized file changes have occurred independent of the application program associated with the file, a search of all computer use logs might reveal the use of a Superzap program, but this is unlikely if the perpetrator anticipates the possibility. Occasionally, there may be a record of a request to have the file placed online in the computer system if it is not typically in that mode. Otherwise, the changes would have to occur when the production program using the file is being run or just before or after it is run.

Superzapping may be detected by comparing the current file with parent and grandparent copies of the file. Exhibit IV-1-5 summarizes the potential perpetrators, methods of detection, and sources of evidence in superzapping abuse.

SCAVENGING

Scavenging is a method of obtaining or reusing information that may be left after processing. Simple physical scavenging could involve searching trash barrels for copies of discarded computer listings or carbon paper from multiple-part forms.

EXHIBIT IV-1-5   Detection of Superzapping

Potential Perpetrators	Methods of Detection	Evidence
• Programmers with access to Superzap programs	• Comparison of files with historical copies	• Output report discrepancies
• Computer operation staff with applications knowledge	• Discrepancies in output reports, as noted by recipients	• Undocumented transactions
	• Examination of computer usage logs	• Computer usage or file request logs

More technical and sophisticated methods of scavenging include searching for residual data left in a computer, computer tapes, and disks after job execution.

Computer systems are designed and operators are trained to preserve data, not destroy it. If computer operators are requested to destroy the contents of disks or tapes, they most likely make backup copies first. This situation offers opportunities for both criminals and investigators.

In addition, a computer operating system may not properly erase buffer storage areas or cache memories used for the temporary storage of input or output data. Many operating systems do not erase magnetic disk or magnetic tape storage media because of the excessive computer time required to do this. (The data on optical disks cannot be electronically erased, though additional bits could be burned into a disk to change data or effectively erase them by, for example, changing all zeros to ones.)

In a poorly designed operating system, if storage were reserved and used by a previous job and then assigned to the next job, the next job might gain access to the same storage area, write only a small amount of data into that storage area, and then read the entire storage area back out, thus capturing data that was stored by the previous job.

Detection of Scavenging

Exhibit IV-1-6 lists the potential perpetrators of, methods of detection for, and evidence in scavenging crimes

TROJAN HORSES

The Trojan horse method of abuse involves the covert placement or alteration of computer instructions or data in a program so that the computer will perform unauthorized functions. Typically, the computer still allows the program to perform most or all of its intended purposes.

Trojan horse programs are the primary method used to insert instructions for

---

EXHIBIT IV-1-6   Detection of Scavenging

Potential Perpetrators	Methods of Detection	Evidence
• Users of the computer system • Persons with access to computer or backup facilities and adjacent areas	• Tracing of discovered proprietary information back to its source • Testing of an operating system to reveal residual data after job execution	• Computer output media • Type font characteristics • Proprietary information produced in suspicious ways and appearing in computer output media

other abusive acts (e.g., logic bombs, salami attacks, and viruses). This is the most commonly used method in computer program-based frauds and sabotage.

Instructions may be placed in production computer programs so that they will be executed in the protected or restricted domain of the program and have access to all of the data files that are assigned for the program's exclusive use. Programs are usually constructed loosely enough to allow space for inserting the instructions, sometimes without even extending the length or changing the checksum of the infected program.

Detecting and Preventing Trojan Horse Attacks

A typical business application program can consist of more than 100,000 computer instructions and data items. The Trojan horse can be concealed among as many as 5 million or 6 million instructions in the operating system and commonly used utility programs. It waits there for execution of the target application program, inserts extra instructions in it for a few milliseconds of execution time, and removes them with no remaining evidence.

Even if the Trojan horse is discovered, there is almost no indication of who may have done it. The search can be narrowed to those programmers who have the necessary skills, knowledge, and access among employees, former employees, contract programmers, consultants, or employees of the computer or software suppliers.

A suspected Trojan horse might be discovered by comparing a copy of the operational program under suspicion with a master or other copy known to be free of unauthorized changes. Although backup copies of production programs are routinely kept in safe storage, clever perpetrators may make duplicate changes in them. In addition, programs are frequently changed for authorized purposes without the backup copies being updated, thereby making comparison difficult.

A program suspected of being a Trojan horse can sometimes be converted from object form into assembly or higher-level form for easier examination or comparison by experts. Utility programs are usually available to compare large programs; however, their integrity and the computer system on which they are executed must be verified by trusted experts.

A Trojan horse might be detected by testing the suspect program to expose the purpose of the Trojan horse. However, the probability of success is low unless exact conditions for discovery are known. (The computer used for testing must be prepared in such a way that no harm will be done if the Trojan horse is executed.) Furthermore, this testing may prove the existence of the Trojan horse but usually does not identify its location. A Trojan horse may reside in the source language version or only in the object form and may be inserted in the object form each time it is assembled or compiled—for example, as the result of another Trojan horse in the assembler or compiler. Use of foreign computer programs obtained from untrusted sources (e.g., shareware bulletin board systems) should be restricted, and the programs should be carefully tested before production use.

EXHIBIT IV-1-7 Detection of Trojan Horses and Viruses

Potential Perpetrators	Methods of Detection	Evidence
• Programmers with detailed knowledge of a suspected part of a program and its purpose as well as access to it	• Program code comparison	• Unexpected results of program execution
	• Testing of suspected programs	• Foreign code found in a suspected program
• Employee technologists	• Tracing of unexpected events or possible gain from the act to suspected programs and perpetrators	• Audit logs
• Contracted programmers		• Uncontaminated copies of suspected programs
• Vendor programmers	• Examination of computer audit logs for suspicious programs or pertinent entries	
• Computer operators		

The methods for detecting Trojan horse frauds are summarized in Exhibit IV-1-7. The exhibit also lists the occupations of potential perpetrators and the sources of evidence of Trojan horse abuse.

COMPUTER VIRUSES

A computer virus is a set of computer instructions that propagates copies of versions of itself into computer programs or data when it is executed within unauthorized programs. The virus may be introduced through a program designed for that purpose (called a pest) or through a Trojan horse. The hidden virus propagates itself into other programs when they are executed, creating new Trojan horses, and may also execute harmful processes under the authority of each unsuspecting computer user whose programs or system have become infected. A worm attack is a variation in which an entire program replicates itself throughout a computer or computer network.

Although the virus attack method has been recognized for at least 15 years, the first criminal cases were prosecuted only in November 1987. Of the hundreds of cases that occur, most are in academic and research environments. However, disgruntled employees or ex-employees of computer program manufacturers have contaminated products during delivery to customers.

Preventing, Detecting, and Recovering from Virus Attacks

Prevention of computer viruses depends on protection from Trojan horses or unauthorized programs, and recovery after introduction of a virus entails purging all modified or infected programs and hardware from the system. The timely detection of Trojan horse virus attack depends on the alertness and skills of the victim, the visibility of the symptoms, the motivation of the perpetrator, and the sophistication of the perpetrator's techniques. A sufficiently skilled perpetrator with enough time and resources could anticipate most known methods of protection from Trojan horse attacks and subvert them.

Prevention methods consist primarily of investigating the sources of untrusted software and testing foreign software in computers that have been conditioned to minimize possible losses. Prevention and subsequent recovery after an attack are similar to those for any Trojan horse. The system containing the suspected Trojan horse should be shut down and not used until experts have determined the sophistication of the abuse and the extent of damage. The investigator must determine whether hardware and software errors or intentionally produced Trojan horse attacks have occurred.

Investigators should first interview the victims to identify the nature of the suspected attack. They should also use the special tools available (not resident system utilities) to examine the contents and state of the system after a suspected event. The original provider of the software packages suspected of being contaminated should be consulted to determine whether others have had similar experiences. Without a negotiated liability agreement, however, the vendor may decide to withhold important and possibly damaging information.

The following are examples of possible indications of a virus infection:

- The file size may increase when a virus attaches itself to the program or data in the file.
- An unexpected change in the time of last update of a program or file may indicate a recent unauthorized modification.
- If several executable programs have the same date or time in the last update field, they have all been updated together, possibly by a virus.
- A sudden unexpected decrease in free disk space may indicate sabotage by a virus attack.
- Unexpected disk accesses, especially in the execution of programs that do not use overlays or large data files, may indicate virus activity.

All current conditions at the time of discovery should be documented, using documentation facilities separate from the system in use. Next, all physically connected and inserted devices and media that are locally used should be removed if possible. If the electronic domain includes remote facilities under the control of others, an independent means of communication should be used to report the event to the remote facilities manager. Computer operations should be discontinued; accessing system functions could destroy evidence of the event and cause further damage. For example, accessing the contents or directory of a disk could trigger the modification or destruction of its contents.

To protect themselves against viruses or indicate their presence, users can:

- Compare programs or data files that contain checksums or hash totals with backup versions to determine possible integrity loss.

- Write-protect diskettes whenever possible, especially when testing an untrusted computer program. Unexpected write-attempt errors may indicate serious problems.
- Boot diskette-based systems using clearly labeled boot diskettes.
- Avoid booting a hard disk drive system from a diskette.
- Never put untrusted programs in hard disk root directories. Most viruses can affect only the directory from which they are executed; therefore, untrusted computer programs should be stored in isolated directories containing a minimum number of other sensitive programs or data files.
- When transporting files from one computer to another, use diskettes that have no executable files that might be infected.
- When sharing computer programs, share source code rather than object code, because source code can more easily be scanned for unusual contents.

The best protection against viruses, however, is to frequently back up all important data and programs. Multiple backups should be maintained over a period of time, possibly up to a year, to be able to recover from uninfected backups. Trojan horse programs or data may be buried deeply in a computer system—for example, in disk sectors that have been declared by the operating system as unusable. In addition, viruses may contain counters for logic bombs with high values, meaning that the virus may be spread many times before its earlier copies are triggered to cause visible damage. The perpetrators, detection, and evidence are the same as for Trojan horse attacks (see Exhibit IV-1-7).

SALAMI TECHNIQUES

A salami technique is an automated form of abuse involving Trojan horses or secret execution of an unauthorized program that causes the unnoticed or immaterial debiting of small amounts of assets from a large number of sources or accounts. The name of this technique comes from the fact that small slices of assets are taken without noticeably reducing the whole. Other methods must be used to remove the acquired assets from the system.

For example, in a banking system, the demand deposit accounting system of programs for checking accounts could be changed (using the Trojan horse method) to randomly reduce each of a few hundred accounts by 10 cents or 15 cents by transferring the money to a favored account, where it can be withdrawn through authorized methods. No controls are violated because the money is not removed from the system of accounts. Instead, small fractions of the funds are merely rearranged, which the affected customers rarely notice. Many variations are possible. The assets may be an inventory of products or services as well as money. Few cases have been reported.

Detecting Salami Acts

Several technical methods for detection are available. Specialized detection routines can be built into the suspect program, or snapshot storage dump listings could be obtained at crucial times in suspected program production runs. If identifiable amounts are being taken, these can be traced; however, a clever perpetrator can randomly vary the amounts or accounts debited and credited. Using an iterative binary search of balancing halves of all accounts is another costly way to isolate an offending account.

The actions and lifestyles of the few people with the skills, knowledge, and access to perform salami acts can be closely watched for deviations from the norm. For example, the perpetrators or their accomplices usually withdraw the money from the accounts in which it accumulates in legitimate ways; records will show an imbalance between the deposit and withdrawal transaction. However, all accounts and transactions would have to be balanced over a significant period of time to detect discrepancies. This is a monumental and expensive task.

Many financial institutions require employees to use only their financial services and make it attractive for them to do so. Employees' accounts are more completely and carefully audited than others. Such requirements usually force the salami perpetrators to open accounts under assumed names or arrange for accomplices to commit the fraud. Therefore, detection of suspected salami frauds might be more successful if investigators concentrate on the actions of possible suspects rather than on technical methods of discovery.

Exhibit IV-1-8 lists the methods of detecting the use of salami techniques as well as the potential perpetrators and sources of evidence of the use of the technique.

TRAPDOORS

Computer operating systems are designed to prevent unintended access to them and unauthorized insertion of modification of code. Programmers sometimes insert code that allows them to compromise these requirements during the debugging

---

EXHIBIT IV-1-8 Detection of Salami Acts

Potential Perpetrators	Methods of Detection	Evidence
• Financial system programmers	• Detailed data analysis using a binary search	• Many small financial losses
• Employee technolgists	• Program comparison	• Unsupported account balance buildups
• Former employees	• Transaction audits	• Trojan horse code
• Contracted programmers	• Observation of financial activities of possible suspects	• Changed or unusual personal financial practices of possible suspects
• Vendor's programmers		

phases of program development and later during system maintenance and improvement. These facilities are referred to as trapdoors, which can be used for Trojan horse and direct attacks (e.g., false data entry).

Trapdoors are usually eliminated in the final editing, but sometimes they are overlooked or intentionally left in to facilitate future access and modification. In addition, some unscrupulous programmers introduce trapdoors to allow them to later compromise computer programs. Furthermore, designers or maintainers of large complex programs may also introduce trapdoors inadvertently through weaknesses in design logic.

Trapdoors may also be introduced in the electronic circuitry of computers. For example, not all of the combinations of codes may be assigned to instructions found in the computer and documented in the programming manuals. When these unspecified commands are used, the circuitry may cause the execution of unanticipated combinations of functions that allow the computer system to be compromised.

Typical known trapdoor flaws in computer programs include:

- Implicit sharing of privileged data.
- Asynchronous change between time of check and time of use.
- Inadequate identification, verification, authentication, and authorization of tasks.
- Embedded operating system parameters in application memory space.
- Failure to remove debugging aids before production use begins.

During the use and maintenance of computer programs and computer circuitry, ingenious programmers invariably discover some of these weaknesses and take advantage of them for useful and innocuous purposes. However, the trapdoors may be used for unauthorized, malicious purposes as well.

Functions that can be performed by computer programs and computers that are not in the specifications are often referred to as negative specifications. Designers and implementers struggle to make programs and computers function according to specifications and to prove that they do. They cannot practicably prove that a computer system does not perform functions it is not supposed to perform.

Research is continuing on a high-priority basis to develop methods of proving the correctness of computer programs and computers according to complete and consistent specifications. However, commercially available computers and computer programs probably will not be proved correct for many years. Trapdoors continue to exist; therefore, computer systems are fundamentally insecure because their actions are not totally predictable.

Detecting Trapdoors

No direct technical method can be used to discover trapdoors. However, tests of varying degrees of complexity can be performed to discover hidden functions used

---

EXHIBIT IV-1-9 Detection of Trapdoors

Potential Perpetrators	Methods of Detection	Evidence
• Expert application programmers	• Exhaustive testing • Comparison of specification to performance • Specific testing based on evidence	• Computer performance or output reports indicating that a computer system performs outside of its specifications

---

for malicious purposes. The testing requires the expertise of systems programmers and knowledgeable applications programmers. Investigators should always seek out the most highly qualified experts for the particular computer system or computer application under suspicion.

The investigator should always assume that the computer system and computer programs are never sufficiently secure from intentional, technical compromise. However, these intentional acts usually require the expertise of only the technologists who have the skills, knowledge, and access to perpetrate them. Exhibit IV-1-9 lists the potential perpetrators, methods of detection, and sources of evidence of the abuse trapdoors.

LOGIC BOMBS

A logic bomb is a set of instructions in a computer program periodically executed in a computer system that determines conditions or states of the computer, facilitating the perpetration of an unauthorized, malicious act. In one case, for example, a payroll system programmer put a logic bomb in the personnel system so that if his name were ever removed from the personnel file, indicating termination of employment, secret code would cause the entire personnel file to be erased.

A logic bomb can be programmed to trigger an act based on any specified condition or data that may occur or be introduced. Logic bombs are usually placed in the computer system using the Trojan horse method. Methods of discovering logic bombs are the same as for Trojan horses. Exhibit IV-1-10 summarizes the potential perpetrators, methods of detection, and kinds of evidence of logic bombs.

ASYNCHRONOUS ATTACKS

Asynchronous attacks take advantage of the asynchronous functioning of a computer operating system. Most computer operating systems function asynchronously

---

EXHIBIT IV-1-10 Detection of Logic Bombs

Potential Perpetrators	Methods of Detection	Evidence
• Programmers with detailed knowledge of a suspected part of a program and its purpose as well as access to it • Employees • Contracted programmers • Vendor's programmers • Computer users	• Program code comparisons • Testing of suspected programs • Tracing of possible gains from the act	• Unexpected results of program execution • Foreign code found in a suspected program

---

on the basis of the services that must be performed for the various computer programs executed in the computer system. For example, several jobs may simultaneously call for output reports to be produced. The operating system stores these requests and, as resources become available, performs them in the order in which resources are available to fit the request or according to an overriding priority scheme. Therefore, rather than executing requests in the order they are received, the system performs them asynchronously on the basis of the available resources.

Highly sophisticated methods can confuse the operating system to allow it to violate the isolation of one job from another. For example, in a large application program that runs for a long time, checkpoint/restarts are customary. These automatically allow the computer operator to set a switch manually to stop the program at a specified intermediate point and later restart it in an orderly manner without losing data.

To avoid the loss, the operating system must save the copy of the computer programs and data in their current state at the checkpoint. The operating system must also save several system parameters that describe the mode and security level of the program at the time of the stop. Programmers or computer operators might be able to gain access to the checkpoint restart copy of the program, data, and system parameters. They could change the system parameters such that on restart, the program would function at a higher-priority security level or privileged level in the computer and thereby give the program unauthorized access to data, other programs, or the operating system. Checkpoint/restart actions are usually well documented in the computer operations or audit log.

Even more complex methods of attack could be used besides the one described in this simple example, but the technology is too complex to present here. The investigator should be aware of the possibilities of asynchronous attacks and seek adequate technical assistance if suspicious circumstances result from the activities of highly sophisticated and trained technologists. Evidence of such attacks would be discernible only from unexplained deviations from application and system spec-

---

EXHIBIT IV-1-11 Detection of Asynchronous Attacks

Potential Perpetrators	Methods of Detection	Evidence
• Sophisticated advanced system programmers • Sophisticated and advanced computer operators	• System testing of suspected attack methods • Repeat execution of a job under normal and secured circumstances	• Output that deviates from expected output or logs containing records of computer operation

---

ifications, in computer output, or characteristics of system performance. Exhibit IV-1-11 lists the potential perpetrators, methods of detecting, and evidence of asynchronous attacks.

DATA LEAKAGE

A wide range of computer crime involves the removal of data or copies of data from a computer system or computer facility. This part of a crime may offer the most dangerous exposure to perpetrators. Their technical act may be well hidden in the computer; however, to convert it to economic gain, they must get the data from the computer system. Output is subject to examination by computer operators and other data processing personnel, who might detect the perpetrators' activity.

Several techniques can be used to secretly leak data from a computer system. The perpetrator may be able to hide the sensitive data in otherwise innocuous-looking output reports—for example, by adding to blocks of data or interspersing the data with otherwise routine data. A more sophisticated method might be to encode data to look like something else. For example, a computer listing may be formatted so that the secret data is in the form of different lengths of printer lines, number of characters per line, or locations of punctuation; is embedded in the least significant digits of engineering data; and uses code words that can be interspersed and converted into meaningful data.

Sophisticated methods of data leakage might be necessary only in high-security, high-risk environments. Otherwise, much simpler manual methods might be used. It has been reported that hidden in the central processors of many computers used in the Vietnam War were miniature radio transmitters capable of broadcasting the contents of the computers to a remote receiver. These were discovered when the computers were returned to the United States.

Detecting Data Leakage

Data leakage would probably best be investigated by interrogating IS personnel who might have observed the movement of sensitive data. In addition, computer

EXHIBIT IV-1-12 Detection of Data Leakage

Potential Perpetrators	Methods of Detection	Evidence
• Computer programmers	• Discovery of stolen information	• Computer storage media
• Employees		• Computer output forms
• Former employees	• Tracing computer storage media back to the computer facility	• Type font characteristics
• Contracted workers		• Trojan horse or scavenging evidence
• Vendor's employees		

operating system usage logs could be examined to determine whether and when data files have been accessed. Because data leakage can occur through the use of Trojan horses, logic bombs, and scavenging, the use of these methods should be investigated when data leakage is suspected.

Evidence will most likely be in the same form as evidence of the scavenging activities described in a preceding section. Exhibit IV-1-12 summarizes the detection of crimes resulting from data leakage.

SOFTWARE PIRACY

Piracy is the copying and use of computer programs in violation of copyright and trade secret laws. Commercially purchased computer programs are protected by what is known as a shrink-wrap contract agreement, which states that the program is protected by copyright and its use is restricted.

Since the early 1980s, violations of these agreements have been widespread, primarily because of the high price of commercial programs and the simplicity of copying the programs. The software industry reacted by developing several technical methods of preventing the copying of disks; however, these have not always been successful because of hackers' skills at overcoming this protection and because they are seen as inconvenient to customers.

The software industry has now stabilized and converged on a strategy of imposing no technical constraints to copying, implementing an extensive awareness program to convince honest customers not to engage in piracy, pricing their products more reasonably, and providing additional benefits to purchasers of their products that would not be obtainable to computer program pirates. In addition, computer program manufacturers occasionally find gross violations of their contract agreements and seek highly publicized remedies.

Malicious hackers commonly engage in piracy, sometimes even distributing pirated copies on a massive scale through electronic bulletin boards. Although criminal charges can often be levied against malicious hackers and computer intruders, indictments are most often sought against educational and business institutions, in which gross violations of federal copyright laws and state trade secret laws are endemic.

EXHIBIT IV-1-13 Detection of Software Piracy

Potential Perpetrators	Methods of Detection	Evidence
• Any purchasers and users of commercially available computer programs • Hackers	• Observation of computer users • Search of computer users' facilities and computers • Testimony of legitimate computer program purchasers • Receivers of copied computer programs	• Pictures of computer screens while pirated software is being executed • Copies of computer media on which pirated programs are found • Memory contents of computers containing pirated software • Printouts produced by execution of pirated computer programs

Detecting Piracy

Investigators can most easily obtain evidence of piracy by confiscating suspects' disks, the contents of their computer hard disks, paper printouts from the execution of the pirated programs, and pictures of screens produced by the pirated programs. Recent court decisions indicate that piracy can also occur when programs are written that closely duplicate the look and feel of protected computer programs, which includes the use of similar command structures and screen displays. Exhibit IV-1-13 summarizes the potential perpetrators, detection methods, and evidence of computer program piracy.

COMPUTER LARCENY

The theft, burglary, and sale of stolen microcomputers and components are increasing dramatically, a severe problem because the value of the contents of stolen computers often exceeds the value of the hardware taken. The increase in computer larceny is becoming epidemic, in fact, as the market for used computers in which stolen merchandise may be fenced also expands.

It has been suggested that an additional method of protection be used along with standard antitheft devices for securing office equipment. If the user is to be out of the office, microcomputers can be made to run antitheft programs that send frequent signals through modems and telephones to a monitoring station. If the signals stop, an alarm at the monitoring station is set off.

Investigation and prosecution of computer larceny fits well within accepted criminal justice practices, except for proving the size of the loss when a microcomputer worth only a few hundred dollars is stolen. Evidence of far larger losses (e.g., programs and data) may be needed.

EXHIBIT IV-1-14 Detection of Simulation and Modeling

Potential Perpetrators	Methods of Detection	Evidence
• Computer application programmers	• Investigation of possible computer use by suspects	• Computer programs
• Simulation and modeling experts	• Identification of equipment	• Computer and communications equipment and their contents
• Managers in positions to engage in large, complex embezzlement		• Computer program documentation
• Criminal organizations		• Computer input
		• Computer-produced reports
		• Computer and data communications usage logs and journals

Minicomputers and mainframes have been stolen as well, typically while equipment is being shipped to customers. Existing criminal justice methods can deal with such thefts.

USE OF COMPUTERS FOR CRIMINAL ENTERPRISE

A computer can be used as a tool in a crime for planning, data communications, or control. An existing process can be simulated on a computer, a planned method for carrying out a crime can be modeled, or a crime can be monitored by a computer (i.e., by the abuser) to help guarantee its success.

In one phase of a 1973 insurance fraud in Los Angeles, a computer was used to model the company and determine the effects of the sale of large numbers of insurance policies. The modeling resulted in the creation of 64,000 fake insurance policies in computer-readable form that were then introduced into the real system and subsequently resold as valid policies to reinsuring companies.

The use of a computer for simulation, modeling, and data communications usually requires extensive amounts of computer time and computer program development. Investigation of possible fraudulent use should include a search for significant amounts of computer services used by the suspects. Their recent business activities, as well as the customer lists of locally available commercial time-sharing and service bureau companies, can be investigated. If inappropriate use of the victim's computer is suspected, logs may show unexplained computer use.

Exhibit IV-1-14 lists the potential perpetrators, methods of detection, and kinds of evidence in simulation and modeling techniques.

SUMMARY

Computer crimes will change rapidly along with the technology. As computing becomes more widespread, maximum losses per case are expected to grow. Ultimately, all business crimes will be computer crimes.

Improved computer controls will make business crime more difficult, dangerous, and complex, however. Computers and workstations impose absolute discipline on information workers, forcing them to perform within set bounds and limiting potential criminal activities. Managers receive improved and more timely information from computers about their businesses and can more readily discern suspicious anomalies indicative of possible wrongdoing.

Although improved response rates from victims, improvements in security, modification of computer use, reactions from the criminal justice community, new laws, and saturation of the news media warning of the problems will cause a reduction of traditional types of crime, newer forms of computer crime will proliferate. Viruses and malicious hacking will eventually be superseded by other forms of computer abuse, including computer larceny, desktop forgery, voice mail and E-mail terrorism and extortion, fax graffiti, phantom computers secretly connected to networks, and repudiation of EDI transactions.

Investigating Computer Abuse

MARK TANTAM

Computer abuse is the collective term used to describe several types of activity that all have one common feature: the exploitation of the computer and its connecting networks. For many purposes, the diverse nature of the activities is irrelevant. When the organization is deciding how to approach the resulting investigation, however, these differences are crucial. Therefore, before discussing the steps that an investigator should take when faced with an incident, the classes into which acts of computer abuse can be placed must be identified.

This chapter identifies three classes of computer abuse:

- *Fraud.* Fraud is the abstraction of money, information, or other property, which presumes an attempt by the abuser to place the money, information, or property into a place of form in which the abuser can use it.
- *Invasion of privacy.* Invasion of privacy (e.g., hacking) is different from fraud in that it entails only the overcoming of security controls within the system.
- *Malicious damage.* As its name implies, this form of abuse damages a system. The damage can be either negligible (e.g., a benign Trojan horse or trapdoor) or disastrous (e.g., a malicious time bomb or virus).

A particular act of abuse may actually fall into two or more classes. For example, a hacker may transfer money from one account to another and then plant a program that wipes the audit trail from the computer's memory. It is important to identify the abuser's motive—fraud, invasion of privacy, or damage—to give the investigator a place to begin the investigation.

This chapter first examines each class of computer abuse from the viewpoint of origin or cause investigation. Evidence, interviewing techniques, and audit tools are then discussed.

FRAUD

Acts of fraud are generally noticed immediately—because, for example, money has been paid to an unknown entity or for an unauthorized purpose or because security procedures have deliberately been breached. Occasionally, however, the victim is aware of what has happened but does not think it is a fraud, perhaps assuming that a wrong account number was entered or someone forgot a password. In either case, the investigation is conducted in the same manner.

The first step is to print out the audit trail for the relevant time to:

- Identify the instructions entered or the routine that was run that resulted in the fraud.
- Establish which terminal was used to input the instructions or initiate the routine.
- Examine the history of activity at that terminal to assess whether the abuser was a legitimate user of that terminal or, if not, an authorized user of the system and to identify any other abusive activities that person may have committed.

The investigation then follows the same course as any outside the computer domain. The legitimate users of the terminal concerned should be interviewed, as well as other people in that area who could have piggybacked onto the system. Documents produced to facilitate the fraud should be analyzed and circumstantial evidence (e.g., notes of the system kept on disk) collected. There should be no difficulty preserving the evidence. (The integrity of the audit trail should be maintained at all times as a matter of course.) Documents and disks should be seized and stored in appropriate conditions to prevent their deterioration.

INVASION OF PRIVACY

Fraud and invasion of privacy often overlap, because persons who commit fraud often must break into the system to commit their crimes, and hackers often try to gain access to systems to remove information. However, these criminals approach their task in different ways. After gaining access to the system, a person intent on committing fraud goes directly to the specific file, account, or area that needs to be accessed to perpetrate the fraud. Once the fraud is completed, the abuser typically leaves the system without further ado. In short, this abuser does nothing more than that which is required to achieve the fraud.

A hacker, on the other hand, typically goes through a process of learning what the system is before trying to do something dishonest. For example, the hacker usually attempts to obtain system user status, look at directories to see what else is on the system, and examine account names and passwords.

The difficulty for the investigator is that, in contrast to a case of fraud, it may not be obvious that an invasion of privacy has occurred. Moreover, the signs in the computer system of what is happening may be trivial and easily explained as the acts of an incompetent rather than malicious user. This is illustrated by the case of hacking described in *The Cuckoo's Egg*; in this case, the only evidence that anything was amiss was a 75¢ accounting imbalance. Many organizations would have ignored this error. Ironically, it was the only lead to a ring of hackers who were supplying the KGB with sensitive information.

Once the investigator decides to take the matter seriously and examines the audit trail, it is often immediately evident that a hacker is active. The hardest part is not recognizing that a hacker is present but persuading management to begin investigating what is happening on the system.

Once the investigation has been justified, the next hurdle the investigator faces is identifying the origin of the attack. A hacker internal to the organization concerned can clearly be tracked in the same way as the perpetrator of a fraud. If the hacker (or, for that matter, the perpetrator of a fraud) is external; however, all that the audit trail will show is the point of entry to the system, not the source terminal.

In this case, it is necessary to enlist the services of the providers of the communications network from which the attack emanated. If only one network is concerned and it is digital, the provider may be able to trace the communication back to its source immediately after the abuser comes online. If it is a data network, the victim may be able to strip off the routing information sent with the message to determine the source. However, if there are many networks or if some are analog in part, serious complications start to arise. When the hacker uses a telephone network, whether digital or analog, tracing is only possible while the abuser remains linked to the system. In other words, the victim must encourage the hacker to stay online for as long as possible if the network provider is to identify the source of the call. That obligation leads many organizations to choose not to venture any further than the boundaries of their own system in investigating a hacking incident.

MALICIOUS DAMAGE

Malicious damage is the form of abuse that poses the most problems to the investigator because the information stored in the computer may have been tampered with, corrupted, or destroyed before anyone knows that something is amiss. For example, the damage caused to the system may have included destruction of the evidence of its cause (e.g. the audit trail or the rogue program itself). Furthermore, the systems department may have needed to manipulate the system or even disinfect it to get it up and running again.

Damage can be caused in such a myriad of ways that the systems staff tends to consider the possibility of abuse only after it has tested several other theories. That means that the investigator may not be approached for some time after the event. This may force the investigator to make assumptions about the state of the system at the time of the incident (e.g., that the system was substantially the same then as it is now).

In fact, the only reliable evidence may be the users' recollection of what the system did at the time of the incident and of what was left in the system afterward, which may or may not be enough for the investigator. Viruses have certain characteristics that invariably make it plain where they have struck; a message typically appears on screen saying, for example, "Your PC is stoned" or appears on an ominous day such as Friday the 13th. A logic bomb often discloses the identity of the abuser by the way it acts—for example, it may detonate on the day that the name of a particular employee has been deleted or it may destroy a set of programs developed by a certain contract programmer.

If the audit trail is intact, it can be consulted in the same way as is done with other forms of abuse. Most important of all, the system's backup disks must be restored. The backups are the most useful source of information for determining the time that the rogue program was added, its source, and its workings.

Because these abusers are not attempting to obtain anything from their actions, they can afford to use indirect means to attack and damage the system (e.g., by way of viruses, worms, or logic bombs in source code) and it does not matter to them if the program they created does not work in the way that they planned. In several cases, a rogue program caused damage but acted in a completely different way from what the creator of the program intended. Therefore, in malicious damage cases, it is important that investigators not assume that the person who added the program was acting deliberately. Rather, investigators must reconstruct what happened to see whether the program alleged to have constituted the abuse was, indeed, responsible.

EVIDENCE OF COMPUTER ABUSE

There are several sources of evidence that may need to be tapped in a case of computer abuse:

- Oral (i.e., evidence obtained from witnesses).
- Written (i.e., original documentation).
- Computer generated (e.g., audit trails).
- Video or audio (e.g., a videotape of the crime).

Each of these is addressed in the following sections.

Oral Evidence

Evidence from witnesses should be relatively easy to obtain and protect. There are two ways in which it can be rendered worthless, however. First, the witness may be threatened; however, this seldom happens in computer abuse cases, because the perpetrators usually face only a light sentence.

More pernicious is the second way that oral evidence can be rendered useless: passage of time, which can rob witnesses of the details of what happened and persuade them to say "I think" rather than "I know." This is why it is important for investigators to interview all those who could have relevant information and take down a statement from them as soon as possible after the incident has occurred. This may enable witnesses to refresh their memory at a later stage, if necessary, and resolve any doubts the witnesses may have.

Written Evidence

Written evidence may be relevant—for example, the forged input that caused the money to be transferred or a note kept by the security guard of the times that certain people went in or out of the building concerned. Such evidence as forged input is clearly relevant and admissible in court, subject to a witness who can explain what it is and where it was found. The original must be produced, and a witness must be available to prove that it has not been tampered with or changed.

The second type of physical evidence (i.e., the security guard's notes) is different in that it is technically hearsay. In the words of US Federal Rules of Evidence 801(c), hearsay is "a statement, other than one made by the declarant [while] testifying at the trial or hearing, offered in evidence to prove the truth of the matter asserted." More simply, evidence can be said to be hearsay when it is secondhand, such as when a person who did not see or hear what happened relates an account received from someone else.

The law precludes the admission of such evidence because it cannot be probed and tested in court by cross-examination to see whether it is partial, inaccurate, fabricated, or otherwise flawed. A document is similarly hearsay because although it is not evidence produced by a witness, it is still secondhand.

The implications of such a rule are startling. Bank transactions could be proved only by a bank official who could personally remember them taking place. Entries in the books of the bank or in bank statements would be ignored. This situation has caused the legislatures in both the United States and the United Kingdom to introduce exceptions to the hearsay rule, the one most pertinent to this discussion being the business records exception. The US Federal Rules of Evidence 803(6) allows a court to admit a report or other document

> made at or near the time by, or from information transmitted by, a person with knowledge, if kept in the course of a regularly conducted business activity, and if it was the regular practice of that business activity to make the [report or document], all as shown by the testimony of the custodian or other qualified witness, unless the source of information or the method or circumstances of preparation indicate lack of trustworthiness."

Therefore, a business record can be produced if a witness gives evidence as to how the document came into existence and proves that all the requirements are

709

satisfied. With regard to the example of the security guard's list of attendances, it would be debatable whether that would be a business record for the purposes of the Federal Rules of Evidence. If not, those concerned would have to revert to the general law and hope that the security guard could remember who went in and out.

Computer-Generated Evidence

Computer-generated evidence is an intelligible representation of what is stored on the computer. In other words, a printout is the data stored in a computer translated into human-readable form. The printout of the audit trail, for example, could be seen as the recollection of the computer as to what happened. To that extent, a computer printout does not meet the best-evidence rule, which maintains that a document can be admitted only when it is the original unless the original is not in existence.

As with the hearsay rule, this was felt to be unduly onerous and so has been expressly removed in the case of computer-generated evidence by the US Federal Rules of Evidence 1001(3). This allows a printout of the system to be admitted as evidence of, for example, the state of the hard disk after a virus attack. The US Senate had the prescience to make data compilation the subject of Federal Rules of Evidence 803(6), so the business records exception applies even when the contents of the memory are adduced as statements of fact.

The same restrictions that apply to written evidence pertain to computer-generated evidence. In addition, according to Federal Rules of Evidence 803(6), the custodian of the records or another qualified witness who is able to authenticate the evidence must produce the computer-generated evidence in court. Several cases have considered this rule, concluding that the witness must:

- Have custody of the records in question on a regular basis.
- Rely on those records in the regular course of business.
- Know that they were prepared in the regular course of business.

Although none of these requires an understanding of the workings of the computer system, it is preferable if the person concerned is knowledgeable about the procedures followed in processing the relevant information, because the courts may want to scrutinize them in detail to ensure that the evidence is accurate and reliable.

Finally, it should be remembered that computer-generated evidence is not produced only by computers. The listings of calls made through a private automated branch exchange and the tally reel from an adding machine fall within this category and are subject to the same rules of admissibility as applies to the more obvious forms of computer-generated evidence.

Video or Audio Evidence

As with written evidence, there are two types of video or audio evidence: that generated at the time of the abuse, and that generated restrospectively. Examples of the first would be film from security cameras recording what was happening at the crime scene at the time or a tape storing conversations between suspects and their accomplices. The second type covers such things as film of the layout of the desks and the terminals a few hours after the abuse has occurred or of the physical configuration of the computer system.

With respect to both, a witness must explain why, how, and when the evidence was obtained. The witness then must state why the evidence is helpful and not misleading. For example, when there is film of the computer system, the witness must show that the system was the same at the time of filming as it was at the time of the abuse.

The evidence must be protected against tampering, corruption, and deterioration, as with computer-generated evidence. In addition, it should be stored in a suitably constructed, locked cupboard and the key kept by a responsible person.

INTERVIEWING TECHNIQUES

A computer cannot ever prove a case; it can only provide evidence. Therefore, no matter how strong a case seems after examination of the audit trail or other records, investigators must always confirm their conclusions by interviewing potential witnesses and examining other sources of evidence (e.g., documents created by the abuser). The purposes of the interviews are:

- To uncover the information necessary to reconstruct what happened at the relevant time as accurately and in as much detail as possible.
- To persuade the persons responsible to admit their guilt.

It has been held that a confession obtained through persistent questioning that puts pressure on the suspect may render any confession the suspect makes involuntary and therefore inadmissible in a criminal trial. Therefore, the second purpose must not be pursued too vigorously unless the victim feels that it is essential to remove the threat to the system as quickly as possible at all costs. This is not to suggest, however, that pressured questioning is merited or even necessary. Initial inquiries carried out at the start of an investigation frequently elicit a confession—sometimes before abuse has even been suspected.

Interviews should be conducted in three phases, which may be seen as a funnel. The first set of interviews is wide-ranging and open, and the last set is directed and to the point. This funnel analogy could also apply to the population of the interviewees. At the start, the interviewees include all those people who could have relevant information. By the end, they have been narrowed down to the suspects in the case. The following sections discuss interviewing phases and techniques in more detail.

The Preliminary Phase

The preliminary phase is designed to establish what was happening at the time the crime occurred in the department where the terminal used for the abuse was situated. An investigator should conduct this initial phase of interviewing with a totally open mind, whether or not any particular person has been identified as the culprit. Any hypotheses as to who could have been to blame or how the abuse occurred can be tested; however, investigators should keep in mind that too many cases have foundered because interviewers were not open to anything that contradicted their own surmises.

The interviewer should make note of the demeanor of the subject during questioning as well as the answers to all questions. Ideally, these observations should be supported by a tape recording or a shorthand note. If the suspect admits guilt at this stage, the program of interviews can be terminated. However, evidence should be sought to corroborate what the culprit has said.

The Intermediate Phase

During the intermediate phase, further interviews are conducted to clarify points or to ask for more detail. Further interviews are typically necessary as more information is revealed during the investigative process. In addition, further interviews may be necessary if there are contradictions among various individuals' accounts of the incident or if individuals initially have gaps in their recollections. Interviews in the intermediate phase should rarely be designed to put pressure on individuals suspected of being involved; this should be done only once the investigators are sure they know all the facts, usually during the final phase.

The Final Phase

When the bulk of the evidence comes from the computer, it may not be possible for the investigator to make any conclusions beyond saying that this person matches the profile of the abuser built up from the audit trail (e.g., the suspect was at the right place at the right time and had the right level of knowledge). This makes the final phase of interviews crucial to the success of the investigation. The interviewer should aim to confront those people who could have been responsible, telling them the results of the investigation to monitor their reaction and, more important, to see if they will confess.

Interviewing is not a skill that can be learned through hours of study. Rather, it is a skill that grows gradually from an awareness of how people answer questions and, consequently, how questions should be asked. Open questions that suggest no answer allow a subject to address a wide range of issues. Closed questions force the subject to deal with just one issue. In practice, many fit somewhere in between.

Generally, the first interview would be made up mostly of open questions, because the investigator does not want to prejudge anything. If the subject wanders into irrelevant areas or has difficulty in answering a simple question, however, closed questions may be used. The final interview should be made up of closed questions, because by now, the investigator should know the facts. An open question may be used at the final interview to allow the investigator to observe a suspect's demeanor or to highlight the implausibility of the account given.

A criminal court will reject any confession made to a police officer that is involuntary. Any other provision would deprive a person of the right to remain silent. Moreover, any confession that was made under circumstances that could render it misleading—for example, if the person was inebriated—may also be ruled inadmissible. Although, strictly speaking, these rules are aimed at police or similar investigators, they should be followed in spirit by all investigators, because their aim is to protect the innocent.

On a more practical note, interviews should be conducted by a team of two: one interviewing and the other observing.

AUDIT TOOLS

Various audit tools can be used to help the investigator:

- Follow a record through the processing cycle to make sure that the system is working properly and has not been tampered with.
- Check the characteristics of a live file against its backup copy to ensure that it has not been changed or corrupted.
- Identify exceptions that arise during processing.
- Analyze the audit trail.

These tools provide an efficient way to examine the information stored on the system to establish what has happened. In addition, they can provide a warning sign if they are used by the systems department or internal audit to probe the system for malfunctions (e.g., exceptions that arise during the processing cycle). Investigators benefit the most from using such tools when they need to isolate changes to the system made by the abuser or to examine the entire system to determine what has happened as a result of an attack.

INVESTIGATIVE REPORT WRITING

In the report on an investigation of computer abuse, it is important to include all of the evidence rather than only those parts that are consistent with the overall conclusion. Otherwise, those reviewing the investigation are not given the opportunity to differ from the conclusions of the investigator, and if new evidence comes to light, they may not give it the appropriate attention.

The report should be set out in the following way:

- *Background*. This includes what happened in the incident, who was brought in to deal with the matter, what action they took, and what is proposed to be done to prevent this abuse from happening again.
- *Sources of information*. This should set out what sources have been consulted (e.g., staff members or particular documents).
- *Interviews*. A summary of the interviews conducted should be provided, setting out, if possible, an account of the incident that was consistent among those interviewed, with any discrepancies between accounts highlighted.
- *Analysis of documentary evidence*. Any observations that can be made about the evidence generated by the computer and other documentary evidence should be provided.
- *Preliminary or final conclusions*. At the preliminary stage, the report should set out the interview program and the forensic analysis of the documents that need to be undertaken. If there are any suspects, they should be referred to (albeit obliquely, so as not to defame any of them). Finally, this section should provide some indication of the prospects of success of an investigation into the abuse, the likely remedies that will be available to the victim, and the resources required. When the final report is submitted, this section evolves into a final conclusion.

Both investigators and their immediate superiors must be committed to the production of regular reports to ensure that an investigation is pursued only when it is cost-effective to do so. Such a course gives investigators some protection if their work yields unsatisfactory results and enables their superiors to have some control over what is happening. The reporting cycle depends on the size of the job. Essentially, an initial report should be submitted as soon as the investigator has had a chance to take a preliminary view of what has happened; the report should be updated at regular intervals (e.g., once a month or once every six months) until a final conclusion is reached.

SUMMARY

When attempting to establish the origin or cause of an incident of computer abuse, investigators must first try to determine the motive of the perpetrator (i.e., fraud, invasion of privacy, or damage). This helps share the course of action the investigation should follow. This chapter helps investigators establish the origin or cause of an attack by discussing the signs that distinguish one type of abuse from another and outlining the different investigative strategies that can be adopted.

Whatever the nature of the investigation, the audit trail commands an important place in the investigator's inquiries. Therefore, investigators must protect the audit trail as much as possible against deletion, corruption, or alteration. Such acts may not necessarily be malicious. Many investigations have been jeopardized because people trying to minimize the damage caused by the attack or investigating anomalous behavior (i.e., before an attack is suspected) consequently damage evidence. Investigators can do nothing about such activities.

What investigators can do, however, is ensure that the primary sources of evidence are identified and adequately protected once the investigation begins. This chapter provides guidance on the rules that investigators should follow in identifying and protecting evidence and outlines the laws that determine the admissibility and weight given to particular types of evidence.

Negligence, Litigation, and Information Security

PETER C. GARDINER

Organizations and their managers may be successfully sued by those who have suffered damages as a result of the failure of an information system to ensure—within reason—the confidentiality, integrity, or availability of the information it contains. Under the standard of due care, managers and their organizations have a duty to provide for information security even though they may not be aware they have such obligations.

These obligations arise from the portion of US common law that addresses issues of negligence (the law of torts). If managers take actions that leave their information systems unreasonably insecure or if they fail to take actions to make their information systems reasonably secure and as a result someone suffers damages when those systems are penetrated, the managers and their organization may be sued.

Information security is still largely an unknown entity to most people, including lawyers. Managers can and often do ignore sound advice offered by information security professionals for a variety of reasons. In the past, when the confidentiality, integrity, or availability of an organization's information systems was breached and damages occurred, most damages were internal and were simply absorbed by the organization. However, information systems and their services are experiencing rapid growth and now reach far beyond the boundaries of the organization providing them. They are relied on by a rapidly increasing number of people outside the organizations providing the services. These systems affect the lives, livelihood, property, and privacy of more and more individuals.

As a result, an increasing number of users and third-party nonusers are being exposed to and are now actually experiencing damages as a result of failures of information security in information systems. For example, a company specializes in keeping and reporting on consumer credit ratings may experience a breach of information security as a result of negligence. The individual damaged in such instances could be the person being reported, who is neither the keeper of the credit reports nor the person seeking the credit report.

Because these individuals are outside organizational boundaries, they are under no obligation to simply absorb damages. Instead, many may turn to litigation.

Therefore, managers must proactively provide reasonable information security for their information systems.

This chapter presents an overview of the fundamentals of negligence and suggests ways that negligence may increasingly form the basis for lawsuits when information security has been breached. Basic concepts are presented from a non-legal point of view; this chapter is not intended as a comprehensive, legal presentation. Rather, the intent is to inform the security professional about the concepts of negligence and the ways an understanding of these concepts may help owners and operators of information systems develop a standard of due care. This chapter should help the security professional alert managers to their legal obligation to provide for reasonable information security, convince them to meet these obligations by pointing out the possible consequences of failing to provide reasonable information security, and obtain sufficient background knowledge and understanding to work with in-house or external legal counsel.

THE LAW OF TORTS

Simply stated, a tort is an action that violates the civil duty people have to each other. Negligence is one type of tort. The law of torts makes courts the decision maker for private disputes when the negligent actions of one person injures another person. The court decisions are designed to find out who was wrong and then to correct the wrong.

Once courts entered into disputes between individuals, rules were developed and used to help standardize court proceedings and to help different courts reach similar decisions in similar situations. One of the rules developed dealt with the concept of liability. In its simplest terms, liability means responsibility. To say a person is liable is the same as saying a person is responsible or can be held responsible. If a person is liable, that person has tort liability. There are three possible ways a person can acquire tort liability:

- By doing something intended to cause harm.
- Through negligent conduct that creates an unreasonable risk of unintentionally causing harm.
- Through conduct subject to strict liability, without intent or negligence, to the extent that it has survived from the early law or has been reestablished by modern ideas of policy.

In this chapter, the focus is on negligent conduct in instances in which, by failing to provide for reasonable security in their information systems, managers and organizations can be held liable and may be sued when their systems are breached and damages occur.

NEGLIGENCE

If someone has engaged in negligent conduct and has caused harm or damages to another, that person can be charged in court by the person harmed. The person bringing the charge of negligence is called the plaintiff. The person being charged is called the defendant. In a court setting, the word *negligence* is used to describe the conduct of the defendant.

A legal charge of negligence cannot be based solely on negligent conduct. Negligent conduct by one person may create a risk of harm to others; if no one is actually harmed, however, a charge of negligence will not stand up in court. A plaintiff charging negligence must prove the existence of each of the following five elements of negligence in order to win a court case:

- *Duty*. A person must act, or may not fail to act, in a way that prevents exposing others or their property to an unreasonable risk of harm.
- *Breach of duty*. This occurs when a person fails to act in ways that meet his or her duty.
- *Cause*. Cause is established by determining whether the conduct of an individual (i.e., the defendant) has resulted in or caused the damages suffered by another (i.e., the plaintiff).
- *Proximate cause*. Proximate cause (sometimes called natural cause) defines the limits in tracing the link between a given cause and its claimed effect. When the link between cause and effect cannot be traced, liability stops.
- *Damages*. The actual losses suffered by one person (i.e., the plaintiff) when injured as a result of the negligent acts of another (i.e., the defendant).

The following sections discuss these elements in greater detail.

Duty

Although many people are not aware of it, everyone has the duty to act (or not fail to act) in a way that will not expose others or their property to an unreasonable risk of harm. In other words, everyone must conform to a certain standard of conduct. Managers of information systems have a common-law duty (as opposed to a contractual duty) to prevent exposing those who use these systems to an unreasonable risk of harm.

Breach of Duty

Negligence may be charged when a person has a duty to another and breaches that duty. Interestingly enough, a defendant may engage in negligent behavior but not be liable if there was no duty to the plaintiff. To successfully charge negligence with respect to duty and breach of duty, a defendant must have a duty to the plaintiff and then have breached that duty.

Unfortunately, it is not simple to determine. It involves several factors:

- Foreseeability (i.e., whether the harm that occurs could be reasonably anticipated.
- Determining what a reasonable and prudent person would do in similar circumstances.
- The existence of sufficient probability that harm will occur as the result of a particular act, such that a reasonable person would take action to avoid it.
- Balancing anticipated harm with the expense and inconvenience of reducing the anticipated harm.
- The standard of due care.

The following sections discuss these factors in more detail.

Foreseeability. In the definition of negligence, a person is obliged to avoid exposing others or their property to unreasonable risks of harm, but not all risks of harm. One of the key tests to determine whether a risk is reasonable or unreasonable is whether or not the resulting harm could have been anticipated. If the harm that occurs to one person as a result of the acts of another could not reasonably have been anticipated, there is no liability for that harm. On the other hand, if the harm could have been reasonably anticipated, there is liability.

For example, in an 1856 case that helps define what courts mean by foreseeability, there was a severe frost in England. During that frost, a fire main installed by a water company burst and flooded a nearby house. The owner sued the Waterworks Co. for negligence. The court found that the company could not have anticipated such a severe frost, as determined by the average temperature in preceding years.

In information systems, there are a wide variety of well-identified threats that are known to exist that can result in failures of data confidentiality, integrity, and availability, which in turn could cause damages to people and organizations. Some organizations (e.g., the American Bar Association and the National Center for Computer Crime Data) publish such information periodically. For example, according to some estimates, between 20% and 25% of information security breaches are caused by insiders (i.e., disgruntled employees or dishonest employees). About 3% to 5% are caused by outside hackers. There are published accounts of what happens when an information system is attacked by either of these threats. If a reasonable and prudent person would foresee these threats, anticipate how these threats might expose others to harm, and therefore act to establish countermeasures to reduce an information system's vulnerability to them, so must a manager of an information system.

Reasonable and Prudent Person. The courts have insisted that the reasonable and prudent person is a hypothetical person of ordinary prudence, not an overly cautious individual with no human frailties and who is constantly preoccupied with the idea that danger may be lurking in every direction at any time. This hypothetical nature is important: one case was reversed when the judge erroneously told the jury members that they were reasonable and prudent persons and that as such they could ask themselves whether the defendants did anything that, under the same circumstances, they would or would not have done. The jury must not be asked what they would do but what they think this hypothetical person would have done under the circumstances in the case, which is always a judgment call left entirely up to the jury.

If a jury decides that a person acting reasonably and prudently would have acted as the defendant did, the defendant is not liable for harm. If, on the other hand, the jury decides that a person acting reasonably and prudently would not have acted as the defendant did, the defendant is liable for harm.

Probability. Foreseeability is not determined by probability. As discussed in *Gulf Refining Co. v. Williams* (183 Miss. 723, 185 So. 234 (1938)), one way defendants have attempted to show that harm is not foreseeable is to argue that it was a low-probability event and therefore was not foreseeable. The argument is that if the harm that occurs to a person is the result of an unusual, extraordinary, and improbable occurrence, there is no way that a person acting reasonably and prudently could have anticipated that harm.

It is true that there is no liability when the harm that occurs is unusual, extraordinary, and improbable. However, improbable does not just mean that the probability of the harm occurring is less than the probability of the harm not occurring. In fact, courts take the position that if the probability of harm is sufficiently serious that an ordinary person would take precautions to avoid it, failure to do so is negligence. If a jury concludes that a reasonable and prudent person in similar circumstances would anticipate harm and act accordingly and the defendant did not so act, the defendant will most likely lose regardless of the probabilities involved.

The implication for information security is clear. A manager may avoid acting to improve information security because a risk analysis shows that the known threats are all of low probability, the resulting annual loss estimates are low, and therefore the proposed countermeasures are not cost-effective. Although this is a reasonable position to take from an economic perspective, it is not a sound position from a legal perspective.

For example, a risk analysis identifies a threat in which a disgruntled employee might gain unauthorized access to confidential personnel data and release it publicly to embarrass the company. The risk analysis may show this threat has a probability of 0.001 for a given year. Management therefore decides to save the expenses associated with installing countermeasures to protect against this low-probability threat. If this threat occurs and employees are damaged by the release of confidential data, however, a lawsuit charging negligence is likely. During the trial, the court will not be interested in management's rationale that counter-measures were not needed because the threat was of low probability. The court will make its decision on the basis of the actions of the reasonable and prudent person in similar circumstances, not the balance of probabilities.

Balancing Foreseeable Harm with the Expense and Inconve-nience of Reducing It. The courts have recognized that everything people use cannot be made absolutely safe. In many settings, the benefits enjoyed by people occur because they are able to use technology and machines that can inher-ently and foreseeably cause harm. The use of such technology is permitted be-cause the benefits gained are large and the potential harm is small. However, as the potential for harm increases and begins to outweigh the benefits of use, the public has a right to demand that a technology be made safer.

A balancing act occurs in the courts between beneficial use, harm, and safety. Courts do not require that a technology be made absolutely safe. No court will require safety measures that are so expensive and inconvenient that they reduce the benefits of using the technology out of proportion to the harms that might occur without such efforts. In each case, the test for the balance between the public benefit, the anticipated harm to the public, and the expense and inconve-nience of making something safer is what the reasonable and prudent person would do in similar circumstances. The bottom line is that an organization's bud-get is not the determining factor in whether or not money should be spent to make something safer.

In information security settings, managers often defer expenditures for counter-measures, claiming that the recommended countermeasures cost too much. How-ever, the results of a financial analysis should be only one of many factors consid-ered in deciding whether or not to implement certain countermeasures. The decision should also balance the benefits gained with the potential for harm to the public. In fact, many information security countermeasures are relatively inexpen-sive when viewed with respect to the public good.

For example, a large vendor of microcomputer software examines the costs of installing an antivirus countermeasure to make sure that all software packages shipped are free of viruses and decides it is too expensive. A virus then infects the company computer used to make the master software disk, which is then used to make all copies for shipping. Every software program shipped then has the virus. Every user who purchases the program, uses it, and suffers damages from the virus may have a basis for suing the software vendor for negligence.

Standard of Due Care. In helping to enhance the understanding of what duty one person may have to another, the courts have developed the concept of a standard of due care. In effect, this standard dictates what a person must know and what care a person must exercise with respect to another person. An individual cannot escape liability just because ignorance is claimed. Under the standard of due care, a defendant may not be able to claim ignorance; there are certain things defendants simply must do whether they know it or not. The standard of due care relates back to what the reasonable and prudent person would do in similar circumstances.

One way defendants attempt to defend against a charge of failing to meet the standard of due care is to claim that what was done in the defendant's organization is exactly what everyone else in the same industry is doing under similar circumstances. This does not hold up in court. Courts take the position that "what usually is done may be evidence of what ought to be done, but what ought to be done is fixed by a standard of reasonable prudence, whether it usually is complied with or not" [*Texas & Pac. Ry. Co. v. Behymer* (189 US 468, 470 (1903))]. In addition, courts have taken the position that industry practice may not be the most effective way to make something safe, and when that is the case, there is a duty to adopt a more effective way if the technology is available, could be known, and would be adopted by a reasonable and prudent person. Expert evidence may be sufficient to prove a better way even if the industry is not using it. In essence, it is possible to be held to a standard of care that should be used in an industry, even if no one is using it at the time.

This aspect of duty could be particularly troubling for information security, because it basically says that some countermeasure may be insufficient. For example, static, user-generated passwords are widely used in systems as a means of access control. However, there are lists containing 600 to 800 common passwords that, it is claimed, can access a high percentage of systems in the United States. It is also widely argued that as a countermeasure to unauthorized access, use of passwords by themselves is now an obsolete countermeasure. Many experts recommend the use of any two of the three major methods available for providing access control: passwords, handheld tokens, and biometrics. If unauthorized access attempts are foreseeable (which they are) and the only countermeasure in place is a system that allows users to generate their own static passwords, and better technologies are available that are not excessive in cost or inconvenience, the door to a negligence charge is wide open when damages occur.

Cause

Sometimes called cause in fact, cause is the element in negligence that determines whether the conduct of the defendant has caused the plaintiff's damages. When negligence is charged, it is insufficient for the defendant to claim that the damages would have occurred even if the defendant had not been negligent. The court's reasoning is that when the negligence "greatly multiplies the chances of accident to the plaintiff and is of a character naturally leading to its occurrence, the mere possibility that it might have happened without negligence is not sufficient to break the chain of cause and effect between the negligence and the injury" [*Reynolds v. Texas & Pac. Ry. Co.* (Court of Appeals of La., 37 La. Ann. 694 (1885))]. On the other hand, the mere fact that an act by the defendant could have caused injury is not sufficient. In addition, there are situations in which there could be multiple causes (i.e., concurrent causes) of damages.

In information security, the focus is on whether a breach of security was the direct cause of a plaintiff's damages. If, for example, a prime contractor's information system was breached and proprietary information was released about a subcontractor's product, which immediately upon its release caused most of the subcontractor's other clients to cancel orders for that product, the subcontractor might charge negligence and initiate litigation.

Proximate Cause

Most courts take the position that there must be practical limits on how far to go in attempts to establish a link between a given cause and a claimed effect. The real challenge involves deciding how to take into account intervening acts (i.e., of other people or of nature) that occur after the original negligent act and before damages occur to a defendant. The more intervening acts, the harder it is to show that the effects were caused by an original negligent act. In addition, effects may be distant in time or geography from an original negligent act asserted to be the cause.

Courts look for cause and effect only within the scope of ordinary human understanding. Every person is responsible for damages that are the proximate results of his or her own acts. When courts cannot trace the link between cause and effect any further, liability stops.

Proximate cause is important because it involves a decision as to where the limits to liability end. In information security, proximate cause is important because in many situations in which countermeasures are absent or inadequate, there may be many intervening acts and large gaps between the time of the security breach and the time the plaintiff suffers damages. The ability to trace and connect the link between the original negligent act and the damages that occur varies from case to case.

For example, a subcontractor's clients cancel orders for a product after a leak of proprietary information about the subcontractor's products. The case may not be so clear, however, if the cancellations had occurred 10 months after the release of the information and all the clients were overseas, and furthermore if there were intervening events (e.g., announcements about new products that compete successfully with the subcontractor's products or a slowdown in the international economy). In some cases, it is not simple to determine whether the defendant's action (or lack of it) was the proximate cause of the plaintiff's damages.

Damages

Damages are the actual losses that the plaintiff suffers as a result of the negligent act of the defendant. Even if defendant has committed negligent acts, the defendant cannot be held liable for negligence if the plaintiff was not harmed. In other words, without damages, there is no case for negligence.

ADDITIONAL LEGAL CONCEPTS AFFECTING LITIGATION

There are three additional legal concepts that, together with the concepts of negligence, should alert information security managers to the potential for litigation. These concepts are summarized as follows:

- *Negligence per se*. A violation of a statute or regulation is negligence as a matter of law when the violation results in injury to a person or persons protected by the legislation and when the harm is of the kind that the statute or regulation was passed to prevent. Violating the statute is conclusive evidence of negligence and is called negligence per se.
- *Res ipsa loquitur (i.e., the thing speaks for itself)*. Res ipsa loquitur allows a jury to consider the circumstances of a given case and, in the absence of a satisfactory explanation by a defendant, conclude that an accident occurred from the defendant's negligence provided that:
  —The accident was one that ordinarily does not occur without someone's negligence.
  —The accident was caused by something within the exclusive control of the defendant.
  —The plaintiff did not voluntarily act or contribute to causing the accident.
- *Respondeat superior*. This doctrine states that employers are liable for the negligence of their employees when the employees are acting in the scope of their jobs regardless of what employers do to prevent such negligent acts.

The following sections discuss these concepts in more detail.

Negligence Per Se

In negligence per se, all that need be proved is that a violation of statute occurred. In *Osborne v. McMasters* (S.Ct. of Minn., 40 Minn. 103, 41 N.W. 543 (1889)), it is pointed out that if a statute or municipal ordinance, for example, imposes a specific duty on a person for the protection or benefit of others, neglecting to perform the duty makes that person liable to anyone who is injured as a result of that neglect. In general, "A violation of a statute or regulation constitutes negligence as a matter of law when the violation results in injury to a member of the class of persons intended to be protected by the legislation and when the harm is of the kind that the statute or regulation was enacted to prevent" [*Stachniewicz v. Mar-Cam Corp.* (S.Ct. of Oregon, 259 Oregon 583, 488 P.2d 436 (1971))]. Duty in such instances is imposed by statute so that proof of violating the statute is conclusive evidence of negligence, which is called negligence per se.

This is of direct interest to the information security professional because so many state statutes have now been passed in addition to federal statutes with respect to computer and high-technology crime. Moreover, there are now various statutes that deal with privacy of information. Any number of negligent actions by people in an organization can lead to violations of privacy. For example, some companies institute the practice of saving paper by using both sides of paper for printing output. There have been instances when output has been printed on paper with employee payroll information on the reverse side. Another violation of privacy may occur if computer terminals face the doors in offices so that passersby can look in and view another employee's payroll information on the screen. Furthermore, access control systems are often bypassed during the morning rush to begin work because there are so many people trying to gain access simultaneously that it would be very time-consuming to check each one individually.

Res Ipsa Loquitur

In some instances, it may not be possible to clearly link someone's damages or injury directly to another's negligent act. It may even be impossible to provide any direct evidence about what has caused the damage. In such cases, res ipsa loquitur may be used to construct a causal link between a defendant's inferred act and a plaintiff's actual damages. Res ipsa loquitur is used only to make inferences from events that cannot be explained otherwise. In general, res ipsa loquitur permits a jury to consider the circumstances of a given case and, in the absence of a satisfactory explanation by a defendant, conclude that an accident occurred from the defendant's negligence.

In information systems, for example, res ipsa loquitur may be applicable in security breaches in which a file containing previously correct information about someone is discovered to have been altered to show incorrect data. The file has existed exclusively within a company's information system, and only the company's employees can access it. The changes made to the data subsequently damage that person. There is an audit trail showing that company employees accessed that file recently but that there have been no other access attempts. In such a situation, res ipsa loquitur might be used to try to link the damages to negligent acts of the company or its employees.

Respondeat Superior

Sometimes called imputed negligence or vicarious liability, *respondeat superior* means to ask the higher level to be answerable. Under this doctrine, an employer is liable for the negligence of employees committed while they were acting in the scope of their job. This is an especially troublesome doctrine because, for example, an organization that played no part in an employee's negligent act did nothing to encourage the negligent act and in fact may have taken precautions to prevent the negligent act nevertheless becomes a defendant charged with negligence just as if the organization had committed the negligent act itself. Employers cannot protect themselves from liability even if they impose safety rules or instruct their employees in expected behavior on the job, no matter how specific and detailed their orders may be.

For example, employees in an information systems department violate specific written orders of the organization that state that no external modems are ever to be used. They connect modems to their personal computers and leave them on 24 hours a day so that they can dial in from home at any time and access the mainframe at the office. As a result, a hacker breaks into the mainframe and causes damages to a third party outside the organization when information about the third party is compromised. The third party could charge negligence and hold the employer liable under respondeat superior regardless of what the written orders were.

IMPLICATIONS FOR INFORMATION SECURITY

Once they understand negligence and the three related legal doctrines presented in the preceding section, most information security professionals react with great concern. It is relatively easy for them to see that if a person suffers damage as a result of a security breach in an information system that has inadequate countermeasures, the organization is vulnerable to negligence litigation, which can be costly.

It can be argued that the entire purpose of information security is to protect the confidentiality, integrity, and availability of information. The managers and employees who provide information systems and their services to users have a duty to prevent others or their property from being exposed to unreasonable risks of harm. This duty is unavoidable. The exact duty with respect to confidentiality, integrity, and availability is still evolving in the courts; when these duties are required by contract or by statute, however, they are clear.

For example, when a company advertises the secure characteristics of its information services, it will be held to the standard it advertises. Absent contracts, statutes, and advertisements, the duty with respect to availability, integrity, and confidentiality may well be defined through lawsuits brought into the court system.

If a company is to rely on the integrity of its information without the proper information security safeguards in place to ensure integrity, it is an invitation for anyone who has been damaged by the lack of integrity to sue for negligence for failure to exercise the standard of due care.

As more people experience information system–related damages, it is likely that more negligence litigation will occur. One key to proving breach of duty in negligence cases is to show that insufficient countermeasures are in place for threats that are foreseeable. Many threats are now well-known.

For example, the National Center for Computer Crime Data published a document summarizing computer crime and information system crime statistics. This report shows the number of computer crimes in various jurisdictions, the demographic makeup of the computer criminals, and average losses. The national media have presented extensive coverage on some of the more newsworthy threats: viruses, hackers, and worms, which account for an estimated 2% to 5% of the threats to information security. Yet, as shown in Exhibit IV-1-15, employee accidents and error account for 55% of known threats; dishonest or disgruntled employees account for 25%; and natural disasters, fire, floods, and earthquakes account for 20%. Although these represent a vastly higher percentage of known security threats, they receive little attention beyond information security literature.

Threat analyses are typically published along with recommended countermeasures and consequently are known and therefore foreseeable. When available countermeasures are not in place against foreseeable threats and a person is damaged as a result, litigation is increasingly likely to occur.

Unfortunately, many of the currently available countermeasures against known threats are simply not used. They range from the simple (e.g., changing the vendor-supplied password for a mainframe user) to the complex (e.g., encryption on a voice and data network). If currently available countermeasures are known and not used against threats that are foreseeable, it would appear that organizations simply hope that no one is damaged as a result of negligent acts.

Although the law is still evolving with respect to civil litigation over information system–related losses, it seems reasonable to suggest that the standard of due care will remain the same as in other negligence cases: what would the reasonable and prudent person have done in similar circumstances? If a reasonable and prudent person would have foreseen the threat and placed a known countermeasure in place regardless of what the current industry practices are, that may be the context in which a system's negligence will be judged.

EXHIBIT IV-1-15 **Information Security Threats**

Threat	Percentage of Known Threats (%)*
Accidents and Errors	55
Employee Dishonesty	15
Employee Revenge	10
Fire	15
Flood Damage	3
Earthquake and Other Natural Disasters	2

Note:
*This table does not include an estimate of the threat from hackers and outsiders, which many estimate at from 2% to 5% of all threats.

SOURCE: Executive Information Network, as reproduced in *Commitment to Security, The Second Statistical Report of the National Center for Computer Crime Data* (Santa Cruz CA: National Center for Computer Crime Data, 1989).

Damages and Their Causes

With respect to information system–related losses resulting from breaches of security, there are two main kinds of damage that may occur, either individually or in combination. Damages can be direct (which are easy to identify and count) or indirect (which are much more difficult to assess). For example, damages that are measured in terms of immediate client loss could be considered direct. However, as news about the loss of clients spreads, other potential clients may simply shop for services elsewhere. These would be considered indirect damages.

Direct and indirect damages can involve loss of money, loss of goods, disruption of service, loss of system integrity, loss of confidentiality, loss of opportunities, and loss of reputation. For example, more and more transactions among vendors and clients are being done through the use of electronic data interchange (EDI) and faxes, which use neither encryption nor authentication to verify information or orders. Significant damages can occur when legitimate organizations are impersonated by others issuing false information or orders for materials or services.

HEADING OFF NEGLIGENCE LAWSUITS

One of the emerging tasks of the information security professional is to avoid lawsuits charging negligence. In other industries, notably in the manufacturing industry, product liability lawsuits arising as a result of negligence are teaching managers and organizations an expensive lesson: lawsuits charging negligence cannot be fended off by simply ignoring them. Some proactive measures are required.

The organization should assemble a team to design and develop an information security program and recovery plans and to recommend appropriate insurance covering lawsuits. The security program and the recovery plans must then be implemented.

Taking these proactive steps will not necessarily prevent an organization from being charged with negligence lawsuits. At the least, however, it can reduce the organization's risk of losing such lawsuits. Exhibit IV-1-16 summarizes the steps. The following sections discuss the main steps in more detail.

Assembling an Information Security Team

A team must be assembled to design and implement a systematic information security team. This team should be interdisciplinary: not only must engineering, management, and human resources experts be involved, but attorneys must participate from the start. Attorneys bring a unique and important perspective to the program because they do not argue for effective engineering or human factors or

---

EXHIBIT IV-1-16 Steps to Avoiding Negligence Lawsuits

Step 1: Assemble An Information Security Team:
- Appoint interdisciplinary members and attorneys.
- Charter the team to design and implement an information security program.

Step 2: The Team Designs the Information Security Program, which:
- Identifies foreseeable threats and countermeasures for those threats.
- Identifies standards of due care and the organization's duties to users (including those required by statute).
- Identifies the countermeasures for those threats identified, according to what a reasonable and prudent person in similar circumstances would implement.

Step 3: The Team Develops Recovery Plans and Makes Insurance Recommendations.

Step 4: The Organization Implements the Security Program.

for cost-effective solutions. Rather, they argue for preventive legal actions that will make it unlikely for anyone to prove negligence in court.

Designing the Program

The information security program should contain several components. First, it must identify foreseeable threats as well as countermeasures for those threats. Second, it must identify the standards of due care and the organization's duties to its users, including those required by statute. These duties should be identified at the start of the project and updated periodically. Finally, the program must make recommendations on implementing the countermeasures for those threats that have been identified.

Because risk cannot be reduced to zero, the organization must be prepared to argue that it acted as a reasonable and prudent person would act in similar circumstances. The organization must be prepared to argue that its countermeasures are on the correct side of the balance between a duty to provide for the public good and the cost and inconvenience of the countermeasures.

Developing Recovery Plans and Obtaining Insurance

An effective information security program identifies the organization's duties and the proper safeguards; however, implementing these safeguards is not enough. Under the doctrine of respondeat superior, a negligent act of one employee in the course of his or her duties can expose the organization to a charge of negligence. Therefore, it may be insufficient if the program puts in place information security precautions, policy precautions, hardware and software precautions, education and training awareness precautions, precautions in advertising, and precautions through testing and control. Negligent acts may still occur and cause damages.

In operational settings, where it is simply impossible to eliminate every negligent act that may cause damages, the ultimate strategy is to develop recovery plans and obtain insurance as part of the lawsuit avoidance program. Although recovery plans do not necessarily alleviate threats to information systems, they can minimize or mitigate resulting damages. For example, if viruses circumvent anti-virus programs and wipe out a hard disk, a complete virus-free backup can permit recovery without interruption to a user.

As a last resort, an organization should consider obtaining lawsuit insurance. Most manufacturers, doctors, and other professionals have had to turn to insurance companies to cushion the blow of civil lawsuits charging negligence. The vicious cycle of escalating jury awards and escalating insurance premiums has not yet started in the information systems arena, however.

SUMMARY

Currently, there is considerable debate over whether charges of negligence will result in a significant amount of litigation over information system–related losses. Some believe that an explosion of litigation is inevitable. Others feel that it will be hard to prove the elements of negligence in court, however, particularly with respect to proximate cause.

In addition, some argue that the joining of information technology, information security, and negligence is so foreign to most users, attorneys, and courts that it will be a long time before such cases are filed. For the moment, it appears too early to tell which path negligence litigation will take in information system–related losses. It seems, however, that some cases may make their way into the court system and draw considerable attention in the process. In addition, the risk of such cases being filed may be increasing.

There are two implications for the information security professional with respect to the potential for litigation over information system–related losses resulting from negligent acts. First, the potential for negligence litigation is another arrow in the quiver of information security professionals as they attempt to persuade line managers to take the proper action to secure their information system against foreseeable threats.

Second, regardless of the current state of affairs with respect to civil litigation charging negligence, it seems prudent to act as though such litigation were a highly likely scenario that should be planned for strategically. If a high volume of lawsuits does not emerge (as some argue), the worst that could happen to an organization is that it spends more than it otherwise would have on information security. If so, from a security perspective, it could be argued the organization has done the right thing for the wrong reason. If, on the other hand, lawsuits do appear and increase in frequency, the organization will probably have spent less on increasing information security than it otherwise might have lost in court without it.

In either event, the organization will have increased the confidentiality, integrity, and availability of its information and at the same time protected itself from an emerging epidemic of negligence lawsuits.

Glossary

abend An error condition that abnormally terminates a program.

abort Program termination when a malfunction, mistake, or other unrecoverable error occurs.

acceptable risk Management's acceptance of a level of risk to an asset, based on empirical data and supportive technical opinion that the overall risk is understood and that the controls placed on the asset or environment will lower the potential for loss. Any remaining risk is recognized and accepted as an accountability entity.

acceptance testing The formal testing conducted to determine whether a software system satisfies its acceptance criteria, enabling the customer to determine whether to accept the system.

access The ability or the means necessary to read, write, modify, or communicate data or otherwise make use of any system resource.

access authorization The granting of authority to an individual or system, to perform specific functions on data or other resources.

access category One of the classes to which a terminal, transaction, user, program, or process in a computer-based system may be assigned, based on the resources or groups of resources that each is authorized to access. This term refers primarily to IBM RACF systems but applies to other systems as well.

access control The prevention of unauthorized use of a resource.

access control list (ACL) A list of entities, together with their access rights, that are authorized to have access to a resource.

access control mechanism A hardware, software, or firmware feature of an operating and management procedure designed to detect and prevent unauthorized access and to permit authorized access to a computer system.

access control model Organizes a system into objects, subjects, and operations with rules that specify which operations can be performed on an object by which subject.

access list A list of users, programs, and processes and the specifications of the access categories to which each is assigned.

access period A segment of time during which access rights are in effect.

access type The nature of access granted to a particular device, program, or file (e.g., read-only access and read-write access).

accountability The property that ensures that the actions of an entity can be traced uniquely to that entity.

accreditation Formal management authorization and approval granted to an automated information system to use information and resources in a developmental or operational environment. Accreditation is made on the basis of a certification by designated technical personnel that the design and implementation of the system meets specified requirements. The accrediting authority assumes responsibility for residual risk.

active threat The immediate possibility of a deliberate, unauthorized change to a system state.

ADCCP The advanced data communications control procedure developed by ANSI; a bit-oriented protocol.

add-on security The retrofitting of protection mechanisms, implemented by hardware, firmware, or software.

administrative security The management constraints, operational and accountability procedures, and supplemental controls established to provide adequate protection of sensitive data.

AFIPS American Federation of Information Processing Societies.

alphabetic test A test of whether an element of data contains only alphabetic or blank characters.

alpha test Initial test in the laboratory environment. Frequently used synonomously with unit test.

annualized loss expectancy (ALE) *See* loss.

ANSI American National Standards Institute, a standards-setting body.

ANSI X9.9 FIMAS Standard The ANSI standard for the protection of electronic funds transfers (EFTs). FIMAS stands for Financial Institution Message Authentication Standard.

antivirus software Detects, identifies, isolates, and eradicates viruses.

application program A computer program written for or by a computer user that causes a computer system to satisfy defined needs.

applications programmer One who designs, develops, debugs, installs, maintains, and documents applications programs.

ASCII American Standard Code for Information Interchange; an information coding technique for asynchronous communications.

ASIS American Society for Industrial Security.

assembler A computer program that translates a source program written in assembly language into machine language.

assembly language A low-level source program language that includes symbolic statements (macros) that the assembler translates to machine language.

assertion A logical expression specifying a program state that must exist or a set of conditions that program variables must satisfy at a particular point during program execution.

asset valuation A quantitative and qualitative assessment of the physical resources of the facilities, information, the sensitivity of the information, the operational impact of loss or denial of support, and the automated information systems resources providing that support. Qualitative valuation is usually expressed in nonmonetary terms (e.g., weighted averages), and quantitative valuation is expressed in monetary terms.

assurance   A measure of confidence that the security features and architecture of an automated information system accurately mediate and enforce the organization's security policy.

asymmetric encryption algorithm   A cryptographic algorithm that uses one key for the encryption of data and a different key for the decryption of data. Knowledge of the encryption key does not necessarily imply knowledge of the decryption key and vice versa. An asymmetric algorithm is sometimes referred to as a public-key algorithm.

asynchronous   Communications or other functions not based on standard time intervals. Typically, this requires start, stop, and perhaps other commands to initiate, control, and terminate the functions.

asynchronous attacks   Taking advantage of the asynchronous nature of a computer operating system to commit an unauthorized act.

audio response system   A system whose output consists of audible signals and transmitters that simulate spoken language.

audit   The performance of an independent review and examination of system records, operational procedures, and system activities to test for the adequacy of system controls, to ensure compliance with established policy and procedures, and to recommend any necessary changes in controls, policy, or procedures.

audit trail   A record of system activities that is sufficient to enable the reconstruction, review, and examination of the sequence of environments and activities surrounding or leading to each event in the path of a transaction, from its inception to output of final results.

authentication   The act of verifying the identity of a station, originator, or individual to determine the right to access specific categories of information. Also a measure designed to protect against fraudulent transmission by verifying the validity of a transmission, message, station, or originator.

authority   An entity recognized by a set of secure systems as a trusted source of security information. An authority may be online as an authentication service or offline as a certification authority.

authorization   The granting of the right of access to a user, terminal, transaction, program, or process.

autodialer   An automatic device that can emulate the dialer of a telephone.

automated information system (AIS)   An assembly of computer hardware, software, and firmware configured to collect, communicate, process, and control data.

automated information system security   *See* computer security system.

automated information system security engineering team   A team established by management to develop, implement, and integrate the automated information system security requirements methodology as an integral developmental and operational process.

availability The property that a given information resource will be usable by authorized persons or programs when needed and in the form needed. To be usable, the resource must be accessible, timely, and of acceptable integrity.

backup operation A method of operation implemented to complete essential tasks (as identified by risk analysis) following the disruption of an IS facility and continuing until the facility is either restored or permanently relocated.

backup procedures Provisions made for the recovery of data, software, and hardware following a system failure or disaster.

backup site agreement A contract to provide off-site emergency computer services on short notice.

baseline A generally accepted state of status to be strived for, from which deviations may be made or planned.

baseline security controls A basic set of controls that meet a minimum set of standards that should be in place in all properly run data centers.

batch control An information processing technique using control totals to provide a basis for validating processing results.

baud A unit of signaling speed that refers to the number of times the state or condition of a line changes per second. It is the reciprocal of the length (in seconds) of the shortest element in the signaling code. In a binary system, a bit is the smallest unit of information. Therefore, the baud rate is equal to the bit rate if each signal element represents one bit of information. In communications, each character requires 10 bits for its representation.

baud rate The speed at which modems exchange information. Common speeds are 300, 1,200, or 2,400 baud (30, 120, and 240 characters per second respectively).

Bell-La Padula model A formal-state transition model of computer security policy that describes a set of access control rules. The entities in a computer system are divided into sets of subjects and objects. The notion of a secure state is defined, and it is proved that each transaction preserves security by moving from secure state to secure state. The system is secure if the only access by subjects to objects is in accordance with a specific security policy. The sensitivity authorization of the subject is compared with the sensitivity classification of the object to determine whether a specific access is allowed.

beta test The test of an application in its true operating environment. This term is used synonymously with system test.

biometric authentication The authentication of an individual on the basis of a unique and measurable physical characteristic, such as a fingerprint.

biometric measurement The measurement of specific physical attributes of an individual (e.g., fingerprints, voice patterns, or signature dynamics) for purposes of identification.

blue box Equipment used fraudulently to synthesize signals and gain access to the toll network so that telephone calls can be placed without charge.

boot Refers to the initial commands to load an operating system. Commonly used to indicate any startup operation, such as starting a microcomputer system.

bps Bits per second. The rate at which bits are transmitted through a serial device.

browsing The searching of computer storage to locate or acquire information without necessarily knowing whether the information exists or what its format is.

bug An error in a coded program statement.

bulletin board A private telecommunications utility employing an application program that turns a computer into a terminal for receiving data from and transmitting data to distant computers through the telephone system.

business continuity planning *See* contingency plan.

business recovery planning *See* contingency plan.

callback A procedure that verifies the identity of a terminal dialing into a computer system or network by disconnecting the terminal, verifying the caller's ID against an automated control table, and then reestablishing the connection, if authorized, by automatically dialing the telephone number of the caller.

capability An immutable ticket (e.g., a token) used as an identifier for a resource. Possession of the ticket, which cannot be forged, confers access rights for the resource.

capability table A table that identifies objects (e.g., files) and specifies the access rights of subjects (e.g., users) who possess the capability to perform a particular operation on the object.

CCITT International Telephone and Telegraph Consultative Committee, an international standards-setting body.

certificate Security information signed by an authority. Certificates are generally signed using public-key technology.

certification The technical evaluation, made before and in support of the accreditation process, that establishes the extent to which a particular computer system or network design and implementation meets a specified set of requirements, including federal, state, and local requirements for government-regulated systems.

Certified Information Systems Security Professional (CISSP) Designated by the International Information Systems Security Certification Consortium after successfully completing a specified amount of experience in the field of information security and passing an examination on the common body of knowledge of the profession.

Certified Protection Professional (CPP) The CPP designation is awarded to individuals who pass an ASIS-sponsored program of coursework and tests.

channel An information-transfer path.

check digits One or more digits appended to a unit item of information that are used to verify the accuracy of other digits in the unit.

cipher lock A combination lock containing buttons that open the lock when pushed in the proper sequence.

cipher system A system in which cryptography is applied to plaintext elements.

ciphertext Unintelligible data produced through encryption. Ciphertext ideally has no available semantic content and can be processed in very few meaningful ways, although other types of data (e.g., compressed data) often exhibit similar properties.

classification   Separation of information into two or more categories that have different protective requirements.

cleartext   Plaintext, or intelligible data, which has an available semantic content.

code system   Any system of communication in which groups of symbols represent plaintext elements of varying length.

cold site   One or more computer rooms, frequently equipped with communnications lines, that are ready to receive hardware for disaster recovery.

COM   Computer output microfilm; microfilm containing data that is generated directly from computer-generated signals.

communications security   Protection that ensures the integrity and authenticity of communications transmissions by applying measures that deny unauthorized persons access to information in a communications system.

compartmentalization   The isolation of the operating system, user programs, and data files from one another in main storage to protect them against unauthorized access or concurrent access by other users or programs; in addition, the breaking down of sensitive data into small, isolated blocks in order to reduce the risk to the data.

compromise   A violation of the security policy of a system that may result in a loss of data or process integrity, a denial of service to authorized users, or unauthorized disclosure of sensitive information.

computer abuse   The misuse of computer technology in a manner through which a victim suffers or could suffer a loss.

computer crime   An illegal act for which the knowledge of computer or data communications technology is required or in which computer equipment is an integral element.

computer security   The protection of a computer system against internal failure, human error, attack, and natural catastrophe with the goal of preventing improper disclosure, modification, or destruction of information or the denial of service.

computer security model   A mathematical description of subjects, objects, and other entities of a system for the purpose of analyzing the security of the system.

computer security system   The technological safeguards and managerial procedures applied to computers and networks—including related hardware, firmware, software, and data—in order to protect organizational assets and privacy.

concealment   A method of keeping sensitivie information confidential by embedding it in irrelevant data.

confidentiality   The property that ensures that information is not made available or disclosed to unauthorized individuals, entities, or processes. The degree to which sensitive data about both individuals and organizations must be protected.

configuration management   Control of changes to a system's hardware, software, firmware, or documentation throughout the system life cycle.

consistency constraints Rules that determine whether a given data base state is consistent in context of a given application. The relational model provides for entity and referential integrity constraints as well as domain and dependency constraints.

contingency plan A plan for emergency response, backup operations, and post-disaster recovery maintained as part of the security program. The purpose of this plan is to ensure the availability of critical resources and facilitate the continuity of operations in an emergency situation.

control A protective action, device, procedure, technique, or other measure that reduces exposure.

control break A point in program processing at which some special processing event takes place—for example, a change in the value of a control field in a data record.

control objective The protection goal expressed at the policy level that results in establishment of an information security requirement.

control policy Senior management decisions that determine how certain security-related concepts will be interpreted as system requirements.

control signals Computer-generated signals for the automatic control of machines and processes.

control totals Numeric data fields that are used to check the accuracy of input data, data being processed, or output data.

control unit A component of the central processing unit that evaluates and executes program processing.

control zone An area around a sensitive area that is subject to physical and technical controls to protect against unauthorized entry or compromise.'

copy protection A mechanism for preventing the duplication of software or other electronically recorded information.

correctness The extent to which software is free from design and coding defects; also, the extent to which software meets its requirements and user objectives.

cost/benefit analysis The determination of the financial advantages of developing a system based on a comparison of its projected costs and its expected benefits.

countermeasure Any action, device, procedure, technique, or other measure that reduces the vulnerability of or threat to a system.

covert channel A communications channel that allows a process to transfer information in a manner that violates the system's security policy.

credentials Data that is transferred to establish the claimed identity of an entity.

criticality The condition in which serious consequences may result if a critical requirement is not satisfied. A system is critical if any of its requirements are critical.

cryptanalysis The process of converting encrypted messages into plaintext without knowledge of the key employed in the encryption algorithm.

cryptographic checksum Information that is derived by performing a cryptographic transformation on a message. Frequently used to authenticate that message.

cryptographic system The documents, devices, equipment, and associated techniques that together provide a means of encryption.

cryptography The process of creating unintelligible ciphertext and converting encrypted messages into intelligible plaintext. The discipline that embodies principles, means, and methods for the transformation of data in order to hide its information content, prevent its unauthorized modification, or prevent its unauthorized use.

cryptology The field of study that encompasses both cryptography and cryptanalysis.

CSMA/CD Carrier-sense multiple access with collision detection. CSMA/CD is a network transmission method in which multiple workstations access a transmission medium (i.e., multiple access) by listening until no signals are detected (i.e., carrier sense) and transmitting while checking to see if more than one signal is present (i.e., collision detection). Each workstation tries to transmit when it senses the network is free. If a collision occurs because of simultaneous transmissions, each workstation attempts to retransmit after a preset delay selected by random number.

custodian A designated person who has authorized possession of information and is entrusted to provide proper protection, maintenance, and usage control of the information in an operational environment.

data A representation of information, knowledge, facts, concepts, or instructions that is being prepared or has been prepared in a formalized manner and is intended to be stored or processed, is being stored or processed, or has been stored or processed in a computer. Data may be embodied in any form, including but not limited to computer printouts, magnetic or optical storage media, and punchcards, or it may be stored internally in computer memory.

data base An organized file of related data.

data capture The process of collecting and encoding data for entry into a computer system.

data communications The transmission of data between physical sites by means of public or private communications channels or lines.

data contamination The deliberate or accidental compromising of data integrity.

data-dependent protection The safeguarding of data at a level commensurate with the sensitivity of the individual data elements rather than the entire file.

data dictionary A file, document, or listing that defines all items or processes represented in a data flow diagram or used in a system.

data diddling The willful act of changing data, using fraudulent input, or removal of controls. *See also* hacking.

Data Encryption Standard (DES) An encryption algorithm that has been endorsed by both the US National Institute for Standards and Technology (NIST) and the American National Standards Institute (ANSI) as providing adequate security for unclassified sensitive information.

data element The smallest unit of data accessible to a data base management system; also, a field of data in a file processing system.

data flow analysis A graphic analysis technique designed to trace the behavior of program variables as they are initialized, modified, or referenced during program execution.

data integrity The assurance that computerized data is the same as its source document form—that is, that it has not been exposed to accidental or malicious modification, alteration, or destruction.

data management system System software that supervises the handling of data required by programs during execution.

debugging The process of correcting static and logical errors in program code.

decipher To convert ciphertext into plaintext using a decryption key.

decipherment Decryption. *Decipherment* is the preferred term in international documents, although the term *decryption* is more commonly used in the US.

decrypt To convert encrypted text into plaintext by means of a decryption key.

dedicated processing The operation of a computer system so that the central processing unit, peripheral devices, communications facilities, and remote terminals are used and controlled exclusively by a group of users in order to process specific types and categories of information.

degauss To erase or demagnetize magnetic recording media (usually tapes) by applying a variable, alternating current.

denial of service The prevention of authorized access to resources; also, the unauthorized delay of time-sensitive operations.

DES *See* Data Encryption Standard.

detective controls Such mechanisms as audit trails, intrusion detection systems, and checksums, which are implemented as a complement to protective controls to provide awareness of violations or attempted violations of physical, technical, or administrative security measures.

dial-up access Access to a computer system using telephone lines and a modem.

digital signature Data appended to or a cryptographic transformation of a data unit that allows a recipient of the data unit to verify the source and integrity of the data unit and thereby protect against forgery.

disaster Any interruption of computing services that adversely and significantly affects user operations.

disaster recovery plan *See* contingency plan.

discretionary access control A means of restricting access to objects on the basis of the identity of subjects or groups to which they belong. The controls are discretionary in the sense that a subject with certain access privileges is capable of passing that privilege (perhaps indirectly) on to any other subject; it is often employed to enforce need-to-know or need-to-withhold policy. Access control may be changed by an authorized individual.

diskless workstation A workstation that has no self-contained storage medium. Files are stored on a server with appropriate access control mechanisms.

distributed processing A form of system-to-system communications in which an application is divided among two or more systems in a fixed design. The decision as to where work will be done is made during the design stage and is bound during implementation. The computer system is designed for multiple users and provides each user with a fully functional computer. A distributed system is designed to facilitate communications among the linked computers and shared access to central files. In personal computer environments, distributed processing takes the form of local area networks.

domain The list of objects that a user can access.

down link The transmission path from a satellite to earth.

downloading The process of transferring a file from a host computer to the user's system.

dumpster diving The process of searching waste receptacles for information (e.g., password lists or system authentication procedures) that can be used to attack a system.

dynamic analysis The execution of program code to detect errors by analyzing the code's response to input.

dynamic processing The technique of swapping jobs in and out of computer memory. This technique can be controlled by the assignment priority and the number of time slices allocated to each job.

eavesdropping The unauthorized interception, through methods other than active wiretapping, of transmitted signals that contain data.

echo The display of characters on a terminal as they are entered into the system.

ECMA European Computer Manufacturers Association, a standards-setting body for the European market.

EDI Electronic data interchange. The interchange of electronic forms of business documents, (e.g., purchase orders and invoices) between multiple organizations' computers.

edit To inspect a line of text, a field, or a data element to verify its accuracy.

electronic vaulting Automatic backup to a secure off-site location.

emanations Electromagnetic waves from a computer system that may convey data and that, if intercepted and analyzed, could allow disclosure of information being processed by that system.

emanation security The practice of denying unauthorized interception and analysis of sensitive data contained in electromagnetic emanations.

emergency response The planned reaction to such disturbances as natural disasters (e.g., fires and floods) and terrorist activities to protect lives and minimize damage to property and interruption of operations.

encipher The process of encoding plaintext by means of a cipher system.

encipherment Encryption. *Encipherment* is the preferred term in international documents. The term *encryption* is more commonly used in the US.

encryption The transformation of data by cryptographic techniques to produce ciphertext.

encryption algorithm A set of mathematically expressed rules for encoding information by the methodically prescribed application of a key.

end-to-end encryption Encryption of data within the source end system, with decryption occurring only within or at the destination end system.

entrapment The deliberate planting of apparent flaws in a system to detect attempted penetrations; also, confusing an intruder about which flaws to exploit.

evolution checking Testing to ensure the completeness and consistency of a software product at different levels of specifications when that product is a refinement or elaboration of another.

exception report A management report that highlights abnormal business conditions. Usually, such reports prompt management action or inquiry.

executive state A privileged status that allows a program to perform functions not normally allowable (i.e., the bypassing of security controls). Also known as supervisor state.

exposure A potential for loss or harm (e.g., erroneous record keeping, unmaintainable applications, or business interruptions) that could affect an organization's profitability or ability to operate normally.

external consistency The consistency of data in a computer system with the real-world environment that the data represents.

fail safe The automatic termination and protection of programs or other processing operations when a hardware, software, or firmware failure is detected in a computer system.

fail soft The selective termination of nonessential processing in cases of hardware, software, or firmware failure in a computer system. Also, the termination of secured information processing when security fails.

failure access Unauthorized and usually inadvertent access to data resulting from hardware, software, or firmware failure in a computer system.

failure control The methodology used to detect and provide fail-safe or fail-soft recovery from hardware, software, or firmware failure in a computer system.

fault A weakness in a computer system that allows circumvention of controls.

fault tolerance The capability of a computer system to cope with internal hardware problems without interrupting the system's performance. Fault-tolerant designs typically use backup systems that are automatically brought online when a failure is detected.

feasibility study An investigation of the legal, political, social, operational, technical, economic, and psychological effects of developing and implementing a computerized system.

federal computer fraud act The Counterfeit Access Device and Computer Fraud and Abuse Act of 1986, which outlaws unauthorized access to the federal government's computers and to certain financial data bases protected under the Right to Financial Privacy Act of 1978 and the Fair Credit Reporting Act of 1971.

Federal Privacy Act A federal law that allows individuals to discover what information pertaining to them is on file and how it is being used by government agencies and their contractors.

fetch protection A system-provided restriction that prevents a program from accessing data in another user's segment of storage.

file maintenance The alteration of a master file by either changing the contents of existing records, adding new records, or deleting old records.

file protection The processes and procedures established to inhibit unauthorized access to and contamination or elimination of a file.

file updating The posting of transaction data to master files or the maintenance of master files through record additions, changes, or deletions.

FIPS Federal Information Processing Standard.

flow control Ensures that information at a given security level flows only to an equal or higher level.

Foreign Corrupt Practices Act A federal law that requires public companies to maintain books, records, and accounts in sufficient detail to accurately reflect the transactions and dispositions of its assets and to maintain a system of internal accounting controls.

formal analysis The application of rigorous mathematical techniques to the analysis of a system solution. The algorithms employed may be analyzed for numerical properties, efficiency, and correctness.

formulary A technique for allowing the decision to grant or deny access to be made dynamically at the time of the access attempt rather than at the time the access list is created.

front-end processor A computer to which input and output activities are off-loaded from a central computer so that the central computer can operate primarily in a processing mode.

functional specification The chief product of systems analysis; the detailed logical description of a new system. The specification contains input, processing, storage, and output requirements that detail the functions of the system.

functional testing The application of test data derived from the functional requirements.

hacker Initially used to describe any person who spent a great deal of time exploring the capabilities of a computer, this term has come to mean a person who engages in such activities to gain unauthorized access to a computer system.

hacking An unauthorized attempt to access a computer system and the data that it supports.

handshaking procedures A dialogue between a user and a computer or between computers or programs whose purpose is to identify and authenticate the identity of a user. Identification and authentication are accomplished through a sequence of questions and answers that are based on information either stored in the computer or supplied to it by the initiator of the dialogue.

hot site A computer service facility that is fully operational with the appropriate hardware and communications and that is ready to support a disabled computer center with a compatible configuration. Commonly accessible only when a long-term lease has been completed before the disaster.

identification The recognition of users or resources as those previously described to a computer system, generally through the use of unique, machine-readable names.

identity-based security policy A security policy based on the identities or attributes of users, groups of users, or entities acting on behalf of users. This type of security policy is often implemented using access control lists.

impersonation An attempt to gain access to a system by posing as an authorized user.

incomplete parameter checking Inadequate checking of system parameters by the operating system for correctness and consistency, resulting in system exposure to unauthorized access.

inductive pickup coil A wiretap device that makes use of a coil placed around or near a telephone line or instrument. It operates on the principle of electromagnetic induction.

inference The ability of users to gather information that is not explicitly available. An inference presents a breach of secrecy if more highly classified information can be inferred from less classified information.

information asset Valuable or sensitive information in any form (i.e., written, verbal, or electronic).

information security The practice of protecting information from accidental or malicious modification, destruction, disclosure, or denial of service. The term is similar to *data security* but implies a broader scope, encompassing both electronic and nonelectronic information.

input controls Techniques and methods for verifying, validating, and editing data to ensure its accurate entry into a computer system.

inquiry processing The process of selecting a record from a file and displaying its contents.

inspection A formal analysis technique that involves manual review of program requirements, design, or program code for errors.

instrumental input The process by which machines capture data and store it in a computer.

integration testing The progressive testing of software and hardware in a system until all intermodule links have been deemed compatible and workable.

integrity The property of data, processes, or information resources that have not been improperly altered or destroyed.

integrity checking The testing of programs to verify the soundness of a software product at each phase of its development.

integrity check value A known function of all the protected bits in a packet that is encrypted to provide integrity services for digital data. An intruder can modify a packet and compute the correct integrity check value of the modified packet but cannot encrypt the integrity check value. Therefore, alteration of the packet can be detected.

internal consistency The self-consistency of interdependent data in a system (e.g., a file containing a monthly summary of transactions must be consistent with the transaction records themselves).

intrusion detection A method for the real-time or after-the-fact identification of all types of security violations.

ISDN Integrated services digital network. ISDN is designed to provide switched communications capabilities for the world's public voice and data networks. Users are provided with digital circuit-switched voice and data services as well as packet-switched data services.

intrusion detection system An expert system designed to track users while they are using the system and, on the basis of their personal profile, determine whether their current activities are consistent with their normal activities.

ISO International Standards Organization.

isolation The separation of users, processes, and resources in a computer system from one another as well as from the controls of the operating system.

ITSEC Information Technology Security Evaluation Criteria. The harmonized criteria of France, Germany, the Netherlands, and the United Kingdom.

job accounting system Software that tracks the services and resources used by a computer system's account holders.

journaling The logging of activities external to the operations environment or internal to the automated systems.

kernelized operating system An operating system in which there is an isolated section of code, or a hardware system that protects itself from tampering and enforces security controls for all processes.

key A sequence of symbols that controls the operations of encryption and decryption. For block ciphers, this is the value used to select a particular transformation from among the many available. For stream ciphers, the key may refer to the actual key stream, not just to the values used to initialize the cryptographic algorithm.

key generation The creation of a key or a distinct set of keys.

key management The generation, storage, distribution, delection, archiving, and application of keys in accordance with an established security policy.

key-pair encryption The use of two keys in three applications of an encryption algorithm whereby the data is first encrypted with one key, the result is decrypted using the second key, and the result is again encrypted using the first key. Key-pair encryption is used to extend the effective key length of algorithms.

label The marking of an item of information to reflect its level of sensitivity, criticality, or security classification. An internal label reflects the classification and sensitivity of the information within the confines of the medium containing the information. An external label is a visible, readable marking on the outside of the medium that reflects the category and classification of the information within the medium.

LAN Local area network.

language translator System software that converts programs written in assembly or a higher-level language into machine code.

least privilege The principle that requires that each subject be granted the most restrictive set of privileges needed for performance of authorized tasks. The application of this principle limits the damage that can result from accident, error, or unauthorized use.

limit check An input control test that assesses the value of a data field to determine whether it falls within a set limit or given range.

linkage The combination of data from two systems in order to derive additional information.

link-by-link encryption The individual application of encryption to data on each link of a communications system, whether a logical link or a physical connection. In general, the term is used to indicate encryption that is not end-to-end.

link encryption The application of online cryptography to a communications link so that all data passing through the link is encrypted.

Local area network (LAN) The linkage of personal and other computers (e.g., workstations, front-end processors, controllers, switches, and gateways) within a limited area by high-performance cables so that users can exchange information and programs, share peripherals, and draw on the resources of a massive secondary storage unit (e.g., a file server).

lock/key protection system A system that safeguards data and resources by matching a supplied key or password with that specified in the access requirements.

lockword A code that is associated with a resource such as a file or program; a form of password.

logical error A programming error in an otherwise syntactically valid program that causes processing to take place incorrectly.

logical operation A comparison of data values in the arithmetic logic unit to determine whether a value is greater than, equal to, or less than another value.

logic bomb Code covertly inserted in a computer system that is designed to cause damage or delay when a predefined logical event takes place.

log-off Procedure followed to terminate a terminal session.

log-on Procedure followed to initiate a terminal session.

log-on identification A unique set of characters used to identify an individual who is initiating a terminal session.

loophole An error of omission or oversight in software, hardware, or firmware that allows circumvention of the access control process.

LU6.2 A logical unit for peer-to-peer communications between nodes with user-defined data streams. LU6.2 is the most commonly known logical unit and is used as the access protocol for IBM's Advanced Program-to-Program Communication facility.

magnetic card An identification tool commonly used for credit or access control that contains a magnetic strip read by various devices.

mandatory access control A means of restricting access to objects on the basis of the sensitivity (as represented by a label) of the information contained in the objects and the formal authorization (i.e., clearance) of a subject to access such information.

mandatory policy *See* rule-based security policy.

masquerade An attempt to access a system by pretending to be an authorized user.

master file A file containing control information that is used by multiple programs and is updated by transactions during file maintenance processing.

memory bounds The limits in a range of storage addresses assigned to a protected region in memory.

message authentication code A code calculated during encryption and appended to a message. If the message authentication code calculated during decryption matches the appended code, the message was not altered during transmission.

multilevel system A system or network that incorporates the mode of operation that allows two or more sensitivity levels of information to be processed simultaneously within the same system when some users are not cleared for all levels of information present.

mutually suspicious Term pertaining to interactive processes in systems or programs that are designed to extract certain data from one another while protecting their own sensitive data.

nak (negative acknowledgment character) attack A technique that seeks access to systems whose operating systems leave them unprotected during asynchronous interrupts.

National Computer Security Center (NCSC) A division of the Department of Defense concerned with certifying the level of security mechanisms in vendor computer products.

need to know A policy of supplying to a person or group of persons only the sensitive information necessary for that person or group to perform assigned work. The default state is no information supplied.

need to withhold A policy of withholding from a person or group of persons only the sensitive information necessary to achieve a purpose of confidentiality. The default state is no information withheld.

network A telecommunications medium and associated components responsible for the transfer of information.

NIST National Institute of Standards and Technology, formerly the National Bureau of Standards (NBS). A US federal standards organization.

nondisplay mode A terminal setting whereby characters entered on the terminal are not shown on screen.

notarization In financial standards and certain NIST publications, a technique for deriving a key-encipherment key using a master key and additional information. In communications standards documents, notarization is the registration of data with a trusted third party—the notary—which later ensures the accuracy of the data, including its content, origin, time, and delivery. Notarization is often considered a mechanism for nonrepudiation.

NSA National Security Agency.

numeric test An input control method designed to verify that a data field contains numeric digits only.

object A resource (e.g., service or information) that is accessed in a passive role and that contains or receives information.

offline hardware Equipment (including terminals) that is not actively connected to a host processor.

off-site storage A secondary storage location that is not adjacent to or within the primary facility.

one-way encryption An encryption algorithm that cannot be reversed.

Orange Book Alternate name for the Department of Defense Trusted Computer System Evaluation Criteria.

OSI model Open systems interconnection model, established by the International Standards Organization. Intended to provide a network design framework that allows equipment from different vendors to communicate with each other.

output controls Techniques and methods for verifying that processing results meet expectations and that they are communicated to authorized users only.

overwriting The destruction of magnetically stored data by recording different data on the same surface.

owner The individual manager or representative of management (frequently the originator of the information) who is responsible for making and communicating judgments and decisions on behalf of the organization with regard to the use, identification, classification, and protection of a specific information asset.

passive threat A means of unauthorized disclosure of information that does not change the state of the system (e.g., eavesdropping on microwave transmissions).

password Confidential authentication information in the form of a string of characters used as proof of identity.

password generator A product that creates a password either as a function of time or in response to a challenge code.

penetration Unauthorized access to a computer system.

penetration profile A list of the activities required to gain access to a computer system.

penetration signature A description of a set of conditions in which unauthorized system access might occur.

penetration testing An attempt by special systems analysis teams to access a system through security weaknesses to identify those weaknesses.

performance monitor Systems software that tracks the service levels of a computer system.

personal identification number (PIN) An individual's access code commonly used to authenticate the bearer of a magnetic card or other physical identification device; logically equivalent to either a user identification code or a password.

personnel security Procedures established to ensure that all personnel who have access to automated information systems resources have the required authorizations, the need to know, and all appropriate security clearances.

phased conversion A procedure for installing new systems in place of old systems that involves incremental implementation of the modules of the system.

physical security Measures that provide physical protection of resources.

piggyback entry Unauthorized access to a computer system by means of another user's legitimate connection.

PIN *See* personal identification number.

pirate bulletin board An electronic bulletin board containing messages about how to obtain unauthorized copies of copyrighted software.

pirating Unauthorized copying of copyrighted software or hardware.

plaintext Text or signals that can be understood without decryption.

policy A high-level statement that indicates management's intentions, providing broad direction or goals.

policy guideline An example of how a policy might be applied to a specific situation. An outline or checklist of detailed procedures recommended to satisfy a policy.

polyinstantiation The simultaneous existence of multiple data objects with the same name but different access classes.

postimplementation review An evaluation of a system after it has been in operation.

Preferred Products List A list of commercially produced equipment that meets TEMPEST and other security requirements prescribed by the National Security Agency. This list is included in the NSA Information Systems Security Products and Services Catalogue, issued quarterly and available through the Government Printing Office.

preventive control A control designed to avoid the occurrence of unwanted security-related events.

principal An accessing entity for the purposes of authentication and access control. Principals can be persons, applications, or systems.

principle of least privilege *See* least privilege.

print suppression The elimination of character printing in order to preserve secrecy (e.g., the characters of a password as it is entered by a user are not displayed on screen).

privacy The ability of an individual or organization to determine whether, when, and to whom personal or organizational information is released. The right of individuals to control or influence information that is related to them in terms of who may collect or store it and to whom that information may be disclosed.

privacy protection The establishment of administrative, technical, and physical safeguards to ensure the confidentiality of data by protecting it against anticipated threats of disclosure. Inadequate privacy protection may put an organization at legal risk.

private key An encryption or decryption key that is paired with a public key and is kept secret.

privileged instructions A set of instructions generally executable only when a computer system is operating in the executive state (e.g., while handling interrupts). These instructions typically are designed to control the security features of a computer system.

procedural language A computer programming language that requires that the programmer determine the logical sequence of program execution and processing.

process control The monitoring and control of production and manufacturing processes.

process description A formal narrative that describes in sequence the processing activities and procedures of a computer system.

processing controls Techniques and methods to ensure that processing produces accurate results.

program analyzer A software tool that modifies or monitors an application program to allow the automatic collection of information on the program's operating characteristics.

program development process The activities involved in the development of a computer program, including problem analysis, program design, process design, and program coding, debugging, and testing.

proof of correctness The inference, based on mathematical logic techniques, that a relation assumed true at program entry implies that another relation between program variables holds true at program exit.

protection ring. One of a hierarchy of privileged modes in a computer system. Certain access rights are granted to users, programs, and processes according to the mode in which they are authorized to operate.

pseudocode Program processing specifications written as structured, English-like statements that can be converted into source code.

pseudoflaw A false loophole embedded in an operating system to snare unsuspecting intruders.

public key   An encryption or decryption key that is paired with a private key and is publicly known.

public-key encryption   An encryption algorithm in which information is encrypted with a public key but can be decrypted only with a corresponding private key.

purging   The orderly review and removal of inactive or obsolete data files.

qualitative risk assessment   A risk assessment that uses labels (e.g., high, medium, and low) to characterize the anticipated level of risk to automated information system resources.

quantitative risk assessment   A risk assessment that requires the use of actual numbers, calculations of annual loss expectancy, and mathematical probabilities to characterize the anticipated level of risk to automated information systems resources.

real-time processing   Online processing that allows the system to reflect the actual status of records as they are updated.

real-time reaction   For security purposes, the detection, diagnosis, and reporting of a penetration attempt as it occurs.

recovery   Restoration of an information processing facility and related resources following physical destruction, damage, or interruption of services.

recovery procedures   Those actions required to restore a system's data files and computational capability following system failure or penetration.

regression testing   The running of test cases that have previously executed correctly in order to detect errors that may have been created during software correction and modification.

remanence   The residual magnetism that remains on magnetic storage media after degaussing.

repudiation   Denial of receipt of a message.

residual risk   A qualitative or quantitative substantiation of potential loss that remains after a safeguard has been implemented and is operational.

residue   Data left in memory after processing operations but before erasing or rewriting.

resource   Any function, device, or collection of data in a computer system that can be allocated for use by users or programs.

resource sharing   The concurrent use of a computer system resource by more than one user, job, or program.

risk   The probability that a particular threat will exploit a particular vulnerability of the system.

risk analysis   A formal examination of an organization's information resources, controls, and vulnerabilities in both manual and automated systems. Risk analysis assesses the loss potential for each resource or combination thereof together with its probable rate of occurrence in order to establish a potential level of damage in dollars or other assets.

risk assessment Identification and evaluation of types of risks, their probability of occurrence, and their potential adverse impact for an automated information system.

risk management The total process of identifying, controlling, and eliminating or minimizing uncertain events that may adversely affect system resources. It includes risk analysis, cost-benefit analysis, and an overall system security review as well as the selection, implementation, testing, and evaluation of safeguards.

risk profile A view of the overall state of vulnerability of an organization. It may be either a full enumeration (by asset or type of risk) of all the events that may endanger the assets, or a collected value (often an annual loss expectancy).

risk range The difference between the person with the lowest security clearance who can have access to the system and the highest classification of information in it.

Rivest-Shamir-Adleman algorithm *See* RSA algorithm.

RJE Remote job entry. In remote job entry, a remote device is configured over a communications line to appear to a system as its primary or secondary input/output.

rotation of duties The principle of periodically changing job assignments to interrupt the opportunity for users to collude for fraudulent purposes.

routing control The application of rules during the process of routing to choose or avoid specific networks, subnetworks, links, or intermediate relay systems.

RSA algorithm A public-key encryption algorithm (named after its developers—Rivest, Shamir, and Adleman) that can be used as an alternative to or in conjunction with the DES algorithm.

rule-based security policy A security policy based on global rules imposed on all users. These rules usually rely on a comparison of the sensitivity of the resources being accessed and the possession of corresponding attributes or clearances by the accessing entities. This type of security policy is also called a mandatory policy.

safeguard A security control designed to prevent system compromise.

salami technique The process of removing assets in such small amounts over time that a significant amount can be taken without detection.

sanitizing The degaussing or overwriting of sensitive information stored on magnetic or other electronic media.

scavenging The process of searching physical and electronic media for remanent (e.g., abandoned or discarded) data that may contain information of value.

scheduling program Systems software that schedules and monitors the processing of production jobs by the computer system.

secure operating system An operating system that effectively controls hardware, software, and firmware functions in order to provide a level of protection commensurate with the value of the data resources it manages.

security audit An evaluation of the adequacy of data security procedures and measures and of their compliance with policy and other security requirements.

security control architecture A composite system of security controls, requirements, and safeguards planned or implemented within an automated information system environment to ensure the integrity, availability, and confidentiality of system resources.

security controls Techniques and methods to ensure that only authorized users can access the computer system and its resources and that the IS environment ensures the integrity, availability, and confidentiality of system resources.

security domain A single domain of trust, which shares a single security policy and a single management.

security filter A set of software or firmware routines and techniques that prevent the automatic forwarding of specified data across unprotected communications links or to unauthorized persons.

security kernel The security-relevant parts of a system, and the only parts of the system that need to be trusted. Specifically, the hardware, firmware, and software elements of a trusted computing base that implement the reference monitor concept. It must mediate all accesses, be protected from modification, and be verifiable as correct.

security label The marking bound to a resource (which may be a data unit) that names or designates the security attributes of that resource. It is often used to indicate the sensitivity level relative to rule-based policy.

security level Assigns a level of access or privilege to a subject, or a classification level or sensitivity label to an object.

security policy The set of laws, rules, and practices that regulate how an organization manages, protects, and distributes sensitive information.

security software System software that controls access to data in files and allows only authorized use of terminals and related equipment. Control usually is exercised through various levels of safeguards, which are applied according to user need.

sensitive information Information that must be protected because its unauthorized disclosure, alteration, loss, or destruction will cause substantial damage.

sensitivity A measure of the harm that could result from the observation, modification, destruction, or unavailability of information.

separation of duties A control that separates a process into component parts and requires different users to perform different parts in order to complete the process. This requires collusion to breach security.

serial processing The processing of records according to their physical sequence in a file or through an input device.

sign-off *See* log-off.

sign-on *See* log-on.

simulation The use of an executable model to represent the behavior of an object. During testing, the computational hardware, the external environment, or the coding segments may be simulated.

754

simultaneous processing The simultaneous execution in a multiprocessing environment of two or more program instructions.

smart card A device about the size of a credit card which contains encoded information and sometimes a microprocessor and a user interface. The information in the code, or the information generated by the microprocessor, is used to gain access to a facility or a computer system.

SNA Systems Network Architecture, developed by IBM Corp. A collection of designs for how terminals and systems will communicate with each other. It is intended to maximize connectivity while hiding application dependences.

software life cycle The period from the conception of a software product to the end of its usability. The software life cycle typically is separated into phases, including requirements, design, programming, testing, conversion, operation, and maintenance.

software piracy The illegal copying of copyrighted software.

source document The form in which data is recorded before its entry into a computer system.

source program A computer program that is coded in assembly or a higher-level programming language.

spoofing The act of assuming the characteristics of another computer system or user for the purpose of deception.

spooling A technique that maximizes processing speed through the temporary use of high-speed storage devices. Input files are transferred from slower, permanent storage and queued in the high-speed devices to await processing, or output files are queued in high-speed devices to await transfer to slower storage devices.

standard of due care Processes covering the implementation of that are considered prudent by most organizations in similar circumstances or environments.

state The collected set of values of the attributes of all the entities in a system. In risk analysis, the state includes the elements required to calculate a numerical single value for the risk profile.

statement testing A method of satisfying the criterion that each statement in a program be executed at least once during program testing.

static analysis The analysis of the form and structure of a software product that does not require its execution. Static analysis can be applied to the requirements, design, or code.

subject The principal that takes the active role in requesting access to an object.

supervisor state *See* executive state.

superzapping The process of using a utility that operates in executive state to perform bit manipulation in RAM or on recording media.

swapping A method of computer processing in which programs not actively being processed are held in virtual memory and alternated in and out of memory with other programs according to priority.

symmetric key Symmetric-key cryptographic algorithms make use of a single key shared by both the originator and the receiver of the data. The key is used to both encrypt and decrypt the data.

synchronous A method of transmitting data. Enables the transmission of data at very high speeds using circuits in which the transfer of data is synchronized by electronic clock signals. Synchronous communications are used within the computer and in high-speed mainframe computer networks.

system integrity The state of a computer system when there is complete assurance of the logical correctness and reliability of the operating system and the logical completeness of the hardware, software, and firmware that implement the protection mechanisms and data integrity.

system integrity procedures Procedures established to ensure that hardware, software, firmware, and data in a computer system retain integrity and are not tampered with by unauthorized personnel.

system-specific security requirements Detailed security requirements that are applicable to a specific automated information system and are derived through risk management and analysis.

TCP/IP Transmission Control Protocol/Internet Protocol. A transport and internet protocol developed by the Department of Defense and widely used in research and government applications. Used in business for internetworking.

technical security Includes fault-tolerance mechanisms (e.g., hardware redundancy, disk mirroring, and application checkpoint/restart), electronic vaulting, access control software, and other mechanisms or measures.

technical threat One that attempts to exploit flaws or oversights in the design, implementation, or configuration of the system.

technological attack An attack perpetrated by circumventing or nullifying hardware, software, or firmware access control mechanisms rather than by subverting system personnel or users.

teleprocessing Information processing and transmission performed by an integrated system of communications, computers, and user-system interface equipment.

teleprocessing security The practice of protecting a teleprocessing system from deliberate, inadvertent, or unauthorized disclosure, acquisition, manipulation, or modification of information.

TEMPEST The term used by the Department of Defense to describe systems that control electromagnetic emanations according to given specifications.

terminal identification Establishment of the unique identification of a terminal by a computer system or network.

test data Data that simulates operational data in form and content and is used to evaluate a system or program.

test data generators Software tools that help generate data files that are used to test the execution and logic of application programs.

testing The execution of a program or system, fully exercising its processing capability on sample data sets to determine whether it meets processing specifications.

threat An event or method that can potentially compromise the integrity, availability, or confidentiality of automated information systems.

threat agent An individual entity, real or perceived, that may initiate, enhance, or otherwise support a threat occurrence.

threat monitoring The analysis, assessment, and review of audit trails and other data collected to identify system events that may constitute violations of information security or precipitate incidents involving data privacy.

threshold alarm An alarm status reached when a specified event is detected following a predetermined number of occurrences within a defined period of time.

time-dependent password A password that is valid only at a certain time of the day or during a specified period.

token A physical device used to convey privilege or a capability (e.g., a handheld password generator).

topology The geometric arrangement of nodes and cable links in a local area network.

traffic analysis The inference of system information from the observation of traffic flows in a system (e.g., presence, absence, amount, direction, and frequency).

traffic flow security The protection that results from those features in some cryptography equipment that conceal the presence of valid messages on a communications circuit, usually by causing the circuit to appear busy at all times or by encrypting the source and destination addresses of those messages.

traffic padding Adding extraneous messages or elements of messages to transmissions to protect data characteristics (e.g., message length, frequency, or destination) from being analyzed by an intruder.

transactional processing The processing of transactions as they occur rather than in batches.

transaction file A collection of records containing data generated from business activity.

trapdoor Code written into system or application software to grant special access without the normal methods of access authentication; also called a backdoor. A programmer's device to enable testing and debugging or to gain access in the event of problems with access routines. Trapdoors pose a security threat if not removed before the system goes into production.

Trojan horse A computer program with an apparent or actual useful function that contains additional, malicious hidden functions. For example, a Trojan horse can contain a virus or a worm.

trusted system A system that employs sufficient hardware and software assurance measures to allow its use for simultaneous processing of a range of sensitive or classified information.

trustworthiness A combination of security with safety and reliability as well as the protection of privacy, which is already considered part of security.

uninterruptible power supply (UPS) A system designed to ensure the constant supply of conditioned power regardless of the status of the commercial power source.

unit testing The testing of a module for typographic, syntactic, and logical errors, as well as for correct implementation of its design and the meeting or its requirements.

update The altering of master records to reflect the current business activity contained in transaction files.

UPS *See* uninterruptible power supply.

user People or processes accessing an information system either by direct methods (e.g., data entry at a terminal) or indirect methods (e.g., receipt of output data or preparation of software).

user identification code A code that uniquely identifies a user.

validation A procedure of review, analysis, and testing applied throughout the software life cycle to uncover errors, verify that functions operate as specified, and ensure the production of quality software.

value added network (VAN) A public data communications network that provides basic transmission facilities (generally leased by the VAN vendor from a common carrier) plus additional, enhanced services (e.g., computerized switching, temporary data storage, protocol conversion, error detection and correction, or electronic mail service).

verification The demonstration of software consistency, completeness, and correctness between each stage of the development life cycle.

verify To ensure that transcribed data has been accurately entered by keyboard.

view A virtual relation that is derived from base relations and other views.

virtual memory A method of extending computer memory by using secondary storage devices to store program pages that are not being executed.

virus A sequence of code inserted into other executable code so that when those programs are run, the viral code is also executed. A virus reproduces itself by attaching to another program. It can be designed to merely replicate itself, replicate and post messages, or damage data and degrade system performance. *See also* logic bomb *and* worm.

vulnerability A weakness in system security procedures, system design, implementation, and internal controls that could be exploited to violate system security policy.

vulnerability analysis The systematic examination of systems in order to determine the adequacy of security measures, identify security deficiencies, and provide data from which to predict the effectiveness of proposed security measures.

walkthrough A manual program analysis technique in which a designer or developer describes a program's structure and logic to colleagues.

well-formed transaction A security and integrity principle that restricts or constrains the ways a user can manipulate data in order to ensure the integrity of that data.

wide area network (WAN) A wide area network is one that links computers located beyond a single metropolitan area and may even be worldwide in scope.

wiretap To attach a communications device, such as a terminal, to a communications circuit to obtain access to data. The unauthorized monitoring or recording of data while it is being transmitted over a communications link.

worm An independent program that reproduces by copying itself from one system to another while traveling from machine to machine across network connections. A worm may degrade system operation by repeatedly copying itself to the same machine or machines.

X.25 The CCITT's packet-switching protocol for connecting open, heterogeneous systems. CCITT X.25 is the most widely used communications architecture.

Recommended Reading

Section I-1. Fundamentals of Security Management

Denning, D.E. "Responsibility and Blame in Computer Security." *Proceedings of the NCCV* (New Haven CT, 1991).

Denning, D.E.; Neumann, P.G.; Parker, D.B. "Social Aspects of Computer Security." *Proceedings of the 10th National Computer Security Conference* (Baltimore MD, 1987).

Denning, P.J., ed. *Computers Under Attack: Intruders, Worms, and Viruses* (New York: ACM Press, 1990).

Forcht, K.A.; Myong, A. *Ethical Use of Computers* (Harrisonburg VA: James Madison University, 1989).

Hoffman, L.J., ed. *Rogue Programs: Viruses, Worms, and Trojan Horses* (New York: Van Nostrand Reinhold, 1990).

Lunt, T.F. "Automated Audit Trail Analysis and Intrusion Detection: A Survey." *Proceedings of the 11th National Computer Security Conference* (Baltimore MD, 1988).

Menkus, B.; Ruthberg, Z.G., eds. *Control Objectives—Controls in a Computer Environment: Objectives, Guidelines, and Audit Procedures* (Carol Stream IL: EDP Auditors Foundation, Inc., 1990).

National Research Council. *Computers at Risk: Safe Computing in the Information Age* (Washington DC: National Academy Press, 1990).

Neumann, P.G. "The Computer-Related Risk of the Year: Computer Abuse." *Proceedings of COMPASS (Computer Assurance)* (June 1988).

———. "The Computer-Related Risk of the Year: Distributed Control." *Proceedings of COMPASS (Computer Assurance)* (June 1990).

———. "Computers, Ethics, and Values: Inside Risks." *Communications of the ACM* (July 1990).

———. "Illustrative Risks to the Public in the Use of Computer Systems and Related Technology." *SEN* 16 (January 1991).

———. "The Roles of Structure in Safety and Security." Position paper for an IFIP Workshop on Reliability, Safety, and Security of Computer Systems: Accidental vs. Intentional Faults (Grand Canyon, 1991).

Neumann, P.G.; Parker, D.B. "A Summary of Computer Misuse Techniques." *Proceedings of the 12th National Computer Security Conference* (Baltimore MD, 1989).

Parker, D.B., et al. *Ethical Conflicts in Information and Computer Science, Technology and Business* (Wellesley MA: QED Information Sciences, Inc., 1990).

Spafford, E. "Are Computer Hacker Break-ins Ethical?" *Journal of Systems and Software* 17 (January 1992).

Section I-3. Risk Management

Gilbert, I.E. *Automated Risk Management Software Tools*. Report by NIST Computer Systems Laboratory (March 16, 1992).

————. *Guide for Selecting Automated Risk Analysis Tools*. NIST Special Publication 500-174 (October 1989).

The National Computer Security Center's Evaluated Products List, as described in *Information Systems Security Products and Services Catalog*. (Washington DC: Government Printing Office, updated quarterly).

Section I-5. Security Awareness

BloomBecker, J.J. *Spectacular Computer Crimes* (Homewood IL: Richard D. Irwin, 1990).

Computer Security: Virus Highlights Need for Improved Internet Management. GAO Report GAO/IMTEC-89-57 (June 1989).

Wells, R.O. "How to Wake Up the 'Non-Believers.'" *Proceedings of the 8th Annual ISSA Conference for Information Security Professionals* (San Diego CA, 1991).

Section II-1. Secure Systems Design and Development

Clark, D.D.; Wilson, D.R. "A Comparison of Commercial and Military Security Policies." *Proceedings of the 1987 IEEE Symposium on Security and Privacy* (April 1987).

Commission of the European Communities. *Information Technology Security Evaluation Criteria (ITSEC), Provisional Harmonised Criteria*, Brussels, Belgium, June 1991.

————. *Information Technology Security Evaluation Manual (ITSEM)*. Draft V0.2. Brussels, Belgium, April 1992.

Department of Defense Trusted Computer System Evaluation Criteria. DOD 5200.28-STD. National Computer Security Center, December 1985.

Government of Canada, Communications Security Establishment, Canadian System Security Center. *The Canadian Trusted Computer Product Evaluation Criteria* (April 1992).

National Computer Security Center. *Trusted Database Management System Interpretation of the Trusted Computer System Evaluation Criteria*. NCSC-TG-021 (April 1991).

————. *Trusted Network Interpretation Environments Guideline*. NCSC-TG-011 (August 1990).

National Institute of Standards and Technology. *Proceedings of the Workshop on Integrity Policy in Computer Information Systems* (1989).

Spafford, E. "The Internet Worm: Crisis and Aftermath." *Communications of the ACM* (June 1989). (Reprinted in *Computers Under Attack: Intruders, Worms, and Viruses*. ed. P.J. Denning. New York: ACM Press, 1990.)

Trusted Information Systems, Inc. *A Proposed Interpretation of the TCSEC for Virtual Machine Monitor Architectures* (August 1992 and earlier drafts).

Section II-2. Systems and Operations Controls

Chalmers, L.S. "What Users Should Know About Microcomputer Security." *Data Security Management* (New York: Auerbach Publications, 1991).

Jacobson, R.V. "Microcomputer Virus Control." *Data Security Management* (New York: Auerbach Publications, 1992).

Section II-3. Data and Applications Controls

Gasser, M. *Building a Secure Computer System* (New York: Van Nostrand Reinhold, 1988).

Korth, H.F.; Silberschatz, A. *Database System Concepts* (2d ed. New York: McGraw-Hill, 1991).

Pfleeger, C. *Security in Computing* (Englewood Cliffs NJ: Prentice Hall, 1989).

Section II-4. Access Controls

Anderson, J.P. "Computer Security Threat Monitoring and Surveillance" (Fort Washington PA: James P. Anderson Co., 1980).

Lunt, T.F.; Jagannathan, R. "A Prototype Real-Time Intrusion Detection Expert System." *Proceedings of the 1988 IEEE Symposium on Security and Privacy* (Oakland CA, 1988).

Neumann, P.G., moderator. *The Online Risks Forum: Forum on the Risks to the Public in Computer Systems* 5 (July 1987).

Sebring, M.M., et al. "Expert Systems in Intrusion Detection: A Case Study." *Proceedings of the 11th National Computer Security Conference* (Baltimore MD, 1988).

Whitehurst, R.A. "Expert Systems in Intrusion-Detection: A Case Study." Menlo Park CA: Computer Science Laboratory, SRI International, 1987.

Section III-2. Communications Security

Bocker, P. *The Integrated Services Digital Network: Concepts, Methods, Systems* (Berlin, Germany: Springer-Verlag, 1988).

International Standards Organization. *International Standard Security Architecture.* ISO 7498-2-1988(E) (Geneva, Switzerland, 1988).

Miles, J.B. "Encryption Products." *Government Computer News* (July 8, 1991).

Nechtvatal, J. "Public-Key Cryptography." NIST Special Publication 800-2 (April 1991).

"A Proposed Federal Information Processing Standard for Digital Signature Standard (DSS)." Federal Register Vol. 56, No. 169 (August 1991).

"Security Requirements for Cryptographic Modules." NIST Draft FIPS Publication 140–1 (July 1991).

Stallings, W. *ISDN: An Introduction* (New York: Macmillan, 1989).

Verma, P.K., ed. *ISDN Systems, Architecture, Technology and Applications* (Englewood Cliffs NJ: Prentice Hall, 1990).

Section IV-1. The Legal and Regulatory Environment

Arkin, S.S., et al. *Prevention and Prosecution of Computer and High Technology Crime* (New York: Matthew Bender, 1991).

BloomBecker, J.J., ed. *Commitment to Security.* The Second Statistical Report of the National Center for Computer Crime Data (NCCCD), Santa Cruz CA, 1989.

Prosser, W.L.; Wade, J.W.; Schwartz, V.E. *Torts: Cases and Materials* (8th ed. Westbury NY: The Foundation Press, Inc., 1988).

Stoll, C. *The Cuckoo's Egg* (New York: Doubleday, 1989).

Tantam, M. *Computer Abuse Investigator* (Oxford UK: Elsevier Scientific Publishers, 1991).

Index

O

P

Q

R